PRINCIPLES OF STRATEGIC MANAGEMENT

Acknowledgements and Dedication

I wish to record my great debt to my wife Barbara and son James, who have given me their unstinting support during the writing of this book.

I acknowledge with grateful thanks the assistance of the following:

- Ian Smith - Senior Process Engineer and Six Sigma Master Black Belt, Huntsman Tioxide Ltd, UK.
- Justin Roe - Process Engineer and Six Sigma Master Black Belt, Huntsman Tioxide Ltd, UK.
- Terry Collins - Director of Neighbourhood Services, City of York, UK.
- Britta Steinriede and Sybille Weber of the University of Applied Sciences, Bielefeld, Germany.
- Christine Woolway, who read the book's initial typescript.

I wish to thank Marion Fisher who prepared the final manuscript of this book. It has been a pleasure to work with her on this project.

Finally, I must acknowledge the great wisdom, encouragement, and care of Gareth Vincenti during very difficult and demanding times for myself and my family.

Principles of Strategic Management
Third Edition

TONY MORDEN
University of Teeside, UK

ASHGATE

Published by
Ashgate Publishing Limited
Gower House
Croft Road
Aldershot
Hampshire GU11 3HR
England

Ashgate Publishing Company
Suite 420
101 Cherry Street
Burlington, VT 05401-4405
USA

Ashgate website: http://www.ashgate.com

British Library Cataloguing in Publication Data
Morden, Tony, 1946-
   Principles of strategic management. - (Innovative business
   textbooks)
   1. Strategic planning
   I. Title
   658.4'012

Library of Congress Cataloging-in-Publication Data
Morden, Tony, 1946-
   Principles of strategic management / by Tony Morden.
      p. cm. -- (Innovative business textbooks)
   Includes index.
   ISBN: 978-0-7546-4474-3 1. Strategic planning. I. Title.

   HD30.28.M6462 2007
   658.4'012--dc22

                                                            2006034157

ISBN: 978-0-7546-4474-3

Printed and bound in Great Britain by MPG Books Ltd, Bodmin, Cornwall.

Contents

INTERNATIONAL BUSINESS STRATEGY

List of Figures

List of Tables

Introduction and Book Plan

This textbook offers a comprehensive and reader-oriented treatment of the principles of business planning and strategic management.

The book will be suitable for undergraduate, conversion-type masters, postgraduate diploma, post-experience, MBA, and professional students on full-time, part-time, and distance-learning courses in business, enterprise, and management. It will also be relevant to students on courses for example in tourism or hospitality management, information technology, healthcare, or engineering which contain a significant element of business and management studies, for instance on a major-minor modular basis.

It will be suitable for access or mature students studying on a vocational, self-developmental, or life-long basis.

The book will also be of use to practitioners in industry, commerce, the public, the healthcare, and the not-for-profit sectors.

The book retains the reader-friendliness of its earlier editions. The presentation is clear, concise, focused, and very much to the point. The chapters are broken down into manageable sections. The text introduces, defines, and analyzes the relevant concepts and theories. These concepts and theories are applied to appropriate issues and contexts, and illustrated with a variety of examples. The text is based on a non-prescriptive and objective analysis.

The book's chapters are grouped into four main parts. Each chapter opens with an introductory overview. There are assessment questions for the review and reinforcement of learning. There are questions for case study and case analysis. And most chapters contain a project assignment or assignments for active or experiential learning purposes.

The book retains the international perspective that characterized the earlier editions.

LEARNING OBJECTIVES

The format and text of this book can be used to fulfil any or all of the following *generic learning objectives*:

❑ developing **awareness** - by which the reader becomes informed of the existence and nature of a particular idea, entity, concept, theory, or application.

❑ **definition** - by which the reader becomes able to express the *precise meaning* of a particular idea, entity, concept, theory or application. Having understood the definition, the reader should then be able to make use of this concept, theory or application in the wider process of study, learning or practice.

❑ **conceptualization** - by which the reader develops an understanding of the nature and character of an idea or entity such that it becomes a useful or applicable concept. This concept may underlie a theory or application, so an understanding of the concept is an essential pre-requisite to understanding or making use of that theory or application.

❑ **understanding** - by which the reader grasps the meaning of an idea, a concept or a theory; and can make sense of the concept and its implications.

❑ **contextualization** - by which the reader becomes able to place a concept, theory or application into a particular context, circumstance or situation. For instance, the reader comes to understand how a particular concept or theory can be used to analyze an issue or problem, or is in some way relevant to providing a structure for its explanation.

❑ **analysis** - by which the reader examines the nature and construction of the concept or entity, breaking it down into its separate components or features so as better to understand and use it; and to be able to explain it to others.

❑ **reflection** - by which the reader thinks about what he or she has conceptualized, analyzed and understood. The process of reflection will deepen the reader's understanding and bring into play insights and perceptions that make the concept or entity richer and more useful. Reflection requirements in this book are associated with the Review Questions to be found at the end of each chapter.

❑ **comparison** - by which the reader puts ideas, concepts or theories together to ascertain the degree to which they are like or unlike each other, or agree or disagree with each other. The process of comparison is often associated with the requirement to **contrast** two or more entities, that is to demonstrate the ways in which they are like or unlike each other.

❑ **explanation** - by which the reader defines, describes and *communicates to others* (i) an understanding of an entity, (ii) the implications of the idea or concept upon which that entity is based, and (iii) the context in which the entity is in this particular case to be found; *such that* *someone else clearly understands what has been explained to them, and understands how it has been analyzed by the reader.*

❑ **synthesis** - by which the reader develops an understanding of whole contexts, structures or frameworks *into which a number of entities are integrated.* The study of business planning and strategic management cannot be separated from wider or "holistic" conceptualizations of external political economies, environments, cultures, knowledge bases, strategic, governance and performance evaluation paradigms, financial management, technologies, and so on.

❑ **application** - by which the reader puts to use the ideas, concepts, and theories he or she has learned and understood, so as to deal with a practical issue or problem associated with a reality.

BOOK PLAN (WHAT THIS BOOK IS ABOUT)

This book offers a comprehensive but reader-friendly treatment of the principles, processes, and practices of strategic management, leadership, and business planning. The book has a structure of four main parts. The purpose of each part is described below, and its chapter titles are listed.

Chapter 1 - Strategic Management

Chapter 1 sets the scene for the book. It looks at some of the key issues of strategic management and business planning that this book deals with. It defines the concept of strategic management, and tells you about the *strategic management approach* that is used to structure the contents of the book.

Part One - Concepts and Techniques of Strategic Analysis

Part One of this book deals with the process of strategic analysis. It contains two interrelated issues. The first issue is the appraisal of the internal circumstances and resources of the enterprise, its capability (what it can do), its ability to generate value, and its sources of comparative or competitive advantage. The second issue is the summary analysis of the relevant external environments and competitive contexts within which the organization operates. Part One contains the following chapters:

Chapter 2   -   Corporate Appraisal
Chapter 3   -   Financial Appraisal

Chapter 4   -   Sources of Competitive or Comparative Advantage,
                Resource Management, Capability, Value Generation, and
                Critical Success Factors
Chapter 5   -   Competitive Analysis
Chapter 6   -   Environmental Analysis

The *appraisal techniques* described in this first part of the book include:

- the analysis of internal strengths and weaknesses based on corporate and financial appraisal.
- the financial health-check.
- the analysis of critical success factors.
- performance gap analysis.
- the analysis of capability and capacity.
- the analysis of value addition, and the value chain.
- the identification of sources of comparative or competitive advantage.
- the analysis of external opportunities and threats based on environmental appraisal.
- competitive analysis.

Part Two - Business Planning, Risk Assessment, Forecasting, the Strategic Management of Time, and Crisis Management

Part Two of this book deals with selected components of the process of strategic and business planning. Business planning and forecasting activities provide contexts for the formulation of strategy and the implementation of decisions described in later chapters of the book. Risk assessment provides a further parameter for these processes, which are also likely to be based on the analysis and management of the relevant time dimensions. Part Two ends with a description of crisis planning and business continuity management. Chapter 10 looks at some of the possible consequences for the strategic management of the enterprise of such emergencies, crises, and disasters that might with a certain degree of likelihood befall it. Part Two contains the following chapters:

Chapter 7   -   The Strategic Management of Time
Chapter 8   -   Risk Assessment
Chapter 9   -   Business Planning and Forecasting
Chapter 10   -   Crisis Management

Part Three - Strategy Formulation, Leadership, Governance, Strategic Decision-Making, and Performance Evaluation

Part Three of this book deals with the inter-related processes of strategy formulation, leadership, governance, strategic decision-making, and performance evaluation. This is sometimes termed "the strategy process".

Part Three defines the concepts of mission, purpose, objectives, and strategy. It identifies the roles and interests of shareholders or stakeholders as beneficiaries or recipients of the activities of the organization. It examines the inter-related issues of business ethics, values, environmentalism, and social responsibility that may influence the formulation of enterprise mission and objectives, and which may shape the implementation of strategy. It analyzes key issues of corporate governance, financial strategy, financial evaluation and performance management. It looks at *who* formulates strategy and makes strategic decisions; and it looks at *how* these processes are carried out. It analyzes the role of leadership in the processes of governance and strategic management. Part Three looks at the relationship between planning style, strategy formulation, and the structure of the organization. And it describes a variety of criteria by which the strategies chosen and implemented by the enterprise may be appraised and evaluated.

In summary, Part Three *looks at what strategy is.* It deals with how strategies and plans are formulated, how decisions are made, and how the results are assessed. It also looks at the related issues of who formulates strategies and plans, who makes decisions, and why. Part Three contains the following chapters:

Chapter 11 - The Concepts of Mission, Objective, and Strategy
Chapter 12 - Business Ethics, Environmentalism, and Social Responsibility
Chapter 13 - Financial Strategy and Management
Chapter 14 - Strategy Formulation, Governance, and Strategic Decision-Making
Chapter 15 - Planning Style and Strategy
Chapter 16 - Performance Evaluation, Performance Management, and Excellence
Chapter 17 - Leadership and Strategy

Part Four - Strategy Choice and Implementation

Part Four of this book analyzes a variety of alternative strategies from which enterprise management may choose in order to fulfil the mission and achieve the objectives described in Part Three. Part Four also deals with key implementation issues.

Decision-makers will have to decide what is the best choice of strategy from the various options available to them, given the findings of the strategic analysis described in Part One; given an understanding of the relevant critical success factors; and given the features of the knowledge, the technology, and the competition strategies described in Part Four that provide the *strategic foundations* of the enterprise itself.

The enterprise will then have to implement its choice of strategies within the parameters identified by the process of strategic analysis; and given the prevailing context of the structure, the relationship architecture, the competencies, and decisions on resource application that have been established by the organization.

Decisions on strategy choice and implementation will therefore be informed by the process of strategic analysis described in Part One. Strategy choice will have closely to be related to enterprise capability, to its ability to generate customer value, and to its sources of comparative or competitive advantage. Strategy choice will also have to be closely related to enterprise understanding of its critical success and its limiting factors; and to its understanding of the nature of the constraints imposed by the relevant external and competitive environments.

The nature and outcomes of strategy choice and implementation will be determined by the processes of time management, risk assessment, forecasting, and business planning analyzed in Part Two.

The nature and outcomes of strategy choice and implementation will also be determined by the processes of leadership, governance, strategy formulation, strategic decision-making and performance evaluation analyzed in Part Three.

Part Four is divided into three sections. The *first section* is entitled **Strategic Foundations**. This section deals with fundamental issues of structure, relationship architecture, knowledge, technology, competence, the character of resource use, and competition strategy. The formulation and implementation of enterprise strategy is dependent on decisions about these issues. Enterprise capability, its ability to generate value, its leadership success, its competitive or comparative advantage, and its operational or financial performance may all depend on the knowledge, the technology, the competence, and the possible patterns of resource use available to the organization. And it may depend on the effectiveness of the management of these key variables over the time horizons described in Chapter 7.

These variables are therefore likely to determine the degree to which the enterprise will be able to fulfil its purpose and achieve its objectives. The first section contains the following chapters:

Chapter 18 - Structure, Architecture, Culture, and Supply Chain Management
Chapter 19 - The Strategic Management of Knowledge, Technology, and Innovation
Chapter 20 - Core Competencies
Chapter 21 - Resource Stretch and Leverage
Chapter 22 - Competition Strategy

The *second section* deals with **Business Strategies**. These are the detailed and practical means by which the enterprise attempts to achieve its competitive, product-market, financial, and performance objectives. Decisions about business strategy in particular cover product-markets and product-market position, brands, reputation, and business development.

Such decisions depend directly on issues of resource capability, value generation, competitive advantage, leadership, and the strategic foundations analyzed in earlier chapters. The enterprise will make decisions about its business strategy that most effectively exploit its strengths and its resources, its sources of competitive or comparative advantage, its knowledge, its technology, its capability, and its competencies such that competitive, market, performance and financial objectives, or objectives for value addition, are achieved. The second section contains the following chapters:

Chapter 23 - Volume and Cost-Based Strategies
Chapter 24 - Differentiated, Focus, and Niche Strategies
Chapter 25 - Brands, Reputation, and Corporate Identity
Chapter 26 - Product-Market Development Strategies
Chapter 27 - Business Development Strategies and Strategic Alliances

The *third section* deals with **International Business Strategy**. This section deals with corporate decisions about key implementation issues associated with the internationalization of business strategy. And it deals with issues of globalization and localization, in which the enterprise has to make decisions about how and why it may choose variously to operate on a local, a regional, or an international basis. The third section contains the following chapter:

Chapter 28 -   International Business Strategy

WHAT SOME REVIEWERS SAID ABOUT THE PREVIOUS EDITION OF THIS BOOK

"the importance of strategic thinking and planning cannot be overstated. That is why I welcome this ... stimulating book. It offers a clear guide to developing a strategic approach; and it provides valuable keys to understanding the nature of a business, identifying goals and achieving them. With lively analysis ... Tony Morden gives useful insights into the concepts and practical techniques of strategic management and planning aimed at enabling businesses to maximize their potential and rise to the challenge of change" - **The Right Honourable Sir Leon Brittan QC, formerly Vice-President of the European Commission.**

"the student is taken carefully, logically and lucidly through the labyrinth of strategic management" - **Professor Emeritus George Thomason CBE, University of Cardiff, UK.**

"Morden succeeds in bringing together the underlying conceptual framework, develops the management theme with good real life reference to actual companies, and facilitates the understanding of the subject with a style which is concise and enjoys clarity of purpose ... this edition is 'must have' essential reference material" - **John Jeffers, International Business Manager, AMEC plc, UK.**

"a clearly structured and reader-friendly book from which one can easily find individual strategic issues for both studies and practical work. The book gives an excellent total picture of strategy and planning" - **Heidi Toivola, Product Manager, L'Oréal Finland.**

TECHNIQUES OF CASE STUDY AND ANALYSIS

The use of case study and analysis has long been associated with the subject and practice of strategy, planning, and strategic management. The use of case study and analysis is regarded as a particularly effective method for the application of conceptual or theoretical frameworks such as those described in this book, and for the reinforcement of the reader's learning about them. It can be used to develop the personal technique and judgement required to deal with the realities of the situations represented by these case studies. Techniques of case study and analysis are for instance associated with:

❑ company or organization analysis.
❑ the identification and analysis of strategic, planning, or performance management issues.
❑ the identification and analysis of strategies, or strategic choice.
❑ the identification of strategic dilemmas or problems.
❑ the selection and recommendation of courses of action from a number of available alternative options.
❑ processes of leadership, strategy formulation, decision-making, and performance evaluation.
❑ the exercise of personal judgement and discretion in dealing with issues, and making decisions about them.

Skills Developed by Case Study and Analysis

Case study and analysis develops a number of personal skills. These include:

Intellectual and cognitive skills - involving the recognition, categorization, evaluation, re-organization, and synthesis of information. These intellectual processes require logical and methodical thinking. They also call for the appropriate work and information processing methodologies, especially where the reader is faced with:-

• a large volume of information, which may or may not be clearly laid out or internally consistent.
• information whose lack of clarity or inherent dilemmas reflect the reality of the situation which the case writer faced in researching and recording his or her material and writing up the case study.
• the need to summarize.
• dealing with the case study under examination conditions.

Application skills - in which concepts, theories, prior learning (and personal experience where appropriate) need to be applied in order to analyze the case study and to answer the questions set. This intellectual, conceptual, and maybe experiential basis provides both the principles and the framework by which the case analysis may be carried out.

Creativity, discretion, and the exercise of judgement - necessary to identifying alternatives, suggesting solutions to dilemmas or problems, dealing objectively with opinions and value judgements, and making decisions. The exercise of judgement is also important where issues of implementation form a key part of the requirement, or where presentation must include persuasion and the making of a case (or business case) for the proposals being put forward.

Communication skills - necessary to the construction and presentation of written reports or oral presentations.

How to Do a Case Study

There are a number of simple steps to follow when dealing with a case study. These are listed in the section below. But before you follow them, you should clear your mind of irrelevant thought and distractions! Concentrate only on the matter in the case study and empathize with it. Remember, the case study is for the time being a *reality* with which you must deal, and about which you may have to make decisions.

PROCESS (WHAT YOU MIGHT DO)

1. Read the case study quickly to gain an overview of its contents.
2. Read and understand the case requirements or the questions you have to answer. Also, read and understand the assessment criteria where this is relevant.
3. Read the case study a second or third time. Study the detail. Attempt to build up a broad understanding of:-
   - purposes, objectives, and strategies being implemented by the organization or organizations in the case study.
   - strategic issues, intentions, dilemmas, or problems.
   - question marks and areas of concern.
   - key personalities, personal motivations, or leadership issues.
4. Carry out a *strategic analysis* of the enterprise or enterprises in the case study, if this is required. The process of strategic analysis is described in detail in **Parts One and Two** of this book.

5. Identify possible scenarios, future circumstances, or time-related issues that the case organization might face within its forecast time horizons. This is dealt with in **Part Two** of this book.

6. Identify and analyze processes of *strategy formulation, leadership, strategic decision-making and performance evaluation*, where the necessary information is available in the case study, or where this is possible. These processes are described in detail in **Part Three**.

7. Identify and analyze strategies currently being proposed or implemented. Be prepared to comment on them or to evaluate them. Are they appropriate? Are they consistent with the strategic analysis and forecasts carried out in steps 4 and 5 above? What degree of risk do they contain? What might their consequences be for the organization within the foreseeable future? The case writer's objective here is to get the student to think about:-

   - what the stated objectives and strategies of the enterprise are.
   - why it has made such strategic choices.
   - how it is proposing to implement these strategies, and what the potential consequences or performance outcomes of its strategic choice might be.

   The processes of *strategic choice* and *strategy implementation* are described in detail in **Parts Three and Four**.

8. Where you are required to suggest solutions to issues, dilemmas, or problems; or to recommend future strategies or courses of action to be implemented, you may have to:-

   - identify, analyze, compare, and justify alternative courses of action available to the enterprise (i) that would allow it to fulfil its purpose, achieve its objectives, or deal with the issue which is the subject of the case study; (ii) that accord with its critical success factors, its philosophy, and the constraints under which it operates; and (iii) that are likely to be feasible given its resources, capability, and attitude to risk.

   - identify and analyze implementation issues relevant to the choice from amongst the alternatives described immediately above. Implementation issues may be associated with leadership, organization structure, and corporate culture; management process; the need to meet customer, shareholder or stakeholder expectations; performance management; or the need to develop specific skills and competencies (and so on).

   - identify and empathize with the role requirements and responsibilities of influential individuals, decision-makers, or stakeholders.

- give your reasoning or justification as to how or why the strategies or courses of action that you propose will most appropriately deal with the requirement that you have been set by the case writer or the assessor.

9. You will need to decide on the degree to which the case requirement calls for the exercise of *judgement* in suggesting courses of action or desired outcomes. This will be regarded as a proper objective for the case writer to set the student.

10. Similarly, you may need to be clear about the extent to which the case requirement calls for *decisions* to be made. Case studies sometimes call for the exercise of judgement in decision-making. This may also be a prime objective of the case writer. Once you have identified and ranked the alternatives you may be required to choose between them. It may not be possible to prevaricate or to obfuscate, or "to sit on the fence", or to give yourself the luxury (?) of "analysis-paralysis"! The making of decisions may have the effect of sending clear signals to customers, competitors, shareholders and investors, employees and stakeholders, government agencies, and so on.

11. As a result, you may have to be prepared to justify the course of action or the strategies that you have recommended. You may not be able to shift the responsibility by simply stating that "the Managing Director should do so-and-so". Why should he or she do it? You may have to be prepared to outline:-

- the relative advantages and disadvantages of your proposal; *or*
- the relative costs and benefits; *or*
- the relative risks involved; *or*
- the relevant performance management issues; *or*
- why the suggested outcomes to your proposal are likely to be the most desirable, and how decision-makers may be persuaded to adopt and implement your proposals; *or*
- how the organization might be able to implement your proposals, achieve the outcomes, and measure the result.

12. Remember, finally, that organizations do nothing. It is their people who do everything! Don't ignore the people in the case study. Put yourself in their shoes. Look at what you are proposing from their viewpoint.

Chapter 1

The Strategic Management Concept

This opening chapter sets the scene for the book. It tells you what the book is about. It looks at some of the major *principles* that the book will deal with. It defines the concept of strategic management, and tells you about the strategic management approach that is used to structure the contents of the work.

STRATEGIC MANAGEMENT AND STRATEGIC PLANNING

This book is about strategic management and strategic planning. The establishment of strategies, the making of plans, and the implementation of those strategies and plans are key management decision-making processes in any kind of enterprise. The strategic decision-making process takes place, in some form or other, in most kinds of organization. The process may be formalized and systematic. Or it may be informal, opportunistic and *ad hoc* in nature.

The formulation of strategies and plans is a prime responsibility of entrepreneurs in small to medium-sized businesses (or "SMEs"); and of leaders, chief executives, presidents, directors, and managers in private and public companies.

Business planning and the formulation of strategy is also a prime responsibility of managers and administrators in such public sector and not-for-profit organizations as hospitals, government agencies, police and security agencies, schools and universities, charities, and fund-raising institutions.

This book, like its predecessor then entitled *An Introduction to Business Strategy* and published in 1999, takes a *strategic management* approach to the subject of strategic decision-making and business planning. The strategic management approach was first described by Kenneth Andrews (1980). This approach is practical and comprehensive. It also corresponds with the realities of life in enterprises and organizations as you may experience it. It is widely used by practitioners, managers, and academics.

Kenneth Andrews' Definition of Strategic Management

Andrews comments that 'strategy is the pattern of decisions in a company that determines and reveals its objectives, purposes or goals, produces the principal policies and plans for achieving those goals, and defines the range of business the company is to pursue, the kind of economic and human organization it is or intends to be and the nature of the economic and non-economic contribution it intends to make to its shareholders, employees, customers and communities ... the strategic decision contributing to this pattern is one that is effective over long periods of time, affects the company in many different ways and focuses and commits a significant portion of its resources to the expected outcomes. The pattern resulting from a series of such decisions will probably define the central character and image of a company, the individuality it has for its members and various publics, and the position it will occupy in its industry and markets. It will permit the specification of particular objectives to be attained through a timed sequence of investment and implementation decisions and will govern directly the deployment or redeployment of resources to make these decisions effective.

Some aspects of such a pattern of decision may be in an established corporation unchanging over long periods of time, like a commitment to quality, or high technology, or certain raw materials, or good labour relations. Other aspects of a strategy must change as or before the world changes, such as product line, manufacturing process or merchandising and styling practices. The basic determinants of company character, if purposefully institutionalized, are likely to persist through and shape the nature of substantial changes in product-market choices and allocation of resources ...'

WHAT IS STRATEGIC MANAGEMENT?

Strategic management is concerned with the character and direction of the enterprise *as a whole*. It is concerned with basic decisions about what the enterprise is *now*, and what it is to be in the *future*. It determines the *purpose* of the enterprise. It provides the framework for decisions about people, leadership, customers or clients, risk, finance, resources, products, systems, technologies, location, competition, and time. It determines what the enterprise should be capable of achieving, and what it will not choose to do. It will determine whether and how the organization will add value, and what form that added value should take.

Strategic management is also concerned with management planning and decision-making for the medium to long-term future. It is concerned with the anticipation of that future, and with the establishment of a vision or view of how the enterprise should develop into the future that it must face.

Missions, Objectives and Strategies

The process of strategic management is used to establish missions, objectives, and strategies for the organization. Statements of *mission* specify what the enterprise is about, what its values are, and what its purpose is to be. The mission of the Walt Disney Company is for example to develop global entertainments that "bring happiness to millions". *Objectives* are statements of the major goals that the organization is aiming to achieve. Objectives specify or quantify the targets towards which leadership, effort, investment, and willpower are to be directed. Objectives might for instance be specified in terms of market share, profitability, the number of new products developed, the cost of government services, or the number of patients treated. *Strategies* are the means or the "game-plan" by which enterprise mission is put into practice, and objectives achieved. For instance, a manufacturing company might wish to compete on the basis of making available very high quality and reliable products sold under a strongly promoted brand name such as Mercedes-Benz, Hewlett-Packard, Orange, or Cadbury. Others might choose to compete by making products or services available at the lowest possible price, which means that they are going to have to keep their costs down to a minimum. A hospital or healthcare system might instead be based on public funds and state provision (as in the UK), or it might be based on market competition between private healthcare companies (as in the USA).

The identification of mission, objectives, and strategy depend on understanding the basic nature and purpose of the enterprise. The process of strategic management and business planning therefore requires us to understand *what business we are in.*

WHAT BUSINESS ARE WE IN?

In a classic work on the fundamentals of strategic management, Theodore Levitt (1960) argued that it was essential for any organization to base its strategic decision-making on a clear understanding of what business it is in. Levitt suggested that this understanding must be based on the view or voice of the *customer or client*, rather than on an inward-looking or "production-oriented" view of the purpose of the enterprise. How does the customer perceive the enterprise, its products, or its services? What *benefits* or *values* does the enterprise provide the customer, and how does it fit into the client's scheme of things?

For instance, strategic decisions about missions and objectives could be described as follows:

- *Nike shoes* - is Nike merely a supplier of specialized footwear? Or does it instead sell image and prestige to brand and fashion-conscious buyers?
- *healthcare* - does a healthcare system cure people who have become ill or need surgery? Or is it instead concerned with the health of the nation as a whole, and should it aim to prevent sickness and disease occurring in the first place?
- *Marks and Spencer UK food halls* - Marks and Spencer plc sells high quality convenience foodstuffs in its UK food halls. Many of these food halls are situated in city centres. Is Marks and Spencer simply selling food? Or is it selling convenience to busy working people who are short of time?

Think about the following examples. What businesses are these organizations in?

- Orange or Vodaphone cellular telecom.
- Coca Cola or Pepsi Cola.
- if you are a student, the college or university where you are studying.
- DaimlerChrysler automotive.
- breakfast cereal manufacturers.
- toothpaste manufacturers.
- the builder of a new house or apartment on an executive housing estate or property development.
- your local soccer or football club (whatever the rules!).

❑ Heathrow or Schiphol airport (or another large airport near where you live, such as JFK New York, Paris CDG, Frankfurt, Singapore, Hong Kong, or Chicago O'Hare).

THE STRATEGIC MANAGEMENT PROCESS

The concept of strategic management is illustrated in Figure 1.1. It has *four component processes*. These are:

❑ strategic analysis and planning.
❑ strategy formulation and strategic decision-making.
❑ strategic choice.
❑ strategy implementation.

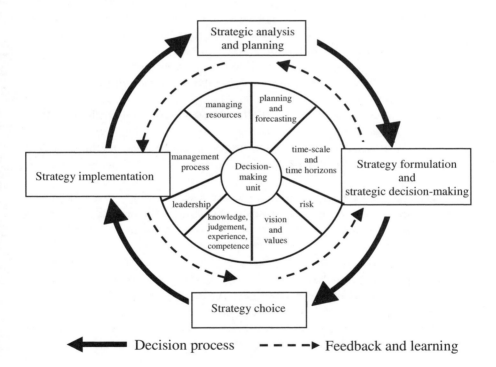

Figure 1.1 The Strategic Management Process

Strategic Analysis and Planning

Strategic analysis is a process by which the enterprise examines its own internal or corporate characteristics and capabilities; and identifies the most important features of the external environment within which it must operate. The process is used to identify and understand such variables as:

❑ the internal operational and financial strengths and weaknesses of the organization.
❑ the external or environmental constraints, opportunities, and threats facing the enterprise.
❑ the competitive environment within which the enterprise must operate.
❑ the political and institutional environments within which the enterprise must operate.
❑ the nature of the resources, capacity, leadership, willpower, and capability that the enterprise possesses, or that are needed so that the enterprise may be able to achieve its objectives (that is, "what the organization must be able to do").
❑ the sources of value addition available to the enterprise.
❑ enterprise sources of comparative or competitive advantage.
❑ enterprise sources of political advantage.
❑ factors which are critical to enterprise survival and success ("critical success factors").
❑ factors which instead will place limits or constraints on the potential achievements of the enterprise.

Strategic analysis is used to inform the processes of strategy formulation, strategic decision-making, and strategic choice described in a later section of this chapter. Strategic analysis is described in detail in Part One of this book.

The *planning process* may variously be described in such terms as "strategic planning" or "business planning". The difference between these two terms is a matter of degree. Both are concerned with how the enterprise proposes to map out and to manage its necessary engagement with, or involvement in the future time horizons to which it is committed. The planning process is described in this book on the basis of the following variables:

❑ the analysis of time.
❑ the analysis of risk.
❑ the analysis of forecasting processes.

❑   the description of the business planning process.

The planning process is used to inform and to structure the processes of strategy formulation, strategic decision-making, strategic choice, and strategy implementation.

The planning process is described in Part Two of this book. Part Two also includes an analysis of *crisis management*. The inclusion of this new chapter reflects the contemporary need for organizations, irrespective of the sector in which they operate, to be prepared for the occurrence of extreme events or damaging conditions caused by severe and direct external threat to the enterprise and to its people.

Strategy Formulation and Strategic Decision-Making

Processes of strategy formulation and strategic decision-making are used to establish enterprise mission, objectives, and strategy. Mission, objectives, and strategy will derive from the *vision* and *values* of the enterprise, of its leaders, of its decision-makers, and of its stakeholders. The enterprise will have to decide how to formulate its strategies and plans; to decide who is to be involved in this process; and to decide how to make decisions about the allocation of finance and resources that are required to put these strategies and plans into operation. Decision-makers will have to know how to identify and describe the alternative courses of action that are likely to be available to the enterprise, given the findings of the process of strategic analysis and business planning described in Parts One and Two. They will also have to put in place criteria by which to judge whether these alternative courses of action are feasible and appropriate, and whether they can afford to put them into practice.

Strategy formulation and strategic decision-making are analyzed in Part Three of this book.

Strategy Choice '

The process of strategy choice is used to identify the alternative courses of action that, given its available resources, its capability, its willpower, and its sources of comparative or competitive advantage, are likely to be available to the enterprise (i) over the time scale and time horizon to which it operates; and given (ii) its attitude to risk.

For example, should the enterprise remain a national supplier, or should it go international? Should it aim to achieve a large market share? Should it make very high quality products? Should it aim for high margins or does it want to be a low-cost supplier? How long will it be able to wait before its investment projects pay for themselves? Can it think long term, for instance in the matter of research and development, skills development, or new product development? Must it meet demands from its shareholders for a consistent and substantial annual flow of dividends? Is it required by the state to meet targets for performance in the provision of healthcare or public services? Or does the organization have to catch and convict terrorists, and how is it to do so?

Decision-makers will have to select those strategies from the alternatives they have identified that they consider will best or most effectively enable the enterprise to fulfil the mission and achieve the objectives it has formulated for itself (or which have instead been laid down for it). This decision will require skill and judgement. It will entail the risk that decision-makers may make the wrong choice, or make decisions that take the enterprise in directions for which it is not prepared. Decision-makers will have to think through the resource allocation implications of their strategic choice. Can the enterprise afford to do what is being proposed? Has the organization got the right people, the right leaders, the right skills, and the right assets? And what kind of market, financial, or political returns will decisions on strategic choice bring?

Strategy choice is analyzed in Part Four of this book.

Strategy Implementation

The process of putting the enterprise's chosen strategies and plans into practice takes place within the internal context and constraints of the people, the leadership, the structure, the resources, the capability, and the culture of the organization. Strategy implementation also takes place within the context and constraints of the external, political, and competitive environments. The implementation of strategic choice will in addition take place within the context of those people and organizations external to the enterprise but with whom it has any form of operational, partnership, supply or trading relationship.

Strategy implementation will depend on the nature of the knowledge, technology, and competence resources available to the enterprise. It will also depend specifically on the nature of decisions about financial and competition strategy. The implementation of strategies will be constrained by the need to make the best use of the available resources, to meet financial obligations, and to ensure survival in the face of the increasingly harsh demands of (i) competitive international trading environments; or (ii) performance-orientated public sector decision-makers.

Strategy implementation is analyzed within Part Four of this book. Reference to implementation issues is also made in Parts One, Two, and Three where this reference is appropriate, and will develop or reinforce the reader's understanding of the principles being described.

The Four Components of the Strategic Management Process

The four elements of the approach to the study and practice of strategic management and business planning described in this book are *inter-related and inter-acting*. Each informs and influences the other, for instance through the processes of *communication, feedback, learning,* and the accumulation by individuals and organizations of *knowledge, judgement, experience,* and *competence*.

At the same time, decisions about strategic choice cannot be taken without careful thought as to their implementation. Strategies or plans that cannot with any degree of certainty be implemented, or for which the necessary finance or resources are unavailable, are not realistically likely to be selected. Strategic choice must be feasible as well as appropriate to the requirements of the situation.

REVIEW QUESTION

Describe the strategic management approach to the study and practice of strategy and planning. What are its components? Why are they inter-related and inter-acting?

References

Andrews, K.R. (1980) *The Concept of Corporate Strategy*, Irwin, Homewood, Illinois.
Levitt, T. (1960) 'Marketing myopia', *Harvard Business Review*, July-August.

PART ONE

CONCEPTS AND TECHNIQUES OF STRATEGIC ANALYSIS

Part One of this book deals with the process of strategic analysis. Part One contains two interrelated issues for study.

The first issue is the appraisal of the internal circumstances and resources of the enterprise, its capability (what it can do), its ability to generate value, and its sources of comparative or competitive advantage.

The second issue is the summary analysis of the relevant external environments and competitive contexts within which the organization operates.

Part One contains the following chapters:

Chapter 2

Corporate Appraisal

This chapter looks at the analysis of the internal strengths and weaknesses of the organization as a part of the strategic analysis process of "corporate appraisal". It outlines some of the criteria by which corporate strengths and weaknesses may be identified and explained. It describes techniques of performance gap analysis and Management By Wandering Around (MBWA). The chapter concludes by commenting on the use of corporate appraisal techniques within the wider processes of strategic decision-making and strategic choice.

CORPORATE APPRAISAL

An initial requirement of the process of strategic analysis is the *appraisal and analysis of the condition in which the enterprise currently finds itself*. For instance, does the enterprise have *internal strengths* upon which it can base its choice of strategies; and thereby better serve its customers, clients, or patients; or alternatively gain competitive advantage in its markets? Is it in a strong operational position? Or does it instead have *internal weaknesses* which may place it at a disadvantage, and which it may have to remedy before it can make decisions on its choice of strategy? Are there *gaps in performance* between what it would like to achieve, and what it is actually achieving at present?

The process of corporate appraisal requires enterprise management to maintain and update its knowledge (or "diagnosis") of the internal position and condition of the organization. This process has a number of components. Some of these are described in this chapter. The parallel process of *financial appraisal* is dealt with in Chapter 3.

ANALYSING CORPORATE STRENGTHS AND WEAKNESSES

It may be useful to start the process of corporate appraisal by analyzing corporate strengths and weaknesses. These can be used as criteria by which to make basic judgements about the position and condition of the organization.

The identification of corporate strengths and weaknesses is a part of the "SWOT" technique for company appraisal (and case study analysis). The acronym "SWOT" stands for Strengths, Weaknesses, Opportunities, Threats. Corporate strengths and weaknesses are dealt with in this chapter. Financial strengths and weaknesses are analyzed in Chapter 3. Opportunities and threats are discussed in Chapter 6.

An Example of a Corporate Strength

The Air Products, Linde and British Oxygen companies both maintain strong competitive positions through their international reputations as a leaders in technologies associated with cryogenics (the science of cold), industrial and medical gases, and the application of advanced physics. Their competitive strength lies in the ability to develop and apply high-technology science to their business activities.

An Example of Corporate Weakness

Some retail companies or small and medium sized enterprises ("SME's") choose to position a very specific or limited range of products on restricted "niche" markets. Such companies may be particularly vulnerable to conditions of trading recession or change in their market because they have nothing else to fall back on.

Some Criteria for Identifying Corporate Strengths and Weaknesses

Corporate strengths and weaknesses may be identified by *functional area*, or by *key issue*. Each is analyzed in turn.

Functional Area

Corporate strength and weakness criteria may be identified and analyzed on the basis of the main functional areas to be found in any business, service, healthcare, public or non-profit organization. For instance:

❑ *marketing* - variables may include market position and market share; reputation in the community; client or patient perceptions; status as market leader or follower; mix and depth of product or service portfolio; relative position on product life cycle; new product development capability; negotiating, sales and promotional competence. *Example:* Coca-Cola's strong market position in the soft drinks sector.

❑ *financial* - variables may include relative profitability; return on capital employed (ROCE); earnings per share (EPS); cash flow; relative efficiency of use of assets; margin of safety; financial structure (ownership, mix of equity and loan capital); financial management skills and competences. *Example:* the potential financial performance of a well-established, well-located, and well-managed hotel whose popularity and positive reputation may generate a significant degree of both profitability and cash flow from its high occupancy rate.

❑ *operational* - variables may include the type, location, age, and productivity of operational assets; operational flexibility; success rates in treating patients; capacity for rapid response or just-in-time (JIT) requirements; quality and reliability of output; relationship with suppliers; cost-effectiveness; type and use of information and communication technology (ICT) or management information systems (MIS). *Example:* Toyota's "lean" manufacturing process.

❑ *technology* - variables may include the type and complexity of technology; ability to manage changing technology; degree to which technological competencies offer efficiency gains or competitive advantage; need for continuing investment in innovation, research and development (R&D), and new product development (NPD). *Examples:* 3M's ability continuously to develop new technologies and new products; Boeing's development of the "7" range of aircraft (707, 727, 737, 747, 757, 767, and 777); ongoing developments in surgical and drug treatments.

❑ *human resources* - variables may include employee type, competence, quality and productivity; ease of recruitment and retention; staff skill and flexibility; staff education, training and experience; staff attitude and culture; expectations; employee relations history and attitude to management; degree of customer service orientation; capacity for response, change and creativity; cost-effectiveness (etc). *Example:* Virgin Atlantic airline cabin crew's high degree of customer orientation and customer service provision.

❑ *processes and systems* - variables may include the type and complexity of processes and systems; flexibility and speed of operation; capacity for parallel processing (doing several things at the same time); service capabilities and cost-effectiveness; external networks and dependencies; information and communication technology features. *Examples:* "lean" or "just-in-time" manufacturing processes; internet or telephone based banking systems; reduced cycle times.

❑ *leadership and management* - variables may include the depth of leadership experience and management skill; quality of management training and development; degree of service and customer orientation; attitude towards innovation and change; appropriateness and effectiveness of management style and culture; capacity for knowledge and technology management; cross-cultural capability. *Examples:* the benchmark quality of management at such companies as the General Electric (GE) Corporation, British Petroleum, Unilever, Procter & Gamble, or the Sony Corporation.

Key Issue

The analysis of corporate strengths and weakness may also be based on key issues. Some examples are given below:

❑ can the organization *actually do what it wants to do* with the resources and assets available or accessible to it? The key issue of enterprise *capability* and *capacity* is dealt with in detail in Chapter 4.

❑ ownership structure and the processes of strategy formulation. Who owns the enterprise? Who makes the decisions? What do they want? These issues are dealt with in detail in Part Three of this book.

❑ the possession of special skills; and distinctive or core competences. Rolls Royce is, for example, known for making aircraft engines of a very high quality and reliability.

❑ the character of the knowledge base. What does the enterprise know? Kodak and Canon for instance probably know more about imaging technology and the imaging business than anyone else.

❑ quality of entrepreneurship (or "intrapreneurship") within the organization. Are staff encouraged to do things in new ways, or to search for new lines of business? Or are they instead discouraged by senior managers from "thinking for themselves", and from being creative or innovative in their work?

❑ the quality and character of risk management. Can the enterprise manage the risk associated with its business? Does it take on risky projects from which it can learn or develop competitive advantage; or does it instead avoid such projects? For example, starting a new airline is considered highly risky. Richard Branson (successfully) decided to take the risk of establishing Virgin Atlantic even though he knew the new airline would have to compete with well-established and aggressive competitors like British Airways and American Airlines. The key issue of risk is dealt with in Chapter 8.

❑ the possession of specific unique selling propositions or product USPs. Daimler-Chrysler and BMW, for instance, have created ranges of prestige high-performance cars that have come to dominate the car markets of many countries.

❑ the offer of quality, reliability, service and value for money (QRSV). The reliability and value for money characteristics of for instance Seiko brand watches has put their manufacturer into a dominant global position in the watch market.

❑ operational scale or "critical mass". Operational viability is often dependent upon the achievement of a minimum operational size, for example for reasons of economies of scale; or a heavy burden of fixed, overhead, or research and development (R&D) cost. This is the case for instance in healthcare and the automotive sectors.

❑ the capacity to develop and manage international or global activities. Does the enterprise have the resources and the skills to operate on a global scale; and does it possess cross-cultural capabilities (that is, can people from different cultures work together to achieve company objectives)?

PERFORMANCE GAP ANALYSIS

A variety of types of appraisal information may be obtained from a corporate analysis of strengths and weaknesses, and also from the examination of the financial state of the organization that is the subject of Chapter 3. This information may be used *for the purpose of comparison*. It can be compared with:

❑ the current plans and objectives of the organization.
❑ the analysis of the performance, strengths, and weaknesses of comparable organizations as *benchmarks*.
❑ the future plans and intentions of the organization.

The process of comparison or "benchmarking" may lead to the identification of "gaps" between what was intended (or what was planned), and what actually happened. These are sometimes called *plan-performance gaps*. In the case of Figure 2.1, a performance gap is shown between the actual (lower) level of sales achieved by a company, and the planned (higher) level of sales called for by the company's market share objective. This gap may be quantified. It acts as a pointer towards the kind of strategies and actions that are required to "close the gap".

For example, UK universities have on a number of occasions suffered a reduction of the per capita funding they received from the state for each of the students they recruited. Each time this happened a gap opened up between the actual funding available and the revenue required to teach the students at a proper level of quality. The solution lay in increasing the numbers of students recruited, or increasing the cost of student fees, or seeking other forms of income such as research grants or consultancy. The additional revenue gained closed the gap between actual and required, such that each university could remain financially solvent.

The identification of performance gaps can also be used to evaluate the quality of the organization's forward strategic and business planning. The continuous discovery of performance gaps may indicate that unrealistic targets are being set, or that the assumptions upon which these targets are being based are incorrect. The gap will have revealed something about the organization's capacity for effective strategic planning and management, as much as about its operational performance.

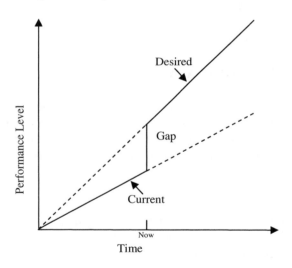

Figure 2.1 A Performance Gap

MANAGEMENT BY WANDERING AROUND (MBWA)

Any process of analysis and appraisal calls for an open mind. The people involved in the process of corporate appraisal may need to be prepared to consult, to listen, and to avoid making premature judgements. Management by wandering around, or MBWA may provide a structure for this process.

Under a system of MBWA, leaders, managers, and planners are involved in a process of listening and consultation. Policy and decision-makers, in particular, are required to hear comments and criticisms, to open their minds to both the internal and external environment, and for instance to hear what employees, customers and suppliers have to say.

The process of MBWA assumes that the organization operates within the framework of an *open system*. This means that the system will be "open" (or subject) to *external influences* from its environment, and from other people and other organizations.

The process of appraisal within a framework of MBWA may therefore be an uncomfortable one. Staff may say what they think. Comments will be made about other people's performance. Customers will criticize the efforts of the company. The mistakes of managers will become evident. Nevertheless, MBWA can be an effective route to the establishment of an honest and thorough appraisal.

THE USES OF CORPORATE APPRAISAL WITHIN STRATEGIC MANAGEMENT

The process of internal appraisal as described in this chapter analyzes:

❑ corporate strengths and weaknesses.
❑ performance gaps that have been identified.
❑ the openness of the organization and its staff to the appraisal process.

This process of corporate appraisal may then be used:

❑ to concentrate the choice of strategies in areas of corporate or resource strength.
❑ to select strategies that exploit, build upon, or develop corporate and resource strengths.
❑ to select strategies that address, remedy, or minimize the potential impact of corporate weaknesses which would otherwise place the enterprise at a disadvantage within its market or its environment.

TECHNIQUES OF CASE STUDY AND ANALYSIS

1. Identify corporate strengths of the case organization and analyze their implications.
2. Identify corporate weaknesses of the case organization and analyze their implications.
3. Identify performance gaps (if any are evident) and analyze their implications.

PROJECT ASSIGNMENT

Part One Project Assignment - The Strategic Analysis of a Company or Organization

Component One: Using available information carry out an analysis of the strengths, and also of the weaknesses or performance gaps (if any) of an organization that is of interest to you.

Chapter 3

Financial Appraisal

Finance is a key resource of any organization. The availability of finance underpins the operational capability of the enterprise. A second key requirement of the process of strategic analysis is therefore the appraisal of the financial condition in which the enterprise currently finds itself. This chapter summarizes some of the criteria by which the process of financial appraisal may be carried out. It also analyzes and illustrates the concept of zero based budgeting.

The chapter concludes by commenting on the use of financial appraisal techniques within the wider processes of strategic decision-making and strategic choice.

FINANCE AS A KEY RESOURCE AND CAPABILITY

Finance is a key *resource* of any organization. Finance is rarely if ever unlimited. It may constitute a *constraint* on, or a *limiting factor* for decision-making in the organization (the concepts of the "constraint" and the "limiting factor" are described in Chapter 4). *The enterprise can only do what its available financial resources (and the quality of its financial management) will permit it to do.*

Finance as a resource underpins the operational *capability* and *capacity* of the enterprise. That is, it may determine what the enterprise is able to afford to do, and is therefore able to achieve. This is because the available funds will determine what kind of assets and people the enterprise can afford to use, and therefore what kind of output it can produce. Wealthier football clubs for instance can afford to build bigger stadiums (which can hold more paying customers), and can pay the salaries of the best managers and the more expensive international players (who together should win more games for the club, win championships, and attract big crowds who will be prepared to pay higher entrance charges than anywhere else because they are seeing the best and most successful teams in the land).

The *financial performance* of the organization is crucial. *Financial performance means the financial results achieved by the enterprise*, for instance in terms of profitability, cash flow, budgetary and cost management, dividends paid (and so on). Financial performance is a *critical success factor* (the concept of the "critical success factor" is described in Chapter 4). It is for example a critical success factor from the viewpoint of the providers of finance. Investors will expect a proper return on their investment. Banks will require interest and the repayment of loans. Family members will depend for their livelihoods on the financial performance of a family business. The state will expect public agencies, schools, or hospitals to act as efficient stewards of the taxpayers' money they receive in order to meet their obligations.

The financial state of the enterprise (and the capability and capacity it represents) may be analyzed by the technique of the "financial health check".

THE FINANCIAL HEALTH CHECK

The financial health check is used (i) to analyze the financial condition of the organization, and (ii) to analyze the capability and capacity that this financial condition represents. It comprises:

❑   the analysis of published accounts and accounting ratios.
❑   the analysis of the margin of safety.

The financial health check is likely to be used to augment the process of internal corporate appraisal described in Chapter 2.

ANALYZING PUBLISHED ACCOUNTS AND ACCOUNTING RATIOS

Where the financial accounts of a business are available in the public domain, the process of financial appraisal may be based upon the analysis of *accounting ratios*. These ratios can be categorized under a number of appraisal headings, as follows.

Performance, Profitability and Asset Utilization

The analysis of financial data under this heading is used to show how well a business is being run. Key ratios include:

$$\text{Profit margin} = \frac{\text{Net profit before interest and tax}}{\text{Sales}}$$

$$\text{Return on capital employed (ROCE)} = \frac{\text{Net profit before interest and tax}}{\text{Capital employed}}$$

$$\text{Return on net assets (RONA)} = \frac{\text{Net profit before interest and tax}}{\text{Net assets}}$$

$$\text{Return on equity (ROE) } or \text{ Return on shareholder capital (ROSC)} = \frac{\text{Net profit after interest and tax}}{\text{Shareholders' capital}}$$

$$\text{Profit per employee} = \frac{\text{Net profit before interest and tax}}{\text{Total number of employees}}$$

$$\text{Asset turnover} = \frac{\text{Sales}}{\text{Net assets}}$$

$$\text{Stock turnover} = \frac{\text{Sales}}{\text{Stock}}$$

$$\text{Debtor turnover} = \frac{\text{Sales}}{\text{Debtors}}$$

$$\text{Average collection period} = \frac{\text{Debtors}}{\text{Average daily sales}}$$

$$\text{Effectiveness of administration} = \frac{\text{Cost of administration}}{\text{Sales}}$$

These ratios indicate the level of return being generated by the assets and people being employed by the organization. They show how fixed assets are used to generate profit, and how working capital is used in the process of generating sales and cash flow. They also show the speed and efficiency with which the business completes its transactions with customers.

Solvency and Liquidity

Indicators of solvency and liquidity are vital to the process of financial appraisal. These indicators show whether the enterprise can pay its suppliers (creditors) for goods and services received. They show whether it is in a position to pay interest on loan finance, or to repay loan capital. They show whether it has adequate working capital upon which to base its current or planned level of business activity. And they indicate whether the enterprise is generating its own funds for investment and business development.

The appraisal process under this heading will also be used to identify management actions that may overstretch the organization's finances and lead it into conditions of "overtrading". Overtrading means trying to operate a level of business activity that exceeds the financial capacity of the organization to operate that business. Any business or service organization must ensure that it has adequate cash resources by which to pay its way, and a proper cash flow on which to base its operations.

Two critical accounting ratios are used to indicate the degree to which the enterprise can finance its operations and pay its debts. These are the:

$$\text{Current ratio} \quad = \quad \frac{\text{Current assets}}{\text{Current liabilities}}$$

$$\text{Acid test} \quad = \quad \frac{\text{Liquid assets (cash + debtors)}}{\text{Current liabilities}}$$

Where the acid test indicates that liquid assets do not cover the cash debts implicit in the figures for current liabilities, the appraisal process should seek some kind of compensating factor, such as a high level of cash sales (as in retailing or the fast moving consumer goods sectors). Otherwise, the appraisal process may have to look very closely at the organization in case there is any risk of insolvency.

Ownership, Capital Structure and Debt Management

Published accounts are required to show information about capital structure, which comprises the various sources of finance used in a business. Funds may come from shareholders, institutional investors or trusts, banks, or the state. The process of corporate appraisal examines the relative importance of, or balance between these different sources, and how the expectations of their providers can be met.

$$\text{Gearing ratio} \quad = \quad \frac{\text{Short + long term debt ('borrowings')}}{\text{Capital employed}}$$

$$\text{Long term debt ratio} \quad = \quad \frac{\text{Long term debt}}{\text{Capital employed}}$$

The analysis of ownership and debt management is an important element of the appraisal process. Shareholders will expect dividends and capital growth. The use of debt and credit entails fixed obligations. Interest must be paid. Debt must be repaid.

Companies borrow money at a given interest rate and invest it in their business. They hope that it will yield a return greater than the cost of the interest. This process may "gear up" or "leverage" the business activity. It *may* increase the return to shareholders if a positive differential between the cost and the return results from the investment.

This form of financing, however, contains significant risk. The process can go into reverse. A combination of high or increasing interest rates, declining returns from the business activity, and recession may lower returns to shareholders. This may have the effect of lowering share valuations as well as dividends. And the greater the debt burden, the less the profit there is to distribute to shareholders in the form of dividends, and the less attractive the shares become to investors. A downward spiral or "vicious circle" may be the result, leading to the loss of confidence or potential for hostile acquisition or takeover described in a later chapter.

The working of this vicious circle was brutally illustrated in the UK and USA in the late 1980s and early 1990s when companies became too highly geared. They had become dangerously over-dependent on large sums of debt finance at a time of high interest rates, deep recession, and emerging global competition.

Stock Market Requirements

Stock Market assessment of a company's trading performance will be based on an interpretation of the trends over time of the following ratios:

$$\text{Earnings per share (EPS)} = \frac{\text{Profit after tax}}{\text{Number of ordinary shares issued}}$$

$$\text{Price / earnings ratio (PE)} = \frac{\text{Market price per share}}{\text{Earnings per share}}$$

$$\text{Dividend yield} = \frac{\text{Dividend per share}}{\text{Market price per share}}$$

$$\text{Dividend payout} = \frac{\text{Dividends paid}}{\text{Profit after tax}}$$

Analysis of these four ratios is used, among other things, to indicate:

❑ stock market evaluation and acceptance of the company as an investment.
❑ the relationship between earnings retained in the business, and dividends paid to investors.
❑ the degree to which retained earnings are being used to provide funds by which to finance the business. A low payout from a healthy firm may indicate that earnings are being reinvested for growth, or that the business wishes to minimize its dependence on other sources of capital.

Cover

The analysis of cover deals with the adequacy of the margin of profit over and above a required rate of dividend payment, or the ability to pay interest on loan finance, thus:

$$\text{Dividend cover} = \frac{\text{Earnings per share}}{\text{Dividend per share}}$$

$$\text{Interest cover} = \frac{\text{Profit before interest and tax}}{\text{Loan interest}}$$

In this case, the appraisal process looks at the capacity of the organization to meet its immediate commitments to shareholders and lenders.

The analysis of cover is also extended to the capacity of the organization to repay the capital of the loan by the due date. Similarly, banks and institutional investors are interested in the value of the assets against which a loan may be secured. This is a particular issue for the small to medium sized enterprise (the SME), the private company, or for the riskier venture.

Financial Strength and Capability

The financial appraisal of the organization may reveal something about the strength of its financial capability and capacity. For instance, it may indicate the degree to which it already possesses funds for use in the business; or is instead likely to be able to obtain new monies, from whichever source. It may indicate how easy (or otherwise) it would be to obtain these additional funds. The analysis of financial strength may therefore demonstrate such features of capability and capacity as:

❑ the feasibility of growth or development strategies, since the availability of finance is essential to their implementation.
❑ the capacity of the organization to self-finance itself, without the need for additional share issues or external borrowing, whilst at the same time meeting shareholder dividend expectations, debt service commitments (etc).

Trends, Growth Rates, and Comparisons

The use of published accounting information and ratio calculations is likely to be most effective when taken over a number of years. The analysis of a series of ratios will reveal *trends over time*. These trends will show whether the company is growing, stagnating, or declining. They may confirm the existence of the strengths or weaknesses described in Chapter 2. They might instead hint that the company is ripe for hostile acquisition or takeover.

Similarly, the use of accounting ratios as a tool of corporate appraisal may be at its most effective where comparisons can be made with other organizations in the same operational or industry sector. These comparisons are used as *benchmarks* by which to evaluate current levels of performance. Interfirm or inter-organization comparisons are for instance available on commercially available databases, from "benchmarking clubs" or benchmarking groups, or from subscription services such as PIMS (the *Profit Impact of Market Share* database described in a later chapter).

Different Appraisal Viewpoints

The interpretation placed upon published financial information, accounting ratios, trends, and interfirm or benchmarking comparisons may depend on the particular viewpoint of the person carrying out the appraisal. For instance:

❑ *the investor* may focus on trends in annual or short-term performance and profitability, share and asset valuation, cash flow, and growth potential.
❑ *the supplier* as creditor is interested in short-term cash flow, the ability to pay debts, long term enterprise viability, and evidence of the systematic avoidance of conditions of overtrading.
❑ *the potential acquirer* monitors trends in relative performance, efficiency and profitability (for instance against industry benchmarks), potential for growth and efficiency gains, and share valuation (especially if the present stock market valuation is perceived to be too high or too low). So-called "asset strippers" or "corporate raiders" will instead be looking for undervalued assets whose real value they think they can realise at a profit if they can acquire them.
❑ *management and employees* are concerned with short and long-term viability and performance, with comparisons with competitors and benchmark companies in the sector, and with the potential for unwelcome or hostile takeover bids.
❑ *the state* will be concerned with the effectiveness and efficiency with which public sector organizations use the financial resources that they have been allocated, relative to the objectives set. In recent years in the UK this has meant a requirement to demonstrate the achievement of "Best Value" performance against pre-established service targets, performance benchmarks, and Performance Indicators ("PI's"). It has also meant adapting to rigorous government policies of the "resource stretch and leverage" process described in Chapter 21.

Published accounting data and ratio calculations are variously used as an appraisal guide, to identify issues, and to provoke questions. They augment and enhance the picture of the organization being built up as the process of corporate appraisal takes shape.

The role of accounting data in identifying the potential for *corporate failure* is analyzed in more detail in Chapter 13.

ANALYZING THE MARGIN OF SAFETY

Margin of safety calculations may be an important part of the *internal* appraisal of the enterprise. Data on a company's margin of safety is normally never made available on an external basis.

Margin of safety calculations are based on the use of *contribution accounting*. "Contribution" is calculated within management accounting as:

$$\text{Contribution} \quad = \quad (\text{Sales revenue - variable cost})$$

Contribution accounting allows the enterprise to calculate *break-even* values, whether by *sales value*, where:

$$\text{Break-even} \quad = \quad \text{Fixed cost} \quad x \quad \frac{\text{Sales}}{\text{Contribution}}$$

or by *sales volume*, where:

$$\text{Break-even} \quad = \quad \frac{\text{Fixed cost}}{\text{Contribution per unit}}$$

Where these break-even calculations are available per product or product line, the margin of safety (M/S) can be calculated. This is:

$$\text{M/S} \quad = \quad \frac{\text{Actual sales - Sales at break-even point}}{\text{Actual sales}} \times \frac{100}{1}$$

The margin of safety is represented by the level of sales in excess of the break-even point. For instance, the Elliott Company sells 1000 widgets per month but has calculated its widget break-even point at 600 per month. It therefore presently enjoys a margin of safety of 40 per cent, thus:

$$\text{M/S} \quad = \quad \frac{1000 \text{ units - 600 units}}{1000 \text{ units}} \times \frac{100}{1} \quad = 40\%$$

The appraisal value of the margin of safety calculations stems from knowing that *the greater the margin of safety, the less the company is vulnerable to a decline in sales of that product or product line*. In the case given above, the Elliott Company can withstand a 40 per cent drop in sales and still achieve break-even. The reverse is also true. The smaller the margin of safety, the more the company is vulnerable to a decline in sales and the closer it is pushed towards its break-even point. Two implications follow from this reasoning. These are that:

❑ the company needs to monitor the gap between actual and break-even sales on a continuing basis. Performance gap analysis was described in Chapter 2.
❑ it may need to control (or to reduce) its fixed cost burden so as to keep its break-even point as low as possible.

The operation of assets such as hotels and commercial passenger aircraft are for instance particularly sensitive to margin of safety calculations. These assets represent a high fixed cost and need a certain minimum level of occupancy in order to break even. Once they are (say) 70 percent full then virtually every unit of extra revenue represents contribution to profit. Variable costs per customer are marginal; most of the costs are fixed irrespective of volume. The hotel or aircraft costs a certain amount of money to operate whether or not it is full.

The analysis of margin of safety calculations is also of importance where information technology-based systems of *direct product profitability analysis* and *customer profitability analysis* are in use. These systems facilitate the close or "real-time" monitoring of sales to customers of individual products or product lines. They for instance permit the frequent adjustment or fine-tuning of distributor or retailer stockholding levels and inventory. Such systems can as a result produce erratic and unpredictable movements in channel purchasing and manufacturing volume patterns. They can erode the profit buffer represented by the margin of safety.

Given the uncertainty and requirement for flexibility implied by these systems, and their widespread use, the appraisal process may focus on the degree to which the enterprise (and in particular a supplier) pursues strategies which have the effect of maximizing its margin of safety, minimizing its fixed cost burden, and minimizing its break-even points.

ZERO BASED BUDGETING (ZBB)

Zero based budgeting (ZBB) is a formalized system for reviewing the process of setting budgets for the activities of an organization. *Zero based budgeting examines each activity as if it were being performed for the first time, that is from a "zero base".* A number of alternative levels of provision for each activity are identified, costed, and evaluated in terms of the benefits to be obtained from them. Zero based budgeting is sometimes also called "priority-based budgeting".

ZBB may be used within the appraisal process because it is based on the belief *that management should be required to justify existing activities and existing resource allocations* in exactly the same way as new proposals. The appraisal process will compare established activities with alternative potential applications of the resources that are to be committed during the planning period in view. Implicit in ZBB, therefore, are the concepts of:

❑ *opportunity cost* - how may the available resources now best be used?
❑ *priority* - do past and current commitments of resources reflect or match present strategic priorities?

Business organizations and public sector institutions normally use *incremental budgeting* over time. Budgetary planning is based on current or immediate past practice. Existing budgets are updated for the planning period ahead by applying expected price, volume, inflation or operational changes. The main justification for next year's expenditure is last year's expenditure. The fact of the allocation of resources to the activity is taken for granted. It is assumed that the activity will continue its right to a claim on resource allocation because it is already there.

The use of ZBB within the process of corporate appraisal challenges these assumptions. It can be used to question the implied right of existing activities to receive a continuing allocation of resources. It may be used to ask such questions as:

❑ what are the current objectives of the activity being appraised?
❑ to what extent are these objectives being achieved, and how relevant are they now to today's circumstances?
❑ is the activity now really necessary?
❑ is there now an alternative way of achieving the same objective, for instance by re-engineering or outsourcing the processes involved in it?
❑ are any of the alternatives more cost-effective?
❑ what would be the consequences (in terms of costs and benefits) if the activity were now to be discontinued?

Implementing ZBB

The organization and its departments must be divided into identifiable and manageable locations of activity, for which costs can clearly be identified and allocated, operating benefits and results described, and meaningful comparisons made.

An analysis of costs, results, and benefits is then undertaken for each identified sphere of activity. This analysis is carried out *from a zero base*, on the assumption that no activity has an established right to command the use of resources. The process may call for the development of a series of alternatives for each decision area, based on the following:

- ❑ a description of the activity, function or department.
- ❑ a statement of the objectives of the activity.
- ❑ performance assessment and measurement criteria for the activity.
- ❑ the alternative methods and costs of performing the activity.
- ❑ the potential results and benefits to be achieved at different levels of funding.
- ❑ the consequences of *not funding* the activity.

The effect of this process for corporate appraisal can be illustrated by an example. Assume that a railway network has four operating divisions. These are illustrated in Figure 3.1. Each division may be funded at any one of five levels, from "high" to "low". It can currently afford to spend a total of 14 units of resource. As Figure 3.1 shows, the priorities of this railway network are clearly concerned with "track and signalling" and "intercity" passenger.

The use of ZBB in the process of corporate appraisal can however, in this case, focus management attention on the consequences of:

- ❑ an upward shift in the gross available resource level, say from 14 to 17.
- ❑ desired changes in the priority of resource allocation within the total service provision, say towards "intercity freight", given a static level of resource availability (that is, 14 units).
- ❑ new priorities, such as customer demand for new electrification schemes or urban rapid transit systems, neither of which are allowed for in the current budget allocation.

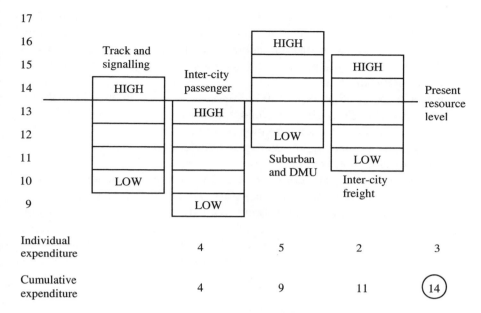

Figure 3.1 Implementing ZBB

The use of ZBB within the appraisal process can therefore be used to clarify the consequences of decisions on funding, whether current or planned. It forces the organization to review the basic reasons underlying what it is currently doing; to confront the consequences of continuing as it is; or to make changes to its priorities.

THE USES OF FINANCIAL APPRAISAL WITHIN STRATEGIC MANAGEMENT

The process of financial appraisal as described in this chapter analyzes:

- the financial state and health of the enterprise.
- financial capability and capacity (what the enterprise can afford to do).
- financial strengths and weaknesses.
- performance gaps.
- the application of the zero base concept.

This process of corporate appraisal may then be used to:

❏ concentrate the choice of strategies in areas of financial capability and strength. *Example:* the exploitation of high margins of safety and low break-even points in markets subject to wide or cyclical variations in demand and profitability, such as those for capital equipment or building construction.

❏ select strategies that exploit, build upon or develop financial capability and strength. *Example:* the trend for companies to re-purchase their shares in order to reduce commitments to paying dividends and to offer the smaller number of remaining shareholders a better return, thereby boosting shareholder value.

❏ select strategies that address or remedy financial weaknesses which would otherwise place the enterprise at a disadvantage. *Examples:* taking steps to improve cash flow; reducing costs; increasing company profitability; lowering the level of corporate indebtedness by reducing long-term borrowing; seeking Best Value performance enhancements that will offset the need for a local government authority to seek higher local taxes.

TECHNIQUES OF CASE STUDY AND ANALYSIS

Where the appropriate information is available in the case study:

1. Identify the financial capacity of the case organization. What is the enterprise financially capable of achieving? What are its financial limitations?
2. Analyze the financial condition of the case company. For instance:-
3. Identify financial strengths and analyze their implications.
4. Identify financial weaknesses and analyze their implications.
5. Identify gaps in financial performance and analyze their implications.

PROJECT ASSIGNMENT

Part One Project Assignment - The Strategic Analysis of a Company or Organization

Component Two: Using available information carry out an analysis of the financial capability, financial strengths, financial weaknesses, financial performance, and financial performance gaps (if any) of an organization that is of interest to you.

References

Brealey, R.A. and S.C. Myers (1996) *Principles of Corporate Finance*, McGraw-Hill, London.

Morden, A.R. (1986) 'Zero-base budgeting: a potential revisited', *Management Accounting*, October.

Sizer, J. (1989) *An Insight into Management Accounting*, Penguin, London.

Thomas, A. (1996) *Introduction to Financial Accounting*, McGraw-Hill, London.

Chapter 4

Sources of Competitive or Comparative Advantage, Resource Management, Capability, Value Generation, and Critical Success Factors

'The word "impossible" is not in my dictionary'.
Napoleon Bonaparte

This chapter develops from, and broadens the description of the process of corporate appraisal and financial appraisal described in Chapters 2 and 3. It defines competitive or comparative advantage. It describes and analyzes some of the key sources of competitive or comparative advantage available to the enterprise. It deals with the issue of capability; and it analyzes the generation of value from the use of resources that this capability represents. The chapter then reviews features that are critical to the success of the enterprise; or instead act to constrain the choices available to it.

COMPETITIVE OR COMPARATIVE ADVANTAGE DEFINED

Competitive or comparative advantage is a concept which describes the degree of *relative advantage* possessed by an enterprise within its sector or markets as compared with other organizations with which it directly or indirectly competes; or with which its use of people, finance, and resources must be compared.

M.E. Porter (1985) comments that 'competitive advantage is at the heart of a firm's performance in competitive markets' (p. xv). He suggests that 'potential sources of competitive advantage are everywhere in a firm. Every department, facility, branch office, and other organizational unit has a role that must be defined and understood. All employees, regardless of their distance from the strategy formulation process, must recognize their role in helping a firm achieve and sustain competitive advantage' (pp. xvi-xvii).

USING CORPORATE APPRAISAL

The techniques of corporate and financial appraisal were described in Chapters 2 and 3. Enterprise management may for example use this process of appraisal to identify the relative, comparative, or competitive advantage that may be obtained from:

❑   the application and exploitation of enterprise strengths.
❑   the application and exploitation of financial strength and capability.
❑   identifying and exploiting the relative weaknesses of competitors, or instead those of benchmark comparators such as other hospitals, schools, or local government authorities.

At the same time, a decision *may* have to be made as to the degree to which *enterprise weaknesses* ought to be remedied or eliminated. This will depend on whether or not these internal weaknesses, such as an uncompetitive cost base, or an inadequate investment in new process or product development, can be exploited by competitors to gain an advantage. This decision will require careful judgement.

Kay (1993) comments that it may be more profitable to reinforce or to develop existing strengths, rather than to commit extensive resources to a significant process of eliminating anything but the most critical weaknesses. Existing strengths will be based on the possession of some particular *capability*, *capacity*, or *competence*. Weaknesses will reflect a lack of such capability. Kay suggests that the attempt to turn weaknesses into strengths may be disproportionately costly where the enterprise has to create new capabilities from the outset, or instead to purchase them at a premium (for instance by acquiring other companies). Kay's view is that the enterprise should as a priority concentrate instead on developing the capabilities and competences that underpin its areas of strength; and attempt to make these sources of competitive advantage sufficiently unique that competitors will be unable to copy them or to compete from the same position of strength. At the same time, it could *outsource* its strategic, operational, or functional areas of weakness to another organization to whom this activity is a *core competence*. The concepts of core competence and outsourcing are analyzed in this and later chapters.

RESOURCE MANAGEMENT AND THE RESOURCE BASE

The *resource base* of the enterprise comprises such factors as people (and their energy and skills), capital, facilities, and land. The resource base will in practical terms be represented by human assets and skill, leadership and management capability, cash and finance, brands, reputation, machinery and equipment, buildings, operational processes, information and communication systems, and so on. It will also be represented by the knowledge, experience, technology, competencies, and relationships described in detail in this and later chapters.

The use of this resource base should *generate some kind of value, or "added value"* for the enterprise and for its customers or clients. It may also be used to yield competitive or comparative advantage which can be exploited by the choice of strategy analyzed in a later part of this book. *The choice of strategy, and the nature of the asset and resource base that will be required to implement that strategy must therefore both be closely related.*

In any case, finance and resources are not unlimited. *The resource base of the enterprise therefore acts as both an opportunity and a constraint.* Strategic decisions will need to be based on the requirement to make the best possible use of the finance and resources available. This may mean:

❑ maximizing or optimizing the value generated or value added by the use of those resources in achieving enterprise objectives; *and*
❑ maximizing or optimizing the comparative or competitive advantage generated by the use of these resources in achieving enterprise objectives.

Resource use, and the concepts of resource "stretch" and resource "leverage" are analyzed in later chapters.

Strategic decisions about the choice of objective and strategy analyzed in later parts of this book need to be related to the character of the resource base, and to the *capability and capacity* that this resource base represents. Otherwise, decisions may be made that cannot be supported by the available resources, and cannot therefore be implemented without additional investments. Resource investment and financial return are analyzed in Chapter 13.

The character of the resource base will also determine the capability and capacity of the enterprise to which reference was made immediately above. The nature and character of the resource base will in consequence shape the potential value generation, comparative advantage, or competitive advantage that the use of this capability and capacity will yield.

CAPABILITY AND CAPACITY

If the organization operates in a competitive environment, or in one where the use of benchmarked comparators in the formulation of strategy is the norm, it must have some kind of relative advantage in order to survive in that environment.

This advantage might for example be based on an ability to do something better than competitors or comparators, or to do it at a lower cost than them. Or instead, the enterprise might add more value to its products or services. Customers or clients will get a better deal as they receive more value for their money or for their taxes. A business organization may generate more revenue or profit than its competitors, and is therefore a more attractive proposition to investors. A hospital may have a better or more cost-effective treatment record than another. Or a local or provincial government authority may deliver its statutory services more effectively and efficiently than others in its benchmark group.

All of this begs the question of capability. What can the enterprise do? What kind of people, leadership, assets, and resources does the organization have? What can these people, assets, and resources be used to achieve? Do they add value to the operations of the enterprise?

It is no use setting objectives that the organization has neither the resources nor the capability to achieve. Issues of capability, and the competitive or comparative advantage (if any) associated with it, are therefore crucial to the process of strategic management.

Enterprise value generation, and competitive or comparative advantage will therefore depend on the relative *capability* and *capacity* upon which the organization can draw. *Strategic decision-making depends on knowing what the organization is (or is not) capable of using its resources to achieve.* Some enterprises for example are capable of mass producing consumer goods to a very high and consistent quality. Their products rarely, if ever go wrong. The reputation for manufacturing reliability that firms such as Seiko or Toyota have built up is a key source of their competitive advantage. The capability and capacity of the organization is represented by:

❑ the character and productivity of its resource base and assets. Does it for instance have up-to-date equipment or the most modern technology?

❑ its leadership capability, and its organizational and managerial culture.

❑ the character of its knowledge base and knowledge management. Does it exploit its own knowledge (*what it knows*) to its own advantage?

❑ its operational capabilities or capacities, for instance to deliver the required *quality, reliability, customer service,* or *value for money* to its customers. For example, the US retailer Walmart is known world-wide for the value for money it offers to its customers. In the UK, Walmart-Asda's "George" clothing operation has become a market leader in mass value for money clothing retail.

❑ its management of the character of the technology changes or dynamics with which it will have to deal. Microprocessor technology, for instance, changes so rapidly that product life cycles may be of less than a year's duration for any particular model of computer or type of software.

❑ the potential or threat of obsolescence in either or both of its knowledge or technology base. Will its knowledge get out of date? Might its products or services become unsaleable?

❑ its experience. Has the enterprise got accumulated wisdom and experience that will give it an advantage relative to less experienced competitors?

❑ its "core competencies". Hamel and Prahalad (1990, 1994) suggest that core competencies are represented by the collective and accumulated learning and experience of the organization and its staff. An example is Boeing's ability to specify and design aircraft (such as the 747) which exactly meet the needs of its international airline customers. Core competencies include the co-ordination, integration, and management of technologies; the application and management of knowledge and experience; leadership, managerial, organizational and operational skills; the ability to use enabling or facilitating mechanisms; capacities to manage change and innovation; and the application of an accurate understanding of customers, markets and their potential; (etc). The core competence concept is analyzed in Chapters 20, 26, and 27 of this book.

VALUE GENERATION

The enterprise is concerned with the capabilities its chosen use of resources currently confer upon it. *What can it do and what can it achieve?* And in particular, it will be concerned with:

❑ *the value that this chosen use of resources adds to the final output created or produced* (which for instance contributes to the revenues and profit margins that can be gained by a business organization from the sale of these outputs in the market). For example, a pharmaceutical company that produces a popular drug (such as "Valium" or "Pro-Zac") that attains widespread acceptance as a medical treatment will have achieved an enormously valuable output from the use of its research, manufacturing and marketing resources. Its capability and resources will in such a case have generated a large amount of value for its customers and for its shareholders.

❑ how effective and efficient this use of resources is judged to be, in particular when compared with external benchmarks in its sector (such as the "best in class", "best in group", "market leader", or "world class"). Toyota for example is often taken as a benchmark by which other car manufacturers judge the effectiveness and productivity of their own operations.

❑ the relative or competitive advantage derived from its capabilities and use of resources, when compared with other organizations in its sector or market. For instance, in what ways can the enterprise create, perform or deliver its outputs *better* than its competitors or comparators (for example in terms of cost, quality, reliability, service, perceived or best value for money, innovation, differentiation, security, patient treatment outcomes, customer perceptions, etc).

❑ the *opportunity cost* of using these resources (relative to alternative available uses or investment of these resources). Could the resources be better invested elsewhere, and how?

❑ the future potential of the use of these resources. For example, in what ways may the capabilities of the enterprise be developed or expanded? Or instead, how may resources be redeployed, for instance by the use of the technique of zero based budgeting as described in Chapter 3; or by re-engineering processes; or by the use of the knowledge management described in a later chapter?

Porter states that 'competitive advantage grows fundamentally out of the value a firm is able to create for its customers' (p.xvi). He comments for instance that 'it may take the form of prices lower than competitors' for equivalent benefits, or the provision of unique benefits that more than offset a premium price' (p.xvi).

THE VALUE CHAIN

The process of :

❑ making, distributing and selling a product or service, or of providing medical treatment or a public service (etc); *and*
❑ the creation of value as a result of the market or supply transaction between the provider of the goods or service and the final customer or client

can be viewed as *a chain of related activities*. These activities require the investment or use of resources in order to create the capability needed to carry them out. They generate an increasing amount of value as the process is undertaken and the product or service moves towards its final exchange or consumption outcome. *This chain of related and value generating activities has become known as the "value chain"*. The value chain is a conceptual framework that may be used for the purposes of:

❑ classifying broad areas of the organization's activity; *and*
❑ analyzing the capability and capacity that the resources invested in these activities represent; *and*
❑ identifying the process of value generation or value addition outcome yielded by this capability and capacity.

The process represented by the value chain:

❑ can take place mainly within one organization (the "integrated", "aggregated" or "monolithic" value chain described in Chapter 18); *or*
❑ can take place across units or locations within any number of independent organizations acting as suppliers within a network or supply chain, as the process of creation of the goods or service moves towards its final exchange or consumption outcome (the "de-integrated" or "disaggregated" value chain described in Chapter 18).

The simplest representation of a business organization's value chain is the McKinsey Company "business system" which views the firm as a series of closely-linked groups of activity. This simplified business system is shown in Figure 4.1.

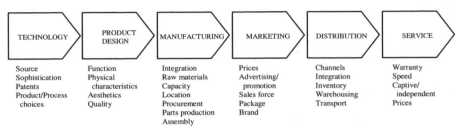

Figure 4.1 The McKinsey Company Business System

M.E. Porter instead describes a value chain which distinguishes between "primary activities" and "support activities" in a commercial organization, as shown in Figure 4.2.

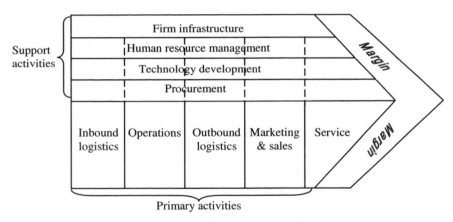

Figure 4.2 M.E. Porter's Value Chain

Porter (pp. 39-40) describes five value generating "primary activities" in his original manufacturing business value chain model to be:

❑ *inbound logistics* - activities associated with receiving, storing, and disseminating inputs to the product, such as materials handling, warehousing, inventory control, vehicle scheduling, and returns to suppliers.

❑ *operations* - activities associated with transforming inputs into the final product form, such as machining, packaging, assembly, equipment maintenance, testing, printing, and facility operations.

❑ *outbound logistics* - activities associated with collecting, storing, and physically distributing the product to buyers, such as finished goods warehousing, materials handling, delivery vehicle operation, order processing, and scheduling.

❑ *marketing and sales* - activities associated with providing a means by which buyers can purchase the product and inducing them to do so, such as advertizing, promotion, sales force, quoting, channel selection and distribution, channel relations, pricing, and retail.

❑ *service* - activities associated with providing service to enhance or to maintain the value of the product, such as installation, training, parts supply, product adjustment or repair.

Porter's value chain model describes these "primary activities" to be *underpinned* by four "support activities" described as follows:

❑ *firm infrastructure* - which comprises the structure and systems by which the enterprise and its processes are organized and managed. Firm infrastructure is sometimes described by the term "architecture", which is defined in a later section of this chapter.

❑ *human resource management (HRM)* - which consists of the recruitment, training, motivation, leadership, management, development, reward, and retaining of enterprise staff.

❑ *technology development* - which involves the management, application and development of the knowledge and technology base of the enterprise. This may include the processes of research and development (R&D), new product or process development, or process re-engineering.

❑ *procurement* - which involves the purchasing of inputs to the value chain, the management of supplier and supply chain relationships; and quality management processes associated therewith.

The value chain model can of course be applied to the creation and marketing of commercial *services* as well as to products. It can also be applied to the provision of healthcare and public services, and in this context is now used within the UK and Australia.

Subsequent criticisms of Porter's original 1985 value chain model point out (among other things) that the so-called "primary activities" should also include the activities of market creation and marketing strategy, customer service, and distribution. In value chain terms, this heading should therefore include the value generated by the marketer's "4P's" or "7P's" summarized in a later section of this chapter.

The model is also criticized for describing the procurement activity as being a "supporting" one. The importance for cost management and quality assurance of effective procurement and supply chain management has meant that Porter's concept of procurement should now be seen as a "primary" activity within the value chain.

Comparative or competitive advantage may be obtained from the use of enterprise resources to create the most effective capability and capacity to carry out the discrete activities described by the value chain, whether these be design, manufacture, management of the supply or distribution chain, selling, customer service provision, treating patients, making public services available, or optimizing management processes. This competitive or comparative advantage is indicated by *value creation*. Porter notes that 'value activities are the discrete building blocks of competitive advantage ... the value chain displays total value, and consists of *value activities* and *margin*. Value activities are the physically and technologically distinct activities a firm performs. These are the building blocks by which a firm creates a product valuable to its buyers. Margin is the difference between total value and the collective cost of performing the value activities' (p.38).

VALUE CHAIN LINKAGES

Discrete value-generating activities are not independent. *They are inter-related and inter-dependent within the value chain.* Porter notes (p.48) that 'value activities are related by linkages within the value chain. Linkages are relationships between the way one value activity is performed and the cost or performance of another'. The Benetton Company's extensive value chain or *value-adding network* for instance links design, manufacture, marketing, distribution and retail activities world-wide, but relies on interpersonal and information system linkages between a large number of independent suppliers, sub-contractors, agents and franchise holders to achieve its cost and distribution advantages.

Porter suggests that enterprise competitive advantage derives as much from the nature of the linkages among activities as it does from the activities themselves. Comparative advantage may here derive from:

❏ *the optimization of the use of the resources and capabilities required to create and activate linkages.* This means seeking more efficient and effective ways of achieving these linkages, for instance through electronic mail and the internet, through high speed computerized information processing, or through ICT-based systems such as electronic data interchange (EDI), electronic point of sale (EPOS), or "chip and pin".

❏ *co-ordination* between the discrete activities that are inter-related by the linkages. Porter notes that 'on-time delivery, for example, may require coordination of activities in operations, outbound logistics, and service ... better coordination ... can reduce the need for inventory throughout the firm ... much of the recent change in philosophy towards manufacturing and towards quality - strongly influenced by Japanese practice - is a recognition of the importance of linkages' (pp. 48-49).

Porter suggests that 'identifying linkages is a process of searching for ways in which each value activity affects or is affected by others' (p. 50). He notes that 'exploiting linkages usually requires information or information flows that allow optimization or coordination to take place. Thus, information systems ... are vital to gaining competitive advantage from linkages'. He also comments that 'exploiting linkages ... requires optimization or coordination that cuts across conventional organizational lines'.

This *cross-functional* or *inter-disciplinary* approach subsequently became a key feature of the re-engineering and teamwork concepts popularized by Hammer and Champy (1993 and 1995), and others. It is now an established feature of "best value" and other forms of public sector service provision in the UK.

More generally, linkages can be described to exist within an organization's value chain; and between that value chain and the value chains of suppliers, distributors, and network partners (etc). These linkages are similar in character - for instance the way that supplier or channel activities are performed affects the cost, quality, or performance of the firm's activities (and vice versa). Suppliers provide a product or service that a firm employs in its value chain, whilst the character of its distributor's value chain will affect the firm's ability to supply the desired outcome values (specification, price, availability, service, etc) to the final customer or client.

The linkages between the value chain of a business organization, and those of its suppliers or its distribution channels provide opportunities for a firm to enhance its competitive advantage. It is possible to configure the value chain system so as to optimize the performance of the total activity, or to improve co-ordination within it. Gains in efficiency and effectiveness that take the form of reduced cost; improved specification, quality and performance, better time management; and better customer service (etc) may result from this process.

However, in commenting on the need for co-operation and partnership within a value chain system, Porter comments that 'independent ownership of suppliers or channels or a history of an adversary relationship can impede the coordination and joint optimization required to exploit ... linkages. Sometimes ... linkages are easier to achieve with coalition partners or sister business units than with independent firms' (p. 52).

The issue of relationships and architecture are dealt with in a later section of this chapter, and in Chapter 18.

VALUE OUTCOMES

The value generated by the value chain and the linkages that it contains may for example be identified on the basis of such *performance or measurement criteria* as the following.

Business and Commercial Organizations:

❑ customer service.
❑ quality and reliability of product or service offer.
❑ customer value.
❑ sales revenue.
❑ cash flow and enterprise liquidity.
❑ cost effectiveness.
❑ credit-worthiness.
❑ profit margin or contribution generated.
❑ Profitability.
❑ shareholder value.
❑ employment stability.

The performance measurement of business and commercial organizations is analyzed in Chapters 3 and 16.

Public Sector, Healthcare and Not-For-Profit Organizations:

❑ customer or client service.
❑ quality and reliability of service offer.
❑ patient treatment outcomes.
❑ customer or client value.
❑ contribution to client health or welfare.
❑ public safety or security.
❑ reduction in the incidence of crime.
❑ cost-effectiveness or Best Value performance.
❑ stakeholder value.
❑ taxpayer value for money.
❑ perceived success in the implementation of government policy.

Reference to the performance measurement of public sector organizations is made in Chapter 16. The concept of the "stakeholder" is analyzed in detail in Chapters 11 and 12.

VALUE GENERATION AND THE ESTABLISHMENT OF COMPETITIVE OR COMPARATIVE ADVANTAGE

The process of value generation being analyzed in this chapter is concerned with the relative value that may be created from the use of:

❑ the corporate strengths described in Chapter 2.
❑ the financial strengths and capability described in Chapter 3.
❑ the enterprise resource base described in this chapter.
❑ the capability and capacity being described in this chapter.
❑ the core competences described in this and later chapters.
❑ the value chain described in this chapter.

The more effective the use by the organization of these resources and capabilities, the greater may be the value generation relative to competitors or comparators. This relative value outcome may then become *a key source of competitive or comparative advantage* to the enterprise.

For instance, customers, clients, shareholders or stakeholders may come to perceive that the organization is capable of using its resources and competences to create and deliver its outputs better, more reliably, or more cost-effectively than its competitors or comparators. They will come to regard this organization as their preferred supplier of the goods or services they seek, ignoring the offer of other suppliers or agencies.

At the same time, the relative performance of the organization will make it increasingly attractive to:

❑ investors who are seeking to optimize the shareholder value they receive. Individuals may have stock market investments upon which they rely for their income. Institutional investors such as life assurance companies or pension funds need instead to satisfy their own customers and clients. Effective value generation may be rewarded by stock market favour, and by the increasing share value that may result.

❑ suppliers, distributors or providers of finance who wish to align themselves with the best companies in the market, in order to stabilize and secure their own business activity. Customers or clients of such suppliers, distributors or sources of finance may in turn be in a strong position to negotiate preferential prices, rates of interest and contracts, thereby adding further value to their own output.

❑ the state (using taxpayers' money) or the providers of healthcare finance (such as medical insurance companies) who will be looking for the generation of optimal or best value outcomes from the public agencies, hospitals, medical practitioners, prisons, local or provincial government authorities, suppliers of security or weapons systems (etc) that they fund.

❑ any institution to whom as customer, client or sponsor, the level of quality, reliability, safety or customer value received from suppliers or contractors is of absolute and over-riding importance. This is likely to be so in the case, for example, of weapons and defence systems, avionics, security systems, body armour, safety equipment, lifts and elevators in buildings, surgical equipment (etc) upon which people's lives depend. Soldiers whose rifles jam in action, or police officers who receive stab wounds because of faulty body armour are unlikely to be impressed by the performance of the suppliers of these essential items! The concept of the *critical success factor (CSF)* is described later in this chapter.

Issues of the relationship between comparative value generation, and the *mission*, *objectives*, and *strategic choice* of the organization are dealt with in later chapters of this book.

KAY'S ANALYSIS OF VALUE ADDITION

Kay contends that a significant indicator of corporate success is that of *added value*. Added value is defined by Kay as the difference between (i) the value of outputs made available to stakeholders (customers, shareholders and other sources of finance, etc); and (ii) the relative cost of the inputs and processes required to create them in the value chain. Enterprise performance in adding value can be measured either or both by:

❑ an added value statement (for instance as shown in Figure 4.3); *and / or*
❑ accounting ratios associated with performance, profitability and asset utilization, cash flow, and stock market requirements as described in Chapter 3. Kay comments that the process of adding value underpins the creation of financial returns, and provides a basis for the future development of the enterprise.

Table 4.1 Added Value Statement: Glaxo 1990

Relationships with	Financial Flow	Value (m.Ecus)
Customers	Revenues	3,985
Labour	Wages and salaries	901
Investors	Capital costs	437
Suppliers	Materials	1,528
	Added value	1,120

Kay comments (p. 24) that 'adding value is the central purpose of business activity. A commercial organization which adds no value - whose output is worth no more than the value of its inputs in alternative uses - has no long-term rationale for its existence'.

Kay therefore contends that a basic source of competitive advantage lies in the ability of the enterprise to add value to its processes and to its transactions with customers, shareholders and other sources of finance, and the wider community. The basic strategy of an enterprise should be to maximize the added-value that can be generated by the development and application of the particular (or "distinctive") capability that it possesses in the relevant segments, sectors or markets.

Kay notes (p. 196) that 'in a contestable market ... the added value earned by firms reflects the value of their competitive advantage'. He states that 'where no explicit comparator is stated, the relevant benchmark is the marginal firm in the industry. The weakest firm which still finds it worthwhile to serve the market provides the baseline against which the competitive advantage of all other firms can be set' (p. 195).

KAY'S ANALYSIS OF COMPETITIVE ADVANTAGE

Kay's thesis is that market or sector position and corporate success derive from the possession of competitive advantage which is based on the use of people and resources that create particular or distinctive capabilities and relationships *that add value* within and around the enterprise. This corporate success will, to a degree, depend on developing capabilities and relationships that are *unique to the company*, and *sustainable* in the medium to long term. Kay identifies four main sources of competitive advantage under the heading of relationships and capabilities. These are:

❑ *architecture* - which is defined as the structure of relationships within the organization; and between the organization and its customers, clients, suppliers, and investors or sources of finance. The successful enterprise is one which (i) creates a distinctive character within the structure of these relationships; (ii) creates uniqueness within these relationships (such that it can attain results that competitors cannot achieve, or cannot achieve so easily); and (iii) creates conditions in which the value that can be derived from these relationships is maximized by the enterprise, its customers, and its partners. *Example:* Benetton's value chain relationships.
❑ *innovation* - which is defined as a capability and a culture that supports and encourages innovation. Additionally, competitive advantage may be achieved by an architecture that is capable of sustaining a process of *ongoing* innovation (which architecture, unlike any single innovation or new product, may be difficult, or even impossible for competitors to

imitate). *Example:* the 3M Company's strategy of continuous innovation and new product development.

❑ *brand* - the strategic and distinctive capability to develop, sustain, and exploit successful brands and brand identity is seen as a key source of sustainable long term competitive advantage to the firm. *Example:* the various derivatives of Richard Branson's "Virgin" brand name (such as Virgin Megastore and Virgin Atlantic).

❑ *corporate reputation* - the strategic capability to develop, sustain, and exploit successful corporate reputation is seen as a key source of sustainable long term competitive advantage to the firm. *Example:* the international Price Waterhouse Coopers or KPMG Peat Marwick accountancy and consultancy companies.

In addition, Kay identifies the possession of what he defines as *strategic assets* to be a fifth significant source of competitive advantage and corporate success. Strategic assets result from the possession by the enterprise of a particular market position or strategic feature that is unavailable or inaccessible to competitors. Competitive advantage will, for instance, derive from the possession of patents such as those held by Polaroid for instant film; or from the development and sustaining of a unique knowledge or skill base, whether it be technical, marketing or managerial, as in the case of Microsoft.

SYNERGY

"Synergy" is an indicator of *joint effect*. The concept of synergy is based on the assumption that the process of combining resources, capabilities, or value chains may yield an output which is greater than the sum of those input resources. This may constitute a significant source of competitive advantage. Such synergy may be represented by the equation:

$$2 + 2 = 5 \text{ (or more)}$$

The combination of resources represented by this equation may achieve a level of outcome which could not be attained by those two individual sets of capabilities on their own. For instance, take two companies who are involved in innovation and new product development. Each faces a limit to what its resources and its capability can achieve. Each faces a limitation to the amount of additional value it can create out of the innovation and new product development process. Together, however, the two companies may be able (i) to combine their knowledge, their experience and their ideas; and (ii) to combine their capability and resources in order to create outcomes which would be beyond the capability of any one of them. This is how new aircraft are designed and built. An aircraft such as the Airbus 380 can only be created and built by a consortium of companies. The project is too large and complex for any one company on its own. The consortium is the source of the synergy needed to build such a large product.

The combining of resources may thus take the constituents of the relationship to a point that neither could ever achieve without the other. Or it may be the combining of diverse ideas that is the source of competitive advantage. For instance, the personal or microcomputer concept, and the distributed processing that it permits, has revolutionized the way people and organizations work. It depended on the coming together of (i) developments in computer specification; (ii) the development of high powered microprocessors such as Intel's Pentium chip; and (iii) the writing of suites of appropriate software such as Microsoft Windows or Lotus Notes. Without the synergy of this coming together of ideas and technologies the concept could not have been made to work.

THE MARKETING MIX, THE 4Ps, AND THE 7Ps

It has long been established that competitive or comparative advantage may be obtained through the effective specification, implementation, and management of the *marketing mix*. This is as much true for the public, healthcare, or not-for-profit sectors as it is for business organizations or SMEs. The marketing mix represents a specific or distinctive use of resources, capability and capacity to achieve value generation or value addition through the value chain. The "4P" marketing mix comprises value addition and competitive advantage that derives from effective:

❑ *product* (or service) specification, positioning, and management.
❑ *pricing* of goods or services.
❑ *placing* of goods or services in locations and channels of distribution.
❑ *promotion* of goods or services through advertizing, selling, or sales promotion.

The "7P" marketing mix comprises value generation and competitive advantage that derives from three variables additional to the 4Ps listed immediately above. These three extra variables are represented by effective:

❑ *personal persuasion or selling* that is often needed to sell intangible products or services such as those associated with finance, insurance, or leisure activities.

❑ *people selection and management*, particularly where a high level of customer service is required or where strategies of relationship marketing are in place to try to retain customers and obtain repeat purchases from them.

❑ *physical evidence* that is needed to provide a tangible quality to intangible products or services such as travel or hospitality, financial services, education and training, medical care (etc).

OTHER SOURCES OF COMPETITIVE ADVANTAGE

Peters (1992) identifies the following additional sources of competitive advantage:

❑ *speed and time* - by which the enterprise develops the capability to reduce or compress the time taken to accomplish its activities; and uses time most effectively by co-ordinating and synchronizing multiple events (for instance by "parallel processing"). The ability to develop new products and to bring them to market more rapidly than competitors is one example of this capability. The strategic management of time is analyzed in Chapter 7.

❑ *flexibility* - by which the enterprise can rapidly get into activities, and out of activities; and maximize its capability to cope with the variability of events that it meets within its internal and external environments. Event characteristics are analyzed in Chapter 8.

❑ *quality and design* - quality, functionality, "fitness for purpose", aesthetics, the service environment, and user friendliness are all key sources of competitive advantage. The PIMS findings (Buzzell and Gale, 1987) show *the crucial relationship between quality and market share*. Optimum quality can now be regarded as a prerequisite to a continued presence in markets such as those for cars, trucks, consumer electronics products, or oil exploration equipment.

❑ *use of information technology* - which underpins a wide range of developments and improvements associated with the value generating processes, cost management, re-engineering and relationship architecture described in this and later chapters.

❑ *the ability to form alliances and partnerships* - such that the process of value generation may be optimised throughout the value chain and the relationship architecture it represents. The issue of partnerships and strategic alliances is dealt with in later chapters.

❑ *the ability to sustain continuous improvement* - which requires the continuous development and upgrading of the enterprise knowledge, skill, and competence base. This capability will have significant implications for the human resource management (HRM) process, and for the character of the relationship architecture used to implement and sustain the improvement.

❑ *the ability to act as a service business* - such that the enterprise offers added-value service as an integral part of its market offer; and is perceived by its customers to be strongly sensitive to market needs. *Example:* are airlines or railway networks selling personal transportation or reliability? Customers have come to expect predictable and punctual journey times, even across long-haul flights between continents.

❑ *the ability to manage structure and scale* - by which the enterprise is simultaneously capable of (i) managing activities which require large scale, taking advantage of any economies of scale that may be associated with them; and (ii) making use of 'cohesive, focused, multi-function unit(s) of moderate size (not tiny, not huge)' that will be capable of a flexible and innovative response to external conditions. Peters suggests that 'the notion of smallish, self-contained units within very big firms, or big networks composed of specialist pieces of firms of various sizes' are likely to take on an increasing importance.

CRITICAL SUCCESS FACTORS

"Critical success factors" (CSFs) *are key determinants of corporate success*. Critical success factors, however they are defined, *have a predominant impact on the achievement of (or failure to achieve) enterprise objectives*. Hence, the achievement of proper performance under these headings is of great importance to the enterprise. The identification and achievement of critical success factors will therefore take priority in the management of the organization's affairs.

For example, the need to meet *annual shareholder expectations* for dividend, share price, and growth in share value is in particular a critical success factor for business corporations in Anglo-Saxon countries such as the UK and the USA (this issue is dealt with in later chapters). A school, a college, or a university will define *annual recruitment* as its most important CSF. Failure to meet its recruitment target will place all of its other objectives and strategies at risk of failure, and eventually threaten the long-term survival of the institution.

A hospital's reputation may instead depend on the *success of its treatment outcomes* relative to other hospitals in its benchmark group. Additionally, in the UK, medical services financed by the National Health Service are increasingly required by the state to be able to demonstrate *cost-effectiveness* in their use of taxpayer's money.

The understanding of critical success factors is a key input to processes of strategic decision-making and strategic choice. A failure to identify, to understand, or to respond to CSFs is instead likely to be correlated with a disproportionate degree of risk and the potential for enterprise failure.

LIMITING FACTORS

Limiting factors *are those influences which directly shape, or impose limits on the leadership, strategies, strategic choices, decisions, and operations of the enterprise.* Typically these limitations on the enterprise derive from:

❑ *internal features* associated with financial, cash flow, operational and human resource capabilities. These features are for instance of particular importance for management in the SME (the small to medium sized enterprise) which may lack finance or managerial skill; or in large public sector service organizations such as schools or hospitals which operate with fixed annual budgets.

❑ *external features* associated with regulatory, distributional or market limitations. Some countries, for example, impose direct quotas on the number of Japanese automobiles that they will allow to be imported. Others will insist on a certain degree of local supply sourcing or manufacture of international products. Channels of distribution may instead vary widely on a global basis in terms of their ownership, openness, and sophistication, such that there will be significant differences in the level and quality of customer service they are likely to offer.

IDENTIFYING CONTINGENCIES AND CONSTRAINTS

There are likely to be a variety of *contingencies* and *constraints* within which the enterprise must operate. These may include:

- [ ] issues deriving from the distinctive character of the *locality* in which the enterprise is operating.
- [ ] national laws that as a *regulatory framework* for instance determine the ownership structures or systems of corporate governance to which an international company must adhere while operating in that territory.
- [ ] local laws or customs that as a *regulatory framework* for example determine the nature and content of marketing communications; or determine the required patterns of distribution (such as in Japan).
- [ ] tax or excise duty impositions made by the state or the province (or both, as in Canada) that will affect enterprise financial and pricing policies.
- [ ] the demands of shareholders and other sources of finance - the need to meet the demands of shareholders and other sources of finance (such as banks or family trusts) will shape enterprise policies towards *the required rate of return* on investments, and to the *time scale* associated therewith. This issue is dealt with in more detail in later chapters.
- [ ] more generally, the wider demands of *stakeholders* who have some kind of interest in the enterprise (an issue also dealt with in later chapters).
- [ ] time management and time scale issues associated with *time* as a determinant variable. Different cultures take different approaches to the use or management of time. Ask a German or Mexican or North American or Spanish or Dutch colleague about their attitude to time! Have you ever had a traditional French "business lunch" and could you do any work afterwards?! The issue of time management is dealt with in Chapter 7.
- [ ] the level of risk tolerance - what level of *business risk* will boards of directors and institutional shareholders tolerate? Is the management of the company risk-averse or risk-tolerant? The issue of risk assessment is dealt with in Chapter 8.
- [ ] culture variables, such as those for example determining the local priority of customer service standards (for instance as between Europe and North America).
- [ ] people and their skill, knowledge, experience, motivation, and ambition. Has the organization got the right people? Can it recruit enough of them to meet its operational needs?

- ❑ technology - does the enterprise need to sustain continuous investment in upgrading its processes and products over time?
- ❑ Organization, leadership and management - can the enterprise actually manage its affairs effectively? Do its decision-makers understand what the process of strategic management involves?
- ❑ processes and systems - for instance, whilst it is in theory possible to achieve the fine tuning of cash flow management by the instant transfer of funds between bank accounts as a result of a customer purchase, top-up of an account, or a business transaction, the reality is that banking systems often introduce delays of several days between the payment and transfer of funds. They smooth out the flows of cash within the banking system in their own interest. But if you are a full-time student it may mean that a generous parent or relative cannot quickly clear your overdraft! So your bank may not allow you to withdraw any money for several days because, as far as they are concerned, you remain temporarily overdrawn even though a cheque has already been paid into your account.

These contingencies and constraints may determine how the enterprise may have to operate. Or they may shape what it is able (or not able) to achieve.

THE POSITIONING OR "FIT" OF COMPETITIVE ADVANTAGE WITHIN MARKET OR INDUSTRY

The enterprise needs to understand (i) the nature and relative power of its sources of competitive advantage; (ii) the nature of its critical success factors; and (iii) those factors which constrain it, as described in preceding sections of this chapter.

It must then apply its sources of competitive or comparative advantage to appropriate markets, business activities, or sector environments. This is because sources of competitive or comparative advantage are dependent for their value on an appropriate positioning on the relevant markets or sectors.

That is, there needs to be a degree of "fit" (or "congruence") between the character of the competitive or comparative advantage and the context in which it is to be applied. The competitive advantage may be irrelevant elsewhere. Hence, a key enterprise skill lies in its ability (i) to understand and segment its markets or sectors; (ii) to develop and put into operation the most appropriate capacities and capabilities; (iii) to position products and services on its market segments or sectors; and (iv) to put in place the most effective product-market, competition, and business development strategies (as described in later chapters) that allow it to exploit its sources of competitive advantage.

At the same time, Kay suggests that the degree of value addition (and hence the ultimate profitability) of which a business enterprise is capable will be a function of both:

❑   the competitive advantage that the firm holds relative to the other firms in the sector; *and*
❑   the relative profitability of the sector itself. Thus, for instance, if there is excess capacity in an industry (such as automobile manufacture) then even the possession of a large competitive advantage may not yield substantial profitability.

That is, it will be *the nature of the competitive environment* on which the enterprise has positioned itself that will in part determine the degree to which added value can be created, and profitability delivered. The nature of the competitive environment is analyzed in Chapter 5.

THE USES OF THE ANALYSIS OF COMPETITIVE ADVANTAGE, VALUE GENERATION, AND CRITICAL SUCCESS FACTORS WITHIN THE STRATEGIC MANAGEMENT PROCESS

The process of appraisal described in this chapter analyzes:

❑   the resource base.
❑   enterprise capability and capacity.
❑   sources of competitive or comparative advantage.
❑   value generation and value addition.
❑   critical success factors.
❑   limiting factors, contingencies and constraints.

This process of appraisal may then be used:

❑   to identify factors that (i) are critical to the success of the organization; that (ii) determine what the nature of enterprise objectives will have to be; and (iii) that will ultimately determine whether or not the organization may be able to achieve these objectives.
❑   to concentrate decisions about the choice of strategies in critical (or the most important) areas of capability and competitive advantage.

❑ to concentrate the choice of strategies in areas in which the enterprise can add or generate most value.

❑ to select strategies that most effectively build upon or exploit the enterprise resource base, capability, synergy, value generation, and competitive or comparative advantage.

❑ to take account of prevailing limiting factors, contingencies and constraints.

❑ to select strategies that address or remedy those corporate weaknesses whose continuing existence may place the enterprise at a competitive disadvantage within its markets or sectors of activity.

REVIEW QUESTIONS

1. What is competitive or comparative advantage? Why is it important to the process of strategic management?
2. What is the significance of enterprise capability and capacity to the process of strategic decision-making and strategic choice?
3. Describe and explain the value chain concept.
4. What is the significance of value generation and value addition to the process of strategic decision-making and strategic choice?
5. How may an enterprise in the public, healthcare, or not-for-profit sector generate or add value?
6. What is synergy? Illustrate your answer with your own examples.
7. Summarize and categorize the sources of competitive advantage available to a business enterprise.
8. Summarize and categorize the sources of comparative advantage available to a public sector, healthcare, or a not-for-profit organization.
9. What are critical success factors? What are their significance to the process of strategic decision-making and strategic choice?
10. In what ways may the process of strategic decision-making and strategic choice be limited and constrained?

TECHNIQUES OF CASE STUDY AND ANALYSIS

1. Identify and analyze the capability and capacity of the case study organization. What is the enterprise capable of doing? What can it do best?
2. Identify critical success factors.

3. Identify and analyze the character of the relevant value chain (or value chains) described in the case study.
4. Identify sources of competitive or comparative advantage that are apparent from the case study.
5. Identify and analyze how (if at all) the enterprise generates or adds value.
6. Identify limiting factors, contingencies and constraints.
7. Identify sources of competitive weakness or competitive disadvantage.

PROJECT ASSIGNMENT

Part One Project Assignment - The Strategic Analysis of a Company or Organization

Component Three: Using available information, carry out an analysis of the capability, competitive or comparative advantage, and value-generating capacity of an organization that is of interest to you. What are its critical success factors? What limitations and constraints affect its strategic choice?

References

Buzzell, R.D. and B.T. Gale (1987) *The PIMS Principles*, Free Press, New York.
Davidson, H. (1987) *Offensive Marketing*, Penguin, London.
Grant, R.M. (1991) 'The resource-based theory of competitive advantage: implications for strategy formulation', *California Management Review*, Vol 33 No 3.
Hamel, G. and C.K. Prahalad (1994) *Competing for the Future*, Harvard Business School Press, Boston, Mass.
Hammer, M. and J. Champy (1993) *Reengineering the Corporation*, Nicholas Brealey, London.
Hammer, M. and J. Champy (1995) *Reengineering the Corporation (Revised Edition)*, Nicholas Brealey, London.
Kay, J. (1993) *Foundations of Corporate Success*, Oxford University Press, Oxford.
Morden, A.R. (1993) *Elements of Marketing*, DP Publications, London.
Peters, T.J. (1992) 'The search for new bases for competitive advantage', *Business Age*, July.
Porter, M.E. (1985) *Competitive Advantage*, Free Press, New York.
Prahalad, C.K. and G. Hamel (1990) 'The core competence of the corporation', *Harvard Business Review*, May-June.

Chapter 5

Competitive Analysis

This chapter describes the role of competition analysis within the process of strategic analysis and strategic management. A key requirement of strategic analysis is the appraisal and understanding of the competitive situation which faces the enterprise in its sectors or markets.

The choice of strategies is influenced by the competitive situation facing the enterprise. The organization needs to establish a clear picture and understanding of the identities and activities of its competitors. This is particularly important if proposals are being made to enter new markets or to operate internationally.

This chapter analyzes some of the main competition variables; outlines a well-known competition model; and describes the sources and management of competitor information. It illustrates some of the means by which competitors may be analyzed and evaluated. And it examines the issue of potential competitor response to market initiatives.

MARKETS, INDUSTRIES AND COMPETITION

Kay (1993) suggests that the basic or "core" business of the enterprise comprises that market (or set of markets) in which the firm's capability gives it the greatest competitive advantage. Kay suggests that a particular capability becomes a source of competitive advantage only when it is applied in the most appropriate market. This is because competitive advantage is relative. A firm can enjoy competitive advantage only by reference to other suppliers in the same market. Matching competitive positioning and product-market activities appropriately to the capabilities of the enterprise is a key element in establishing competitive advantage. *The enterprise must therefore define and understand its competitive arena.* Kay contends that the enterprise must identify:

❑ *its sector or market(s)* - as defined by customer and segment characteristics, usage contexts, and demand factors. *Example:* electrical power generating equipment.

❑ *its industry* - defined as groups of products or services between whose supply there is some market-relevant association (such as technology, distribution patterns, brand categories, corporate identity or external perceptions). *Example:* electrical engineering.

❑ *its strategic group* - defined as those firms identified as primary competitors within the relevant sector or markets, having broadly similar aims and strategies. *Examples:* international electrical engineering companies who manufacture power generating equipment include ABB, GE Corp, CGE Alcatel Alsthom, Siemens.

THE LOCATION OF COMPETITION

Kay comments that the generation of competitive advantage and added value (as described in Chapter 4) is a function of the competition and competitive behaviour within:

❑ any one market, industry, or strategic group; *and*
❑ any one country; *and*
❑ any one trading bloc.

given (i) the relative degree of *freedom of entry* for newcomers (whose arrival may cause disturbance or turbulence within the market, the industry, or the strategic group); and given (ii) the character and strength of national or international policies on the encouragement or limitation of competition (*competition policy*). For instance:

❑ the European Union (EU) and the North American Free Trade Area (NAFTA) espouse policies that facilitate and encourage free trade, in particular within the framework of the World Trade Organization (WTO) agreements.

❑ the USA has tough anti-trust (anti-monopoly) laws that are based upon a philosophical and constitutional belief in the merits of open competition and free market capitalism.

❑ Japanese and South Korean competition policy has been based upon the encouragement of "competitive oligopoly" between local companies within a framework of national protectionism.

❑ "Rhineland capitalism" (for instance as described by Michel Albert, 1993) places competition policy within the wider framework of the concept of the "social market". Free market competition is permitted or constrained according to its impact on employment conditions, and on the general welfare of society. Competitive behaviour is judged by the degree of its social responsibility.

Kay comments that aggressive competition policies or free trade arrangements may encourage newcomers to enter national markets in which they were not hitherto represented. Their arrival may "disturb" the existing parameters of local competition, increase market instability, reduce profitability, and increase the prevailing level of business risk. The arrival of large international or multinational corporations may in particular give rise to a level of competitive pressure that may change the nature and "rules" of the competitive arena, and overwhelm (or destroy) smaller or less efficient local suppliers.

THE ANALYSIS OF MARKET COMPETITION - THE "FIVE FORCES" MODEL

A widely used technique for the analysis of market competition is the *"five forces" competition model* of M.E. Porter (1980). Porter suggests that market competition is a function of five major groups of variables or "forces". These are:

❑ the extent of industry rivalry.
❑ the bargaining power of buyers.
❑ the bargaining power of suppliers.
❑ the threat of new entrants.
❑ the threat of substitutes.

These five groups of variables are inter-related. They are illustrated by Porter's five forces competition matrix shown in Figure 5.1.

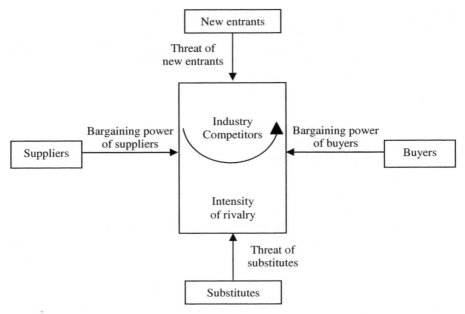

Figure 5.1 M.E. Porter's "Five Forces" Competition Model

EXTENT OF INDUSTRY RIVALRY

The extent of industry rivalry is determined by such factors as:

❑ the number and diversity of competitors, and the degree of balance (or equality) between their relative market strengths. This factor includes the *degree of concentration* within the industry. British grocery retailing is highly concentrated, while the British tourist industry is highly fragmented.

❑ the degree to which the industry can be defined as "young" or "mature". Growth prospects are, in particular, limited in a mature and slow-growing industry. This may prompt intense competition among the participants. It may also harden their resolve to hold on to market share. This situation characterizes the foodstuffs industry in the UK, in which competition centres on maintaining or increasing market share.

❏ the degree to which *product differentiation* is effective. The harder it is to differentiate the product or service, or the more difficult it is to establish an effective brand acceptance, the more competitive the market is likely to become. *Example:* financial and banking services in the UK have become relatively standardized. There is some competition between the suppliers of financial and banking services in terms of customer service, but it is becoming increasingly difficult to maintain a strong degree of brand identity and loyalty. Customers perceive that they are in control and tend to shop around for the best deal

❏ the degree to which operational capacity is "lumpy", that is only increased in large increments. The addition of large increments of operational capacity may lead to the risk of over-supply in the market, and the emergence of price competition. *Example:* the 1990s were characterized by a global oversupply of semiconductors, with depressed microchip prices. Large extra increments of capacity came on stream throughout the 1990s and saturated the market.

❏ the incidence of *high burdens of fixed cost* associated with market operations. Price competition may increase the risk that fixed costs cannot be recovered, particularly where the margin of safety is relatively low. Competition may as a result be so intensified by the major players that weaker contestants give up altogether and leave the industry, or potential newcomers are strongly discouraged from entering the sector. *Example:* the automotive industry is one in which it is increasingly difficult (and expensive) to establish a foothold in new locations. Even if they are successful, newcomers may not be able to achieve a reasonable return on their investment in such a market.

❏ high *exit barriers* causing companies to remain in a market, however unattractive it is, because (i) of the costs and risks attached to leaving it (what else are these companies going to do, and how will they develop or obtain the necessary new capabilities and competencies?); or (ii) because of the existence of "sunk costs" (fully depreciated past investments) that give competitive advantage to existing suppliers but which newcomers would have to finance. If a company is heavily committed to, or dependent on a market, it is unlikely to be willing to leave it except in the direst of circumstances. And the more dependent it is upon any particular market, the more competitive its behaviour may become. *Example:* the automotive industry, in which existing players are likely to defend their current position and market share at all costs against their competitors and against the threat of new entrants.

BUYERS' BARGAINING POWER

The relative bargaining power of buyers is determined by such factors as:

❑ the degree of buyer concentration relative to suppliers. A classic example of the exercise of "buyer power" that can result from such buyer concentration is to be found in the UK grocery market. This is dominated by a very small number of very large retail chains whose combined purchases as a strategic group exceed 70 percent of the total in the sector.

❑ the relative volume of the buyer's purchases in that market, combined with the relative importance of the purchase to that buyer. *Example:* clothing retailers such as Arcadia, George at Asda, or Marks and Spencer have immense buying power over their suppliers, who are often heavily dependent on such buyers for their custom.

❑ the availability of close substitutes. *Example:* home entertainments, such as DVDs, videos and computer games like "Nintendo" and "Game Boy". The availability of close substitutes and a significant degree of choice increases the power of the buyer relative to the supplier.

❑ the standardized or "commodity" nature of the products or services in the market, which makes it difficult to differentiate the supplier's offering. This puts the buyer in a strong position. Commodity products could include general forms of insurance, financial services, industrial paint or lubricants, telephone services, and staple foodstuffs. It is virtually impossible to differentiate these products effectively. In the 1990s the UK British Telecom's expensive promotional campaigns to differentiate its telephone services had the result of extending the telecommunications market for everyone else's benefit. At the same time, however, other telecommunications suppliers who are competing on price were left for a number of years with a free hand to carve out their UK market share unhindered by direct competition from the largest operator! Many UK telephone subscribers are only interested in price - they assume that the service is all the same - and so will shop around for what they consider to be the best deal.

❑ the degree of threat of *backward integration* by buyers wishing to control their sources of supply more closely, or wishing to gain competitive advantage over their own competitors by controlling that supply. *Example:* attempts by French electronics companies to dominate the supply of advanced computer software in order to optimize their competitive position.

❑ the relative *cost of switching* ("switching cost") between alternative suppliers. The easier or cheaper it is for the buyer to switch between suppliers, the more competitive is the market. Suppliers will therefore attempt to "lock-in" their customers to unique supply conditions or deals in order (i) to reduce the opportunity for switching, or (ii) to increase its cost. Credit and finance packages often have this effect in business-to-business markets, as do information technology (IT) based ordering, transaction or electronic data interchange (EDI) systems which "direct" customer orders to favoured suppliers. The objective will be to limit the range of options which appears to be available; or to make it expensive for customers to switch between alternative offerings. This will reduce the degree of buyer power.

❑ the degree to which buyers are *price-sensitive*. Price-sensitive buyers are likely to "shop around" and to switch allegiance between suppliers to a greater extent than those buyers to whom quality and reliability of supply are more important.

❑ the degree to which buyers wish (or need) to build up effective *long-term relationships* with suppliers to ensure the quality and reliability of supply within the architecture of their value chain. This may reduce the buyer's bargaining power. It may also reduce his or her price sensitivity, and provides the supplier with an effective form of product or service differentiation. It also illustrates how the architecture of the value chain may be used to yield advantage within the prevailing competitive context. This issue is dealt with in Chapters 4 and 18.

SUPPLIERS' BARGAINING POWER

Supplier bargaining power is determined by such factors as:

❑ the degree to which suppliers are effectively able to differentiate their product or service. This will increase their bargaining power relative to customers. Differentiation may, for instance, be based on product or service specification, possession of unique selling propositions, strong brand identity, or corporate reputation for quality, reliability and customer service. *Example:* the position of the UK Northern Foods company as a supplier of high quality foodstuffs to Marks and Spencer and other grocery retailers. The power of these retailers is in part offset by Northern Foods' own reputation as a preferred supplier.

❑ the degree of supplier concentration. The fewer the suppliers, or the scarcer or the more important the product they supply, the greater will be the competition among buyers to secure their supplies. This dependence strengthens the supplier's market position. *Supplier power* within the market is further enhanced where the possession of a strategic asset such as proprietary knowledge or effective patent protection means for example that the supplier is in a monopoly position to provide the product, or to licence others to manufacture it. *Example:* the computer industry, in which companies such as Intel (microprocessors) and Microsoft (software) are in a strong position relative to manufacturers. It is the hardware that has become the commodity, not the microprocessor or the software.

❑ the relative importance to the buyer of the product or service being purchased from the supplier. The more important the product or service, the stronger the bargaining power of the supplier.

❑ the availability (or otherwise) of close substitutes as satisfactory inputs to the buyer's requirement. *Example:* tramway systems are beginning to return as pollution-free forms of urban rapid transit. These are expensive because of their need for tracks in the road and special signalling systems. The electric trolley bus achieves the same purpose but with simpler technology, no special signalling and no track. This weakens the bargaining position of the suppliers of tramway systems.

❑ the degree of *forward integration* by suppliers, wishing more closely to control their own market outlets. Hence, for example, the traditional control of UK retail outlets by companies in the brewing and vehicle fuel sectors. Ownership and control of retail outlets by UK brewers has, in particular, been the subject of significant government intervention seeking to reduce the market power of brewing companies and to increase competition in the licenced trade.

THE THREAT OF NEW ENTRANTS

The degree of competitive threat posed by newcomers to the market will be determined by *the relative ease of entry to that market*. This, in turn, will be a function of the relative strength of *barriers to entry* to that market. These barriers to entry include:

❑ the effectiveness of product differentiation and the strength of customer loyalty to the brands of existing suppliers in the market. Strongly brand-loyal customers may ignore new market offerings, however attractive they may be.

❑ the ability of would-be entrants to gain access to the necessary channels of distribution. This is a vital issue for companies planning to expand their operations on an international basis. Daewoo's entry into the UK car market was strongly resisted by the motor trade. At first, no existing automotive dealer would touch the company's cars. Daewoo had to set up its own distribution network from scratch.

❑ the ability of would-be entrants to obtain access to the necessary value chain inputs, capability, operational experience; or instead to develop the required corporate credibility. *Example:* the entry of UK building societies into the market for unsecured personal loans after financial deregulation in 1986. This market had hitherto been dominated by the clearing banks. Unsecured personal lending is a risky business. The building societies had little prior experience of this market. They had to move down a long and expensive learning curve in order to develop their ability to manage the risk involved.

❑ the capacity of existing competitors to deter new entrants by the offensive (attacking) use of price reduction tactics or the offer of extra discounts to existing customers. The choice of *competition strategies* is described in Chapter 22.

❑ the possession by existing competitors of *absolute cost advantages* deriving from economies of scale or a pre-eminent position on the industry's "experience curve". The strategic importance of the experience curve is described in Chapter 23. A newcomer could not match the cost position of an incumbent supplier. This is a strategy used by companies such as Du Pont in the bulk international chemicals market.

❑ the absolute size of the capital cost to be incurred in establishing a presence in the market. Given the likely return on investment on such an investment in a highly competitive market, it may simply not prove to be worthwhile entering a market by "starting from scratch". A preferred strategic choice may be to merge with, or to acquire (take-over) an existing supplier, *if this option is available* (many companies have found it difficult, for instance, to gain a foothold in the Japanese market, since take-overs of Japanese companies are difficult to achieve).

❑ the difficulty for newcomers in building effective brand loyalty, corporate reputation, or positive customer perceptions about quality or service offer, especially where existing suppliers are at their strongest in these areas. *Example:* the reputation and position of the UK Prudential and Standard Life companies in the long-term personal investment and pensions markets. The issue of corporate reputation is dealt with in Chapter 25.

❑ government policy discouraging further entry into the market, for instance to protect home suppliers against the entry of more efficient foreign suppliers. Post-war Japanese and South Korean governments have for instance effectively restricted entry to foreign companies in order to build up a powerful home base of *world class* companies capable of global marketing and supply.

THE THREAT OF SUBSTITUTES

The competitive threat posed by the availability of *substitute products or services* will be determined by such factors as:

❑ buyer propensity (willingness) to substitute between the products or services on offer. Are buyers actually willing to change their customary purchase behaviour? This is related to:-

❑ the relative price of existing and substitute products. Which is perceived to be more expensive? This is also related to:-

❑ the relative price-performance perception held by customers. Does the substitute product match up to the existing offer? Does the substitute perform better? Does it offer better value for money?

❑ the relative cost and perceived risk involved in switching between the existing and substitute products or services. What will it cost to change products, and what are the likely risks involved?

The significance of the threat posed by substitute products or services depends on the ease with which customers, existing suppliers, and potential newcomers can (i) identify substitutes and (ii) identify the nature of the competitive threat they imply. Is it obvious that substitutes are available?

This, in turn, raises the issue of clearly defining the market, the industry, or the strategic group for which the competitive analysis is being carried out. This issue was analyzed above.

THE NATURE OF COMPETITION

Porter suggests that the nature and intensity of competition within a market will depend on *the relative strength and interaction of the five forces* described above. The effect of this competition may then take such actual (visible) forms as:

- ❑ *price competition*, which may reduce industry margins and profits and drive some businesses out of the market. The global semiconductor industry had for instance reached a dangerous over-supply situation by 1998. Margins and profits had collapsed, and companies such as Siemens left the sector.
- ❑ *non-price competition*, such as that characteristic of mature markets. This is based on product and brand differentiation, the offer of "value-added" products or services, promotion, and so on. *Example:* consumer electronics goods, which tend to compete on the basis of specification, brand and innovatory features.
- ❑ *"locking in"* customers or distribution channels by the use of discounts, credit and preferential financial arrangements, or preferential service agreements. *Example:* the construction equipment market in which manufacturers provide financing packages to assist the lease or purchase of heavy capital plant by construction companies and plant hire agencies.
- ❑ *mergers with, or take-overs of competitors or newcomers* so as to consolidate and protect market position. BMW, for instance, acquired the Mini brand as a result of its purchase of the UK Rover car group. Ford took over Jaguar and Land Rover in order to achieve a stronger position in the premium car market.
- ❑ *direct government regulation and intervention* put in place in order to shape and control the nature of competition. For instance, the governments of a number of countries (such as France, Germany, Japan, and the USA) may not permit the take-over by foreign companies of local enterprises which they regard as being of national importance in terms of contribution to the economy, security, employment, value addition, or national competitive advantage. The objective of government policy is to ensure that the knowledge base, technology, capability and competence of such enterprises stays within (and remains available to) the nation.

COMPETITOR INFORMATION

Accurate competitive analysis requires an adequate input of competitor information. Without this information, competitor analysis (for instance against Porter's five forces model) may not be effective. Companies may therefore choose to establish some kind of *competitor intelligence system.* Such a system may be based on a mix of *field* and *published* data sources, as follow.

Field data sources include:

❑ sales force.
❑ distribution channels, customers and buyers.
❑ suppliers.
❑ trade association data.
❑ commissioned market research studies and market surveys.
❑ company analysts; commissioned consultant's reports.
❑ commercial clipping services providing information about competitors.

Published data sources include:

❑ annual company reports and accounts.
❑ interfirm comparisons.
❑ commercially published sector/industry reports e.g. *Mintel, Economist Intelligence Unit, Financial Times* in the UK; *Financial Post*, and *Globe and Mail* 'Report on Business', in Canada.
❑ newspapers, trade journals, and business magazines.
❑ academic journals.
❑ job advertisements, which may give a clue to some forthcoming competitor initiative.
❑ public speeches, media interviews, etc.
❑ public patent records.

This competitive intelligence needs effective information management so that an accurate competitor database can be used to inform the processes of strategic choice and decision-making. Such an information management process is illustrated in Figure 5.2.

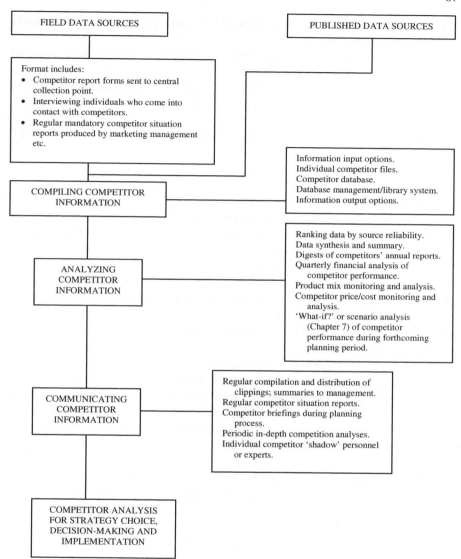

Figure 5.2 A Competitor Information Management System

EVALUATING COMPETITORS

Competing organizations may be subjected to the kind of appraisal process being described in part one of this book. Using information derived from the company's competitor database:

❑ competitor capabilities, strengths, and weaknesses may be identified by functional area and key issue.
❑ competitor sources of comparative advantage may be identified and categorized.
❑ financial status may be analyzed where published financial data is available; or the calculation of estimates of margin of safety can be attempted.
❑ performance gap analysis may be carried out.

Key indicators about competitors would include assessments of:

❑ leadership capability.
❑ market position and apparent market-place objectives.
❑ customer perceptions of competitor QRSV (quality, reliability, service, and value for money offered).
❑ the relevant critical success factors.
❑ capabilities and asset profile.
❑ knowledge and technology base (described in Chapter 19).
❑ core competencies (described in Chapter 20).
❑ other significant sources of competitive advantage.
❑ sources of weakness.
❑ opportunities available to competitors (see Chapter 6).
❑ potential threats to competitors (see Chapter 6).
❑ cost structure, cost advantage, or cost disadvantage.
❑ financial position, financial strength, and apparent financial objective.
❑ capacity to sustain competitive position and competitive advantage in the medium to long term.
❑ growth potential.
❑ apparent capacity to respond to market, technological, financial, or macro-economic changes within the external environment.
❑ apparent management attitudes and perceptions towards the market and the competition in it.
❑ competition strategies apparent (described in Chapter 22).

POTENTIAL COMPETITOR RESPONSE

M.E. Porter also suggests that the process of competitor analysis must involve *an assessment of potential competitor response* to events within the market place or the competitive environment. This assessment may deal with such issues as:

❑ the apparent level of competitor satisfaction with current position (*status quo*) and the strength of desire to avoid unnecessary competition. To what extent are competitors content with their present position? Or do they instead wish to increase their market share at someone else's expense? Will they defend their ground against newcomers? Will they try to pre-empt new competition (or will government competition policy make such a course of action unacceptable)? Can they defend their position if a powerful multinational company enters the market?

❑ competitor perceptions of the need or priority of making some kind of competitive response to changes in the competition situation. For example, reference has already been made above to the attempts by the UK motor trade to make Daewoo's life as a new entrant as difficult as possible.

❑ the alternative courses of action that competitors *perceive* to be available, and the relative attractiveness of each of these courses of action. What can competitors do to deal with the situation; and what will be the costs and benefits of the course of action chosen? Nestlé's entry into the breakfast cereal market was, for instance, met by a predictably robust (and expensive) defensive response by the market leader, Kellogg.

❑ perceptions of corporate strength or vulnerability relative to other participants in the market when being faced with the need to respond to competitive initiatives. How strong is competitive position relative to other companies? For example, Clarke's Ice Cream made a disastrous foray into the UK ice cream market. Clarke's Ice Cream, a small player relative to the industry giants, went out of business within about a year as a result of entering that market.

❑ the likely effectiveness of retaliatory action. If for instance the enterprise proposes to attack Coca-Cola head-on in the soft drinks market it had better know what it is going to let itself in for (and it had better have plenty of money to spend on promotion or law-suits too, as the UK grocer Sainsbury found out when it used "look-alike" packaging for its own brand cola drink!).

❑ the nature of events or initiatives that may provoke retaliatory action; and the *threshold* at which this action will be triggered. For instance, the development by the UK company EMI of the CAT body-scanner created an enormous new medical electronics market. Existing competitors within that market, such as the General Electric (GE) Corporation of America, Philips, and Siemens were stung into action. They recognized that the body-scanner would become a crucial constituent of the demand for high-tech medical electronics. Immense investments were made by these companies to get into the technology, and EMI was "out-spent" until it could no longer compete. It was forced to get out of that market, selling off the rights to its invention to its stronger competitors.

❑ the place, the time, and the form of competitive response. For example a competitor, forced into a *competition strategy* response which it considers it can both control and win, will select its "battlefield" with care. It may attack its competitors where they are at their weakest, not their strongest. Its attack may for instance come in an *offensive* form of a price war, technological innovation that its competitors cannot match or copy, or the further reinforcement of an already powerful brand image or reputation. Or the competitor may instead force on its rivals a reaction that gives rise to *internal conflicts* or *goal uncertainty*. For instance, the retailing at a discount of a full range of manufacturer brand foodstuffs and household products puts pressure on those grocery retail chains that prefer to stock the "own brand" or "own label" products which are more profitable to them. Given the use of a discount pricing policy for these manufacturer brands, other grocery chains cannot conclusively argue that their own-brands offer better value for money. After all, many grocery customers consider that manufacturer-branded products offer superior quality, and can be obtained at discount retailers as cheaply as own-brands elsewhere. At the same time, own-brand orientated grocery retailers will be forced carefully to monitor the balance between the own-label and manufacturer-branded products that they stock, remaining sensitive to external promotions that cast doubt about their commitment to ranges of own-label products. After all, "if it doesn't say Kellogg's *on* the packet, it isn't Kellogg's *in* the packet!"

Ultimately, Porter suggests that 'the ideal is to find a strategy that competitors are frozen from reacting to, given their present circumstances. The legacy of their past and current strategy may make some moves very costly for competitors to follow, while posing much less difficulty and expense for the initiating firm' (p. 70).

For instance, the manufacturers of electric motors, batteries, and control systems for electrically powered trams, trolley buses, cars and vans may eventually displace the makers of internal combustion engines in some segments of the road transport market. The manufacturers of petrol engines, in particular, are becoming increasingly vulnerable to the pollution regulation and legislation that may eventually create new markets for electrical engineering companies and battery manufacturers.

Competition strategies are analyzed in Chapter 22.

THE USES OF COMPETITION ANALYSIS WITHIN THE PROCESS OF STRATEGIC MANAGEMENT

This chapter has analyzed competition on the basis of:

❑ sectors, markets, and industries.
❑ the location of competition.
❑ Porter's "five forces" model.
❑ the nature of competition.

The process of competition analysis requires inputs of information about competitors and their market activity. This information may be used:

❑ to construct a detailed competition analysis for the sector, segment, or market; or for the strategic group; or for the industry.
❑ to carry out a detailed evaluation of individual competitor activity.
❑ to forecast potential competitor response to market initiatives.

Competition analysis may then be used:

❑ to identify the competitive and marketing implications of the internal corporate appraisal described in Chapters 2 and 3, particularly building upon corporate strengths and financial position to gain competitive advantage.
❑ to identify the implications of the sources of competitive advantage described in Chapter 4, particularly building on resource capabilities and the ability to generate value.
❑ to identify, rank and select strategies which will yield competitive advantage; and alternatively:-
❑ to identify strategies whose implementation would instead place the enterprise at a competitive disadvantage relative to its competitors.

The selection of appropriate strategies is dealt with in Part Four of this book.

REVIEW QUESTIONS

1. Why is competitive analysis a key part of the process of strategic analysis?
2. Describe and comment on the five major groups of "forces" or variables which make up M.E. Porter's competition model. How are these variables inter-related?
3. Describe and comment on some of the main sources of competitor information.
4. In what way may an enterprise appraise or evaluate its competitors?
5. How may the enterprise assess potential competitor response to a planned market initiative?

TECHNIQUES OF CASE STUDY AND ANALYSIS

1. Identify the relevant industry and market.
2. Identify the key competitors (the "strategic group") in the case study.
3. Carry out a "five forces" competition analysis.

PROJECT ASSIGNMENT

Part One Project Assignment - The Strategic Analysis of a Company or Organization

Component Four: Using available information, carry out a competitive analysis of an organization that is of interest to you. Use M.E. Porter's "five forces" competition model as the framework for your analysis.

References

Kay, J. (1993) *Foundations of Corporate Success*, Oxford University Press, Oxford.
Porter, M.E. (1980) *Competitive Strategy*, Free Press, New York.
Albert, M. (1993) *Capitalism Against Capitalism*, Whurr Publishers, London.

Chapter 6

Environmental Analysis

**'The pessimist sees difficulty in every opportunity.
The optimist sees opportunity in every difficulty.'**
Winston Churchill

An important requirement of the process of strategic analysis described in Part One of this book is the appraisal of the *external environment* within which the enterprise operates. This is because the choice of strategies and the means by which they are implemented are, in part, determined by the character of this external environment.

It is therefore necessary for enterprise management to understand the characteristics, variety, and complexity of the *external forces* that shape strategy formulation and decision-making. The organization needs to be aware of the extent to which it must be prepared to adapt to influences that derive from these external forces.

This chapter describes and illustrates a variety of the components of the external environment. These are defined as "external environments". Most commercial, public sector, and not-for-profit organizations will have to take the effect of these external environments into account in their planning and decision-making.

The chapter examines the degree of *environmental stability*. The *threats* and *opportunities* that may derive from external forces are placed in a simple conceptual framework. The "SWOT" technique is described and its role explained. The chapter concludes on the role of environmental appraisal within the process of strategic analysis and strategic management.

ANALYZING EXTERNAL ENVIRONMENTS

The process of strategic analysis includes the assessment of a variety of external environments within which the enterprise operates. This assessment process is sometimes called the "scanning" of the external environment.

The process of analyzing the external environment is sometimes described as a "PEST" analysis. The acronym PEST stands for "Political, Economic, Social, and Technological" factors within the external environment. The concept of the PEST analysis is of course simplistic. There is a wider range of variables to consider than the four covered by the PEST analysis. The analysis of the external environment might for instance identify the fact that:

❑   business, commercial and public sector organizations within the European Union (EU) operate in a competitive but significantly regulated environment. They face increasingly well-informed and "energetic" customers, determined legislators, and electorates who have become environmentally aware.

❑   companies and organizations in Central and Eastern Europe have faced a critical period in adapting to market and political conditions that have developed at breakneck speed since the 1990s. They have faced extraordinary pressures for change.

❑   Japanese companies (and the Japanese government) continue to remain resistant to the global pressure on them to open up markets that have hitherto been largely inaccessible to foreign companies.

Some key external environments are analyzed below.

Demographics

Basic demographics underlie all market and economic trends. The external environment within which the enterprise operates depends on how the population is made up and who it contains. Business and public sector enterprises in the West, for instance, are having to adapt to major changes in population structure including an ageing population. Demographics affect the type and characteristics of consumer behaviour, marketing and promotion, staff recruitment, the development of enterprise capability and competence, and the wider process of forward strategic planning.

National and International Economic Conditions

The enterprise will attempt to analyze and to evaluate the potential consequences (both for the sector and for the organization) of the economic conditions it faces. It may for instance examine:

❑   trends in economic growth and Gross Domestic Product (GDP).

- relative rates of inflation.
- interest rates.
- international variations in relative currency values.
- employment levels and prospects.
- unemployment trends.
- trends in the management of international trade.

The policies of governments and international institutions are vital determinants of these prevailing economic conditions.

Of equal importance to international trade is the relative state of global economic development. To what extent, for instance, are the developing economies of the world breaking free of the problems of disease and over-population, degraded environment, political tyranny, internal instability, debt, or poverty?

Industry and Sector Structure

Strategic planners need to be fully aware of the structure of the trade or industry in which the enterprise operates. While the enterprise may have an intimate knowledge of its domestic context, it may have to research the structure of overseas markets in which it has a developing interest.

Analysis of sector structure may for example reveal the processes of concentration; government sponsorship of "competitive oligopoly" as in Japan or South Korea; or EU attempts to increase competition through restricting manufacturer control of distribution channels. UK companies are still coming to terms with the consequences of the privatization of former nationalized industries. Alternatively, the UK local government and public healthcare sectors have gone through a lengthy sequence of establishing "internal markets", of the implementation of compulsory competitive tendering contexts for purchasing activities, and of the subsequent introduction of Best Value or comparative methodologies for performance evaluation.

Markets

The markets within which the enterprise operates are a key constituent of the external environment. Whether the enterprise is a business organization, a public sector body, or a not-for-profit institution, there will be a need for effective market analysis as a fundamental input to the process of strategy formulation and strategic decision-making. This is because the nature and behaviour of markets determines or constrains both the choice of strategies, and the means by which they are to be implemented. The process of market analysis comprises:

- ☐   market research.
- ☐   the assessment of business risk (Chapter 8).
- ☐   sales and market forecasting (described in Chapter 9).
- ☐   the analysis of consumer and buyer behaviour.
- ☐   market segmentation (described in more detail immediately below).

Market Segmentation

To know a market implies segmenting that market. Market segmentation can be defined as *the analysis of a particular market demand into its constituent parts, so that sets of buyers can be differentiated and targeted.* Having carried out the process of market analysis described immediately above, the enterprise can segment and analyze its target markets. It will use the results of its market research, the analysis of consumer or buyer behaviour, and the forecasts it has made in order to produce detailed descriptions of its chosen market components and their likely behaviour over the planning period in view.

This means identifying the characteristics of different sets of buyers within the market. These sets of consumers or buyers need to be differentiated so that:

- ☐   they may be used as marketing targets against which appropriate products or services may be *positioned* exactly to meet segment customer demand; *and*
- ☐   a promotion and distribution mix appropriate to that particular segment may be selected.

What then follows is that the enterprise needs to choose a method of segmenting the market that most effectively allows it to understand that market and its customer needs.

How to Segment Markets

There are two main sets of criteria by which a market can be segmented or analyzed. These are (i) the characteristics of consumer or user; and (ii) product or benefit segmentation. Each is analyzed below.

Consumer or user characteristics - customer segments are differentiated by such criteria as:-
- geographic distribution or location.
- demography.
- life-style.
- consumption or usage rate.
- customer size.
- industry classification.

Product or benefit segmentation - this focuses on how consumers or buyers themselves perceive, differentiate, and group together the available products or services. This technique is used where people:-
- seek the benefits that the product provides, rather than the product itself (e.g. analgesics or proprietary pain-killers for the relief of headaches or pain); *or*
- consider the available alternatives from the viewpoint (i) of the *usage context* with which they have experience, or (ii) of the specific application that they are considering. For instance, business travel may be looked at primarily in terms of convenience, speed, and frequency of service. This may imply frequent high-speed rail or air-shuttle services in which ticket price is a secondary consideration.

Product or benefit segments can be differentiated by such criteria as:-
- principal benefit sought within perceived usage context.
- vendor requirements, that is the usage requirements of the customers of the organization being supplied.
- contribution per unit of limiting factor, such as square metres of retail floor space.

Segmentation criteria for consumer, and industrial or business-to-business markets are summarized in Table 6.1.

The Entrepreneurial Environment, and Attitudes to Risk

Prevailing attitudes towards *entrepreneurship* and *risk-taking* form a key context within which the organization's values and objectives are formulated. These attitudes are a function of such variables as:

- culture.
- tradition.
- experience.
- education.

Table 6.1 Segmentation Criteria

Segmentation criteria

	Consumer markets	Business-to-business markets
Consumer/user characteristics	Geographic distribution. Demography (age, sex, socio-economic group, occupation, income, family characteristics etc). Life-style. Personality (significant in the diffusion of new products). Consumption rate.	Geographic distribution. Customer size (the marketing process may have to vary with customer size, especially for very large industrial concerns). Usage rate. Industry classification (e.g. for steel marketing).
Product segmentation	Principal benefit sought within perceived usage context.	Principal benefit sought within perceived usage context. Vendor segmentation (usage requirements of customers of firms supplied). £ contribution per unit of limiting factor (such as square metres of supermarket floor space).

Prevailing culture, tradition, experience, and education may combine to provide an environmental context that is either (i) *positive to*, or instead (ii) *hostile towards* entrepreneurial activities. The organization's values will then determine the internal priority given to risk-taking, new business development, and so on.

Attitudes to entrepreneurship and risk-taking are also a function of the *perceived priorities* within the institutional community. Short-term expectations of profit and capital growth dominate stock market oriented financial environments. This may discourage risk-taking activities whose payback period may be perceived to be too long. The longer-term financial focus to be found in Germany and Japan, on the other hand, may encourage enterprise and initiative. Long-term perspectives and the minimization of stock market pressures may be essential to the long-term risk management involved in innovation and market development.

Similarly, the transition from centrally-planned to market-based economies in Russia, Central, and Eastern Europe has depended, in part, on the speed with which a degree of enterprise culture could be developed. These countries had limited prior experience of (legal) enterprise. It took a while for the capacity to manage risk to develop.

Technology

Strategic and operational decision-making depend on prevailing technological conditions and, increasingly, on the rate of change in the knowledge and technology base of the external environment. Competitive position and technological adaptation are closely related in such markets as electronics, computing, telecommunications, fast-moving consumer goods, data management, and security services.

Social and Cultural Factors

Social and cultural factors have a direct impact upon people's attitudes, consumer and business behaviour. Social trends, changes in education or the attitudes to work and leisure, and changing expectations all affect the operation of the organization. The enterprise does not work as a closed system. It is an open system that is subject to the changes that take place within its external environment. So, for instance, it may be directly affected by changes in family structure; by changing attitudes to racism, disability, ageism, and sexism; by changes in the role of women in society; or by varying attitudes towards personal saving and corporate investment (etc).

More fundamentally, the organization's values are shaped by the ethics and standards that characterize society. Attitudes and behaviour patterns are based upon the ethical and moral standards of the time. Changes in these ethical and moral standards must be reflected in the organization's own functioning. Otherwise it will eventually be subject to the sanction of the wider society of which it is a part.

"Environmentalism" and the "Green Revolution"

Western societies have become increasingly aware of, and sensitive to the effect of industrial and consumer society on the physical and psychological environments within which people live. There is increasing global concern about climate, disease, deforestation, and the exploitation of the natural environment. These concerns, and the more visible issues of pollution, waste, poverty, and the destruction of tropical rainforests are bound to influence the perceptions of individuals and institutions towards their external environment. This means, eventually, that their behaviour as consumers and buyers will be affected.

The issues of "environmentalism" and the "green revolution" are examined in more depth in Chapter 12.

The Political and Legislative Environment

Issues from the external environment find their ultimate expression within the political and legislative arena. The environment within which the enterprise operates could be shaped by political judgements or regulatory decisions for instance made:

- ❑ at local or national government level.
- ❑ in the European Union or the North American Free Trade Association (NAFTA).
- ❑ in the political scenarios developing in Central and Eastern Europe, Russia, the countries of the former USSR, and China.
- ❑ in changing Japanese and South Korean attitudes to the entry of foreign competition.
- ❑ in global negotiations over tariffs and trade.

Political decisions affect economic and social trends, markets, industrial structure and employment law. The enterprise needs to understand the political and legislative environments of all the countries within which it operates. And it needs to anticipate what their direct impact will be on the management of its affairs. The process of environmental forecasting is analyzed in Chapter 9.

ANALYZING ENVIRONMENTAL STABILITY AND CHANGE

The external environments described in this chapter may be analyzed in terms of *the degree of stability* and the *rate of change*.

It is advisable for enterprise management to understand the degree to which the relevant external environments are subject to variation and change. This variation and change can be classified as being any of:

- ❑ stable.
- ❑ moderately dynamic.
- ❑ turbulent.
- ❑ turbulent with increasing rates of change.

Each is described below.

Stable - variables within the external environment show little or no change over long periods of time. Organizations and their stakeholders have adapted to each other's needs (stakeholders are people or institutions who have some particular interest in the enterprise. They include customers, investors, distributors, suppliers, employees and trade unions, etc). Organizations and stakeholders will have reached, and are able for the time being to maintain a satisfactory accommodation with each other. An example might be a market during the mature stage of the product life cycle.

Moderately dynamic - variables within the external environment show a limited degree of change over time. Organizations and stakeholders face some problems of adapting to each other's needs and requirements, and may experience difficulties in reaching mutually acceptable accommodations. There might be some entry of newcomers, or increasing competition. Moderately dynamic conditions might also be represented by minor changes in the knowledge or technology base, or in the legislative context. The major environmental variables, however, remain unchanged or at most change slowly.

Turbulent - environmental variables now show a significant degree of change over time. There are very substantial problems of adaptation. The difficult situation may be exacerbated (i) by the entry of new competitors, new "players" or new stakeholders; and (ii) by the disappearance of others. There may be significant changes to the knowledge or technology base, or to the legislative context in which the major environmental variables operate. UK examples of turbulent environments have included:

- the enactment of the 1986 Building Societies Act and Financial Services Act which deregulated the markets for financial services, and gave rise to extensive new product ranges, customer service opportunities and increased competition.
- the introduction of the "internal market" into the National Health Service, based (i) upon budget holders (the purchasers of healthcare services such as General Practitioners); (ii) suppliers (self-governing hospital units, staffing agencies, and private sector companies); and (iii) the use of the processes of performance measurement described in Chapter 16 of this book.

Turbulent with increasing rates of change - environmental variables show an increasingly rapid rate of change. This may give rise to significant additional problems of adaptation. It may threaten the survival of existing operators or stakeholders. For instance, the markets for consumer electronics; computer and information systems; security and personal identification systems; information, communication and telecommunications (ICT) technologies (etc) have all shown this pattern of turbulence. There is a consequent need for constant innovation and investment in research and development (R&D) by companies in order to survive such conditions.

PERCEPTION AND INTERPRETATION

Environmental analysis is subject to the nature of processes of perception and interpretation. Perception and interpretation may either be objective or subjective. Where subjectivity occurs, the process of environmental analysis may be subject to the effect of:

❑   value judgement.
❑   variable attitude and opinion.
❑   "agenda forming" and influence.
❑   direct or indirect attempts to shape decisions (and their likely outcomes) in particular directions.

Perception and interpretation are dependent on *who* is carrying out the analysis of the issue at hand. For instance, differences may emerge between the perceptions and interpretations of:

❑   enterprise leadership.
❑   people in different parts of the enterprise, or at different levels of the management hierarchy.
❑   people within the enterprise in general.
❑   stakeholders.
❑   people within the trade or sector.
❑   relevant interest or pressure groups.
❑   so-called "experts" or "pundits" who possess influence.
❑   the news media.

The enterprise may choose to examine and compare a variety of the perceptions of an issue in question in order to obtain a broad view of how that issue is seen by different people, and in order to identify their relative interest in it. The enterprise may then weight these inputs as sources of interpretation according to their degree of credibility, interest, and influence.

The issue of *crisis management* is analyzed in Chapter 10.

IDENTIFYING OPPORTUNITIES AND THREATS

The strategic planner and decision-maker needs to treat the enterprise as an open system that is affected by the features of the external environment being described in this chapter. The influence of this external environment may either be positive or negative. At the same time it may offer external *opportunities*, or it may contain external *threats*.

Hence it is customary for the process of environmental appraisal to be used to identify those external opportunities and threats that may impact directly on the enterprise.

Opportunities

Features of the external environments within which the enterprise operates may present opportunities of which the organization may be able to take advantage. Some examples could include:

❑ the removal of barriers to international trade, allowing greater access to markets.
❑ EU or NAFTA harmonization - products or services from one country may now be saleable across the whole of the free trade zone.
❑ The economic development of China.
❑ the emergence of wealthy "grey" population cohorts aged 50 years and over who have significant personal disposable income (no longer having any children to support!). This income may be spent on expensive cars, second homes, or international travel (etc).

Threats

Features within the external environment may instead present some kind of threat to the continued operation of a particular activity. Worse, they may pose a threat to the continued existence of the enterprise itself. Some illustrative examples could include:

❑ demographic trends moving against the traditional customer base of the enterprise. For instance, the low birth rates in Western Europe have reduced demand for products associated with the feeding, clothing, and care of babies and young children.
❑ changing social or cultural factors moving against the pattern upon which the existing business of the enterprise is based. The wearing of

animal fur is widely perceived in the UK to be "politically incorrect". Fewer people in the UK eat red meat.

❑   global recession or restraint on trade.

❑   political uncertainty and acts of terrorism, caused for instance by conflicts in the Middle East or by tension between different ethnic or religious groups.

❑   free trade developments likely to encourage powerful new entrants into a market.

❑   free trade zones encouraging manufacturers to move to low-cost manufacturing locations such as Mexico or Poland.

THE USES OF ENVIRONMENTAL ANALYSIS WITHIN THE PROCESS OF STRATEGIC MANAGEMENT

The process of environmental appraisal described in this chapter has analyzed:

❑   the characteristics and the influence of the relevant external environments.

❑   the degree of environmental stability.

❑   specific external opportunities and threats.

This process of environmental appraisal may then be used:

❑   to forecast and assess likely future trends in the external environment that are of concern to the enterprise; *and*

❑   to select strategies that may best adapt enterprise activity to the developing characteristics of these relevant environments, thereby enhancing the degree of "fit" between the two; *and*

❑   to take advantage of specific opportunities that derive from the external environment; *or*

❑   to shape enterprise response to specific external threats.

THE "SWOT" ANALYSIS

The appraisal process described in Chapters 2 and 3 of this book analyzed the concepts of corporate and financial strengths and weaknesses. This chapter has identified the need to analyze opportunities and threats that may be present in the external environment. The process of strategic analysis may then most simply be based on a combined analysis of strengths, weaknesses, opportunities, and threats (the so-called "SWOT" analysis). To recap, this technique comprises:

❑ the analysis of internal strengths and weaknesses based upon corporate and financial appraisal; *and*
❑ the analysis of external threats and opportunities based upon environmental appraisal.

STRATEGIC ANALYSIS

The process of enterprise strategic analysis may however be rendered more systematic and more valuable if it also includes:

❑ performance gap analysis (Chapter 2).
❑ the financial health-check (Chapter 3).
❑ the analysis of capability, capacity, value addition, and the value chain (Chapter 4).
❑ the identification of sources of competitive advantage (Chapter 4).
❑ the analysis of critical success factors (Chapter 4).
❑ competitive analysis (Chapter 5).

REVIEW QUESTIONS

1. How may decision-makers analyze the external environments in which the enterprise operates?
2. Describe and comment in detail on any one external environment which can shape or influence strategic decision-making and choice.
3. Explain and comment on the different degrees of environmental stability with which the organization may be faced. How might dynamic or turbulent external environments affect enterprise strategy formulation?
4. How might the organization identify opportunities and threats from the external environment? Why is it important to scan the environment for these potential opportunities and threats?

TECHNIQUES OF CASE STUDY AND ANALYSIS

1. Identify the external forces and external environments described in the case study that may directly influence enterprise decision-making in the case study company.
2. Identify the nature of these external forces and external environments; and assess their potential impact on enterprise decision-making in the case study company.
3. Assess the relative stability or instability of the external environment and its component parts. What rate of change (if any) is evident?
4. Identify potential opportunities or threats (if any) that derive from the external environment, and assess their implications for the case study company.

PROJECT ASSIGNMENT

Part One Project Assignment - The Strategic Analysis of a Company or Organization

Component five: Using available information, carry out an environmental analysis for an organization that is of interest to you.

PART TWO

BUSINESS PLANNING, RISK ASSESSMENT, FORECASTING, THE STRATEGIC MANAGEMENT OF TIME, AND CRISIS MANAGEMENT

Part Two of this book deals with selected components of the process of strategic and business planning. Business planning and forecasting activities provide contexts for the formulation of strategy and the implementation of decisions described in later chapters of the book. Risk assessment provides a further parameter for these processes, which are also likely to be based on the analysis and management of the relevant time dimensions.

Part Two ends with a description of crisis planning and business continuity management. Chapter 10 looks at some of the possible consequences for the strategic management of the enterprise of such emergencies, crises, and disasters that might with a certain degree of likelihood befall it.

Part Two contains the following chapters:

- *its sector (or market)* - as defined by customer and segment characteristics, usage contexts, and demand factors. *Examples:* electrical power generating equipment.
- *its industry* - defined as groups of products or services between whose supply there is some market-relevant information (such as technology, distribution patterns, brand categories, corporate identity, or external perceptions). *Example:* electrical engineering.
- *its strategic group* - defined as those firms identified as primary competitors within the relevant sector or markets, having broadly similar aims and strategies. *Example:* international electrical engineering companies who manufacture power generating equipment include: ABB, GE Corp, CGE, Alcatel Alsthom, Siemens.

THE LOCATION OF COMPETITION

Key concepts that the generation of competitive advantage and added value (as described in Chapter 4) is a function of the competition and competitive behaviour within:

- any one market, industry, or strategic group, *and*
- any one country, *and*
- any one trading bloc.

given (i) the relative degree of *freedom of entry* for newcomers (whose arrival may cause disturbance or turbulence within the market, the industry, or the strategic group); and given (ii) the character and strength of national or international policies on the encouragement or limitation of competition (*competition policy*). For instance:

- the European Union (EU) and the North American Free Trade Area (NAFTA) espouse policies that facilitate and encourage free trade, in particular within the framework of the World Trade Organization (WTO) agreements.
- the USA has tough anti-trust (anti-monopoly) laws that are based upon a philosophical and constitutional belief in the merits of open competition and free market capitalism.
- Japanese and South Korean competition policy has been based upon the encouragement of *competitive oligopoly* between local companies within a framework of national protectionism.

Chapter 7

The Strategic Management of Time

The first chapter of Part Two of this book deals with attitudes towards time, and to its management. Time is a key variable in the process of strategy formulation, strategic choice, strategic decision-making, and business planning in the enterprise, but it may be subject to a wide variety of different conceptualizations. Some of these different conceptualizations are described and illustrated in this chapter.

TIME AS RESOURCE

Time is a key resource for any and all types of organization, irrespective of what these organizations do, or what sector they operate in. Western analysis assumes that *time as a resource is finite*. That is, time is as limited as is any other resource used by enterprise management to carry out its business. Time may as a result be conceptualized in terms of *capability*. Capability was described in Chapter 4. The enterprise can only achieve what its capacity will permit given the amount of time available to it. Time, like all other resources, may therefore be seen to have its *opportunity cost*. Opportunity cost may in this case be described in terms of the "optimum return" that may be derived from the investment by the organization of the time available to it, as compared with the potential alternative uses of that time.

TIME AS CRITICAL SUCCESS FACTOR (CSF)

The concept of the critical success factor (CSF) was defined in Chapter 4 as a key determinant of corporate success. Critical success factors are likely to have a predominant impact on the achievement of (or failure to achieve) the organization's objectives.

Time may act as a critical success factor where decision-making or investment (such as in additional process capacity, new process development, or new product/service development) has to react to, or respond to external conditions such as customer demand that is *time-dependent* or time-limited. For instance, client demand for improved surveillance or security facilities in the face of terrorist threat will have to be satisfied before the customer believes himself, herself, or itself to be likely to be under any increased threat of attack.

Time may instead act as a CSF when the required outcome or output must be created *at an exact given moment*. The success of a restaurant, for example, depends on its ability consistently to deliver the exact selection of food from the menu to its customers, properly cooked, and served at the right temperature within an acceptable period of delay from the taking of orders. This implies an appropriate investment in catering expertize, cooking facilities, and staffing. This will especially be the case where the restaurant is catering simultaneously to a large number of diners, as in the hotel, wedding, or conference trade.

Time may also be a critical success factor where the provision of resources is *time sensitive*. For instance, capacity decisions about the level of provision in any service-based activity will have to be based on an estimate of the maximum level of demand likely to occur at any particular time. For example, medical treatment capacity needs to be available when it is required. Urgent or emergency treatment cases cannot easily be stored, or placed in a queue until the appropriate level of resource becomes available to deal with them! Nor may a hospital be able to refuse to deal with a sudden epidemic on the grounds that the infection was unexpected!

TIME AS LIMITING FACTOR

Limiting factors were described in Chapter 4 as those influences that directly shape and limit the strategies, strategic choices, and operations of the enterprise. Chapter 4 noted that limiting factors could derive either from internal or external features.

The effect of such limits may be seen where the strategic management process is shaped by fixed or predictable time horizons. For instance:

❑ a school or a university must teach and assess students within absolutely fixed (and known) time horizons, and produce an acceptable outcome (for instance in terms of pass-rates or grades) at a given level of quality within that fixed time, irrespective of the character, capability, and motivation of any particular year's student cohort.

❑ a local or provincial government authority may instead have to manage its responsibilities within a fixed financial planning period of one year only, since decisions on taxation levels (and hence income) are continually subject to political pressure, and hence likely to vary from one year to another.

TIME AS CONTINGENCY OR CONSTRAINT

Prevailing contingencies and constraints were defined in Chapter 4 as being likely to determine how the enterprise may have to operate. They may instead shape what the organization is able (or unable) to achieve.

Time-related *commitments* may constitute a key example of such a contingency or constraint. The organization may be committed to courses of action (whether resulting from the making of past or present decisions) that are time-related or time-sensitive. Government decisions on investments in healthcare or social welfare provision will for instance be shaped by such contingencies as the time scales associated with the age structure and life expectancy of the population for which it must provide finance and benefits from the resources of taxpayers' money and the contracted private sector or insurance funding available to it. Past investment decisions, similarly, constrain a company's current and likely future strategic choices, since the enterprise will have to live with the present consequences of past resource commitments made by it. This is likely to be particularly critical where these resource commitments were long term in nature, as in the oil, steel, or petrochemical sectors.

SHORT AND LONG TERM ORIENTATION TO TIME

Hofstede (1997) notes the national cultural difference between societies that take a *long term* view of time and events, and societies that take a *short term* view. The difference between short termism and long termism is of course a matter of degree. Both are at opposite ends of a time (or "term") continuum. Oriental and South East Asian societies have tended to take a long term view towards the evolution of society or the economy, for instance making long term investments in technology development, education, competition strategy, or business development that may not pay off for many years to come. Anglo-Saxon and European societies, or the USA are instead characterized by a preference for short-term results and outcomes, for instance as a result of investments that they have made.

Impatience may be seen to be as much a virtue as patience, given the relentless drive of short-termist societies for rapid progress, continuous economic growth to meet stock market expectations, continuous innovation, continuous novelty of experience, personal self-gratification, and media stimulation. Short-termist societies may however be vulnerable to issues that demand a long term view, such as the future levels of personal pension provision, technology and process innovation, or public spending on infrastructure provision, healthcare, education, or social welfare support.

HAMPDEN-TURNER AND TROMPENAARS' ANALYSIS OF TIME DILEMMAS

Hampden-Turner and Trompenaars (1994), and Trompenaars and Hampden-Turner (1997) suggest that the nature of enterprise value systems, and the value judgements associated with them (such as the strategic conceptualization and management of time being analyzed in this chapter) appear to depend on a series of what they call "value dilemmas". Hampden-Turner and Trompenaars contend that these value dilemmas, and the varying solutions that may be found to resolve them, permit the understanding of key cultural differences between the approach taken by different nationalities to the various practices and processes of management. Value dilemmas associated with the strategic management of time are described as follows.

Making Rules and Managing Exceptions

The organization must to some degree formalize, standardize, or codify its operations. There exists a minimum (or "requisite") level of bureaucracy without which enterprise activities cannot be consistent, systematic, or predictable. Strategies, policies, plans, procedures, rules, and routines are seen to provide the basic framework for organized work over time.

This basic framework is a part of enterprise technology (Chapter 19); and is also a part of the relationship architecture described in Chapters 4 and 18.

At the same time, however, the value system needs to facilitate the recognition and management of time-related exceptions, and the inevitable need for change or innovation to which they may give rise. Enterprise leadership and organizational modes of strategy formulation, strategic choice, and strategic decision-making may need at the same time to be capable of any or all of the following:

❑ time management that is consistent with the relevant or chosen time horizons, for instance associated with business or public sector planning (Chapter 9), risk assessment (Chapter 8), or financial management (Chapter 13).

❑ short term adjustment (in order to deal with exceptional, new, or unexpected eventualities).

❑ longer term evolution.

❑ rapid and wholesale change (for instance when there is a sudden redefinition or shift in the knowledge, technological, or market base, such as has happened with the development and integration of information, computing and telecommunications technologies).

Deconstructing and Constructing

The "deconstruction" of concepts and phenomena is based on the process of analysis (breaking things down into their component or constituent parts). The "construction" of concepts and phenomena is based instead on the process of integration or synthesis, in which concepts are combined or aggregated into larger entities or wider systems. Analysis and integration are the opposite ends of an intellectual process.

Anglo-Saxon societies tend to analyze (that is, to "deconstruct"). Eastern societies (and the Germans) tend to seek wider and cohesive patterns (to "construct" or integrate).

The process of the strategic management of time may however call for both of (i) the analysis or breaking-down of time-related concepts, phenomena or events into their constituent parts; and (ii) the integration or synthesis of these time-related concepts, phenomena or events into whole patterns, relationships, systems, and wider contexts in time.

The strategic management process may also require the enterprise to be able to deconstruct and reconstruct its attitudes, its values, its concepts, its knowledge, its technology, its products and services, and its processes over time. It may have to be capable of combining the two intellectual processes of analysis and synthesis in order to be able to re-conceptualize, redefine, re-engineer, adapt, improve or change these attitudes, values, knowledge resources, concepts, technologies, products, processes and services as the time-related contingencies and constraints described in an earlier section determine or dictate at that moment.

Time as Sequence and Time as Synchronization

The enterprise may perceive an activity in terms of a single *linear sequence* of events that it has to carry out in order to achieve the objectives associated with that course of action. Time will be conceptualized (i) in terms of the time consumed by any one single event; and (ii) in terms of the total duration of the sequence of events. This duration might be illustrated by the sequence that represents a critical path in an activity network. The enterprise may then conceptualize the process of the strategic management of time in terms of concentrating its efforts and resources on finding the fastest way of completing that series of events, for instance by simplifying it by some process of re-engineering, or by exploiting the value chain linkages described in Chapters 4 and 18. Time is perceived in terms of a focus on carrying out individual activities as quickly as is feasible, which will result in the achievement of the shortest possible total sequence of time.

Alternatively, the enterprise may perceive activity in terms of achieving the synchronization of events (or of sequences of events) over time such that the completion of those events is co-ordinated coterminously (at the same time) or in parallel with other events that are related within a wider system or context. Hampden-Turner and Trompenaars give the example of Toyota's system of kanban and lean manufacturing. This is a flexible approach that depends for its success on the synchronization of a coterminous series of procurement, quality management, supply, and production events rather than the speed of their individual execution. Once this synchrony has been achieved, improvements in the required value outcomes may in any case follow, as in the case of just-in-time (JIT) processes where supply chain management, quality management, manufacturing, and cost management activities may all be optimized together on the basis of parallel processing and reduced cycle times.

Linear and Cyclical Conceptualizations of Time

The previous section comments that the organization may perceive activity in terms of a linear sequence of events over time. Time-related processes of the analysis and the integration of knowledge, events, or phenomena may be based on a linear conceptualization of time, moving forwards in a straight line into the future from the past and the present. This linear view of time for example underlies the marketer's idea of the dynamics of product management (which, confusingly for our purposes here is known as the "product life cycle"). Concepts based upon linearity are "logical" and "tidy" in the terms of deconstructionist Western analysis.

The use of such arbitrarily linear concepts may however be counterproductive to the development of the apparently more successful incremental, adaptive, and evolutionary approaches to the development of attitudes, values, knowledge, competences, technologies, resources and processes favoured for instance by the Japanese and the Germans. Western thinking may categorize an entity at a certain point on a linear sequence as being in "decline" or becoming "obsolete". The entity is seen as having little or no future potential. This conceptualization may blind the thinker to possible alternative cyclical views of the entity. Features of the entity may comprise a continuing resource to be recycled from the past or present into the future. It may be adapted and used within a wider long-term context of ongoing capability, competence, tradition, or market management. For instance, see Figure 7.1.

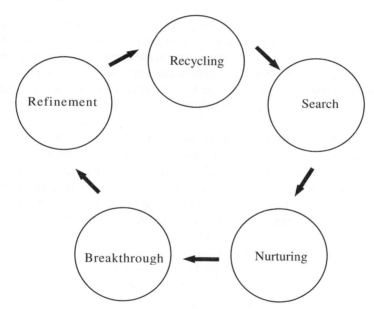

Figure 7.1 Tatsumo's Mandala of Creativity

Tatsumo's cyclical mandala of creativity demonstrates the Japanese belief in the evolutionary nature of society. Society is seen as being subject to continuing change. It is also amenable to improvement (*kaizen*), particularly as people accumulate experience, refine it, and hand it on over time across the generations.

The Japanese take a synchronous and long-term view of time rather than the linear, sequential and short-term approach of the West. The passage of time is associated with cycles. These cycles affect individuals, generations, entities, processes, and society generally. The present underpins the future, and lays its foundations. This is illustrated by the long-term and synchronous view taken towards technology. Developments now will, as progenitors, yield generations of products in the future. The development of technologies may be synchronized over time to achieve "fusion". This may firstly take the form of the hybrid technologies for which Japan is famous. Secondly, it may take the form of newly synthesized technologies, such as those based on the properties of the laser (Hampden-Turner and Trompenaars, 1994, pp. 147-150).

MONOCHRONICITY, POLYCHRONICITY, AND TIME

Lewis (1992, 1999) differentiates "monochronic" and "polychronic" cultures. *Monochronic* cultures behave in a focused manner, concentrating on one activity at a time within a set or planned time scale. Lewis for example categorizes the Germans, the Finns, and some North Americans as being monochronic. To such people time is a scarce resource which has the opportunity cost described in an earlier section, above.

Polychronic cultures are flexible and unconstrained by concerns with time. Polychronic people do many things at the same time, maybe in an unplanned or opportunistic sequence. They are not interested in time schedules or concepts of "punctuality". They consider that the "reality" of events and opportunities is more important than adherence to what they perceive to be intellectual or artificial constructs of planning, schedules, and appointments. Time is not seen as a resource. Nor is time seen to have any opportunity cost. Matters can always be settled tomorrow. Or fate may intervene instead. Lewis suggests that, for example, Indians, Polynesians, Latin Americans, and Arabs tend to be polychronic.

Monochronic cultures may in this context be more likely than polychronic ones to conceptualize time:

❑ in systematic or requisite terms, being subject to the need for proper procedures to deal with any exceptions to the rule that may emerge. Examples might include the use of standard times in service delivery; or the implementation of budgetary planning and control that is variable or flexible in terms of the time horizon to which it applies.

❑ primarily in deconstructionist (analytical) terms, prior to any necessary subsequent constructionism (integration or synthesis). Network analysis and the derivation of critical paths for instance depend on the effective breaking down of time into its activity components, and re-assembly on the basis of processes of synchronization and optimization.

❑ in terms of linear sequence, with the possibility of the optimization and synchronization of the use of time being achieved through deliberate, logical, planned, or systematic organizational process or procedure.

❑ in terms of incremental potential, by which change, improvement, or adaptation may rationally or deliberately be pursued by inter-relating time, capability, performance, and external contingencies as the relevant variables. This may be illustrated by any or all of the strategies of reduced cycle time, accelerated "time to market" processes of new product or new service development, or improved customer service described in the next section of this chapter, below.

There are parallels between the work of Lewis and that of Hampden-Turner and Trompenaars, whose analysis of time was described in an earlier section. The degree to which the enterprise is characterized by monochronicity or polychronicity may also affect the *time basis of strategy formulation* of which its decision-makers are capable. The basis of strategy formulation is described in Chapter 11. Monochronic cultures may be capable of any or all of the methods analyzed in that chapter. Polychronic cultures might instead be restricted to any of:

❑ "emergent" or "opportunistic" approaches to strategy formulation.

❑ a loose or ineffectively integrated process of "incrementalism", based upon unpredictable or poorly adapted step changes over time.

❑ a limited and inflexible form of "rationalistic" or "deliberate" form of "planning down" (described in Chapter 15), driven by a strongly centralized corporate centre characterized by high power distance, hierarchy, low trust, and a locus of control that as an architecture are collectively sufficient to extract organizational and staff compliance, and to force activities to happen within the time parameters prescribed.

The mixing of monochronic and polychronic cultures may give rise to culture clash and disagreement. It may call for the establishment of modes of co-operation and co-ordination between the two types about how time should be conceptualized and managed. On the other hand, the mixing of these two cultures may also yield synergies. Features of each cultural type may be complementary to the other. For instance, the greater flexibility of the polychronic may facilitate on-going developmental processes that are subject over time to unpredictable internal variation or external change, making it easier for the monochronic to modify plans and schedules in order to adapt. As such, therefore, the mixing of the two types may be a source of the "requisite variety" and "genetic diversity" in the organization that are described in a later chapter of this book, preventing stagnation and entropy, and acting as a potential source of creativity and value addition.

TIME MANAGEMENT AS SOURCE OF COMPETITIVE ADVANTAGE

Time may be used as a competitive weapon. Commenting on his use of rapid movement and manoeuvre as a campaign strategy, Ries and Trout (1986) note of Napoleon that 'his troops, he claimed, could march two miles to the enemy's one. "I may lose a battle", said Napoleon, "but I shall never lose a minute"'. The effective use of time may be a competitive determinant in such activities as:

❑ the *reduction of cycle time* associated with operational or developmental activities. Reduced cycle time might be for instance be associated with processes of manufacturing; supply chain management; the treatment of patients; teaching, learning, and assessment methods; or the management of working capital. Or the achievement of improvements in cycle time might instead be the objective of institutional programmes of re-engineering, excellence, or Six Sigma described in Chapter 16.
❑ *new product development time* (or "time to market"). Competitive advantage will be gained by bringing effective new products or processes to the market or client more quickly than competitors.
❑ *on-time performance* within the quality and reliability parameters specified for product or service delivery. On-time performance is for instance just as crucial to the provision of healthcare, policing, or security services as it is to systems of just-in-time supply, to running an airline service, or to delivering the right products on a mail order basis.
❑ *customer response*, in which competitive advantage may be gained by those organizations that respond most speedily to customer demand, or make them wait the shortest time for service. The timing of response to customer or client is as much a key issue in the provision of healthcare,

fire fighting, or police services as it is in the marketing of business or consumer services.

A preceding section of this chapter noted Hampden-Turner and Trompenaars' contention that time can be viewed as either or both sequential and synchronous. Competitive advantage may be gained by enterprises that can:

❑ conceptualize and plan workflows, systems, or procedures to contain fewer sequential steps through time than their competitors. For instance, the Russian eye ship carried out eye surgery on a flowline out-patient basis, requiring no hospital accommodation and maximizing the output of the most valuable resource (and limiting factor), the services of the eye surgeon. Even the processing of revenue transactions was simple. Clients paid in hard currency by cash or credit card before they left the ship!

❑ conceptualize workflows, systems, or procedures as synchronous as well as sequential through time. The simultaneous or parallel execution of sequential steps will reduce the total time taken for the process (that is, it will shorten the sequence). The logical consequence is then to eliminate some of the original steps, thereby reducing the length, complexity, and cost of the sequence. There are many examples of this process. They include (i) the synchronous manufacture of car specification variants (Hampden-Turner and Trompenaars use Toyota as an illustration); (ii) the mass flowline production of bread variants through the "Chorleywood" manufacturing process; and (iii) simultaneous or real time electronic payments, funds transfer, and inventory management systems.

SHAREHOLDER VALUE, TIME, AND COMPETITIVE DISADVANTAGE

The enterprise will have to decide on its term-orientation, and on the length of its future time horizons. These will depend upon the basic definition of the objective of the institution, and may be driven by the demands of owners, shareholders, sources of finance, taxpayers, (etc) as stakeholders for results and returns ("stakeholders" are defined in Chapter 11 as people and institutions both internal and external to the organization who have an investment in it, or who instead have some kind of involvement or interest in it, or who are directly affected by its activities or its processes).

Anglo-Saxon companies whose shares are publicly listed (and openly available) on stock exchanges may find that there is a large proportion of their shares being held by institutional investors such as insurance and investment companies, or pension funds. These large institutional shareholders are likely to require the management of the companies in which they hold shares to maximize shareholder value on a short-term or an annual basis. This is needed so that these large investors may satisfy their own customers, for instance in terms of personal pension or investment income. Such pressure for the continuous delivery of shareholder value is likely to grow as the population in Anglo-Saxon countries ages, with more and more people being dependent on institutional investment returns for their retirement income.

Japanese, Swiss, and German companies may on the other hand be able to take a longer-term view of their business than many of their American, British, or Anglo-Saxon competitors. Companies in Japan, Germany or Switzerland are for a number of reasons under less pressure to maximize short-term shareholder value. Investment returns may instead be measured over a period of years, "taking one year with another". This may especially be the case where these companies are family-owned, private, or their shares are "close-held" or "cross-held" and therefore unavailable for purchase on the open market. This may give them significant competitive market and technological advantages, for instance (i) in the long-term development of new products or processes, or in business development; (ii) in the capacity to "pick global sector winners" for the long-term; and (iii) in the long-term development of leadership, management, staff, capability, and competence.

The issues of short and long-termism, shareholder value, and competitive advantage are given more detailed treatment in Chapter 13 of this book.

OTHER TIME-RELATED ISSUES OF STRATEGIC MANAGEMENT

Other time-related issues of strategic management are analyzed in the following chapters:

- □ time and risk assessment - Chapter 8.
- □ planning horizons and forecasting - Chapter 10.
- □ financial strategy and management - Chapter 13.

REVIEW QUESTIONS

1. Why may time be classified as a resource, and what is its opportunity cost?
2. Why may time be a critical success factor?
3. Why may time be a limiting factor?
4. In what ways may time act as a contingency or a constraint?
5. Compare, contrast, and comment on short and long term orientations to time. Give examples of each.
6. Summarize Hampden-Turner and Trompenaars' conceptualization and analysis of time dilemmas. Comment on the implications of these time dilemmas for the strategic management process.
7. Compare and contrast monochronic and polychronic approaches to the management of time.
8. In what ways may the strategic management of time be used to achieve value generation or competitive advantage?

TECHNIQUES OF CASE STUDY AND ANALYSIS

1. Identify and comment on any of the characteristics of the strategic management of time that are apparent in the case study.
2. How, if at all, is the case organization (or case organizations) making strategic use of the time management process to add value or to achieve competitive advantage?

PROJECT ASSIGNMENT

Using available information, analyze and comment on the attitude towards, and use of time inherent in the strategy, plans, and operations of an organization in which you are interested.

References

Hampden-Turner, C. and F. Trompenaars (1994) *The Seven Cultures of Capitalism*, Piatkus, London.
Hofstede, G. (1997) *Cultures and Organizations (revised edition)*, McGraw-Hill, London.
Lewis, R.D. (1999) *When Cultures Collide*, Nicholas Brealey, London.
Lewis, R.D. (1992) *Finland: Cultural Lone Wolf - Consequences in International Business*, Richard Lewis Communications, Helsinki, Finland.

Ries, A. and J. Trout (1986) *Marketing Warfare*, McGraw-Hill, Singapore.
Trompenaars, F. and C. Hampden-Turner (1997) *Riding the Waves of Culture*, Nicholas
    Brealey, London.

Chapter 8

Risk Assessment

"Put your trust in God, my boys, and keep your powder dry"
Oliver Cromwell (attributed)

This chapter analyzes risk assessment as a component of strategic management and business planning. It deals with the management of the risk and uncertainty associated with processes of strategy formulation, strategic choice, and strategic decision-making within the organization. The chapter concludes with a summary analysis of selected implementation issues.

RISK AND UNCERTAINTY

The process of risk assessment and risk management has two components. Each is summarized below.

Risk Defined

The concept of *risk* may be defined for the purpose of this chapter in terms of strategic decision-making and strategic choice that is to some degree characterized (i) by a knowledge of the alternatives available to the decision-maker; *and is in addition* characterized (ii) by some knowledge of the probability of occurrence of the various alternative outcomes. That is, the likelihood of achieving any one of the available alternatives may at least be estimated, or a forecast created. Forecasting techniques are analyzed in Chapter 9.

Uncertainty Defined

The concept of *uncertainty* may be defined for the purpose of this chapter in terms of strategic decision-making and strategic choice that is to some degree characterized (i) by a lack of knowledge of the likely alternatives available to the decision-maker; *and is in addition* characterized (ii) by a lack of knowledge of the probability of occurrence of the various alternative outcomes that might be identified. That is, the likelihood of attaining any one of the potential alternatives may be difficult or even impossible to predict or to forecast.

THE ROLE OF RISK ASSESSMENT IN THE STRATEGIC MANAGEMENT PROCESS

The assessment of risk and uncertainty is a key input to the processes of strategy formulation, business planning, and strategic management being described in this book. Risk assessment is used in the creation of estimates of the likelihood or probability with which desired strategic outcomes (the objectives and strategies defined in Chapter 11) may be achieved. It is also used to identify the possible consequences of strategic decision-making about these desired outcomes for the financial, human, and other resources being committed to the strategic choice of the enterprise. As such, risk assessment is therefore a key part of:

❑   the business planning and forecasting process described in Chapter 9.
❑   the process of financial management described in Chapter 13.
❑   the processes of strategy formulation and strategic decision-making described in Chapter 14.
❑   the process of leadership described in Chapter 17.

CATEGORIES OR SOURCES OF RISK AND UNCERTAINTY

Risk and uncertainty may derive from either or both of internal and external sources. These sources may be categorized as follows.

Internal Sources of Risk and Uncertainty

Which may be identified through the strategic analysis processes of organizational, asset, resource, and capability appraisal, for instance as described in Chapters 2, 3, and 4 of this book. Risk and uncertainty might derive from any or all of capability and capacity issues; managerial, architecture or systems issues; information flow issues; weaknesses; unpredictable or irrational leadership behaviour or decision-making (as sometimes happens in SMEs or family firms where the use of executive power is strongly centralized and unquestioned); or the emergence of strong or politicized forces driving change from within; (etc). Other internal sources of risk and uncertainty might include potential internal threats of business interruption or failure; or security issues associated with assets, resources, staff, or finance.

External Sources of Risk and Uncertainty

Which may for instance be identified through the strategic analysis processes of external, competitive, and environmental appraisal described in Chapters 5 and 6. They may also be understood from an analysis of the time dynamics described in Chapter 7; and through the use of some of the forecasting techniques analyzed in Chapter 9. Risk and uncertainty might for example derive from any or all of contingencies associated with time; with market or competitive dynamics; environmental behaviour or change; government policy-making; the emergence of new external paradigms, comparators, or benchmarks; the emergence of powerful forces driving innovation; or the emergence of strong forces driving change. Other external sources of risk and uncertainty might include:

❑ potential external threats of business interruption or failure.
❑ mandatory areas of compliance or liability associated with external legislation or regulation.
❑ the potential for criminal intervention or damage (such as fraud or terrorism).
❑ physical or psychological risk associated with location (such as political instability, civil unrest, lawlessness, etc). This issue is also dealt with in Chapter 28.
❑ risk and uncertainty associated with prevailing national culture variables (such as a low degree of *uncertainty avoidance* in which there is a relatively more relaxed attitude to business risk and to the potential for shareholder or stakeholder loss).

Emergencies, Crises, and Disasters

Whose incidence may pose severe risk and uncertainty to the continued viability of the organization. The issue of crisis management is dealt with in detail in Chapter 10.

RISK, AND THE DEFINITION OF EVENT CHARACTERISTICS

The risk and uncertainty inherent in the strategic management processes of strategy formulation, strategic choice, strategic decision-making, and strategy implementation will, in part, depend on *the definition of the characteristics of the events* about which judgements or decisions have to be made. These event characteristics include the following. Each may be a source of risk or uncertainty.

Ambiguity - by which the event is characterized by a variety of potentially conflicting definitions or interpretations, and therefore presents alternative meanings from which the decision-maker may have to choose.

Change - by which the event, and the variables which make it up, are subject to a pattern or dynamic that is characterized by any or all of ongoing originality, novelty, variation, alteration of parameters, inconsistency, or instability. There may be no relevant past experience or precedent by which to make judgements about the event, whose interpretation may in any case be ambiguous.

Complexity - by which the components of the event are characterized by a wide variety of inter-related variables, each of which (*and* the inter-relationship between them) must be considered in the process of evaluation and decision-making.

Economic value implications - the event may possess economic value characteristics whose potential outcome will shape processes of interpretation, judgement, and decision-making. Decisions based upon financial calculations, accounting conventions, investment proposals, discounted value methodologies, and value-chain concepts, (etc) may be characterized by risk or uncertainty.

Entropy - by which the nature and outcomes of the event are likely to be characterized by risk and uncertainty because negative features such as stagnation, decline, deterioration, or criminal intervention are present. Systems theory states that open systems that do not receive and apply an adequate (or "requisite") variety or quantity of relevant or new information and stimulus from the external environment may be subject to entropy.

Inconsistency - by which the event is likely to act as a source or risk or uncertainty by failing to demonstrate similar or predictable features over time. There may be a lack of reliable precedent by which to make judgements about the event.

Instability - by which the characteristics of the event demonstrate a random or unpredictable degree of variation around the norm. Political systems (and hence government decision-making) are often characterized by such instability, making it difficult to make long-term predictions about the likely course of public policy. Markets for fast moving consumer goods (FMCG) based on a high fashion content (such as clothing, toys, electronic games, or popular media entertainment) may also demonstrate short-term instability.

Originality, novelty, or innovation - by which event characteristics present new features for which the organization possesses no precedent for risk assessment or decision-making. Conditions of originality, novelty, or innovation may give rise to risk and uncertainty because they will require new modes of thinking, new experience, or the development of new capability and competence before the enterprise is in a position to make effective judgements and decisions about them.

Unpredictability - by which the nature or likely occurrence of the event may not easily be anticipated and forecast in advance. The event demonstrates characteristics of the unexpected or the unknown. This unpredictability acts as a source of risk and uncertainty.

Values implication - the event may possess value (or "value-laden") characteristics whose potential implications may shape processes of interpretation, judgement, and decision-making. Risk and uncertainty may characterize decisions based upon features of social architecture, organization culture, organizational value-sets and attitudes, values-based management, or national culture variables.

Variety and diversity - by which risk and uncertainty derive from the degree of variation or diversity of events or experience to which strategic management processes are subject. It may reasonably be assumed that the greater the degree of the variety or diversity of events, (i) the greater the need for effective evaluation and judgement; (ii) the more important it will be to be able to identify, categorize, and differentiate the various or diverse features of the event; (iii) the greater or more complex will be the decision-making load to be undertaken; (iv) the more critical becomes the need for an organizational capability to deal with, or possess experience of diverse events; and (v) the potentially greater the degree of risk and uncertainty that enterprise management will face.

Volume - the degree of risk and uncertainty associated with strategy formulation and decision-making may vary proportionately with the volume of events faced by decision-makers. The greater the volume of events, (i) the greater the task associated with making judgements and decisions; (ii) the greater the risk of decision-maker overload, time delay, or process confusion; and (iii) the greater the risk of prioritization, filtering, or simplification of decision-making processes based on artificial or conventional criteria that are selected for their expediency or convenience at the time, irrespective of their actual relevance to the events being experienced. For example, one way for an overburdened state health service to simplify decision-making in conditions of excessive patient load is to reduce all decisions about risk and uncertainty to a cost-effectiveness basis. Decisions on strategy and patient care may simply be made on the basis of prioritizing courses of action which are seen to be most cost-effective in the general scheme of things.

RESOURCES AND RISK ASSESSMENT

The degree of risk to resource allocation and resource use that is inherent in any particular strategic choice or strategic decision may be a function of such variables as:

❑ the total value of the resources involved in the implementation of the chosen strategies and plans.
❑ the length of time during which resources are committed, and therefore at risk.
❑ the relative risk inherent in any one venture.
❑ the proportion of the total available resource committed to any one venture.

Resource risk assessment is analyzed below.

The Risk of Value Loss

Where the implementation of a chosen strategy involves the combination and use of enterprise resources, the objectives may include:

❑ *the generation of customer value* from the application and use of these resources, thereby satisfying a customer, client, or market need; and justifying the selection of the strategy.
❑ *the adding of value* as a result of the combination and use of resources in the value chain described in Chapter 4, such that a positive return may be obtained from the investment in these resources over the time during which they are in use. This return may be measured in outcome terms such as positive contribution earned, profit margin, return on investment, payback, net present value (NPV) or internal rate of return (IRR), patient treatment success rates, voter satisfaction, and so on.

❑ *the maintenance of the real value of the resource* invested in the implementation of the chosen strategy. *Example:* if you have an investment in shares or unit trusts, are they worth more or less than last year? Or, if you know someone who has their own business, is it worth more than they invested in it, or less? If the former, they have gained value. If the latter they have lost value.

However, in evaluating the choice of current and future strategies, the enterprise needs to remain aware that any investment of resources that it makes in the implementation of its plans *may give rise to the risk that those resources may lose their value or even disappear altogether.* The potential for loss of value may occur as a result of the internal sources of risk and uncertainty listed in an earlier section, above. Examples might include any of the following:

❑ ineffective or inadequate staff capability.
❑ poor forecasting or decision-making capacity.
❑ the direct loss of staff competence (for instance through the "poaching" or "head-hunting" of key managers, technologists, engineers, or decision-makers).
❑ inadequate investment; poor financial management or overtrading; depreciating assets; or the actual damage to or deterioration of physical assets. For instance, such was the neglect of its plants in Akron, Ohio by the former US Firestone Tyre Company that it became unable to produce tyres to world class standard. Firestone was taken over by the Japanese Bridgestone Tyre Company, who subsequently had to invest heavily in refurbishing Firestone's US manufacturing capability.
❑ ineffective leadership; or the loss of leadership motivation and willpower.

The potential for loss of value may instead occur as a result of external sources of risk and uncertainty listed in an earlier section above. Examples might include shifts in the external market or environment deriving from:

❑ sudden or drastic changes in demand pattern or volumes (such as have affected international sales of British beef).
❑ the impact of technological change (the Boeing 707 killed off the transatlantic ocean liner at a stroke), for instance as described in Chapter 19.

❑ the interaction of innovation dynamics, new product or process development, and product or process obsolescence, for instance as described in Chapter 19.

❑ the impact of powerful government, environmental, or environmentalist influences on demand (for instance on the attitude towards the consumption of cigarettes or alcoholic drinks), or on operational process (for example the generation of electricity by means of the use of nuclear or wind power, or the burning of fossil fuels).

❑ the emergence of powerful criminal or terrorist influences.

Risk and Time Scale

The proportionate risk of negative financial return or value loss may be a function of the *duration* and *time scale* of the resource commitment. For instance:

❑ the longer the time scale, the more probable it will be that the enterprise may suffer exposure to the risks described in previous sections, above.

❑ the longer the time scale, the less certain may be any of (i) the generation of the requisite customer or client value; (ii) the generation of added value, and the return on the investment of stakeholders; (iii) the maintenance of the real value of the assets involved; or even (iv) the actual survival of those assets.

❑ the longer the time scale, *the proportionately greater may be the eventual requirement* for the generation of value, and for the return on the resources invested by stakeholders. Long term investments, for instance in oil exploration in the Caspian Sea, or airline purchases of aircraft, may raise the *dilemma* that (i) obtaining a return on investment may be uncertain and unpredictable over such a long time frame; whilst (ii) at the same time it may become increasingly difficult to convince shareholders or stakeholders of the viability of the strategy being proposed, and to persuade them to fund the necessary investment in it. This syndrome was amply demonstrated by the Anglo-French Channel Tunnel project, which is unlikely ever to fulfil the investment returns once promised for it.

Financial strategy and management are analyzed in Chapter 13 of this book.

Risk and Resource Commitment

The risk of negative return or value loss may be related to the proportion of total available resources being committed to any one venture. This is an "eggs in the basket" argument. Do you put all your eggs in one basket? What then happens if you drop the basket?! The greater the proportion of its resources that the organization commits to the implementation of any one strategy, the more pronounced may be the consequences if the strategy is unsuccessful. This lack of success may be clearly demonstrated in terms of losses to investors and stakeholders; in terms of a loss of institutional credibility; and in the form of criticism of enterprise leadership. This was the case for the UK Marconi Company whose decisions on product-market strategy proved disastrous during the late 1990s.

A more positive example of the potential consequences of the high level of strategic commitment being analyzed in this section is that of the Boeing 747 aircraft. Boeing had to commit much of its available resource to the design, manufacture, and certification of the first "jumbo" jet. If airlines had not decided to buy the 747 it is likely that the Boeing company itself would have collapsed. As it was, the accuracy of Boeing's reading of the market meant that the company attained a dominant position in the supply of long-haul passenger aircraft that lasted for many years. The 747 project catapulted Boeing into the number one position in the aircraft market.

MATRIX RISK ASSESSMENT METHODOLOGIES

The process of risk assessment may be represented in diagrammatic form by the use of *risk matrix* methodologies. Such methodologies may encompass such variables as:

- ❑ risk category or event characteristics, as described in earlier sections, above.
- ❑ the potential impact on, or consequences for the organization of the risk or event.
- ❑ the likelihood or probability of the risk or event occurring, for instance as expressed in terms of relative frequency.

For instance, the matrix shown in Figure 8.1 may be used to categorize particular types of risk or events in terms of "high", "medium" or "low" values. The nine cells of the matrix might then for the sake of illustration be weighted on a score of, say, 2 (very low) to 32 (very high) to indicate the potential seriousness of the risk to the enterprise.

RELATIVE IMPORTANCE/ POTENTIAL IMPACT/ DEGREE OF RISK ⟍ PROBABILITY, LIKELIHOOD, FREQUENCY	HIGH SCORES	MEDIUM SCORES	LOW SCORES
HIGH INCIDENCE	32	16	8
MEDIUM INCIDENCE	16	8	4
LOW INCIDENCE	8	4	2

Figure 8.1 A Risk Assessment Matrix

STRATEGIES FOR MANAGING RISK

Risk management mechanisms might include any of the following.

Risk Avoidance

Risk avoidance may be based on a strategy of altering the organization's risk profile by changing or improving the nature of its process or practice. For instance, a pharmaceutical company might replace the testing of substances on live animals with computer modelling methodologies which yield a similar result. A company might instead increase its level of security so as better to avoid the risk of fraud or criminal intervention. Alternatively, use may be made of the appropriate competition strategies described in Chapter 22, whereby the enterprise avoids "head-on" or other high risk forms of competition with companies or organizations who have a lower level of risk aversion; or whose absolute level of resource availability (or "deep pockets") may permit them to outspend others over long periods of time in order to maintain or increase market dominance. Remember, the Biblical David was only able to take on Goliath because the giant wasn't wearing full body armour! If Goliath had had leg and body pads, a cricket helmet with visor, and a bat to execute a square cut, then David and his stone wouldn't have had a chance! The Israelites would have had to come up with another battle plan!

Co-operation and Partnership

The adoption of strategies of co-operation, resource-sharing, and partnership is described in later chapters. These strategies include the use of the de-integrated value chain incorporating network structures or value adding partnerships analyzed in Chapters 18 and 22; making use of the strategies of "stretch and leverage" described in Chapter 21; or incorporating the strategic alliances described in Chapter 27. Such changes to the relationship architecture and structure of the enterprise may be used (i) to widen the resource base available to the organization; (ii) to focus on what each constituent or partner does best; and thereby (iii) to spread risk among the participants. This is how aircraft are designed and manufactured by the various companies that make up Europe's Airbus consortium.

Risk Transfer

Risk management may be based on a strategy of transferring risk to third parties, for instance by subcontract, or by insurance through the facilities of agencies such as Lloyds of London.

Risk Reduction

Risk management is based in this case on the reduction of potential risk by (i) changing or improving the nature of enterprise capability, process, or practice (for instance by specifying organizational capability to comply exactly with health and safety regulation, or with prevailing legislation dealing with such employment issues as conditions of work, disability, diversity or equality); or by the process of "target hardening" described immediately below.

Target Hardening

Obvious sources of risk are identified and "hardened" against intervention, criminal impact, or failure. For instance:

- buildings, assets, people, knowledge, intellectual property, and systems may be made secure.
- processes and practices may be specified to conform exactly with external requirements for compliance, whether by legislation, regulation, insurance requirements, or with the ethical standards described in Chapter 12.
- strategic management processes of leadership, risk assessment, strategy formulation, and business planning may be subjected to effective forms of *scrutiny* before decision-making, the assumption of risk, and the commitment of resources by the enterprise is permitted. The objective

here is to minimize the potential for ineffective decision-making that will increase the risk profile of the organization, not decrease it. Such a process of scrutiny may be a required component of the processes of stakeholder analysis, corporate governance and leadership described in Chapters 11, 13, 14 and 17.

Risk Retention

The organization accepts the responsibility of independently accepting and managing the potential consequences of its risk profile, for instance because this risk cannot be subcontracted or insured. The process of risk management will in consequence have to include the target hardening described immediately above, the preparation of appropriate contingency plans, and the identification of the resources that would need to be made available to cover the costs of failure, emergency, crisis, disaster, or subsequent litigation.

Log Keeping

In this case, the organization maintains detailed minutes and formally validated records of communication and decision-making processes associated with risk planning and risk management, and with the emergencies, crises, and disasters described in Chapter 10. Such records may provide vital explanation or evidence in any subsequent inquiry or litigation procedures.

Media Management

The process of risk management in any particular situation may be complicated by the organization's need to deal with the print and broadcast media. Decision-makers dealing with conditions of known risk or uncertainty, or the emergencies, crises or disasters described in Chapter 10, are likely to have to meet the requirements of the representatives of such media. This may complicate the process of organizational response by adding an additional layer of complexity in which the external agendas of others may be dominant.

The need for media management may therefore call for a carefully planned and controlled accumulation and dissemination by the organization of accurate, credible, and up-to-date information flows for external media consumption. It may call in turn for effective media training, and the prior simulation of communication strategies, press briefings, and media relationships.

IMPLEMENTATION ISSUES

SOME ISSUES ASSOCIATED WITH RISK ASSESSMENT

Risk assessment may be affected by *the inter-related cognitive processes* of:

- ❏ perception.
- ❏ conceptualization.
- ❏ interpretation.
- ❏ the derivation of meaning.

That is, what does the perceived type and level of risk *imply* to the person or people making the assessment? And how will that assessment influence judgements, or shape decisions that have to be made on the basis of those judgements?

Issues Associated with the Analysis of Risk

Issues associated with the analysis of risk might include any of all of the following:

Attitude to risk - the outcomes of processes of strategy formulation and strategic decision-making may depend on the national culture variable of *uncertainty avoidance*, and on whether enterprise leadership is (i) *risk tolerant* or (ii) *risk averse*. This issue is for instance dealt with in Chapter 13, in which perceptions of risk are related to issues of financial strategy, investment, required returns, capital structure, and financial management. It is also dealt with in Chapters 19 and 22. Attitude to risk is related to:-
The perception of risk as opportunity or threat - decision alternatives may be viewed as giving rise to opportunity or threat dependent upon the prevailing attitude of decision-makers to the risks that they perceive they face. *One person's threat may be an opportunity for another*. This is for instance true of potential changes in the knowledge or technology base described in Chapter 19, or for the choice of competition strategies described in Chapter 22.

Ability to exploit risk - perceptions of risk may be related to the ability of decision-makers to manage and to exploit that risk. This ability to manage and to exploit risk may be a function of the attitude to uncertainty already described above. It may also be a function of the degree to which the enterprise has been able to build-up and retain the necessary knowledge and experience of such activities (i) as target hardening and security management; or (ii) the implementation of the competition strategies, new product or process development, new business development, and internationalization described in Part Four of this book.

The choice of opportunistic strategies - decision-makers may deliberately select the opportunistic strategies described in Chapter 11. In this case, strategic choices and strategic moves are contingent (dependent) upon the opportunities that emerge or become available. Competitive advantage in this situation may then derive from the possession of an agile, responsive, flexible, and adaptive capability; a high degree of risk tolerance; and the ability to exploit risk already described above. The use of opportunistic strategies may be illustrated by the aggressive and successful competitive behaviour of some Japanese, South Korean, and Chinese enterprises.

Entrepreneurship - situations that are perceived by existing players to be unacceptably risky may be a key source of entrepreneurial opportunity for others. Entrepreneurs may for instance be able to make use of new knowledge, new technology, or security issues as the basis of a new business that has been rejected by more risk-averse competitors. This was the case of Sony's decision to use the newly created transistor in order to develop solid-state radios and electronic goods. Western suppliers were resistant to the fundamental design change this represented, and saw no need to invest in it. This proved to be a fatal decision for such electronic component manufacturers as Mullard, which soon disappeared.

Intrapreneurship - the term "intrapreneurship" is used to describe the implementation of entrepreneurial attitudes and risk-tolerant behaviour within existing organizations. Intrapreneurs may be charged with developing new products, new processes, new markets, or new businesses. The process of intrapreneurship may confront the enterprise with a need to accept and understand attitude to risk assessment from a variety of different viewpoints, such that intrapreneurial activity may actually be allowed to take place. The potential conflict to which this may give rise is sometimes resolved by separating intrapreneurial, "newstream", or new business development activity from current mainstream activities. This issue is dealt with in detail in the author's text *Principles of Management*, also published by Ashgate.

The "paralysis by analysis" syndrome - the rationalization and systematization of the process of risk assessment may be carried out by individuals or organizations to such a degree that planning for risk becomes the *end*, not the *means*, of strategic management. In such a sense, strategic managers *plan*; they do not *act*. Wisdom, intuition, common sense, and proposals for action are overwhelmed by intellectual process. Or they are neutralized by reasons not to take action. This "plan it, not do it" syndrome may then be exacerbated by any or all of the following behaviours.

The "irrationality syndrome" - in which apparently rational techniques are used to identify and to "confirm" the risk assessment that is deemed to be "most correct" in terms of, or "most consistent" with the existing value set, presuppositions, or prejudices of decision-makers. The risk assessment will prove what decision-makers want it to prove, irrespective of its relevance to the actual situation in hand. For instance, the British Government did not believe in the 1940s that jet propulsion would in the foreseeable future be used for commercial passenger aircraft and instead invested in the ill-fated "Brabazon" project. This left the door wide open for US plane makers to reinforce their lead in transport aircraft such as the DC3, and resulted in American dominance of the civil aviation market for decades to come.

Control obsession - in which decision-makers use the process of risk assessment to rationalize and "to make certain" circumstances or situations that *cannot in fact* be fully understood or fully rationalized. Decision-makers try to fit risk and uncertainty into a "fixed" model, irrespective of whether that model is appropriate to the use to which it is being put. To what extent can police or security services, for instance, ever be expected to be able fully to rationalize and to anticipate in advance the threat posed by random and changing forms of criminal or terrorist activity? An obsession with rationalization and control may in particular be a feature of national cultures characterized by high levels of uncertainty avoidance and high power distance.

Fictionalization - by which the processes of risk assessment are taken to such extremes of "pseudo-exactness" that they become meaningless in terms of the reality of what may be achieved. The internal needs of the operation of sophisticated planning procedures (perhaps encouraged by the availability of powerful computer modelling capability) may come to displace the purpose for which those procedures were intended in the first place. This syndrome was characteristic of the era of "corporate planning" in UK central and local government. Complex plans and risk assessments were created, but by the time they were published they had lost any meaning or relevance to the situations for which they had been developed. They had become intellectually challenging, but futile academic exercises.

REVIEW QUESTIONS

1. How may risk be defined?
2. How may uncertainty be defined?
3. Describe and comment on some of the categories or sources of risk and uncertainty (also see Chapters 9, 10, and 13).
4. In what ways may an analysis of event characteristics be used to indicate the potential risk associated with enterprise decision-making?
5. In what ways may the process of strategy formulation and strategic decision-making place the finance and resources of the enterprise at risk? (Also see Chapter 13).
6. What are matrix risk assessment methodologies?
7. In what ways may the enterprise manage the risk associated with the formulation and implementation of its chosen strategies and plans? (Also see Chapters 9, 10, and 13).
8. Describe and comment on some of the limitations to the risk assessment process.

TECHNIQUES OF CASE STUDY AND ANALYSIS

1. Identify and comment on the potential risk(s) associated with the strategies, decisions, and plans being described in the case study (also see Chapters 9 and 13).
2. How, if at all, is the case company (or case companies) managing the risk(s) that you have identified in Question 1 above (also see Chapters 9 and 13).

PROJECT ASSIGNMENTS

1. Using available information, analyze and comment on the apparent risks inherent in the strategy and plans of a SME or any other type of organization in which you are interested. How is risk being managed by this organization? (Also see Chapters 9 and 13).
2. Using available information construct a risk matrix, or a set of matrices according to category of risk, for a SME or any other type of organization in which you have an interest.

References

Borodzicz, E.P. (2005) *Risk, Crisis and Security Management*, Wiley, Chichester.
Mintzberg, H. (1994) *The Rise and Fall of Strategic Planning*, Prentice Hall, London.
Morden, A.R. (2004) *Principles of Management (2nd Edition)*, Ashgate, Aldershot.
Nottingham, L. (1996) "Integrated risk management", *Canadian Business Review*, Summer.
Weston, J.F. and E.F. Brigham (1980) *Managerial Finance*, Holt, Rinehart & Winston, London.

Chapter 9

Business Planning and Forecasting

"Fail to plan ... then plan to fail"   Anon.

"Don't let *your* failure to plan ahead become *my* crisis!"   Anon.

This chapter analyzes the process of business planning and forecasting. Business planning is a way of managing time, and of anticipating the future. Business forecasting is a basic ingredient of this planning process. Forecasting is an attempt to visualize the way in which market or other external environmental variables might behave during the planning period (or "time horizon") within which the enterprise is working.

The chapter defines and describes the processes of planning and forecasting. It analyzes the role of forecasting within the business planning process. It describes a variety of forecasting techniques, and it looks at the choice of forecasting method. The material builds on the contents of Chapter 7 (the strategic management of time) and Chapter 8 (risk assessment).

STRATEGIC, BUSINESS AND BUDGETARY PLANS

The next major component of this book, Part Three, describes a variety of concepts and techniques of strategy formulation and strategic decision-making. These concepts and techniques of strategy formulation and strategic decision-making are used by enterprise management to chart the progress of the organization through time and through risk into the future.

Processes of strategy formulation and strategic decision-making described in Part Three will determine the nature of the objectives the enterprise is to pursue over time, the directions in which it will move, the degree of risk it can manage, the capability and resources it will require, and the means *(strategies)* by which it will achieve its goals.

An end product (or manifestation) of the strategy process being described in this Book will be *strategic and business plans*. These *plans* will be based on the chosen objectives and strategies of the enterprise. They provide the *framework* by which these objectives and strategies are to be implemented and achieved. They provide the *time scale* for the implementation process. And they will be based on the chosen degree of *risk tolerance* or *risk aversion* of the organization.

The enterprise plans that result from the processes of strategy formulation, strategic decision-making and strategic choice may be categorized as follows.

Enterprise Plans

Strategic plans - which are constructed with, say, a two to five year planning horizon into the future. Strategic plans are used to implement and achieve the broad strategic purpose (or "strategic intent") of the organization, for instance as described in Chapters 11, 12, 13, and 15 of Part Three. Strategic plans may also be referred to as "corporate" or "long-range" plans.

Business plans - which are constructed with, say, a one to three year planning horizon into the future. They are used to shape the detailed operational and business unit activities required to implement the strategic plans described immediately above. They are likely to contain mechanisms of monitoring, feedback, and review to ensure the achievement of the necessary performance outcomes. Achievement will in turn be measured by the appropriate performance indicators such as sales, or profit, or the number of patients successfully treated.

Business planning is now widely used. It has become mandatory in the UK public sector. Virtually all UK institutions (such as local government authorities and agencies, the uniformed services, hospitals, schools, and universities) that are in receipt of public funds are required to compile detailed business plans and to monitor their performance against the objectives set down therein.

The issues of performance evaluation and performance management are analyzed in Chapter 16 of this book.

Budgetary plans - which operate on the basis of an annual cycle. Budgetary plans provide a detailed financial framework by which to manage the implementation of the business plans described immediately above. They will be associated with mechanisms of monitoring, feedback, and review to ensure the achievement of the necessary performance outcomes. Achievement will be measured by the use of detailed performance indicators such as departmental operating cost, numbers of staff employed ("headcount"), or sales revenue per employee (etc).

The effectiveness of the planning process will itself in part be dependent on the process of *business forecasting*. The forecasting process is analyzed in the remaining sections of this chapter.

The planning process is summarized in Figure 9.1.

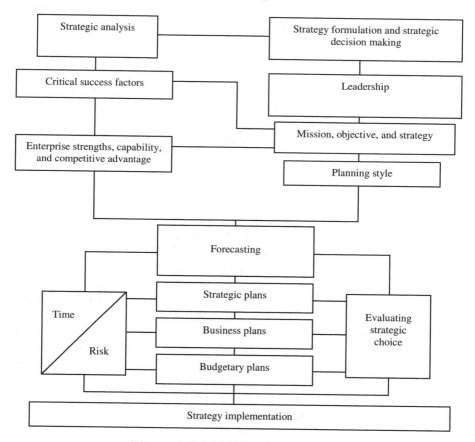

Figure 9.1 The Planning Process

BUSINESS PLANNING AND FORECASTING

Forecasting is an important input to enterprise planning and strategy formulation. Forecasting and planning are inter-related. An enterprise cannot plan ahead without making forecasts, and it cannot make forecasts without having some kind of plan to act as framework for the forecasting process.

The process of forecasting attempts to produce a picture of the kind of *future risk and future environment* in which enterprise plans and activities are likely to be implemented. It makes assumptions about the future conditions that are likely to determine the success of these plans. And it attempts to predict the outcome from the implementation of these plans.

The Need for Planning and Forecasting

It is inadequate (and dangerous) for the enterprise to be responsive only to its present environment. Any enterprise, whether business, public sector, or not-for-profit, needs to plan for the future. Enterprise management needs to attempt to anticipate the future environments within which the organization will operate. *Planning for tomorrow is as important as making decisions for today.* There are two reasons for this.

Firstly, the making of plans and forecasts, and their eventual review, forces managers *to think ahead*. The organization should know what are at least some of the likely consequences of both its *existing commitments* and the *future plans* it is implementing. And it ought to be able to describe some of the most probable *scenarios* that it is likely to face over the next few years. A "scenario" is a prediction of what is more or less likely to happen in the future. There is no reason why the enterprise should not limit the risk and uncertainty implicit in the future to those most unpredictable events that are almost always impossible to forecast.

Secondly, the making of plans and forecasts involves *systematic thought and analysis*. Such an intellectual process may be of value in itself, particularly in organizations that have a tendency to 'be long on action but short on thought'.

Planning Assumptions and Future Expectations

Planners will base forecasts on *planning assumptions* and *future expectations*. Planning assumptions are predictions about the likely environments in which plans are expected to be implemented. In some cases, such assumptions might be described in terms of the *probability* with which their occurrence may be predicted. For instance, while it is *quite likely* that there will be further rises in the price of crude oil, it is *almost certain* that UK households will pay significantly more for their water supply as river and lake pollution is cleaned up, new reservoirs are constructed to augment supply, water quality is improved, and sewerage systems upgraded over the next decade. The question is whether water bills will rise by 20 percent, or 40 percent, or more?

Decisions based upon these assumptions then become *forecasts of future expectations.* The enterprise calculates probable ranges of revenues, costs, cash flows, or profits which may result from the conditions that are forecast to occur. These expected outcomes result from the planning assumptions that form the basis of the forecasting process for a business organization for instance shown in Figure 9.2.

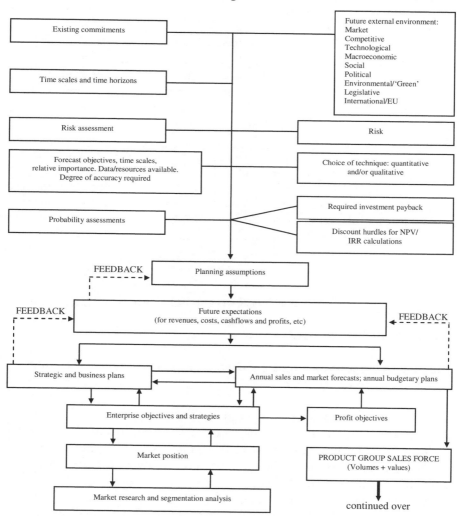

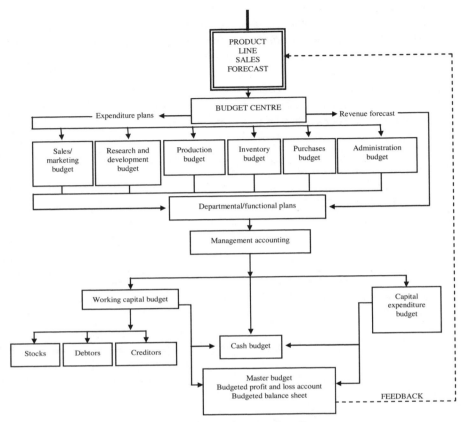

Figure 9.2 The Forecasting Process

WHAT IS BEING FORECAST?

The forecasting process ultimately deals with *volumes* and *values*. Volumes to be forecast could include:

☐   sales volume per customer, per territory, or per segment.
☐   numbers of customers, clients, or patients to be dealt with. How will hospital, pension, and welfare systems cope with the increasing numbers of old people in Western countries in the next few decades?
☐   volume at target market share.
☐   volume to be shipped or distributed.
☐   production or workload volume to be handled; and in consequence the operational capability required.

❑ the number of staff to be employed.
❑ the amount of sub-contracting or outsourcing that will be required. Can sub-contractors be found; and could they handle the quality and quantity of work needed?

Commercial values to be forecast could include:

❑ sales revenues per customer, territory or segment.
❑ revenue at target market share.
❑ costs of production, distribution, or service.
❑ cash flows per customer or segment.
❑ customer or segment profitability. Will the forecasted returns be enough to keep shareholders happy?
❑ the cost of staff to be employed. Would Mexican employees be cheaper than American ones; and what will be the potential consequences for the location of factories in North America?
❑ the cost of sub-contracting or outsourcing. Is it likely to be cheaper to run IT-based transaction systems in Paris or in India (assuming location is irrelevant to the operation)? Where do you carry out the large-scale writing of standard software?

Volume forecasts will for instance be used to determine the level of operational capacity required by the organization in the future, whether it be to manufacture cars, to provide electricity to homes and industry, or to treat patients.

Forecasts of value will for example be used to assess the financial consequences of planned operations; to identify the necessary level of investment required to finance this planned level of operation; and to predict the likely financial returns to be obtained. Financial performance ratios were described in Chapter 3.

SALES, MARKET, AND OPERATIONAL FORECASTING; AND BUDGETARY PLANNING

The purpose of sales, market, and operational forecasting is to assess:

❑ the likely sales or operational volume and value during the time horizon ahead.

❑   potential changes in market or environmental determinants that are likely to affect the enterprise and its operations. *Example:* increasing expectations of the quality and timeliness of healthcare treatment.

❑   possible cost changes that are likely to affect prices, and the profit or contribution margins that are dependent on them. *Example:* reduced labour costs that result from the outsourcing of an activity to a low labour cost location facilitating lowered prices or increased profitability for the enterprise.

Sales, market and operational forecasts are a key part of the planning process in any commercial, public sector, or not-for-profit organization. These forecasts contribute to medium to long-term planning, say for the next two to five years ahead. In particular, however, they are a driving force of the annual process of budgetary planning. Budgetary planning and control provide the basic framework for detailed operational and departmental planning and control, thus:

❑   a *budget* may be defined as a quantitative and financial plan of the activity to be pursued during the forthcoming financial year to achieve that year's objectives.

❑   the *budgetary planning and control process* may be defined as the establishment of budgets that relate the responsibilities of departments and individuals to the requirements of strategies and plans; and the continuous monitoring and comparison of actual results with the budgeted targets, so that these targets may be achieved or amendments made to the objectives upon which they were made.

The preparation and compilation of budgetary plans requires the input of a forecast of sales or operating volume and value. This forecast becomes the basis upon which is constructed a series of inter-related departmental, functional, and financial budgets. These culminate in a forecast of cash flow, cost, and profit or surplus. The sales and market forecast is illustrated in Figure 9.2.

OTHER FORECASTING TECHNIQUES

There is a wide variety of forecasting techniques. These can be divided into two main categories, namely *quantitative* and *qualitative*. Each is described below.

QUANTITATIVE FORECASTING TECHNIQUES

Quantitative forecasting techniques comprise three main groups, namely:

❑ Subjective.
❑ Statistical.
❑ Explanatory.

Subjective Forecasting Techniques

Sales force composite method - combined sales force and sales management view of customer or territory sales, or market share to be obtained during the next forecast period.

Juries of executive opinion - a combination and compilation of informed and expert opinion about market or operational trends, and future scenarios within the sector.

Surveys of buyer intention - a compilation of expected purchases by major customers in the sector during the forecast period ahead.

Statistical Forecasting Techniques

Moving averages - forecast for Time (t + 1) is based on an average of several past values of the actual variable (e.g. sales, cost, etc) achieved. Of short term use, applicable to less than one year.

Exponential smoothing - forecast for Time (t + 1) is based on an exponentially decreasing set of weights, so that the more recent years receive more weight than earlier ones. Of short term use, applicable to less than one year.

Time series analysis - this projects past or historical trends forwards into the future. It assumes stable economic, environmental, market, distribution, and organizational conditions. The forecaster searches past time-series of data for *consistent* evidence of seasonal variations, cyclical variations, variations which can be attributed to the occurrence of identifiable and non-random events, and longer-term (or "secular") trends and their likely degree of permanence.

Trend extrapolation and curve fitting - which is based on past time-series of data, using statistical techniques to project trends forward for periods of two or more years ahead. Extrapolated trends or projected curves may be varied to allow for unstable environmental conditions, variations in risk or outcome probability, etc.

Explanatory Forecasting Techniques

Operational Research (OR) models - which are *abstractions* of real systems or processes used to represent the basic *constant* and *variable* features that make up these systems or processes. Their purpose is to allow exploration and explanation of the behaviour of the system or process, for instance:-

- as the values of the variables are changed, for example on a "what would happen if" or "what if " (*sensitivity*) basis.
- as the system or process operates through time or risk.
- as it is affected by the incorporation of variations in the probability with which events are forecast to occur. What, for instance, is the probability of the UK joining the Euro currency in the next few years? Is it 10 percent or 50 percent or 100 percent?!

Operational Research models are used to *simulate* the workings of a real-life system or structure, so that the planner can identify or "experiment" with alternative patterns or behaviours. Forecasting examples could include:-

- *production scheduling* - modelling inventory, cash flow, and capacity management for a manufacturing activity involving a wide variety of large complex engineering work carried out on a unit, small batch, or just-in-time basis in conditions of variable market growth and uncertainty. Such modelling may be of particular value in determining the scale and necessity of proposed investments in additional manufacturing capacity, especially where market demand is likely to be subject to a pattern of variable peaks and troughs, and where outsourcing is likely to be a viable alternative.

- *promotional mix* - the optimizing of promotional mix expenditure required to achieve and maintain the sales growth needed to meet the revised revenue and profit targets of next year's business plan.

Management System Dynamics - which is used to model time-varying behaviour, for instance of markets; operational, production and distribution systems; cash and financial flows. It is particularly suited to modelling *dynamic* forecasting situations based upon feedback processes and information systems. It can be used to model complex behaviours over long time-spans, if this is appropriate.

QUALITATIVE FORECASTING TECHNIQUES

Three qualitative forecasting techniques are analyzed, namely:

❑ Scenario development.
❑ Delphi techniques.
❑ Cross-impact analysis.

These techniques are summarized below.

Scenario Development

Scenario development involves the construction of a number of alternative possible forecast "future scenarios" or outcomes. These future scenarios are used to describe the particular variables under consideration, and to indicate how they might develop under a range of different future circumstances. Often, three scenarios are constructed. These are the *pessimistic*, the *most likely*, and the *optimistic*. Probabilities may be assigned to each scenario. The most likely scenario will be based on a projection of known and stable trends; may incorporate statistical extrapolation; and represents a relatively "surprise-free" outcome. The other two scenarios will be developed around this first one, representing a more optimistic and a more pessimistic outcome respectively.

An example of scenario planning is the mounting European concern with car ownership and traffic volumes. Governments are constructing alternative scenarios which for example model (i) the effects of increasing traffic volumes on the adequacy (or otherwise) of road networks, (ii) the potential consequences of increasing pollution, and (ii) the potential costs of further investment. Such scenarios are giving rise to a variety of alternative suggestions as to how to deal with the problem. These solutions might propose higher taxes on motorists, more investment in public transport, road tolls, or the banning of private cars from city centres. They also point to the likely potential for the development of electric commuter cars, "park and ride" facilities, tramway systems, trolley buses, and urban rapid transit systems.

Delphi Techniques

Delphi techniques are based on the combined views (or "executive opinion") of a number of experts, perhaps drawn both from inside and outside of the organization. Each member of the panel provides his or her views about the forecast issue, *working independently* from the other panel members. These initial opinions are collected and compiled, and fed back to the panel. Certain ideas are then eliminated, by mutual consent. With the remaining information to hand, each panel member makes a further assessment until, after this iterative process has been repeated a number of times, some convergence of opinion may appear. The forecast is thus based on a synthesis of mutually informed and developed opinion, and is characterized by a certain level of agreement among panel members which has been brought about by the iterative process used.

Cross-Impact Analysis

Cross-impact analysis is a methodology for exploring and analyzing the actual or potential *inter-relationship* or *interaction* between events or circumstances. Two or more variables are taken and their relationship analyzed. Potential cross-impacts between these variables are then sought. For example:

❑   the development of computer technology called for the parallel development of printer and cable technologies.
❑   the development of computer technology affected the market for typewriters, ultimately rendering them obsolete with the emergence of the word processor. Subsequent development of information and communication technologies (ICTs) have had a massive impact on the nature and organization of clerical and administrative work, transaction processing, data management, telephony, or office accommodation (etc).
❑   political developments in Eastern Europe and the Near East may affect the long-term development of the European Union. Eventually, for example, the EU may have to deal with applications for membership from Israel, Serbia, and the Ukraine?

The problem for the forecaster is two-fold. Can the most likely or the most important cross-impacts be identified? And can the probability of their occurrence be estimated with any degree of accuracy?

The Application of Qualitative Forecasting Techniques

Qualitative techniques in general are used to give a *broad shape* to the issues being forecast. They are used to put quantitative forecasts, such as for market share or required capacity, into a wider or environmental context. The qualitative forecasting process may also be used to supplement the quantitative techniques described in earlier sections, above.

Qualitative forecasting provides a means of analyzing the wider potential opportunities, risks, and threats contained within the external environment. In terms of the strategic management of time (Chapter 7) the process is usually relevant to medium and long-term and planning. Two illustrations are given below.

Illustration One - Macro-political Forecasting

A large international financial institution might construct a variety of alternative macro-political scenarios describing the different degrees of (i) economic, (ii) monetary, and (iii) political unification that may occur within the European Union over the next decade. Three such scenarios might be developed, as follow.

First scenario - the lowest level of co-operation and unification foreseeable. There are "fast track" members such as Germany, France and The Netherlands; with "slow track" members such as the UK and Denmark following reluctantly. Poland becomes a powerful voice in promoting the interests of the newer Central and Eastern European members.

Second scenario - the likely level of co-operation realistically to be foreseen in the newly expanded EU.

Third scenario - the most optimistic level of co-operation possible, with a high degree of economic and monetary union, a high degree of political and inter-government co-operation, and European policies on international trade. Countries such as the Ukraine, Serbia, Israel, Switzerland, and Turkey join as "associate members". NAFTA and the EU commence negotiations to establish an Atlantic Ocean free trade zone between them.

The forecaster might then attempt to rank these scenarios in the order of probability of occurrence. Probabilities might be assigned thus:

Scenario (1) = 0.3
Scenario (2) = 0.6
Scenario (3) = 0.1

Strategic decisions on future business development in Europe might then be based on scenarios (1) and (2) only, with scenario (3) ignored for planning purposes for the time being.

Illustration Two - Technological Forecasting

Technological forecasting deals with the projected impact of scientific developments on the future state of technology. The process attempts to examine how such developments may affect a company's products, processes or markets. For instance, the high rate of scientific and technological development in the fields of electronic semiconductors, microprocessors, and optical light-transmitting gallium arsenide technology during recent decades affects companies manufacturing electronic and telecommunications products, computers, and so on. Technological forecasting has become a crucial part of the strategic planning process in such companies. There is a direct link between technological development, new product specification and development, research and development expenditure, brand, price, profitability, and the company's standing and reputation in the marketplace.

Issues of knowledge and technology management are analyzed in Chapter 19 of this book.

CHOICE OF FORECASTING METHOD

The choice of forecasting method will depend on a number of factors, including any or all of the following:

Forecasting objectives - these may be to quantify the annual process of budgetary planning and control; or instead to look ahead for major changes likely to occur within the organization's external environment, and so on.

Time scale - the various forecasting methods have been described as having different value according to the time scale for which they are being applied. Commonly, sales and market forecasting for a period of one or two years ahead is differentiated from other types of forecast, and especially those dealing with longer-term or more uncertain issues.

The importance of the forecast - the more important the forecast, the more informed must be the choice of method, and the more likely it will be that several forecasting methods will be used and combined. The use of several different forecasting methods may serve to minimize the risk of any one forecast being inaccurate. Ultimately, the enterprise may subject its forecasts to a process of review, evaluation, qualification, and synthesis by the periodic use of Delphi panels.

The degree of accuracy required - the sophistication and cost of the forecasting process, and the eventual use of comparison of forecast with actual performance achieved, determines the accuracy of that process. *Feedback* on the relevance and accuracy of forecasting over a number of years is an essential ingredient of the forecasting process.

Availability of data - there are limits to the kinds of information available for use in the forecasting process, and especially that associated with competitive analysis. As in all commercial calculations, the cost of obtaining information and carrying out forecasts needs to be balanced against the likely benefits to be obtained from that process. There may come a point where it is preferable to carry out a *limited trial or experiment* to see *what actually happens*, rather than to hypothesize about what might happen if that experiment was to be undertaken.

Access to forecasting skills and experience - the quality and accuracy of the forecasting process will in part be a function of the skills and experience available. So, the more that the enterprise can develop staff skills, information systems, and feedback on actual results compared with forecast, the more successful may be its forecasting capability. And the more effective is its forecasting "track record", the more willing may the enterprise be to undertake the high risk experiments or trials with new products, new processes, or new methods that are a significant source of competitive advantage. Knowledge management issues are dealt with in Chapter 19. Issues of core competence are analyzed in Chapter 20.

REVIEW QUESTIONS

1. Why should an enterprise plan ahead?
2. What different types of plan are there? Compare and contrast these different types of plan.
3. What is forecasting? Why is forecasting important to the process of strategy formulation and business planning?
4. What is the role of the sales and market forecast in the process of business planning?
5. Describe and explain the use of any one quantitative forecasting technique.
6. Describe and explain the use of any one qualitative forecasting technique.

TECHNIQUES OF CASE STUDY AND ANALYSIS

1. State your interpretation of information (if any) in the case study that gives an indication of future eventualities likely to impact on the case company or companies.
2. Suggest alternative scenarios for these future circumstances, given the information in the case study *(but don't make things up - stick to the case study information only)*. What are the implications of these scenarios for the strategy of the case company or companies?

PROJECT ASSIGNMENTS

1. Using available data, construct a three-year quantitative and qualitative forecast for a market, a sector, or an industry in which you have an interest.
2. Using available data, construct a detailed two-year quantitative and qualitative forecast for a market segment of interest to a client company or SME. Present your findings.

References

Hampden-Turner, C. and F. Trompenaars (1994) *The Seven Cultures of Capitalism*, Piatkus, London.
Higgins, J.C. (1980) *Strategic and Operational Planning Systems*, Prentice Hall International, London.
Morden, A. R. (1993) *Elements of Marketing (3rd Edition)*, DP Publications, London.
Morden A .R. (2004) *Principles of Management (2nd Edition)*, Ashgate, Aldershot.

Chapter 10

Crisis Management

'No company, no matter how financially successful, powerful or reputable, is immune to crisis' Regester and Larkin (2002, p. 105)

'A badly managed crisis can severely damage a company, its reputation, and its brand' Curtin *et al* (2005, p. 28)

Borodzicz (2005) comments that the 'concepts of "major incident", "emergency", "crisis", "disaster", "accident" (and) "catastrophe" … are all examples of terms used to describe events capable of rupturing our social world and devastating our physical one' (p. 76).

EMERGENCIES DEFINED

Borodzicz defines an emergency as a situation which requires 'a rapid and highly structured response where the risks for decision makers can, to a relative degree, be defined' (p. 79). He suggests that 'in organizational terms, an emergency could represent a situation of danger that can be responded to (by) using … procedures … laid down … in a management plan' (p. 79). As such, emergencies 'are situations requiring rapid application of an organization's existing policies and procedures' (p. 83).

CRISES DEFINED

A crisis may be categorised as 'a serious threat to the basic structures or the fundamental values and norms of a social system'.

Borodzicz defines a crisis as a situation requiring an urgent diagnosis and response but in which the risks for decision-makers may be 'difficult to define owing to an ill-structure in the situation. It is typical for such situations that the effect of a response is, or appears to be, unclear' (p. 79).

Such a crisis may in addition 'not be immediately apparent to those decision makers responding to the situation' (p. 80). Borodzicz suggests that 'crises are ill-structured situations ... in terms of technical, social and cultural contexts. The greater the degree of ill-structure ... the more difficult the incident becomes for recognition and management; more agencies become involved and hence more social agendas become juxtaposed ... this spiral ... can lead to disaster' (p. 81).

Regester and Larkin add that a crisis may become: 'an event which causes (an organization) to become the subject of widespread, potentially unfavourable attention from the national and international media and ... (stakeholder) groups such as customers, shareholders, employees and their families, politicians, trade unionists and environmental pressure groups who, for one reason or another, have (an) interest in the activities of the organization' (p. 120).

DISASTERS DEFINED

Nudell and Antokol (1988) define a disaster as 'an overwhelming ecological disruption occurring on a scale sufficient to require outside assistance' (p. 3). A disaster might result from a natural occurrence, a serious accident, or some kind of criminal or terrorist activity. Disasters may be caused for example by industrial accidents, fires, crashes, floods, hurricanes, earthquakes, volcanic eruptions, landslides, avalanches, famines, epidemics of disease, political instability, government incompetence, anarchy, armed conflict, criminal intervention, or concerted terrorist attack. As a result, Borodzizc suggests that any process of disaster management may, *inter alia*, have to be concerned with the circumstances associated with such "unexpected and unwanted" events, as well as with the practical consequences of "picking up the pieces" thereafter.

Borodzizc notes that despite being categorized as "freak events" or "acts of God" in the past, disasters are now seen to have *causes* which may be identified and understood. This is important because: 'the notion of a causal agent suggests that blame may be identified ... (in) public enquires, an exhaustive amount of time and expense may be focused on establishing causality and (therefore) responsibility' (p. 76).

Borodzizc defines a disaster as a systematic 'collapse of cultural precautions for dealing with socio-technical phenomena' (p. 82). He suggests that 'a disaster can be defined as a cultural construction of reality. Disaster is distinct from ... emergency and crisis only in that physically it represents the product of the former ... fundamental to (this) understanding is that specific socio-technical systems affected by disasters will have been indelibly challenged, possibly leading to inquiries at the highest social and cultural levels ... the public inquiry in the UK is an example of this' (pp. 81-82). A disaster may be overwhelming, as expressed in terms of human costs, lives lost, financial loss, or damage to social structures. That is, there may in terms of the event characteristics described in Chapter 8 be a degree of severity or danger which differentiates disaster conditions from emergencies or crises.

INDUCED CATASTROPHE DEFINED

Nudell and Antokol define an induced catastrophe as a category of crisis, emergency or disaster that results directly from the *intentional activities* of individuals or groups. Two types of induced catastrophe are identified under this heading.

Non-Security Type

These are ecological, human, social, political, financial, corporate, or business emergencies, crises or disasters that result from the incidence of negative or hostile external conditions or event characteristics; or instead result from such features as ineffective leadership, personal or political misjudgement, precipitate action, mismanagement, ineffective government policy, greed, incompetence, or anti-social, unethical or illegal practice.

Security Type

These are emergencies, crises or disasters that are associated with such illegal features as extortion, fraud, corruption, the tampering with or contamination of product or process, sabotage, arson, kidnapping, bombing or other forms of violent attack or terrorist activity.

CRISIS AND CATASTROPHE ILLUSTRATED

Regester & Larkin comment that evidence from the 1990s showed that key categories of crisis and catastrophe in the UK and the USA included:

❑ product or process faults.

❑   organizational mismanagement, incompetence, and ineffective leadership.
❑   executive dismissals and payoffs (the "fat cat" syndrome).
❑   cases of discrimination and staff harassment.
❑   lawsuits and litigation.
❑   industrial and labour disputes.
❑   fraud.
❑   sabotage and extortion.

Borodzicz gives the following specific examples of crisis and catastrophe:

❑   fire and smoke sweeping through densely crowded buildings.
❑   fires or explosions in complex chemical plants or storage facilities.
❑   accidents associated with the transportation of people or hazardous products.
❑   incidents associated with nuclear installations.
❑   other events with a potential to damage operational reputation or brand values.
❑   incidents associated with crime or terrorism as sub-sets of illegal activity.

Borodzicz also describes a general category of events which arise out of a lack of congruence (that is, a mis-match) between management processes associated (i) with operational or technological systems, and (ii) with human and information systems within their context of the social architecture described in Chapters 4 and 18 of this book. This lack of congruence or mis-match may arise from any of the following:

❑   interdependency.
❑   complexity.
❑   vulnerability to disturbance, unplanned events, or external intervention.
❑   system failures.
❑   excessive pressures for profit generation or cost reduction which have the unplanned consequence of taking operational activities below a safe or critical threshold, for instance in terms of prevailing health and safety criteria. A controversial example in the UK has been rail crashes resulting in loss of life, which *inter alia* were caused by ineffective track maintenance processes.
❑   a failure to match positions of leadership and operational responsibility with the requisite personal intellectual capacity described by Elliot Jaques in Chapter 17.

Curtin *et al* define three types of crisis or catastrophe. The *first type* results from events or accidents which happen unexpectedly or unpredictably. Examples include air accidents and crashes, the contamination of products or processes by others, or the loss of staff by injury or death.

The *second type* result from the escalation of the first. For instance, Curtin *et al* give as an example the destruction by explosion of the Chernobyl nuclear power plant, on which catastrophe 'the green groups were quick to seize ... as a means of attacking the nuclear industry throughout the world' (p. 3).

The *third type* is created, perhaps inadvertently. For instance, in 1991 the UK entrepreneur Gerald Ratner described his products as "total crap" in a speech to the UK Institute of Directors. Regester and Larkin comment that Ratner's 'upmarket audience thought the joke was funny and true. It was the next day's tabloids, notably the *Sun*, which devoted five pages to the story ... which tore Ratner apart for his mocking insincerity towards the customers who had made him his fortune' (p. 104). The third type of crisis may also be deliberately manufactured by people or organizations who believe that they can exploit the circumstances for their own ends. Curtin *et al* give the example of the Brent Spar oil rig which 'would have caused no controversy for Shell had Greenpeace not become involved' (p. 3). A pressure group may thus seize 'on a cause and escalate it into a crisis' (p. 3).

Regester and Larkin cite other examples of crises and catastrophes. These are quoted below:

❑ product-related crises which 'range from outright failures as in the case of the widget which resulted in millions of cans of Carlsberg-Tetley bitter (beer) being withdrawn from the (UK) market in 1995, to (the) unanticipated side effects illustrated by cases of asbestosis and thalidomide' (p. 101). The accidental or deliberate contamination experienced by the manufacturers of products such as the drug Tylenol (1982), Perrier Water (1990), and Lucozade (1991) come into this category.

❑ 'advancing technology, which the public has often come to believe to be foolproof, forms ... another category ... (which) includes the 1979 "incident" at the (US) Three Mile Island nuclear reactor ... and Chernobyl (in April 1986) ... more recently, the world was stunned ... (by) the fatal (2000) Concorde crash' in Paris (p. 102). Similarly, in 1912 the "unsinkable" transatlantic ocean liner *Titanic* was lost with extensive loss of life after colliding with an iceberg; whilst in 1937 the *Hindenburg*, the world's largest rigid airship, exploded in full view of the world's media as she arrived at her destination in the USA.

❑ fraudulent behaviour which 'has led to the demise of some major businesses' such as Barings and the BCCI banks (p. 103).

❑ business crises which 'are often caused by mismanagement of the company - injudicious expansion or diversification - evident in such (UK) cases as Brent Walker, Next, Saatchi and Saatchi ... and Ferranti International' (p. 103).

Regester and Larkin also comment that 'it is major crises such as airplane, (railway), and ferry disasters involving ... loss of life which lead to (the) greatest public interest. It is this type of crisis which leads to the most visible and measurable erosion of public confidence' (p. 101).

Precipitate Action and Leadership Complacency

Crisis and catastrophe may result directly from precipitate management action or leadership complacency. Such causes might for instance include any of the following:

❑ the making of hasty or unconsidered strategic decisions.

❑ irrational, unstable, or unpredictable leadership behaviour; perhaps associated with:-

❑ excessively centralized and individualistic decision-making, characterized by very high power distance and a lack of scrutiny or sanction, for instance as described in Chapter 8.

❑ the desire of designated leaders, political appointees, or chief executive officers to "leave their mark" on an organization, or to be known for bringing about change even if such change is made solely for its own sake. This syndrome may have become as much a feature of the UK public sector as it is of business and commerce?

❑ the acceptance of critical decisions based on inappropriate or "one size fits all" methodologies for instance sold to clients by management consulting companies.

❑ the making of strategic decisions motivated by perceptions of an over-riding need to "optimize" short-term financial performance (for instance as described in Chapters 13 and 16) at the expense (i) of other performance indicators and (ii) of the long-term viability and survival of the enterprise.

❑ the making of decisions (for instance associated with the company mergers, acquisitions, and divestments described in Chapter 27 as forms of business development) which are primarily motivated by personal ambition and individual financial greed, and in which there is an absence (i) of any real strategic or business logic, or (ii) of the corporate social responsibility analyzed in Chapter 12. Young and Scott (2004) give a graphic account of such "corporate raider", "robber baron", or "fat cat" capitalist behaviour in the UK.

Regester and Larkin also comment that 'in our experience, some executives have difficulty admitting … that their companies could face a crisis because in doing so they would have to question the excellence of their company and, in some cases … their own professionalism. Others subscribe to the fallacy that well-managed companies simply do not have crises' (p. 117).

HOW TO CREATE A CRISIS

Curtin *et al* suggest that some crises may be exacerbated or even created for their own purposes by pressure groups or by the media. *This process may be deliberate.* It would be undertaken in order to further some particular objective or purpose. And the process may be opportunistic. Pressure groups and the media may be highly skilled at rapidly exploiting the sudden emergence of situations or incidents which become the "trigger" events for creating the story to be associated with external perceptions of the developing crisis. Curtin *et al* suggest some characteristics of a manufactured crisis. These might include any or all of the following.

Simplicity of concept - a crisis may be created if it can be defined in very simple or unequivocal terms. Curtin *et al* comment that 'this allows sides to be taken, particularly by the media. So for Brent Spar, the issue of sea dumping was bad and recycling of the structure on land (as advocated by Greenpeace) was good. GM (genetically modified) foods are bad … organic foods are good' (pp. 19-20).
Scientifically complex - 'paradoxically, the science surrounding the crisis must be … complex and impenetrable to the ordinary person. This is essential (because) otherwise people would be able to make reasoned decisions on what is right and what is wrong' (p. 20). This syndrome was clearly illustrated in the UK agricultural cases (i) of BSE in cattle (and its potential connection with CJD in humans), and (ii) in the incidence of foot and mouth disease.
Data rich - corporate and governmental environments in Anglo-Saxon countries are characterized by a large variety, diversity, and volume of

information that is openly available to anyone who wishes to access it, and who may wish to use it to create external perceptions (or "spin") about issues or events in which they have an interest. Curtin *et al* comment that 'in environmental issues there is no truth, only data. From this data one can manufacture ... information, perspectives and assumptions (which may) be accepted by (other) people ... as knowledge' (p. 21).

The law of the absolute - scientifically complex and data-rich events make ideal environmental issues. There has, by definition, to be an element of uncertainty and doubt within any controversy about such events. The more people think they know about something, the less they actually know. This is the "law of the absolute". As science advances, it throws new light but also shows up the imperfection of existing understanding. As a result, anything may be categorized as potentially unsafe or dangerous if someone wishes to make such a case, even if the risks are actually miniscule. Curtin *et al* for instance comment of the Perrier water case that 'to the question "can you categorically assure me that drinking mineral water with tiny traces of benzene will never harm me?" the categorical answer "no" is not available' (p. 22).

Slogan-ability - people should be able to summarize or encapsulate the crisis and its meaning in a few succinct words. For instance, genetically modified crops may be used to manufacture "Frankenstein foods"! The deep-sea disposal of the Brent Spar facility (the experts' chosen option) was akin to "dumping an old car in the village pond"! Curtin *et al* comment that 'slogans like this are hard to argue with - generally because they have enough truth in them to make them credible, and they have no "small print" to qualify them ... for the media there is no choice: the words to be used are those that are the most understandable ... or those that shock the most' (pp. 21-22).

THE WORKING OF MURPHY'S LAW

The triggering of crisis or catastrophe may be made harder to identify, or more difficult to deal with where Murphy's law comes into play. Murphy's law states that *if something can go wrong, it will go wrong*. For instance, in the case of incidents that as trigger events could lead to the development of a crisis:

❏   the necessary people will not be in the right place at the right time to deal with unfolding events.

□ the crisis will happen late at night, during the weekend, or during a public holiday.
□ the unpredictable will happen.
□ people and systems that normally operate to the highest efficiency will suddenly or inexplicably fail.
□ things will get worse before there is any chance of them getting better.

Curtin *et al* comment that 'it is uncanny that when a crisis strikes, it always seems to be at ... the time of holidays, weekends or when people are not prepared'. They suggest that pressure groups who are creating or developing a crisis will use this syndrome to good effect, choosing "their timing with deadly accuracy" (p. 23).

CONTINGENCY PLANNING AND MANAGEMENT

The occurrence of crises may be infrequent, but their impact may be highly significant for the enterprise. In consequence, Nudell and Antokol comment that "crisis management is not just anticipating what is likely to happen; it is thinking the unthinkable before it happens" (p. 3). They suggest that there may be very significant legal, financial, human resource, marketing, insurance and other penalties attaching either or both to (i) a failure to anticipate, or (ii) an actual lack of preparation for a crisis, emergency, or disaster. This is especially the case where it could be established that a *prudent person* could (or should) have foreseen the possibility or the potential for that crisis, emergency, or disaster. That is, "a crisis is not the time for *ad hoc* responses" (p. 2).

Worse, Borodzicz notes that 'decision makers may ... have to operate with less information than the media ... it is ... not unusual for a crisis to receive heavy and close monitoring...with modern communication facilities, the media (may be) more up to date than the decision makers who are attempting to respond ... the image portrayed by the media may have to be dealt with at the same time as the crisis itself; sometimes this can even pose the greatest difficulties' (p. 33), as in the case of Shell's Brent Spar incident.

The process of assessing and planning for at least the most likely forms of emergency or crisis may therefore be a necessary precaution, or an essential form of insurance. The risk to the enterprise posed by the occurrence of emergencies, crises, induced catastrophes, or disasters may therefore be lessened by *proactive prior assessment and planning*, and the anticipation of contingent "measures that (may) enable the organization to co-ordinate and control its responses" (p. 20).

Nudell and Antokol take the view that crises may not necessarily happen without some kind of prior warning or intimation. A decision may therefore have to be made as to whether certain types of situation might with the use of appropriate information, policy, and forethought either or both (i) be anticipated in advance, or (ii) actually be pre-empted or prevented. For instance, the risk of accidents and emergencies may be estimated in probability or scenario terms on a "what might happen if?" or "what if?" basis. These techniques were analysed in Chapter 9 of this book. Nudell and Antokol comment for example that decision-makers working in potentially dangerous industries or who are "responsible for the transportation or storage of hazardous materials should ... recognize the statistically greater possibility ... of being involved in a major accident" (pp. 10-11). There is widely available information, knowledge, advice, past precedent, and experience available from official, expert, trade, and insurance sources (i) about accidents and emergencies, (ii) on how to assess the risk inherent in them, and (iii) how to plan for them.

Disasters may similarly follow established patterns of occurrence. There may be common causes, or types of location or situation in which certain categories of disaster are more likely to occur than elsewhere. There may again be experience or past precedeat from which learning and pre-planning may take place, and from which forecasts of potential or probability may be constructed. Nudell and Antokol note that there are established bases of relevant information available from government, environmental, or statistical institutions; specialist and expert agencies; universities (etc).

The occurrence of induced catastrophes may also show patterns of prior indication or prior warning. Nudell and Antokol comment that 'regardless of the sub-category of induced catastrophe, such emergencies rarely occur out of a clear blue sky. Areas of terrorist activity are continually tracked by governments ... law enforcement agencies around the world maintain records about criminal activity within their jurisdictions' (p. 14). Nudell and Antokol define terrorism as a highly visible category of induced catastrophe in terms of 'the threat or use of violence for political purposes' (p. 11). They suggest that contingency planning in such cases must be based on an awareness and acceptance of the possibility that the 'organization may become the target of an induced catastrophe - whether for political reasons, criminal reasons (or) as a result of a labour dispute' (p. 11).

Borodzicz comments that 'organizations are under pressure to respond to crisis situations for two reasons. First, a crisis will affect an organization's ability to trade, with potential implications for profit, reputation and survival; the (Arthur) Anderson case was an example of this. Second, a crisis can ... descend into media speculation about organizational dealings and affairs, making it impossible to function normally' (p. 99). Matters may be exacerbated where the crisis is of an unpredictable nature and threatens to overwhelm decision-makers by the speed of its onset, by its apparent lack of structure, and by the problems of definition and interpretation it may pose.

The result is the preparation and implementation of *risk or contingency plans*, perhaps based on the matrix-type methodologies described in Chapter 8. Risk and contingency plans that are specified to deal with emergencies, crises, disasters, or induced catastrophes are to be found in many large-scale organizations. The construction of such plans is mandatory for much of the UK public sector, as noted in Chapter 8. Such processes of contingent planning for emergencies, crises, disasters, or induced catastrophes may be called "crisis management". It may also be termed "continuity management" or "business continuity planning". Borodzicz notes that 'business continuity planning is about achieving a balance between preparing for situations in which contingency plans will have to be used, whilst at the same time doing everything conceivable to stop them ever having to be used' (p. 87).

Key issues in the processes of business continuity planning or crisis management are (i) the capacity of the organization to recognize and to absorb the consequences of emergencies, crises, and disasters; and (ii) its ability to deal with them once they have occurred. The issue of *capability* was dealt with in Chapter 4. How resilient will the organization and its staff be when confronted by events that are unthinkable, feared, unwelcome, and unwanted? Can the enterprise continue to function effectively under such circumstances? Or will its survival be threatened?

Borodzicz's Analysis of Continuity Planning and Crisis Management

Borodzicz suggests that the process of planning for emergencies, crises, and disasters has at least three key components. These are described below.

Technology and systems - in which a focus is placed on the continuing viability, protection, target hardening, and backing-up of technology systems vital to organizational performance. This includes ICT-based systems, critical operational and financial systems, or systems specified for health, safety, and security purposes (etc).

Compliance - in which management processes and systems are specified to achieve absolute compliance with corporate governance and regulatory parameters, and with the formalized auditing procedures associated therewith. Such compliance may be required in respect of issues of health and safety; managerial and financial probity; the protection of shareholder and stakeholder interests; or the standards of performance in such activities as the military or security and policing, healthcare, the care and protection of the elderly or the disabled, child care, the treatment of prisoners, the social services and social welfare, education, local or provincial government, transportation (etc).

Organization, leadership, and management - in which a focus is placed on whatever features of organization, leadership, management process, or internal and external architecture that are judged to be relevant to dealing with (or surviving) the extraordinary conditions imposed by emergencies, crises, induced catastrophes, and disaster. Such features might include:-

- leadership quality.
- the degree of inner or outer directedness.
- issues of national and organizational culture.
- the degree of centralization and decentralization.
- the distribution of responsibility and authority.
- vulnerability.
- capacity.
- competence.
- capability.
- resilience.
- the degree of adaptability and flexibility.

Issues of organization, leadership, and management process are analyzed at length in the author's companion text *Principles of Management* (Ashgate, 2004).

REACTIVE APPROACHES TO CRISIS MANAGEMENT

A *reactive approach* to crisis management or continuity planning would be characterized by a failure to think the unthinkable, or a refusal to prepare any meaningful contingency plans by which to deal with potential emergencies, crises, induced catastrophes or disasters that the organization might face. Enterprise management would "ride its luck" in the face of the risks that occur. Emergent events would be treated in an *ad hoc* manner. The organization might emerge from the crisis unscathed, or it might not. Crisis management would have become a matter of serendipity.

Nudell and Antokol suggest that any crisis may represent a potential threat if the leadership of the organization takes such a reactive response to it. Not only may the enterprise suffer the consequences of the crisis, but it may be perceived by the relevant external stakeholders and publics to have failed properly to manage its affairs. Such a stigma of failure may then persist long into the future, casting a blight on strategic intent and reputation for years to come. Nudell and Antokol give the example of the potentially catastrophic melt-down at the US Three Mile Island nuclear power plant during 1979, which resulted in lasting global damage to public faith in nuclear energy. People's fears were only made worse by, and attitudes hardened as a result of the subsequent induced catastrophe at Chernobyl.

PROACTIVE APPROACHES TO CRISIS MANAGEMENT

Nudell and Antokol comment that the taking of a *proactive approach* to crisis management or contingency planning may result not only in the limiting of actual damage, but lead to positive external perceptions of the manner in which the organization conducts its affairs. The enterprise will have been seen to be *responsive and responsible* in its behaviour. Nudell and Antokol suggest that a proactive approach to contingency planning for crisis or continuity management might include any or all of the following processes by which the enterprise chooses to:

❑ identify the types of emergency, crisis, induced catastrophe, or disaster to which the organization might be exposed.

❑ attempt to make some kind of assessment or forecast of the probabilities with which such events might occur.

❑ create scenarios of what might happen if such events occurred; suggest the kinds of dangers or threats to which they might give rise; and identify the most potentially obvious consequences for the organization (the concept of scenario planning was analyzed in Chapter 9).

❑ identify which people, assets, corporate reputations, locations, operations, or processes (etc) could be most at risk.

❑ identify and locate leadership and management responsibilities for specific features of the crisis management process. Nudell and Antokol contend that 'effective planning should include proactive mechanisms that have been tested and revised over time, and that can be implemented by personnel who are carefully selected, properly trained, and secure in their authority and procedures' (p. 14).

❑ create feasible or plausible polices, plans, procedures, and responses to deal with specific threats.

❑ identify or locate the resources that will be needed to implement these contingent polices, plans, procedures, and responses.

❑ create prior preparedness to deal with damage to people, assets, reputations, locations, operations, or processes (etc) if or when it occurs.

❑ analyze the remit, validity, and adequacy of the organization's insurance. Is the coverage appropriate to the scenarios being forecast? What are the key restrictions or exceptions written into the insurance policies held by the enterprise? What does the *small print* say?

❑ estimate the *potential cost* of any emergency, crisis, induced catastrophe, or disaster to which the organization might be exposed.

❑ estimate the *potential loss of value* of any emergency, crisis, induced catastrophe, or disaster to which the organization might be exposed. The concept of value loss was analyzed in Chapter 8.

❑ make an assessment of the *aftermath*. Will the organization be able to resume what had been its customary pattern of work? When might this be, and how is it to be achieved?

❑ put in place mechanisms of *feedback*, so that the leadership and management of the enterprise can be sure (i) to learn from the past (and potentially very costly) experience of emergency, crisis, or catastrophe; and (ii) to feed that experience forward into contingency planning so as more effectively to reduce future probabilities and risk faced by the organization.

Litigation

Nudell and Antokol note that the risk of *litigation* may have to be assessed in terms of the effectiveness of enterprise planning for, and the actual response to emergencies, crises, induced catastrophes, or disasters. Litigation for instance became the over-riding feature in the aftermath of the Bhopal disaster (in the case of the Union-Carbide corporation), or the Exxon Valdez oil spill. Nudell and Antokol comment that 'regardless of the type of emergency, organizations that neglect advance preparations risk becoming targets of lawsuits. And, should the emergency prove to have been avoidable or, if unavoidable, mishandled, then the ramifications of such lawsuits, coupled with ... adverse publicity can trouble the organization for years after the event' (p. 26).

Curtin *et al's* Guidelines for Managing a Crisis

Curtin *et al* suggest the following guidelines for managing a crisis once it has occurred:

- monitor events carefully and honestly.
- identify the worst case scenarios.
- assume that Murphy's Law will operate.
- assume that matters will get worse before they get better.
- estimate potential damage to key outcome variables such as market position, financial results, reputation, brand, or public confidence (etc).
- prioritize response in terms of what is most important, and what must be done first.
- assume, at least for the time being, that (i) the enterprise will lose control of events; and (ii) that others will for their own purposes try to exploit any vacuum or opportunity that emerges as the situation develops.
- be prepared to accept responsibility for events quickly, and do not try to "pass the buck" to someone else.
- overcompensate by making strong and positive moves to placate or shape external opinion.
- be open and transparent in dealings with stakeholders, publics, the media, and interest groups that are affected (or otherwise have for whatever reason become involved).
- do not behave like the proverbial ostrich who buries its head in the sand and hopes that the problem will go away. This will only make the situation worse for the organization and its leadership.

Curtin *et al* suggest that 'ideally, senior ... managers should have a working knowledge of politics, the media, reputation and brand values, (stakeholder management), and corporate (social) responsibility' (pp. 17-18) in order most effectively to manage a crisis situation. Some of these issues are dealt with in later chapters of this book.

REVIEW QUESTIONS

1. Define an emergency.
2. Define a crisis.
3. Define a disaster.
4. Define an induced catastrophe.
5. Describe and analyze features of the process of contingency planning for emergencies, crises, disasters or induced catastrophes.
6. Describe and comment on the potential consequences of a reactive approach to crisis management.
7. Describe and comment on features of a proactive approach to crisis management.

PROJECT ASSIGNMENTS

1. Using available information, research and write a case study example of a crisis, disaster, or induced catastrophe in which you have an interest. Present your findings.
2. Construct a methodology by which an organization might plan for, and deal with a future crisis, disaster, or induced catastrophe. What kinds of capabilities and resources might be needed to deal with this crisis?

References

Borodzicz, E.P. (2005) *Risk, Crisis, and Security Management*, Wiley, Chichester.
Curtin, T., Hayman, D. & N. Husein (2005) *Managing a Crisis*, Palgrave Macmillan, Basingstoke.
Nudell, M. and N. Antokol (1988) *The Handbook for Effective Emergency and Crisis Management*, Lexington Books, Mass.
Regester, M. and J. Larkin (2002) *Risk Issues and Crisis Management (2nd edition)*, Kogan Page, London.
Young, D. and P. Scott (2004) *Having Their Cake...*, Kogan Page, London.

Additional Reading

Farazmand, A. (ed.) (2001) *Handbook of Crisis and Emergency Management*, Marcel Dekker, New York.

PART THREE

STRATEGY FORMULATION, LEADERSHIP, GOVERNANCE, STRATEGIC DECISION-MAKING, AND PERFORMANCE EVALUATION

Part Three of this book deals with the inter-related processes of strategy formulation, leadership, governance, strategic decision-making, and performance evaluation. This is sometimes termed "the strategy process".

Part Three defines the concepts of mission, purpose, objectives, and strategy. It identifies the roles and interests of shareholders or stakeholders as beneficiaries or recipients of the activities of the organization. It examines the inter-related issues of business ethics, values, environmentalism, and social responsibility that may influence the formulation of enterprise mission and objectives, and which may shape the implementation of strategy.

It analyses key issues of corporate governance, financial strategy, financial evaluation, and performance management.

It looks at who formulates strategy and makes strategic decisions; and it looks at how these processes are carried out. It analyses the role of leadership in the processes of governance and strategic management.

Part Three looks at the relationship between planning style, strategy formulation, and the structure of the organization. And it describes a variety of criteria by which the strategies chosen and implemented by the enterprise may be appraised and evaluated.

In summary, Part Three looks at what strategy is. It deals with how strategies and plans are formulated, how decisions are made, and how the results are assessed. And it looks at the related issues of who formulates strategies and plans, who makes decisions, and why.

Part Three contains the following chapters:

Chapter 11

The Concepts of Mission, Objective and Strategy

"Everything on the earth has a purpose, every disease an herb to cure it, and every person a mission."

American North West Coast Salish Indian saying.

This chapter describes and illustrates the concepts of mission, objective, and strategy as key outcomes of the process of strategy formulation and strategic decision-making in the enterprise. The components of strategy are explained. The basis of strategy formulation is categorized and analyzed. The influence of stakeholders on the process of objective setting and strategy formulation is summarized.

Objective setting, strategy formulation, and strategic decision-making are sometimes described, for the sake of summary and convenience, as the "strategy process".

THE STRATEGY HIERARCHY

The processes of strategy formulation, strategic decision-making, and strategy implementation take place at three main levels. These are:

- ❑ the strategic
- ❑ the tactical
- ❑ the operational

These three levels are shown as the *strategy hierarchy* in Figure 11.1.

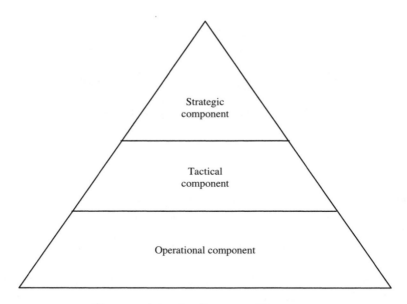

Figure 11.1 The Strategy Hierarchy

The *strategic level* at the top of the hierarchy contains *three key components*. These components are:

❑   enterprise mission
❑   enterprise objectives
❑   enterprise strategies

Each is described in the first three of the five main sections that make up this chapter.

SECTION ONE - MISSION

THE CONCEPT OF MISSION

Enterprise mission is a *fundamental statement of purpose and direction, which defines the place of the organization within its environment.* The Walt Disney Company's mission for example is "to entertain and to bring happiness to millions".

This statement of purpose and direction distinguishes the enterprise from others of its type, and separates it from its competitors. It can be used to define the scope of the organization in terms of location and positioning; its approach to people; and its strategies towards markets, operations management, quality, and service. It may shape the image that the enterprise seeks to project; and reflects how the people who run the organization wish to be viewed by others in the external environment. It may reflect the values and culture of founder and decision-makers as these have evolved over the life of the organization. Mission statements may be defined to derive from any or all of five inter-related components, as follow:

- ❑ enterprise purpose
- ❑ enterprise vision
- ❑ enterprise values
- ❑ core ideology
- ❑ enterprise ethos

Each is described below.

Enterprise Purpose

Purpose is defined by Argenti (1974) as 'the reason why the organization was formed or why it now exists. All organizations are originally formed to provide a specific benefit for specific groups of beneficiaries' (p. 39). Enterprise purpose will shape the formulation of mission and objectives within the enterprise.

Argenti argues that purpose will typically be decided by those people who have power and influence within the organization. Within business or service organizations these people may be entrepreneurs; founders or families; shareholders, chief executive officers, boards of directors, or non-executive directors; managers or management committees. Or they may be elected representatives or appointed officials within public sector or not-for-profit organizations. The "benefits" that the enterprise was established to provide could include:

- ❑ utilities, values, need or want satisfaction, products, services, customer service (and so on). These are provided for *primary recipients* such as customers, clients, patients, local residents, or taxpayers; *and*
- ❑ rewards or returns to *owners, proprietors, or beneficiaries*, whether these be an entrepreneur, a family, shareholders, a bank, a charity, or members of the general public as voters, taxpayers, local residents, or members of the community.

Enterprise Vision

Vision can be defined as 'a long term pattern of communal possibility to which others can be drawn into commitment' (Morden, 2004). The OED defines vision as 'a mental concept of a distinct or vivid kind; a highly imaginative scheme or anticipation ... something not actually present to the eye; an insight or foresight displayed in the mind'. Vision acts as a "glue" which holds together sets of value judgements and ideologies in the value system of the enterprise. It can be used 'to build bridges from the present to the future of the organization' (Bennis and Nanus, 1985). The Eastman Kodak Company's vision statement has stated that "our heritage has been and our future is to be the World Leader in imaging".

Enterprise Values

Values are moral principles or core beliefs. Enterprise values may act as a driving force or as "animating principles" (*l'élan vital*) that underpin the organization's activities. Values create or give rise to required standards and expectations of behaviour within the enterprise. In particular they shape attitudes as to *how things should be done* within the enterprise; how the enterprise should deal with people and relationships; and how it should deal with external stakeholders and its wider environment.

Values derive from prevailing ethical principles. Ethics are defined in Chapter 12 as "a conception of right or wrong conduct". They indicate the basic standards and parameters for making decisions. The Eastman Kodak Company's values were for example listed as being based on:

- respect for the dignity of the individual
- integrity
- trust
- credibility
- continuous improvement and personal renewal

The value set of the enterprise underpins its *core ideology* and its *ethos*.

Core Ideology

Collins and Porras (1995) define enterprise mission in terms of "core ideology". Core ideology comprises the basic values and sense of purpose that guide and inspire people whether internal or external to the enterprise. Collins and Porras suggest that this core ideology should remain stable and fixed for long periods of time. Table 11.1 shows selected examples of core ideologies from Collins and Porras' study.

Table 11.1 Core Ideologies

Company	Core ideologies
Boeing	<ul><li>being on the leading edge of aeronautical; being pioneers.</li><li>tackling large challenges; taking large risks.</li><li>product safety and quality.</li><li>integrity; using ethical business practices.</li></ul>
Johnson & Johnson	<ul><li>the company exists 'to alleviate pain and disease'.</li><li>the company 'has a hierarchy of responsibility: customers first. Employees second, society at large third, shareholders fourth'.</li><li>belief in individual opportunity, and reward based on merit.</li></ul>
Merck Pharmaceuticals	<ul><li>the company 'is in the business of preserving and improving human life'.</li><li>honesty and integrity.</li><li>corporate social responsibility.</li><li>science-based innovation.</li><li>unequivocal excellence in all aspects of the company.</li><li>profit from work that benefits humanity.</li></ul>
Walt Disney	<ul><li>the company aims 'to bring happiness to millions' and to celebrate, nurture, and promulgate 'wholesome American values'.</li><li>no cynicism allowed.</li><li>continuous progress via creativity, dreams, and imagination.</li><li>fanatical control and preservation of Disney's 'magic' image.</li><li>fanatical attention to detail and consistency.</li></ul>

Enterprise Ethos

Argenti defines ethos as 'how an organization behaves towards its employees and all other people or groups ... with whom it interacts. These include ... the state, the local community, employees, suppliers and so on ... the way in which it has decided to behave constrains and modifies the means it uses to achieve its purposes' (p. 39).

The ethos of the organization acts to constrain the activities it chooses to undertake. The ethos of the organization may therefore impose restrictions on the choice of objective or strategy. Ethos recognises that the formulation of mission and objectives must take into account the needs and desires of people who are not the main beneficiaries of the original enterprise purpose. Ethos is a recognition that people who are not defined as primary beneficiaries or owners must nevertheless have some right or capacity to influence or shape decision-making within the organization.

For example, the ethos of many enterprises is based on the simple premise of "doing no harm". They will refuse to countenance activities which for instance would lead to damage or pollution of the environment, or injuring people or animals as a result of carrying out their business.

STRATEGIC INTENT AND DIRECTION

Hamel and Prahalad (1994) describe the concept of *strategic intent*. Strategic intent defines the *nature of the direction* that needs to be taken in order to attain the long term strategic position that the enterprise wishes to achieve for inself. Hamel and Prahalad argue that if enterprise management can clearly define and communicate this strategic intent, the activities of the organization should be characterized by a clear and consistent purpose. Hamel and Prahalad contend that strategic intent comprises:

❑ a sense of direction
❑ a sense of discovery
❑ a sense of destiny

Each is summarized below.

A Sense of Direction

The enterprise needs a meaningful, consistent, and unifying sense of purpose. It also needs some degree of consensus that this purpose is worthwhile (or is at least essential or unavoidable). Otherwise 'with no particular point of view about long-term corporate direction, the definition of "core" business changes every few years, acquisitions and divestments are made with no logic other than short-term financial expediency, and market and product development efforts are often hamstrung by a lack of ' consistency and an overwhelming 'orthodoxy' or 'installed base' of thinking (p. 131).

The sense of direction indicates the *where* and *why* of the long-term strategic intent of the enterprise.

A Sense of Discovery

Hamel and Prahalad suggest that people may be motivated by the opportunity to do something new and challenging, or to explore the unfamiliar. People may be less likely to be energized and motivated by an uninspiring mission or purpose (such as that which deals solely with generating returns to shareholders). Strategic intent could offer the prospect of new destinations, new horizons, or better ways of doing what has to be done.

A Sense of Destiny

Strategic intent may have to be deemed worthwhile and to command respect. It may have to inspire or enthuse people. Hamel and Prahalad comment that 'too many mission statements fail entirely to impart any sense of *mission*' (p. 133). In this sense, strategic intent is in particular as much about the creation of meaning for *employees* as it is about the establishment of direction. Hamel and Prahalad comment that 'when queried as to his job, a stonemason at work on St Paul's in London replied "I build cathedrals". How many corporate stonemasons today feel they are building cathedrals, we wonder?' (p. 133). Such sentiments are echoed by Collins and Porras in their 1995 study of what are described as *visionary companies*, to which reference is made above, and in Chapter 17 on leadership and strategy.

Hamel and Prahalad contend that the "scoreboard" of top management in stockholder corporations, that is return to shareholders, is likely to exert little if any positive emotional pull on employees several levels removed down the hierarchy. Enterprise strategic intent may aim instead to inspire vision and engender commitment (however this may be achieved). The more inspired and committed the employee, the less are pay and Herzberg's other "hygeine factors" likely to be the main sources of motivation and satisfaction. Turning strategic intent into reality requires that all those involved in the enterprise understand the way in which their contribution is important to the achievement of that long-term intent. That is, the enterprise needs to make its purposes directly relevant to the work of each person throughout the value chain by which activities are accomplished. In other words, is an employee to be defined as a "construction worker", or instead "a builder of cathedrals"?

SECTION TWO - OBJECTIVES

THE CONCEPT OF OBJECTIVE

Enterprise objectives follow from the specification of mission and strategic intent described above. Objectives specify and quantify the goals or targets towards which leadership, willpower, effort, the investment of resources, and the use of enterprise capability are to be directed such that mission and strategic intent are achieved.

Objectives are likely to specify (i) the *time scale* or *time frame* analyzed in Chapters 7 and 13; and (ii) the level of *risk tolerance* described in Chapter 8. Objectives may be based on the forecasting process analyzed in Chapter 9. Objectives may be *quantitative*, or *qualitative*, or both. Examples of corporate objectives might include:

Published targets for the required institutional or "best value" performance of public agencies - such agencies may include central, regional, provincial, and local government organizations; the police and security services; agencies associated with the enforcement of drug-related legislation; the provision of educational and training opportunities; or the implementation of equal opportunity or diversity policies. The UK and Australian concept of "best value" is described in a later chapter.

The local or international market position or market share that the enterprise wishes to develop - for instance, the US Southwest Airlines company was established as a focused and high performance business. It was set up with a simple service concept built around low-cost coach class flights of a limited duration between cities. It does not provide free meals. It does not belong to any airline reservation system (so customers or their travel agents have to contact the airline direct). Its costs per seat-mile are about two-thirds of the industry average, enabling it to sustain low fares. It only operates in North America, where it considers there to be untapped scope for growth in its business.

The level of customer service and satisfaction required - for instance, it is the objective of the Hyatt Hotel chain to provide a consistently high level of standardized US style service wherever its hotels are located in the world. The service and the environment are always the same, so customers know in advance what they are getting. American guests also know that there will be an ice machine along the corridor! Similarly, the performance of healthcare organizations such as hospitals or health agencies may be measured against clear targets set for the volume, time-scale, and relative success of patient treatment; or instead for the control of unhealthy practices such as smoking, drug abuse, or the excessive consumption of alcohol.

Perceptions of leadership or "World Class" status that are to be developed or maintained. Kodak's objective to be a world leader in imaging has already been given as an illustration.

The perception that the enterprise is an élite employer capable of attracting and retaining the very best staff on a world wide basis. Companies such as Unilever or Procter and Gamble obtain significant advantage from the high quality of staff that they can recruit.

The target financial rate of return on capital employed to be achieved - Goldsmith and Clutterbuck (1997) noted the comment of Martin Ellis, General Manager of UK Healthcare at the UK Rentokil Initial company that 'the key thing for me is focus - 20 percent profit growth for ever. The message has never changed in all the time since I started with the company as a technician. People here talk about it all the time. The next bit after the 20 percent profit is important - forever. You can achieve good results for a while cutting costs, but you can't sustain it forever. That forces managers to motivate their people, not simply to take a knife to the business when they're having problems' (p. 50).

Targets for innovation, new product development (NPD), new market development, or new business development (NBD) - the UK Siebe company for instance spent an average of 4.5 percent of its turnover on research and development, but 10 percent in its high technology businesses. Like some of the leading US innovation companies (General Electric or 3M), Siebe aimed to obtain 50 percent of sales over a five year period from products developed during those five years. It focused attention on this goal by requiring all operating companies to have at least five new product launches per year.

SECTION THREE - STRATEGY

THE CONCEPT OF STRATEGY

Strategies are *the means by which the enterprise achieves its objectives.* They describe the chosen "paths to goal", or "routes to achievement" or "plans of campaign".

Strategies act as "ground-rules", and define the nature and occasion of the decisions needed to achieve enterprise objectives. Strategies have their time scale and their risk content, as described in earlier chapters.

In summary, strategies determine how the enterprise intends to carry out its activities during the time horizons to which it is working, in order to achieve its objectives.

WHAT IS STRATEGY?

Mintzberg (1987a) defines strategy in terms of *5Ps*. These 5Ps are:

1P *Perspective* - which is the basic business concept or idea, and the way in which that concept or idea is put into practice (or implemented). Polytechnic, *écoles polytechniques*, or *fachochschule* type institutions of higher education concentrate on creating directly marketable vocational learning outcomes based on a mixture of theory, application, and practice.

2P *Plan* - which is a direction, a guide, or a course of action from now (or from the past) into the future, however that "future" is defined and whatever the time horizons associated with it.

3P *Pattern* - which is the consistency of enterprise decision-making over time. Goldsmith and Clutterbuck comment of the UK Boots company (a retailer of cosmetics, pharmaceutical, and personal care products such as soaps and shampoos) that it aspires to achieve a strong degree of homogeneity about its retail stores. People want to have the same shopping experience when they go into these stores. Boots believes that "familiarity breeds sales" wherever the customer may travel.

4P *Position* or *positioning* - by which the enterprise "locates" itself within its external and competitive environments; and by which it positions specific products or services (and therefore the resources and capabilities required to produce them) against the demands of the market segments it serves. The UK's Asda and its US parent the Wal-Mart company are for instance both large-scale retailers of grocery and household goods competing in their respective geographic markets on the basis of value for money and convenience. They sell to working people and their families.

5P *Ploys* - which are the competitive moves or competition strategies designed to maintain, reinforce, achieve, or improve the relative competitive position of the enterprise within its sector and markets. US film makers for example long ago realized the critical importance of film distribution to the success of their business. In the case of the UK, the distribution and showing of movies has been in part controlled by American companies since the 1920s.

Two further Ps may be added to Mintzberg's original list. These are:

6P *Using power* - within internal and external environments.

7P *Politics* - that is, using legitimate political behaviour and power to further the cause of the enterprise or its sector. The use of political mechanisms and political power may take the form of *lobbying*, or of influence on *standards institutions* and *regulatory bodies*.

Power and Politics

The ability to *use power*, and to *manage political behaviour* has always been a key part of the process of strategic management. For instance, Kay (1993), in discussing the need to sustain the sources of competitive advantage described in Chapter 4, comments that the possession of key strategic assets (such as a radio or television franchise; or the rights to exploit some natural resource) is likely to be strongly defended by enterprise management. However, the possession of, or access to such strategic assets may be at risk where (i) changes in allocation or ownership; or (ii) changes in regulation, technology, or market conditions are taking place.

For the enterprise that depends on the competitive advantage that derives from the possession of a particular strategic asset, skills in handling (or influencing) public policy, and lobbying skills may be as important as those of business management. For example, the management of a campaign for market deregulation or market liberalization (such as that for air travel in Europe) may, according to Kay, require the combination of an effective political argument with an effective technical one.

Kay comments that companies in the UK vary widely in the sophistication with which they, or their trade association, handle issues of public policy. This competence is of increasing importance in the contemporary environment created by the fashion for deregulation; and in the growth of regulatory power in Brussels (EU), Geneva (GATT/WTO), and potentially in NAFTA, at the expense of traditional relationships in national capitals.

STRATEGY FORMULATION IN THE LARGE COMPANY OR ORGANIZATION

It may be convenient to divide strategy formulation in the large company into two inter-related components. These components are:

❏   *Corporate strategy* - which deals with issues of strategic management at the level of the enterprise as a whole. Such issues will include the basic character, capability, and competence of the enterprise; the direction in which it should develop its activity; the nature of its internal architecture, governance and structure; and the nature of its relationships with its sector, its competitors, and the wider environment

❏   *Business strategy* - by which the enterprise establishes strategies for specific business or organizational activities, specific sectors and markets, and specific *divisions* or *business units* into which operations are allocated.

STRATEGY FORMULATION IN THE SME

Strategy formulation in the *small to medium sized enterprise* or *SME* is unlikely to differentiate corporate and business strategy. The corporate strategy of the enterprise is its business strategy, at least until the SME grows to a sufficient size to have to think about issues of corporate development and external relationships.

THE BASIS OF STRATEGY FORMULATION

In a famous series of journal articles, Mintzberg and colleagues (1985a, 1985b, 1987b; also see Mintzberg 1989 and Mintzberg *et al* 1995) categorize the basis of strategy formulation under the following headings:

- ❑ the forced or the self-imposed
- ❑ the required
- ❑ the rationalistic
- ❑ the deliberate
- ❑ the logically incremental
- ❑ the emergent and the opportunistic

Each is summarized below.

Forced or Self-Imposed Strategies

Strategies may be *forced* on enterprise decision-makers, or of necessity imposed upon them (*self-imposed*) as a result of the *internal* or *external* conditions described below.

Internal conditions that are for instance characterized by:

- ❑ a significant lack of leadership expertize and managerial continuity, or an unsustainable turnover of senior managerial staff, or an unclear strategic intent and direction, or excessive "short-termism".
- ❑ a significant lack of effective strategic management capability or competence.
- ❑ a significant level of institutional weakness, or lack of capability or competence.
- ❑ a significant lack of competitive advantage.
- ❑ an enforced recognition of the need for significant enterprise change, as in conditions of inadequate value generation (or actual value loss), operational crisis, re-centralization, or "turnaround".

Example - limitations on strategic choice predicated by a lack of the necessary technological, operational, financial or managerial capacity and competence. The enterprise is simply not capable of doing certain things. Shortages of finance may in particular force require the self-imposition of certain strategy limitations on the firm.

Irresistible external conditions or threats that are characterized for instance by:

❑   significant market or environmental development and change.
❑   significant change in prevailing competition policy, competitive context, competitive strategy, or competitive conditions.
❑   significant technological change, or the emergence of the technological "discontinuities" described in Chapter 19.
❑   pressure from environmentalist, "single interest" groups.
❑   determined or aggressive political behaviour; *perhaps leading to*
❑   legislative or regulatory developments and change; *or to*
❑   significant change in prevailing macro level fiscal and economic management; *or to*
❑   significant change in prevailing social, consumer behaviour, cultural, or ethical contexts.

Example - external and legislative pressures for environmentally responsible behaviour already described above, and analyzed in detail in Chapter 12. Enterprise management may be forced by legislation to adopt environmentally responsible policies; or instead may consider that external perceptions of unethical behaviour would be highly damaging to the market reputation of the company.

Required Strategies

A particular choice of strategies or strategic decision may (i) be perceived to be required; or (ii) require to be self-imposed, for instance:

❑   as a result of a perceived need for consistency with the enterprise's capability and competence, choice of mission, strategic intent, purpose, perspective, and objectives as described above; and as a result of the need to meet the requirements of its shareholders or its stakeholders. Stakeholders are described in a later section of this chapter.
❑   as a result of the choice of position and positioning within the relevant external, market, operational, or competitive environments.
❑   as a result of the choice of competition strategies or ploys.
❑   because of the prevailing organizational attitudes to risk aversion and uncertainty avoidance. Strategic choice might vary on a continuum from highly risk averse and short-termist at one extreme, to the risk maximization of the highly opportunistic entrepreneur at the other.

❑ because of the effect or influence of prevailing critical success factors, limiting factors, or contingencies and constraints to which the enterprise is subject, or with which it must deal.

❑ as a result of the need to use power or to undertake political behaviour, as already described above.

❑ because of the character and influence of enterprise values, value set, and culture.

❑ because of prevailing perceptions of the issues and influence of ethics, environmentalism, and social responsibility described Chapter 12.

❑ because of the need to bring about adaptation in reacting to changing internal or external conditions.

Example - shareholder corporations may select a variety of strategies whose objective is to meet stockholder expectations over any particular number of years. These strategies will cover the generation of the appropriate financial returns described in Chapters 3 and 13 of this book. They will also aim to create an institutional reputation for being aware of the need consistently to meet the wider demands of the financial community. They will develop the ability to communicate with shareholders and financial institutions in a manner which most effectively supports the fulfilment of the stewardship obligations they perceive to be required of them as recipients of investment finance.

Rationalistic Approaches to Strategy Formulation

Rationalistic strategy formulation implies a planned, systematic, and centralized approach in which:

❑ the chief executive officer (CEO) or president of the organization, and his or her colleagues at the "corporate centre" are dominant forces in the process of strategic management.

❑ strategic and business plans tend to be "handed down" (or "thrown over the wall") from the corporate centre to subordinates for implementation. Subordinates *may* be consulted but their lack of status or their lack of relevant information precludes them from detailed participation in the process of strategy formulation and strategic decision-making.

This approach is sometimes described as "corporate planning" or "strategic planning".

Rationalistic approaches to strategy formulation are characteristic of traditional French management styles. Rationalism is described in the author's *Principles of Management* (2004), a companion book to this text.

Deliberate Approaches to Strategy Formulation

Under this approach to strategy formulation there is an attempt to realize strategies exactly as intended because management perceives (or believes) that:

❑ the enterprise can formulate precise intentions and unambiguous objectives.
❑ organizational staff and resources can be shaped exactly to "fit" the realization of these objectives (that is, they can be led and managed so as to be totally congruent with them).
❑ external environmental or competitive forces are unlikely to be able to distort any of the processes of strategy formulation, implementation, and realization.

Example - the widespread use of acquisition and takeover as a strategy for market share protection, business growth, and diversification as described in Chapter 27. This strategy has dominated the thinking of boardrooms in Anglo-Saxon companies during recent decades. A takeover is made. It is then up to others to make it work. If it is unsuccessful then that is a fault of implementation. It may instead of course have been a bad idea in the first place, with no synergies likely between the parties to the acquisition however hard any one tries to develop them.

Logically Incremental Approaches to Strategy Formulation

Strategy is described under this heading as *evolving on a dynamic basis over time* in response to the internal and external contingencies that emerge to confront the enterprise. *Strategy evolves in response to what decision-makers perceive to be the best course or choice of action at the time.* Strategies may for the time be consistent with enterprise mission or objectives. Or instead, mission, strategic intent, and enterprise objectives may themselves be adapted on an evolutionary basis to meet new challenges that are emerging to confront the organization.

Quinn (in Mintzberg *et al*, 1998) comments that logical incrementalism is a *step-by-step approach* to strategy formulation. The approach recognises the existence of:

❑ the risk, uncertainty, inconsistency, and unpredictability of the event characteristics for instance as described in Chapter 8.
❑ limitations on forecasting capability and foresight.
❑ the need for flexibility of response to changing circumstances, and the necessity to be prepared to change directions.
❑ the existence of multiple (and potentially inconsistent) values and goals; and the potential impact on strategic choice of internal bargaining processes, internal negotiation, management power plays, and organizational politics (etc).

Quinn suggests that decisions about strategic choice may emerge from a series of sub-processes or steps, each of which deals with specific strategic issues (e.g. structure and architecture, business development, financial strategy, and so on); and which are then blended incrementally and opportunistically into a wider cohesive strategic pattern.

Strategy tends to evolve as internal decisions and external events flow together to create a consensus about the need for action among members of the decision-making group. Feedback on past and existing decisions will be incorporated into the process of strategy formulation and decision-making for future events.

Commitments are kept broad and generalized (for instance in the form of core values or core competencies), and are subject to periodic review and appraisal.

Decisions may be deliberately delayed until the last possible moment, when the information available will be as relevant as it is likely to get before the decision has to be made. Quinn comments that 'some companies ... have formalized this concept into "phase programming planning systems". They make concrete decisions only on individual phases (or stages) ... and postpone final ... commitments until the latest possible moment'. At the same time, 'they often purposely delay initial decisions, or keep such decisions vague, in order to encourage lower-level participation, to gain more information from specialists, or to build commitment to solutions' (p. 109).

Quinn states that 'executives link together and bring order to a series of strategic processes and decisions spanning years. At the beginning of the process it is literally impossible to predict all the events and forces which will shape the future of the company. The best that executives can do is to forecast the most likely forces which will impinge on the company's affairs and the ranges of their possible impact. They then attempt to build a resource base and a corporate posture that are so strong in selected areas that the enterprise can survive and prosper despite all but the most devastating events. They consciously select market/technological/product segments which the concern can "dominate" given its resource limits, and place some "side bets" ... in order to decrease the risk of catastrophic failure or to increase the company's flexibility for future options.

They then proceed incrementally to handle urgent matters, start longer-term sequences whose specific future branches and consequences are perhaps murky, respond to unforeseen events as they occur, build on successes, and brace up or cut losses on failures. They constantly reassess the future, find new congruencies as events unfurl and blend the organization's skills and resources into new balances of dominance and risk-aversion as various forces intersect to suggest better - but never perfect - alignments. The process is dynamic, with neither a real beginning nor end' (pp. 113-114).

Quinn concludes that strategy 'involves forces of such great number, strength and combinatory powers that one cannot predict events in a probabilistic sense. Hence logic dictates that one proceeds flexibly and experimentally from broad concepts towards specific commitments, making the latter concrete as late as possible in order to narrow the bands of uncertainty and to benefit from the best available information. This is the process of "logical incrementalism"' (p. 114).

Example - Quinn describes the disorderly development of Honda's US motorcycle strategy. Honda had tried to introduce its large motor cycles into America during the late 1950s. This strategy was not initially successful. Honda had in 1960 introduced a small 50cc motorcycle (the "Super Cub") with a step-through construction as much suitable for women as men. It was Honda's retailers who subsequently focused Honda's attention on the strong reaction of US customers to these new bikes. Honda was still trying to improve sales of its larger models, but radically changed its strategy when it realized that it had on its hands the unexpected leader of a new market that it had unwittingly helped to create.

Emergent and Opportunistic Approaches to Strategy Formulation

Strategic choices and strategic moves *may be contingent upon the corporate and business opportunities that emerge and become available to the enterprise*. The use of an emergent or an opportunistic approach to the strategic management process implies that:

❑ the organization continuously scans the business and market environment for emerging opportunities; *and as a consequence*
❑ maintains a flexible resource base and an agile capability (for instance by making use of external sub-contracting, or the outsourcing of operational, manufacturing or service activities) such that the enterprise can quickly adjust to take advantage of those opportunities it finds attractive.

Example - former Second World War pilots suddenly found in the late 1940s and early 1950s that transport planes being sold off cheaply by the military could be converted to carry European holiday makers to sunshine destinations such as Spain or Italy. Thus was the air package tour industry born from an opportunity seized by airmen turned entrepreneurs.

SECTION FOUR – STAKEHOLDER ANALYSIS

THE CONCEPT OF THE STAKEHOLDER

Stakeholders may be defined as people and institutions both internal and external to the organization who have an investment of some kind in it; or who instead have some kind of involvement or interest in it; or who are directly affected by its activities or its processes.

Stakeholder analysis identifies three broad categories of stakeholder. These stakeholders can be described as:

❑ stakeholders internal to the organization
❑ stakeholders immediately external to the organization
❑ other external stakeholders

These stakeholders are illustrated within their environmental context in Figure 11.2.

Stakeholders may, to a varying degree according to their relative power, be able to exercise influence over the formulation of mission, objectives and strategy, and over the strategic management of the organization.

Three Categories of Stakeholder

Internal stakeholders - include the chief executive officer (CEO) or president; the board of directors, management board, or board of governors; non-executive directors representing shareholders; shareholders, family, or trust members who work within the enterprise; or elected representatives. This group of internal stakeholders are owners or proprietors; or act on behalf of the owners; or act as stewards of the interests and investments of the owners or providers of funds as primary beneficiaries or representatives of enterprise purpose.

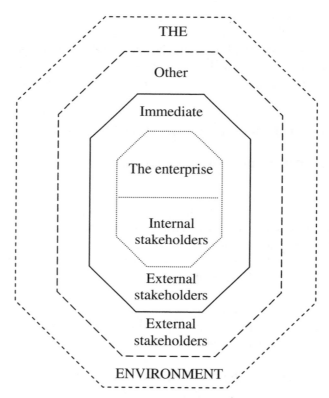

Figure 11.2 Stakeholder Categories

Other internal stakeholders include professional managers or officials, and employees or their representatives.
Immediate external stakeholders - include customers or clients, patients, taxpayers, and so on, as primary recipients of enterprise purpose. This

category also includes those stakeholders with a close or value chain relationship to the enterprise, such as individual and institutional investors; banks, creditors, and other sources of finance; distributors and channel intermediaries; suppliers and value chain constituents; customer or consumer representatives; trade unions; employers' organizations; chambers of commerce.

Other external stakeholders - include professional bodies; regulatory organizations; special interest or pressure groups; the wider community within which the enterprise operates; and elected representatives at local, regional, provincial, and central, EU or NAFTA level (etc) who are able to influence the broad processes of regulation and legislation.

THE RELATIONSHIP BETWEEN STAKEHOLDERS AND THE ENTERPRISE

The capacity of the stakeholder to exercise influence over any of the processes of enterprise leadership; the setting of mission and objective; the process of corporate governance described in Chapters 13 and 14; strategy formulation; strategic decision-making; or strategy implementation may depend upon a number of variables, including the following.

The relative closeness or distance of the stakeholder - from leadership, objective setting, strategy formulation, strategic decision-making and implementation processes. Internal stakeholders are, clearly, likely to have the greatest power and influence in this respect. This is related to:-
The relative power of any particular stakeholder - and the power relativities between the stakeholders as a group.
The character of the relationship between enterprise and stakeholder - whether based on:-

- the use of power, dominance, or control by either party.
- the use of proactive strategies by either party (such as "defining the terms of the relationship", "getting in front of the issue", "managing the stakeholders", or "setting the agenda").
- seeking parity as the minimum basis for the relationship between stakeholders.
- the use of reactive or defensive strategies by which an attempt is made to limit or to constrain the use by other stakeholders of their own power and influence.

The means by which the relationship is implemented - which may be based upon any of the following approaches:-

- prescription, command, or authoritarianism.
- consultation, and the taking of advice from other parties.
- participation, and the involvement of other parties in the process of governance and strategy formulation.
- negotiation between the relevant parties.
- democratic processes among the parties.
- periodic or tactical capitulation to the demands of one or other of the parties; or a strategic withdrawal until a stronger negotiating position can be created.

SECTION FIVE – OTHER RELEVANT ISSUES

CRITICAL SUCCESS FACTORS

Critical success factors were described in Chapter 4 as having a disproportionate effect on the achievement of enterprise objectives (or on the failure to achieve them). Enterprise management will need to understand these critical factors, and ensure that they are taken into account in the process of corporate governance, objective setting, strategy formulation, and strategic decision-making. Critical success factors to which reference is made in this book for instance include the following:

- leadership capability
- staff skill, staff experience, and enterprise competence
- knowledge and technology
- capability and resource efficiency
- financial management
- enterprise scale, scope, volume, and critical mass
- market access and market share.
- product or service quality
- business development and growth
- cost containment and cost management
- value generation, margin, profitability, and return on capital employed

A failure to understand and respond to critical success factors is likely to be correlated with a disproportionate degree of risk and the potential for enterprise failure.

LIMITING FACTORS

Limiting factors were described in Chapter 4 as directly limiting the opportunities available to the enterprise. They are likely to shape and constrain the alternative objectives, strategies and activities from which the enterprise may choose (or which it perceives to be most desirable). Typically these limiting factors derive from:

❑ *Internal features* - for example associated with financial, cashflow, resource, leadership, competence, skill, and operational capabilities.

❑ *External features* - for example, associated with regulatory, distribution, or market limitations. Some countries (such as the USA) have strong competition laws restricting certain types of business development or distribution strategy. Other countries insist on a certain minimum degree of local supply sourcing or manufacture as a condition of inward investment and profit repatriation by foreign companies.

CONTINGENCIES AND CONSTRAINTS

A variety of contingencies and constraints were identified in Chapter 4. The enterprise must operate within the contingencies and constraints that characterize its business or operational environment. The process of objective setting, strategy formulation and strategic management will need to understand the nature and relevance of these contingencies and constraints; and to make appropriate allowance for their influence.

THE TACTICAL COMPONENT OF THE STRATEGY HIERARCHY

Tactical planning determines the *functional* and *departmental* contribution to the achievement of enterprise objectives, and to the implementation of strategies. It shapes detailed decisions as to how the resources and capability of the enterprise will be allocated and organized, whether on the short or medium term, as between these different functional and departmental activities.

For instance, a decision may be made to increase the budgetary allocation of working capital to a particular business unit in order to allow it to meet an unexpected increase in demand. The means by which this additional cash is to be obtained then depends on financial management strategy. This may permit additional borrowing; or may instead insist on the withdrawal of working capital from a budget elsewhere in the organization so as to keep within pre-determined financial targets.

The tactical component lays down the objectives, criteria, and standards for *performance evaluation*, so that performance monitoring, control and review can be carried out. It is at the tactical level that measurements of *effectiveness* and *efficiency* are applied to indicate whether or not the enterprise is implementing its chosen strategies appropriately and within budget. Performance evaluation and management are dealt with in Chapter 16.

Finally, the tactical component includes the formulation of detailed *policies*. Policies are used to establish "contingent decision". Contingent decisions anticipate and lay down the range and type of responses required in pre-specified recurring situations. Thus, for example, there will be policies on how to deal with delayed payment by customers, or on the procedure to be followed in cases of employee discipline or dismissal. Policies are used to guide and to standardize the actions of people and departments, so as to achieve a consistent and predictable pattern of response.

THE OPERATIONAL COMPONENT OF THE STRATEGY HIERARCHY

Operational planning has a number of elements. These include the establishment of:

Programmes and projects - which specify the actions, rules or procedures required to achieve a particular objective. Programmes or projects allocate tasks and responsibilities to individuals and groups, lay down the time scale for their achievement, and establish the required outcomes by which their implementation is to be monitored and assessed.

Procedures - which detail the ways in which specified and recurring issues or problems are to be accomplished. Procedures often comprise a standardized set of rules.

Rules - which are used to specify the particular course of action to be followed in recurring situations in which a consistent response is required, or in which it has been decided that individual discretion should be minimized.

Business and budgetary plans - which were described in Chapter 9. Business and budgetary plans are used as the framework for the detailed quantitative planning required to achieve the projected departmental, functional, or programme results for the forecast period ahead. Budgetary planning then provides the basis for *budgetary control*, by which actual results achieved are compared with plans and performance standards.

The operational component is thus concerned with the detailed quantification, planning, and implementation at functional or departmental level of the chosen strategies and courses of action. From then on, processes of monitoring, feedback, control and review take over, using the plans as standards or benchmarks with which actual performance is compared.

REVIEW QUESTIONS

1. What is the strategy hierarchy?
2. What is enterprise mission? Describe its components.
3. What is strategic intent?
4. What are enterprise objectives?
5. What is strategy?
6. Compare and contrast the various bases of strategy formulation.
7. What are stakeholders? What influence may they have on the strategy process?
8. Why are critical success factors relevant to the formulation of objectives and strategy?

TECHNIQUES OF CASE STUDY AND ANALYSIS

1. Identify enterprise mission. Does the case study organization appear to have a clear purpose?
2. Identify strategic intent and direction. In what direction does the case organization appear to be heading?
3. What objectives are evident from the case study?
4. What strategies are evident from the case study? Can these strategies in any way be categorized as being forced, self-imposed, required, rationalistic, deliberate, logically incremental, emergent, or opportunistic in character?

5. What are the relevant critical success factors? Are the missions, objectives and strategies evident in the case study clearly related to them?
6. Can the key stakeholders be identified from the case study? What are their various interests in the organization?

References

Argenti, J. (1974) *Systematic Corporate Planning*, Nelson, London.
Bennis, W. and B. Nanus (1985) *Leaders: the strategies for taking charge*, Harper & Row, New York.
Collins, J.C. and J.I. Porras (1995) *Built To Last*, Century Business, London.
Goldsmith, W. and D. Clutterbuck (1997) *The Winning Streak Mark II*, Orion Books, London.
Hamel, G. and C.K. Prahalad (1994) *Competing for the Future*, Harvard Business School Press, Boston, Mass.
Kay, J. (1993) *Foundations of Corporate Success*, Oxford University Press, Oxford.
Mintzberg, H. (1987a) 'Five Ps for strategy', *California Management Review*, Autumn.
Mintzberg, H. (1987b) 'Crafting strategy', *Harvard Business Review*, July-August.
Mintzberg, H. (1989) *Mintzberg on Management*, Free Press, New York.
Mintzberg, H. and A. McHugh (1985a) 'Strategy formulation in an adhocracy', *Administrative Science Quarterly*, Vol 30 June.
Mintzberg, H. and J.A. Waters (1985b) 'Of strategies, deliberate and emergent', *Strategic Management Journal*, July-September.
Mintzberg, H; Quinn, J.B. and S. Ghoshal (1998) *The Strategy Process: Revised European Edition*, Prentice Hall International, London.
Morden, A.R. (2004) *Principles of Management (2nd Edition)*, Ashgate, Aldershot.
Peters, T.J. and N. Austin (1986) *A Passion for Excellence*, Fontana, London.
Peters, T.J. and R.H. Waterman (1982) *In Search of Excellence*, Harper & Row, New York.
Quinn, J.B. (1980) *Strategies for Change: logical incrementalism*, Irwin, Homewood, Illinois.
Tichy, N.M. and S. Sherman (1994) *Control Your Destiny or Someone Else Will*, Harper Business, New York.
Wheeler, D. and M. Sillanpää (1997) *The Stakeholder Corporation*, Pitman, London.

Chapter 12

Business Ethics, Environmentalism, and Social Responsibility

People have to decide in life what is the right thing to do. So do companies and organizations. It will all depend on what each defines the "right thing" to be. What decisions are ethical? What actions are environmentally sustainable? What behaviour is socially responsible? Such decisions cannot be cast aside. And they may affect all of us.

This chapter analyzes business ethics, environmentalism, and social responsibility. These concepts are inter-related. They are likely to shape the nature of mission, objective, and strategy described in Chapter 11. They are key variables in the management of the relationship between the enterprise, its stakeholders, and its external environment.

STAKEHOLDERS AND ETHOS

Chapter 11 analyzed mission, objectives, and strategy as the key components of the strategy hierarchy. These three components are the basic building blocks of the process and practice of strategy formulation, strategic decision-making, and strategic management.

As a part of the discussion, Chapter 11 defined and dealt with *values, core ideology*, and *ethos* as key strategic concepts. Chapter 11 also defined and dealt with *stakeholder analysis*. The discussion of the issues of business ethics, environmentalism and green issues, and social responsibility that is the subject of this chapter takes place within a framework of stakeholder analysis; and within the context of the stated ethos and values of the organization.

SECTION ONE – ETHICS

Business ethics issues are described in the first section of this chapter. The establishment of mission, objectives, and strategy may (or may not) accord, or be *congruent* with the culture and values of the wider society within which the enterprise is located. This congruence is a function of the degree to which the process of strategic management is rooted in, and underpinned by prevailing *ethical considerations and ethical frameworks*.

ETHICS IN BUSINESS

Ethics underpin the *ethos* and *values* of the enterprise described in Chapter 11. *Ethics* can be defined as *a conception of right or wrong conduct*. Ethics tell us when our actions are "moral" or "immoral". Ethics provide guides to moral behaviour, or to what is "morally acceptable" or "morally unacceptable". Ethical principles underlie the basic rules of social behaviour that are essential for the preservation and continuing of effective social and organized life. Ethical principles stem from:

❑   religious beliefs or philosophical codes
❑   a society's history, experience and tradition
❑   national culture
❑   kinship, and the family context
❑   educational processes
❑   the influence of peers and reference groups
❑   the influence of opinion leaders and role models

Ethical principles tend to vary from society to society, and from culture to culture across time.

BUSINESS ETHICS

Business ethics can be defined as *the application of general ethical principles to business behaviour*. In order to be considered "ethical", the enterprise and its management must draw concepts of what is proper behaviour from the same sources as everyone else, not constructing its own definitions of what is right or wrong behaviour. People who work in business or administrative organizations are bound by the same ethical principles that apply to others. Ethical and socially responsible behaviour:

❑   is expected by the general public, and by its elected representatives, legislators (etc). Transgressors can eventually expect to be identified, criticised, or punished.

❑   prevents harm to stakeholders, the general public, and society as a whole. One of the strongest ethical principles is stated in common sense terms as "do no harm" (*primum non nocere*). A company that is careless in disposing of toxic chemical wastes that cause disease or death, for example, is breaking this basic ethical injunction.

❑   protects the enterprise from abuse by unethical managers, employees, or competitors. Frederick, Post and Davis (1992, p. 55) give as an example unfair competitive practices based on bribery and corruption.

❑   protects employees from harmful actions by their employer. Such actions might include being forced to work in hazardous or unsafe conditions; or being forced to do something illegal or against their personal convictions or values (such as falsifying an accounting audit or report). Frederick, Post and Davis comment that "businesses that treat their employees with dignity and integrity reap ... rewards in the form of high morale and ... productivity" (p. 56).

❑   allows people to act consistently with their personal ethical beliefs within the employment and organizational context. Frederick, Post and Davis comment that 'most people want to act in ways that are consistent with their own sense of right and wrong. Being pressured to contradict their personal values creates much emotional stress. Knowing that one works in a supportive ethical climate contributes to one's sense of psychological security' (p. 56).

TYPES OF BUSINESS ETHICS ISSUES

Frederick, Post and Davis identify three main categories of business ethics issue. These are:

Face to face ethics - which arise from the interpersonal interactions and transactions that make up day-to-day organizational life. Managers and employees face ethical conflicts when their own personal standards differ from job demands. Frederick, Post and Davis identify as examples 'the giving of gifts and kickbacks to gain business; unfair discrimination in dealing with others; unfair pricing, ... firings and layoffs that harm people, ... unfairness to employees, ... (and) questionable selling practices' (pp. 58-59).

Corporate policy ethics - which affect activities and operations on a company-wide basis. Senior management, boards of directors, CEOs (etc) are likely as a part of their corporate responsibility to have to establish company-wide or governance policies on ethical issues. Such issues might include responding to pressure from competitors to become involved in an industry practice of colluding to fix prices and allocate orders; or the departmental placing of covert restrictions on the management of equality of employee opportunity, diversity, or disability within the enterprise.

Functional area ethics - Frederick, Post and Davis suggest that each business function tends to have its own variety of ethical issues and *ethical dilemmas*. For example:-

- *accounting* - unfair pressure on employees or auditors not to report financial performance honestly and accurately according to the accounting standards and principles laid down; not disclosing information about relationships with people and organizations that should have been made available to stakeholders and the general public; or a failure to adhere to professional standards or codes of conduct.

- *sales and marketing* - the making of false or misleading claims; the use of unethical or high pressure selling practices; unfair or predatory pricing tactics; or the failure to adhere to professional standards or codes of conduct.

- *purchasing and supply* - unfair pressure on suppliers (especially SMEs) to obtain low prices, preferential treatment, or extended credit; the use of bribery and corruption to allocate or gain orders; or the failure to adhere to professional standards or codes of conduct.

WHY ETHICAL PROBLEMS OCCUR IN BUSINESS

Ethical problems occur for a variety of reasons. These include:

Personal gain and selfish interest - in which individual greed or concern for personal gain are placed ahead of all other concerns, irrespective of the potential for harm this may cause other people or the organization. Frederick, Post and Davis describe a manager or an employee who puts his or her own self-interest above all other considerations as 'an ethical egoist ... (who) tends to ignore ethical principles accepted by others, or to believe that "ethical rules are made for others". Altruism ... is seen to be sentimental or even irrational' (p. 63).

Competitive pressures on profits - Frederick, Post and Davis comment that 'when companies are squeezed by tough competition, they sometimes engage in unethical practices in order to protect their profits. This may especially be true in companies whose financial performance is already substandard' (p. 64). Or instead, a single-minded and aggressive drive for profits, regardless of financial condition, may create a climate or culture in which unethical activity comes to be perceived as acceptable. Frederick, Post and Davis also identify price-fixing and the establishment of cartels as a practice that occurs when companies compete vigorously in a limited or static market. Such practices represent unethical behaviour where customers end up paying higher prices than they would under conditions of free competition.

Business goals versus personal values - ethical conflicts may occur where an organization pursues goals, or uses methods that are unacceptable to employees or stakeholders; or clash with their personal values. An ethical dilemma will in particular arise where enterprise goals and methods require employees to follow orders that they believe will harm themselves or other employees, customers, the company, shareholders, or the general public. The individual is then placed in a dilemma between accepting and implementing the unethical practice, or "blowing the whistle" on the organization. Blowing the whistle may pose severe risks of dismissal, the incidence of lawsuits, or even prosecution for breach of contract.

Cross-cultural contradictions - ethical problems are likely to arise as corporations transact business in other societies where ethical standards and practices differ from those in the home country. Frederick, Post and Davis comment that 'the policy-makers and strategic planners in all multinational corporations, regardless of the nation where they are headquartered, face this kind of ethical dilemma' (p. 66).

This cross-cultural contradiction can be reduced to a simple dilemma. *Which ethical standards does the enterprise accept as its benchmark?* Does it accept local standards which are lower than those prevailing at home, and exploit them quite legally within the territory? Or does it instead impose uniform high standards throughout its global operations, thereby operating at a much higher ethical standard than is called for by the law of some of the territories in which it is active? The resolution of this dilemma will for instance affect localized enterprise policies and practices concerning:-

- environmental and ecological protection, as described in the next section of this chapter, below.
- enterprise social responsibility, as described in a later section of this chapter, below.
- the equitable treatment of employees; and in some countries the communication and protection of basic human rights in the workplace.

- the acceptability or unacceptability of bribery, the payment of "commissions", and the making of other forms of questionable payments in international trade.
- the more general adaptation of enterprise operations and management to the prevailing business culture (defined as "the way we do things round here") and the ethical standards that underlie it.

ANALYSING ETHICAL PROBLEMS IN BUSINESS

Frederick, Post and Davis identify three methods by which managers may deal with ethical problems. These are:

Utility: comparing benefits and costs - this approach emphasises the utility (the overall amount of good) that can be produced by an action or a decision. It uses *utilitarian reasoning*. This is based on cost-benefit analysis, in which the costs and benefits of an action, a policy, or a decision, are compared. These costs and benefits may be:-
- economic (expressed in measurable values)
- social (measured by indicators of effect on society)
- human (measured by psychological or emotional impacts)

By comparing the relative costs and benefits, the net cost or net benefit may be apparent. Under this reasoning, if the benefits outweigh the costs the action is ethical, and vice versa.

Rights: determining and protecting entitlements - ethical judgements in this case are based on *human rights concepts*. A right means that a person or a group is entitled to something, or is entitled to be treated in a particular way. Such rights include survival, subsistence, privacy, independence, freedom of choice and opportunity, legal treatment by others, and freedom from arbitrary decision. Denying those rights, or failing to implement or protect them for other people and groups is considered unethical.

This approach to ethical reasoning holds that individuals should be treated as valued ends in themselves just because they are human beings. Using others for your own purposes is deemed unethical if, at the same time, you deny them their own purposes and objectives.

Justice: is it fair? - justice and fairness exist when benefits and burdens are distributed equitably and according to an accepted rule or code. The result is conceptualized in terms of "fair shares" for all, whether it be of benefits, or burdens, or both. If the shares of benefits and burdens appear to be fair according to society's rules, then the action will be deemed to be ethical.

These three approaches to ethical reasoning are summarised in Table 12.1.

Table 12.1 Three Approaches to Ethical Reasoning

Three approaches to ethical reasoning
(Source: W.C. Frederick, J.E. Post and K. Davis, 1992)

Method	Critical determining factor	An action is ethical when …	Limitations
Utilitarian	Comparing benefits and costs.	Net benefits exceed net costs.	Difficult to measure some human and social costs. Majority may disregard rights of minority.
Rights	Respecting rights.	Basic human rights are respected.	Difficult to balance conflicting rights.
Justice	Distributing fair shares.	Benefits and costs are fairly distributed.	Difficult to measure benefits and costs. Lack of agreement on fair shares.

THREE TYPES OF MANAGERIAL ETHICS

Bartol and Martin (1994) identify three approaches to ethical practice taken by organizations or their managements, for instance to the issue of strategic choice. These are:

Immoral management - in which ethical principles are absent, or their application is instead actively opposed. Such an approach to the processes of leadership and strategic management is characterized by an exclusive focus on the personal gain, selfish interest, competitive position, and company profit already described above. There is likely to be an absence of concern about issues of equity and fairness; a view of the law as "not applying to me", or instead constituting an obstacle to be overcome; a willingness to "cut corners"; and active hostility to the environmental or ecological considerations, and the issues of social responsibility described in later sections of this chapter.

Amoral management - which ignores or is oblivious to ethical considerations. Two varieties are identified:-

• *intentional*: in which managers do not include ethical variables in their decision-making and actions because they perceive that general ethical standards are only appropriate to non-business areas of life.

• *unintentional*: in which managers do not include ethical variables in their business dealings because they are inattentive or insensitive to the moral implications of their decisions and actions.

Bartol and Martin suggest that a 'basic principle governing amoral management is "within the letter of the law, can we make money with this action, decision, or behaviour?"' (p. 118). They quote as an example the controversy arising over the supply by Nestlé of powdered baby milk to nursing mothers in poor third world countries.

Moral management - which attempts to follow ethical principles and precepts. Bartol and Martin comment that 'while moral managers also desire to succeed, they seek to do so only within the parameters of ethical standards and the ideals of fairness, justice, and due process. As a result, moral managers pursue business objectives that involve simultaneously making a profit and engaging in legal and ethical behaviours. They follow not only the letter but also the spirit of the law, recognizing that moral management generally requires operating well above what the law mandates. The central guiding principle is: "Is this action, decision, or behaviour fair to us and all parties involved?"' (p. 118). Moral management may also be described as "values-based" management.

SECTION TWO - ENVIRONMENTALISM

ENVIRONMENTALISM

Recent decades have seen increased national and international focus on the *physical, ecological, and psychological environments* in which people live. This focus has resulted from heightened popular concern about the sustainability and impact of industrial and consumer society on the various environments in which it operates. These concerns are for instance visible in:

❑   the potential for climate change and global warming
❑   air and water pollution
❑   the exploitation and the degradation of the natural environment
❑   the loss of animal and plant species

- deforestation
- the effects of commercial forestry
- the effects of urbanization
- the effects of increasing car ownership and road traffic volumes

Morden (2004) comments that 'there is nothing new in public concern for the physical and psychological environment. The UK's National Trusts, for example, have been in the conservation business for many years. However, increasingly severe environmental problems associated with … pollution, toxic waste contamination, and the destruction of tropical rain forests have raised the level of environmental awareness on the part of the public' (p. 462). This awareness has reached a threshold at which people are prepared *to act in some way*. Such action may be based on the exercise of consumer or buyer power, or on voting choice in political elections (for instance as in Germany). Environmental, ecological and "green" concerns appear, therefore, to have pushed their way on to the agenda in:

- the external market and economic environment.
- the technological environment.
- the social and cultural environment, especially among the young people who will have to inherit (and deal with) the legacy their parents leave behind.
- the political and legislative environment. Green concerns have been absorbed into mainstream politics in the West (for instance in Canada and Germany), whilst the democratization of Russia and central Europe has left governments with the job of cleaning up inefficient industries and polluted landscapes.

The increasing level of environmental concern, and the "greening" of markets, contain opportunities and threats for enterprise management. Some products or services have become unacceptable. Processes and practices are being re-engineered. Product specification or packaging may have to be changed. New methods and new technologies are being developed to meet more stringent environment-friendly standards, or to maintain competitive advantage in increasingly environmentally sensitive markets.

At the same time, increasing environmental awareness may decrease the level of the environmental stability described in Chapter 6 of this book. Formerly stable market or technological environments, such as those for agricultural, livestock, or chemical products have become dynamic or turbulent as consumer attitudes change and purchasing habits alter.

Similarly, companies will have to react to influential young people who, as opinion-formers, shape the perceptions of their peers. An increasingly educated and aware youth will eventually become the voters, customers, conservationists, and decision-makers of the future.

GREEN ISSUES

In a pioneering UK study, Elkington and Hailes (1988) identified a series of "green issues" which impact on purchase behaviour, political attitudes, and legislation. These issues may serve to restrict enterprise freedom of action, or to increase the level of turbulence in the external environment. These issues include:

The ozone layer - it is apparent that the thinning and puncturing of the ozone layer has, in part, been brought about by the use of the chemical compounds of the chlorofluorocarbons or CFCs. These chemical compounds have been used in aerosols and packaging; whilst their use in refrigeration and air conditioning plants is being phased out on a global basis in accordance with the Montreal Protocols.

Climatic conditions and the "greenhouse effect" - poor air quality; air pollution; an increasing incidence of asthma in young children; and the potential for unpredictable weather conditions, global warming and global dimming, are in part due to the emission of carbon dioxide, nitrogen oxides, methane, CFCs, and "black smoke" into the atmosphere.

Tropical deforestation - forests are believed to act as "sinks" for carbon dioxide, and return oxygen to the atmosphere. They also darken the surface of the earth and so absorb heat. Tropical deforestation by burning returns carbon dioxide into the atmosphere in enormous quantities, and may thereby contribute to the "greenhouse effect". Where proper agricultural use or re-afforestation do not occur (or "slash and burn" techniques of agriculture continue to be used), the remaining land suffers soil erosion and deteriorates, rivers silt up and cause flooding, and the flora and fauna of the area is lost. There may be a direct effect on climate in the region, as in the Sahel region of Africa. There may also be a direct link between deforestation, reduced rainfall, and desertification.

Acid rain - moisture in the atmosphere combines with such emissions as sulphur compounds and nitrogen oxide to produce acid rain, which can cause extensive damage to soils, trees, lakes and rivers. The most important man-made sources of acid rain are car exhaust emissions and coal-burning power stations. Acid rain is a major environmental problem in Europe and North America.

Water pollution - the pollution of streams, rivers, lakes and seas results in part from:-

- the dumping of wastes and effluents, for instance into the North and Baltic seas.

- uncontrolled intensive farming methods, giving rise to slurry which leaches into local rivers.

- the inefficient use of chemical fertilizers, nutrients and pesticides associated with agriculture and fish-farming, which build up in ground water or escape into local rivers or lakes.

- the use of phosphates and bleaches in household chemicals, which may not be properly treated in the sewage system, and subsequently escape as effluent into rivers and lakes.

Waste - the generation and disposal of large quantities of waste, whether in the form of used packaging or the residues of agriculture, production, or consumption, has now become a major environmental issue. It also represents an inefficient use of scarce resources, and constitutes an unnecessary cost. Elkington and Hailes note two main considerations under this heading, as follow.

Packaging - while packaging is an essential feature of product specification, product protection and the marketing mix, it is highly visible. It has become an obvious and easy target for environmental questioning and criticism. The enterprise may have to consider simplifying or reducing packaging; avoiding the use of non-renewable resources in the manufacture of packaging; or using returnable and re-usable systems or recyclable materials.

Disposal - the disposal of waste may involve the process of incineration. Incineration may give rise to the contentious issue of the safe burning of toxic materials. Or instead, waste may be buried in landfill. Landfill uses up land, and may create what Elkington and Hailes describe as 'a deadly cocktail of domestic, commercial and industrial waste'. Landfill may generate methane gas, which is explosive, and contributes to air pollution. The disposal of waste also uses up finite resources and "loses" the energy associated with the original manufacture or processing.

German companies (under the so-called "Topfer Law") have to ensure that bulk packaging is collected and re-cycled. They are also required under the Duales System Deutschland or "Green Spot" scheme to pay for this process.

The disappearing countryside - in the case of the UK, the spread of urban development, afforestation through the planting of pinewoods, and intensive farming methods have brought about a drastic change in the countryside, for instance in:-

- the loss of traditional woodland
- the loss of lowland grassland and heath
- the loss of hedgerows

At the same time, the loss of moorland valleys to the construction of reservoirs may accelerate as the demand for water increases.

Endangered species - housing development and urban spread, road building, intensive farming (and so on) have all had a severe effect on wildlife and flora in the developed countries. Much wildlife and flora is threatened; other wildlife has become marginalized through loss of habitat or food source.

Excessive fishing in any location can drastically reduce fish stocks. This has the effect of threatening other animals in the food chain that depend on that fish stock. This affects seals, dolphins, whales and birds. Worse, some fishing methods themselves endanger the lives of sea creatures such as dolphins.

The destruction or impoverishment of tropical rain forests and habitats is associated with an acceleration of the pace at which plant and animal species (many still unknown to us) are threatened or have become extinct. Quite apart from the moral and ethical arguments this raises, there are practical implications of such a destructive process. Plants and animals are being lost whose use as potential sources of food and plant strains, pharmaceutical and bio-chemical substances, or natural pesticides, will never be available when otherwise they should have been maintained for posterity.

Animal welfare - there are long and sad international traditions of animal abuse and cruelty associated with:-

- the testing of products and substances.
- the intensive rearing of livestock such as veal calves, poultry and pigs.
- the rearing or killing of animals or birds for fur, skin, feathers or ivory.
- the abuse of beasts-of-burden such as the donkey.

Many commercial organizations are now careful to avoid any association with animal abuse or cruelty, whether as manufacturers or buyers. For instance, they have eliminated from sale any item associated with cruelty or destruction of wildlife. Cruelty-free cosmetics are now widely available. Others have stopped buying from countries with a poor record of promoting animal welfare. Sealskin apparel has become an anathema to many people; whilst the fur trade provides ongoing controversy in Europe and North America.

SUSTAINABILITY

Elkington and Hailes see *sustainability* as a key environmental and ecological issue. A fundamental question is whether the operations of the enterprise are environmentally sustainable. Or does the enterprise exploit its environment on an irrecoverable basis? For instance, look at the two following illustrative comparisons:

Example one - tropical deforestation and short-term agricultural or ranching activities, which may cause soil erosion and desertification, being employed to supply soya, or beef for fast-food outlets. Or instead, the proper management and replanting of tropical hardwoods for the supply of timber, at the same time retaining ecology and habitat.

Example two - the excessive use of chemical fertilisers and pesticides, or the damage to soil structure through monoculture (for instance of wheat or rice). This process may involve the elimination of habitats (birds and bats are nature's pesticides); and place at risk insects, bats and birds that carry out plant pollination. Or instead, the sympathetic use of agro-chemical and organic farming that respects soil structure, maintains the landscape, makes space for flora and fauna, and involves fauna to a proper degree in pollination and pest control.

SOME DETERMINANTS OF STRATEGIC ENVIRONMENTAL CHOICE

Three main determinants of strategic environmental choice and decision-making can be identified. These are described below.

Coercive Pressures

Coercive pressures will force the enterprise to formulate and to adopt environmentally appropriate strategies. These *forced strategies* have as their source:

❑ prevailing government policy and legislation.
❑ EU regulation and policies on environmental, audit, eco-labelling, or eco-management issues, for instance (i) through the use of *life cycle analysis* to assess environmental impact; or (ii) through the concept that "the polluter must pay".

- ❏ the requirement to meet ISO 14000 standards for environmental management systems.
- ❏ market forces caused by green consumerism; and driven for instance by the response of retail chains, distributors (etc) who place pressure on their suppliers to meet the needs of this demand.
- ❏ the requirements of ethical and environmental investment policies marketed by financial institutions.

Normative Pressures

Normative pressures of a sufficient strength may cause the enterprise of its own choice to formulate and to adopt environmentally appropriate strategies. These *self-imposed or required strategies* have as their source:

- ❏ increasing public expectations of environmentally sustainable behaviour.
- ❏ the desire to be seen to be adhering to, or adopting the prevailing standards and expectations of environmental and ethical behaviour; and to be seen to be keeping up to date as these standards change and develop over time.
- ❏ the desire to be seen to respond to environmentalist concerns from pressure and lobby groups, advisory bodies, and government agencies.
- ❏ the requirements of ethical sourcing policies in supply chain management.
- ❏ the requirements of ethical and environmental investment policies marketed by financial institutions.

Pressures to Imitate and Follow

In this case, the ethical and environmental standards set by *market leaders* are copied by competitors; or imitated by suppliers, distributors (etc) who wish to enter a supply or value chain that includes such a leader. The leader sets the environmental or ethical benchmark that others perceive they have little choice but to match (that is, *to impose upon themselves*). For instance, the UK Body Shop retail chain has shaped perceptions of environmentally responsible product specification and retail activity. In so doing, it has influenced the behaviour of a wide variety of cosmetic manufacturers and other retailers in the direction of responsibility, sustainability, a refusal to carry out tests on animals, management style, and so on.

ENVIRONMENTAL STRATEGY CHOICES

A variety of environmental strategy choices are described, for instance by Azzone and Bertele (1994, 1997); *The Financial Times* (1996); Maxwell (1996); and Shapiro (1997). Some of these choices are summarized as follows.

Passive Strategies

Passive strategies imply that the enterprise does little or nothing positive to improve the sustainability of its actions. Such strategies may be adopted by organizations which have a significant vested interest in past or existing operational investments. These organizations may lobby legislative or regulatory bodies in a reactive manner in order to attempt to pre-empt or to reduce the impact of proposed environmental legislation that has the potential (i) to affect the viability of these past or existing operational investments; or (ii) to enforce new investments in more sustainable processes.

Compliance Strategies

In this case, environmental actions are undertaken only in reaction to:

❑ enforcement by regulation or legislation.
❑ market forces that favour environmentally friendly products or processes.
❑ external pressures from environmentalists.
❑ adverse public opinion or media coverage.

Organizations adopting compliance strategies may be categorized as viewing the price of environmental compliance as a negative influence on profit generation; and accordingly limit its application to whatever is perceived by them to be unavoidable. The assumption may also be made that the enterprise should make environmental investments only when everyone else in the sector has been forced to make such investments as well.

Alliance Strategies

Business, commercial, public sector, or administrative organizations may make alliances with environmental groups. Such strategies are characterized by an attempt to balance economic, operational, and ecological goals. The organization may enhance its reputation or brand franchise, and gain increased public credibility. The environmental group may acquire greater influence as well as resources, and be able to achieve greater compliance by other organizations within the sector as a whole.

Proactive Strategies

In this case, the enterprise uses forecasting processes (such as those described in Chapter 9) to put in place forward-looking or proactive environmental strategies which aim to achieve such objectives as:

❑   shaping standards for the rest of the sector, which will then be forced to "catch up" and thereby incur similar (or greater) environmental costs.
❑   conferring market leadership and public credibility as the dominant environmental benchmark for the sector.
❑   yielding competitive advantage.

The success of proactive strategies will be dependent on:

❑   the effectiveness with which likely environmental shifts in legislation and markets can be anticipated, and reactions made to them.
❑   enterprise capacity to influence the setting of standards and benchmarks for the sector (an *architectural* and a *political* capability described in Chapters 4 and 11).
❑   the risk incurred in "first mover" strategies, for which there is no precedent. The *first mover* may make the right move, or it may not (competition strategies such as the "first mover" are analyzed in Chapter 22).

Maxwell (1996) quotes the example of Du Pont. Du Pont was a low-cost manufacturer of CFCs. It supported the Montreal Protocol banning CFCs after investing in the development and production of substitutes. The net result of the inter-government decision was to turn an unprofitable industry into a profitable one during the phase-out of CFCs. Du Pont used this extra profitability to secure its dominant position in the more profitable substitute market. Proactive strategies may be related to, or combined with the innovation strategies described immediately below.

Innovation Strategies

Innovation strategies are for instance described by Azzone and Bertele (1997) in terms of the proactive introduction of 'process innovations implying radical improvements in a company's environmental performance; or product innovations creating ... new market needs'. The successful implementation of environmental innovation strategies may call for highly developed environmental competencies and a strongly positive environmentally orientated culture within the organization. Innovation strategies are described in more detail in Chapter 19.

SECTION THREE – SOCIAL RESPONSIBILITY

STRATEGIC MANAGEMENT AND SOCIAL RESPONSIBILITY

Enterprise management has clearly defined strategic responsibilities for the establishment of corporate objectives, and for the effective use of the financial, material, knowledge, human, and creative resources contributed by stakeholders in achieving those objectives. This is a primary purpose of the process of strategic decision-making and strategic management.

The enterprise must also adhere to operational standards prescribed by law, such as those dealing with health and safety, employment practice, and the merchantable quality of goods sold.

But enterprise management may also be deemed to have a wider *social responsibility* in that its mission, objectives, and strategy should accord with the ethics, values, and culture of the wider society of which it is a part. This implies that management should interact in a *responsible* manner with the various stakeholders with whose interests it is confronted. And it should refrain from unethical or questionable practices.

SOCIAL RESPONSIBILITY AND STAKEHOLDERS

Stakeholders Internal to the Enterprise

There may more than likely be a deeply-rooted expectation on the part of the employees of the enterprise that management will make consistent and strenuous efforts to maintain stable employment prospects and career development opportunities. At the very least, management will be expected to be seen by core employees to show a minimum degree of leadership and concern by attempting to mitigate the effects of recession or market change on the circumstances and conditions of employment.

Management may not be perceived to be socially responsible if its approach to the workforce is predicated purely on short-term considerations, on "spot" contractual terms, or on crude exploitation.

Stakeholders Immediately External to the Enterprise

The customer - customer expectations about socially responsible behaviour may be defined in terms of the degree to which products or services properly satisfy the buyer's needs within "appropriate" availability, supply or purchase contexts; at a "reasonable" or "value for money" price; and are not exploitative.

Morden (2004, p. 459) notes that in this respect 'controversy has surrounded the sale of powdered milk to nursing mothers in Africa, and remains in the sale of tobacco products (in decline in the West) to Third World countries'.

There may also be an expectation that there should be corporate honesty in the communication of messages through advertizing, sales promotion, or techniques of public relations (PR).

The supplier - the relationship, for instance between a large-scale purchaser and a small-scale supplier, may be one in which concepts of commercial advantage and social responsibility come face to face. The management of a large buying organization may have to exercise a significant degree of self-restraint if it is not excessively to dominate, or even threaten the continued existence of supplying organizations over which it is potentially able to exercise crude "buying power".

Other External Stakeholders

Of immediate concern to the enterprise may be professional bodies, and special interest or "pressure" groups, whose power or prestige may be sufficient to extract enterprise behaviour which is defined as socially responsible by the standards of these external stakeholders. These might include professional accountancy, medical, and legal institutions; or consumer organizations capable of direct influence in the affairs of the organization.

More general judgements of what is, or is not, ethical or acceptable behaviour may be made by elected representatives, whether at a local, regional, provincial, national, federal, or supra-national level (such as the

EU). Such representatives may have the capacity *to enforce a legislative perspective* of socially responsible behaviour.

At the same time, the reactions of the wider or general public may depend for articulation on the interpretation and standards of the relevant media (press, radio, television, and internet). Corporate officials responsible for external or public relations (PR) may therefore exercise significant pressure on strategic decision-makers to ensure that the organization at the very least portrays some semblance of widely acceptable behaviour in order to secure favourable media coverage of its affairs. This issue was dealt with in Chapter 10.

The Environment and Environmentalism

The issue of environmentalism was dealt with in an earlier section of this chapter. It noted that public concern over social responsibility has in recent years reached a powerful focus in the adoption of enterprise strategies that are *environment-friendly*. Responsibility towards the *physical, ecological and psychological environment* affects employment conditions, product specification, raw material supply, production, packaging, marketing, and disposal. It can take the form of responsible policies aimed at specifying life-cycle implications (for instance, what happens to the product at the end of its life, and how much of its resource content is recyclable); reducing resource use and pollution; using environment-friendly materials and processes; espousing "green" products whether for cosmetics, packaging, paint, fuel or transportation; or improving the quality of people's lives (etc).

OPERATIONAL ISSUES

The implementation of socially responsible attitudes and practices throughout the organization is likely to be faced by a number of operational issues. These include:

Perceiving expectations - the management of the relationship with stakeholders and the environment may be complicated by the need to obtain a clear perception (i) of the current expectations of stakeholders for ethical and socially responsible behaviour; and (ii) of the standards associated therewith. It may prove difficult to establish an agreed consensus amongst the organization's decision-makers as to what actually constitutes ethical and socially responsible behaviour; by what standards it should be measured; and how it should be measured. *What* exactly *is* defined to be ethical and socially responsible behaviour? *Who* defines it?

Mandatory or discretionary - the issue described immediately above may be exacerbated where managers cannot (or choose not to) decide whether a requirement to be ethical or socially responsive in their behaviour is mandatory or discretionary. The degree to which there is any difference between the two depends on the nature and strength of prevailing ethical, moral, and cultural values; and on how influential these have become in determining what is "acceptable" as opposed to "unacceptable" enterprise decision-making and behaviour.

Stakeholders and contingencies - there is likely to be some kind of relationship between the level of stakeholder interest in the ethical and social responsiveness of the strategic management process, and such contingencies as:-

- company size, type, and technology.
- products and markets involved.
- the scale, scope, and visibility of operations.
- the level or degree of social impact or environmental disturbance.

Morden (p. 461) comments that in general terms 'the larger and more conspicuous the organization, the greater are likely to be the pressures upon it to behave in a socially responsible manner'.

The feasibility and acceptability of compromise - where the organization faces a variety of different stakeholder or environmental expectations about how it should behave, it may produce some kind of operational compromise about how it should respond. Such a compromise might be effective. Or instead it may satisfy none of its stakeholders whilst at the same time alienating at least some of them in the process.

Neutral or proactive? - decision-makers may choose to take a publicly neutral (or non-committal) stance towards their perceived obligations. Or instead they may espouse a proactive position, boldly *defining what they consider to be ethically and socially responsible behaviour* and attempting to promote this as a part of the organization's culture. Such a decision may be accompanied by a clear public declaration within statements of mission and values about how the enterprise proposes to respond to stakeholders and environment. This may be perceived to have considerable value as a corporate communication and marketing message. Kodak's values, for example, were described in Chapter 11.

SOME INTERNATIONAL EXAMPLES OF SOCIAL RESPONSIBILITY ORIENTATIONS

There are a variety of international examples of strategic social responsibility orientations. These include the following.

Hampden-Turner and Trompenaars (1994), Chen (1995), and Redding (1997) comment on a primary role of the Japanese corporation ("kaisha" or in its extended form the "keiretsu"). This is to employ people and develop long term strength or competence for individual people, for the enterprise, and for Japan.

Bloom, Calori and de Woot (1994) describe as key features of European management a *humanistic* orientation to people and their society; and a perceived need for social responsibility in corporate dealings. People are to be served by progress - not the other way round.

Lessem and Neubauer (1994) identify a number of other features of social responsibility within the European context. These include:

❑ a *holistic* view of the place of the enterprise within the context of the needs of the society of which it is a part. Responsibility towards, and co-operation with other components of the whole society are seen as the appropriate relationship by which to achieve social progress.
❑ a *rationalist* orientation to prescribing the role of the enterprise within the wider needs of the economic and political management of society.

Michel Albert (1993) compares Anglo-Saxon with Germanic or "Rhineland" capitalism. He places the role of the enterprise firmly within the context of the needs of the *social market* (or the *civic economy*) and its stakeholders - a concept which underpins broad areas of European Union thinking. The role of business enterprise is conceptualized to be to serve a long-term communal purpose; whilst a "reasonable degree" of annual profitability (and careful financial management) are seen to indicate that value is being created and that resources are not being misused or wasted.

The UK Royal Society of Arts (RSA) "Tomorrow's Company" Report (1995) contends that only through a strengthened relationship architecture with and between employees, customers, suppliers, investors, and the community as stakeholders will companies innovate, adapt and prosper, whilst at the same time maintain public confidence through overtly responsible behaviour. The RSA comments that 'we believe that only by giving due weight to the interests of all key stakeholders can shareholders' continuing value be assured. We describe this as the *inclusive* approach and have developed a framework for its use by Tomorrow's Company' (piii) ... 'it is this *inclusive* approach which differentiates Tomorrow's Company ... the companies which will sustain competitive success in the future are those which focus less exclusively on shareholders and on financial measures of success - and instead include all their stakeholder relationships, and a broader range of measurements, in the way they think and talk about their purpose and performance' (p. 1).

Hamel and Prahalad (1990, 1994) emphasise the importance to competitive advantage of the long-term build-up and sustaining of skills and competencies within the relationship architecture of the enterprise. The development of skills and competencies by organizations will at the same time strengthen the economic factor advantages that the wider society enjoys, and improve the opportunities and skills of its people.

REVIEW QUESTIONS

1. Why are ethics and values relevant to strategy formulation and strategic decision-making? In what ways may they influence the process of strategic management?
2. In what ways does environmentalism influence strategy formulation and strategic decision-making?
3. What are "green issues"?
4. What is "sustainability"?
5. What is social responsibility and why is it relevant to the strategic management process?

TECHNIQUES OF CASE STUDY AND ANALYSIS

Where the appropriate information is available in the case study:

1. Identify enterprise values or value set.
2. Identify actions that are (or are not):-
    *   ethical
    *   environmentally sustainable
    *   socially responsible
3. Comment on the degree to which the enterprise applies ethical principles to the processes of strategy formulation and decision-making.

PROJECT ASSIGNMENTS

1. Using available information, identify a good "corporate citizen".
2. Using available information from a variety of sectors, identify some actual examples of:-
   - ethical strategies
   - environmentalist strategies
   - socially responsible strategies
3. Describe the ethos and value set of an organization that is of interest to you.
4. Using available information, identify some actual examples of:
   - ethical enterprise behaviour
   - good environmentalist practice
   - socially responsible enterprise behaviour

References

Albert, M. (1993) *Capitalism Against Capitalism*, Whurr Publishers, London.

Azzone, G. and U. Bertele (1994) 'Exploiting green strategies for competitive advantage', *Long Range Planning*, December.

Azzone, G. and U. Bertele (1997) 'At last we're creating environmental strategies that work', *Long Range Planning*, August.

Bartol, K.M. and D.C. Martin (1994) *Management*, McGraw-Hill, New York.

Bloom, H., Calori, R. and P. de Woot (1994) *Euromanagement*, Kogan Page, London.

Chen, M. (1995) *Asian Management Systems*, Routledge, London.

Elkington, J. and J. Hailes (1988) *The Green Consumer Guide*, Gollancz, London.

Financial Times (1996) 'Planet Profit' Supplement, 25 September.

Frederick, W. C., Post. J.E. and K. Davis (1992) *Business and Society*, McGraw-Hill, Singapore.

Hamel, G. and C.K. Prahalad (1994) *Competing for the Future*, Harvard Business School Press, Boston, Mass.

Hampden-Turner, C. and F. Trompenaars (1994) *The Seven Cultures of Capitalism*, Piatkus, London.

Lessem, R. and F. Neubauer (1994) *European Management Systems*, McGraw-Hill, London.

Maxwell, J.W. (1996) 'What to do when win-win won't work', *Business Horizons*, September-October.

Morden, A.R. (2004) *Principles of Management (2nd Edition)*, Ashgate, Aldershot.

Prahalad, C.K. and G. Hamel (1990) 'The core competence of the corporation', *Harvard Business Review*, May-June.

Redding, G. (1997) 'Three styles of Asian capitalism', *Financial Times*, 13 January.

Royal Society of Arts (RSA) Inquiry Report (1995) *Tomorrow's Company: the role of business in a changing world*, Gower, Aldershot.

Shapiro, R. (1997) 'Growth through global sustainability', *Harvard Business Review*, January-February.

Chapter 13

Financial Strategy and Management

'For which of you, intending to build a tower, does not first sit down and estimate the cost, to see whether he has enough to complete it? Otherwise, when he has laid a foundation and is not able to finish, all who see it will begin to ridicule him, saying "this fellow began to build and was not able to finish"'.

St Luke's Gospel - Chapter 14, Verses 28-30

You cannot study strategy without studying finance. Finance is a basic resource and constraint upon which the process of strategic management depends. Those who have made funds available to others for business purposes will eventually require a return on their investment. Life almost always comes back to "the bottom line", whether we like it or not.

This chapter deals with a variety of financial management issues, including expected performance, capital structure, risk management, and the avoidance of corporate failure.

The chapter analyzes the role and expectations of the providers of finance as key stakeholders in the organization. It describes and comments on some of the strategies used by enterprise management to satisfy these stakeholder expectations. It explains the "cost of capital" concept, and discusses the relevance of this concept within the context of strategy formulation and strategic decision-making.

Strategy formulation and strategic decision-making processes are analyzed in Chapter 14. Performance evaluation is described in Chapter 16.

THE PROVIDERS OF FINANCE AS KEY STAKEHOLDERS

Individuals, families, institutions, or the state provide the financing of the enterprise. The capital provided may take the form of equity, overdrafts, credit, loans, or funds made available from the public purse. The providers of this finance are *key stakeholders* in the organization. They expect an appropriate return on their investment, or the proper payment of interest and the repayment of capital, or clear evidence of the effective use of monies provided by the state for the public good.   *Shareholders* as stakeholders may, in particular, expect:

❑   consistency and reliability of dividend flows over time.
❑   growth in the real value of these income flows over time.
❑   growth in the capital value of the shareholding that may arise from increasing company profitability and business value.

The UK Hanson Group clearly stated, for example, that *the maximizing of shareholder value* was one of its primary objectives, and shaped its corporate governance, financial strategy, and financial management. Hanson believed that many other companies failed to maximize shareholder value, and as a result under-performed as far as shareholders are concerned. The company believed that such under-performing companies made good acquisition targets for its own business development because once they were purchased, effective and competent management could be put in place to increase the level of shareholder value yielded by the investment. This issue is dealt with at a number of points in this and other chapters.

Shareholders may include individuals, families, investment trusts, holding companies, banks, insurance companies, pension funds, financial institutions, and the state.

RETURNS TO EQUITY

Returns to equity shareholders are commonly measured in terms of:

❑   earnings per share
❑   price-earnings ratio
❑   dividend yield
❑   dividend payout

These ratios were described in Chapter 3.

Meeting Shareholder Expectations

Shareholders may expect the enterprise to provide a return that is *appropriate* to their investment. Enterprise management has to judge what shareholders perceive to be appropriate by using:

- ❑ past performance trends
- ❑ interfirm comparisons and benchmarks
- ❑ current market expectations
- ❑ alternative investments and opportunity cost

At the same time, shareholders may have expectations about the *quality of earnings* that they should receive. Quality of earnings means the *dependability of dividend income streams.* The more dependable the income, and the lower the risk, the more desirable will be the investment. The resulting share price "premium" may protect the company from the threat of takeover, if it is publicly quoted, but places management under pressure to provide consistent dividends, year in and year out (irrespective of fluctuations in trading conditions or the emergence of recession). Major institutional investors, such as pension funds, seek dependable earnings above all else so that they can satisfy the demands of their own customers and investors.

Shareholders may also be concerned about the *asset-backing* of their investment. Assets provide a buffer for share price in the event of the enterprise running into trouble. Ideally, these assets should be easily realizable and unencumbered by securities on loan finance. In this case, the enterprise can realize some of its finance and reassure its shareholders that there is no risk to their investment, thereby lessening the chance of a fall in share price and company valuation.

Shareholders are concerned with *enterprise cash flow.* A shortfall in cash flow may make it difficult to pay dividends. Dividend and interest payments, loan repayments, payments to creditors (etc) may have to be financed through further borrowing or the issue of additional equity capital, which will exacerbate the difficulty. At the same time, a shortfall in cash flow may bring about a drop in company valuation, since the enterprise may have to sell off productive assets or investments in order to make good the cash shortage.

Strong cash flow, on the other hand, makes the enterprise attractive to investors. Cash is available to fund competence building, innovation, business development, and so on. Dividend and interest payments present few problems. The capacity to *internally finance* the chosen development strategies means that the enterprise can seek additional funds from outside investors at competitive rates, since little risk is likely to be involved. And the quality of the investment discourages shareholders from trading their investment. Share values are high and any potential takeover threat may be prohibitively expensive.

Shareholders may also favour a company that has strong *institutional* backing. Large institutional investors, such as insurance companies, pension funds, investment trusts, or unit trusts are often reluctant to withdraw their support for the enterprise. They may view their investment as long term, provided that they receive an appropriate quality of earnings taken one year with another. The presence of key institutional investors may "keep management on its toes", since a fundamental purpose of financial strategy and financial management will be to keep these large investors happy.

Managing Returns to Equity

Earnings per share (EPS) are maximized when the enterprise achieves the greatest possible *sustainable* return over time on the capital employed in the business. EPS can be improved (i) by increasing the return from existing assets (as for instance described in Chapter 21); (ii) by new investments, new acquisitions, or innovation; or (iii) by reducing capital employed but maintaining earnings.

The reduction of capital or assets employed may imply the strategy of *divesting* activities that are no longer considered to be able to meet the minimum target for earnings quality or return on investment. Company management may feel on grounds of opportunity cost that such activities contain no further useful potential for earnings improvement, so wish to invest the funds they represent in a more profitable line of business. Effective, consistent and long-term performance in terms of EPS may have the effect of boosting share prices and keeping share valuations high. This (i) encourages existing shareholders to hold on to their investment; (ii) makes the enterprise less vulnerable to takeover; and (iii) makes it easier for the enterprise to raise additional equity.

Dividend Policy and Retained Earnings

Dividends (and therefore the EPS they represent) may be reduced if profits are low. They may also be reduced if there is a pressing need *to retain funds in the business* for investment in new business development, acquisition or innovation, etc. These *retained earnings* are a widely used source of working capital and investment finance.

Policy decisions therefore need to be taken on the *relative distribution* of available cash and profit to (i) dividend payment or (ii) retention in the business. Dividend policy, in consequence, has two interrelated objectives:

❑ optimizing or maximizing returns to shareholders in the short and the long term; *and*
❑ maintaining the investment that will generate these returns to shareholders within the time-scales appropriate to the sector.

The need to provide a consistent quality of earnings, but at the same time to fund competence development, innovation, new product or process development, or new business development poses decision-makers with a dilemma. They may choose to make the most appropriate *trade-off* between paying out, or retaining profits. They may instead take a short-term view of the business, abandoning longer-term investments in innovation, research and development, business development (etc), despite the likelihood that their competitors will gain competitive advantage from such activities. Or they may use a *mix* of investment funds, including long term loans and income from cash flows, to attempt to satisfy a wide range of strategic, product-market and business development objectives, whether short or long term.

These issues are also dealt with at various other points in this book, including Chapters 11, 12, 14, 15, 16, 17, 19, 20, 21, 22, 27, and 28.

SERVICING LOAN FINANCE

The servicing of loan finance commitments represents a *fixed cost* to the business. Interest payments on loan finance, and capital repayments themselves, cannot normally be waived. Returns to preference shareholders and debenture holders also represent a fixed cost, as these too cannot be waived. Loans and debentures are secured against assets, which reduces the risk to the lender. Default on payment may allow the lender to take control of the company in order that funds can be recovered. And the higher the perceived risk, the higher will be the interest rate charged. On the other hand, loan capital does not carry any ownership rights *per se*, unlike equity capital. And interest payments may be *tax-deductible*, as in the UK.

The need to service loan finance commitments may present the enterprise with a number of policy dilemmas, and with the need to make *trade-offs* or *compromises* between them. Interest payments and capital repayment absorb profit and cash flow. Where profit or cash flow fluctuate, there may be a "knock-on" effect on the earnings available for reinvestment or the payment of dividends. Once interest payments have been made, the profit balance (or residue) could either (i) be shared in some proportion between returns to equity and reinvestment; or (ii) returns to equity may be stabilized to provide earnings quality, leaving funds for reinvestment potentially subject to wide and unpredictable annual fluctuations.

This dilemma may affect the formulation and choice of dividend policy. It may also pose difficulties where the enterprise is committed to heavy and long-term investments in business or technology development, innovation, or new product or process development (etc). Additional sources of investment funds (which need to be financed by dividends or interest payments) may have to be obtained in order to maintain the continuity of innovation, new business development, and so on.

Strategic priority may, therefore, be given to *maintaining stable profit and cash flows*. This may minimize the risk posed by the potential for wide variations in profit and cash flow, described above, in situations where extensive use is made of loan finance within the capital structure of an organization based upon equity ownership.

At the same time it confirms the apparent advantage of structures of ownership and finance in which considerations of maximizing short-term returns to shareholders are displaced by the longer-term objectives for competitive advantage, knowledge management, innovation, business development and market position that for instance characterize many Swiss, French, South Korean, Chinese, and Japanese businesses.

TAXATION

Interest on loan finance is for example tax-deductible in the UK. Therefore its use may be preferred to that of additional equity finance (on which the payment of dividends is not tax-deductible) within the capital structure *if its cost is calculated net of the tax that would otherwise have been paid if dividends to equity finance had been incurred.*

More generally, and depending upon national tax laws, financial strategy may in part be directed towards minimizing or offsetting the level of company or corporation tax that would otherwise be payable on declared profits. Certain types of investment may be made because they attract *investment allowances* against tax. Or additional expenditures may be made on employee welfare, contributions to pension funds, etc, which are tax-deductible, or increase goodwill and help the enterprise to attract better employees.

In the private and SME sector, the objective of financial strategy is often to *minimize* the level of profit declared, rather than to maximize it. Directors may take advantage of company taxation laws that permit allowances against tax for company cars, perquisites, etc. Or they may deliberately undertake additional investments in marketing, market share enhancement, operational, or new product development activities that are calculated to have the effect of eliminating much of the taxation liability that would otherwise have to be financed. They might even purchase potentially loss-making activities like professional football clubs for reasons of prestige or personal ambition.

THE COST OF CAPITAL ("K")

Sizer (1979) comments of the *cost of capital* (or "K") that 'the minimum acceptable return from any project is the rate of interest which the firm is paying for the capital invested in (it) ... a firm draws capital from various sources and each has a different cost ... the objective should be to develop a financing structure which minimizes the firm's weighted average cost of capital' (p. 305).

The variable "K" therefore represents *the notional cost of the capital invested in the firm.* It may be described in terms of the *weighted average cost of capital* or "WACC". This weighted average cost of capital is made up of a series of capital components, obtained from various sources, for each of which a "component cost" may be calculated. Weston and Brigham (1980) for example identified four main component costs within the WACC to be (i) any or all of preference shares or debentures; (ii) loan finance; (iii) retained earnings; and (iv) external equity. Weston and Brigham then calculated the company's weighted average cost of capital using the general formula:

$$K\% = \sum_{(t1)}^{(n)} w(i)\, k(i)$$

at time one *(t1)*, where *(n)* is the number of components, *w(i)* is the weight of the *i'th* type of capital component; and *k(i) is* the cost of the *i'th* component.

This weighted average cost of capital, together with the individual costs of debt and equity components, may for the purpose of illustration be plotted against the debt-equity ratio within the company's capital structure, as in Figure 13.1. *This shows an optimal point x at which the WACC is minimized.*

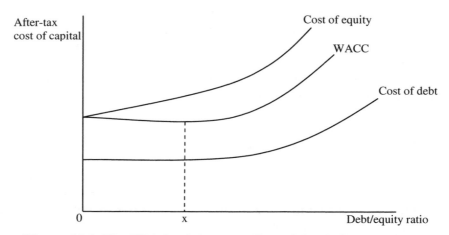

Figure 13.1 The Weighted Average Cost of Capital (WACC)

"K" and the Return from Divisions

Where a company operates on a decentralized, divisionalized, or semi-autonomous basis, the cost of capital "K" may be used as a *tool of strategic integration and control.* This is because neither the cost of capital employed in any one division, nor the return earned on the investment of that capital, can conceptually be permitted by the corporate centre to get "too far out of line" from the cost and return to the organization *as a whole.*

In practical terms this may mean the use of K% as a *threshold figure* in the establishment of divisional performance targets. The financial performance of any one division would be measured against "K" as a minimum yardstick, and divisions would be encouraged to maximize their financial return at or above this figure. Divisions may then be required to *remit* to the corporate centre an annual sum equivalent to K% on their capital employed, perhaps being permitted to retain *residual income* earned in excess of this cost of capital return threshold.

These issues are also dealt with in Chapter 15.

"K" and the Return from Capital Investment

Where the firm is carrying out an appraisal of possible capital investments, the minimum acceptable commercial return may be established as equivalent to the firm's cost of capital. "K" is used as an *appraisal hurdle* or *cut-off rate* against which forecast returns from the alternative investments are compared. Capital investment appraisal will then be based on either of the main methods of *discounted cash flow*.

In the simplest case, the forecasted revenue returns from the investment will be discounted to give their *net present value* or "NPV". The company's cost of capital K% is used as the minimum hurdle or threshold rate against which the expected returns are discounted. Where a positive NPV results, the return from the investment exceeds the cost of capital and the project may be viewed as commercially viable.

Where forecasted revenues can instead be discounted to calculate the *internal rate of return* ("IRR") from the investment alternatives available to the firm, the resultant IRR curve may conceptually be plotted against the curve representing the *marginal cost of capital* ("MCC") that would be required within the firm's capital budget to finance the investment alternatives proposed. This is shown in Figure 13.2.

Figure 13.2 shows that projects *m* to *n* would be undertaken. These projects equal or exceed the threshold cost of capital *a*% of a capital budget *£b*. Projects *n* to *q* would be rejected as their IRR would not cover K% as expressed in the MCC curve, given that *a*% is the hurdle rate below which investments are considered to be commercially unviable.

These issues are also dealt with in Chapter 15.

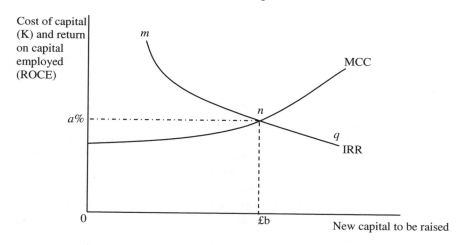

Figure 13.2 IRR and Capital Investment Appraisal

The Relative Level of "K"

Where an investment opportunity exists and the potential returns can be forecast with any degree of relative accuracy, *the lower the cost of obtaining the capital required, the greater the profitability is likely to be.* Competitive advantage *relative to competitors* may be obtained where the enterprise is financially strong, or is in a good position to raise funds, or can obtain funding at the lowest possible cost. The lower the K% cost of adding the value represented by the investment, the more profitable may be the opportunity. This issue is dealt with at various points elsewhere in this chapter and in other chapters of this book. The forecasting process was described in Chapter 9.

MANAGING RISK AND RETURN

Chapter 3 referred to the following *risk-related* appraisal calculations:

❑   current ratio and acid test as indicators of solvency and liquidity.
❑   gearing ratio and long-term debt ratio as indicators of debt management.
❑   dividend cover and interest cover as indicators of ability to meet the requirements of key financial stakeholders.
❑   margin of safety.

Issues of risk management were analyzed in Chapter 8. Chapter 9 dealt with the forecasting process.

Risk and Returns to Equity Capital

Shareholders may (i) expect a return on their equity capital that is above a minimum threshold figure. Otherwise they will invest their money in risk-free fixed interest bonds or deposit accounts (etc). Shareholders may also (ii) have expectations of growth in the capital value of their investment, taken over some "reasonable" period of time. They may therefore be prepared to make some kind of *trade-off* between these two expectations, for instance favouring lower dividends for greater capital growth. Thereafter, the degree to which any particular equity shareholding *meets owner expectations* may determine:

❑   investor attitude to the relative desirability of the investment.
❑   investor willingness to make further investments in the company.
❑   company valuation and share price.
❑   incidence of trading of these shares.

❑ the degree to which acquisition by others is a viable course of action, and hence the potential threat of hostile takeover by a predator.

An earlier section of this chapter has already suggested that shareholders may seek investments that:

❑ contain a minimal risk of achieving a poor rate of return.
❑ maximize the chance of obtaining a satisfactory rate of return.
❑ yield a consistent and dependable quality of earnings.

Such expectations may in consequence shape the choice of business and financial strategies pursued by the enterprise. They may constrain the strategic choice that is perceived to be available where equity capital is a key constituent of the capital structure. And such expectations may play an important part in the formulation of decisions about the nature and direction of the competition strategies described in Chapter 22, and business development strategies discussed in Chapter 27.

The level of risk inherent in the strategic decisions made by the enterprise must therefore, to an appropriate degree, be consistent with the prevailing expectations and experience of equity shareholders. Perceptions of business risk, shareholder expectations, and investor confidence in the enterprise may all be interrelated features of company risk management.

The interrelationship of (i) enterprise risk management strategies and (ii) the maintenance of *investor confidence* is of particular importance in the case of activity proposals that contain higher than usual risk, or whose outcome may prove unpredictable. Higher risk business development, innovation, new product or process development (and so on) must be capable of attracting funds from investors. In such cases, investors may expect that their shareholding:

❑ stands a "reasonable chance" of yielding a high rate of return.
❑ has an "acceptable chance" of achieving a satisfactory rate of return.
❑ contains the minimum acceptable risk of an unsatisfactory rate of return, or the actual loss of value described in Chapter 8.

The formulation of enterprise financial strategy may therefore have to accommodate to the likelihood of investors formulating their own *risk-return trade-offs*. These investor preferences may depend upon:

❑ the level of risk perceived by existing or potential investors (or by their financial advisers).

❑ the effectiveness of corporate communications, and the capacity of the *investor relations activity* (i) to create understanding about the investment proposal and (ii) to generate favourable external attitudes towards it.

❑ the perceived risk posed to the overall valuation of the business that is inherent in the consequences of any particular investment proposal.

Enterprise choice of financial strategy may therefore have to accord with the *performance expectations* and *risk tolerance* of existing and potential investors. The choice of business, product-market, and development strategies described in this book may, of necessity, *have to be informed and constrained by these key investor parameters.* This is particularly true in the case of the traditional UK and US public company, quoted on the stock exchange, dependent on shareholder funding and investor attitude, and potentially vulnerable to the threat of takeover by predators, corporate raiders, or asset strippers.

FINANCIAL OBJECTIVES IN THE FAMILY BUSINESS AND THE SME

Financial strategy within the family business or the SME may be oriented towards the achievement of a particular set of objectives. These objectives include:

❑ survival.
❑ achieving break-even position or maximizing the margin of safety.
❑ making a profit.
❑ optimizing the use of the potential competitive or market share advantage that may arise from the ability to accept low margins on a sustained basis over time.
❑ minimizing tax burden.
❑ managing the potential consequences of (i) unlimited liability; or (ii) the need to give personal financial guarantees; or (iii) the need to secure external sources of funding against valuable personal or family assets such as a house, property or real-estate.
❑ meeting interest payments and repaying loans.
❑ preserving family assets and preserving future income.
❑ continuing the business within the family, or retaining family influence and control over its affairs even when operating as a private or public company.

- ❑ selling off the business to realize or maximize personal wealth.
- ❑ dealing with the consequences of incompetent or poorly motivated members of the family.
- ❑ selling off the business to retire, for instance in the absence of effective management continuity, drive, enthusiasm or interest on the part of younger members of the family.

Goldsmith and Clutterbuck (1985) noted that some of the large family-dominated businesses that they had studied showed particular concerns about *succession.* The successful companies in their study were at pains to point out that family members had to complete difficult and prolonged "apprenticeships" before they could even be considered for management positions. The preservation of asset and business quality and value became a paramount objective, and would-be managers had to prove their worth before getting anywhere near to directing the affairs of the enterprise. That said, it is the large family companies of Mediterranean Europe, South Korea, and the expatriate or Hong Kong Chinese that are well known for the development of long-lasting *dynasties* based on the relationships of kin, marriage, personal allegiance, and partnership under whose strategic direction many successful businesses are run.

FINANCIAL STRATEGY AND FINANCIAL MANAGEMENT IN PRIVATE, CLOSE-HELD, AND CROSS-HELD COMPANIES

Financial strategy and financial management in the private, close-held, or cross-held company may be oriented towards the achievement of such objectives as:

- ❑ preserving personal, proprietorial, family, or stakeholder control and influence over the affairs of the company.
- ❑ preserving the viability and value of personal, proprietorial, family, or stakeholder assets; and ensuring the continuity of future income flows therefrom.
- ❑ eliminating the risk of unwanted or hostile takeover by a predator.
- ❑ maintaining the ownership and control of key strategic assets (Chapter 4) such as property and real estate; brand names; proprietary knowledge or patents (etc); secret processes, formulae or recipes; or personalized features of service provision; and so on.

❑ optimizing the use of the potential competitive or market share advantages that may arise from the ability to accept low (or zero, or negative) profit margins over a sustained period of time.

❑ optimizing the relationship between short-term and long-term rates of return.

❑ the pursuit of strategic objectives such as those associated with (i) optimizing the long-term capability and competence of the enterprise, and optimizing its competitive advantage; (ii) long-term research and development, innovation, new product or new brand development, or new process development; (iii) market positioning; (iv) competitive objectives such as those associated with the pursuit of aggressive competition strategies or market share enhancement; (v) business development; (vi) the pursuit of an aggressive programme of acquiring other companies; or (vii) internationalization or globalization as are described at various points in this book.

❑ fulfilling non-business objectives for instance associated with (i) charitable or socially responsible aims; (ii) the provision of localized medical or welfare facilities; (iii) the development of political affiliations (as in Japan); or (iv) the pursuit of political influence and power (as for example happens in the USA).

❑ optimizing the market value of the enterprise in order eventually to sell it to the highest bidder; and thereby to realize or to maximize the personal, family, or corporate wealth of the owners, proprietors, or stakeholders.

Examples of private, close-held, or cross-held companies include:

❑ the German *mittelstand*.

❑ many such companies in Hong Kong, Switzerland, Lichtenstein, Spain, and Scandinavia (such as those of the Swedish Wallenberg Trust).

❑ the Japanese *keiretsu* groupings.

❑ the South Korean *chaebol* groupings.

❑ the Mexican *grupos* companies.

IMPLEMENTATION ISSUES AND FINANCIAL MANAGEMENT

MANAGING COSTS AND REVENUES

Enterprise financial performance may be indicated by trends in such accounting ratios as ROCE, RONA, or ROSC described in Chapter 3. Such indicators may be used to demonstrate the effectiveness over time of enterprise planning, strategic decision-making, and strategic management. Within the calculation of each of these ratios there are *three key variables*. These key variables are:

❑ *net revenue* and *cost*, because profit = (net revenue - total cost); and
❑ *capital employed* to generate revenue and to incur cost.

The processes of strategic and business planning, financial management, marketing and operations management, (etc), must therefore be concerned with the consequences of making decisions and implementing strategies that will determine enterprise performance under these three basic headings. This is because improved business performance, as indicated by improved profitability, can ultimately only come from the processes of:

❑ increasing revenue.
❑ decreasing costs.
❑ improving the use of capital employed (or decreasing the amount of capital employed whilst increasing its productivity).
❑ *or* a combination of each.

The impact of revenue, cost, and capital employed on business planning and performance is described below.

Revenues

Financial performance (and the results of the strategic management and business planning it represents) depends upon the *net revenues* achieved by the enterprise from its activities. Given any level of customer or segment demand, revenues may for instance depend on:

❑ market, competitive, and environmental conditions over which the enterprise has a greater or lesser degree of control (Part One of this book).
❑ company sources of competitive advantage, and its relative position in the sector or market (Part One).
❑ company competences of foresight and forecasting, over which the enterprise should have a considerable degree of control (Part Two).
❑ competition and product-market strategies, as described in Part Four of this book.

Pricing

Financial performance also depends upon the *pricing competence* of the enterprise. Revenues and pricing are directly related. Morden (1993) suggested that, in addition to knowledge of the level of market demand, the nature of market competition, and the prevailing macroeconomic trends, enterprise capacity for effective pricing depends upon a clear understanding of the impact on available *pricing choices* of:

❑   customer types and market segments.
❑   consumer behaviour and perceptions of price.
❑   the influence of channels of distribution.
❑   the need to cover costs of research and development, innovation and new product or process development, etc.

Pricing policy needs to take into account the implications for establishing *profit margins* of using (i) a percentage mark-up added to costs, or a target percentage rate of return criteria.

Enterprise pricing is also dependent on policy decisions about whether *absorption costing*, or *contribution-based* ("marginal") costing is to be used. In conditions of intense market competition, the use of contribution costing may be seen as the most flexible available pricing technique. This is because it allows the enterprise to set prices (i) that at least cover direct (variable) costs; or (ii) that earn some contribution while not necessarily covering all fixed (overhead) costs incurred; or (iii) that achieve break-even; as well as (iv) to price for profit (where price covers variable cost + fixed cost + required profit margin).

Capital Employed

The assets used to generate revenue, and that give rise to costs may variously be described as *capital employed*, *net assets*, *shareholder capital*, or *total investment* according to the ratio (Chapter 3) being used as a performance indicator. This capital employed is represented by the operational capacity, capability, knowledge, and competence described at various points in this book. It has a direct influence on the generation of revenue, cost, and profit. For instance:

Revenue generation - may be dependent upon:-
•   operational capacity, quality, and volume.

- the capability of the assets to generate competitive advantage, customer service, reputation, or value.
- the situational flexibility or adaptability of the asset profile over time.
- staff knowledge and competence in maximizing the effective use of operational capacity to generate value and revenue over time.

Cost and profit generation - may be dependent upon the level of operational efficiency and productivity. The more efficient is the operational capacity, (i) the higher may be the profit margins obtained relative to competitors; or (ii) the lower is the investment required, since the enterprise is achieving more value per unit of capital expenditure than its competitors.

Cost and profit generation may also be dependent upon the achievement of asset, operational, or staffing *synergies*. Synergy is an indicator of joint or combined effect, and is described elsewhere in this book.

Costs

Business results as indicated by profit performance are likely to depend heavily on *enterprise capacity to manage and control costs*. This for example may imply:

- ❑ optimizing operational and employee efficiency and productivity.
- ❑ minimizing waste.
- ❑ understanding the applicable technologies, and their impact on cost behaviour.
- ❑ making appropriate investments in project and process research and development, innovation, Six Sigma, or reengineering.
- ❑ making appropriate investments in people, knowledge, experience, competence, and skills development, for instance as described in Chapters 19 and 20.
- ❑ implementing appropriate strategies of resource "stretch and leverage" described in Chapter 21.
- ❑ achieving economies of scale, critical mass, or movements down the experience curve described in Chapter 23.
- ❑ Making use of "lowest cost" locations as described in Chapter 28.

MANAGING CAPITAL STRUCTURE

A variety of issues associated with the management of capital structure have already been analyzed in this chapter.

Capital structure was defined in Chapter 3 as comprising the various sources of finance used in the business. Funds may come from investors, lenders, and creditors. Capital structure and ownership are therefore closely linked. Capital structure and business survival are also closely related. Business survival and the potential for corporate failure are examined in the next section below.

Chapter 3 described the gearing ratio and long-term debt ratio as indicators of the health of company capital structure. Long-term debt may be used to "gear up" the business where it is judged that the return from the investment of these funds will be greater than its cost. Holders of equity then "own" the increased value so generated, and may receive the benefit in the form of increased dividend. This benefit may be enhanced where interest payments are tax-deductible, as in the UK.

An earlier section of this chapter however described the risk inherent in using loan capital in this way. This risk comes from:

❑ the requirement to pay interest and to repay the capital. These requirements take precedence over the allocation of funds to make dividend payments. Interest payments have to be made, (i) whether or not rates of interest are subject to unforeseen increases, or (ii) irrespective of conditions of recession when enterprise profitability may be falling. Dividend payments may have to be lowered in order to meet more difficult prevailing circumstances, or be abandoned altogether until trading conditions improve.

❑ the temptation to increase borrowing in order to finance continued trading (for instance when the possibilities of raising further equity capital or external credit have become exhausted), or to finance the payment of dividends in the hope of maintaining share values. This may have the effect of mortgaging the future of the company. The enterprise may become over-reliant on sources of loan finance. It may then become over-committed to a level of interest and capital repayments it cannot sustain. It could then become a candidate for failure, as described in the following section.

BUSINESS SURVIVAL AND CORPORATE FAILURE

It was noted in Chapter 3 that enterprise management needs to keep its financial situation under continuous review. This is essential in order (i) to ensure long-term corporate survival, and (ii) to identify and remedy potential causes of corporate failure.

Classic symptoms of corporate failure

Letza (1992) suggests that there are *three classic symptoms* of corporate failure. These are:

❑ low profitability
❑ high gearing
❑ low liquidity

Each of these three symptoms may be indicated by trends in the company's accounts. The relevant ratios are described in Chapter 3. The symptoms are interrelated, and are shown in Figure 18.3. The classic path to corporate failure starts with the company experiencing *low profitability*. This may be indicated by trends in the ratios for:

❑ profit margin
❑ return on capital employed
❑ return on net assets

A downward trend in profitability will raise the issue of whether, and for how long the enterprise can tolerate a return on capital that is *below* its cost of capital "K". If profitability problems become entrenched, the failing company may seek additional funds and working capital *by increasing its borrowings*, whether in the form of short term or long term debt. This increases the company's gearing, since the higher the proportion of borrowed funds, the higher the gearing within the capital structure. The increased debt burden this represents may then exacerbate the situation, particularly if the causes of the decreased profitability have not (or worse, cannot) be resolved.

The worsening profit situation must now be used to finance an increased burden of interest and capital repayments. In the case of a publicly quoted company this means that fewer and fewer funds will be available to finance dividend payments. It may become impossible to obtain external credit or to raise further equity funds. Confidence in the company as an investment may wither away, leaving the share price to collapse. If the company is basically sound, for instance, but ineptly managed, the best that can be hoped for is a takeover bid for what may be now a significantly *undervalued investment*.

Letza comments that 'a company may at this point not be beyond redemption but unfortunately, more often than not, rescue attempts are not mounted'. This may be because the company's management does not recognize the seriousness of the situation; or is by now too heavily committed or too frightened to admit the truth to its stakeholders; or is instead simply "living on borrowed time" before it must face the inevitable. Letza suggests that 'when the next round of refinancing' (or attempted refinancing) 'occurs and profits fail to cover interest payments' (or capital repayments) 'a *cash flow crisis* occurs. Effectively *the liquidity position* is desperate (and) no more money' can be borrowed. Creditors then withdraw their support and seek to obtain the payment of outstanding debts, thereby hastening the final outcome.

Company solvency and liquidity, as indicated by the current ratio and acid test, now indicate the desperate nature of the situation faced by the enterprise. The patience and goodwill of lenders and creditors becomes exhausted. Stakeholders will be concerned to limit their own losses, and they will petition for the company's *administration, receivership* or *liquidation*. This step may be forced upon the company, or it may seek the end gracefully by voluntary means.

Thus, the financial health check described in Chapter 3 may find its most important application in attempting to predict and avoid the potential for corporate failure. Rescue attempts may fail because they did not recognize the symptoms of potential failure early enough to do anything about the causes.

Worse, shareholders, stakeholders, or external analysts may be the first to recognize the impending potential for failure. The apparent absence of recognition by management of the existence of this potential for failure, or an apparent unwillingness to remedy the causes may itself spark off a loss of confidence amongst stakeholders that may make the eventual failure all the more likely.

Argenti's Corporate Failure Model

Argenti (1983) suggests that corporate failure may instead result from any (or a combination) of:

❑   high gearing

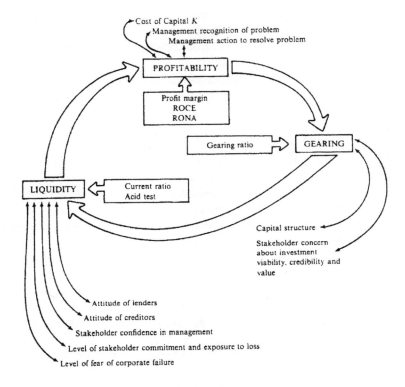

Figure 13.3 The Corporate Failure Cycle

❑ overtrading
❑ investment in large projects

The risks of excessive borrowing and *high gearing* have been described in
the previous section, above. *Overtrading* describes a situation in which the
enterprise attempts to finance a given or increasing level of operational
activity on the basis of inadequate working capital. Where the working
capital base is inadequate, the enterprise runs the risk of becoming
over-reliant on short-term financing from banks and trade creditors. An
increasing reliance upon such funds may eventually lead to a situation in
which there is a significant excess of current liabilities over current assets,
and the threat of the withdrawal of bank and creditor support. *Large
projects* pose a threat to the financial viability of the enterprise where the
investment they represent:

❑   has the effect of decreasing company profitability below an acceptable level, or over an unacceptable time scale.
❑   is financed by excessive borrowing, thereby increasing gearing beyond what is regarded as a safe level.
❑   is the cause of overtrading, especially in the SME.

REVIEW QUESTIONS

1. Why are financial strategies a key component of enterprise strategic choice?
2. Describe and comment on the expectations of the providers of finance as key stakeholders in the enterprise.
3. How may the enterprise satisfy the expectations of financial stakeholders?
4. What is dividend policy and how may it be managed?
5. What is the cost of capital? How may it be formulated?
6. What is the role of the cost of capital concept in strategic choice and decision-making?
7. How may the enterprise manage risk and the return to capital employed?
8. Describe some of the financial objectives of the family business and the SME.
9. What is financial management? Why is it an important feature of the strategic management of the enterprise?
10. How may the enterprise attempt to secure its financial survival?

TECHNIQUES OF CASE STUDY AND ANALYSIS

Where the appropriate information is available in the case study:

1. Identify the role and influence of the providers of finance as key stakeholders.
2. More specifically, how influential are shareholders (and the directors representing their interests) in strategic decision-making and choice?
3. Identify and analyze the financial strategy or strategies (if any) apparent from the case study. Why do you think that the case company is pursuing this strategy?
4. Identify the relationship (if any is apparent) between financial strategy and enterprise strategic choice.

PROJECT ASSIGNMENTS

1. Using published data, analyze the financial and dividend performance of a publicly quoted company. Comment on its apparent choice of financial strategy.
2. Using published data, compare and contrast the financial performance of two or more publicly quoted companies in different countries. Comment as appropriate on the apparent choice of financial strategy within the wider context of enterprise strategic choice.
3. Write a report appraising the financial performance of a client SME or family company. Make appropriate suggestions for future financial strategy within the wider context of enterprise strategic choice. Present your findings.
4. Using trends in ratios calculated from published accounts, prepare an analysis of the financial management of a company of interest to you. Comment on the implications of your findings for the wider strategic management of that company. Present your findings in the form of a report to management.

References

Argenti, J. (1974) *Systematic Corporate Planning*, Nelson, London.
Argenti, J. (1983) "Discerning the cracks of company failure", *The Director*, October.
Goldsmith, D. and W. Clutterbuck (1985) *The Winning Streak*, Penguin, London.
Horngren, C.T. and F. Foster (1991) *Cost Accounting - a Managerial Emphasis*, Prentice-Hall International, London.
Letza, S.R. (1992) "A review of the corporate failure cycle", *ACCA Newsletter*, March.
Morden, A.R. (1993) *Elements of Marketing (3rd Edition)*, DP Publications, London.
Sizer, J. (1979) *An Insight into Management Accounting*, Penguin. London.
Weston, J.F. and E.F. Brigham (1980) *Managerial Finance*, Holt, Rinehart & Winston, London.

Chapter 14

Strategy Formulation, Governance, and Strategic Decision-Making

"If a window of opportunity appears, don't pull down the shade."
Tom Peters.

Chapter 7 analyzed the strategic management of time. Chapter 8 looked at risk assessment. Chapter 9 analyzed business planning and forecasting as a pre-requisite to the strategy process. Chapter 11 defined the concepts of mission, objective, and strategy; and analyzed their purpose. Chapter 12 looked at the impact of ethical issues and values on the establishment of enterprise mission, objectives, and strategy. Chapter 13 dealt with issues of financial strategy and management.

This chapter looks at the issue of who formulates objectives and strategy, and who makes decisions. It analyzes how strategies are formulated, and looks at the generation of strategic alternatives. It looks at process issues associated with strategy formulation. It describes a variety of decision-making roles. It deals with issues of strategic fit or congruence. It comments on target or expected level of achievement. And it summarizes the process of allocating resources that follows the making of enterprise decisions.

STRATEGY FORMULATION, GOVERNANCE, AND DECISION-MAKING

The process of strategic management does not "just happen". Someone has to decide what is best for the enterprise. There may be agreement about what is the best way to proceed; or there may be disagreement. Someone has to identify the alternative strategies and courses of action that are available to the organization to help it achieve its objectives. Someone has to decide whether the enterprise is capable of doing what is being proposed. There may be a consensus about all of these things, or everything may have to be subject to negotiation. There may be conflicts amongst decision-makers, and there may even be "battles in the boardroom". But in the end, somebody or some group of people has to exercise leadership, to make the decisions, and to take responsibility for them.

WHO FORMULATES STRATEGY?

There will be a relationship between the *type of enterprise* and the *people who formulate the strategic component of the strategy hierarchy* described in Chapter 11. The process of strategy formulation depends, in part, on the type of organization in which it is taking place, thus:

The small to medium sized enterprise (SME) - typically owned and controlled by an entrepreneur as proprietor. Strategy formulation and decision-making are in the hands of the owner, and derive from his or her objectives for the business.

The partnership - in which strategy formulation and decision-making are jointly the responsibility of the partners. Strategy formulation will therefore depend on the interpersonal processes used by the partners to establish agreement among themselves. The *prior* joint agreement on the strategies to be pursued by the enterprise may be an essential pre-requisite to management harmony in a UK partnership, given the legal condition that the actions of any one partner are binding on the others.

Partnership as a legal form of enterprise is mandatory in the UK for professional organizations such as legal, accountancy, medical, and some types of consulting organizations.

The private company - in which control is vested in the hands of a relatively small (or restricted) number of shareholders, trustees, or their representatives. Private companies often develop out of successful sole traderships or partnerships; and are a common form for family businesses to adopt. Strategy formulation and decision-making are likely to be controlled by dominant shareholders or family representatives. Ownership, strategy formulation, and operational control are likely to be closely linked.

Private or family companies are a common feature of the business environments in Europe and South East Asia. The Chinese family business (CFB) is a predominant enterprise form world-wide amongst the overseas Chinese.

The public company or shareholder corporation - in which there is commonly the separation of ownership from the processes of strategy formulation and management. A chief executive officer (CEO) or president, and a board of directors (perhaps comprising "executive" and "non-executive" directors) or management board nominally elected by the shareholders, direct and control the affairs of the company. The board may contain employee representatives and people from outside bodies, depending on local company law. One of its main responsibilities is the establishment of the corporate mission, objectives, and strategy described in Chapter 11.

A key issue for a public company is how strategy is to be established, and who is to be involved in the process. In many public companies, for instance, professional managers who do not necessarily hold shares are often involved in the process of strategy formulation. At the same time, there has in recent years been increasing shareholder pressure on Anglo-Saxon companies, through the "corporate governance" movement, to allow independent or non-executive directors (who directly represent the interests of shareholders as key stakeholders and primary beneficiaries) a greater influence on the establishment of corporate objectives and strategies. The corporate governance movement is primarily concerned to increase the *shareholder value* represented by the investment in the enterprise; and typically focuses on short-term profitability and growth in share value. Corporate governance is described in a later section of this chapter.

Co-operatives and commonwealth organizations - as quasi-democratic bodies, members of the co-operative or commonwealth (or their representatives) are to some degree entitled to have a say in the direction of its affairs. For instance, Lessem and Neubauer (1994) describe the workings of the general assembly and general councils of the Mondragon co-operatives in Spain, and the rights of worker-members to be involved in management processes and strategy formulation there. Members of the UK John Lewis Partnership are called "partners" and are represented through branch and central councils in the management of that company's affairs.

In the UK, however, there appears to have been an increasing trend towards the employment of professional managers in co-operatives and commonwealths, and the establishment of professionalized management boards responsible for strategic decision-making within the organization.

Building societies and mutual companies - building societies and mutual companies are legally owned by their members or trustees, and the process of strategy formulation and decision-making is normally the responsibility of an elected management board. This board must seek a mandate from the membership before major strategic initiatives can be undertaken. Nevertheless, as with co-operatives and commonwealths in the UK, the processes of strategic management are becoming increasingly professionalized.

State-controlled, public sector, and not-for-profit institutions - strategy formulation and decision-making in such organizations may involve any (or all) of:-

- elected representatives.
- appointed officers.
- appointed management boards.
- central, federal, provincial, or local government representatives.
- representatives of regulatory authorities (such as the UK's OFTEL, OFWAT, or the Regulator of Railways).
- employee representatives.
- representatives of stakeholders such as customers, clients, or sub-contractors (etc).
- professional managers or administrators.

Strategy formulation and decision-making in such institutions may be highly *politicized*. Strategic management outcomes will be a function of the *process issues* described in a later section of this chapter.

THE INFLUENCE OF FOUNDER AND FAMILY

Goldsmith and Clutterbuck (1985) argue that *founder* or *family* may have considerable influence on objective setting, strategy formulation, and strategic decision-making. The founder of the enterprise shapes the initial perspective and vision of the organization, and sets the tone for much of what is to follow.

Goldsmith and Clutterbuck argue that their sample companies seemed to show that the founder and his or her family successors *may*:

❑ *provide continuity* - family members grow up with the business and understand it intimately. Those that go into it and rise to positions of authority have charge of the family's most important asset. They are likely to wish to maintain the value and standing of that business for the benefit of future generations. The business is the family's most important inheritance.

❑ *provide a long-term perspective* - which it may be difficult for the professional manager from outside to give. One of Goldsmith and Clutterbuck's respondents notes that 'the founder takes a longer view than the professional manager' (p. 133). This longer term view is, of course, helped where private company status or dominant family shareholdings mean that strategy formulation is not subject to the short-term rigours of annual stock market expectations. This year's dividend may be a less pressing issue, and longer-term attitudes to investment, innovation, and staff development may characterize the strategy hierarchy.

Long-term perspective and continuity has been a hallmark of some of the large South Korean conglomerates (the *chaebol*) which remain family controlled.

❑ *have room for wider values than might otherwise be possible* - for instance, when it comes to providing extra employee benefits or staff development opportunities. These, in turn, make the company an attractive employer and may reinforce team spirit and staff loyalty.

❑ *may be able to establish a public identity that reinforces product, service, and brand image* - private or family companies may be able to avoid appearing "faceless" or "uncaring". Goldsmith and Clutterbuck quote the UK example of H P Bulmer; other examples might be Richard Branson's Virgin Group or Paterson and Zochonis (Cussons).

However, family businesses may be at a significant disadvantage from any or all of:

❑ *competence issues* - Goldsmith and Clutterbuck comment on 'the potential for disaster that comes from allowing incompetent family members to assume positions of responsibility' (p. 135). There may be a need for (and the willpower to carry out) the "sidelining" of incompetent family members before they can do any lasting damage to the enterprise. Otherwise the business may experience what is known in the world of the Chinese family business as the "three generation" syndrome. The family business may go "from shirtsleeves back to shirtsleeves" in three generations, the final (third) generation ultimately ruining the success that had taken the two preceding generations to put together!

    Goldsmith and Clutterbuck note of their sample companies that 'most of our successful companies seem to have overcome this by being more severe in their demands of family recruits into management than they are towards outsiders ... (the incompetents) ... are weeded out at an early stage and promotion depends heavily on ability'.

❑ *succession issues* - the private or family enterprise may be confronted by the problem of succession between generations. The search for a successor may reveal a lack of competence or willpower on the part of the available candidates. Or the wealth created by the founder's dynamic efforts may have so corrupted the family's offspring that there is no motivation to carry on the hard work involved in running the business: wealthy entrepreneurs may create "playboy" children whose idleness or fecklessness contrasts starkly with what went before! There may instead simply be no-one to take over the reins of the business.

Succession issues in Italian or South Korean family enterprises are for example widely documented. Able children may be expensively (and internationally) educated and ruthlessly prepared for succession. The prevailing culture will then ensure that they recognize and come to fulfil their duty to others! At the same time, the necessary marriages for the children will be arranged; future heirs will be expected; and family networks proactively reinforced.

❑ *internal rivalries* - a variety of authorities for instance note of the South Korean *chaebol* the incidence of family infighting over control, succession issues, and inheritance. Such internal rivalries may be impossible to deal with, and may have devastating effects on the strategic management process and on management continuity. Family members may not be able to separate their business activities from the interpersonal dynamics (or "stew") of family relationships. Feuds may spill over from one to the other.

❑ *the potential for catastrophic mistakes* - entrepreneurial, family, or private businesses characterized by a concentration of power may operate in an environment where there is no outside or "objective" sanction to the use of that centralized power. The use of unchecked authority (perhaps exacerbated by the existence of a dominant individual or clique, or "groupthink" amongst decision-makers) may lead to the making of catastrophic mistakes that may threaten the continued existence of the enterprise.

❑ *the need to accommodate to professional management* - even where the private or family business recognizes the need to bring in professional management from outside, there may be a lengthy period of accommodation and uncertainty associated with the process of professionalization. There will have to be a necessary delegation and devolution of authority to the newcomers; and a recognition that they must eventually be drawn into the most confidential activities of the enterprise. A changed culture, open communications, and a new trust of "outsiders" will have to be developed before the process of professionalization may succeed.

CORPORATE GOVERNANCE

The concept of "corporate governance" is not new. It may be dated back to the time in the eighteenth and nineteenth centuries when the incorporation of business companies with limited liability became available. A corporation is a legal entity. It is separate and distinct from its owners and managers. Governance issues arise when such a corporation acquires a life of its own, that is, whenever ownership of the entity is separated from its management and control. A change in ownership structure for instance from family or private to public company status (with the opportunity to raise capital through the external sale of stock), separates the owner from the functions of leadership and management. The role of owner may ultimately change from active participant to passive observer.

The Separation of Ownership and Control in Business Enterprises

Thus, one major issue of corporate governance is the separation in business companies of equity holders and owners (as the primary beneficiaries described in Chapter 11) from those who lead and control these business enterprises. The separation of ownership from control, and the wide dispersion of equity ownership amongst shareholders means that the latter may no longer be able to control the leadership and direction of the corporation of which they are the owners. Control shifts to the hands of executives responsible as "agents" or "stewards" for the assets of the shareholders. The rise of professional directors and managers acquiring wide powers in shaping the future strategic direction of the corporation then means that there may be a large body of shareholders who exercise little or no control over the wealth of the enterprise that they own.

The Definition of Corporate Governance

Corporate governance may generally be defined as a process whose purpose is to shape, to direct, and to supervise the actions of an organization. This definition may be applied to any kind of organization; and comprises:

- the setting of strategic intent, purpose, and direction, as described in Chapter 11.
- the selection, development, and compensation of senior management.
- the supervision of leadership and managerial action, for instance in the strategic management process.

❑ the evaluation of the capability, competence, and leadership record of decision-makers and managers. Performance evaluation is dealt with in Chapter 16. Leadership and strategy are analyzed in Chapter 17.

❑ the creation and guarantee of corporate accountability variously to primary beneficiaries such as owners, the providers of finance described in Chapter 13, or other key stakeholders so that the interests of all are properly safeguarded.

The governance role is not concerned directly with the operations of the organization, but instead focuses (i) on the process by which directors or governors (etc) give leadership and direction; (ii) on overseeing and controlling the executive actions of management in achieving enterprise objectives; and (iii) on satisfying the legitimate expectations of shareholders, stakeholders, or other interests within or beyond the boundaries of the corporation for regulation and accountability, as described in Chapters 11 and 12. Corporate governance may in this sense be regarded as a means of safeguarding the interests of, or balancing the relationships between the corporation's constituents, namely the shareholders, banks, other sources of finance, or the representatives of taxpayers; directors, governors, and management; employees; customers, clients, or patients (etc); suppliers and creditors; and other stakeholders including the state and the general public.

The Organization for Economic Co-operation and Development (OECD) defines corporate governance in business organizations as 'the system by which business corporations are directed and controlled. The corporate governance structure specifies the distribution of rights and responsibilities among different participants in the corporation ... and spells out the rules and procedures for making decisions on corporate affairs. By doing this it provides the structure through which the company objectives are set, and the means of attaining those objectives and monitoring performance' (1999).

In addition, the need for the proper co-ordination and integration of the affairs of the organization is seen as a further reason for the presence of an accountable authority and control. Corporate governance may be concerned to ensure that this necessary co-ordination takes place in order to prevent fragmentation and the risk of loss of shareholder or stakeholder value it may represent. This risk was graphically illustrated by the unco-ordinated US public sector response to Hurricane Katrina in New Orleans during August and September 2005, which resulted in severe and long-term losses of a human, social, and financial nature.

Corporate Governance and Stakeholder Interests

The concept of the stakeholder organization or stakeholder corporation is defined to provide for, and to balance the interests of a broad spectrum of stakeholders as beneficiaries. These beneficiaries may include owners, shareholders, taxpayers or their representatives; the relevant sources of finance; appointed officials, decision-makers, or the management of the organization; employees; customers, clients, patients, or voters; suppliers and creditors; the state, and the wider community or its environment (etc). The governance of the public, the educational, and maybe the healthcare sectors in any one country may be characterized by the use of such stakeholder-oriented organizations. The success of such institutions in achieving their objectives may therefore be judged by the degree to which the required service outcomes can be achieved whilst harmonizing or balancing stakeholder interests within the relevant financial and time-related constraints.

Corporate Governance and Shareholder Value

Corporate governance in this case is rooted in the concept of profit maximization for shareholders. Corporate governance in a shareholder corporation may be defined in terms of strategic decision-making that is based on the relationship between the investor, the board of directors of a company, and the management team. Decision-making is founded on the requirement for an accountability towards shareholders that requires the enterprise to focus primarily on maximizing shareholder welfare. This may be described in terms of a model of managerial discipline in which the single most important responsibility of company directors is to ensure that managerial behaviour conforms to the wishes of the company's shareholders. Shareholder value is defined in terms of company earnings, dividend payments, and share price. Its may also mean, controversially, that directors may be discouraged from forestalling a takeover from which shareholders as owners would benefit financially. These issues are dealt with in detail in Chapters 13 and 27.

Governance in a shareholder corporation therefore deals with the ways in which shareholders as the providers of finance assure themselves of getting a return on their investment. Indeed, one view of corporate governance is defined in terms of how investors persuade managers to give them back their money with an added return. This raises the question of how far the performance of a firm should reflect the nature of the capital structure described in Chapter 13. Corporate governance is also understood in this context as a means of dealing with business risk (Chapter 8) for investors, whose interests may not be protected by lenders, suppliers, and customers.

Some International Comparisons of the Corporate Governance of Business Organizations

Significant differences in structures of corporate ownership may be found between different countries. Culture, history, and the legal systems of countries have led to different approaches to corporate governance. In this sense, the concept of corporate governance may be regarded as *equifinal* in nature. This equifinal view states that there is no one "best" system of corporate governance. Each system exists in a different social, political, and legal environment. Each has its own advantages and disadvantages.

Corporate governance systems may differ in the following ways. They may concentrate power in the hands of just a few; or instead distribute influence among several stakeholder groups. They may provide stakeholders with few instruments of influence; or instead provide many such mechanisms. And they may distribute those instruments of influence in a way which is (i) consistent with, or (ii) inconsistent with other factors such as the distribution of power and influence in the organization; prevailing regulation; or perceived needs for the ethical, environmental, or social responsibility described in Chapter 12.

International differences may be illustrated by assigning alternative forms of corporate governance into one or other of two categories. The first category is the "insider system", which is characterized by a high level of ownership concentration, non-liquid capital markets, and a high degree of the close or cross-holding of shares described in Chapter 13. The second is the "outsider system", which is characterized by widely dispersed ownership; liquid stock markets; a low or non-existent level of close or cross-holdings of shares; and an active, competitive, or contestable market for corporate control.

The Anglo-Saxon - this is typically an outsider-controlled and shareholder-oriented system. Historically, Anglo-Saxon countries have tended to adopt a unitary board comprising both executive and non-executive directors. In a unitary board the responsibility for all management and control activities is handled by one single governance body. In the Anglo-Saxon model the interests of shareholders are paramount and the role of corporate governance is to ensure that the defined degree of shareholder value is generated. It is however recognised that shareholder value may only be achieved through the directors having proper regard to the architecture and trust on which company success depends. This architecture includes employees, customers, suppliers, the state, and the community. The Anglo-Saxon model also points to the significance of, and the impact of business decisions on the company's reputation in its relevant environments. Companies in the UK have traditionally resisted mechanisms of co-determination such as supervisory boards or works councils.

The USA - US boards of directors predominantly represent the interests of the owners, and act in the best interest of shareholders to deliver shareholder value. The board of directors of a listed company must consist of a majority of independent directors, and certain committees must consist only of independent directors. Historically US citizens have relied on external regulation and legislation enforced by the state to resolve controversial issues of governance, business ethics, social responsibility, stakeholder interest, and strategic choice. It is unusual to have employee representation on boards of directors.

Japan - the annual general meeting (AGM) and the board of directors may be regarded as ceremonial institutions. Many Japanese companies are not represented on stock exchanges and tend to have few non-executive directors. The system is collegiate, with shareholdings being held by families, or being held by core banks in the *keiretsu* business groupings, or being mutually cross-held by group members or other companies. Chen (1995) notes that 'a Japanese company tends to select shareholders that it wants to acquire its shares. Usually, shares are mutually held among companies and financial institutions that have business relationships ... unless ... two companies which cross-own each other's shares intend to end their relationship, they show little interest in the management of the other company. This practice is a *de facto* ... separation of management from the wishes of the owners ... the management does not have to worry about the interference of the shareholders, and thereby enjoys a high degree of autonomy' (pp. 182-183).

The interests of employees and customers are likely to be rated above those of shareholders for the reason that the system of shareholding means that management does not have to be so concerned with shareholder value issues, or the threat of hostile take over as in the Anglo-Saxon model. Chen notes that 'dividends are paid not as a percent of earnings but as a percent of the par value of shares ... consequently, dividend yields as a percentage of market value ... are relatively low...since dividends are paid as a percent of the par value of shares, a highly profitable company can easily meet its dividend requirements with a small percentage of total earnings. Therefore, the bulk of its earnings can be utilised for reinvestment' (pp. 182-183).

Managerial discipline, decision-making, and control is internalized within the structure of the company. Chen comments that 'as long as the ... shareholders are satisfied with a return on their investment they have very little power in meddling in the company's affairs. The majority of the board of directors ... is made up of inside members, ie the members are selected from the senior executives of the company. As career employees, they become board members as they move up in the executive hierarchy and closely identify themselves with the company ... in cases where the companies are either members of large business groups or (are) heavily indebted to commercial banks, outside directors may be appointed to represent the solidarity of the group or to protect the interests of the bank. Nevertheless, outside directors can neither function as real outsiders ... nor can they constitute a majority' (pp. 182-183).

Germany - the German corporate governance system has traditionally been regarded as a representative example of a stakeholder-oriented and insider-controlled system. As in countries such as France and the Netherlands, companies in Germany are customarily seen as having a social as well as an economic purpose. However, as compared with some other European countries the legal framework (the *grundgesetz* and the *handelsgesetzbuch*) in which German companies operate is highly specific and is strongly enforced.

There is a two-tier system of governance, in which supervisory and control functions are separated. German stock corporations are governed by three separate bodies. These are the shareholders' meeting, the supervisory board, and the management board.

The *shareholders' meeting* controls the actions of the supervisory and management boards; decides the amount of the annual dividend; appoints the independent auditors; carries out certain significant corporate transactions; and elects the members of the supervisory board.

The *supervisory board* (*aufsichtsrat*) appoints (and as necessary removes) the members of the management board and oversees the management of the corporation. The supervisory board is concerned with the interests of the owners and the employees, and is responsible for the long-term well-being of the enterprise. Its objective has not traditionally been to maximize shareholder value, but rather to ensure the stability and growth of the enterprise.

The *management board* (*vorstand*) manages the business of the corporation and represents it in dealings with third parties.

Under German law, simultaneous membership of the supervisory board and the board of management is not permitted so as to separate the supervising and executing components of an enterprise.

The German corporate governance system is based on the premise that it is necessary to involve lenders and employees in the decision-making and strategic management of business organizations. Firstly, banks play an important role in Germany. Borrowing has historically proved more important than equity as a source of external finance. Banks are often represented on the supervisory boards and own large amounts of equity in many listed companies. Secondly, employees are given significant influence in the supervisory board. Employees have rights of co-determination (*mitbestimmung*) in corporate governance as well as the owners or the representatives of banks. Depending on the size of the company, up to 50 percent of the members of the supervisory board may be nominated by employees or their unions.

Typically, the chairperson of the supervisory board, who has a second vote in the case of a tie, will be a representative of the owner or the bank, while his or her deputy will come from the employee side.

In the past, however, investor protection was given lower priority in Germany than for instance in the USA or in Anglo-Saxon countries. This is in part explained by the long-standing dislike of the "speculation" that Germans associate with the buying and selling of company shares as a source of trading profit.

In the past decade there has however been a wave of developments shifting the general structure of German corporate governance towards the Anglo-Saxon model. Germany is adopting elements of US capital market regulation, and there is a trend towards common accounting standards and greater information transparency. There is improved investor protection and stronger monitoring of management performance, for instance in terms of profitability and cost.

However, significant differences between the German and the Anglo-Saxon model remain, for instance in the extent of employee representation on company boards; the role of large or institutional shareholders as compared with banks in corporate governance; and the extent to which stock options and performance-oriented financial incentives (which remain unpopular) are used to motivate managers and employees.

HOW STRATEGIES MAY BE FORMULATED

There are a number of methods by which strategies may be formulated, and strategic decisions made within the enterprise. Any combination of the following may be used:

❑ *appraisal and analysis* - of the results of the processes of the strategic analysis, forecasting, and business planning described in detail in Part One and Part Two of this book; or more generally of emergent gaps, opportunities, and threats that have been identified.

❑ *stakeholder analysis* - by which the requirements of corporate governance described above, and the potential influence of the stakeholders described in Chapters 11 and 13 are incorporated into the process of objective setting and strategy formulation.

❑ *the identification and solution of specific issues and problems* - as identified through processes of scanning, forecasting, appraisal, monitoring, and feedback.

❑ *scenario analysis* - as described in Chapter 9 of this book.

❑ *modelling and synthesis* - for instance using sensitivity or "what if?" analysis of emergent issues or forecast scenarios.

❑ *simplification* - by which unnecessary complications or redundant variables (however these are to be defined) are eliminated from the processes of conceptualization and formulation of the issue at hand. This process of simplification is sometimes described in terms of the application of "Occam's razor". Occam's razor may be used to cut away irrelevant external variations or surface "window dressing" to reveal the heart of the matter that lies within, and about which the decision must really be concerned. The process of simplification may also be used to eliminate the syndrome of paralysis by analysis (or "analysis-paralysis") by which the issue of concern is rendered so complex that decision-makers are unable or unwilling to act. Decision-makers are literally "frozen" into a state of confusion, indecision, and incapacity.

❑ *limited experimentation* - by which the enterprise implements a limited programme of trial and test in order to further develop and understand the type and range of strategies from which it may make an eventual choice.

❑ *consultation* - for instance by taking "expert advice", seeking trade opinion, or employing consultants to identify and specify options and alternatives. The use of a process of consultation assumes that decision-makers are "open" or "sympathetic" to a variety of views rather than just their own.

❑ *participation* - by which any or all of directors, managers, stakeholder representatives, employees, customer representatives, and other value chain constituents are to some degree involved in the process of objective setting and strategy formulation. This would assume a high level of enterprise openness, a low power distance, a low degree of uncertainty avoidance, high levels of trust, open communication networks, and a high level of risk tolerance. Decision-makers would have culturally to be prepared to have their decisions questioned and criticized; and perceived "mistakes" openly discussed and challenged by others.

Participative influences on strategy formulation and decision-making may imply the use of the *high trust cultures* described by Fukuyama (1995), and analyzed in Chapter 18. Or they may imply the use of *consensus based cultures* such as those found in Japanese *keiretsu* companies, or those described by Ouchi (1981) as "Theory Z" in character.

❑ *prescription or command* - by which objective setting and strategy formulation is centralized to the locus of dominant power in the enterprise. Prescriptive or "top down" approaches are typical of entrepreneurial or family type enterprises; or of those enterprises run by a strongly authoritarian leader or "taipan". Prescription or command are features of high power distance and low trust.

❑ *negotiation* - by which strategic choice and strategic management result from negotiations between stakeholders and the relevant sources of power within (and external to) the enterprise.

❑ *compromise* - by which the form of enterprise strategic choice and strategic management is shaped by the perspectives, positioning, parameters, and values upon which most of the participants to the decision-making process can agree. Compromise outcomes are often characteristic of the strategic management of public sector and not-for-profit organizations. The resultant compromise may (or may not) then be relevant to dealing with the conditions faced by the organization.

❑ *vote or quasi-democracy* - by which objective setting or strategic choice are determined by processes which are more or less democratic in form. Such processes may be subject to compromise; or may instead be subject to:-

❑ *lobbying, "persuasion", and politicized processes* - for which the development of the relevant political and lobbying skills may be needed by leaders and decision-makers. This issue was described in Chapters 4 and 11.

GENERATING STRATEGIC ALTERNATIVES

Strategy formulation also depends on the identification of appropriate *strategic alternatives* or choices. E.R. Alexander (1979) suggests for instance that the range and quality of the alternatives or options generated by the strategy process may be a function of two inter-related variables of the search process being used to identify them. These variables are shown in Figure 14.1.

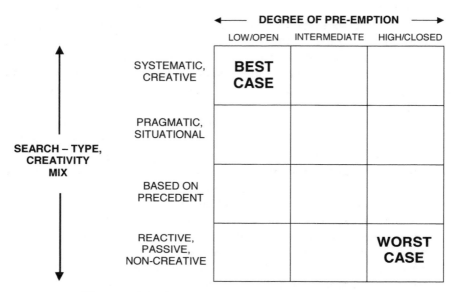

Figure 14.1 Generating Strategic Alternatives

The first variable is the *degree to which the search process is systematic and creative in character*. This is shown on the vertical axis of Figure 14.1 as "search-type, creativity mix". Alexander suggests that search processes have two dimensions. The first dimension is the *level of creativity* inherent in the process. The second dimension is the *type of search*, which may range between:

❑   the systematic and comprehensive (e.g "leave no stone unturned").
❑   the pragmatic, heuristic, or situational (e.g. "do the best you can under the circumstances").
❑   being based on precedent (e.g. "this is how we always do it").
❑   being reactive or passive (e.g. "but what, if anything, can we do about it?").

The second variable is the *degree to which the search process is open, pre-empted, or "closed"*. This is shown on the horizontal axis of Figure 14.1. The variable indicates the extent to which the process of generating strategic alternatives is an open or restricted one. For instance, classic sources of closure (restrictions on the type, range, or novelty of the alternatives generated or permitted) include:

- high power distance, authoritarianism, and the centralization of power ("the boss decides what we do round here; it's up to him").
- low trust of other people or ideas ("well, the … would say that, wouldn't they. But their funny ideas won't work here!").
- negative or hostile value judgements ("it's simply inappropriate; we most certainly can't do that").
- negative or hostile cultural features ("it's not the way we do things here").
- strong or hostile professional, political, or ideological forces ("it's unacceptable! How can you even think of suggesting it?!").
- strong uncertainty avoidance and a high level of risk aversion ("it's too risky for us").
- short-termism ("it won't pay back quickly enough").
- complacency, inertia, and the desire to maintain the status quo ("we've never done things that way; why change now? And besides, it's too much like hard work … how about a nice lunch and a bottle of wine, eh!").
- fear of new ideas or the need for change ("if it ain't broke why fix it?").
- the "not invented here" syndrome ("we didn't invent it, so it can't be any good"!).
- the "we have nothing to learn from them" syndrome ("we know better than them!").

A classic analysis of the closure process is given by Rosabeth Moss Kanter in the 1985 book *The Change Masters* (Routledge).

Alexander suggests that the "best case" is located at the upper left quadrant of the matrix shown in Figure 14.1. Here there is a minimum of pre-emption, coupled with a systematic and creative search process. Alexander suggests that the "worst case" is located at the bottom right quadrant of the matrix. Here there are severe constraints on the type or range of alternatives that it is permissible to identify. At the same time, the search process is reactive or passive and non-creative.

STRATEGY FORMULATION: PROCESS ISSUES

The *process* of strategy formulation and decision-making may be influenced by such variable factors as:

The composition of the decision-making group - the stronger, the more culturally similar, and the more cohesive this group perceives itself to be, the more confident it may be in taking major decisions and risks. Decision-makers who are at the same time owners, key stakeholders, and primary beneficiaries are likely in particular to exercise a dominant influence on decision-making.

Boards of appointed directors or managers may be less sure of their position relative to owners or stakeholders, especially where they perceive themselves to be culturally or functionally varied in outlook, and where they do not enjoy a significant degree of security of tenure in the job. They may feel constrained and risk-averse as decision-makers; and in consequence adopt "conservative", low risk, or short-term policies. This issue is related to:-

The relative organizational power and status of the members of the decision-making group - power and status may be correlated with ownership or a stakeholder role; or with the degree of strength of tenure of an appointed manager or official. Owners, stakeholders, or expert appointees are in a strong position to determine strategy.

The appointed managing director, university vice-chancellor, or health service administrator may instead find that he or she enjoys no such clarity of role, being subject to pressures from institutional investors, non-executive directors, political masters, powerful boards of governors, trade unions, or influential pressure groups. Appointed managers must wait to see whether they can always rely on the unequivocal backing and support of those who were responsible for making the decision to recruit them in the first place (eg "we have every confidence in the manager!").

The role of functional specialists or "strategic planners" - the use of functionally specialised strategic planners to create objectives and strategy, and to determine the allocation of resources within the enterprise, was widespread in large Anglo-Saxon companies until relatively recently. They are still to be found for instance in public sector and healthcare bodies, for example in the UK. However, the concept of strategic or corporate planning as a functional speciality is now out of fashion in Anglo-Saxon companies; and the process of strategic management (at least at the level of the business unit, as described in Chapter 11) is typically delegated to divisional or business unit managers.

Strategic planners as functional specialists are still influential, however, in French and South Korean companies. High prestige and status attaches to the role of strategic planner in French organizations. Chen (1995) notes that 'an outstanding organizational feature of Korean companies is that their vertical and hierarchical control is supported by strong *functional control* from departments like planning, finance and personnel. Korean companies attach great importance to functional specialization, allowing the planning and finance departments to exercise significant functional control under the leadership of the chief executive. Many chaebols have a planning and co-ordination office under the group chairman, which is responsible for allocating major internal resources within the group' (p. 214). The issue of enterprise "planning style" is dealt with in Chapter 15.

The nature of the prevailing political or negotiative process - the processes of establishing objectives and formulating strategy will in part be shaped by the nature of political and negotiative processes within the internal and external architecture of the organization. This point has already been made above. The more politicized the process, the greater may be the need for negotiation, compromise, or mutual adjustment; and the more uncertain or unsatisfactory may be the outcome. At worst, a compromise could result that satisfies none of the parties.

Information flow issues - the process of objective setting and strategy formulation will depend upon the availability, quality, quantity, and distribution of the necessary information. The quality of the process will also depend on the relevance and accuracy of the information that is available. Similarly, the more restricted is the access to the necessary information, the more centralized and "top down" will be the planning style. "Top-down" planning styles are analyzed in Chapter 15.

Time scale, priority, and urgency - the nature of the strategy process and of strategic management may be contingent upon relative priority and the time scale in consideration. This issue was also dealt with in Chapters 7 and 8. The shorter the time scale, or the more urgent the matter, the more that a clear, simple, and decisive outcome is likely to be expected from decision-makers. The longer the time scale, the more it may be assumed that the outcome will be carefully prepared and researched, and consensus about it obtained amongst all the parties involved. This is related to:-

Stakeholder expectations of decision-makers - given any particular contingency that affects the enterprise, decision-makers will have to understand what are the expectations of stakeholders for action, and how strong these expectations may be. For instance, are decision-makers expected to show decisive behaviour in a crisis, being seen to make whatever decisions they deem necessary (however unpopular)? Or should they instead adopt a consultative stance, being seen to listen to as many views as possible before making a "consensus decision"? How opportunistic or entrepreneurial should decision-makers be; and to what extent should they *always* take into account the prevailing level of risk aversion of dominant stakeholders? Indeed, to what extent should decision-makers within the enterprise take a *proactive* stance towards their stakeholders, attempting to shape and influence the values and expectations which provide the context within which decisions are made?

STRATEGIC DECISION-MAKING

The process of strategic decision-making may be analyzed on the basis of Mintzberg's four *decision roles* (1973, 1975, 1989).

The Entrepreneurial Role

In this role the *decision-maker specifies and initiates strategic action or change*. So, for instance, the decision-maker will respond to the process of strategic analysis (and to stakeholder expectations) by positively seeking opportunities which the enterprise can use its sources of value addition or competitive advantage to exploit; and will implement strategies which "best fit" the capability and resources upon which strategy formulation is to be based. The entrepreneurial role is used to shape the perspective, the pattern, the positioning, and the ploys that underpin strategic choice (whether the basis of that choice is perceived to be required, self-imposed, rationalistic, deliberate, logically incremental, emergent, or opportunistic; as described in Chapter 11).

Example: Alan Sugar's decision to enter, redefine, and develop the market for home and small business personal computers (PCs). This emerging market was largely ignored during the 1980s by existing computer manufacturers. It also caught the manufacturers of typewriters unawares. IBM's electro-mechanical "golf ball" typewriters for instance cost in excess of £3000 each at the time in the UK. Office word processors cost £10,000 each. Very soon Amstrad's low-cost computers and word processors (introduced at prices between £500 and £1000 each) had established a position of market leadership. Typewriters became obsolete. And the proprietors of small businesses had reorganized their paperwork around an Amstrad system.

The Disturbance Handler Role

Whereas the entrepreneurial role uses self-initiated or voluntary action to bring about activity or change, the disturbance handler role deals with *involuntary or unpredictable events* (or the *crises* described in Chapter 10) whose origin and timing are beyond the control of the enterprise. These events are judged to require decision-making and action, for instance in terms of:

❏ changing plans, pattern, and positioning.
❏ changing ploys.
❏ using power.
❏ engaging in lobbying or political behaviour.

This decision-making may be perceived to be forced, required, self-imposed, or logically incremental in character, but may also permit opportunistic behaviour. Disturbances may result from:

❏ conflicts internal to the organization, or associated with its stakeholders.
❏ changes in the dynamics of the relationship between the enterprise and other organizations within its architecture or its environment with which it must deal. Disturbances may come from the inter-relationship with customers, competitors, suppliers and partners within the value chain, or from legislative institutions and regulatory bodies (etc).
❏ direct threats of resource loss, or actual reductions in the enterprise asset base.
❏ risks posed by crisis conditions.

Example: the management of the delays and cost overruns associated with the construction and commissioning of the Anglo-French Channel Tunnel; and the re-financing that was necessary to complete the project.

The Resource Allocator Role

As resource allocator, the decision-maker has the authority *to commit the resources of the enterprise* (and in consequence holds the corresponding responsibility for the proper use of those resources, for which he or she may be held to account). Resource allocation is a function of perspective, plan, pattern, and the use of power. It implies:

❑ putting in place the necessary resource base (whatever this is judged to be), on the best available terms and conditions (for instance as described in Chapter 13).
❑ establishing resource allocation priorities, so as to make the best use of those resources for instance in terms of opportunity cost.
❑ authorizing resource disbursement and expenditure.
❑ scheduling time as a critical success factor and constraint.
❑ scheduling work and the programming of tasks and achievement.
❑ monitoring and controlling enterprise activity.
❑ presenting performance-based evidence of the results of resource investment and use to stakeholders (for example as described in Chapter 16).

Example: management decisions about the allocation of hospital budgets in the current resource-constrained context in which the UK National Health Service (NHS) operates. Who is to get what money (and for how long)? Does a healthcare service concentrate its expenditure on treatment? Or should it emphasize prevention (it is much cheaper to stop people becoming ill, or needing to go into hospital). Should you for instance put in place expensive campaigns to discourage smoking and the excessive consumption of alcohol; and what will be the reaction of tobacco and drinks companies (who provide much of any government's revenues) to this threat?

Resource allocation issues are also dealt with in the final section of this chapter.

The Negotiator Role

The enterprise may find itself involved in major, non-routine negotiations with powerful individuals, stakeholders, and other organizations. Such negotiations might for instance result in the signing of major commercial contracts associated with building construction developments or the purchase of a ship; or establish new industry standards through EU or NAFTA institutions. Decision-makers will have to take on *representative and persuasive roles* in carrying out these negotiations. Such roles may include:

❑ acting as negotiator and spokesperson.
❑ providing information and expertize relevant to the negotiation.

❏ adding "weight", credibility, and prestige to the negotiating position of the enterprise.

❏ persuasion, selling, and the use of interpersonal skills; attempting to shape the outcome of the negotiation in the interests of the enterprise.

❏ "selling the deal" to the enterprise and its stakeholders, and creating commitment to it.

The negotiator role may be concerned with any or all of strategy perspective, plan, pattern, and position. It is likely to involve the use of power and political behaviour by the organization.

Example: the negotiation of major capital or defence contracts. High level political and bargaining skills are crucial to the survival of such companies as ABB Asea Brown Boveri Ltd, British Aerospace plc, or the US GE Corporation, who supply large scale capital or defence items to governments, utility companies, and so on.

Example: negotiations between pharmaceutical companies, and the National Health Service as the primary buyer of prescription drugs in the UK, as to what should (and should not) be on the list of drugs from which practitioners may choose when prescribing to patients.

STRATEGIC FIT OR CONGRUENCE

The process of strategy formulation and strategic decision-making is likely to have to take into account the issue of *fit*, *match*, or *congruence*. Firstly, enterprise strategic choice and decision-making should, to the necessary degree, fit, or be congruent with:

❏ the critical success factors that the enterprise has identified for itself (Chapter 4).

❏ the internal corporate and financial condition of the enterprise (Chapters 2, 3 and 13), for instance as described by its strengths, weaknesses, and financial capability.

❏ the findings of gap analysis (Chapter 2).

❏ the enterprise resource base (Chapters 4, 19, 20 and 21).

❏ enterprise capability and capacity (Chapter 4, 19, 20 and 21).

❏ enterprise sources of value generation (Chapter 4).

❏ enterprise sources of comparative or competitive advantage (Chapter 4).

❏ the relevant contingencies and constraints (Chapter 4).

❏   limiting factors (Chapter 4).
❏   time factors (Chapter 7).
❏   risk factors (Chapter 8).
❏   the relevant or necessary issues of financial management (Chapter 13).
❏   the chosen or required performance indicators (Chapter 16).

Secondly, enterprise strategic choice and decision-making should, to the necessary degree, fit or be congruent with:

❏   the findings of competitive analysis (Chapter 5).
❏   the findings of external environmental analysis (Chapter 6).
❏   the apparent opportunities, risks, and threats extant in the external and competitive environments (Chapters 5, 6, 8 and 10).
❏   the findings of the business planning and forecasting process (Chapter 9).

Example: an enterprise that operates in a high-technology market characterized by a turbulent external environment, rapid rates of technological and market change, short product life cycles, and competitive international markets will need to put in place strategies which can adapt the enterprise to rapidly emerging or changing opportunities and threats. The enterprise will have to develop and exploit a capability to put in place the new technologies, new processes, or new products that it will require to survive in such hostile conditions.

TARGET OR EXPECTED LEVELS OF ACHIEVEMENT

The process of strategy formulation may be based on *target* or *expected levels of achievement*. These levels of achievement will be used to provide a benchmark against which the performance measurement and evaluation standards described in Chapter 16 may be set.   A number of levels of achievement may be identified. These are listed below.

Optimization - by which performance levels are for instance established:-
•   on the basis of expectations that are benchmarked against the world's best in the sector (that is, they are "excellent" or "world class").
•   by the use of the systematic "resource optimizing models" of operations management, Six Sigma, or linear programming. These are typically applied to the functions of operations or quality management, manufacturing, supply chain management, logistics, or distribution.

Zero base - which was described in Chapter 3 as looking at each activity as if it were being performed for the first time, that is, from a zero base. Target levels of achievement are based on:-

- current perceptions of priority ("what is important *now?*").
- perceptions of what is *now* desirable relative to current external or competitive benchmarks.
- current opportunity cost ("should we be in this business at all?").
- activities which make the best current use of the "core competencies" of the enterprise (core competencies are described in Chapter 20).

Satisficing - by which "adequate" or "acceptable" levels of performance are deemed satisfactory. Such levels of performance may for instance (i) be benchmarked against competitors in the sector - whatever the competition achieves will be deemed as the necessary standard of performance; or (ii) be based upon the minimum level of provision or service that it is thought that customers can be persuaded to accept.

The concept of satisficing, however, does not fit easily with current demands for the optimization or "excellence" of product or service quality; the achievement of "world class" status described above; or the "stretching" of resource use described in Chapter 21.

Compromise or negotiated outcome - by which performance levels are established on the basis of what can be agreed between the parties to the process of strategy formulation. This has often been the tradition of strategy formulation in public sector bodies. There is no guarantee that compromise or negotiated outcomes will necessarily be the most desirable or the best available; they simply represent the ground upon which at least a minimum level of agreement can be reached.

Muddling through - by which target or expected levels of achievement are established on a *reactive* basis, responding to events as they occur. Muddling through is not a systematic process; and will depend for its effectiveness on luck. Muddling through cannot be used for dealing with long-term performance issues. It is also useless in dealing with strategic management situations that are characterized by an ongoing need systematically to deal at the same time with a large number of inter-related issues or variables (such as the inter-connected issues of UK school leaver qualifications; the access of people with "non-standard" or "access-level" entry qualifications and prior work experience to university places in the UK; university entrance requirements and tuition fees; the appropriateness of vocational and non-vocational degree courses; employer attitudes to graduates and the institutions from which they come; and graduate employment prospects in the UK).

Muddling through is often evident in SMEs where the proprietor is unwilling to delegate and is suffering from work and information overloads.

ALLOCATING RESOURCES

An end product of the strategy hierarchy described in Chapter 11, and of the process of strategy formulation and strategic decision-making being analyzed in this chapter will be the *allocation of finance, people, leadership, willpower, and resources* to those activities by which the enterprise implements its strategies and attempts to achieve its objectives. The processes by which resources are allocated include:

Business planning - by which the annual business plans described in Chapter 9 are drawn up for individual units and functions. These are detailed statements of the objectives to be achieved, the strategies to be employed, the resource requirements for implementation, and the forecasted or proposed outcomes for the planning period ahead. Business plans will show quantifications of forecast sales or market performance, customer or client service activity, revenues, resource requirements, costs, margins, profitability or other value outcomes. They may contain indications as to how the business plan for this year incorporates feedback from last year's performance, or how it improves upon it. The business planning process includes any or all of the following:-
Budgetary plans - described in Chapter 9 as budgetary allocations that relate the responsibilities of departments and individuals to the requirements of strategies and plans. The *budgetary control* process then monitors actual performance within the planning period and compares it with budgeted targets, so that these targets may be achieved or amendments instead be made to the objectives upon which they were based.
Capital budgets - by which capital expenditure is planned and financed. The available financial resources are compared with the demand for capital investment, either or both at the corporate or the business unit level. The capital budgeting process is usually associated with:-
Return targets or thresholds - which represent the cost of capital to the enterprise, and which capital investments must equal or exceed. Chapter 13 noted that return targets or thresholds usually provide the basis for:-
Investment appraisal techniques - whether time-related (payback); or discounted cash flow-based, using DCF or internal rate of return (IRR) computations. Investment appraisal techniques were analyzed in Chapter 13.

The post audit of capital investments - by which actual capital investment performance is monitored and compared with the desired or forecasted outcomes on the basis of which the investment proposal was made. The post audit of capital investments will usually include the use of the investment appraisal techniques described immediately above.

Zero basing - by which resources are applied to an activity as if it were being performed for the first time, that is from a zero base. The resource allocation process may ignore existing resource commitments or methods of operation. This radical approach underlies the *re-engineering* of strategic management resource allocation that has been dominant in Anglo-Saxon organizations during recent years.

The process of allocating resources may be based upon any of the formulation methods analyzed immediately above. In Anglo-Saxon organizations these processes tend at least to some degree to be dominated by:

❑ *competitive bidding* in which the demand for capital and other resources exceeds the available supply, such that managers are motivated by necessity to put forward strong "business cases" in order to have any chance of making a successful bid.

❑ *the formal presentation and discussion* of resource commitment proposals at corporate or board level. This will involve the arguing or making of business cases and the use of persuasive communication methods, *requiring the development of the appropriate communication skills on the part of the presenting managers.*

❑ *negotiation* amongst those who control the allocation of resources and those who seek to invest them. Typically this negotiative behaviour also leads to:-

❑ *political or politicized behaviour* amongst those who control the allocation of resources and those who seek to use or invest them. The use of power and politics within the strategic management context is analyzed at various points in this book, as well as in preceding sections of this chapter.

The development by an individual leader or manager of the requisite *resource allocation process skills* may be of fundamental importance within the broader context of the strategic management processes and competencies being described in this book.

REVIEW QUESTIONS

1. Who is involved in the process of strategy formulation within the enterprise?
2. In what ways may founder or family influence strategy formulation or strategic decision-making?
3. What is corporate governance?
4. How are strategies formulated? By what means may strategic alternatives be most effectively generated?
5. What process issues influence the outcomes of strategy formulation and strategic decision-making?
6. Compare and contrast Mintzberg's four decision roles.
7. Compare and contrast some of the alternative conceptualizations of target or expected levels of enterprise achievement.
8. How may resources be allocated within the organization?

TECHNIQUES OF CASE STUDY AND ANALYSIS

Where the appropriate information is available in the case study:

1. Identify who the decision-makers appear to be in the case company.
2. Identify the key influences on corporate governance, strategy formulation, and strategic decision-making. What are the critical success factors?
3. Identify the target or expected levels of achievement (if any) that are evident from the case study.
4. Identify how strategies appear to be formulated in the case company.
5. Identify how decisions are made in the case company.
6. Identify and analyze the nature of the resource allocation process in the case company or organization, if information is available.

PROJECT ASSIGNMENT

Using available data or key informant interviews, describe the process by which objectives are established, strategies are formulated, and decisions made in an organization of interest to you.

References

Albert, M. (1993) *Capitalism Against Capitalism*, Whurr Publishers, London.

Alexander, E.R. (1979) 'The design of alternatives in organizational contexts', *Administrative Science Quarterly*, Vol 24, September.

Armbrüster, T. (2005) *Management and Organization in Germany*, Ashgate, Aldershot.

Chen, M. (1995) *Asian Management Systems*, Routledge, London.

Daianu, D. and R. Vranceanu (2005) *Ethical Boundaries of Capitalism*, Ashgate, Aldershot.

Fukuyama, F. (1995) *Trust* Hamish Hamilton, London.

Goldsmith, W. and D. Clutterbuck (1985) *The Winning Streak*, Penguin, London.

Lessem, R and F. Neubauer (1994) *European Management Systems*, McGraw-Hill, London.

Mintzberg, H. (1973) *The Nature of Managerial Work*, Harper Collins, New York.

Mintzberg, H. (1975) 'The manager's job: folklore and fact', *Harvard Business Review*, July -August.

Mintzberg, H. (1989) *Mintzberg on Management*, Free Press, New York.

Mintzberg, H. (1994) *The Rise and Fall of Strategic Planning*, Prentice Hall/Financial Times, London

Morden, A.R. (2004) *Principles of Management (2nd Edition)*, Ashgate, Aldershot.

OECD (1999) *Principles of Corporate Governance*, OECD, Paris.

Ouchi, W. (1981) *Theory Z*, Addison-Wesley, Reading, Mass.

Sizer, J. (1979) *An Insight into Management Accounting*, Penguin, London.

Wheeler, D. and M. Sillanpää (1997) *The Stakeholder Corporation*, Pitman, London.

Young, D. and P. Scott (2004) *Having Their Cake*, Kogan Page, London.

Chapter 15

Planning Style and Strategy

Chapter 11 of this book looked at the concepts of enterprise mission, objective and strategy. Chapter 12 looked at the impact of ethical issues and values on the establishment of mission, objective and strategy. Chapter 13 analyzed financial strategy and management. Chapter 14 dealt with issues of strategy formulation, governance, and decision-making.

This chapter deals with the variations in the style (or the approach) by which these components of the strategy process may be put into practice. Planning style, in its own turn, must then be related to issues of organization structure and management style. The chapter gives a brief overview of these "strategy-structure" relationships.

PLANNING STYLE

The approach or planning style by which enterprise management may formulate objectives and strategies can take any of the three following forms:

- ❑ "top down" or "planning down".
- ❑ "bottom up" or "planning up".
- ❑ "negotiated" or "negotiative".

Each is described in turn.

Top Down or Planning Down

Top down or planning down describes a *centralized* approach to strategy formulation in which the corporate centre or head office is predominant. The corporate centre determines mission, strategic intent, objectives and strategies for the organization as a whole, and for all of its parts. It formulates strategy for operating units, irrespective of whether or not they are notionally established as companies or divisions. Unit managers are seen as implementers of pre-specified corporate strategies.

Planning down corresponds to the description by Mintzberg and Waters (1985) and Mintzberg (1987) of a *rationalistic* form of strategy formulation. This was described in Chapter 11 as being a planned, systematic, and centralized approach in which the chief executive officer and his or her colleagues are dominant forces in the process of strategic management. Self-imposed restrictions on the dissemination of sensitive information or confidential planning requirements preclude subordinate staff from participation in the strategy process. Instead, strategic and business plans may be "handed down" (or "thrown over the wall") to subordinates for implementation.

Planning down also corresponds to Mintzberg *et al's* description of a *deliberate* approach to strategy formulation in which there is an attempt to realize strategies exactly as intended because it is perceived by the people at the corporate centre that:

❑   they are capable of formulating precise and unambiguous objectives and strategies; *and*
❑   the staff and resources of the organization can then be made to "fit" the realization of these objectives (that is, their congruence is a function of the management process and therefore of management expertize).

Example one - where a shareholder corporation is strongly oriented towards financial performance and the need to provide consistent returns to shareholders, the corporate centre may impose on its operating units the *required* strategies described in Chapter 11; and implement by applying financial and operations management techniques to its subsidiaries such that they are forced to meet (and then improve on) performance targets specified by the centre. These might, for example take the form of:-

•   minimum levels of profit margin, ROCE, RONA, ROE or ROSC; and other indicators of profitability and asset utilization (for instance as described in Chapter 3).
•   "threshold" corporate cost of capital "K" or weighted average cost of capital (WACC) hurdles which are used as a minimum discount rate in the discounted cash flow (DCF) calculations described in Chapter 13.
•   a minimum internal rate of return (IRR) hurdle.
•   a given (or increasing) residual income target from which a proportion (or an increasing proportion) of unit investment must be met.

Issues of financial strategy and management were dealt with in Chapter 13. Performance evaluation is analyzed in Chapter 16.

Example two - where the corporate centre instead views the enterprise as a *portfolio* of activities, planning down may be used to attempt to "optimize" the sum total of the organization's activities. The portfolio approach to strategic management was described by Buzzell, Gale and Sultan (1975). Enterprise activities or divisions are designated as "business units" or "strategic business units" (SBUs) by the corporate centre. Each is defined as a distinct activity in which resources may be applied or withdrawn, especially where the corporate centre holds and controls the disbursement of all *cash* within the organization. A "balance" between *cash earning* and *cash using* SBUs is sought within the portfolio, such that:-

- sufficient funds are generated across the portfolio as a whole to ensure that an appropriate return is made to shareholders, banks, or stakeholders over time.
- high risk in any one activity or location is offset by low risk activity in another.
- positive cash flows may be allocated to develop any or all of (i) what are described in Chapter 26 as product-market "stars" and "question marks"; or (ii) the continuing processes of innovation, new product development, and business development described in later chapters; or (iii) the "core competencies" described in Chapter 20.

The concern by the corporate centre to optimize the performance of the business as a whole will mean that the process of strategy formulation will be co-ordinated and integrated. The individual preferences of any one subsidiary or division are of secondary importance. Ultimately, the corporate centre may (for instance on grounds of opportunity cost) deliberately sub-optimize or divest the activities of particular business units in order to achieve what it considers to be this optimum performance of the enterprise as a whole.

Bottom Up or Planning Up

Planning up is characteristic of "federal" structures comprising autonomous or semi-autonomous divisions or subsidiary companies in which the corporate centre *does not* conceptualize its strategic role as being directly responsible for determining the mission, objective, or strategies of its operational activities. It may prefer instead to act as a *catalyst, facilitator* and *referee*, keeping things reasonably simple and confining itself to:

❑ establishing *perspective* for the enterprise as a whole.
❑ establishing the broad guidelines of the organization's *strategic intent* described in Chapter 11.
❑ establishing and disseminating core values and culture throughout the organization.
❑ developing competencies, and developing leaders and managers throughout the organization.
❑ establishing systematic strategic planning, strategy formulation, and strategic management processes for the enterprise.
❑ ensuring consistency and co-ordination across the federation *(pattern)* establishing the minimum or requisite performance criteria to be applied throughout the enterprise.
❑ using *power* and undertaking *political behaviour* on behalf of the enterprise in its external environment.

Individual subsidiaries and divisions are responsible for interpreting corporate intent and guidelines, using them to establish and achieve their own objectives and strategies. In this, they are responsible for decisions on the specific *perspective* and *pattern* towards which they are working; and for the *positioning* and *ploy* elements of strategy described in Chapters 11 and 22. They may also be given the authority for the necessary *use of power*, both within and outside of the enterprise, such that they can look after their own interests. Typically, each subsidiary or division establishes its own strategic and business plans, which quantify performance forecasts and resource requirements for the planning period being used. Where the corporate centre acts as a "referee" and banker, these unit plans may also contain bids for additional funds to finance capital and competence development, business development, innovation and new product or process development (etc). The corporate centre may then attempt to question, reconcile, and aggregate the various unit plans by:

❑ negotiating with individual units the actual and forecast financial returns and cash flow, such that the corporate centre is able to satisfy itself that the company will be able to meet shareholder, bank, or stakeholder expectations of the performance of the business as a whole.
❑ dealing with requests for capital investment funding or development monies, for instance allocating resources from the capital budget on the basis of the investment appraisal techniques, return targets and thresholds described in Chapters 11 and 13.
❑ negotiating with, or mediating between the interests of the various managements of the subsidiaries and divisions.

Planning up may be characterized by any or all of:

❑ the use of *logically incremental* approaches to strategy formulation, each strategic step or adjustment being informed by the closeness of the business unit to its market and to the contingencies with which it has developed (and should continue to develop) close experience. In this respect, planning up correlates favourably with the flexibility and adaptability of decentralized structures that are close to their business environment and clientele.

❑ *opportunistic* approaches to strategy formulation and strategic management, predicated (i) on the ability of decentralized structures to respond quickly to emergent opportunities; and (ii) on the freedom to make rules or define exceptions that closely suit the evolving circumstances with which the unit is faced.

Ultimately, planning up treats divisions and subsidiaries as autonomous units largely responsible for their own fate, required only to meet specified targets for operational integrity, adherence to corporate values, financial performance, cash remission or residual income, perhaps taking one year with the next.

Negotiative or Negotiated

The establishment of objectives and the formulation of strategies results in this case from *interactions* between the parties to the negotiation. This approach to strategy formulation was described in Chapters 11 and 14. The outcomes of the negotiation may be determined by any of a number of variables, whether these be the prevailing power relativities, leadership competence and process, access (or otherwise) of the parties to the necessary information, the urgency and importance of the situation, or the negotiating skills being brought into play.

A negotiative style of planning may favour the use of a *logically incremental* approach to strategy formulation. The character of each step in the evolving process will result from each new set of negotiations. At the same time, however, powerful or high status groups with highly developed negotiating competencies may be able to take advantage of this style of planning to achieve outcomes favourable to themselves on an *opportunistic* basis, as circumstances permit. This syndrome is common in the public, state, education or healthcare sectors, where powerful interests are often able to further their own interests at the expense of the weaker, the less skilled, or the disadvantaged.

A negotiative planning style is in particular characteristic of public sector policy bodies associated with local, regional, provincial, federal, national or international government agencies which typically contain multiple interests and multiple stakeholders.

PLANNING STYLE, STRUCTURE, AND STYLE OF MANAGEMENT

The analysis of planning style is dependent on, and correlates with features of *organization structure* and *style of management* as means of implementing strategy. These features are summarized below.

Planning Down

Organization structure - planning down may be associated with the following:

Entrepreneurial structures and family businesses - which tend to be strongly centralized, typically with personalized decision-making power focused on the entrepreneur or family members. This issue was discussed in Chapter 14.

Public service administrative organizations - which are characterized by responsibility to accountable individuals who hold official positions as elected officers, mayors, government ministers, provincial governors, and so on. Their management behaviour is likely to be driven by the need for control of, and accountability for (i) the quality and reliability of operational activity and (ii) the disbursement of public funds that is implicit in achieving objectives.

Planning down in this case is strongly linked to a high degree of centralization. Mintzberg (1983, 1989) comments that the greater the degree of external control of an organization, the more centralized and formalized (*rationalistic* and *deliberate*) will be its management process and behaviour. External (and maybe politicized) authority will:-

- hold the chief executive officer personally responsible for the strategic management process of objective setting, strategy formulation, strategy implementation, and the achievement of results.
- impose requisite core values and standards which must underpin strategy formulation, implementation, and performance evaluation.
- establish a strong control culture and mentality amongst decision-makers and managers within the organization.

Classical hierarchical mechanistic structures - which are characterized by a hierarchy of management roles and offices, embodying the scalar chain. Morden (2004) notes that 'the scalar chain is used to establish a "top-down" unity of command in which instructions flow down and feedback on results achieved flows back up the hierarchy. Communication and control processes are vertical. Decision-making will be centralized, that is carried out at the "top" or "apex" of the organization' (p. 70).

Classical hierarchical mechanistic structures tend to be characterized by a *rationalistic, universalistic,* and *deliberate* approach to strategy formulation in which it is assumed that rational and logical plans, policies, rules, regulations and procedures can be effectively used (i) to implement strategic decisions; (ii) to ensure "fit" between strategy, structure, leadership, capability and resources; and (iii) to deal with exceptions that arise.

It may also be assumed by decision-makers that sufficiently robust and comprehensive rationalistic, deliberate, and universalistic procedures of strategic planning can be put in place by the corporate centre (or by its functionally specialized corporate or strategic planners and advisers) such that exceptional, unpredictable, novel, high risk, or ambiguous events and contingencies (for instance associated with conditions of external change and uncertainty) can in the main be legislated for in advance.

Divisionalized structures - which may be characterized by "controlled" or "co-ordinated" decentralization in which there is strong direction from the corporate centre.

Management style - planning down may be associated with any of:
- Theory X (McGregor, 1960).
- low trust (Fukuyama, 1995).
- high power distance (Hofstede, 1980, 1991).
- high uncertainty avoidance (Hofstede), correlated with centralization and a strong control mentality.
- strong "universalism", which is defined by Hampden-Turner and Trompenaars (1994) as a belief in centralized prescription, codification, formalization, standardization, and regulation. Rules are to be universally applied in order to standardize decision-making; individual discretion is to be denied; and subordinates are seen by their superordinates (bosses) as implementers.
- a strong belief in management by role description, formal hierarchy, and "mechanistic" (regulated, programmed, or prescribed) interaction.

- the use of "role" or "power" cultures (Harrison, 1972, 1995; and Handy, 1985).
- a prescriptive style of leadership (Chapters 14 and 17).

Planning Up

Organization structure - planning up may be associated with the following:

Divisionalized structures - in which there is full divisional or delegated autonomy, empowerment, and responsibility; and where the corporate centre acts as a holding company, banker, mediator or "honest broker" between the various divisions. The corporate centre represents the enterprise externally to shareholders, stakeholders, and the external environment on a federal basis.

Innovative, organic, adhocratic, or network structures - which as fluid and adaptive mechanisms may pursue strategy on an *opportunistic* basis. This will call for a high degree of localized planning autonomy and flexibility.

Management style - planning up may be associated with any of:
- Theory Y (McGregor) or Theory Z (Ouchi, 1981).
- high trust (Fukuyama).
- low power distance (Hofstede).
- low uncertainty avoidance (Hofstede), possibly correlated with high risk tolerance.
- an acceptance of the need for both universalism and particularism. Universalism was defined above. Hampden-Turner and Trompenaars define "particularism" as (i) the acceptance that the enterprise needs to recognize and be capable of dealing flexibly with exceptions to the norm; (ii) to be able to deal with unusual, novel, uncertain or ambiguous exigencies; and (iii) to engage with the need for innovation and change. Decision-makers therefore accept the (universalistic) need for an over-arching structure, architecture and value set; but also accept the (particularistic) need for situational relevance and sensitivity to the need to make adjustments, and to respond flexibly to new ideas and new conditions as contingencies. The relevance of "contingency" to leadership is discussed in Chapter 17.
- a belief in a degree of equality between the operating unit and the corporate centre (Hampden-Turner and Trompenaars).
- the use of task cultures (Harrison, Handy) which are primarily focused on achievement. Attitudes to issues of leadership, direction, authority,

role, expertize, and the locus of decision-making are all shaped by the over-riding need "to get the job done".

- the use of what Tichy and Sherman (1994) define as "planful opportunism". Planful opportunism was a term used by Jack Welch, a former CEO of the US General Electric (GE) company, to describe unit or divisional freedom to pursue its own business opportunities within the wider framework of (i) an overarching set of core corporate values, and (ii) pre-stated corporate performance requirements for market position and financial return that are applied to all business activities.
- a consultative, facilitatory, or enabling style of leadership.

Negotiative

Organization structure - a negotiative planning style may be associated with the following:

Divisionalized structures - in which there is a classic tension between leadership, direction, core values, and control from the corporate centre (centralization); and the demand for divisional autonomy (decentralization) as measured by divisional performance assessment procedures and responsibility criteria.

Matrix structures - in which strategic outcomes may be dependent on negotiative interaction between two equally empowered axes of the matrix making up the structure.

Innovative, organic, adhocratic, or network structures - in which strategy formulation results from a tension between the direction and core values of the corporate centre, and the local need of the unit to respond flexibly and quickly on a *logically incremental* or *opportunistic* basis to changing external, technological, or market conditions.

Management style - a negotiative planning style may be associated with any of:

- Theory Y or Theory Z.
- low power distance.
- low uncertainty avoidance, possibly correlated with high level of risk tolerance and operational flexibility.
- an emphasis on particularism - each case may need arguing on its merits. Rules may be seen "to get in the way". Everything "may be negotiable".
- a belief in equality between the operating unit and the corporate centre (unless either party can obtain an advantage over the other through its

leadership competence, its negotiating skill, its use of power, or its political behaviour!).

- the use of a power or a task culture (Harrison, Handy). For example "get the best people you can employ! Use your power and influence! Attempt to shape the rules of the game in your own favour! Negotiate the best deal you can, from the strongest position you can achieve! Get the job done and do it well! Talk up your success and make sure that you get the credit; then go and use your advantage to negotiate the next piece of business!".
- a transactionally appropriate, or contingent style of leadership.

GOOLD AND CAMPBELL'S PLANNING STYLE ANALYSIS

Goold and Campbell (1987) analyzed the planning styles of a sample of large, diversified UK companies. They found a variety of alternative approaches to strategy formulation and strategic management in these companies. Goold and Campbell focused on two variables, namely:

❑ the degree of involvement of the corporate centre or head office in strategy formulation; *and*
❑ the type of performance controls imposed by the corporate centre.

They then identified five different planning styles. These are illustrated in Figure 15.1, and described below.

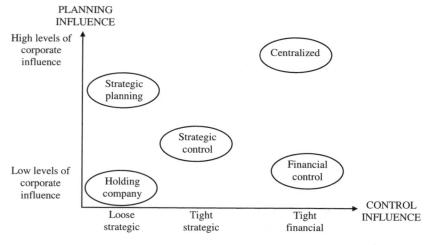

Figure 15.1 Goold and Campbell's Alternative Planning Styles

Holding company style - in which the corporate centre exercises a minimal strategic influence (or none at all). It simply acts as a recipient of profit and cash flow from subsidiaries, from which it pays out dividends to shareholders. This style is currently unfashionable in Anglo-Saxon countries, being perceived to add little value to the process of strategic management.

Centralized style - which corresponds with the planning down already described above. A centralized planning style is for example characteristic of the large South Korean *chaebol* companies.

Strategic planning style - in which a well-informed and powerful corporate centre plays an influential role on the medium to long term time scale in formulating and coordinating the objectives and strategy of business units or divisions. However, the corporate centre does not get involved in issues of implementation and control, which are left to unit management to decide. The strategic planning style combines elements of both planning down and planning up.

Goold and Campbell gave British Petroleum (BP) as an example of a company from their study sample who used this approach to strategic management. A strategic planning style may also be characteristic of French, German, and Japanese companies whose ownership structures and relative freedom from takeover threat facilitates the long-termism that this style may encourage.

Financial control style - in which the corporate centre has a limited involvement in strategy formulation. The financial control style can be regarded as a variant of planning down. The primary influence of the corporate centre in this case lies in the shaping and sanction of short-term business and budgetary plans. Business units and divisions are set quantitative performance and profit targets to achieve. These targets form the basis of annual unit plans. Their achievement is simply and easily monitored. They provide a strong short-term motivation to the managements of business units and divisions:-

- to seek profitable new business, whether by new initiatives or by acquisition and takeover.
- to continually seek to reduce costs, for instance by rationalisation, resource stretch and leverage (described in Chapter 21), business process re-engineering, Six Sigma, or outsourcing.
- to continually seek increases in efficiency and productivity.
- to divest (sell off or close) underperforming or unprofitable businesses.

The corporate centre undertakes a careful and continuous monitoring of unit or divisional performance relative to the annual business and budgetary plans agreed with unit management. There is likely to be rigorous questioning of unit managers responsible for underachievement or for deviations from the performance target.

The result is strong corporate pressure on unit management to optimize short term profit performance. This pressure may be reinforced by the implementation of systems of executive remuneration based upon profit-related performance bonuses, stock purchase schemes, and so on. Alternatively, there may be the periodic "pruning" of business units and managers whose performance fails to meet the target set.

Goold and Campbell suggest that the financial control approach to planning style is seen as appropriate to business activities in mature markets, and to investment projects whose payback is relatively short or medium term.

The financial control approach to planning style may however not be appropriate to business activities in which a longer-term view needs to be taken towards competitive advantage based upon:-

- the development of staff, and the build-up of experience and expertize.
- the development of the knowledge base, knowledge, and technological capability of the enterprise (Chapter 19).
- the development of the core competencies described in Chapter 20.
- the processes of research and development (R&D); innovation; new product, new brand, or new process development; and new market development.
- the establishment of an international or global product-market, brand, image, and competitive position.

Goold and Campbell comment that a principal weakness of the financial control approach to strategic planning and business development is that the emphasis on achieving short-term profit targets (in order to meet annual stock market and shareholder expectations) may result in a corporate and cultural bias against the adoption of strategies and investments which have long lead times and payoff periods, as described in Chapter 13.

This may then render the enterprise vulnerable to competition from rivals who have adopted a longer-term strategic approach (for instance based upon the strategic planning style described above). Examples include the global shipbuilding, automotive, consumer electronics, and machine tools industries where European and North American companies have yielded market position to competitors from South East Asia and the Far East. In the consumer electronics market, for instance, western companies such as GE, RCA, Thorn, and GEC eventually withdrew from well-established segments which were experiencing depressed profitability as a result of competitive incursions (such as those of Sony, Toshiba, and Matsushita), and as a result of the need for continuing and expensive innovation and new product development to which these competitive pressures gave rise. The short term financial focus of these western companies eventually forced them to cede market position to newcomers espousing *long-term competitive strategies* of market share development and market dominance described in Chapter 13, 22 and elsewhere in this book.

Companies who espouse a financial control approach to strategic management in competitive international markets may similarly find themselves at the risk of disadvantage where their rivals:-

- have the long-term support of banks or family interests.
- do not have to meet shareholder or stock market expectations of annual (and preferably increasing) profit and growth in capital value.
- cannot, for whatever reason, be taken over by "predators" seeking to make acquisitions of other companies (acquisitions as a business development strategy are analyzed in Chapter 27).
- have access to state subsidy or protection such that, for instance, companies can undercut their rivals in seeking contracts through the process of competitive tendering; and thereby establish a degree of market dominance.

Strategic control style - which is a hybrid of the strategic planning and financial control styles described above. As such it combines elements of planning down and planning up.

The strategic control approach to planning style aims to balance a degree of unit or divisional autonomy with the requirements of head office control and co-ordination. It may be regarded as a form of controlled decentralization.

The adoption of this compromise planning style may reflect the existence of a tension within the strategic management process between (i) the need to establish medium to long-term competence, competitive advantage, and product-market scope; and (ii) the need to meet short-term financial considerations associated with stock market expectations and the risk of hostile takeover threats.

The use of this approach to strategic management may only be as good as it is appropriate. It may work in stable and mature industries characterized by a degree of oligopoly, strong and effective barriers to entry, a relatively low level of international competition, effective control or ownership of such strategic assets as distribution channels, or effective product and brand differentiation supported by heavy expenditures on marketing and promotion. As with the financial control approach, it may become ineffective (i) where global world class players are pursuing long-term competence development, innovation, quality, and market share objectives with a view to long-term return; and (ii) where the ownership structure or global strength and experience of such players supports the pursuit of such strategies.

REVIEW QUESTIONS

1. What is "planning style"?
2. Describe the top down or planning down style. What are its advantages and disadvantages?
3. Describe the bottom up or planning up style. What are its advantages and disadvantages?
4. Describe the negotiated or negotiative style of planning. What are its advantages and disadvantages?
5. In what ways are planning style, organization structure, and style of management inter-related?
6. Compare and contrast the alternative planning styles of Goold and Campbell.

TECHNIQUES OF CASE STUDY AND ANALYSIS

Where the appropriate information is available:

1. Identify planning style evident in the case study. Analyze its apparent implication for strategy formulation and decision-making in the case organization.
2. Identify any apparent relationship evident in the case study between planning style, processes of strategy formulation, key objectives, key strategies, and critical success factors.

PROJECT ASSIGNMENT

Using available information, carry out a comparative analysis of the planning style of two or more organizations known to you. Try, if possible, to include a variety of different types of organization, proprietorship, and management style.

References

Buzzell, R.D., B.T. Gale and R. Sultan (1975) "Market share: a key to profitability", *Harvard Business Review*, January-February.

Goldsmith, W. and D. Clutterbuck (1997) *The Winning Streak Mark II*, Orion Books, London.

Fukuyama, F. (1995) *Trust,* Hamish Hamilton, London.

Goold, M. and A. Campbell (1987) *Strategies and Styles*, Blackwell, Oxford.

Hampden-Turner, C. and F. Trompenaars (1994) *The Seven Cultures of Capitalism*, Piatkus, London.

Handy, C.B. (1985) *Understanding Organizations*, Penguin, London.

Harrison, R. (1972) "Understanding your organization's character", *Harvard Business Review,* May-June.

Harrison, R. (1995) *The Collected Papers of Roger Harrison*, McGraw-Hill, London.

Hofstede, G. (1980) *Cultures Consequences*, Sage, London.

Hofstede, G. (1991) *Cultures and Organizations*, McGraw-Hill, London.

Lessem, R. and F. Neubauer (1994) *European Management Systems*, McGraw-Hill, London.

McGregor, D. (1960) *The Human Side of Enterprise*, McGraw-Hill, London.

Mintzberg, H. (1983) *Power In And Around Organizations*, Prentice-Hall, Englewood Cliffs, New Jersey.

Mintzberg, H. (1987) "Crafting strategy", *Harvard Business Review*, July-August.

Mintzberg, H. (1989) *Mintzberg on Management*, Free Press, New York.

Mintzberg, H. and J.A. Waters (1985) "Of strategies, deliberate and emergent", *Strategic Management Journal*, July-September.

Morden, A.R. (2004) *Principles of Management (2nd Edition)*, Ashgate, Aldershot.

Ouchi, W. (1981) *Theory Z*, Addison Wesley, Reading, Mass.

Tichy, N.M. and S. Sherman (1994) *Control Your Destiny or Someone Else Will*, Harper Business, New York.

Chapter 16

Performance Evaluation, Performance Management, and Excellence

This chapter identifies a variety of performance management methodologies and performance measurement criteria by which the process and outcomes of strategy formulation, strategic decision-making and strategic choice, strategic management, and strategy implementation may be evaluated. The chapter analyzes a variety of performance benchmarks and performance indicators. It looks at single and multiple variable performance evaluation methodologies. And it makes reference to the concepts of Six Sigma, the Balanced Scorecard, the triple bottom line, Best Value, and performance excellence.

EVALUATING PAST PERFORMANCE

The success of *past* strategic decision-making may be judged from the processes of performance appraisal and performance evaluation. Some examples of these processes are given in Chapters 2, 3, and 13 of this book.

The lessons of past performance, like the wider *history and culture of the enterprise*, have relevance to the process of strategic management in the present and in the future. The current process of strategic decision-making and implementation needs to be informed by *evidence* gained from the past performance of the enterprise and its staff; and by the lessons of the corporate, time, and risk appraisals described in Parts One and Two of this book.

PERFORMANCE MEASUREMENT CRITERIA, PERFORMANCE INDICATORS, AND BENCHMARKS

Performance criteria, performance indicators ("PI's"), benchmarks, and the measurement criteria associated with them, may be stated in:

❑ *quantitative physical* terms such as unit quantities, frequency, time, variation from the norm or quality benchmarks, output, or service provision, etc.

❑ *quantitative financial* terms such as monetary value, revenue, cost, cost-efficiency, added-value, best value, profit, return on investment, etc.

❑ *qualitative* terms such as degrees of relative acceptability, variation between the "positive" and the "negative" in customer attitude towards the quality of service rendered, assessments of intangible service features, the definition and probability of successful patient treatment outcomes, etc.

Performance criteria, performance indicators, benchmarks, and the measurement criteria associated with them should ideally be:

❑ clearly stated and easily understood; *and*
❑ easily interpreted and free from ambiguity; *and*
❑ easily verified.

The achievement of these characteristics may be relatively straightforward in the case of quantitative performance criteria. Their achievement may be more difficult, however, in the case of qualitative performance criteria, for instance associated with the provision of customer or client service, healthcare, hospitality, or service marketing intangibles. As a result, performance criteria, performance indicators, benchmarks, and the measurement criteria associated with qualitative or intangible features are sometimes expressed in terms of *outcomes* or *end results*. For instance, annual statistics for employment stability and labour turnover may be used to evaluate the effectiveness of an organization's recruitment function or the quality of its leadership and its human resource management. Similarly, student pass-fail rates, first employment destination statistics, or the number of books or publications achieved may be used to evaluate the performance of a teaching college or university.

The process of performance evaluation may be readily understood where the comparison of actual performance with the standard or benchmark set for that activity is undertaken using the same measurement criteria for both. For instance, did a hospital meet its treatment targets as expressed in the patient numbers stated in its annual service plan?

Performance criteria, performance indicators, benchmarks, and the measurement criteria associated with them may have instead to be based on previously agreed conversion formulae where transformation between physical and financial measurement criteria is required, or where conversion between the qualitative and the quantitative must be undertaken. This is because complications can arise where one performance criterion must be converted into another. In particular this means conversions from the physical to the financial, and from the qualitative to the quantitative. The value of the criterion as a mechanism of performance evaluation may break down where the basis of the conversion (i) is not properly understood; or (ii) becomes the subject of negotiation or dispute. For instance, difficulties may arise from the use of performance measurement devices of:

❑ contribution calculations within production or service provision and sales mix planning (where "contribution" is defined as the difference between net sales revenue and the variable costs incurred at that volume of output).

❑ the varying approaches to divisional performance measurement and evaluation. For instance, should a corporate centre apply the same cost of capital across all divisions, irrespective of location or product group. Or should variations be permitted according to the relative profitability of different activities in the short and the long term?

❑ public sector service quality where the performance indicators to be applied contain a variety of potentially conflicting qualitative and quantitative measurement criteria. For instance, stated objectives for improvement to social welfare provision for the elderly or the infirm may conflict with pressures on local government or healthcare agencies to improve efficiency or to cut costs.

Performance Evaluation Criteria

Performance criteria, performance indicators, benchmarks, and the measurement criteria associated with them may be specified on the basis of any of the following:

Performance evaluation criteria should be timely and accurate - systems of management control should be capable of indicating deviations from plan or standard promptly and accurately, so that there is no disagreement about the nature and timing of the remedial action that needs to be taken.

Performance evaluation criteria should be understandable - if systems of management control are clearly understood by all of the staff involved in their application, they are more likely to be effectively and speedily implemented.

Performance evaluation criteria should be realistic - where projected plans and standards of performance are seen as being realistic by all those involved in their application, there is a greater likelihood of their being attained. Systems of performance evaluation are instead likely to be treated with scepticism if they are based on unrealistic standards of performance, unrealistic measurement criteria, or unrealistic expectations of corrective or remedial action. This is in particular a problem for healthcare agencies where the level of external expectation may become incompatible with the likely patient treatment outcomes that can be achieved within any given level of available resources.

Performance evaluation criteria should be attainable - systems of management control based upon unattainable objectives or unachievable standards of performance are also likely to be treated with scepticism. The degree to which plans and performance standards are unattainable might for instance be a function of the following:-

- the organizational and communication relationship (or "distance") between planners and implementers. Planners who set objectives and strategies in isolation from the realities of implementation and control may succeed only in establishing unattainable standards. They maximize the "planning-control gap" (for instance as described by Machin and Wilson, 1979). The generals of the first world war, for example, planned military campaigns in isolation from the catastrophic consequences of their implementation on the battlefield. This issue was dealt with in Chapter 11.

- a lack of control over the resources or assets required to meet the standards laid down. Enterprise leadership cannot hope to meet performance standards laid down for operational activities if there is no effective control over the resources needed to achieve these standards.

Performance evaluation criteria should be flexible - performance criteria, performance indicators, benchmarks, and the measurement criteria associated with them may need to be changed as a result of unanticipated or unpredictable events; changes in environmental, market, or operational conditions, etc. The system of performance evaluation in use needs to be adaptable to such changes as, for instance, in the case of the use of flexible budgets within the process of budgetary control.

Performance criteria, performance indicators, benchmarks, and measurement criteria should reflect organization structure, departmental roles, and the responsibilities of management positions - the structure of organization and management is the means by which strategies and plans are implemented. The system of performance evaluation should reflect the reality of this structure. Procedures of management control should be related to the objectives, responsibilities, and roles of departments and managers who are charged with the achievement of these strategies and plans. And their application should be correlated with the requisite authority over resources, assets, and staff by which these strategies and plans are to be achieved.

"Smart"

Performance criteria, performance indicators, benchmarks, and measurement criteria are sometimes summarized in the form of the mnemonic "SMART". This stands for criteria that are:

- ❑ S = specific.
- ❑ M = measurable.
- ❑ A = achievable.
- ❑ R = realistic.
- ❑ T = time-related.

Some Issues Associated with Performance Criteria, Performance Indicators, and Benchmarks

Issues associated with performance standards, performance criteria, performance indicators, and benchmarks may include any or all of the following:

- ❑ *best practice* - issues here concern how criteria of "best practice" are to be specified, and how agreement about them is to be achieved amongst the parties to whom they will apply. Similarly, how is best practice to be evaluated? For instance, what does best practice mean in education, healthcare, government, or social welfare? Or, how is best practice to be defined in the terms of the ethical, environmental, or social responsibility issues analyzed in Chapter 12?
- ❑ *comparing like with like* - the effectiveness of performance evaluation will depend on the degree to which the relevant performance criteria, performance indicators, and benchmarks are standardized or comparable. For instance, the standard cost of a particular kind of patient treatment could be used to compare the cost-efficiency of hospitals to which this benchmark is applied.
- ❑ *service standards* - performance standards, performance criteria, performance indicators, and benchmarks may be applied to the evaluation of service quality, whether in the private, the public, or the

healthcare sectors. This may raise problems of comparability, as described above. It may also raise the question of the degree to which measurement criteria may effectively be standardized where the achievement of homogeneity of performance will by definition be unpredictable, as in the operation of surgical, healthcare, transportation, hospitality management, or customer service activities.

❑ *seamlessness* - the achievement and evaluation of comparable standards of performance may prove a problem in the joint organizational and managerial architectures variously described in Chapters 18 and 27 as de-integrated value chains, partnerships, joint ventures, and strategic alliances. This problem also appears in inter-agency public sector arrangements. The achievement of seamless performance may be difficult where different organizations are working to a variety of different internal methodologies or standards which will require harmonization before joint performance evaluation can be used to indicate the effectiveness (or "seamlessness") of collective outcome achievement. For instance, issues of child welfare, youth crime, or anti-social behaviour may have collectively to be managed by social welfare and healthcare agencies, the police, school authorities, and probation agencies. Each may be working towards separate performance criteria within their own sphere of operation, but will have to align the performance evaluation process with that of the other agencies with which they are in partnership.

❑ *adaptability to requirements for change, innovation, and improvement* - the process of establishing and agreeing performance standards, performance criteria, performance indicators, and benchmarks may over time need to take into account event characteristics (described in Chapter 8) or pressures that will necessitate change, innovation, or improvement in the performance evaluation process. Such adaptability may be required by ongoing changes in customer expectations of the specification or quality of product or service; by pressures for greater cost or resource-efficiency (for instance as described in Chapter 21); or by the competitive, international, and product-market pressures analyzed in Part Four of this book.

SINGLE VARIABLE PERFORMANCE EVALUATION METHODOLOGIES

The process of performance evaluation may be based on the use of *single variable* performance measures or performance indicators based on the:

❑   functional criteria; *and*
❑   financial criteria; *and*
❑   value outcomes

already described in Chapters 2, 3, 4, and 13 of this book.

MULTIPLE VARIABLE PERFORMANCE EVALUATION METHODOLOGIES

The process of performance evaluation may be based on the use of *multiple variable* performance measures or performance indicators, for instance based on the concepts of zero based budgeting, business process reengineering, and Six Sigma. Each is described below.

ZERO BASED BUDGETING (ZBB)

Zero based budgeting (ZBB) was described in Chapter 3 as a formalized system for reviewing the process of setting objectives, strategies, and budgets for the activities of an organization as if these activities were being performed for the first time, that is from a "zero base". A number of alternative levels of provision for each activity may be identified, costed, and evaluated in terms of the benefits to be obtained from them.

ZBB can be used within the process of performance evaluation because it is based on the belief that management should be required to justify existing activities and existing resource allocations in exactly the same way as new proposals. The process of performance evaluation will compare the outputs of established activities with the forecasted outcomes of alternative potential applications of the resources that are to be committed during the planning period in view. Chapter 3 noted that implicit in ZBB, therefore, are the measurement of both:

❑   *opportunity cost* - how may the available resources now best be used to create an optimum outcome, however this optimum outcome is to be defined?
❑   *priority* - do the outcomes of past and current commitments of resources reflect or match present strategic priorities for required performance?

The principle of zero based budgeting is related to the concept of business process reengineering, which is analyzed in the next section below.

BUSINESS PROCESS RE-ENGINEERING (BPRE)

The "business process re-engineering" concept was widely publicized by Hammer and Champy in the 1993 book *Reengineering the Corporation* (revised edition 1995).

Hammer and Champy proposed a business model (and an associated set of techniques) that managers could use to "re-invent" their enterprises in order that they might perform more effectively. To re-invent their companies, Hammer and Champy suggested that managers might have to throw out some of their existing notions about how the enterprise should be organized, and about how its performance might more effectively be evaluated. They might need to abandon some of their established principles and practices of performance management, and create different ones.

Hammer and Champy (1995) define the concept of re-engineering as 'the fundamental rethinking and radical redesign of business processes to achieve dramatic improvements in critical, contemporary measures of performance such as cost, quality, service and speed' (p. 32). They suggest that the implementation of BPRE implies abandoning long-established performance management procedures, and looking afresh at what is needed to create the organization's product or service, thereby delivering the required value to customers, clients, shareholders or stakeholders. BPRE means asking the question "if I were re-creating this company today, given what I know and given current technology, what would it look like?" It involves going back to the beginning and inventing what may be a more effective way of managing performance and doing the necessary work.

Johansson *et al.* (1993) identified three main types of BPRE. These are:

❑ *BPRE that is concentrated on improving the performance of individual business functions* - such BPRE is often aimed at yielding performance improvements that can directly be measured in terms of revenue enhancements or cost reductions (however these may be achieved), for instance as described in Chapter 13. Such improvements may also be achieved by the variations in architecture, or by the use of the strategies of knowledge and technology management, prioritizing core competence, or resource stretch and leverage that are analyzed in Part Four of this book.

❑ *BPRE that aims to achieve comparative or competitive parity* - in which the enterprise uses "best practice" or "world class" benchmarks as performance targets and comparators. This form of BPRE is now widely used in the performance management of the UK public sector. It is in particular applied in the UK local government and healthcare sectors as a means of achieving "best value" (described in a later section of this chapter). This form of BPRE is also used in procurement and supply chain management (Chapter 18) in order to achieve a globally comparable "total cost of acquisition" of inputs to the value chain. The use of competition strategy benchmarks is analyzed in a later section of this chapter.

❑ *BPRE that is used to achieve a "breakpoint" in performance* - where the objective is to identify a level of customer, client, market, or value-generation performance outcome (such as service improvement, speed or flexibility of response, innovation, or product variations offered) that, if achieved by the organization, will yield significant gains in comparative or competitive advantage. Ultimately the achievement of a breakpoint will permit the enterprise to redefine the performance expectations of the environment or market in its own favour. This is what happened when Boeing's customer-orientated rethinking of the civil aircraft specification and design process led to market dominance by the new jet-powered 707, and later with the large size 747. The achievement of a breakpoint in performance may be associated with the emergence of a new technology "S" curve. Technology "S" curves are described in Chapter 19.

SIX SIGMA

Six Sigma may be defined as 'a set of tools for improving processes and products, and as an approach for improving both the process and people related aspects of business performance' (Bertels, 2003, p. 3). Bertels notes the US Honeywell Corporation's description of Six Sigma as a strategy 'to accelerate improvements in processes, products, and services, and to radically reduce manufacturing (or) administrative costs and improve quality' (p. 4). Bertels comments that Six Sigma 'institutionalizes a rigorous, fact-based way to deliver more money to the bottom line through process improvement and process design projects ... that aim to create near-perfect processes, products, and services all aligned to delivering what the customer wants' (p. 3).

Six Sigma and Process

Like business process re-engineering (BPRE) before it, Six Sigma is focused on achieving measurable improvement in process performance. Bertels comments that 'if one takes the view that organizational work is done by people embedded in processes, then a big part of a manager's role is to plan, organize, direct and control *process*. Processes are the instruments by which organizations execute strategy. Processes are the vehicles by which employees carry out their work. It is the effectiveness of processes that drives customer satisfaction. It is the efficiency of processes that drives operating costs. And processes provide the framework around which organizations (may) be constructed ... hence, as organizations embrace Six Sigma, they also embrace process focus and management. This can change organization structure from functional to process-focused. It can change managers' roles from driving employees to driving processes. It can change intra-organizational behaviour from functional competition to process-based collaboration. Six Sigma helps create organizational alignment through use of a common language, process focus, attention to the customer, and leadership development' (pp. 21-22). Ultimately, Bertels suggests (p. 11) that 'the way to become a world-class company is to create superior process performance, as that is what ensures superior products and services for customers. Superior process performance maximizes value for the customer and for the shareholder.'

Six Sigma Outcome Measurements

Jack Welch, the former CEO of the US General Electric Corporation, notes (2005) of Six Sigma that GE 'went from 3000 ... projects in 1996 to 6000 in 1997, when we achieved $320 million in productivity gains and profits ... by 1998, we had generated $750 million in Six Sigma savings over and above our investment and would get $1.5 billion in savings the next year. Our operating margins went from 14.8 percent in 1996 to 18.9 percent in 2000' (p. 335). Outcome measurements claimed for Six Sigma include any or all of the following:

❑ cost reduction (see Chapters 3, 4, 13, 21 of this book).
❑ revenue growth (see Chapter 13 and Part Four of this book).
❑ optimization of the use of capital employed, or the actual reduction in the need for capital (see Chapters 13 and 21 of this book).
❑ improved customer satisfaction (as for instance described in Part Four of this book).

- ❑ improved employee productivity and satisfaction (see Chapter 17 of this book).
- ❑ improved and increased capability (see Chapters 4, 7, 19, 20, 21, 23, 24, and 25 of this book).
- ❑ improved use of time (see Chapter 7 of this book).
- ❑ risk reduction (see Chapters 8, 9, 13 of this book).
- ❑ improved competitive and product-market performance (see Chapters 22, 23, 24, 25, and 26 of this book).

The Cost of Poor Quality (COPQ)

Six Sigma may also be used to evaluate the *cost of poor quality*, or the cost of non-conformance with standard or benchmark. Bertels suggests that the main components of the cost of poor product or service quality may include any or all of:

- ❑ the cost of external failure (that is, failure in the context of customer usage or customer experience) and damage to corporate reputation.
- ❑ the cost of internal failure.
- ❑ the cost of identification, inspection, and appraisal.
- ❑ the cost of remedial action.
- ❑ the cost of prevention.
- ❑ the opportunity cost associated with poor quality and the need for remedial activity.

These costs may be quantified directly in such terms as defect or reject rates, necessary re-work, customer returns, customer dissatisfaction or client complaints, stock unavailability, customer service delays, patient ill-health, and so on. Bertels however adds that 'it is not sufficient to look at the reject rates of final products or customer returns alone. The term "hidden factory"… is used to describe the amount of capacity spent on fixing problems and reworking parts … cost control systems (may) not measure these cost elements' (p. 474). The hidden factory as a category of activity not only fails to add value in value chain terms, but is actually a net consumer of value. Bertels' Figure 24.4 (p. 474) is reproduced in Figure 16.1.

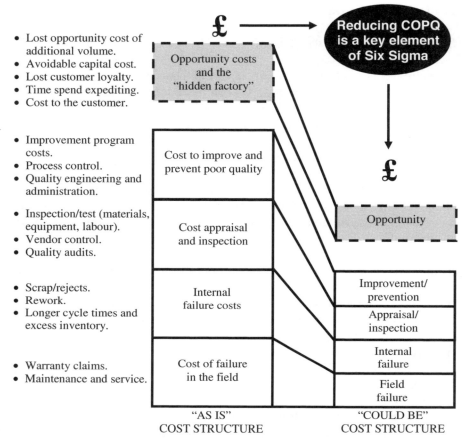

Figure 16.1   Quality and the Cost Structure of the Business

Six Sigma Methodologies

Six Sigma is based on the following components:

- ❑   the DMAIC (Define, Measure, Analyze, Improve, Control) process.
- ❑   listen to the voice of the customer (VOC).
- ❑   the identification of variation.
- ❑   the DFSS (Design For Six Sigma) process.

Each is described below.

The DMAIC Process

The DMAIC acronym stands for:

- *define* the process, problem, or issue under consideration. This definition will to the necessary extent be based *on an agreement about the exact nature of the requirements of the customer or client* (whether internal or external), through ensuring an appropriate organizational exposure to the "voice of the customer" described in the next section below.
- *measure* and quantify the magnitude of the process, problem, or issue under consideration. This measurement might for instance be based on cost-benefit, opportunity cost, or discounted cash flow (DCF) analysis.
- *analyze* the behaviour of key factors and process components in order to establish cause and effect relationships associated with the process, problem, or issue under consideration.
- *improve* the design of the process in order to achieve better performance.
- *control* the process, having implemented the resulting solutions or improvements and monitored their outcomes.

Hear the Voice of the Customer (VOC)

The *voice of the customer* is used early on in the DMAIC or the DFSS elements of the Six Sigma process to specify and to quantify the most critical requirements of the client or customer. The voice of the customer is defined to include either or both of external and internal stakeholders, the parameters and constraints of whose requirements will shape the outputs or outcomes of the particular process under consideration. Bertels notes for example of the Ford Motor Company that it uses the technique 'to identify projects that have the greatest potential to increase customer satisfaction by improving quality and reducing defects' (p. 23).

The Identification of Variation

Six Sigma is based upon the development of a capacity to identify and to measure the efficiency and effectiveness of any particular process in meeting the performance requirements of both customer and the enterprise itself. Six Sigma is used to measure how far the process creates an output that deviates from a norm that can legitimately be described as "perfect" (i) in terms of *the fitness of purpose* for the designated customer or client requirements, and (ii) in terms of the internal performance criteria of the enterprise itself. The technique therefore concentrates on the identification, analysis, and relative degree of necessary reduction of undesirable *variability* from the agreed benchmark of process performance.

This variation may be defined as the sum total of all unwanted, chance, or random events that may occur each time a process is performed, and which may take the level of this performance away from the chosen parameters ("tolerances" or "limits") of its specification for instance in terms of cost, quality, reliability, availability, customer service, patient treatment outcomes, the control of criminal or anti-social behaviour (etc).

Output variability within designated upper and lower specification limits may be accepted. Variation outside of these tolerance levels is instead defined in terms of "defective" performance. A *defect* is produced where the process fails to meet the required performance specification. The incidence of defects needs to be measured and analyzed using the DMAIC methodology, and attempts made to reduce the variation or instead to eliminate it altogether. The target defect rate may be described in terms of a "zero" benchmark. Bertels comments in this respect that a 'central idea behind Six Sigma is that if you can measure how many defects you have in a process, you can (then) systematically figure out how to eliminate them and get as close to "zero defects" as possible' (p. 4).

Six Sigma is based on the statistic that nearly one hundred percent of all outcome values will lie within six standard deviations around the average or mean of a normal distribution curve. This curve is approximately six standard deviations (6σ) wide, and is shown in Bertels' Figure A2 (p. 490), which is reproduced in Figure 16.2.

The nature of the application of Six Sigma methodologies to deal with the incidence of process variation is related to the requirement for fitness of purpose (or *quality*) of the designated customer or client requirements described above. This may be expressed in the formula Q x A = E where:

the quality of the solution (Q) x the acceptability of that solution (A)
= the effectiveness of that solution (E)

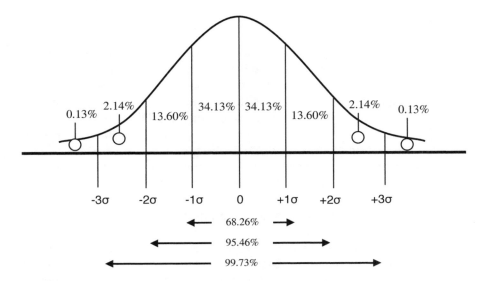

Figure 16.2 Percentages of Values Contained Within One, Two and Three Standard Deviations on a Normal Curve

How the formula Q x A = E is defined is a matter of degree. The chosen outcome is likely to be stated *relative* to the needs for fitness for purpose, not in *absolute* terms. The customer outcome will be determined by the *necessary rigour of the benefit required as compared with the resultant cost that will have to be incurred in achieving it.* For instance, compare the following two examples:

❑ the specification of safety and reliability features in the (necessarily inter-related) processes of the design and specification of commercial civil aircraft; airframe and engine manufacturing, procurement, and supply chain management; and commercial aviation operations. In this case, the variable "E" may have to be specified at a level of 6σ.

❑ airport baggage handling operations, in which losses of passenger luggage, whilst inconvenient, are not life-threatening. The relatively very rare disappearance and loss of passenger luggage will most likely in any case to be subject to compulsory travel insurance arrangements. In this case, the variable "E" might be specified at a level of 2σ.

The DFSS Process

DFSS or *Design For Six Sigma* is focused on process re-specification, process re-design, or new process development that by using the DMAIC and the voice of the customer methodologies will better meet (i) future customer requirements and (ii) ongoing corporate needs for performance improvement, revenue generation, or cost reduction. DFSS may be applied to any or all of processes associated with production, the delivery of services, transaction processing, or innovation (etc).

DFSS may be associated with the knowledge dynamics and the technology "S" curves described in Chapter 19.

Six Sigma, Organizational Improvement, and Learning

Bertels notes that Six Sigma 'builds organizational learning through replication of improvements. Many companies involved in Six Sigma efforts implement knowledge repositories, such as websites that contain case studies and project reports that help spread improvements across an entire (institution). This adds … to design and problem-solving ability, as well as agility' on an organization-wide basis (p. 22). Knowledge management is dealt with in Chapter 19 of this book.

EVALUATING STRATEGIC CHOICE AND PLANS

Enterprise management will need to subject the processes of strategy formulation, strategic choice, planning, and strategy implementation to ongoing review, scrutiny and appraisal. This process of review and appraisal may in part be *objective*, as in the case of the evaluation of the available performance data. It is also likely to be *subjective*, for instance based on the projections, forecasts, and scenarios described in Chapter 9.

The skill with which enterprise leadership is able to make judgements about the likely success of its strategic decisions may depend on such factors as:

❑   its past experience or track record in successfully making these kinds of judgements.
❑   its honesty and willingness to recognize past weaknesses or failures in making effective evaluative judgements about strategic decisions whose resource commitments, risks, and likely consequences take the enterprise forward into the future.

❑   its openness to, or willingness to learn or experiment with new or untried methods of making assessments about the potential outcomes of the courses of action it is proposing.

Current and future strategic choice and plans may be evaluated by such judgemental criteria as:

❑   critical success factors.
❑   desirability.
❑   comparative or competitive advantage.
❑   feasibility.
❑   appropriateness.
❑   knowledge and competence.
❑   fit.
❑   consistency.
❑   facilitating change or innovation.

Each is described below.

Critical Success Factors

Decisions on the suitability of current and future strategies may be based on judgements about the degree to which implementation of the proposed strategies and plans is likely to result in the enterprise meeting the objectives associated with its critical success factors. For instance, did a university's strategy result in the recruitment of the right number and quality of students, and does its reputation allow it to bid successfully for research and consultancy contracts? Student numbers and income generation are critical success factors for a university. All other variables are dependent on them.

Desirability

Decisions on the choice of current and future strategies may be based on judgements about:

❑   the relative desirability (or necessity) to key stakeholders, leaders, managers, and staff *internal* to the organization of proposed enterprise objectives, strategies, and plans.

❑ the relative desirability or necessity of enterprise objectives, strategies and plans in the view of customers, sources of finance, and other key stakeholders *external* to the organization.

❑ the degree to which enterprise purpose is perceived to be responsive towards, or acceptable to broader ethical, environmental, or social concerns such as those described in Chapter 12.

Comparative or Competitive Advantage

Decisions on the choice of current and future strategies may be based on judgements about the degree to which implementation of the selected strategies and plans will permit the enterprise most effectively to exploit its sources of comparative or competitive advantage in achieving its objectives. These sources of comparative or competitive advantage were described in Parts One and Two of this book.

Feasibility

Decisions on the feasibility of current and future strategies or plans may be based on judgements of:

How effective the enterprise is in generating feasible strategic alternatives - for instance as described in Chapter 14. Does the enterprise know what feasible options are actually available to it? Conversely, does it know what is *not* feasible (for instance because of a lack of available finance; or because of internal limitations on capability; or because of external constraints). Examples might include:-

• the non-availability of acquisition targets in countries such as Japan, South Korea, and China because of prevailing ownership structures or the government protection of local industries. Takeovers are in this case not a feasible alternative.

• the requirement to globalize by means of the strategic alliances analyzed in Chapter 27. This may be the only feasible form of business development strategy available to resource-constrained companies who wish to grow their business internationally in a relatively short space of time.

Whether or not the chosen strategy will work - for instance, is the implementation of the chosen alternative viable or realistic? For example, despite its (very expensive) purchase of MCA, who owned a large part of the US film and media industry, Matsushita soon found that it could neither manage nor control its wily new American subsidiary. Matsushita subsequently sold MCA to the Seagram Company.

Whether strategies can be implemented and achieve their desired result within the time-scale laid down - judgements may have to be made about the potential for delays such as those that for instance affected the building and commissioning of the Channel Tunnel on London's new Wembley Stadium. What might be the possible consequences for the organization of such delays?

Whether enterprise objectives, strategies, policies, and plans are properly understood by the people who have to implement them - for example, the "rational" or "deliberate" strategies described in Chapter 11 may have been "thrown over the wall" by those who formulated them to subordinate staff who are perceived to be the "implementers" of strategies and plans. Such people may not have been involved in the process of formulating objectives and strategies; may only have a limited understanding of the implications of what it is their bosses are asking them to do; or may have a low level of motivation and commitment to a process of which they have little ownership.

Whether the leadership, structure, staff, and capability of the organization can actually implement the chosen strategies, and deliver the required results - for instance, can the enterprise actually do what is being asked of it? The French for instance were the first to try to build the Panama Canal towards the end of the nineteenth century. The task proved beyond them given the nature of the technology that was available at the time.

The extent to which the enterprise possesses leadership, managerial, and staff ability - that (i) can effectively carry out the processes of strategic analysis and planning described in Parts One and Two of this book; (ii) can successfully formulate and communicate mission, intent, objectives, strategies, and plans as described in Parts Two and Three of this book; and (iii) can successfully put into effect the implementation and achievement of objectives and strategies, as described throughout this book.

Appropriateness

Decisions on the appropriateness of current and future strategies may be based on judgements about:

Whether the chosen strategies take advantage of - the relevant enterprise strengths, capability, competences, and sources of comparative or competitive advantage; the external opportunities; and prevailing competitor weaknesses.

Whether the chosen strategies address - the relevant corporate weaknesses, external and environmental threats, and competitor strengths.

Whether the strategies formulated clearly represent the best available path or route to achieving objectives and putting statements of mission into practice - that is, are the strategies clearly appropriate to achieving the required objectives? For instance, should an airline that wishes to expand its business concentrate its efforts on a central hub like London, Paris, Beijing, or Chicago, and use feeder flights from regional centres on a "hub and spoke" basis? Or should it instead increase the choice of direct international flights from regional airports? These will by-pass the central hub and cut out the need for the feeder flights, but call for a bigger investment in aircraft and airports than is required by operating from one central hub. The issue of path to goal within a leadership context is analyzed in Chapter 17.

The degree to which the chosen strategies are appropriate to the situation, or are situation-specific - how well do the chosen strategies address the relevant contingencies and constraints, as well as taking into account the relevant critical success factors? For instance, the active development of credit card and credit-based financial operations are appropriate to consumer cultures in which borrowing to spend "now" is acceptable. This is because consumption and personal gratification are a primary value of societies such as the UK and the USA. Credit-based operations may however be inappropriate to societies in which personal saving is encouraged, and in which spending on the basis of credit is frowned upon. Personal saving to cover the uncertainties of tomorrow, to pay for education, or to finance great family events such as weddings, is a prime motivation in such societies.

The issue of situational relevance and contingency within a leadership context is analyzed in Chapter 17.

The degree to which plans and strategies are locationally appropriate - to local or regional implementation; or to international or global operations; or to both. International business strategy is dealt with in Chapter 28.

Knowledge and Competence

Decisions on the choice of current and future strategies will in this case be based on judgements about the degree to which implementation will permit the enterprise to exploit and further to develop its *knowledge base, its competencies*, and its *technology base*. Long-established pharmaceutical companies such as Glaxo-SmithKline for instance use their immense knowledge of human ailments and the medical properties of plants and chemical substances to invent drugs that are increasingly effective in the alleviation and treatment of illness and suffering. At the same time such companies work with healthcare agencies to prevent the incidence of illness or disability, and to reduce the cost of human ailments to society generally.

Knowledge and technology management are analyzed in Chapter 19. The core competence concept is described in Chapter 20.

Fit

Decisions on the choice of current and future strategies will have to be based on judgements as to whether the objectives and strategy to be implemented are congruent with, or *fit* (i) the resource base of the enterprise as represented by its leadership, human, financial, and physical assets; (ii) its knowledge, technology, and competence; (iii) its capability; and (iv) its operational capacity to implement. *In other words, has the organization actually got the capability and the resources to put its chosen strategies into effect such that it can deliver the required results?* For example, it is no use a university or a hospital claiming that it "pursues excellence" in some particular research activity if it does not employ the world's best researchers, or cannot attract them to come to work for it. Its pretence will soon be found out!

Where objectives, strategies, leadership, and the resource base of capability are not congruent, that is, where there is an inadequate degree of fit, the strategic management process will have to find a way to close the gap between the actual and the required capability. This might be achieved by any of:

❑ the upgrading of, or further investment in enterprise capability and competence.
❑ the reconceptualization of capability, competence, process, or technology. This may be achieved by strategies of re-engineering, or of innovation (analyzed in Chapter 19). A classic case was the development of container shipping and handling which, by its standardization of load size and shape, revolutionized freight transportation by reducing and simplifying handling, speeding up transfer, and reducing cost.
❑ the business development strategies described in Chapter 27.
❑ co-operating with other organizations within the relationship architecture, for instance through the de-integrated value chains, value adding partnerships, network structures, or strategic alliances described

in later chapters to achieve the joint effect or *synergy* that was defined in Chapter 4.

❏ making assets work harder, whether by the strategies of "doing more with what you already have" or of "doing more with less", as described in Chapter 21.

At the same time, decisions on the choice of current and future strategies will have to be based on judgements as to whether the objectives and strategy to be implemented are congruent with, or fit the character of the *external environment*. Chapter 12 for instance looked at the issue of ethics and social responsibility. To what extent may the enterprise adopt strategies that are out of step with the ethical standards of the day, or are clearly seen to be socially unresponsive by the wider society? Chapter 6 instead analyzed the relative stability of the external environment. The enterprise will have to adapt its strategic choice to the prevailing conditions of environmental change, or it may run the risk of being left behind by, or being rendered obsolete by those changes.

Consistency

A decision will have to be made as to the degree to which purpose, objectives, strategies, and plans are consistent with each other over time. In other words, do they demonstrate the *pattern* described in Chapter 11. Pattern was defined in that chapter as 'the consistency of enterprise decision-making over time'. Companies such as the UK grocery retailers Tesco, Asda-Walmart, and Sainsbury are known for their consistent and long-term pursuit of quality and value for money market offer. They tend to follow the same policies year in and year out. Customers know what they will get if they shop in the stores of these companies. They have a reputation for consistency.

An alternative to this consistent pattern lies in the making of short-term changes to the basic parameters of the business; or at worst "muddling through" with no pattern and consistency at all. The diversification by the Eastman Kodak Company into pharmaceutical products and household items during the 1980s for instance demonstrated an inconsistency of strategic pattern that was subsequently "corrected" by Kodak's later return to a clear focus on its core imaging business.

Facilitating Change and Innovation

Decisions on the degree to which current and future strategies facilitate the implementation of change or innovation may be based on judgements about:

❑ whether the chosen objectives and strategies are flexible, and are capable of responding to changing internal and external events.

❑ whether the process of formulating and implementing strategies and plans described in Chapters 14 and 15 facilitates innovative or flexible behaviour, and encourages staff and structures to adopt the necessary change. The aggressive use of techniques of centralized planning down analyzed in Chapter 15, on the other hand, may cause leaders and decision-makers to become inflexible and out of touch with reality. Feedback from implementers about negative performance features may in consequence be filtered or screened out until eventually a disaster occurs. This disaster may then force decision-makers to confront unpalatable truths about external or market developments (etc) which hitherto they have been ignoring or denying.

Decisions on the degree to which current and future strategies facilitate the implementation of change or innovation may also be based on judgements about the degree to which the *timing* and *time-scale* of strategy implementation matches with:

❑ the capacity of customers, markets, and environments to absorb and accept change. Can tobacco products be banned altogether in Anglo-Saxon countries? Will electric cars become dominant in urban areas? Or will motorists return to public transport for their journeys to work in order to reduce the effects of congestion and to speed up their travel time?

❑ the capacity of enterprise staff and operational resources to absorb and accept change.

❑ the capacity of the organization's leadership to absorb and to adapt to change. For example, Tichy and Sherman (1994) recounted in detail the story of CEO Jack Welch's epic and controversial battle with the US General Electric Corporation to bring about drastic change in that organization. Welch set out to reduce bureaucracy, to make GE more responsive to the market, and to increase its competitiveness in the face of global competition in its markets. He made drastic changes to the structure and character of that company over a ten-year period.

SINGLE VARIABLE STRATEGIC MANAGEMENT PERFORMANCE EVALUATION METHODOLOGIES

The evaluation of *the strategic management process itself* may be based on any or all of the single variable methodologies listed as follows. The use of these variables can be used to indicate the extent to which the implementation of the strategic management process has delivered the desired performance results in respect of:

❑   the relevant critical success factors (Chapter 4).
❑   the relevant sources of comparative or competitive advantage (Chapter 4 and others).
❑   the achievement of the planned synergies (Chapters 4 and 27).
❑   accommodating the relevant limiting factors, contingencies, and constraints (Chapters 4, 5, and 6).
❑   the effective use of time as resource (Chapter 7).
❑   the effective use of risk management capability (Chapter 8).
❑   the effective use of business planning and forecasting capability (Chapter 9).
❑   the effective financial management of the organization (Chapters 3 and 13).
❑   the implementation and achievement of effective enterprise leadership (Chapter 17).

MULTIPLE VARIABLE STRATEGIC MANAGEMENT PERFORMANCE EVALUATION METHODOLOGIES

The evaluation of the strategic management process may also be based on any of the multiple variable methodologies for strategic performance management and evaluation analyzed in this section.

THE BALANCED SCORECARD

Kaplan and Norton (1996) suggest that enterprise management can use the concept of the "balanced scorecard" (BSC) in order to complement 'financial measures of past performance with measures of the drivers of future performance' (p. 8). Kaplan and Norton comment that 'the Balanced Scorecard translates an organization's mission and strategy into a comprehensive set of performance measures that provide the framework for a strategic measurement and management system. The Balanced Scorecard retains an emphasis on achieving financial objectives, but also includes the performance drivers of these financial objectives' (p. 2).

The objectives and measures of the balanced scorecard are derived from an organization's vision and strategy. The objectives and measures used by the balanced scorecard view organizational performance from four formalized "balanced perspectives". These perspectives are described at various points throughout this book. They are:

❑ the perspective of customer or client.
❑ the perspective of internal business processes, innovation, and change.
❑ the processes of knowledge management, organizational learning, and organizational development.
❑ the financial perspective.

The balanced scorecard has been developed as a synthesis from 'the collision between the irresistible force to build long-range competitive capabilities, and the immovable object of the historical-cost financial accounting model' (p. 7). Kaplan and Norton state that 'breakthroughs in performance require major change, and that includes changes in the measurement and management systems used by an organization. Navigating to a more competitive, technological, and capability-driven future cannot be accomplished merely by monitoring and controlling financial measures of past performance' (p. 6).

Kaplan and Norton argue that the balanced scorecard expands the set of activity performance criteria beyond the summary financial measures for instance described in Chapter 3 of this book. The purpose of balanced scorecard methodology is:

❑ to permit the measurement of how the activities comprising operational performance create value for customers and clients.
❑ to decide how the necessary internal competencies and capabilities, for instance as described in this chapter and also analyzed in Chapters 4, 7, 8, 9, 13, 14, 17, 19, 20, 21, 22, and 28 of this book may be enhanced or developed.
❑ to determine how the enterprise should invest in people, knowledge, systems, and procedures needed to achieve improvements in the capability that underpins current and future performance.

The proponents of the balanced scorecard methodology suggest that the technique may be used to translate the concepts of strategic vision, mission, and leadership being described in Part Three of this book into a balanced set of tangible and measurable objectives. This balanced implementation process is based on four key strategies. These strategies are summarized as follows.

❑ *firstly*, define and establish the nature of the relationship with customers or clients, and decide what value outcomes (or what value chain outcomes) must be achieved in the market or the external environment.

❑ *secondly*, define and establish what internal processes (or process re-engineering, Six Sigma, etc) are necessary to meet customer or client demands, and decide what capabilities and competencies are critical to that achievement.

❑ *thirdly*, establish what processes of employee retention and development, knowledge and technology management, systems development, organizational learning, and architecture development will be needed to put in place the necessary capabilities and competencies (for instance in creating customer value; in product, process, or service innovation; in managing partnerships; or in handling change, etc) as necessary internal processes described immediately above.

❑ *fourthly*, decide what kinds of financial outcomes must be achieved by the interaction of the three strategies listed immediately above, so that shareholder or stakeholder satisfaction may be maintained or improved.

THE TRIPLE BOTTOM LINE

Elkington (1997) proposes the use of "triple bottom line" methodology by which to evaluate the strategic choice and performance of the enterprise in terms of the concepts of business ethics, environmentalism, and social responsibility described in Chapter 12. Elkington suggests that strategic choice and performance should *at the same time* be compared and evaluated on the basis of:

❑ its financial performance, for instance as described in Chapters 3, 13, and 15.

❑ its environmental impact, as described in Chapter 12.

❑ the degree to which it demonstrates ethical and socially responsible behaviour in its business activities, as described in Chapter 12.

The emergence of triple bottom line thinking has resulted in the increasing adoption of social and environmental reporting methodologies in company reports and accounts. UK users include Shell plc, BP plc, and the Body Shop. Pressures for more comprehensive social and environmental reporting are growing within European Union countries generally, with France and The Netherlands for instance now requiring significant levels of statutory compliance by companies.

BEST VALUE

"Best Value" as a multiple variable methodology for strategic performance management and evaluation is applied to public sector activities in the UK and Australia. In the UK for instance, Section Three of the 1999 Local Government Act requires local government authorities 'to make arrangements to secure continuous improvement in the way in which they exercise their functions, having regard to a combination of economy, efficiency and effectiveness' (*DETR Circular 10/99 Local Government Act 1999: Part 1 "Best Value"*).

The UK government has defined Best Value as a duty on the strategic management process in the public and healthcare sectors to deliver services to clear standards for customers and clients as voters and taxpayers. These standards should specify both *cost* and *quality*, and deliver results by the most *economic*, *efficient* and *effective* means available. This has for instance during the last decade presented local government authorities with a challenging framework of performance management. Local government authorities are required:

❑ to consult with residents and the local users of services about their views and priorities.
❑ to publish annual *Best Value performance plans* that report on past and current performance and identify forward activity plans, service priorities, and targets for improvement.
❑ to review all of their functions over a five year cycle.

Best Value requires local government authorities to ask themselves fundamental questions about the underlying objectives and priorities of their work. They must also concern themselves with their operating performance relative to other organizations in the public, private, and voluntary sectors with which they are benchmarked and compared. Some of the principles of Best Value in the UK include:

❑ the requirement *to improve performance* - as measured by the "3Es", which are effectiveness, efficiency, and economy.

❑ the requirement *to make use of the "5Cs"* - which are the strategies of challenge, consultation, comparison, co-operation or collaboration, and competition.

❑ the use of *performance indicators* ("PIs") - as standards and benchmarks by which to judge achievement, and to set targets for improvement.

❑ the pursuit of *visible continuous improvement over time.*

The achievement of Best Value should also be subject to the achievement of *equity* and the sustainability of the *environment*. These are described as the fourth and fifth "Es".

Local government authorities in the UK have been required to publish performance measurement data since 1993. They have done this by using performance indicators specified by the UK government's Audit Commission. These Audit Commission performance indicators (or "ACPIs") have now been superseded as benchmarks by Best Value performance indicators (or "BVPIs") published by the UK government.

EXCELLENCE AS A MULTIPLE VARIABLE STRATEGIC PERFORMANCE EVALUATION METHODOLOGY

Pressures to demonstrate levels of strategic and operational performance that in comparative terms may legitimately be described as "excellent" derive from:

❑ increasingly competitive trading conditions in product-markets, in part deriving (i) from an accelerating pace of globalization, (ii) from the use of the internet, and (iii) from the emergence of China as a manufacturing superpower.

❑ increasingly informed, sophisticated, and selective consumers.

❑ growing pressures from governments, and the taxpayers and voters that they represent, for visibly improved public, educational, and healthcare sector performance.

❑ an increasing acceptance and use of objective benchmarks or standards as valid comparators. Such benchmarks for example are widely used to assess quality, service, patient care, educational achievement, reliability, or cost-efficiency. Their use underpins the methodologies of Best Value described in the preceding section of this chapter.

Excellence as a multiple variable strategic performance evaluation methodology may be described by any or all of the following.

Strategic Management and Leadership Capability

The degree to which the enterprise can in comparative terms be judged to have achieved excellence, and be capable of sustaining this excellence on the long term may be a function of *its strategic management and its leadership capability*. The analysis of these capabilities is a key issue for this book, and is dealt with in detail for instance in Chapters 11, 13, 14, 15, and 17 of Part Three; and throughout Part Four.

Quality, Reliability, Service, and Value (QRSV)

Peters and Waterman analyzed the excellence concept in their pioneering book entitled *In Search of Excellence* published by Harper and Row in 1982. They categorized excellence of customer service in terms of the four variables quality, reliability, service, and value for money. Hence the acronym "QRSV".

This description of excellence was based upon, and foreshadowed the increasing acceptance and use of objective benchmarks or standards as valid comparators described at the beginning of this section of Chapter 16. Only those organizations that could legitimately demonstrate outstanding levels of customer or client orientation and market performance by comparison with widely accepted standards or benchmarks could be entitled to claim excellence, and benefit from the competitive advantage that such a status might confer on them. Such an acceptance is then related to the competition strategy benchmarks described immediately below.

Competition Strategy Benchmarks

Excellence-based benchmarks that may be applied to the formulation and implementation of the competition strategy analyzed in Chapter 22 could include any or all of the following. These would be demonstrated by agreed, objective, and widely accepted external standards:

❑ *world class.*
❑ *excellent.*
❑ *market leader.*
❑ *first in class* or *first in category.*

❏ *model provider* or *"beacon" provider*, a benchmark for instance used in the UK public and healthcare sectors.
❏ *preferred supplier*, for instance in the concept of procurement and supply chain management described in Chapter 18.
❏ *number one*.
❏ *number two* (for instance because "we try harder").

The European Foundation for Quality Management (EFQM) "Excellence" Model

The European Foundation for Quality Management (EFQM ®) is a membership-based, not-for-profit institution whose mission is to help bring about the achievement of sustainable performance excellence in European organizations.

The description of the EFQM Model of Excellence ® given below is based on EFQM documentation, and is reproduced here with permission. The EFQM states that its 'model is a non-prescriptive framework that recognises there are many approaches to achieving sustainable excellence. Within this non-prescriptive approach there are some fundamental concepts which underpin the EFQM model'. These *fundamental concepts of excellence* are listed as follows.

Results orientation – 'excellence is dependent upon balancing and satisfying the needs of all relevant stakeholders (this includes the people employed, customers, suppliers and society in general as well as those with financial interests in the organization)'. Stakeholder analysis was dealt with in Chapters 11, 12 and 14.

Customer focus – 'the customer is the final arbiter of product and service quality. Customer loyalty, retention and market share gain are best optimised through a clear focus on the needs of current and potential customers'.

Leadership and constancy of purpose – 'the behaviour of an organization's leaders creates a clarity and unity of purpose within the organization, and an environment in which the organization and its people can excel'. The issue of strategic pattern and consistency was analyzed in Chapter 11. The process and practice of leadership is given extensive treatment in Chapter 17.

Management by processes and facts – 'organizations perform effectively when all inter-related activities are understood and systematically managed, and decisions concerning current operations and planned improvements are made using reliable information that includes stakeholder perceptions'.

People development and involvement – 'the full potential of an organization's people is best released through shared values and a culture of trust and empowerment, which encourages the involvement of everyone'. These issues are for instance dealt with in Chapter 18.

Continuous learning, innovation, and improvement – 'organizational performance is maximized when it is based on the management and sharing of knowledge within a culture of continuous learning, innovation and improvement'.

Partnership development – 'an organization works more effectively when it has mutually beneficial relationships built on trust, [the] sharing of knowledge, and integration with its partners'. The issues of relationship architecture and partnership are analyzed in Chapter 18.

Public responsibility – 'the long-term interest of the organization and its people are best served by adopting an ethical approach and exceeding the expectations and regulations of the community'. These issues were analyzed in Chapter 12.

The EFQM states that its excellence model 'is a non-prescriptive framework based on nine criteria. Five of these [criteria] are "Enablers" and four are "Results". The "Enabler" criteria cover what an organization does. The "Results" criteria cover what an organization achieves. "Results" are caused by "Enablers". The Model, which recognises that there are many approaches to achieving sustainable excellence in all aspects of performance, is based on the premise that excellent results with respect to Performance, Customers, People and Society are achieved through Leadership driving Policy and Strategy, People, Partnerships and Resources, and Processes'.

This *equifinal* model is reproduced with permission as Figure 16.3. The EFQM states that the arrows in the model 'emphasise the dynamic nature of the model. They show innovation and learning helping to improve enablers that in turn lead to improved results'.

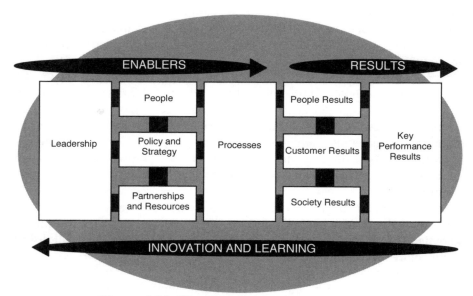

Figure 16.3 The EFQM Excellence Model ®

The nine criteria of the EFQM excellence model are used to monitor or to assess an organization's progress towards the achievement of excellence. The EFQM's definition of the five *enabling criteria* are listed as follows.

Criterion one: leadership - 'how leaders develop and facilitate the achievement of mission and vision, develop values required for long term success and implement these via appropriate actions and behaviours, and are personally involved in ensuring that the organization's management system is developed and implemented'.
Criterion two: policy and strategy - 'how the organization implements its mission and vision via a clear stakeholder-focused strategy, supported by relevant policies, plans, objectives, targets and processes'.
Criterion three: people - 'how the organization manages, develops and releases the knowledge and full potential of its people at an individual, team-based and organization-wide level, and plans these activities in order to support its policy and strategy and the effective operation of its processes'.
Criterion four: partnerships and resources - 'how the organization plans and manages its external partnerships and internal resources in order to support its policy and strategy and the effective operation of its processes'.

Criterion five: processes - 'how the organization designs, manages and improves its processes in order to support its policy and strategy and to fully satisfy, and generate increasing value for, its customers and other stakeholders'.

The EFQM's definition of the four *results criteria* are listed as follows.

Criterion six: customer results - 'what the organization is achieving in relation to its external customers'.
Criterion seven: people results - 'what the organization is achieving in relation to its people'.
Criterion eight: society results - 'what the organization is achieving in relation to local, national and international society, as appropriate'.
Criterion nine: key performance results - 'what the organization is achieving in relation to its planned performance'.

Performance Evaluation

The EFQM model contains a variety of performance evaluation methodologies and performance measures that are used to indicate the degree of organizational progress towards the achievement of excellence. Some of these methodologies, benchmarks, and measures have been discussed in this chapter. The EFQM model categorizes the performance measurement process in terms of the following.

Key performance outcomes - are measures of the 'key results planned by the organization and which, depending on the purpose and objectives of the organization, may include those relating to ... financial outcomes [and] non-financial outcomes [and] activities [that] assist in the preservation and sustainability of resources'.
Performance indicators - these are internal measures 'used by the organization to monitor, understand, predict and improve the performance of the organization and to predict perceptions of society'.

REVIEW QUESTIONS

1. Why may enterprise management undertake the review and evaluation of the past or present strategic and operational performance of the organization?

2. How may enterprise management undertake the review and evaluation of the past or present strategic and operational performance of the organization?
3. What is the purpose of performance measurement criteria, performance indicators, and performance benchmarks?
4. How may enterprise management evaluate its choice of strategies and plans?
5. Analyze and comment on single variable evaluation methodologies for performance management.
6. Analyze and comment on multiple variable evaluation methodologies for performance management.
7. Analyze and comment on single variable strategic management performance evaluation methodologies.
8. Analyze and comment on multiple variable strategic management performance evaluation methodologies.
9. How may a public sector or healthcare organization achieve "Best Value" performance outcomes?
10. How may enterprise management achieve "excellent" performance outcomes?

TECHNIQUES OF CASE STUDY AND ANALYSIS

1. Evaluate the strategies and plans evident in the case study. Use whatever measurement or judgmental criteria you consider to be most appropriate.
2. Identify and comment on whatever process of performance management is evident in the case study.
3. Evaluate whatever process of performance management is evident in the case study. Use the measurement or judgmental criteria you consider to be most appropriate.
4. Identify and comment on whatever process of strategic performance management is evident in the case study.
5. Evaluate whatever process of strategic management is evident in the case study. Use the measurement or judgmental criteria you consider to be most appropriate.

PROJECT ASSIGNMENTS

1. Using available information, evaluate the strategy and plans of an organization in which you are interested.

2. Using published information, evaluate the past or present performance of an organization in which you are interested. Comment on the processes of strategic and operational performance management in this organization.

References

Bertels, T. (ed.) (2003) *Rath and Strong's Six Sigma Leadership Handbook*, Wiley, Hoboken, NJ.

Bicheno, J. and P. Catherwood (2005) *Six Sigma and the Quality Toolbox*, Picsie Books, Buckingham.

Elkington, J. (1997) *Cannibals With Forks: the triple bottom line of 21st century business*, Capstone, Oxford.

Hammer, M. and J. Champy (1995) *Reengineering the Corporation*, Nicholas Brealey, London.

Johansson, H.J., McHugh, P., Pendlebury, A.J. and W.A. Wheeler (1993) *Business Process Reengineering: breakpoint strategies for market dominance*, Wiley, Chichester.

Kaplan, R.S. and D.P. Norton (1996) *The Balanced Scorecard*, Harvard Business School Press, Boston, Mass.

Machin, J.L. and L.S. Wilson (1979) "Closing the gap between planning and control", *Long Range Planning*, Vol 12, April.

McHugh, P.; Merli, G. and W.A. Wheeler (1995) *Beyond Business Process Reengineering*, Wiley, Chichester.

Morden, A.R. (1986) "Zero base budgeting: a potential revisited", *Management Accounting*, October.

Peters, T.J. and R.H. Waterman (1982) *In Search of Excellence*, Harper & Row, New York.

The European Foundation for Quality Management (1999) *The EFQM Excellence Model*, EFQM, Brussels.

Tichy, N.M. and S. Sherman (1994) *Control Your Own Destiny Or Someone Else Will*, Harper Business, New York.

UK DETR Circular 10/99 Local Government Act 1999: Part 1 "Best Value".

Welch, J. (2005) *Jack - Straight From The Gut*, Headline Books, London.

Chapter 17

Leadership and Strategy

"Control your destiny, or someone else will" - Jack Welch

This chapter looks at the role of enterprise leadership within the context of strategic management. It analyzes the process of leadership, and examines in detail the implementation of that process. It looks at leadership as a key strategic competence, as a source of value generation, and as a source of comparative or competitive advantage. It deals with the role of leadership in establishing and sustaining the vision of the organization, and in securing commitment to achieving its purpose.

The contents of this chapter are based on a variety of leadership concepts and models.

LEADERSHIP AND STRATEGY

The European Foundation for Quality Management comments that 'the behaviour of an organization's leaders (should) create ... clarity and unity of purpose within the organization, and an environment in which the organization and its people can excel' (EFQM, 1999).

Warren Bennis suggests that 'leaders are people who do the right things and managers are people who do things right. Leaders are interested in direction, vision, goals, objectives, intention, purpose, and effectiveness - the right things. Managers are interested in efficiency, the how-to, the day-to-day, the short run of doing things right' (quoted in Bennis and Townsend, 1995, p. 6).

Leadership is a key issue for the long-term strategic direction, stability, and survival of the enterprise. The organization's leadership for instance has a strategic responsibility to focus attention towards, and develop the core values, culture, and ideology; the knowledge base; the architecture and relationships; the core competencies; the finance and resources; the sources of value addition and competitive advantage; and the strategic management process upon which the efforts of the enterprise ultimately depend.

Chapters 11 to 16 of this book have analyzed a series of strategic management components whose formulation and implementation will require a leadership input. These components include decisions about:

❑ how the process of strategy formulation and strategic decision-making is to be implemented and facilitated.
❑ understanding and choice of the basis of strategy formulation.
❑ planning style.
❑ perspective - the conceptualization, purpose, and direction of the enterprise.
❑ core values and ideology.
❑ mission.
❑ strategic intent.
❑ ethos and ethics.
❑ how to ensure understanding and consensus about the critical success factors of the enterprise.
❑ objectives.
❑ financial strategy and management.
❑ performance management.
❑ how the enterprise is to move forwards into the future.
❑ how power is to be used within the organization; and how the politics of internal and external relationships are to be managed.
❑ how relationships with key internal and external stakeholders are to be managed within the architecture of the organization.

LEADERSHIP DEFINED

Armstrong (1990) defined leadership in terms of *getting things done through people*. He suggests that leadership happens 'when there is an objective to be achieved, or a task to be carried out, and when more than one person is needed to do it. All managers are by definition leaders in that they can only do what they have to do with the support of their team, who must be inspired or persuaded to follow them. Leadership is therefore about encouraging and inspiring individuals and teams to give their best to achieve a desired result. Leadership is required because someone has to point the way and ... (to) ensure that everyone concerned gets there' (p. 165).

Northouse (2001) defines leadership as 'a process whereby an individual influences a group ... to achieve a common goal' (p. 3). This implies that:

- defining leadership as a *process* means that it is a dynamic interaction or transactional event that occurs between the leader and his or her followers. The leader affects and is affected by followers.
- leadership occurs in a *group context*, that is, leadership involves influencing a group of individuals who are in some way inter-related or interacting in a purposive manner.
- leadership is *goal-directed*. Leadership involves influencing the individual and the group towards accomplishing some objective or task. Leaders attempt to combine all of the available energies and to direct them to achieving this objective or task.

SOME SOURCES OF LEADERSHIP INFLUENCE AND POWER

The exercise of leadership involves the use of *influence*. This is concerned with how the leader affects followers, and is in turn affected by them. There are a variety of sources of leadership influence and power. These include:

Tradition - historically, traditional leaders derived authority from their inheritance by birth or kinship. Kings, queens, and clan or tribal leaders were born to lead the people over whom they held sway. There may be similar leadership expectations (for instance in Spain, Italy, or South Korea) of those who as offspring inherit from their parents or predecessors the assets of family businesses.

Office - leaders in this case derive their authority from the *offices they hold*. These offices or positions may be associated with political and economic power to act on behalf of others, and may be backed up by sufficient authority or force to ensure compliance. For instance, countries such as France and Russia have long histories of powerful (or "absolutist") leadership that to this day influence attitudes to leadership. One consequence of this approach may be *the expectation that hierarchical position and leadership are correlated*. Organizational rank, the right to exercise influence and authority, the expectation of leadership responsibility, and the expectation of compliance from subordinates may all be perceived as components of senior management roles. This may similarly be expressed in terms of the exercise of:-

Legitimate power - which derives from the authority formally vested in a hierarchical position or office held within the organization, the exercise of which by the leader is recognized by subordinates as appropriate and proper.

Reward power - which derives from the authority to decide and to make the allocation of rewards to others. Such rewards may take the tangible form of pay increases, bonuses, or promotion; or the intangible form of recognition, congratulation or praise.

Coercive power - which describes the authority to recommend or impose punishment. The exercise of coercive power might take the form of criticism, the denial or withdrawal of optional conditions or rewards of employment (such as bonuses), demotion, or dismissal.

Expert power - which derives from the leader's special knowledge or skill. Subordinates will comply with the leader's decisions and actions because they perceive him or her to know better, or to be more experienced, or to be more effectively equipped to deal with situations characterized by novelty, uncertainty, or risk.

Referent power or personal "charisma" - which derives from features of the personality or character of the leader, and which can be used to command the respect, admiration, or compliance of others. Followers may wish to identify with the leader, to whom they will refer as a desirable role model or example. The special case of the concept of "charisma" as a source of leadership influence and power is dealt with in a later section of this chapter.

PERSONAL TRAITS AND QUALITIES

Some studies of leadership have focused on the *personal traits or qualities* that appear to be correlated with people's perceptions of effective leadership. Early studies identified such personal traits and qualities as:

- the possession of above average competence.
- the possession of effective interpersonal and social skills.
- the ability to inspire others.
- good health.
- the possession of abundant initiative and enthusiasm.
- the possession of self-confidence and self-assurance.

Later studies place emphasis on such personal traits and qualities as:

The "helicopter factor" - the possession of which describes the ability of the leader to rise above the detail of a situation and to see it as a whole entity within its wider context.

Determination - which Northouse describes as 'the desire to get the job done and includes characteristics such as initiative, persistence, dominance, and drive. Individuals with determination are willing to assert themselves, they are proactive, and they have the capacity to persevere in the face of obstacles. Being determined includes showing dominance at times and in certain situations where followers need to be directed' (p. 19).

Integrity - which indicates personal honesty and trustworthiness. Northouse comments (p. 20) that 'individuals who adhere to a strong set of principles and take responsibility for their actions are exhibiting integrity. Leaders with integrity inspire confidence in others because they can be trusted to do what they say they are going to do' (p. 20).

Intelligence - as for instance indicated by the possession of effective perception, reasoning, judgement, communication, and decision-making skills relative to the needs of the situation and the group.

Self-confidence - by which the individual is self-assured about his or her own capability and competence; and is certain and comfortable in the application of this capability in the leadership situation.

Sociability - Northouse comments that leaders who demonstrate sociability 'are friendly, outgoing, courteous, tactful and diplomatic. They are sensitive to others' needs and show concern for their well-being. Social leaders have good interpersonal skills and create co-operative relationships with their followers' (p. 20). They are therefore likely to possess a high degree of *emotional intelligence.*

Attention to detail - Peters and Waterman (1982) and Peters and Austin (1986) add attention to detail to the list of personal qualities appropriate to leadership. They suggest that leaders may have to be comfortable with detail as well as with broad issues. This is demonstrated by:-

- their ability to perform the detailed tasks that they require their subordinates to carry out; or at least to show an understanding of the relevance of these tasks. This is *leadership by example.*

- their identification and empathy with, and respect for the routines of their subordinates. Leaders who downgrade the importance of detail, or who appear contemptuous of day-to-day routines, may be perceived by subordinates as arrogant. Such behaviour may be perceived to be inappropriate to the requirements of effective leadership.

Other personal traits and qualities might include:

❑ a depth of professional or technical knowledge, experience, and expertize.

❑ an ability to deal or work with a wide variety of different kinds of people and attitudes.
❑ an ability to think and to respond quickly, as circumstances require.
❑ an ability to think laterally or to act unconventionally, as circumstances require.
❑ communication fluency and effectiveness.
❑ effective or persuasive self-presentation.
❑ decisiveness.
❑ effective professional judgement.
❑ originality or creativity of thought and action.
❑ professionalism or professional prestige.

Proponents of trait models of leadership may suggest that the use of personal traits and qualities must be *appropriate to the situation* to which they are being applied. Thus, for example, an individual might exhibit decisiveness and self-confidence in a crisis situation where others expect clear leadership. But where there is a need to make a complex technical judgement in an uncertain situation whose outcome is dependent on the exercise of a wide range of expert power, (i) the leader's professional credibility and prestige, and (ii) his or her ability to maintain or manage close and participative working relationships with and between other professionals may be seen to be the test of leadership competence.

THE STYLE APPROACH TO LEADERSHIP

A STYLE MODEL OF LEADERSHIP BEHAVIOUR

The style approach emphasizes the *behaviour* of the leader. It focuses on what leaders *do*, and on how they *act*. The style approach may be illustrated by the use of Tannenbaum and Schmidt's 1958 model.

Tannenbaum and Schmidt's Authoritarian-Democratic Leadership Model

Tannenbaum and Schmidt proposed a *continuum* along which leadership behaviour choices may vary. At one extreme there will be high power distance, "boss-centred" leadership characterized by high levels of authority, prescription, and control. At the other extreme there will be low power distance, "subordinate-centred" leadership characterized by consultative and facilitatory behaviour.

Tannenbaum and Schmidt identify four distinct styles of leadership behaviour along this continuum. These are:

Style one - the leader *tells*. The leader makes decisions on a unilateral, authoritarian, or absolutist basis and expects his or her subordinates to implement these decisions without question. Subordinates are merely perceived in this case as "tools of implementation".

Style two - the leader *sells*. The leader makes the decisions but tries to persuade subordinates that these decisions are the right ones, and that it is in their best interest to accept them and implement them.

Style three - the leader *consults*. The leader makes the decision after a process of consultation and discussion with the group. It is the leader's responsibility to listen to subordinate opinion and comment. But it is also the leader's responsibility to decide on the value and relevance of that advice to the decision at hand.

Style four - the leader *joins*. The leader or the group, or both, define the issue or problem for resolution. The leader may then have to specify the parameters within which a decision could realistically be made about it. The group then makes the final decision, for instance by establishing a consensus of agreed opinion, or by establishing a majority view in favour of a chosen outcome.

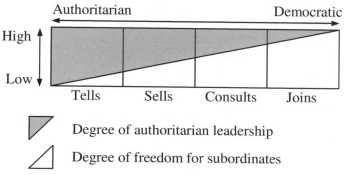

Figure 17.1 Tannenbaum and Schmidt's Leadership Model

Tannenbaum and Schmidt's leadership model is illustrated in Figure 17.1. Tannenbaum and Schmidt suggested that a leader's choice of style across the continuum may depend on the *situation* that he or she faces. Daft (2000) comments that 'for example, if there is time pressure on a leader or if it takes too long for subordinates to learn how to make decisions, the leader will tend to use an autocratic style. When subordinates are able to learn decision-making skills readily, a participative style can be used.

Another situational factor is the skill difference between subordinates and the leader. The greater the skill difference, the more autocratic the leader approach, because it is difficult to bring subordinates up to the leader's expertize level' (p. 507).

The issue of leadership style was also dealt with in Chapter 14.

TRANSACTIONAL APPROACHES TO LEADERSHIP

TRANSACTIONAL LEADERSHIP MODELS

Other leadership models may be categorized as *transactional*. Such models focus on the exchanges or transactions that occur between leaders and followers in the task or goal achievement context within the organization. These exchanges are used *to seek to achieve or to optimize the relative mutual benefit to be secured from the transaction*, for instance in terms of such criteria as:

- organizational performance and productivity in pursuit of objectives; or in terms of the generation of value within value chain analysis.
- organizational capability, competence, or competitive advantage.
- leader development.
- leader motivation and reward.
- subordinate development.
- subordinate motivation and reward.
- the achievement of, or the strengthening of the values to which participants adhere (whether for instance it be service quality, excellence, professional expertize, care and concern for clients, or community welfare, etc).

COMPONENTS OF THE TRANSACTIONAL APPROACH TO LEADERSHIP

The transactional approach to leadership may be described on the basis of the following variables:

- the needs of purpose or the task.
- the necessary relationships and architecture.
- the situation.

❑ contingent circumstances.
❑ the needs, motivations, and capability of the individual, the group, or the team.
❑ the path to goal.

These components are summarized in Figure 17.2, and are described within a strategic management context below.

THE LAYERS OF TRANSACTIONAL LEADERSHIP

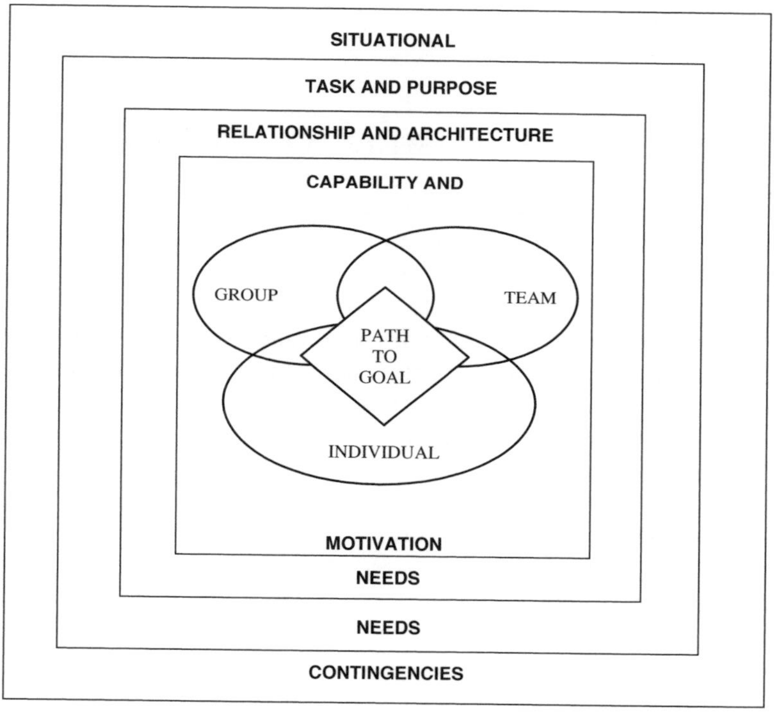

Figure 17.2 The Layers of Transactional Leadership

THE NEEDS OF THE TASK OR PURPOSE

Goal accomplishment is in this case facilitated by *achievement or task-oriented behaviours*. Purpose or task-oriented leadership behaviours direct and assist individuals, the group, and the organization to achieve strategic, operational, or task objectives, so as such these types of behaviour may be categorized as any or all of "result-orientated" or "performance-orientated"; "resource-oriented"; "activity-orientated"; or "operations-oriented". Task or purpose-oriented behaviours include resource allocation; the definition, organization, and structuring of work; the allocation or delegation of responsibilities; and evaluation or control activities that ensure the work gets done to the required standard. These behaviours result from the task requirements of the strategic management process being analyzed in this book, which were defined in Chapter 1 to comprise:

❑   strategic analysis and planning.
❑   strategy formulation and strategic decision-making.
❑   strategic choice.
❑   strategy implementation.

THE NECESSARY RELATIONSHIPS AND ARCHITECTURE

Relationship-oriented leadership behaviours are used to enable and to facilitate the effective performance of the individuals, the group, and the organization within the context of the purpose or task in which they operate. Relationship-orientated behaviours include such activities as the development of architecture and organization; the creation of trust and respect; the development of corporate values and culture; the creation and stimulation of an esprit de corps; team and teamwork building; and staff motivation, management, mentoring and nurturing. Chapter 18 defines the necessary relationships in terms of:

❑   internal and external architecture.
❑   shared values and trust.
❑   the value chain concept.
❑   organization culture.
❑   supply chain relationships.

TASK AND RELATIONSHIP-ORIENTATED BEHAVIOURS

The task or purposive, and the relationship-oriented leadership behaviours described immediately above are likely to have to be based on the premise that the leader's actions towards others *must be implemented on both levels at the same time*. In some situations, the leader needs to be more or less task-oriented; in others he or she needs to be more or less relationship-orientated. A key to effective leadership under these two headings may then be perceived to lie in how the leader understands, inter-relates, balances, and decides to apply these two core behaviours at the same time in any given situation.

THE SITUATION

The transactional approach suggests that leadership behaviour *must be relevant to the situation*. Different situations are likely to call for different kinds of leadership. From this perspective, leadership effectiveness requires the leader *to adapt* his or her style to the demands of the different circumstances faced by the strategic management process. This implies that the leader must:

❑ use the processes of strategic analysis and planning to diagnose and understand the nature or demands of the situation under consideration.
❑ use the processes of strategy formulation, strategic decision-making, and strategic choice to exploit, to manage, or to deal with the conditions faced by the enterprise.
❑ evaluate the likely response of the group and the organization to the implications of strategic choices and decisions made by the leadership.
❑ evaluate the competence of the group and the organization to perform the tasks involved in the process of strategy implementation within that situation.
❑ identify and understand the relative degree of individual, group, and organizational motivation and commitment to perform the tasks involved in that situation.
❑ apply a combination of leadership behaviours that most effectively bring about a congruence (or match) between these variables in order successfully to accomplish the purpose or the task within the situational context that has been specified.

Leadership effectiveness under this heading requires the leader to adapt his or her style to the demands of different conditions or circumstances. That is, leadership choices and decisions are seen to be *contingent* (or *conditional*) on the prevailing circumstances. The situational approach is therefore seen to be *contingency-based*.

CONTINGENT CIRCUMSTANCES

The transactional approach to leadership may next be conceptualized on the basis of the degree of "match" or "congruence" with the prevailing or *contingent circumstances*. It analyzes leadership effectiveness and strategic choice within the context of the degree to which leadership behaviour is seen to be more or less appropriate to the conditions in which that leadership occurs. This is a contingency-based view of the strategic management process.

In order to understand leadership performance, contingency theorists believe it is necessary to diagnose, to understand, and to inter-relate all of the relevant transactional variables being analyzed in this part of Chapter 17 that shape the circumstances in which the leadership process occurs. Leadership in this sense is seen as "contingent" because the approach suggests that leadership effectiveness will depend on how well the leader's style fits the context in which the leadership choices and behaviour are to occur. Effective leadership is seen to be contingent (dependent) on matching, or securing a degree of congruence between the chosen leadership process and the needs of the context in which that leadership is being undertaken.

This section looks at two different contingency models of leadership, namely:

❏ the "best fit" approach.
❏ the "time span of discretion" concept.

The "Best Fit" Approach to Leadership

C.B. Handy (1985) comments that the *best fit* approach to leadership is based on the (*equifinal*) assumption that there can be no such thing as a "right style" of leadership. Leadership is only seen to be effective when there is congruence between the various needs of:

❏ the leader, and his or her objectives; *and*
❏ the requirements of purpose, task or operation; *and*
❏ the situation, context, or circumstances; *and*
❏ the capability, commitment, or expectations of subordinates or the team.

A failure to achieve a degree of harmony between these four variables may render leadership choices or behaviour ineffective. Alternatively, the mismatch between them may be so significant that the leadership outcome may prove to be negative and counterproductive. For instance, there may be significant hierarchical variations in the strategic interpretation of the character and dynamics of conditions of external change faced by an enterprise, whether in markets, technologies, government policy, globalization, or the stability of international political environments. Such conditions of change, uncertainty, and risk may be interpreted by some in the organization to require increasingly varied, flexible, and decentralized management processes in which individuals are locally empowered to drive processes of adaptation and adjustment. Others may however interpret the threats implied by these condition to give rise to a need for aggressive re-centralization; the rigid structuring and control of strategies, priorities and tasks; and assertive and determined prescription by senior management.

Time Span of Discretion

Elliot Jaques' concept of the "time span of discretion" (1976) is based on the premise that a critical feature of leadership capability is the willingness and the capacity to look and think far ahead in time. Long-term time orientation is seen as an indicator of a high level of leadership capacity and status.

Time span of discretion is a feature of the "requisite bureaucracy" described by Jaques. According to Jaques, the proper functioning of social institutions depends (that is, contingent) upon their having at the same time (i) an appropriate organizational and administrative structure, and (ii) the right people to fulfil the roles to which these structures give rise. Only in this way will the objectives, strategies, and tasks that are the purpose of the organization be achieved. This is because (in contingent terms) differing conditions will require different structures and different kinds of leadership.

Jaques contends that organizational structures or heirarchies contain a range of increasingly complicated levels or "strata", each carrying out different levels or complexities of work. Jaques' conceptualization of "level of work" is defined in terms of *the time span for which people are required to exercise discretion* (or the time span for which they carry strategic or decision-making responsibility).

These hierarchical strata are differentiated by time spans of discretion that range from a few weeks, to three or six months, to a year or two, and to the medium or long term (however this is defined). Jaques defines seven such hierarchical strata. These are the:

❑   *immediate* - being day-to-day and reactive to events.

❑ *supervisory* - being responsible for monitoring and controlling operational activities, and responding to events as they occur on a day-to-day basis.

❑ *planning* - being responsible for anticipating and ordering operational events into the future time scales of the organization.

❑ *business management* - being responsible for decision-making associated with the achievement of purposes and objectives established in the planning process, and for maintaining the health and viability of organizational and administrative structures. Business management may be characterized by the need for processes of negotiation at any number of levels, both within the enterprise and external to it.

❑ *strategy management* - being responsible for charting the course and decision-making of the enterprise into the medium to long-term; and ensuring that the organization has the necessary resources, capability, and competence to achieve its purposes over that time span.

❑ *environmental management* - being responsible for dealing or negotiating with wider political, economic, social, and cultural environments external to the institution, and being capable of exercising influence over it.

❑ *visionary management* - being responsible for rethinking, re-conceptualizing, or transforming the purposes and capabilities of the enterprise so as to secure or strengthen its long-term position (or survival) within the external, legislative, regulatory, customer, or market environments it is likely to face.

These hierarchical strata are seen as requisite to the complexity of the task in hand. The complexity of the task will be determined by the number, diversity, duration, rate of change, novelty, uncertainty, risk, and degree of interdependency of the variables and event characteristics that characterize that task.

Jaques contends that these hierarchical strata reflect in social organizations the (statistically predictable) existence of stratification and discontinuity in the nature of human capacity (i) to operate or manage through increasingly intellectual and abstract concepts; and (ii) to deal with increasingly complex circumstances. Thus:

❑ each category of task, interpersonal, and situational complexity is seen to call for a corresponding category of *cognitive capability* (intelligence and competence) in human beings; *and therefore*

❑ complexity in leadership and work behaviour may of necessity have to be matched with an appropriate level of cognitive capability in people in the organizational layer in which that leadership and work requirement occurs.

Leadership aptitude and capability is therefore seen by Jaques to be a function of:

□ personal cognitive capacity and intelligence that is appropriate (or requisite) to mastering the level and degree of complexity to which the prevailing circumstances give rise.

□ the possession of the necessary professional value sets and individual motivation that are consistent with the willingness to deal routinely and in a sustained manner over time with complex (and potentially stressful) situations.

□ the personal capacity (and willingness) to make appropriately skilled use of the knowledge and experience relevant to the circumstances, even if this knowledge is novel, risky, or uncertain.

□ a highly developed personal wisdom about, and experience of dealing with people and entities (this might provide a significant problem for the aggressive, individualistic and self-centred "Type A" personality described in the author's companion Ashgate text *Principles of Management*).

□ a natural and relaxed interpersonal style of behaviour (this might also pose a problem for the "Type A" personality described immediately above).

□ the absence of serious individual defects in personality or temperament, such as an unstable or unpredictable temper, the inability to interact appropriately with people who reasonably question or criticize the received organizational wisdom, poor judgement, inconsistent behaviour, a lack of proper objectivity, an unwillingness to properly share information with others or to delegate, or an inability to work with people from another gender, nationality, or ethnic group. Such defects are likely seriously to damage the leadership credibility of such people in the eyes of colleagues or subordinates.

Jaques suggests that the greater is a person's professional capacity and aptitude, the greater may be the number of variables and the greater the situational complexity that can be coped with. In consequence, the greater may be that person's time horizon and the greater his or her time span of discretion. And the greater, therefore, may be his or her leadership potential.

Jaques comments that the development of personal cognitive capacity is *evolutionary*. Some people reach a final plateau of personal and leadership competence. Others develop an on-going capacity to manage increasing levels of complexity and longer time spans of discretion. As people learn, mature, and develop competence and experience, they may progress through a variety of developmental stages, moving from one level of capacity to the next more complex one until they reach their cognitive (or preferred) limit. This evolutionary pattern may be matched by the increasing levels of necessary complexity to be found in the strata that make up the strategic decision-making and management levels within the hierarchy.

Issues of time and risk were analyzed in Chapters 7, 8, 13, and 14 of this book. The specific circumstances of crisis management were dealt with in Chapter 10.

THE NEEDS, MOTIVATIONS, AND CAPABILITY OF THE INDIVIDUAL, THE GROUP, OR THE TEAM

The transactional approach to leadership requires an assessment and an understanding of the needs, motivations, and capability of individual followers, the group, or the team. This assessment may be based on an analysis of the following variables.

Task Characteristics and Staff Capability

Task characteristics include the degree of:

❑ task familiarity or novelty.
❑ task variety or diversity.
❑ task complexity, task inter-relatedness, and the requirement for processes of co-ordination, integration, or synthesis.
❑ required accuracy, quality, and control.
❑ task ambiguity, risk, or uncertainty.
❑ time duration or sensitivity.

The characteristics of the tasks faced by the leader and the group will determine:

❑ the required staff capacity, capability, and competence.
❑ the operational structures and processes that are deemed to be necessary or required.
❑ role descriptions, work arrangements, and performance indicators.

- the nature of the required communication, co-ordination, and interpersonal relations.
- required staff motivation.
- workgroup norms.

So, for instance, the leader:

- may have to provide strong direction in situations characterized by task novelty, ambiguity, risk, or uncertainty.
- may choose a supportive or an inspirational role in a situation characterized by clear and unambiguous task needs and high trust, since subordinates know what they have to do and know that they can be trusted to get on with the work.
- the leader may have to build workgroup cohesiveness, and reinforce personal motivation and responsibility in cases where group norms are weak or non-supportive, or where the context is presently characterized by excessive personal individualism.

Subordinate Characteristics

The characteristics of followers or subordinates may be described in such terms as preference for, or a dislike of:

- a degree of external or managerial structure and control.
- personal independence and autonomy.
- social affiliation or group consciousness.
- leadership trust of, and identification with subordinates (which may be unacceptable to both parties in a low-trust environment, or in one characterized by high power distance).

These characteristics may determine the degree to which subordinates or followers find the choice of leadership behaviour appropriate or inappropriate to their task needs and work satisfaction. Thus, for instance:

- subordinates who have strong needs for social affiliation may prefer supportive leadership because friendly and concerned leadership is seen as a source of satisfaction. Such a style of benevolent and concerned leadership is described as *amae* in Japanese, and is still seen as fundamental to the maintenance of effective management processes in Japanese organizations.

❑ subordinates who are dogmatic, authoritarian, and low-trust in outlook may prefer a directive style of leadership that provides structure and clarity, especially where the task or context is characterized by a degree of uncertainty.

❑ subordinates who are confident in their own capability, and who prefer autonomy, may prefer a participative or achievement-oriented style of leadership. The use of direction by the leader in such circumstances may be strongly counter-productive to the task performance and work satisfaction of such subordinates.

Subordinate Expectations and Motivation

Vroom and Lawler's concept of *expectancy theory* (in Vroom and Deci, 1970) suggests that the individual, the group, or the team may only be motivated by conditions or circumstances in which:

❑ they believe that they are capable of performing their work to the required standard; *and*

❑ they believe that their efforts will result in the achievement of the required task outcome; *and*

❑ they believe that the rewards or payoffs for doing their work are worth having.

The objective of the leader under this heading will therefore be to select a style and process of leadership that best meets or best fits the motivational, directional, and performance needs of subordinates described immediately above. This may mean adopting leadership behaviours that:

❑ reinforce the positive aspects and conditions of the purpose and task; *and/or*

❑ remedy negative shortcomings of the context or operational situation.

❑ clarify the goals, personal role definitions, and personal role expectations of those involved in achieving objectives or implementing strategy.

❑ make clear and attainable the direction (*the path*) to the desired objective; *and/or*

❑ remove obstacles or impediments to that goal achievement.

❑ increase the number or range of payoffs and satisfactions that are perceived by peers and subordinates to be available from the task or work context.

THE PATH TO GOAL

The *path-to-goal* approach deals with how leaders influence subordinates to achieve their designated objectives. Path-to-goal theory emphasizes the relationship between (i) the leader's style, (ii) the characteristics of the task or work context, (iii) the characteristics, capability, motivation, and behaviour of the subordinates, and (iv) the "path" or *means* to be taken to achieve the desired outcomes.

Path-to-goal theory is therefore specified to show how leaders may help their subordinates along the path towards the desired goal by selecting specific leadership behaviours that are best suited to (or "best fit") the needs and motives of those subordinates in the situation in which they find themselves. These two components of path-to-goal theory are described below.

Leadership Behaviour Choices

Leadership behaviour choices include:

Directive leadership - which is characterized by low-trust and low-confidence type leadership behaviour based (i) on detailed task instruction; (ii) on the setting of clear rules, regulations, and performance standards; and (iii) on the specification, clarification, monitoring and control of required subordinate task performance.

Supportive leadership - which is based on attention to the human and social needs of subordinates, and to their welfare. The objective is to optimize the level of personal and intrinsic satisfaction to be gained by staff from the task and work context.

Participative leadership - which calls for consultative and participative forms of communication, negotiation, and decision-making about issues of purpose, task accomplishment, goal achievement, employee needs (etc).

Achievement-oriented leadership - which is characterized by leadership behaviour choices that challenge subordinates to achieve their objectives at the highest level of productivity and satisfaction within the prevailing context and situation. The leader establishes performance standards characterized by excellence, and seeks a dynamic of continuous improvement. Collins and Porras (1996) describe this behaviour choice in terms of "good enough never is". Achievement-oriented leadership requires a high degree of trust and confidence that subordinates, once trained, capable, and motivated, will be able to achieve challenging goals.

Leaders may demonstrate any or all of these four styles of leadership behaviour, depending upon the characteristics of the subordinates or the requirements of the context or situation. Appropriate adaptation is seen as the key to successful leadership, as different situations and different types of subordinate will call for different leadership behaviour choices. In this sense, path-to-goal theory is seen to contain the features of contingency and "best fit" described in an earlier section of this chapter.

The Path to Goal

Path-to-goal theory is designed to show how leaders may best help subordinates to travel along the chosen path towards the desired goal. The leader has to select specific leadership and subordinate behaviours that are best suited to (or "best fit") the task and social needs of the situation in which they find themselves. This has two implications.

Firstly, the leader (and the followers, as appropriate) need to define the best available path or route to achieving the necessary outcomes. Given that path-to-goal theory is seen as contingency-based, this means that the principle of equifinality will come into play. A decision has to be made about what exactly is the best path or approach to take, given the circumstances at the time. There can be no fixed rule about the path to choose. Different circumstances may call for different approaches at different times to goal-achievement.

Secondly, the leader may have to take on the specific role of choosing a style of leadership or subordinate behaviour appropriate to dealing with obstacles or impediments that get in the way of the successful achievement of tasks and goals. It will be the leader's job to remove or reduce these obstacles, or to take the responsibility of helping subordinates to get around them. The requirement to deal with such obstacles may take the leader into a situation characterized by the need to develop skills of problem diagnosis and analysis, problem solving, negotiation, lobbying, political behaviour, and persuasion, for instance as described in Chapter 14.

CHARISMA

CHARISMATIC LEADERSHIP

The concept of charismatic leadership is described by House (1976). The term "charisma" is used in a leadership sense to describe characteristics that enable individuals to exercise influence over others by force of personality, reference, or charm. Such charismatic people may be capable of demonstrating exceptional powers or, with the help of their followers, being able to achieve extraordinary accomplishments. Charisma may be described as "a fire that ignites followers' energy and commitment, producing results above and beyond the call of duty". The charismatic leader may be able to inspire and to motivate people to do more than they would otherwise do, in spite of the obstacles to progress that all may face, and despite the need for some degree of personal sacrifice. Followers may over-ride their own self-interest for the sake of the leader, the purpose, the department, or the organization (etc).

In order for this charisma to be effective, it must be recognized and accepted as *valid* by followers in order for them to accept the leader's influence.

Ultimately, charismatic leaders may succeed in transforming the self-concepts, values, and ideologies of followers into those that they themselves hold or promote. In the case of organizations and corporations, this may mean forging strong links between (i) the individual identity of the followers, and (ii) the collective identity of the institution led by the charismatic leader. Followers internalize and take ownership of the values and ideologies of the enterprise and its leaders, identifying with them in preference to alternatives (such as individualism or personal self-actualization) that might otherwise be available to them.

Charismatic leaders may however be unpredictable. Their leadership behaviours may be associated with a higher degree of risk than the other types of leadership being analyzed in this chapter. Their behaviour may become obsessive, overly focused and unreasoning; it may become incapable of adapting to changing circumstances or ideas that do not conform to the leader's mind-set, wishes, or values. This is sometimes a problem in entrepreneurial businesses where the founder is committed to his or her ideas or inventions, and is unable to adapt to external change affecting these ideas. This syndrome is described by Drucker (1985).

Examples of business and political leaders often quoted as being charismatic include, or have included, the following:

- Anita Roddick (founder of the UK Body Shop retail chain).
- Richard Branson (Virgin Group).
- Frank Stronach (Magna International).
- Sir Winston Churchill.
- President John Kennedy.
- Martin Luther King (for example, the "I have a dream" speech).

❑ Mohandas Ghandi, who focused the hopes of his people for nationhood, but insisted on non-violent means of civil disobedience to achieve India's independence.

Charismatic leadership may achieve positive outcomes from which individuals or the organization may benefit. But it may also be used to achieve the leader's self-serving purposes of the deception, manipulation, and exploitation of others, ultimately resulting in the evil done by the likes of so-called charismatic leaders such as Adolf Hitler, Idi Amin, or Benito Mussolini.

Cole (1990) concludes that 'the difficulty with charismatic leadership is that few people possess the exceptional qualities required to transform all around them into willing followers' (p. 214). Nor may it be possible to acquire or develop these qualities by any form of training or developmental activity?

A charismatic model of leadership might possess the features that are described in Table 17.1.

Table 17.1 A Charismatic Model of Leadership

Personality Characteristics	Leadership Behaviours	Effects On Followers
❑ Personal determination and dominance. ❑ Strongly held values and views. ❑ Strong desire or motivation to influence others. ❑ Strong personal self-confidence and self-belief.	❑ Clearly articulate and communicate a vision of a desired or imagined future with which followers may identify, and of which they may wish to take ownership. ❑ Clearly articulate and communicate the values, value system and culture to which they wish to secure follower adoption and adherence. ❑ Clearly articulate and communicate objectives. ❑ Demonstrate personal skill and competence. ❑ Set strong role models for the beliefs and values they want followers to adopt. ❑ Communicate high expectations for their followers. ❑ Develop trust in subordinates' capability and willpower. ❑ Stimulate the output of follower motivation, energy and commitment.	❑ A developing identification and empathy with the leader. ❑ Developing trust in the leader's values and ideology. ❑ A developing coalescence and congruence between the values and beliefs of leader and followers (until they become the same). ❑ Increasing commitment to the leader's goals; and increased allocation of willpower, energy and resources to the achievement of these goals. ❑ Increasingly, the leader's goals become the followers' goals. ❑ Increasing follower self-confidence and motivation. ❑ Ultimate development of an acceptance (maybe unquestioning?) of leadership ideology and behaviour.

TRANSFORMATIONAL LEADERSHIP

TRANSFORMATIONAL LEADERSHIP ANALYZED

The concept of "transformational leadership" was developed by Burns (1978). The concept is based on a process of accessing the needs and motives of followers as well as those of leaders in order better to achieve the purpose of the organization and the goals of the leader. This implies that the leader engages in a dynamic with subordinates that may create an increased motivation and performance through a positive change in the values, attitudes, and willpower of those followers.

Daft suggests that transformational leaders 'are distinguished by their special ability to bring about innovation and change. Transformational leaders create significant change in both followers and the organization. They have the ability to lead changes in the organization's mission, strategy, structure, and culture, as well as to promote innovation in products and technologies. Transformational leaders do not rely solely on tangible rules and incentives to [manage] transactions with followers. They focus on intangible qualities such as vision, shared values, and ideas to build relationships, give larger meaning to diverse activities, and find common ground to enlist followers in the change process' (p. 522). Two examples of leaders often quoted as transformational are described as follows.

The first example is Percy Barnevik, formerly chief executive officer of Asea Brown Boveri Ltd (ABB). Barnevik created ABB out of the merger between AB Asea of Sweden, and BBC Brown Boveri of Switzerland. He transformed the company into a successful global engineering multinational. The development of ABB is described in detail by Barham and Heimer (1998).

The second example is Jack Welch, formerly CEO of the US General Electric (GE) Corporation, whose transformation of GE led to the development of an aggressive and profitable international player, occupying top market spots in many of its businesses. Jack Welch's leadership is described in detail by Tichy and Sherman (1994).

The analysis of transformational leadership in this section is based on the work of Bass (1985, 1990), Bennis and Nanus (1985), Bass and Avolio (1994), Tichy and Sherman (1994), Collins and Porras (1996), and Avolio (1999).

Bass argues that the transformational approach to leadership motivates followers *to do more than the expected* by raising followers' levels of consciousness about the relative priority or importance of the goals (such as customer service excellence, patient care, or zero defect manufacturing) with which they are being presented by the leader. It is the leader's responsibility to persuade followers to transcend their own self-interest for the sake of the team or the organization. In return, the leader will attempt to facilitate a move towards satisfaction of the higher order personal needs of followers, for instance in terms of feelings of self-worth or esteem; the accomplishment of challenging tasks from which experience may be gained; or occupational self-actualization.

Bennis and Nanus studied ninety successful US public figures. They identified four key strategies used by these leaders to transform their organizations. These are:

The creation and communication of a vision that others can believe in and adopt as their own - "vision" is defined in this sense as an imagined or perceived pattern of communal possibilities to which others can be drawn into commitment. Bennis and Nanus suggest that this vision must derive from the needs of the organization (and not just the leader), and that those involved in this organization must take ownership of these needs. As a result, the vision might have to be desirable, realistic, and credible to all concerned. It might have to be simple, understandable, and obviously beneficial. It would also have to be capable of releasing willpower, and creating motivation amongst the people involved. Such a vision might be expressed in terms of quality, care, or service; encompass progress through creativity, innovation, continuous improvement or competition; or in some way be dependent on staff development, experience, or empowerment.

The use of concepts of social architecture - by which the leader actively influences or shapes the nature of internal relationships, trust, and structure; values, culture, social norms, and accepted patterns of behaviour; and perceptions of purpose and identity. So, for instance, an averagely performing service organization, local or provincial government authority, or hospital might be transformed into an excellence-based sector leader. Percy Barnevik's reconstruction of the architecture and values of ABB has been widely documented, demonstrating what innovations and transformations can be achieved on a global scale.

The creation of a high degree of trust within the organization - which may be achieved by the clear demonstration of leadership integrity, and by a relationship architecture characterized by open and honest exchange within the enterprise. Ultimately, all parties to any communication relationship must feel able, at least from their own point of view, to speak as they think best, to talk about things as they see them, and to know that criticism will be constructively given and positively received.

The creative use of personal competence - by which leaders demonstrated and proved their capability in furthering the purposes of the organization and the goals of the people associated with it. Leaders were strongly identified with their work, and their competence and confidence "cascaded" down to their subordinates, who demonstrated their own feelings of confidence and self-worth on a reciprocal basis. Northouse comments that 'in addition, leaders in the study were committed to learning and relearning, so in their organizations there was consistent emphasis on education' and training (p. 143). Transformational leaders may therefore be associated with the "learning organization" concept.

Bass and Avolio describe a model based on their suggested *four "i's"* of transformational leadership. These four "i's" are summarized thus:

Idealized influence - which describes a leadership capability to act as an influential role model for followers, and to command their respect. Such leaders are seen "to do the right thing" (Warren Bennis) and to represent appropriate values or ethics. Such leaders may use this capability to communicate, to instil, and to empower both vision and mission into the group and the organization (for instance to be number one in the sector; to be the best hospital or university; to offer social progress to an electorate, etc). Such a leadership style is likely to create a high level of trust, or to operate in a high trust context.

Inspirational motivation - which describes a leadership capacity to articulate and to communicate high performance expectations to followers, inspiring them to share and to become committed to the achievement of the vision and mission of the organization, thereby creating a total effort that goes beyond self-interest. Murphy (1996) suggests that the transformational leader should function as a 'synergizing force', releasing and combining capabilities and energies amongst those they lead. Ultimately, the leader may develop the ability to create 'a state of achievement far beyond what individuals, teams and organizations ever dreamed possible' (p. 5), for instance by using the resource management strategy of stretch and leverage described by Hamel and Prahalad (1994) that is the subject of Chapter 21.

Intellectual stimulation - which describes a leadership capability that stimulates positive values of creativity or innovation within the organization, and permits the analysis and challenge of received wisdom or established mindsets. The leader is able to create a high trust environment in which the fear of experimentation and failure are eliminated, and in which mistakes are categorized as "learning experiences".

Individual consideration - which describes a leadership capability to create a supportive climate within which colleagues can operate at their best. Leaders might use the maximum delegation of responsibility and authority to empower those subordinates and groups who seek autonomy, advising or coaching them in their work in order to develop their capabilities. Other staff might prefer clear direction and structure; or require guidance on how to fulfil their responsibilities. At the same time, the leader may have to negotiate resolutions to interpersonal or inter-group conflicts that may arise, or to be seen sympathetically to attempt to heal any wounds that may have been inflicted by change. Elliot Jaques also comments that successful leaders are likely to exhibit integrity, empathy, and care. The effective social skills that characterize these leaders may be based on a developed but natural interpersonal style, and personal wisdom about people as well as extensive experience of dealing with them. Jaques adds that effective and trusted leaders are unlikely to be characterized by serious individual defects in personality, stability, or temperament. This issue was dealt with in an earlier section, above.

Collins and Porras' study *Built To Last* was published in the UK in 1996. Collins and Porras suggest that their study identifies the main leadership characteristics of what they term "visionary companies". These companies were all American, with the exception of the Sony Corporation. These companies are described as being characterized by *leadership excellence.* Collins and Porras define such companies, which include 3M, Hewlett-Packard, Johnson and Johnson, and Boeing, as 'premier institutions - the crown jewels - in their industries, widely admired by their peers and having a long track record of making a significant impact on the world around them ... visionary companies prosper over long periods of time, through multiple product life cycles and multiple generations of active leaders' (pp. 1-2).

The Visionary Company

Collins and Porras propose a model of leadership excellence in a visionary company. This model is characterized by:
Clock building, not time telling - by which the organization itself is the ultimate creation. The builders of such organizations take an architectural approach and concentrate on developing the key organizational traits of the visionary company. Building a vision and an organization that can prosper

far beyond the presence of any single leader and through multiple life cycles is described as "clock building".

More than profits - leadership in the visionary company is driven by a powerful internal core ideology, which comprises core values and a sense of purpose that extend beyond simply making money. This attitude of "pragmatic idealism" towards the process of corporate governance and strategy formulation described in Chapter 14 guides and inspires people, and remains relatively fixed for long periods of time. The core ideology is seen as a primary element in the historical and cultural development of the visionary company, and as a source of its long-term success.

Preserve the core but stimulate progress - leaders in the visionary company protect and preserve the core ideology, but put in place a relentless drive for progress that implies development and change in all of the activities inspired by that core ideology. Visionary companies are characterized by strong drives for exploration and discovery, for creativity and innovation, for improvement, and for change.

"Big hairy audacious goals" (or "BHAGs") - the leaders of visionary companies will deliberately set audacious and risky objectives, some of which will "bet the company" (Deal and Kennedy, 1988). Such objectives (for example the development of the Boeing 747) will challenge the whole company and force change upon it, as well as reinforcing the market leadership typically enjoyed by these premier companies.

Cult-like cultures - the company's core ideology is translated into clear cultural and behavioural patterns. These cultural and ideological patterns are imposed on people in the organization, who are screened and indoctrinated into conformity and commitment to them. There are high levels of expected commitment; those who cannot accept the prevailing culture will leave or be fired. Visionary companies tend to be more demanding of their employees and managers than other companies. But those who can cope may develop a strong sense of working for an élite organization, which in turn has an effect on the calibre of people who can be attracted and recruited. Visionary companies may be regarded as ultimate employers who are in a position to recruit "the best" of the right kind of people.

Try a lot of stuff and keep what works - visionary companies exhibit high levels of action and experimentation, whether unplanned or emergent in character, that produce new or unexpected paths of progress. This evolutionary progress may be opportunistic and equifinal in character; accepts the value of trial-and-error and chance discovery; and rejects "not invented here" limitations for instance on the strategic management of knowledge, technology, process, innovation, or change. Individual employees are encouraged and empowered to seek new paths and new ways of doing things.

Home grown management - the leaders of visionary companies select, develop, and promote managerial talent from inside the company to a greater degree than other organizations. This brings to senior levels only those who have spent considerable time being socialised into, and internalizing the core ideology of the company. This has the effect of preserving and reinforcing the core ideology, and bringing about continuity. For instance, in commenting on the track record and succession planning of the US General Electric (GE) Corporation, Collins and Porras comment that 'to have a Welch-calibre CEO is impressive. To have a century of Welch-calibre CEOs all grown from inside … that is one key reason why GE is a visionary company' (p. 171).

Good enough never is - the visionary companies are characterized by an ethic of continuous self-improvement, with the aim of doing better and better in the future. This helps to stimulate progress. The search for improvement becomes a way of life - a habit of mind and action. Collins and Porras suggest that excellent performance comes naturally to the visionary company as a result of a never-ending cycle of self-stimulated improvement and investment for the future. One consequence of this ethic is that leadership in visionary companies tends to install powerful mechanisms to create discomfort and to obliterate complacency. As a result, such companies may not be "comfortable" or "easy" places in which to work!

Tichy and Sherman's Analysis

Tichy and Sherman's account of the US General Electric (GE) Corporation was published in the UK in 1994. This in-depth and influential work describes the transformation of the GE Corporation under its former CEO, Jack Welch, and sparked a major renewal of academic and practitioner interest in corporate leadership. This section of Chapter 17 is based upon direct quotations from Tichy and Sherman and from Jack Welch.

Jack Welch and leadership:-

'Welch's six rules:
- control your destiny, or someone else will.
- face reality as it is, not as it was or as you wish it were.
- be candid with everyone.
- don't manage, lead.

- change before you have to.
- 'if you don't have a competitive advantage, don't compete' (p. 15).
- 'you don't get anywhere if you keep changing your ideas. The only way to change people's minds is with consistency. Once you get the ideas, you keep refining and improving them; the more simply your idea is defined, the better it is. And you keep communicating. Consistency, simplicity, and repetition is what it's all about' (pp. 255-256).

Vision and leadership:-

'Somehow, the leader and the led have to define a vision that everyone can share' (p. 181).

'A company should define its vision and destiny in broad but clear terms' (p. 298).

'Look at Winston Churchill and Franklin Roosevelt: they said, "this is what it's going to be". And then they did it. Big, bold changes, forcefully articulated. When you get leaders who confuse popularity with leadership, who just nibble away at things, nothing changes' (p. 298).

'In the new culture, the role of a leader is to express a vision, get buy-in, and implement it. That calls for open, caring relations with employees, and face-to-face communication. People who cannot convincingly articulate a vision won't be successful' (p. 248).

Vision and emotional energy:-

'In the years ahead, corporations will sort themselves out into those that can compete on the playing field of global business, and those that either sell out or fail. Winning will require the kind of skill, speed, and dexterity that can only come from an emotionally energised work force. Bureaucratic corporations instead respond sluggishly to environmental changes. Businesses organized on the old scientific model still build their best ideas into systems instead of encouraging employees to think for themselves. You can recognize such companies by the listlessness of their workers, who lack the conviction, spirit, and drive that characterizes champions in any field of endeavour' (p. 73).

'The old managerial habit of imposing ideas on employees transforms concepts into rules, stripping them of their vitality. Workers change their behaviour but not their minds' (p. 73).

'The world ... will not belong to "managers" or those who can make the numbers dance. The world will belong to passionate, driven leaders - people who not only have enormous amounts of energy but who can energise those whom they lead' (p. 182).

'Executives have substantial power over employees, but they can't tell people what to believe. Creating the pumped-up, turned-on ... workforce that Welch envisions requires an honest intellectual exchange between bosses and subordinates - conducted as a dialogue of equals. Welch calls this "leading while being led"' (p. 75).

'One of Welch's main goals ... has been to stimulate positive emotional energy in subordinates. He says he wants "turned on people"' (p. 62).

The values represented by the vision:-

'The goal was to implant and nourish the values Welch cherishes: self-confidence, candour, and an unflinching willingness to face reality, even when it's painful' (p. 4).

'The new organisation at GE ... depends on shared values ... the values-based organisation ... derives its efficiency from consensus: workers who share their employer's goals don't need much supervision' (p. 4).

'The most effective competitors in the twenty-first century will be the organisations that learn how to use shared values to harness the emotional energy of employees. As speed, quality, and productivity become more important, corporations need people who can instinctively act the right way, without instructions, and who feel inspired to share their best ideas with their employers. That calls for emotional commitment. You can't get it by pointing a gun. You can't buy it, no matter how much you pay. You've got to earn it, by standing for values that other people want to believe, want to identify with, and by consistently acting on those values' (p. 195).

'Welch pushes values because that's the way to get results. Delegating more of the control function to individuals ... reduces the need for reports, reviews, and other external mechanisms. A boundaryless organization can achieve the same level of control as a hierarchical one - but at less cost, with less friction, and faster' (p. 195).

OTHER LEADERSHIP ISSUES

REPRESENTATIONAL LEADERSHIP ROLES AND CHAMPIONING

The leader may also have to fulfil *representational* and *championing roles* within the strategic management process. These include the following.

Acting as a Champion within the Organization

A prime strategic role of any leader will be to develop and to reinforce a culture in which the values and mission of the enterprise can take root and prosper, and in which the purpose of the institution can be achieved. The leader may be responsible for protecting the organization's culture from negative influences, whether internal or external. At the same time, the leader as champion will want (as appropriate) to encourage or to protect such behaviours as:

❑ the development of the knowledge base and technology of the enterprise.
❑ experimentation.
❑ unconventional thinking.
❑ creativity and innovation.
❑ risk-taking.
❑ the positive implementation of necessary change.

The leader may also need to manage the incidence and consequences of *failure*. Failures are inevitable in any organization, particularly where tasks are characterized by ambiguity, novelty, risk, or uncertainty. Leadership may have to create a climate and a culture in which the fear of risk-taking and failure are removed; and failure conceptualized as a learning process on an incremental path of evolving experience and progress towards the future. This issue has been dealt with in earlier sections of this chapter. It is also analyzed in Chapter 19.

Acting as a Role Model and Exemplar within the Organization

The leader may serve as a *role model* for the organization's staff, embodying the values, culture, and purpose of the institution. The leader may constitute the benchmark for what the enterprise (i) wants its staff to emulate, and (ii) to put into practice in daily work and interpersonal relationships.

At the same time, the leader may act as an *exemplar*, especially to subordinate staff, to candidates for staff development or promotion, and to newcomers. In this sense, the leader can be perceived to be in an analogous position to that of a "parent". Subordinates and newcomers may view the leader's behaviour as an example from which they should learn or which they might wish to emulate. Or instead, they may reject the leader's behaviour because they think that the role model or values being offered are inappropriate. The leader's behaviour provides a standard or yardstick against which to measure their own perceptions of what it is desirable to emulate. Handy notes that 'we cannot avoid the role of model once we have any importance in the world. Since modelling is thrust upon us it would be well for us to consider what forms of behaviour, what attitudes and values we represent. If we are seen as effective then these behaviours and values will be imitated, if ineffective they will be shunned. Either way we influence behaviour' (p. 113).

Acting as Ambassador, Figurehead, and Representative within the Enterprise

The leader may act as a *symbol* for the group, thereby providing a focus for group unity. At the same time, as ambassador and representative the leader represents the purpose, the task, and the group:

❑   to peers in the organization.
❑   to superordinates.

The leader may attempt to negotiate with peers and superordinates *outcomes* that are best for the task and for the group. These outcomes should in path-goal terms (and from the viewpoint of the leader) provide the minimum level of constraint on the working of the group, maximize group discretion and freedom, and facilitate group achievement. At the same time, the leader may try to filter out any obstacle or threat from negative influences external to the group, thereby facilitating (or "easing") its task performance, its movement along the chosen path, the creation of its outputs, and the visible achievement of its required performance measures.

Group effectiveness may then in turn be a function of subordinate perception of the leader's influence with peers and superordinates. The more effective is the leader perceived by group members to be in *championing* the group and its task, attaining favourable decisions and achieving rewards, the more motivated may be the group and the more respected the leader.

Similarly, the success of the group in meeting or exceeding its performance criteria may depend on the effectiveness of the leader in representing the group to peers and superordinates. As a result of the leader's activities, superiors may come to perceive the group in a positive light. They may come to believe that the leader and the group can be left alone "to get on with the business". At the same time, they may favour the group with additional resources. The group and its task will be managed by the leader into a stronger position than other groups who are not represented so effectively, and who do not enjoy the same level of superordinate trust.

Acting as Ambassador, Figurehead, Champion, and Representative within the Organization's External Environment

The leader may represent and champion the organization, its path to goal, its values, and its reputation within the wider external environment.

The leader may champion the interests of the enterprise; or act in a persuasive or negotiating role in dealings with customers, clients, stakeholders, government or the wider community. This may require the leader to develop the necessary negotiating skills to undertake such a role; and to engage in appropriate forms of political and lobbying behaviour to further the interests of the enterprise. Such behaviours are, for instance, closely associated with the workings of the European Union, the North American Free Trade Association, NATO, and the World Trade Organization (etc).

LEADERSHIP AS STRATEGIC ASSET

A strategic asset was defined in Chapter 4 as a feature of competitive advantage that is unavailable or inaccessible to competitors. It may prove impossible to copy or replicate this asset. The competent implementation of strategic leadership may come into this category.

Leadership may in terms of the content of this chapter become strategic assets where leaders are able to demonstrate any or all of the following:

❑ the effective inter-relationship and synthesis of the various requirements of the strategic management and leadership processes being described in this book.
❑ the appropriate choice and implementation of leadership model or methodology.
❑ the appropriate understanding of, and adaptation to the relevant contingent variables.
❑ the appropriate implementation of leadership influence, style, and process.
❑ the creation of motivation and commitment on the part of others towards the vision, values, purposes, and tasks of the organization.
❑ the representation and championing that is pre-requisite to successful strategy implementation within the enterprise.

Such leadership may create conditions of commitment and progress within the enterprise that other organizations, however similar their stock of human, financial and physical resources, cannot match. It is the leadership of the enterprise that differentiates it from its competitors, and creates a level of competitive advantage that it may be impossible for those competitors to match.

Leaders who, however controversial their decisions, might be categorized as strategic assets include Jack Welch of the US GE corporation, George Davies (the founder of the UK's "Next" clothing retail chain), Richard Branson of the Virgin Group, Philip Green of the UK Arcadia clothing retail chain, Soichiro Honda (the founder of Honda Motors), Anita Roddick of the "Body Shop", Alan Sugar of "Amstrad", Konosuke Matsushita (founder of the Matsushita Electric Industrial Company), or Sir Arnold Weinstock of the former UK GEC company. The leadership of these individuals was, or remains, a key source of competitive advantage to their enterprises.

REVIEW QUESTIONS

1. What is leadership? Why is leadership a key component of the processes of strategy implementation and strategic management being analyzed in this book?
2. Describe some of the sources of leadership influence and power.

3. What personal traits and qualities are stated to be associated with leadership capability?
4. What is transactional leadership? Analyze and comment on the transactional conceptualization of leadership, and on some of its components. How may the transactional approach to leadership be applied in a strategic management context?
5. Explain and comment on the relevance of Elliot Jaques' concept of "time span of discretion" to the conceptualization of leadership and strategic management.
6. Describe and comment on the concept of charismatic leadership within a strategic management context.
7. What is transformational leadership? Analyze and comment on the transformational conceptualization of leadership. How may the transformational approach to leadership be applied in a strategic management context?
8. Describe and comment on the representational and championing roles of the leader.
9. In what ways may enterprise leadership become a strategic asset?

TECHNIQUES OF CASE STUDY AND ANALYSIS

Where the appropriate information is available:

1. Are any leaders evident in the case study?
2. If so, what is their apparent role? In what ways do they provide leadership?
3. What impact does this leadership appear to have on the strategic management of the case company?
4. What impact does this leadership appear to have on the performance or success of the case company?

PROJECT ASSIGNMENT

Research, analyze and comment on the leadership contribution of a named individual in a company or organization in which you have an interest. Use published information or key informant interviews.

References

Armstrong, M. (1990) *How to be an Even Better Manager*, Kogan Page, London.
Avolio, B.J. (1999) *Full Leadership Development: building the vital forces in organizations*, Sage, Thousand Oaks, CA.
Barham, K. and C. Heimer (1998) *ABB: the dancing giant*, Pitman, London.
Bass, B.M. (1985) *Leadership and Performance Beyond Expectations*, Free Press, New York.
Bass, B.M. (1990) "From transactional to transformational leadership: learning to share the vision", *Organizational Dynamics*, Vol 18, pp. 19-31.
Bass, B.M. and B.J. Avolio (1994) *Improving Organizational Effectiveness Through Transformational Leadership*, Sage, Thousand Oaks, CA.
Bennis, W. and B. Nanus (1985) *Leaders: the strategies for taking charge*, Harper & Row, New York.
Bennis, W. and R. Townsend (1995) *Reinventing Leadership*, Piatkus, London.
Burns, J.M. (1978) *Leadership*, Harper and Row, New York.
Cole, G.A. (1990) *Management: theory and practice*, DP Publications, London.
Collins, J.C. and J.I. Porras (1996) *Built To Last*, Century Business, London.
Daft, R.L. (2000) *Management*, Dryden, Fort Worth, TX.
Deal, T. and A.A. Kennedy (1988) *Corporate Cultures*, Penguin, London.
Drucker, P. (1985) *Innovation and Entrepreneurship*, Heinemann, London.
Goldsmith, W. and D. Clutterbuck (1997) *The Winning Streak Mark II*, Orion Books, London.
Hamel, G. and C.K. Prahalad (1994) *Competing for the Future*, Harvard University Press, Boston, Mass.
Handy, C.B. (1985) *Understanding Organizations*, Penguin, London.
House, R.J. (1976) "A theory of charismatic leadership", in J.G. Hunt & L.L. Larson (eds), *Leadership: the cutting edge* (pp. 189-207), Southern Illinois University Press, Carbondale.
Jaques, E. (1976) *A General Theory of Bureaucracy*, Heinemann, London.
Morden, A.R. (2004) *Principles of Management (2nd Edition)*, Ashgate, Aldershot.
Morden, A.R. (1997a) "Leadership as competence", *Management Decision*, Vol 35, No 7.
Morden, A.R. (1997b) "Leadership as vision", *Management Decision*, Vol 35, No 9.
Morden, A.R. (1997c) 'Built to Last': paradigm or panacea?' *International Journal of Value-Based Management*, Vol 10, No 1.
Murphy, E.C. (1996) *Leadership IQ*, Wiley, New York.
Northouse, P.G. (2001) *Leadership: theory and practice*, Sage, Thousand Oaks, CA.
Peters, T. and N. Austin (1986) *A Passion for Excellence*, Fontana, London.
Peters, T. and R.H. Waterman (1982) *In Search of Excellence*, Harper & Row, New York.
Tannenbaum, R. and W. Schmidt (1958) "How to choose a leadership pattern", *Harvard Business Review*, March-April.
The European Foundation for Quality Management (1999), *The EFQM Excellence Model*, EFQM, Brussels.
Tichy, N.M. and S. Sherman (1994) *Control Your Own Destiny or Someone Else Will*, Harper Business, New York.
Vroom, V.H. and E.L. Deci (eds), (1970) *Management and Motivation*, Penguin, London.

PART FOUR

STRATEGY CHOICE AND IMPLEMENTATION

Part Four of this book analyses a variety of alternative strategies from which enterprise management may choose in order to fulfil the mission and achieve the objectives described in Part Three. Part Four also deals with key implementation issues.

Decision-makers will have to select the best choice of strategy from the various options available to them, given the findings of the strategic analysis described in Part One; given an understanding of the relevant critical success factors; and given the features of the knowledge, the technology, and the competition strategies described in Part Four that provide the strategic foundations of the enterprise itself.

The enterprise will then have to implement its choice of strategies within the parameters identified by the process of strategic analysis; and given the prevailing context of the structure, the relationship architecture, the competencies, and decisions on resource application that have been established by the organization.

Decisions on strategy choice and implementation will therefore be informed by the process of strategic analysis described in Part One. Strategy choice will have closely to be related to enterprise capability, to its ability to generate customer value, and to its sources of comparative or competitive advantage. Strategy choice will also have to be closely related to enterprise understanding of its critical success and its limiting factors; and its to understanding of the nature of the constraints imposed by the relevant external and competitive environments.

The nature and outcomes of strategy choice and implementation will be determined by the processes of time management, risk assessment, forecasting, and business planning analysed in Part Two.

The nature and outcomes of strategy choice and implementation will also be determined by the processes of leadership, governance, strategy formulation, strategic decision-making, and performance evaluation analysed in Part Three.

Part Four is divided into three main sections.

The *first section* is entitled **Strategic Foundations**. This section deals with fundamental issues of structure, relationship architecture, knowledge, technology, competence, the character of resource use, and competition strategy. The formulation and implementation of enterprise strategy is dependent on decisions about these issues. Enterprise capability, its ability to generate value, its leadership success, its competitive or comparative advantage, and its operational or financial performance may all depend on the knowledge, the technology, the competence, and the possible patterns of resource use available to the organization. And it may depend on the effectiveness of the management of these key variables over the time horizons described in Chapter 7.

These variables are therefore likely to determine the degree to which the enterprise will be able to fulfil its purpose and achieve its objectives. The *first section* contains the following chapters:

Chapter 18 - Structure, Architecture, Culture, and Supply Chain Management
Chapter 19 - The Strategic Management of Knowledge, Technology, and Innovation
Chapter 20 - Core Competencies
Chapter 21 - Resource Stretch and Leverage
Chapter 22 - Competition Strategy

The *second section* deals with **Business Strategies**. These are the detailed and practical means by which the enterprise attempts to achieve its competitive, product-market, financial, and performance objectives. Decisions about business strategy in particular cover product-markets and product-market position, brands, reputation, and business development.

Such decisions depend directly on issues of resource capability, value generation, competitive advantage, leadership, and the strategic foundations analysed in earlier chapters. The enterprise will make decisions about its business strategy that most effectively exploit its strengths and its resources, its sources of competitive or comparative advantage, its knowledge, its technology, its capability, and its competencies such that competitive, market, performance and financial objectives, or objectives for value addition, are achieved. The *second section* contains the following chapters:

Chapter 23 - Volume and Cost-Based Strategies

The *third section* deals with **International Business Strategy**. This section deals with corporate decisions about key implementation issues associated with the internationalization of business strategy. And it deals with issues of globalization and localization, in which the enterprise has to make decisions about how and why it may choose variously to operate on a local, a regional, or an international basis. The *third section* contains the following chapter:

Chapter 18

Structure, Architecture, Culture, and Supply Chain Management

Chapter 14 looked at the process of strategy formulation. That chapter dealt with the inter-related issues of who formulates strategy and how decisions are made within the organization. Chapter 15 analyzed planning style. It made reference to issues of organizational centralization and decentralization, and to the location of power to formulate strategy and make decisions. Chapter 15 looked at the relationship between planning style, strategy formulation and strategic decision-making, organization structure, and style of management.

This chapter deals with structure, social architecture, and organization culture as key strategic foundations of the enterprise. These foundations provide the context within which strategies are formulated and implemented. The chapter looks at the issue of relationships and trust within enterprise architecture. It describes integrated and de-integrated value chains. It looks at organization culture as a key determinant of the way in which strategic decisions are made, and of the way in which structure and architecture will work. The chapter concludes with an analysis of the related issue of supply chain management.

SOCIAL ARCHITECTURE AND RELATIONSHIPS

Rosabeth Moss Kanter's influential book *When Giants Learn to Dance* (1990) described what she calls the "post-entrepreneurial corporation". Such organizations are held to be appropriate to the competitive conditions prevailing in international markets. Kanter puts forward the view that in order to succeed, Western companies need (i) to act like smaller, more flexible and more focused organizations whose mission has to be innovative and entrepreneurial; (ii) to do more with the same or fewer resources (as described in Chapter 21); and (iii) to do it in close *collaboration* with employees, suppliers, and distributors as partners.

This collaboration implies the strategic prioritization of co-operative relationships and partnerships. These organizational relationships and partnerships are sometimes described as *social architecture*. The concept of architecture was introduced in Chapter 4.

Bennis and Townsend (1995) suggest that a key to competitive advantage lies in the capacity of enterprise leaders to create an architecture that is capable of generating intellectual and social capital, and thus be able to add value. This social and intellectual capital will be manifest in the value addition that results from the generation and development of ideas, knowledge, experience, expertize, innovation, intrapreneurship and entrepreneurship. This architecture is likely to be based on high levels of *co-operation* and *trust*.

ARCHITECTURE

Kay's (1993) analysis of architecture as a source of competitive advantage was described in Chapter 4. Kay suggests that the enterprise is defined by its relationships and contracts with others. Enterprise management will establish relationships and contracts with and among its employees. This is its "internal architecture". It will also establish relationships and contracts with customers, suppliers, and distributors; and with institutions engaged in related activities. This is its "external architecture".

Kay suggests that added value is created by successful collaboration and partnership, so it is the quality and distinctiveness that enterprise management can bring to its internal and external relationships and contracts that will determine the amount of value addition (and hence the degree of competitive advantage and corporate success).

The value adding potential of enterprise architecture will derive from the ability of those who establish that architecture successfully to create and sustain:

❑ organizational knowledge, capability, and competence.
❑ experience.
❑ leadership.
❑ internalized disciplines of motivation, quality, improvement, and control.
❑ flexible and adaptable responses to changing circumstances.
❑ open and useful exchanges of information and information flows.
❑ effective management of external value chain relationships and contracts.

An important feature of Kay's analysis is his contention that architecture (and the intellectual and social capital it represents) can only be created, sustained, and protected from imitation by competitors if it is contained within a framework of collaborative behaviour, partnership, and community. Architecture therefore depends:

❑ on the willingness and ability of enterprise leadership to build and sustain long term relationships characterized by trust and the pursuit of mutual benefit (as described in the next section, below); *and*
❑ on the willingness and ability of enterprise management to establish an environment that discourages (or makes unnecessary) "opportunistic" and short-term behaviour. Opportunistic behaviour by individuals is likely by definition to be counter-productive to the achievement of long-term value generation by the organization (especially where the individual has been able personally to appropriate some of the value he or she has generated). This is also described below.

Long term enterprise relationships may therefore have to be mutually profitable, for instance taking the form of the offer of 'noticeably fatter paychecks' (Tichy and Sherman [1994] p. 217), employment guarantees, high quality pension schemes, or significant length of service based bonuses, in return for personal flexibility and commitment. They might instead take the form of long term supply, distribution, or service contracts framed within the partnership agreements or network arrangements described later in this chapter.

SHARED VALUES AND TRUST

Fukuyama (1995) suggests that the most effective architecture and relationships are likely to be based on *a community of shared values*. Such communities of shared values do not require extensive contractual or legal regulation of their relations and social architecture because a strong moral consensus gives members of the group a basis for *mutual trust*. Fukuyama comments that 'social capital has major consequences for the nature of the industrial economy that society will be able to create. If people who have to work together in an enterprise trust one another because they are all operating according to a common set of ethical norms, doing business costs less. Such a society will be better able to innovate organizationally, since the high degree of trust will permit a wide variety of social relationships to emerge. Hence ... the sociable Americans pioneered the development of the modern corporation ... (whilst) the Japanese have explored the possibilities of network organizations ... by contrast, people who do not trust one another will end up co-operating only under a system of formal rules and regulations, which have to be negotiated, agreed to, litigated, and enforced (if necessary by coercive means). This legal apparatus, serving as a substitute for trust, entails ... "transaction costs". Widespread distrust in a society, in other words, imposes a kind of tax on all forms of economic activity, a tax that high-trust societies do not have to pay' (pp. 27-28).

Fukuyama suggests that a high degree of trust increases economic efficiency by reducing these transaction costs that would otherwise be incurred, for instance in:

❑ maintaining and sustaining an effective enterprise relationship architecture.
❑ holding together large scale and impersonal organizations or networks whose relationships must have a wider basis than that restricted to family or kin.
❑ dealing with inter-party disputes.
❑ finding trustworthy and reliable suppliers, buyers, or creditors.
❑ negotiating and implementing contractual arrangements.
❑ complying with government, trade, or environmental regulations.
❑ identifying, and dealing with malpractice, fraud, or corruption.

Such transactional arrangements are made easier (and less expensive) if the relationship architecture is characterized by trust and honesty. For instance:

❑ there will be a need for fewer control mechanisms within the management process.
❑ there will be less need to specify matters contractually (which imposes a cost of bureaucracy).
❑ there will be fewer grounds for dispute; and hence fewer disputes.
❑ there will be less need for litigation (which consumes wealth but adds little or no value; destroys relationships; and reduces trust).
❑ there will be less need to hedge against unpredictable issues and unexpected events.

At the same time, Fukuyama contends that societies manifesting a high degree of communal solidarity and shared values may be more efficient than their more individualistic counterparts in that they may lose less value from "free riders". Free riders benefit from value generation by an organization or society, but do not contribute proportionately (or at all) to the effort by which that value is generated. The free rider problem is a classic dilemma of social or group behaviour.

One solution to the free rider problem involves the group imposing some sort of coercion or discipline on its members to limit the amount of free riding that they can do. This might classically involve the use of frequent and close monitoring or control (which is expensive; and which as a form of control may be resented by the "non free riders" in the community who *are* pulling their weight).

Equally, but more efficiently, the incidence of free riding could instead be mitigated if the group possesses a high degree of social solidarity. People become free riders where they put their individual interests ahead of the group. But if they strongly identify their own well-being with that of the group, or put the group's interests ahead of their own in the relative scale of priorities, they may be less likely to shirk work or avoid responsibilities. Hence, within work organizations, emotionally competent leaders may attempt to establish a culture of pride, equality, a sense of belonging, a sense of *ésprit de corps*, vision, and a sense of mission amongst their employees such that these people believe that they are part of a worthwhile enterprise which has a valuable purpose.

Lean Manufacturing as High Trust Workplace

Fukuyama describes and compares *high trust* and *low trust* societies. He describes the various types of architecture and structure associated with each type.

Fukuyama identifies *lean manufacturing*, for instance as found in the automotive industry, as an example of the architecture and relationships of a high trust workplace. This can be contrasted with the classic low trust system of high-control operations management identified and developed by F.W. Taylor and the school of scientific management (for instance, see Morden, 2004). Lean manufacturing systems require a high level of trust because, for example:

- ❏ the fragility of the system, which can easily be disrupted, calls at all times for responsible behaviour throughout the network of relationships upon which it is based. This requirement applies equally to employees and suppliers.
- ❏ people are trusted to deal with problems where and when they happen, at source. This is because:-
- ❏ people are trusted with high levels of responsibility and discretion at all points of the supply and operational process. This implies a significant

degree of the delegation of authority and responsibility throughout the supply chain and the workforce.

❑ the use of collective and team or cell based operational structures means that free riding behaviour becomes unacceptable. Group norms become dominant (particularly if pay is also based on them) over individualistic priorities.

❑ the abandonment by employees of traditional lines of demarcation and trade union involvement in the establishment of work practices must be reciprocated by management. This may mean making available the necessary multi-skill and quality assurance training; providing employment guarantees (at least to core workers); implementing single employee status; downgrading or eliminating hierarchical privilege; increasing remuneration as a result of increased productivity; and so on.

❑ there will be an expectation of totally co-operative and trustworthy behaviour by suppliers and intermediaries throughout the value chain. This is related to the requirement that:-

❑ open information flows are needed to make the system work. The free exchange of information will only occur where there is adequate trust between the parties to that exchange. This is particularly true of the network or de-integrated structures and supply chain management process described in later sections of this chapter.

THE VALUE CHAIN CONCEPT

The value chain concept was described in Chapter 4 as a *chain of related activities* from which value is generated, and from which competitive advantage may be obtained.

M.E. Porter (1985) describes issues of architecture, relationship, and trust in terms of the concept of value chain *linkages*. Chapter 4 noted that value generating activities are not independent but inter-dependent. Porter writes that 'value activities are related by linkages within the value chain. Linkages are relationships between the way one value activity is performed and the cost or performance of another ... identifying linkages is a process of searching for ways in which each value activity affects or is affected by others' (pp. 48-50).

The nature and *depth* of the activities and linkages that characterize the architecture and relationships of the value chain will depend on the *scope* or variety of that value chain. A number of *scope and depth alternatives* can be described. They include:

❑ the "core business" or "sticking to the knitting" concept. This is described by Hamel and Prahalad (1994) as summarized in Chapter 20, and by Peters and Waterman (1982). In this case both scope and depth are strictly limited, whilst an attempt may be made to achieve very high levels of competence within a relatively restricted field of activity. This concept is analyzed in detail in Chapters 26 and 27 of this book.

❑ "concentric" or "related-constrained diversification". This is described by Ansoff (1968), Channon (1973), and Rumelt (1974). Scope and depth are limited to a clearly inter-related set of competences and product-markets between which there may be extensive synergies. This concept is also described in Chapters 26 and 27.

❑ "vertical integration" (as described by Ansoff) in which competence and competitive advantage are focused on a vertically deep but relatively limited scope of activity, such as in the petrochemical industry described in a later section below. This concept is also described in Chapters 26 and 27.

❑ "conglomerate diversification" (as described by Ansoff) in which the enterprise attempts to achieve both a depth and a variety of activity. This concept is also described in Chapters 26 and 27.

These value chain scope and depth alternatives are summarized in Figure 18.1.

Chapter 4 noted that the value chain may be *integrated* (that is "monolithic" or "aggregated"); or it may be *de-integrated* ("disaggregated"). Each category is described below.

THE INTEGRATED VALUE CHAIN

The value chain may be "integrated", "monolithic" or "aggregated" in structure. In this case, key value generating activities take place mainly within one organization; or instead within a group of closely inter-dependent and inter-related organizations functioning routinely and seamlessly as an integrated value chain (such as those companies that combine to provide the UK rail service, the US Amtrak, or the Canadian VIA Rail network).

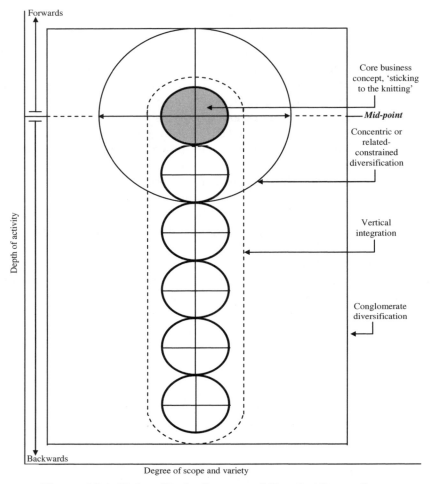

Figure 18.1 Value Chain Scope and Depth Alternatives

Examples of the most extensive integrated monolithic single company value chains are to be found in vertically integrated petrochemical companies which, over a period of many years, have built up a depth of high level internal competences in extractive, manufacturing, logistics, and distribution activities associated with the discovery, extraction, processing, and supply of petrochemical products and services. Such a depth of competence would be difficult (if not impossible) for a newcomer to replicate; contains enormous "sunk" costs; and constitutes *both* a barrier to entry and key source of competitive advantage.

Some advantages of an integrated value chain include:

- the maximizing of value appropriation (no one else's profit margins have to be allowed for!).
- optimal control over, and harmonization of the activities of the value chain.
- optimal security and the maintenance of secrecy and confidentiality, for instance in knowledge-based, high-technology, innovative, or creative activities. For example, "Star Trek" films were made in-house by the staff of Paramount Studios in Hollywood, so as to avoid any "leakage" to the competing film makers of the latest plot, script, or design features.

Some disadvantages of an integrated value chain include:

- the need to develop a range of competencies relevant to the required depth or scope of activity shown in Figure 18.1. This may be expensive and time consuming. It may also constitute a severe limiting factor or constraint where the required competencies are in short supply and would be difficult to attract.
- the maximizing of complexity - for example the formerly monolithic value chains of such companies as IBM and Eastman Kodak were huge entities, characterized by problems of communication, inertia, decision-making delay, ineffective focus, and bureaucracy.
- the risk of "groupthink" and conformity. Closed monolithic structures may suffer from a lack of "requisite variety" and "genetic diversity" such that new ideas or new stimuli from outside are ignored or rejected. Such structures run the risk of obsolescence and entropy (that is, running down or deteriorating as a result of a lack of novelty and an unwillingness to adapt to changing circumstances). This issue is dealt with in Chapter 19.

THE DE-INTEGRATED VALUE CHAIN

The value chain may instead be "de-integrated" or "disaggregated" in structure. Key value generating activities take place across units or locations within any number of independent organizations acting as agents, suppliers, or distributors within a network architecture or structure as the progress of creation of the product or service moves towards its final exchange or delivery outcome.

Johnston and Lawrence (1988) describe the de-integrated value chain as a *value adding partnership* or VAP. A value adding partnership is described as 'a set of independent companies that work closely together to manage the flow of goods and services along the entire value-added chain'.

McHugh *et al* (1995) develop the de-integrated value chain concept by describing the application of business process reengineering (BPRE) to the constituents of the value or supply chain, treating them as a part of the total value generating process. They describe the de-integrated value chain in terms of *holonics* and *holonic networks*. McHugh *et al* describe a holonic network as a set of companies (or partners) that act in an integrated and organic manner. Each company in the network provides a different process capability and is termed a *holon*. Companies are selected to become constituents of the network on the basis of their operational competence and process excellence. The network may be re-configured to manage each emerging business opportunity presented by the network's customer base. Each configuration of process capability within the holonic network may be described as a *virtual company*. An early description of the concept of the virtual company is given by Davidow and Malone (1992). By synergistically combining the capabilities (or the core competencies described in Chapter 20) of many individual companies within the network, each virtual company may be more powerful and flexible than the participating members alone could be.

Some advantages of a de-integrated value chain include:

❑   the minimizing of organizational complexity and bureaucracy. The network may have a simple linear, cyclical, or sequential structure.

❑   the opportunity for any one constituent or link in the network to concentrate and specialize only on its own capability or core competence.

❑   the potential to combine a high level of these individual capabilities or competencies across the constituents, for instance to a world class benchmark or standard as a condition of entry to the network, so as to achieve either or both the depth and scope of activity shown in Figure 18.1 above.

❑   flexibility - the ability to change constituents of the network according to particular customer needs. Ultimately, the virtual company will comprise a network of organizations constituted to meet one only customer need (such as the making of a film or theatre production; or a construction engineering project). The network will be re-constituted as appropriate each time a new contract has been negotiated.

❑ the ability to use specialized supply chain management information and communication technologies (ICTs) to optimize the performance of the whole entity.

Some problem issues affecting a de-integrated value chain include:

❑ the need for trust and shared values amongst the partners.
❑ the need to harmonize cultures, systems, procedures, and processes across the entities that make up the network.
❑ the need to establish effective control mechanisms across the network, often requiring complex ICT based systems.
❑ the need to establish common languages and protocols, especially where the network is international in constitution.
❑ the need to agree or negotiate the relative distribution of value generated between the constituents. What margins will be payable to whom, and how are these to be agreed across the network?
❑ the need for erstwhile competitors to collaborate. Competitors may also have to be partners. Co-operative and competitive attitudes may be difficult to combine and reconcile in organization cultures that were once predominately or traditionally competitive in orientation.

ORGANIZATION CULTURE

Morden (2004) defines organization culture as *the collective mental programming of the enterprise and of its members*. Organization culture is apparent "in the way we do things around here" (as compared with the way things are done in any other organization). Organization culture is represented diagramatically in Figure 18.2.

Some Components of Organization Culture

Organization culture can be analyzed on the basis of five main variables. These variables are inter-related. They are described as follows.

Value judgements - behaviour and decision-making in the organization are shaped by individual and collective judgements about enterprise mission, intent, and ethos. Such judgements are based upon *values*, such as those prioritizing customer, client, patient, taxpayer, stakeholder, or shareholder interests; those favouring quality or excellence in levels of output or customer service; choosing either or both competitive or collaborative values; or deciding between integrated or de-integrated value chains. These values and value judgements shape the priorities of the strategy process described in Part Three of this book.

Vision - defined in Chapters 11 and 17 in terms of patterns of communal possibility to which others can be drawn into commitment and motivation. Vision may act as a "glue" by which to hold together sets of value judgements and ideologies within the prevailing value system.

Value systems - the sum total of the value judgements and vision described immediately above comprises the value system of the culture. The value system provides a wider framework or core ideology by which missions, ethos, strategies, and behaviours are defined and implemented within the organization.

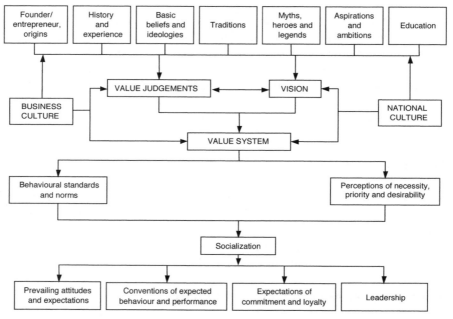

Figure 18.2 Organization Culture

The sum total of the value judgements and vision that make up the value set then shape:

Behavioural standards and norms - which determine the attitudes, behaviours, and "style" of enterprise staff, for instance as leaders or decision-makers.

Perceptions of necessity, priority, and desirability - as reflected in the processes of strategy formulation, strategic decision-making, and strategic choice being described in this book. Such perceptions will, for instance, determine the relative priority of targets for:-

- sales, market share, quality, service levels of patient treatment, the level of crime detection or prevention, taxpayer value for money, or profit performance (etc).
- management control of the value chain.
- increasing the international scope of enterprise activity.
- managing or taking risks.
- acting in an ethically, environmentally, or socially responsible manner.
- acting within the confines of long-established core values and ethics.
- leadership capability.

Sources of Organization Culture

Sources of organization culture include:

National culture - as described in Chapter 28.
Business culture - as described in Chapter 28.
Founder, entrepreneur, or origins - the values, vision, and ideology of the original founder(s) or early leaders may permeate through the later history of the organization.
History and experience - organization culture is continuously shaped over time by the developing experience and learning of the staff who make up the enterprise.
Basic beliefs and ideologies - organization culture is shaped by the basic beliefs and ideologies that underlie the value judgements and value systems already described above. Chapter 22 for instance compares competitive and co-operative ideologies that underpin competition strategy.
Traditions - patterns of individual, leadership, and communal tradition are likely to influence the evolution of organization culture. For instance, a tradition of authoritarian leadership or high power distance management may make the introduction of de-integrated value chains, or the contemporary paradigm of the *"Theory Z" empowered team* and *team-leader based* organization structure and architecture difficult to achieve. The organization will have to make a major transition to a value system based upon a low power distance and high trust style of management of which it has no previous tradition or experience, and with which it may have little cultural sympathy.

Myths, heroes, and legends - organizations tend over time to build up a rich array of legends and myths about the exemplary (or instead infamous) acts of individuals or groups. Such myths or legends serve to rationalize, sensationalize, focus, and communicate the heroic deeds of export sales representatives, paramedics, field engineers, university lecturers (!), police, emergency services or armed forces personnel, credit controllers, debt collection agents, sanitary engineers, or wheel clampers such that they become examples for future generations, or instead targets for others to beat. At the same time, myths and legends have the effect of binding people to the organization, directing their energies and commitment more strongly to its purpose.

Aspiration and ambition - the aspiration and ambitions of founder, entrepreneur, leader, family, president, director, politician, manager, administrator, or employee are powerful forces shaping the values and character of the enterprise. Forceful leaders, motivated staff, or committed teams have driven many enterprises to the "number one position" in their field; or achieved the goal of "being the best in the business". Others have sought to become model or ethical employers; or known for the creativity and originality of their work.

Education - organization values and culture will be shaped by the prevailing type and level of education experienced by founders, leaders, managers, and employees. Educational curricula may (or may not) develop a clear historical, ethical, or international context within which society's evolution may be placed. Education systems may serve to help (or hinder) the development of vocational, scientific, business, leadership, entrepreneurial, quantitative, literary, communication, or information technology skills and competencies.

Educational systems may emphasize academic analysis. They may be based on the evaluation and criticism of traditional and separate subject "disciplines". Or they may instead prioritize integration and synthesis. They may be "inter-disciplinary". They may place an emphasis on local and national preoccupations. Or they may foster the development of language competence and an international view of the wider environment.

Visible Signs of Organization Culture

Organization culture is manifest in a number of ways. These include:

Patterns of socialization - members of the organization are socialized into the prevailing culture over a period of time. Personal and corporate behaviour patterns are modified so as to bring attitudes and values into some degree of accord with the expectations and standards contained within the culture. This process of socialization may affect any or all of:-

- individual personality.
- individual attitude and behaviour.
- group attitude and behaviour.
- corporate behaviour, corporate "style", and corporate identity.
- decision-making and the strategy process described in Part Three of this book.

Prevailing attitudes and expectations - which are shaped by the value system that underpins the organization's culture. For instance, attitudes towards, and expectations of leadership style and managerial performance in decision-making within the strategy process will in part be culturally determined. This may in turn shape the process described in Chapter 14 by which strategic alternatives are generated, and from which choices must be made.

Conventions of expected behaviour and performance - for instance in determining the processes and patterns of leadership, decision-making, and planning style described in Part Three. Centralized and hierarchical structures are for example more likely to be characterized by expectations of an autocratic and top-down style of leadership and decision-making than will be decentralized ones characterized by low power distance, local autonomy, and habitual consultation.

Expectations of commitment and loyalty - prevailing value systems, expected standards of behaviour, and perceptions of strategic, operational, and managerial necessity are likely to give rise to an expectation that individuals and groups will develop some degree of commitment and loyalty to the enterprise and its aims. Equally, processes of management development and promotion to senior positions may depend on (and constitute a reward for) a significant history of personal commitment to shaping and implementing the values, objectives, and strategies of the organization. It is commonly perceived to be in the interest of the organization to reward those who most closely identify with it; and who most closely represent its value system in the strategy and decision-making process.

Leadership - leadership processes promote and protect enterprise ideology and values, and reinforce its culture. The style and character of leadership are likely to be key determinants of the process of strategy formulation and strategic decision-making. Leadership and strategy were analyzed in Chapter 17 of this book.

STRUCTURE, ARCHITECTURE, AND CULTURE AS STRATEGIC ASSET

The concept of the strategic asset was defined in Chapter 4 as a feature of competitive advantage that is unavailable or inaccessible to competitors. It may prove impossible to copy or to replicate this asset. The structure, architecture, and culture of the enterprise described in this chapter may be developed into a powerful strategic asset for instance where:

❑   it is sensitive to customers or clients, and is adaptable to changing circumstances.
❑   it is structured effectively to meet the strategic needs of the enterprise and its external environment.
❑   it can attract and retain (i) the best staff and (ii) the most effective knowledge management, experience, and competence.
❑   its relationships are characterized by strongly positive values, trust, and a high level of long-term commitment.
❑   it has the most appropriate styles of leadership and management.
❑   it generates a consistently high level of value.

Kay comments that whilst competitors may imitate products or processes, it may be impossible for them:

❑   to replicate the structure, architecture, and culture of the enterprise.
❑   to replicate the *reputation* that such an architecture may have been able to generate for itself.

This source of competitive advantage may be strengthened where the structure, architecture, and culture of the enterprise being discussed in this chapter are reinforced by the *leadership competence* analyzed in Chapter 17.

Collins and Porras (1996) give examples in their *Built to Last* study of firms who have created a powerful strategic asset from their structure, architecture, and culture. One such example is Johnson and Johnson, the international manufacturer of healthcare products such as the "Band Aid". Similarly, the capability afforded by the structure, architecture, and culture of the international 3M and Hewlett-Packard companies to sustain a market-leading strategy of continuous technology development and product innovation is widely quoted. The *Built to Last* study was described in Chapter 17.

SUPPLY CHAIN MANAGEMENT AND THE PROCUREMENT PROCESS

The process of *procurement and supply* links (i) organizations who as customers are purchasing goods and services required for their business activity; and (ii) enterprises that supply these goods and services. The customers might be manufacturing companies, hospitals, distributors, government agencies providing services, or public utilities. The suppliers might produce raw materials, may manufacture parts and sub-assemblies, make entire sections or major components such as engines or generators, or provide services of some kind. The components of the supply chain are shown in Figure 18.3.

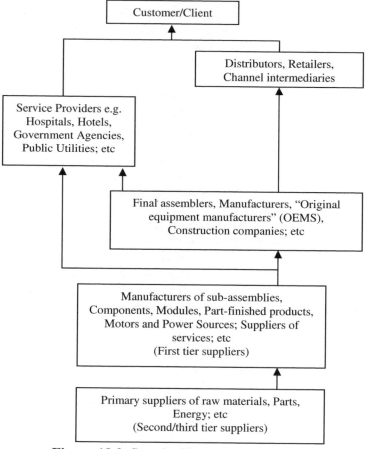

Figure 18.3 Supply Chain Components

In some business sectors it has become apparent that in the case of the manufacturers of *final* or *finished* industrial or consumer goods (such as cars, consumer electronics goods, or electrical engineering products), the process of procurement and supply now assumes major importance. *Between 30-70 percent of the added value produced by these manufacturers is contributed by their suppliers.* In the case of Toyota, this figure is as high as 75 percent. So it has become vital that the process by which this added value is generated (and which mainly depends on outside firms), is carefully organized. This process of procurement and supply is now termed *supply chain management.* The supply chain management issue has become a *critical success factor* to many organizations, whether in the private or the public sector.

The supply chain management concept represents the re-thinking or re-engineering of the procurement and supply process. It implies for instance the positive and strategic management of the relationship between the final manufacturers described immediately above, and suppliers in their value chain. These final manufacturers are sometimes called Original Equipment Manufacturers or OEMs.

This proactive and strategic management of the relationship between the final manufacturers and the suppliers in their value chain may for instance imply:

❑ seeking to improve the managerial and operational performance of each supplier. This may be achieved by the final manufacturer through its use of processes of supplier education and training, business process re-engineering, or Six Sigma. The final manufacturer would make use of its own knowledge base or competence to assist this process of improvement. It might use leadership skills and exhortation to persuade its suppliers. Or it might instead communicate a more or less subtle reminder about the supplier's dependence on it for its livelihood in order to achieve the necessary degree of compliance! That is, it may make use of its *buyer power* to exercise leverage over the supplier. Subsequent improvements in the supplier's own performance and profitability may in turn reinforce the motivation to co-operate with this process of change.

❑ sharing the benefits of the improvements achieved throughout the supply chain as a whole, in order to reinforce (or to give incentive to) the commitment to the supply chain management concept.

IN-HOUSE SUPPLY

Companies such as Nestlé, IBM, and Unilever seek to a significant degree to own, to manage, and therefore directly to control the assets, resources, and processes that make up their value chain. Such companies make use of the *integrated or monolithic value chain* described in an earlier section of this chapter, above. Such companies are *backwards* or *forwards integrated* (or both), maybe even controlling sources of primary materials, manufacturing all of the components or inputs they need, making their own manufacturing equipment, or controlling the channels of distribution they use.

This strategy is based on the perceived need for *control*. For example, Eastman Kodak's film and printing paper manufacturing processes are carried out entirely in-house, and the company acts as its own supplier, only buying in raw materials such as cellulose, paper, and silver compounds. It retains highly developed quality management and Six Sigma skills. It believes that in-house supply and manufacturing is (i) the only way to guarantee the product quality upon which its reputation depends; and (ii) is the only way to protect the valuable proprietary knowledge required to make such a consistently high quality product on a global volume basis.

Co-operation and partnership with external suppliers, in the form of close inter-relationship through the value chain, may be rejected because of the fear of loss of control of (i) the valuable proprietary knowledge, (ii) the experience and expertize, and (iii) the core capabilities, skills, and competencies upon which value addition and competitive advantage are seen to depend.

This strategy may be viable (and may constitute a significant source of competitive advantage) where the enterprise has built up an abundance of capabilities and competencies in-house; and can at the same time exploit these individual competencies, and the relationship between them. Such an abundance of capabilities is likely to represent:

- ❑ a lengthy period of investment.
- ❑ sunk cost advantages.
- ❑ the development and application of proprietary knowledge from which competitive advantage is obtained.
- ❑ effective knowledge retention, knowledge combination, and knowledge management, as described in Chapter 19.
- ❑ a lengthy and consistent process of core competence development and management, as described in Chapter 20.

SUPPLY CHAIN MANAGEMENT - THE DE-INTEGRATED VALUE CHAIN OR VALUE ADDING SUPPLY PARTNERSHIP

This section analyzes the purpose and workings of the *de-integrated value chain based supply chain, or value adding supply partnership*. Such supply chains are based on linkages and co-operation between independent buyers and suppliers acting as partners within the de-integrated value chain described in an earlier section of this chapter.

Strategic Purpose

The strategic purpose of the de-integrated value chain or value adding supply partnership (VASP), based on the concept of mutual advantage, includes:

❑   adding value.
❑   generating competitive advantage.
❑   optimizing such customer or outcome values and performance indicators as quality, cost, delivery, innovation, time to market, and customer or client satisfaction.

At the same time, the value adding supply partnership may be used to optimize the creation and application of core *knowledge*, *competence*, and *technology* across the partnership, thereby obtaining the benefits of synergy, combination, synergy, and resource leverage described in Chapters 19, 20, and 21.

How the De-integrated Value Chain or Value Adding Supply Partnership Works

A received strategic wisdom of recent years has been for organizations to identify and to focus on their key capabilities as a means of optimizing the generation of value and competitive advantage. This implies concentrating on the issues of knowledge and technology management described in Chapter 19, core competence described in Chapter 20, and resource leverage described in Chapter 21. Core knowledge and competence underpin enterprise technology, operational process, market offer, or client provision. Increasingly, activities that are not considered to be core, or in which no advantage is possessed, are being *outsourced* to organizations in the supply chain. Such activities might include specialisms such as distribution or transportation, data processing, call centre operations, product or service testing, or the writing of software. Or they might include the manufacture of components or sub-assemblies which may benefit from the economies of scale and experience effect analyzed in Chapter 23, and exploited by the high volume based manufacturers described in that chapter.

What is Outsourcing?

Outsourcing generally refers to the practice by which one organization engages another to undertake certain services or to make particular products for it. Typically this is done when a company determines that it cannot be, or should not be involved in an activity that other firms can do better or at a lower cost. There is a realization that the value generation or the competitive advantage enjoyed by the organization may otherwise be eroded if it attempts to be "all things to all people".

Optimizing Supply Chain Outcomes

There may therefore be a strategy of concentrating operational activity in the component of the supply chain that is most competent to perform that activity. Each component of the supply chain will represent one of the knowledge and technology resources, and one of the core competencies of that supply chain. Thus, in theory at least, the value adding supply partnership should be able to optimize the application of its knowledge, competence, and technology *taken as a whole*. In consequence:

❑   excellent or world class status may be achieved where all of the components of the supply chain possess (and operate to) excellent or world class levels of capability or competence; *and*

❑   the excellent or world class suppliers in the VASP may be used as benchmarks up to whose operating standards other organizations in the supply chain may be brought. Suppliers who cannot (or will not) upgrade their competence and reputation will be dropped from the supply chain.

The use of the de-integrated value chain or value adding supply partnership may lead to the supply chain becoming more substantial or dense in scope. For instance:

❑   it may encompass products, processes, or activities in which the final customer or original equipment manufacturer *would never before have been directly involved.* Car makers do not make sheet steel or plastic, nor do they make tyres. But they are dependent on the quality, specification, delivery, performance, and reliability of such key products. Hospitals do not make the drugs that they depend upon to treat their patients.

❑   it may increasingly include activities that were formally carried out in-house but which decision-makers have chosen to outsource to external suppliers. For instance, some large scale UK brewers have outsourced the bottling, packaging, labelling, and physical distribution of their products. These brewers now concentrate only on the large scale brewing, marketing, and bulk supply of product, outsourcing what are now perceived to be all "non-core" activities.

Once the supply chain is established, necessary knowledge and skills may be transferred from buyer or OEM to supplier. The purpose of this transfer is to make sure that suppliers understand and will be able to deliver their contribution exactly as specified by the customer. They may not otherwise, for example, have access to proprietary knowledge or skills that are required to complete some particular activity which has now been outsourced to them. Large manufacturers or service organizations may also find that they have to upgrade the management processes and quality systems of their much less sophisticated suppliers in order to make the VASP work.

Recent experience shows that the dissemination of final manufacturer or OEM expertize has occurred in major programmes of cost analysis, cost reduction, quality and delivery improvement, project management, and process innovation. Such programmes focus on knowledge and competence related issues of supplier technology and operations management, production engineering, operational productivity, and cost efficiency. There have been a variety of examples in the automotive industry which is particularly sensitive to factors of cost and quality. UK companies such as Corus (formerly British Steel) and Marks and Spencer also have extensive experience of cost analysis and cost reduction programmes involving their suppliers.

One result of the establishment of the de-integrated value chain or value adding supply partnership may be a *reduction of the number of suppliers in the value chain.* The fewer suppliers that remain are likely to be amongst the best in their field. Their weaker brethren, unable to cope with the increasing demands of their customers, will fall by the wayside; operating at the margins of the business or leaving it altogether. The reduced number of suppliers will receive larger, longer-term orders from their customers in the supply chain. This may enhance final quality, and reduce the transaction costs of procurement. It may also increase the margin available to the supplier to re-invest in the process and product improvement, innovation, and management competence required to maintain the position of *both* themselves and their final customer in increasingly competitive markets. The more that the VASP becomes de-integrated, and the greater the inter-dependencies of its relationship architecture, the more is the final customer or OEM dependent for its own success on (and exposed to) the effectiveness of the companies and organizations in that supply chain.

The principle being described in this section may then be taken to its logical conclusion. There will be *single or dual supplier agreements* in which the buyer voluntarily becomes dependent on one or two only suppliers or outsources. In return it will (i) demand absolute guarantees on quality, delivery, price; and (ii) more generally monitor the management, reliability, and reputation of these suppliers at the highest level.

Some Advantages of the De-integrated Value Chain or Value Adding Supply Partnership

A variety of advantages of the co-operative de-integrated value chain or value adding supply partnership model are suggested. These include:

Knowledge, competence, and synergy - the incremental development and build-up of experience through the value chain, the combination of knowledge and competence, and the access of supply chain participants thereto, have already been described above.

Synergy was described in Chapter 4. The interaction between suppliers and the final customer or OEM forms a key part of the relationship structure of the whole value chain. Supply chain management, if conducted effectively, may create synergies between the partners. In this way, more can be done with the existing resources available; or more can be done with less. These concepts are discussed in Chapter 21.

Interaction - the VASP may be characterized by frequent communication, interaction, and the build-up of experience between customer and supplier, at all stages of the procurement and supply process. People talk to each other, and facilitate rapid problem-solving at whatever level is required. Multi-disciplinary teams may be set up between partners, for instance on a project management or Six Sigma basis, in order to deal with issues that need resolution, to carry out joint specification and design activities or production engineering, and to solve emergent problems.

Applying insight and creativity - organizations in a supply chain may bring fresh insights to bear on the issues at hand. This may reduce the potential impact of any self-imposed limitations in the final customer's current "installed base of thinking" (a concept described in Chapters 19 and 20). The various supply chain participants may be able to introduce diversity into the processes of thought and conceptualization by which products or services are specified. This was the case for cycle manufacturers, who were able with the assistance of their component suppliers, to re-conceptualize the bicycle into such variants as the mountain bike or the lightweight racer.

Differentiation - the features of the supply chain may permit the final customer more effectively to differentiate its product. Differentiation as a business strategy is analyzed in Chapter 24. Product or process differentiation may for instance be achieved on the basis of the quality of supplier outputs, particularly where those suppliers (such as the Cummins Diesel Engine company) are themselves excellent or world class in status.

Or the diversity of the supply chain described immediately above, may permit the final customer to market a variety of offerings superior in specification to anything else on the market. This is the case for example of world class suppliers of automotive and consumer electronics products; or of computer manufacturers who use Intel as a supplier of microprocessors.

Quality - a co-operative supply partnership may be used to achieve an improving level of product or service quality. Benchmarks may be applied to participants, and those who cannot meet them will be dropped. Similarly, long-term supply contracts may provide the incentive and the resources required to meet the OEM or final customer's needs for the rising input quality that is driven by the increasing expectations of global customers.

Flexibility - the supply chain may be specified and assembled so that it is capable of speedy and flexible response to changing customer needs. The short life cycles of computer products or toys, for example, call for rapid changes to the specification of manufactured components.

At the same time, the supply chain may be set up to operate on a just-in-time or JIT basis. This has now become standard in the automotive sector.

Cost - the achievement of cost reductions, cost-efficiency, and resource leverage has been a key driving force behind the development of the co-operative de-integrated value chain or value adding supply partnership model being analyzed in this chapter. This model of supply chain management is being used to achieve:-

- increasing value generation per unit of supply; *or*
- decreasing costs; *or*
- both of the above.

The supplier may be in a position to access the benefits of volume production and experience described in Chapter 23. Longer production runs will reduce costs, and eliminate the need for inventory (the supplier knows what it is going to sell and when this product is needed by the customer). If the customer's demand is sufficient the supplier may set up a dedicated operation for that customer. This may be established to supply on a just-in-time basis. Either way, the supplier may then be in a position further to reduce price. This is also a feature of the automotive industry.

Risk - the final customer may be able to transfer some of its business risk backwards to its suppliers or forwards to its distributors. For instance, it may require some of its suppliers to get involved in the financing of new product or process development if they themselves are likely to benefit as a result. This is a feature of the automotive and aircraft industries.

The final customer or OEM may make use of the specialist knowledge and experience of its suppliers in order to deal with issues with which it is unfamiliar. This lessens the risk of dealing with events (such as those associated with the technological changes described in Chapter 19) characterized by novelty, uncertainty, or unpredictability. The expertize of these suppliers will be regarded as a part of the total knowledge base of the VASP as a whole, available for transfer to companies throughout the de-integrated value chain.

Advantages to the supplier - the establishment of a trust-based relationship between customer and supplier may mean that the supplier can look forward to some stability of demand, and can plan ahead. Where the relationship is based on the "open book" negotiation and agreement of supplier costs, margins and prices, the supplier will know how much finance may become available for re-investment in continuous improvement, innovation, and business development for instance as required by the customer. The customer wants improvements or innovation from the supplier. The supplier now knows how much it can afford to invest in the foreseeable future in this process of improvement or innovation.

Some Disadvantages of the De-integrated Value Chain or Value Adding Supply Partnership

There appear to be two key disadvantages to the de-integrated value chain or value adding supply partnership concept.

Firstly, the final customer will experience increasing dependence on, and exposure to a relatively small number of key suppliers. The effective operation of the supply chain depends on the efforts of these key suppliers, and on their continuing commitment and ability to meet the required (and probably increasing) standards required of them.

Secondly, there may be a risk of losing control of proprietary knowledge, skills, capability, or competence (and their application potential) as these are disseminated to supply chain members. Where this knowledge or capability is a key source of value addition or competitive advantage it may be highly undesirable to give suppliers access to it. This may be tantamount to giving the secrets of your business away for nothing! The in-house monolithic value chain based supply process, described in an earlier section, may be necessary for the production of inputs that require such knowledge or competence. This is particularly the case in sectors (such as high-technology electronics or engineering, the creative or media industries, design, advertizing, consultancy, and accountancy) in which knowledge, technology, competence, human intelligence, ideas, and experience *are* the basis of the business.

REVIEW QUESTIONS

1. What is architecture? Why may it be a source of competitive advantage?
2. Why may the relationship architecture of an organization need to be characterized by trust?
3. What are the advantages and disadvantages of an integrated value chain?
4. What are the advantages and disadvantages of a de-integrated value chain?
5. What is organization culture? Why is it important to the process of strategic management?
6. What is supply chain management?
7. What is outsourcing? What are its advantages and disadvantages?
8. In what ways may the process of procurement and supply add value and generate competitive advantage?
9. Describe and comment on the de-integrated supply chain or value adding supply partnership concept. What is its purpose? What are its advantages and disadvantages?

TECHNIQUES OF CASE STUDY AND ANALYSIS

Where the appropriate information is available:

1. Identify features of structure, architecture, and culture evident in the case study.
2. Analyze the apparent implications of these features for strategy formulation and decision-making in the case organization.
3. Analyze the apparent implications of these features for strategy implementation in the case organization.

PROJECT ASSIGNMENTS

1. Using appropriate information, analyze and describe the structure, architecture, and culture of an organization that is of interest to you. In what ways does this structure, architecture, and culture yield value and competitive advantage for the enterprise? How does this structure, architecture, and culture shape strategic management, the strategy process, strategic choice, and strategy implementation in the enterprise?
2. Using appropriate information (and key informant interviews if possible), analyze and describe the culture of an organization that is of interest to you.
3. Analyze and describe your own example of a high trust organization.
4. Analyze and describe your own example of an integrated value chain. What are its advantages and disadvantages?
5. Analyze and describe your own example of a de-integrated value chain. What are its advantages and disadvantages?
6. Using published information, key informant interviews or personal work knowledge, research and write up an actual case study of supply chain management. Comment on the effectiveness of this supply chain.

References

Ansoff, H.I. (1968) *Corporate Strategy*, Penguin, London.
Bennis, W. and R. Townsend (1995) *Reinventing Leadership*, Piatkus, London.
Bertels, T. (ed.) (2003) *Rath & Strong's Six Sigma Leadership Handbook*, Wiley, Hoboken, NJ.
Bowles, D. (1995) "Strategic partnership between manufacturing industry and its supply chain: a key to global competitive advantage", *Unpublished MBA Dissertation*, University of Teesside, Middlesbrough, UK.
Brindley, C. (ed) (2004) *Supply Chain Risk*, Ashgate, Aldershot.
Channon, D. (1973) *Strategy and Structure of British Enterprise*, Macmillan, London.
Collins, J.C. and J.I. Porras (1996) *Built to Last*, Century Business, London.
Corbett, M.F. (1996) "Outsourcing as a strategic tool", *Canadian Business Review*, Summer.
Davidow, W.H. and M.S. Malone (1992) *The Virtual Corporation*, Macmillan, London.

Fukuyama, F. (1995) *Trust: the social values and the creation of prosperity*, Hamish Hamilton, London.

Hamel, G. and C.K. Prahalad (1994) *Competing for the Future*, Harvard Business School Press, Boston, Mass.

Handy, C.B. (1985) *Understanding Organizations*, Penguin, London.

Johnston, R. and P.R. Lawrence (1988) "Beyond vertical integration - the rise of the Value Adding Partnership", *Harvard Business Review*, July - August.

Kanter, R.M. (1990) *When Giants Learn to Dance*, Routledge, London.

Kay, J. (1993) *Foundations of Corporate Success*, Oxford University Press, Oxford.

McHugh, P., Merli, G. and W.A. Wheeler (1995) *Beyond Business Process Reengineering*, Wiley, Chichester.

Morden, A.R. (2004) *Principles of Management (2nd Edition)*, Ashgate, Aldershot.

Peters, T.J. and R.H. Waterman (1982) *In Search of Excellence*, Harper & Row, New York.

Porter, M.E. (1985) *Competitive Advantage*, Free Press, New York.

Rumelt, R. (1974) *Strategy, Structure and Economic Performance*, Graduate School of Business Administration, Harvard University.

Tichy, N.M. & S. Sherman (1994) *Control Your Destiny or Someone Else Will*, Harper Business, New York.

Chapter 19

The Strategic Management of Knowledge, Technology, and Innovation

The heart of an organization is its knowledge, its experience, and its technology. These are key strategic foundations.

This chapter starts by analyzing *knowledge management* in organizations. Knowledge is recognized as a strategic asset with a potentially enormous worth. It is seen at a strategic level as a vital source of value generation and competitive advantage. The chapter defines knowledge, the knowledge base, and experience. It relates knowledge management to issues of structure, relationships, and trust. And it looks at the creation and sharing of knowledge within the organization, in order to achieve enterprise objectives.

The chapter then goes on to deal with *the strategic management of technology and innovation*. It defines the concepts of technology and innovation. It describes technology and innovation as critical sources of competitive advantage, and analyzes some of the sources of innovation. And it discusses the strategic management of new technologies and the dynamics that may be associated with them.

KNOWLEDGE MANAGEMENT

THE KNOWLEDGE BASE

The knowledge base of the enterprise comprises:

❑ concepts.
❑ theories and methodologies (which determine how the enterprise goes about its business or manages its affairs).
❑ prevailing paradigms.
❑ accumulated experience.
❑ received wisdoms ("this is the usual way we do this").

❑   technologies or "ways of doing the work".
❑   values and cultures.
❑   mindsets and attitudes.

Knowledge underpins enterprise:

❑   capability, competence, and skills.
❑   technology.
❑   leadership and management process.
❑   structure and systems.
❑   capability to innovate.
❑   capability to facilitate and manage change.

Knowledge may be:

❑   *"tacit"* - that is, a rich, complex and (to a degree) *inarticulable* entity developed and internalized by an individual over a long period of time; *or*
❑   *"explicit"* - that is a structured and *articulated* entity accessible to many people.

Tacit and explicit knowledge are defined in more detail below. The management of the knowledge base may be:

❑   *proactive* - such that knowledge is continuously updated and maintained at the forefront of its development.
❑   *reactive* - by which the enterprise updates its knowledge base incrementally or opportunistically in response to, or under pressure from external opportunities or threats.
❑   *non-existent* - such that updating (if it takes place at all) is haphazard and unplanned, responding only to direct threats. Enterprise management either does not understand the significance of the knowledge base in the strategic management process; or is instead complacent about it.

Knowledge may become obsolete, leaving an enterprise that fails to understand the need to update and manage its knowledge and technology base in a potentially disastrous (or even fatal) situation. Knowledge (and the *knowledge management* and *technology management* associated with it) may be a key source of comparative or competitive advantage. At the same time, the possession of knowledge may constitute a powerful barrier to entry to a sector or market.

KNOWLEDGE AS ASSET

Knowledge may be perceived to be a key corporate asset. Davenport and Prusak (1998) comment that 'what an organization and its employees *know* is at the heart of how the organization functions' (p. x). *Knowledge, personal intellectual resources, and the organization's knowledge base* underpin the experience, capability, capacity, and competence of the enterprise. Knowledge, personal intellectual resources, and the knowledge base are key sources of value generation, value enhancement, and comparative or competitive advantage.

The management of technology and innovation analyzed in later sections of this chapter will depend on the knowledge base of the organization described immediately above. What does the enterprise know? What knowledge and *experience*, for instance about managing its technology or its product-markets, can it bring to bear in carrying out its activities? Is it able to do new things, and can it innovate? Has it accumulated knowledge about its past and current experience; and does it take positive steps *to retain (and if necessary to protect) this proprietary knowledge?*

The base of knowledge and accumulated experience of the enterprise and its staff may be conceptualized as *social capital* or *intellectual equity*. It may be valued as the difference between the total or market worth of a company, and the net worth of its tangible assets as described on the balance sheet. Caulkin (1997) commented that 'human capital comprises the knowledge and talents that reside only in the human brain - the stuff that goes down in the lift each evening. This kind of capital is rented, not owned, and must be managed accordingly. When Microsoft went public in 1981, it was not to raise money to build new productive assets (it didn't need any): it was to tie the human capital to the firm by monetising its stake ... at the end of 1996, Bill Gates' firm had a market value of $85.5 billion and net fixed assets of just $930 million. A mere one-hundredth of its valuation is captured in the familiar balance sheet' (p. 29).

KNOWLEDGE DEFINED

Davenport and Prusak define knowledge as 'a fluid mix of ... experience, values, contextual information, and expert insight that provides a framework for evaluating and incorporating new experiences and information. It originates and is applied in the minds of knowers' (p. 5). Knowledge is in part a function of values and beliefs that derive from:

❑ the individual's own value set and context; *and*
❑ the value system, culture and context of the organization described in other chapters of this book.

Knowledge management differentiates *tacit* and *explicit* knowledge. These may be compared on the basis of the degree of judgement, interpretation, personal discretion, and value that they contain. Tacit is *high*; explicit is *low* on such a basis.

Tacit Knowledge

Tacit knowledge is a rich and complex knowledge developed and internalized by an individual person over a long period of time. It incorporates accumulated judgement, learning, and experience. Tacit knowledge may be difficult to:

❑ observe in use or application.
❑ articulate.
❑ document.
❑ teach.
❑ render useful for another person or for the community that is the organization.

Nonaka (1991) suggests that: 'tacit knowledge is highly personal. It is hard to formalize and, therefore, difficult to communicate to others ... tacit knowledge is also deeply rooted in action and in an individual's commitment to a specific context - a craft or profession, a particular technology or product market, or the activities of a work group or team. Tacit knowledge consists partly of technical skills - the kind of informal, hard-to-pin-down skills captured in the term "know-how". A master craftsman after years of experience develops a wealth of expertise "at his fingertips". But he is often unable to articulate the scientific or technical principles behind what he knows. At the same time, tacit knowledge has an important cognitive dimension. It consists of mental models (values), beliefs, and perspectives so ingrained that we take them for granted, and therefore cannot easily articulate them. For this ... reason, these implicit models profoundly shape how we perceive the world around us' (p. 98).

Explicit Knowledge

Explicit knowledge is structured, expressed, and accessible to the community that is the organization. Explicit knowledge may be:

- observable in use or application.
- articulated (expressed or written down).
- schematic.
- documented.
- teachable.
- useable by any number of people.

Explicit knowledge is established and applied in policies, procedures, processes, rules, programmes of socialisation and training (etc).

Nonaka comments that 'explicit knowledge is formal and systematic. For this reason, it can be easily communicated and shared, in product specifications or a scientific formula or a computer program' (p. 98).

EXPERIENCE

Experience is a key component of knowledge. Our experience is what we (individually or collectively) have done and what has happened to us in the past. We build up experience by iterative processes of repetition, trial and error, feeling, observation, analysis, interpretation, categorization, evaluation, learning, application (practice) and feedback.

Experience and *judgement* are related. The greater the accumulation of knowledge and experience the more effective may be judgements about:

- repeated situations of which we have had some past experience; *and*
- new situations characterized for example by novelty, ambiguity, risk, uncertainty, complexity, or unpredictability.

Experience may lead to the build up of *intuition* on the part of individuals or groups. Intuition is the compression and internalization of knowledge and experience that permit rapid evaluation, judgement about, reasoning, and decision-making about stimuli or events (such as driving a car; or interacting with a stranger; or carrying out some kind of negotiation, or managing sensitive interpersonal relationships within the organization).

Expertize is knowledge that has been tried and tested by experience. Experience and expertize may serve to change theories or ideas about *what should happen* into knowledge or intuition about *what is actually likely to happen* in reality. Thus, experience can be used to decide what course of action is more likely to work, or less likely to work in any particular situation.

Experience also allows us to recognize and to deal with *variety and complexity*. The greater the accumulated knowledge and experience, the greater may be the variety and complexity that can be dealt with by the individual, the team, or the organization. Hence the need to retain experience and expertize within the organization so that it can be applied to future situations, whether these situations are understood, novel or unknown. For instance, how should the enterprise react to technological changes described in a later section of this chapter, particularly if these changes are of a fundamental nature and indicate a major shift away from an existing technology to a completely new one? Past experience of innovation, and extensive experience with identifying and managing changes in technology may permit the organization to make the right judgements about how to identify and react to the new circumstances.

Reference was made in Chapter 17 to Elliot Jaques' concept of the "time span of discretion", and to the role of cognitive capability, personal intelligence, and personal experience in dealing with the relative level of situational complexity as a key contingency faced by decision-makers.

KNOWLEDGE, STRUCTURE, RELATIONSHIPS, AND ARCHITECTURE

Structure and architecture were analyzed in Chapter 18. Knowledge and experience are "located" in tacit form in individuals, teams, departments, organization structure, and relationships within and outside of the enterprise. Individual members of staff accumulate and apply their knowledge on the basis of their learning and experience. Groups of staff come to share common knowledge that they use to interact with each other in order to do their work. Or the enterprise accumulates wisdom through its dealings with customers or clients, and with those external suppliers, distributors, or intermediaries with whom it maintains the relationship architecture described in earlier chapters, and upon whose efforts it has chosen to be dependent.

Knowledge and experience are also located in explicit form in written documents, programmes, operating procedures and rules, libraries, databases and systems (etc).

There is a key inter-relationship between the knowledge base of the enterprise, its leadership, the knowledge management process, organization structure and relationship architecture, management style, and management process. Each requires knowledge and experience; or is instead a product of that knowledge and experience. The fluid structure of the organization and relationship architecture of Microsoft, for instance, is based on the perceived need in that company for open and dynamic communication and feedback between staff; for organizational learning; and for the continuous and rapid build-up of experience about the company's products that can be fed into the next generation of software that it is writing.

Similarly, knowledge management provides a necessary facilitation and integration of the working of the architecture and relationships represented by the value chain. But effective knowledge management is in particular critical to the operation of the de-integrated value or supply chain, holonic network, or virtual company described in Chapter 18. Communication and feedback processes are central to the integration of such structures, but depend on the definition of how the knowledge held by the different partners that is required to make the structure work should be recognized, categorized, harmonized, disseminated, and applied across the whole.

Trust

Effective knowledge management needs a high level of trust. This implies putting in place the high trust working environment described in Chapter 18. The conception of knowledge and the accumulation of experience by individuals and groups is a sensitive and creative process. It is easily damaged. People will need to feel that the knowledge and experience that they can bring to bear in their work is valued, and that the enterprise places reliance on this knowledge as well as on them.

It may need a sharing of values, such that people involved in a task believe in the same culture or objective, and seek to develop knowledge and experience in approximately the same direction as others in order to achieve that objective.

It also requires *care or the application of emotional intelligence*, for instance about the work and the personal circumstances of others within the relationship architecture. People who are not trusted, or who feel unimportant in the scheme of things, may not bother to learn and accumulate wisdom about what they do. They may see no point or usefulness in personal learning or the development of experience, performing their daily tasks in a mentally-detached or "brain suspended" state! Or instead they may exploit what they have learned for their own purposes, appropriating to themselves a proportion of the organizational value represented by that knowledge and experience.

And hence the likely damage caused to the knowledge base and enterprise experience, for instance as sources of value addition and competitive advantage, from the crude tactics of restructuring and downsizing described in a later section below.

INDIVIDUAL AND COMMUNAL ORIENTATIONS, AND THE SHARING OF KNOWLEDGE

The knowledge management process may in part be conceptualized on a continuum between "individual" and "community" orientations within the enterprise. This is shown in Figure 19.1. The more that there is a community orientation (i) the more that the knowledge and experience of the enterprise are *shared*, and the more it will create intellectual equity and enterprise value; but (ii) the greater the *trust* that must prevail within the community in order to achieve that sharing.

The reverse may also be true. The lower the trust, the less widespread or effective will be the process of sharing information; and the more that valuable tacit knowledge may be withheld (particularly if the articulation, or making explicit of that knowledge by the individual who holds it is easy for him or her to control or to prevent).

A key strategic issue therefore lies in how the enterprise is to achieve an effective dissemination and sharing of knowledge, at the same time as providing conditions by which individuals and groups may be able (and will be motivated) to create and accumulate that knowledge and experience in the first place. This implies putting in place the high trust working environment described above. Such an environment implies widespread trust and openness; and the provision of a workplace characterized by an emphasis on personal and collective creativity and empowerment.

Caulkin comments in this respect that a 'dialogue between individual intelligences centring on tangible issues - whether cutting costs in assembling an offshore oil platform or making better welds - will recombine to produce usable knowledge. The chief resources required for this kind of knowledge work are time and space for the conversations to develop ... and crucially, the community of interest to provide the spark that makes things happen. If the design principles are right, then knowledge sharing is the most natural thing in the world. One of the best-known examples of this kind of knowledge management is 3M. Powered by multiple overlapping scientific networks (communities of enquiry), the "15 percent rule" (which allows employees to spend that amount of time on their own projects), and the governing principle that 25 percent of company turnover must come from products introduced in the last four years, 3M scientists in hundreds of divisions produce an endless stream of new products, sometimes based on brand new knowledge, more often by recombining existing knowledge in different and creative ways' (p. 32).

Snowden (1998) comments that 'tacit knowledge is ... powerful, in that its use by a truly knowledgeable person enables rapid and sophisticated decision-making in complex environments. However, it requires a high degree of trust in the owner(s) of tacit knowledge to be deployed. If that trust does not exist in the degree they feel is necessary, then ... (enterprise) decision-makers will fall back to explicit knowledge which is slower and less responsive, but is lower risk'.

On the other hand, the individual who holds (and can control) valuable tacit knowledge needs to feel that the sharing of that knowledge with others will pose no threat to his or her own personal and career circumstances. Otherwise they may be tempted to remove that knowledge and experience from the enterprise, thereby appropriating the value it represents. They may instead attempt to market this knowledge and experience as a proprietary product or service (for instance as an independent entrepreneur or consultant) on an outsourcing, partnership, or de-integrated value chain basis. Entrepreneurs may of course be well aware that specialist knowledge and experience on the one hand, and *personal reputation* on the other, may relatively easily be inter-related by their clients, particularly if that entrepreneur is already well-established (or "networked") within the relationship architecture of the sector (the issue of reputation as a source of value enhancement and comparative or competitive advantage is dealt with in detail in Chapter 25).

Knowledge management therefore requires the enterprise to manage *in a strategic manner* the conditions in which knowledge is created, shared, and sustained. *Knowledge, trust, and architecture need to be conceptualized as inter-dependent.* They are all a part of the same thing. The strategy is demonstrated in Figure 19.1. The objective should be to move the knowledge curve K to the right. Position K2 is more productive for everyone than position K1.

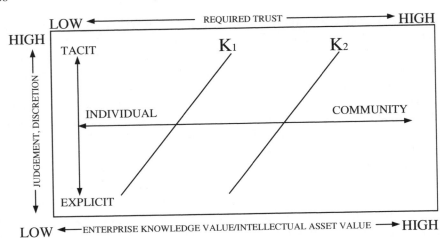

Figure 19.1   Individual and Communal Orientations to Sharing Knowledge

KNOWLEDGE AND COMPARATIVE OR COMPETITIVE ADVANTAGE

Tacit and explicit knowledge, personal and collective intellectual resources, experience, expertize and intuition are key sources of comparative or competitive advantage. Davenport and Prusak suggest that companies may increasingly differentiate themselves on the basis of what they know, and how they can apply that knowledge to do new things or to gain advantage.

Davenport and Prusak comment that 'in their search for new efficiencies, global corporations have outsourced much of the labour of manufacturing to countries where the cost of labour is relatively low ... the knowledge-based activities of developing products and processes are becoming the primary internal functions of firms and the ones with the greatest potential for providing competitive advantage' (p. 13).

This is reinforced by the syndrome of *self-cancelling technological advantage*. It is now difficult to prevent competitors from copying, creatively imitating, or improving on new products, processes, or brand images developed by others. Organizations exist in an era characterized by mobility, the free flow of ideas and information, reverse engineering, and widely available access to technology. Technology *on its own* may disappear as a sustainable source of competitive advantage, because it may eventually become available to everyone. This point is also made by Kay (1993) and is further discussed in later sections of this chapter.

Davenport and Prusak comment however that 'knowledge, by contrast, can provide a sustainable advantage. Eventually, competitors can almost always match the quality and price of a market leader's current product or service. By the time that happens, though, the knowledge-rich, knowledge-managing company will have moved on to a new level of quality, creativity, or efficiency. The knowledge advantage is sustainable because it generates increasing returns and continuing advantages. Unlike material assets, which decrease as they are used, knowledge assets increase with use: ideas breed new ideas, and shared knowledge stays with the (originator) while it enriches the receiver. The potential for new ideas arising from the stock of knowledge in any firm is practically limitless - particularly if the people in the firm are given opportunities to think, to learn, and to (communicate) with one another ... knowledge resources - ideas - have unlimited potential for growth' (p. 17).

This point is also made by Hamel and Prahalad (1994) in respect of the *core competence concept* that is of necessity underpinned by tacit and explicit knowledge. The core competence concept is analyzed in Chapter 20.

At the same time, the possession of knowledge and expertize may constitute a significant (or even insuperable) *barrier to entry* to a sector or market. An effective enterprise knowledge management strategy will protect and reinforce this barrier to entry. The knowledge and experience of high volume feature and television film making, and the creation of popular Hollywood produced "soap operas" and serials has for instance put US film producers in an almost unassailable competitive position in the film industry in the West. Similarly, British producers of popular and rock music use their expertize in writing, marketing and producing music, and managing the careers of popular music artists in order to create demand and maintain market leadership.

KNOWLEDGE AS A STRATEGIC ASSET

Knowledge, the enterprise knowledge base, and the experience and competence that derive from them, may be a *strategic asset*. Kay's analysis of competitive advantage, described in Chapter 4, would categorize knowledge and experience as a strategic feature that may be unavailable to competitors (who will therefore be unable to imitate or copy it) if that knowledge and expertize *is properly retained, protected, and managed.*

Competitive advantage would therefore prevail if competing firms are unable to apply or replicate the tacit or the proprietary explicit knowledge of the enterprise; or must instead pay to use it.

Reference has already been made to the use of tacit experience and expertize by Microsoft, and its control of copyrighted proprietary explicit knowledge to maintain its dominant position in the computer market. Knowledge is Microsoft's strategic asset.   Its control of the creation, selling, and installation of its products is a key source of its market valuation.

The analysis of organization culture provides another illustration of knowledge as a strategic asset. Harrison (1972, 1995) and Handy (1991) identify person-based or individualistic organization cultures. Handy describes them as "Dionysian". He comments that these cultures appear 'where it is the talent or skill of the individual which is the crucial asset of the organization. This is the culture preferred by professionals. They can preserve their own identity and their own freedom, feeling owned by no man'. In such cultures, the individual is assumed to be (or demands to be) in charge of his or her own destiny. The unrestricted freedom to work and create, or to push out (or "stretch") the boundaries of what is known; the low power distance; the absence of external or hierarchical control; and the internalization of personal and organizational control may make such an operating environment just the right place for pioneering (or mould-breaking) creativity and innovation. This may lead to the achievement of large increments in value, or the obtaining of an unassailable knowledge-based market position that are described by Hamel and Prahalad in terms of the strategies of "stretch" described in Chapter 21 of this Book.

KNOWLEDGE MANAGEMENT AND RESTRUCTURING

Management Today commented in 1997 of *re-structuring* that 'knowledge management picks up on and crystallises several of the decade's most compelling management propositions. The first is the 1990s obsession with organizational learning. One result of de-layering and downsizing was meant to be less bureaucracy, more knowledge sharing, faster decisions. In some cases it was. More often, the result was a forgetting, not a learning organization as companies flattened their stock of experience along with the hierarchy and found they had outsourced the ability to make the wheel, let alone invent it' (p. 29).

Knowledge and experience are identified in this chapter as key sources of capability, proprietary and strategic asset, value enhancement, and competitive advantage. This implies therefore that short-term cost-cutting programmes of de-layering, downsizing, rationalization, and staff redundancy (the "restructuring" process described by *Management Today*) are likely to have the potential for severely damaging in a random and unpredictable manner:

❑ the base of enterprise knowledge and experience.
❑ the trust upon which effective knowledge management depends.
❑ the source of capability and competence represented by knowledge and experience.
❑ the source of value enhancement and competitive advantage represented by knowledge and experience.

Processes of random and short-termist restructuring may therefore be described as a potential source of long-term *competitive disadvantage*. These processes are likely to weaken the enterprise and to disseminate its expertize to others who may be able to make competitive use of it. Ultimately, processes of random and short-termist restructuring might be categorized as acts of significant strategic incompetence and leadership failure.

THE STRATEGIC MANAGEMENT OF TECHNOLOGY AND INNOVATION

TECHNOLOGY DEFINED

Technology is defined as 'belonging to or relating to, or systematically characteristic of a particular art, science, profession or occupation ... also pertaining to the mechanical arts and applied science, the science of industrial arts' (*Oxford English Dictionary*). Technology defines *how things are done,* for instance 'in the manner of performance in the mechanical or industrial arts, skill or capacity' (*OED*), or in 'the appliance of science' (Zanussi!). Technology *widely defines* processes, products, services, or the manner in which an organization completes its tasks or carries out its business. It is not a narrow technical or scientific concept.

INNOVATION DEFINED

The *Oxford English Dictionary* defines innovation in terms of 'something newly introduced, a novel practice or method; the alteration of what is already established; a change made by innovating; a renewal, something that favours change'.

Kanter (1985) suggests that 'the term "innovation" makes most people think first about ... new products and new methods for making them. Typically, the word "innovation" creates an image of an invention, a new piece of technical apparatus, or perhaps something of conventionally scientific character'. She argues that 'fewer people would mention new tax laws or the creation of enterprise zones ... quality circles or problem-solving task forces; (but) ... those are innovations too' (p. 20). In commenting that 'many "productivity improvements" rest ... on innovations that determine how jobs are designed or how departments are composed', she goes on to define innovation in terms of a comprehensive 'process of bringing any new, problem-solving idea into use. Ideas for reorganizing, cutting costs, putting in new budgeting systems, improving communication, or assembling products in teams are also innovations. Innovation is the generation, acceptance, and implementation of new ideas, processes, products, or services ... application and implementation are central to this definition; it involves the capacity to change or adapt' (p. 21).

INNOVATION AS A KEY SOURCE OF COMPARATIVE OR COMPETITIVE ADVANTAGE

The capacity to innovate is a fundamental source of comparative or competitive advantage. Innovation may be closely associated with:

Change in the knowledge base - a dynamic of change or development in the knowledge base may give rise to the opportunity for innovation; or instead give rise to a threat of obsolescence.

The knowledge management process - already described in preceding sections of this chapter.

Changing customer expectations - once they are familiar with the advantages made available to them by new products or processes, customers are usually unwilling to continue their patronage of existing products or processes that have not kept up with innovative competitors. Steam lorries for example gave way to the superior performance and economy of the diesel truck in the UK during the 1930s. Road hauliers abandoned steam as an obsolete technology. Those steam lorry manufacturers who would not change simply went out of business.

Shareholder and stakeholder expectations - both shareholders and stakeholders will expect enterprise management to invest in the development of technology where markets or sectors are characterized by innovation. Innovation constitutes a key source of value addition, from which continuing returns may be obtained. It also represents a means to achieve credibility and survival in such markets.

Life-cycle dynamics - innovation and technology development give rise to new products and new processes, new life cycles, and obsolescence. Do you remember the tub, washboard and mangle (for washing clothes); the typewriter; the logarithmic slide rule (for doing calculations); or 9mm cine film?

Value generation - innovative products may generate significant value, particularly in the early stages of their life cycle, or where proprietary patent protection makes it impossible for competitors to copy them. Proprietary drugs such as "Zantac" or "Diazepam" have generated substantial profits for pharmaceutical companies, and are used to finance further drug research and development.

Cost management through the value chain - process innovations may be used to reduce costs or to increase cost-efficiency. Bulk transaction processing based on data transmission, for instance, has become faster and cheaper with the introduction of information and communication technologies (ICTs). Issues of cost management through the value chain are dealt with in Chapter 23.

Product-market differentiation - innovation is widely used to differentiate products or services from their competitors. Customer service and in-flight entertainment innovations have for example been a key feature of the competitive advantage of the Virgin Atlantic airline. Issues of product-market differentiation are dealt with in Chapter 24.

Entrepreneurial opportunity - innovation is often a key source of new business development. Entrepreneurs develop new markets with innovatory new products or processes. George Eastman for instance transformed photography into a mass consumer pastime with his easy-to-use Kodak cameras and roll film.

The re-engineering or restructuring of business processes or systems - process innovations, for instance associated with project management or information and communication technology developments, lie at the heart of the re-engineering of operational and service activities.

The strategic management of core competencies - as described in Chapter 20.
The process of resource stretch and leverage - as described in Chapter 21.

SOME SOURCES OF INNOVATION

Customers and Markets

M.E. Porter (1990) comments that *market competition* acts as a key stimulus to the innovation process. He states that innovation is stimulated by:

❑   the type, sophistication, and expectations of customer demand within the market.
❑   the level of domestic competition prevailing in the market. Intense competition may give rise to vigorous innovation as a means of maintaining or improving market position.

In both cases, market sensitivity and customer orientation are prime motivators of the innovation process. That is, *successful innovation responds to market needs*. Where, for instance, potential customers are involved in the process of research and development, the needs of the customer and the market are most likely to be properly determined and understood. Peters and Waterman (1982) note that many innovations come from users themselves, not their manufacturers. They quote scientific and control instrumentation, and control systems as examples. Other innovations are developed with the potential customer. Boeing's record of success, e.g. with the 727 and 737 as compared, say, with the British BAC 1-11, can be attributed to its close and continuing communication with its customers, and to its dependence upon the competitive world of commercial aircraft. Unlike some of its competitors, it did not enjoy the relative "security" of major contracts with government defence agencies or nationalised airlines. Its survival is dependent upon effective and customer-orientated innovation.

Closeness to the market may require particular attention to be paid to *leader customers*. The business or institutional customer who is in the vanguard of his or her own market may be years ahead of the current staple demand, particularly in high technology industries such as avionics and aerospace, process control systems, virtual reality, or biotechnology. Innovators who work with such customers will eventually be able to develop and to diffuse their experience into more mundane markets, gaining competitive advantage there from the competence that they have acquired.

Demographics

Demographic variables define the population in terms of size, composition, age structure, income, employment, socio-economic status, etc. Demographic sources of innovative opportunity are almost unique, in that the changes they represent are often unambiguous and predictable. This is because demographic patterns have known lead times and almost certain dynamics. For example, all of the people who will reach retirement age by the year 2030 in the UK are already in the UK labour force, making some kind of pension, healthcare, or retirement provision (or not, as the case may be). This demographic certainty provides a major opportunity for the financial services sector, for instance in the markets for personal pension and investment products.

Demographic variables have a major impact on what is bought, by whom, when, and in what quantities - and hence create opportunities for innovation. Innovation potential can be illustrated by purchase patterns and consumer behaviour in age cohorts and the family life cycle. For instance:

❑ *18-25 years* - fashion and life-style innovations derived from life-style segmentation and marketing; personal financial products based upon some degree of family financing of higher education studies, whether at undergraduate or postgraduate level.
❑ *65 plus* - sheltered and other innovatory housing for the elderly; personal security and communication systems; public and private sector medical and healthcare; financial service products based upon the security of capital gains associated with home ownership.

Where demographic changes occur rapidly, as they did in the massive nineteenth century migration from Europe to the Americas, they may give rise to extensive opportunities for innovation, whether it be in infrastructure developments, communications, transportation, distribution, real estate, agriculture or manufacture.

Industry and Market Structures

Opportunities for innovation may arise from basic changes in industry, sector, or market structures. In the UK consumer goods distribution and retailing sector, for instance, changing customer attitudes to shopping, life-style changes, the use of the internet, and retail concentration have combined to yield opportunities in distribution systems, retailing methods, retail management, merchandizing, purchasing techniques and stock control (with their associated data recognition and ICT developments).

Changes in Perception

Substantial changes in the *personal perceptions* upon which consumer or buyer behaviour is based may give rise to opportunities for innovation. When such changes in perception take place, the facts associated with them do not necessarily change. *What changes is their meaning to people.* Changes in perception and attitude may result from behavioural factors, from the views of opinion-leaders, or from consistent and effective promotion. One example is changing western perceptions and attitude to personal health and fitness. Greater health and fitness awareness have given rise to a plethora of new product and service innovations. Similarly, the increasing public concern over environmental issues is creating innovative opportunities in such disparate fields as personal and public transportation, forestry, biotechnology, air treatment, pollution control, waste disposal, and recycling.

Incongruities

Drucker (1985) describes an "incongruity" in terms of the difference between (i) a reality; and (ii) that reality *as it is assumed to be*. For instance, the manufacturers of lawn fertilizer specify an exact unit measure per square metre of lawn by which the product is to be distributed. Originally there was no actual means to achieve the accuracy of "dosage", since the gardener had to broadcast the product by hand! Which of course meant that the correct dosage and distribution could not be obtained. It was only when simple wheeled distributors were invented that the correct dosage could be achieved, and nasty burn marks (from hand-delivered over-concentrations of fertilizer) were eliminated, to obtain the spotless and "striped" lawns shown glowing on the fertilizer bag!

Similarly, the economics of cargo-vessel operation depend not so much on the *actual speed* of a ship on the high seas, but on the *total journey time*. Total journey time includes *time in port*, and modern port operations, based upon the use of container ships or roll-on, roll-off ferries, are designed to minimize the amount of time when the ship is not actually at sea, and maximize the revenue earning time it spends travelling to its next destination. At the same time, this realization enabled ship designers to optimize the fuel efficiency and running cost of marine engines, which would otherwise consume fuel oil in vast quantities in order to power vessels at unnecessarily high speeds across the oceans.

Process Need

Innovative opportunity in this case stems from a need within a process or operation, and takes the form of a task or job to be done. Examples include:

❑ automatic digital electronic telephone switching systems and exchanges that have increased telecommunications potential well beyond the restricted capacity of manually or electro-mechanically operated switchboards.
❑ inexpensive postage stamps and frequent postal services; daily newspapers; subscriber trunk (direct) telephone dialling and fax services; international news gathering and transmission; radio, television, broadband, and internet services. Each development has facilitated fast and comprehensive national and international communication, and eliminated barriers imposed by geographical distance and location.
❑ instalment-based buying and purchase on mortgage or credit, which has stimulated purchasing in housing, and in consumer goods markets (especially of consumer durables such as cars, and electrical "white" or "brown" goods).

The industrial revolution, and subsequent waves of technological and economic development, are a rich source of examples of this kind of process innovation, going right back to early process needs involved in power generation, textile manufacture, transportation, and distribution. In each case, a *weak* or *missing link* could be identified and described; a specification for its solution drawn up; and an opportunity for innovation thereby created for which the appropriate technology or system was eventually developed.

The Unexpected

The *unexpected* may provide sources of innovative opportunity. Firstly, an *unexpected success*, if recognized as such, can be followed up to provide new business opportunities. The critical problem for the enterprise is the recognition and acknowledgement of the success, and the organization's response to it. Examples include the taking up by IBM of commercial demand for the "computer", a machine originally designed for defence and scientific applications; or the emergence of BMW from a position of relative obscurity to becoming a front rank producer of high performance prestige cars; or the recognition by Akio Morita of Japan's Sony Corporation of the electronic potential of the transistor invented in the USA but initially ignored there. Secondly, innovation opportunities may result from an *unexpected outside event*, which again must be recognized, understood, and its implications developed. The major manufacturers of computer and office systems were unprepared for the explosion of demand for inexpensive microprocessors, personal computers, and word processors that occurred after 1980.

New Knowledge

The development and convergence of new knowledge may give rise to innovative opportunities. Innovation may depend upon the eventual combination of several different kinds of new knowledge, whether it be scientific, organizational, or marketing. Advances in telecommunications, for instance, depend upon developments in solid-state silicon and gallium arsenide processing technologies, fibre-optics, and techniques of manufacturing and quality assurance connected with their installation. American success in constructing the Panama Canal, when compared with the French failure that preceded it, depended upon a combination of advanced railroading and earthmoving technologies, the maintenance of efficient hygiene and preventative medicine for construction workers, effective organization, and detailed operations management.

THE STRATEGIC MANAGEMENT OF NEW TECHNOLOGY

Technology was defined in an earlier section above as encompassing processes, products, services, or the manner in which the enterprise completes its tasks or carries out its business. Innovation was defined as the generation, acceptance, and implementation of new ideas affecting processes, products, services, or the manner in which the organization functions.

Current strategic decisions may be based on the assumption that tomorrow's knowledge and technology will be similar to that of today; or that change in the knowledge and technology base will occur slowly or at most at a predictable and controllable rate.

As a result, *proactive strategies* of knowledge management, innovation, or new technology, product or process development may be seen by enterprise management to be more risky than committing resources *to defending the existing business, its knowledge, and its technology.* This raises a fundamental strategic dilemma. Does the organization invest in *today's knowledge and technology,* or does it also commit itself to *the knowledge and technology of tomorrow* (whatever this might eventually prove to be) as the means of exploiting innovation opportunities or responding to competitor initiatives?

The Technology "S" Curve

The dynamics of technological evolution and innovation may be described by the "S" curve, an example of which is shown in Figure 19.2. Foster (1987) describes the "S" curve as 'a graph of the relationship between the effort put into improving a product or process, and the results one gets back for that investment' (p. 31). The shape of the "S" curve shows *learning curve effects* (and the build-up of *experience)* at the lower left-hand end of the curve, and it shows the onset of diminishing returns at the upper right-hand end, as *technological limits* are reached.

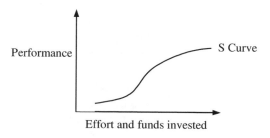

Figure 19.2 A Technology "S" Curve

Technological Limits

The "S" curve implies *technological limits.* As the enterprise approaches a technological limit, the cost of making progress may accelerate dramatically. Eventually, it may reach a point beyond which no further worthwhile gains in performance can be achieved. Being close to a limit means that all of the important opportunities to improve a business by improving knowledge and technology have been used up. Thereafter, other factors (such as the efficiency of marketing, supply chain management, manufacturing, and cost management) may for a time determine the success of the business.

Limits determine which knowledge, technologies, products, or processes run the risk of *obsolescence*. Some understanding of potential limits is therefore essential if a company is to anticipate change, and to stop committing resources to knowledge and technology that will yield few further gains in performance.

Once a limit is reached, *new concepts and knowledge* may determine future success, and there may be no reason why other organizations, as well as those already in the business, cannot attempt to develop them or apply them. Management's *strategic ability to recognize limits* may, in consequence, be crucial to the determination of the success or failure of enterprise investments in innovation. The recognition of limits provides a vital clue as to when or how the company needs to develop or adapt to new technologies.

The recognition of innovative opportunity may thus depend upon the capacity to recognize limits, and on the perceived degree of proximity to the potential obsolescence of knowledge and technology. This recognition, however, may be hindered by an organizational unwillingness to accept or to confront the existence of potential limits. After all, there is no guarantee that the enterprise will have access to, or be prepared to listen to insiders or outsiders who as *limit analysts* (i) may possess the ability to recognize limits, or (ii) who could predict the initial forms of technologies which would take the enterprise on to a new S curve, or (iii) who might then be able to advise what to do about the situation.

Limit analysts use a variety of techniques to test the received technological wisdom and to try to predict the new. These techniques might include lateral thinking, qualitative forecasting based upon delphi or cross-impact analysis (described in Chapter 9), brainstorming, "imagineering", or team efforts (etc). They may attempt to arrive at solutions that draw on or develop new ideas, *but which use existing knowledge and process capacity*. By so doing, they may avoid the "great leap forward" whose enhanced risk derives from dependence upon a combination of ideas or technologies that may not yet be fully developed or tested.

Foster quotes an example of the application of limit analysis. The component miniaturization and integration of electronic circuitry was for a time held up by the problem of wiring connections between the components. Wiring technology had been pushed to the limit. The problem was overcome by the use of silicon-based microchips that at the same time were designed to include (i) electronic components and (ii) semi-conducting paths that provided the circuit connections between the components. The integrated circuit, with no internal wiring, allowed component miniaturization and combination to proceed along its new S curve.

Technology Discontinuities

A discontinuity *is a period of change from one prevailing technology to another*. There is a break between the "S" curve of the prevailing technology, and the new curve that begins to develop. "S" curves may therefore come in sequential pairs, as illustrated in Figure 19.3 The right-hand curve of the pair represents the new technology. This new technology may be a development of the old, or instead derive from an entirely new knowledge base. For instance:

❑ electronic vacuum tubes were replaced by discrete germanium-based components, which in turn were replaced by solid state silicon based semiconductors as the mainstream electronic component technology.
❑ propeller aeroplane propulsion was replaced (i) by turbo-prop, prop-jet, jet, or fan-jet propulsion in large passenger-carrying commercial aircraft; and (ii) in high performance jet-powered military aircraft.
❑ metal structures have in some cases been replaced by entities made from composites based on plastics and carbon fibre.

Discontinuities brought about by technological change may then give rise to opportunities for innovation. These may *cause* changes in market expectation or demand. Or instead they may *follow* from them. Alternatively, they may derive from wider socio-economic or political changes such as a rapid rise in vehicle fuel or water prices; the introduction of more effective environmental controls; or changes in public attitude towards accessible and "high tech" preventative care and health treatment within public or private health-care agencies.

The emergence of a discontinuity (and the limits it thereby confirms) may also present major philosophical and practical problems of adaptation to an established market leader who suddenly discovers that competitors have been the first to adopt and master the introduction of a new technology. For instance:

❑ the market for electro-mechanical cash registers (dominated by NCR) virtually disappeared during a four-year period 1972-1976 under the onslaught from electronic cash registers introduced by manufacturers such as Burroughs.

❑ reference was made in an earlier section to the UK market for heavy steam-powered road transport vehicles. This market lasted from 1898 until it came to an abrupt halt in 1934. Technical obsolescence, coupled with legislation that in 1933 restricted the unladen weight of certain types of vehicle, resulted in the rapid dominance of oil and diesel engines as the basic motive power for heavy road transport vehicles then being introduced by newcomers to the industry.

The exploitation of innovative opportunities represented by such discontinuities may depend upon leadership and management skills not well developed in current market leaders. Or it may instead be "hidden from view" by inertia, conventional thinking, the "not invented here" syndrome, or complacency within role-based or bureaucratic structures.

The management of technology discontinuities may call for adaptive and flexible operation, and a philosophical acceptance that the enterprise may have little choice but to invest in risk (by investigating alternative technologies, undertaking limit analysis, etc). In undertaking the strategic management of discontinuities, enterprise leadership may have *at the same time* to learn (i) how to manage or develop its technology within the dynamics of an existing "S" curve, and (ii) how successfully to cross discontinuities indicated by the appearance of a new "S" curve.

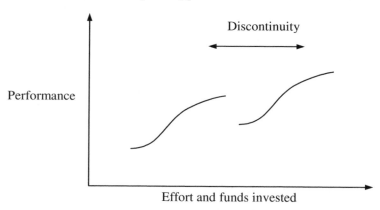

Figure 19.3 A Technology Discontinuity

JAPANESE INNOVATION PROCESSES

Hampden-Turner and Trompenaars (1994) describe Japanese innovation processes as being characterized by a combination of:

❑ processes of incremental refinement.
❑ processes of continuous re-specification and improvement (*kaizen*).
❑ processes of the recycling of past and existing knowledge and experience (*sairiyo*), as described by Tatsumo's mandala of creativity shown in Figures 7.1 and 19.4 (below). Morden (2004) notes that 'concepts based upon life cycles (such as the marketer's product life cycle) are "tidy" and "logical" in the (linear) terms of western analysis. Such concepts may however be counterproductive to the development of the apparently more successful evolutionary, adaptive and incremental approaches to the development of technologies and processes favoured by the ... Japanese. What we consider "obsolete" may to them ... be a resource to be recycled and adapted within a wider context of prevailing competence, tradition and market awareness' (p. 38).
❑ processes of hybridization, integration, and fusion in which elements of existing and new technologies are blended. International examples variously include (i) mechantronics, which is the combination of reliable, proven and robust electromechanical technologies with electronic ones; (ii) the electronic manipulation of chemical based photographic images (and vice-versa); (iii) the fusion of oriental and western food recipes and approaches to cooking; and (iv) the jet-prop, which combines propeller and jet technologies to give efficient and reliable high performance engines for medium-sized short haul passenger aircraft.

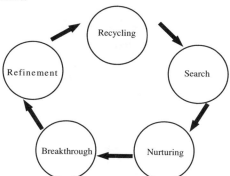

Figure 19.4 Tatsumo's Mandala of Creativity

SOME IMPLEMENTATION ISSUES ASSOCIATED WITH INNOVATION AND TECHNOLOGY

Two implementation issues are described in this section. A more detailed analysis of implementation issues associated with the process of innovation can be found in the first and second editions of the author's text *Principles of Management*.

Enterprise Architecture

Architecture and structure were analyzed in Chapter 18. Kay's (1993) description of the importance of innovation as a source of comparative and competitive advantage was noted in Chapter 4. Kay suggests that comparative or competitive advantage may be obtained from:

The direct capability to manage knowledge, technology, and innovation - this implies a clear understanding of the knowledge base and of the processes of knowledge and technology management described in earlier sections of this chapter. It also implies an understanding of the issues associated with the concept of core competence described in Chapter 20.

An architecture that is capable of sustaining a process of ongoing innovation - it may eventually be possible for competitors to copy any one innovation (or to "get round" the protection of patents or design registration). But it may be impossible for competitors to imitate the innovator's architecture, its knowledge base, its processes of knowledge and technology management, and the capability this represents. In such a case, it is the architecture as much as the innovation that is the key source of competitive advantage.

An innovative capability and an architecture that is supported and reinforced - for instance by other distinctive capabilities such as brand management; or protected by complementary or strategic assets such as an effective patent law system like that of the USA. Imitation of any one innovation (even if possible) is now no longer enough for competitors to match the firm's competitive advantage. A whole series of variables (some of which it may be impossible to exploit or copy) will have now been brought into play by the innovator.

Requisite Variety and Genetic Diversity

The enterprise is likely to need to be exposed to a critical level (or critical mass) of incoming *external stimuli*. These external stimuli may as new or challenging knowledge:

❑ establish the requirement for innovation in the minds of decision-makers.
❑ provide the priority and direction for that innovation.
❑ establish the parameters or substance for investigation, research, and application.

This critical level of external and novel stimuli will provide the necessary level of:

❑ *requisite variety*; and
❑ *genetic variety*.

by which sufficient new ideas, paradigms, and concepts are introduced that will have the effect of:

❑ offsetting obsolescence and entropy (deterioration) in the enterprise knowledge and paradigm base.
❑ facilitating ongoing creativity, innovation, and change in the knowledge base and the processes of knowledge and technology management.
❑ updating, refreshing, or challenging enterprise thinking about its markets, technologies, and processes.

REVIEW QUESTIONS

1. What is knowledge management? Why may it be a source of value addition and comparative or competitive advantage?
2. What is the knowledge base, and what is its significance for the strategic management of enterprise technology?
3. Compare and contrast "tacit" and "explicit" knowledge.
4. How may knowledge be shared in an organization? What factors may influence this sharing and dissemination of information?
5. Why is trust necessary to the knowledge management process?
6. What is technology?

7. Why is technology a key source of comparative or competitive advantage?
8. How may the enterprise manage its technologies?
9. What is innovation?
10. Describe and comment on some of the sources of innovation.
11. Why is the capacity to innovate a key source of competitive advantage?

TECHNIQUES OF CASE STUDY AND ANALYSIS

1. Identify the knowledge and technology base that underpins the capability and competence of the case organization. To what extent do knowledge and technology constitute sources of competitive advantage?
2. What knowledge management strategies, if any, are apparent in the case study?
3. How, if at all, is it apparent that the case company manages its knowledge and experience to innovate or to generate value and competitive advantage? Does it use its knowledge and experience? Is it creative?
4. Where the appropriate information is available, identify technology and innovation dynamics (if any) evident in the case study. To what extent do these dynamics present opportunities or threats to the case company?

PROJECT ASSIGNMENTS

1. Using published information and (where possible) key informant interviews, research and write up an actual case study of a knowledge management programme or project.
2. Carry out an analysis of the technological evolution of an industry or product-market in which you are interested. Can you make predictions about the likelihood of the emergence of technological limits or discontinuities within the foreseeable future?
3. Describe and evaluate an innovatory process, product, service, or institution with which you are familiar. Comment on its success or failure as an innovation.
4. Identify an opportunity for innovation. Specify a process, product, service, or concept that would create or satisfy the need implied by that opportunity.

5. Using published information, (i) analyze, explain and describe one or a series of actual successful innovation implementations; then (ii) compare these with one or a series of actual unsuccessful innovation implementations. What differences can you discern between the two analyzes? Why do you think that the unsuccessful companies failed to adapt to or adopt the necessary changes?

References

Cadbury, D. (2003) *Seven Wonders of the Industrial World*, BBC/HarperCollins, London.

Caulkin, S. (1997) "The knowledge within", *Management Today*, August.

Davenport, T.H. and L. Prusak (1998) *Working Knowledge*, Harvard Business School Press, Boston, Mass.

Drucker, P. (1985) *Innovation and Entrepreneurship*, Heinemann, London.

Foster, R.N. (1987) *Innovation: the attacker's advantage*, Pan Macmillan, London.

Fukuyama, F. (1995) *Trust: the social values and the creation of prosperity*, Hamish Hamilton, London.

Goldsmith, W. and D. Clutterbuck (1985) *The Winning Streak*, Penguin, London.

Goldsmith, W. and D. Clutterbuck (1997) *The Winning Streak Mark II*, Orion Books, London.

Hamel, G.C. and C.K. Prahalad (1994) *Competing for the Future*, Harvard Business School Press, Boston, Mass.

Hampden-Turner, C. and F.Trompenaars (1994) *The Seven Cultures of Capitalism*, Piatkus, London.

Kanter, R.M (1985) *The Change Masters*, Routledge, London.

Kay, J. (1993) *Foundations of Corporate Success*, Oxford University Press, Oxford.

Meek, M. (2003) *There Go The Ships*, The Memoir Club, Spennymoor.

Morden, A.R. (1989a) "Innovation: sources and strategies", *Management Decision*, Vol 27, No 1.

Morden, A.R. (1989b) "Innovation: people and implementation", *Management Decision*, Vol 27, No 3.

Morden, A.R. (1993) *Elements of Marketing*, D P Publications, London.

Morden, A.R. (1996) *Principles of Management*, McGraw-Hill, London.

Morden, A.R. (2004) *Principles of Management (2nd Edition)*, Ashgate, Aldershot.

Nonaka, I. (1991) "The knowledge-creating company", *Harvard Business Review*, November-December.

Nonaka, I. amd H. Takeuchi (1995) *The Knowledge-Creating Company*, Oxford University Press, New York.

Peters, T.J. and N. Austin (1986) *A Passion for Excellence*, Fontana, London.

Peters, T.J. and R.H. Waterman (1982) *In Search of Excellence*, Harper & Row, New York.

Porter, M.E. (1990) *The Competitive Advantage of Nations*, Macmillan, London.

Rendall, I. (1988) *Reaching for the Skies*, BBC Books, London.

Snowden, D. (1998) "Alignment of intellectual capital and corporate strategy - new model consultancy in computer services", *Proceedings of the Dynamics of Strategy Conference*, Surrey European Management School, Guildford, April.

Chapter 20

Core Competencies

This chapter is extensively based on the work of Gary Hamel and C.K. Prahalad (1990, 1994) who contend that the strategic management process should focus on the long-term identification, development, and exploitation of the "core competencies" of the organization. This chapter analyzes and illustrates the core competence concept. Hamel and Prahalad suggest that leaders and managers in organizations have to rethink the concept of the corporation, its mission, and its approach to strategic management as a consequence of espousing the core competence perspective that they describe in their work.

The copyrights of the material upon which this chapter is based are held variously by Gary Hamel and C.K. Prahalad, Harvard Business School Press, and the President and Fellows of Harvard College. Their permission to reproduce this copyright material is gratefully acknowledged.

RETHINKING THE CORPORATION

A received Anglo-Saxon wisdom of recent decades, based upon varying interpretations of (i) Rosabeth Moss Kanter's (1990) dictum of "doing more with less"; and (ii) the concept of re-engineering described in Chapter 16, has been that the structure of the organization and the process of management should be "restructured", "decluttered", "delayered", "made lean", and if necessary "rightsized" or "downsized" in order to achieve improvements in performance, profitability, or cost-effectiveness.

This interpretation of the direction in which the strategic management process should be taken by chief executive officers (CEOs) and senior executives has been a widespread one. It is based on *short-termist* and *cost-cutting* responses to conditions of recession and increasing global competition, for instance from Eastern Europe and South East Asian countries.

Hamel and Prahalad, in an influential Harvard Business Review article of 1990, and in the 1994 book *Competing For The Future*, contend that management should instead be focusing on the longer term identification, development, and exploitation of *core competencies* that make business development and growth possible. They suggest that as a result leaders will have to rethink the concept of the corporation, its mission, and its management.

Hamel & Prahalad (1990, p. 81) comment that 'the survivors of the first wave of global competition, Western and Japanese alike, are all converging on similar and formidable standards for product cost and quality - minimum hurdles for continued competition, but less and less important as sources of differential advantage'. In the long run, Hamel and Prahalad maintain that competitiveness will derive from an ability to build core competencies that will enable companies:

❑ to make use of the knowledge, experience, creativity, and technology development described in Chapter 19.
❑ to introduce new technologies, processes and products.
❑ to create new customer demand.
❑ to respond to changing opportunities and conditions.
❑ to create 'what isn't' (Pascale, 1994, p. 20).

The realization of this concept of comparative advantage and competitive positioning will depend on management's ability appropriately to configure and consolidate organization-wide knowledge, technologies, skills, experience and creativity into the basic competencies required for strategic progress.

Hamel and Prahalad's premise is that competition between firms is now as much a race for mastering and developing competence as it is for market position and market power. They maintain (1990, p. 83) that 'successful companies have stopped managing themselves as bundles of businesses' only making products or positioned on product-markets. They suggest that 'Canon, Honda, Casio, or NEC may seem to preside over portfolios of businesses unrelated in terms of customers, distribution channels, and merchandising strategy ... but looks are deceiving. In NEC, digital technology, especially VLSI and systems integration skills, is fundamental. In the core competencies underlying them, disparate businesses become coherent. It is Honda's core competence in engines and power trains that gives it a distinctive advantage in car, motorcycle, lawn mower, and generator businesses. Canon's core competencies in optics, imaging, and microprocessor controls have enabled it to enter ... markets as seemingly diverse as copiers, laser printers, cameras, and image scanners. Philips worked for more than 15 years to perfect its optical-media (laser disc) competence, as did JVC in building a leading position in video recording. Other examples of core competencies might include mechantronics (the ability to marry mechanical and electronic engineering), video displays, bioengineering, and microelectronics. In the early stages of its competence building, Philips could not have imagined all the products that would be spawned by its optical-media competence, nor could JVC have anticipated miniature camcorders when it first began exploring videotape technologies'.

However, Hamel and Prahalad comment (1994, p. 221) that 'the core competence perspective is not a natural one in ... companies. Typically, the most basic sense of corporate identity is built around market-focused entities ... rather than around core competencies ... whereas it is entirely appropriate to have a strong end-product focus in an organization, this needs to be supplemented by an equally explicit core competence focus. A company must be viewed not only as a portfolio of products or services, but a portfolio of competencies as well'.

WHAT IS A CORE COMPETENCE?

Competencies are capabilities represented by the collective and accumulated knowledge, learning and experience of the organization and its staff. *Core competencies* are those capabilities that are most fundamental to the successful operation of the enterprise. They represent activities that the organization must be good at performing, or be "excellent" or "world class" in achieving if it wishes to attain its objectives.

A school for instance must be able to maintain proper discipline, and teach its pupils consistently and effectively. These are two fundamental competencies in education. Where the school's performance is measured on the basis of the examination results of its students (as in the UK), then the staff have also got to be able successfully to teach examination technique to their pupils.

A business organization needs instead to be able to promote, market and sell its products or services. These activities are basic. Companies operating in open and competitive markets will not survive without the appropriate competencies in sales and marketing. At the same time, the company must be consistently able to produce its products or services to the required quality. In global markets that simply means one thing - total quality and zero defects. Nothing else will do. Total quality management is a fundamental competence.

Where an organization is operating in an international environment, similarly, its staff must have the necessary language skills. Even if people can speak good English or French, Spanish or Chinese they will still expect product documentation and technical explanations in their own local language. And managing ordinary employees in local situations will require local language skills; the possession of international languages will not be enough.

Core Competence Defined

Hamel and Prahalad (1994, pp. 202-203) define a competence as 'a bundle of skills and technologies rather than a single discrete skill or technology … a core competence represents the sum of learning across individual skill sets and individual organizational units. Thus, a core competence is … unlikely to reside in its entirety in a single individual or small team'. Core competencies comprise the co-ordination, integration, and management of such variables as:

❑ leadership, managerial, and organizational skills.
❑ structure and relationship architecture.
❑ knowledge and experience.
❑ operational skills.
❑ technologies.
❑ innovation capabilities.
❑ understanding of customers, clients, markets and their potential.
❑ creativity.
❑ cultures and value sets.
❑ capacities to manage change and innovation.

Hamel and Prahalad suggest that enterprises might identify between five and fifteen core competencies. They give as examples of such core competencies:

❑ package tracking (Federal Express).
❑ fast cycle-time specification and manufacturing (Motorola).
❑ engine specification and manufacture (Honda).

THREE TESTS OF CORE COMPETENCE

Hamel and Prahalad suggest that there are *three tests* by which the enterprise may identify its core competencies. These are:

Test One: Customer Value

The core competence will make a significant contribution to the customer benefits and value of the end product. Core competencies provide the capability to deliver this fundamental customer benefit and value which, when compared with competing offers, most effectively defines, fits or satisfies the customer requirement. Hamel and Prahalad note that the greater the contribution of the core competence to creating customer value, the greater may be the competitive advantage provided by that core competence.

Example: the manufacturing quality of high value consumer durable goods. German products have a world class reputation for robustness and durability. People are prepared to pay premium prices for products that they perceive to be highly specified, well made, and unlikely to go wrong. Would you be prepared to tolerate a freezer that keeps breaking down when it is full of frozen food? Or an unreliable car that has a habit of breaking down on a cold winter's night on the motorway!

Test Two: Competitive Uniqueness

A core competence should be competitively unique, and difficult for competitors to imitate. The unique features provide key sources of product or service differentiation in the market place. This test corresponds with Kay's (1993) analysis of non-imitatable innovation capability as a key source of enterprise competitive advantage, described in earlier chapters. The imitation of a core competence, or the relationship architecture within which it is contained, will be difficult if for example it comprises a complex integration of, and a harmonization between:

- tacit and explicit knowledge.
- staff skills.
- operational capabilities.
- technologies.
- organizational experience.
- networks of relationships and personal friendships (see below).

A rival might be able to acquire some of the technologies that make up the core competence, but may find it impossible to replicate patterns of internal architecture, structure, co-ordination, learning, employee expertize, and individual idiosyncracy.

Example: Richard Branson's Virgin companies have a relationship architecture and culture that its competitors may find difficult to imitate, particularly where these competitors have had a tradition of bureaucratic, arrogant, or hierarchical leadership in which ordinary employees are neither trusted nor accorded any significant status. At the same time, Richard Branson's personality and charisma (and for instance his ballooning exploits!) as a strategic asset are a key source of reputation and publicity which cannot easily be replicated by his competitors.

Test Three: Extendability

A core competence will provide increasing or extended access to a wide variety of applications and markets. Hamel and Prahalad comment (1994, p. 207) that 'a core competence is truly core when it forms the basis for entry into new product markets'. They suggest for instance that the core competence should be a key source of new applications, new technologies, new products, and new processes. Part of the process of managing and developing the core competencies of the enterprise will be to search for new configurations and new concepts which may be derived from these core competencies.

Example: the development by Philips of the optical laser-disc or CD has already been described above. The origination of the laser disc led to a variety of later developments associated with computer data storage. Similarly, the development of adhesives technology by 3M has given rise to a host of applications associated with paper tape, Post-It® notes, and abrasives for building construction or materials finishing.

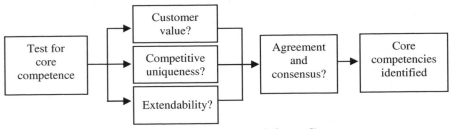

Figure 20.1 The Three Tests of Core Competence

CO-ORDINATING AND INTEGRATING CORE COMPETENCES WITHIN THE ENTERPRISE

Hamel and Prahalad suggest that the co-ordination and integration of core competences within enterprise architecture and structure may imply:

❑ a long-term strategic vision and intent on the part of enterprise leaders to create, to sustain, and to protect the organization's necessary competencies.

❑ an appropriate culture and value set, focused on the development of co-operation and competence across the organization.

❑ shifts in the priority of resource allocation and skill deployment across the institution. The management of the core competences of the enterprise needs to be based on their *opportunity cost* and their *capacity to generate value*. This implies:-

❑ a willingness (or an obligation) to share resources and skills across the enterprise. It also implies:-

❑ the weaning of key employees off 'the idea that they belong in perpetuity to any particular business' or product-market. Hamel and Prahalad suggest (1990, p. 91) that 'early in their careers, people may be exposed to a variety of businesses through a carefully planned rotation programme. At Canon, critical people move regularly between the camera business and the copier business, and between the copier business and the professional optical products business. In mid-career, periodic assignments to cross-divisional project teams may be necessary, both for diffusing core competences and for loosening the bonds that might tie an individual to one business even when brighter opportunities beckon elsewhere. Those who embody critical core competences should know that their careers are tracked and guided ... competence carriers should be regularly brought together from across the corporation to trade notes and ideas. The goal is to build a strong feeling of community among these people. To a great extent, their loyalty should be to the integrity of the core competence area they represent, and not to particular businesses'. At the same time, 'in travelling regularly, talking frequently to customers, and meeting with peers, competence carriers may be encouraged to discover new market opportunities'.

❑ that the skills and resources that constitute core competence should coalesce around individuals and activities whose efforts are not so narrowly focused that they cannot recognise, or access opportunities for blending their functional expertize and operational experience in new

and interesting ways with those of other individuals and activities in the architecture of the value chain.
- that the development and maintenance of core competences requires communication about, acceptance of the need for, and involvement in work that takes place across organizational boundaries and levels.
- the establishment of managerial and administrative mechanisms for selecting and concentrating in one place or in one project the necessary people, skills, and resources that are currently dispersed elsewhere across other businesses or activities. Hamel and Prahalad (1990, p. 87) note in this context that 'western companies have traditionally had an advantage in the stock of skills they possess'. But they have not necessarily been able to reconfigure these skills quickly in order to be able to respond to new opportunities. Hamel and Prahalad comment that 'Canon, NEC, and Honda have had a lesser stock of the people and technologies that compose core competencies but could move them much quicker from one business unit to another to exploit opportunities'. This implies:-
- that core competences are regarded as corporate and not functional, divisional or business unit resources. They may as such be reallocated by senior management according to their opportunity cost and value generating potential. Indeed, Hamel and Prahalad (1990, p. 90) suggest that 'each year in the strategic planning or budgeting process, unit managers must justify their hold on the people who carry the company's core competencies'. They note that 'when Canon identified an opportunity in digital laser printers, it gave (unit) managers the right to raid other (units) to pull together the required pool of talent'.
- the targeting of *strategic alliances* as mechanisms by which to access experience and competence currently external to the enterprise, but whose internalisation is considered essential to the development of core competencies. Hamel and Prahalad note the intensive use by the Japanese of such mechanisms in order to achieve knowledge, experience and technology transfer; and to develop and refine core competences. The use of such mechanisms has also obviated the need to incur large research and development expenditures, or developmental costs.

THREE CASE EXAMPLES

Hamel and Prahalad (1990) describe three case studies. These are:

NEC (Nippon Electric Company)

Hamel and Prahalad (pp. 79-80) comment that NEC has emerged as a 'world leader in semiconductors and as a first-tier player in telecommunications products and computers ... NEC conceived of itself in terms of core competencies ... early in the 1970s, NEC articulated a strategic intent to exploit the convergence of computing and communications, what it called "C&C". Success, top management reckoned, would hinge on acquiring competencies, particularly in semiconductors. Management adopted an appropriate (relationship architecture) ... and then communicated its intent to the whole organization and the outside world during the mid-1970s.

NEC constituted a "C&C Committee" of top managers to oversee the development of core products and core competencies. NEC put in place co-ordination groups and committees that cut across the interests of individual businesses. Consistent with its (relationship architecture), NEC shifted enormous resources to strengthen its position in components and central processors. By using collaborative arrangements to multiply internal resources NEC was able to accumulate a broad array of core competencies.

NEC identified three interrelated streams of technological and market evolution. Company management determined that computing would evolve from large mainframes to distributed processing; components from simple IC's to VLSI; and communications from (electro-mechanical) cross-bar exchange(s) to digital systems ... as things evolved further, NEC reasoned, the computing, communications, and components businesses would so overlap that it would be very hard to distinguish among them, and that there would be enormous opportunities for any company that had built the competencies needed to serve all three markets'.

3M (Minnesota Mining and Manufacturing Company)

Founded in 1902, the 3M company has developed specialist expertize in adhesives, film and coatings. Hamel and Prahalad note (p. 82) that 'in dreaming up businesses as diverse as "Post-it" notes, magnetic tape, photographic film, pressure sensitive tapes, and coated abrasives, the company has brought to bear widely shared competencies in substrates, coatings, and adhesives; and devised various ways to combine them. Indeed, 3M has invested consistently in them. What seems to be an extremely diversified portfolio of businesses belies a few shared core competencies'.

Honda

Honda perceive the design and manufacture of high specification automotive engines as a core competence. Hence its large commitment to Formula One motor racing. Honda develops, combines and applies its engine-related technologies in a wide range of product-markets from cars to portable generators to motor cycles to lawn mowers.

IMPLEMENTATION ISSUES: SOME MANAGERIAL IMPLICATIONS OF IGNORING THE CORE COMPETENCE CONCEPT

There would appear to be a number of significant managerial implications of ignoring the core competence concept as proposed by Hamel and Prahalad. These implications include:

The inability to respond to new opportunities or change - Hamel and Prahalad (1994, pp. 221-222) suggest that, even where someone in the organization identifies new business opportunities or understands the necessity to bring about change, 'if the competencies that are needed to respond ... lie in another business unit, there may be no way to redeploy the people who "carry" (the required competences) into the new opportunity (or change) arena ... the result is imprisoned and under-leveraged competencies'.

The risk of fragmentation - Hamel and Prahalad (1994, p. 222) comment that if an enterprise 'divisionalizes and fractures into (an increasing number of) business units ... competencies may become fragmented and weakened. Business unit boundaries may make cross-application difficult and slow the cumulative learning processes through which competencies are enhanced'. Worse, Hamel and Prahalad warn that it may be the case that any one business unit could even become unable to sustain the investment needed to maintain the existing levels of competence upon which its current business depends, let alone build new core competences.

Cutting out development prospects - an enterprise that fails to invest adequately in new core competencies is likely to diminish its long-term growth and development prospects. Hamel and Prahalad (1994, p. 222) comment that 'tomorrow's growth depends on today's competence-building. Investment in new core competencies provides the seeds for tomorrow's product harvest'.

At the same time, an enterprise failure to invest in maintaining or developing basic competences will have a direct and personal impact on the knowledge, skill and experience base of unit management and staff. The negative consequences of a deteriorating, obsolete or out-of-date knowledge, skill and experience base will be most graphically illustrated where competitors are carrying out the systematic benchmarking comparison of the competences of their rivals. A perceived failure to maintain or develop the enterprise competence base will be a key strategic weakness that competitors may make strenuous efforts to exploit in their own interest.

Divestment risk - Hamel and Prahalad (1994, pp. 222-224) suggest that 'companies insensitive to the issue of core competence may unwittingly relinquish valuable skills when they divest an under-performing business ... (in order) to protect core competencies, a company must be able to distinguish between a bad business and the potentially valuable competencies buried within that business'.

IMPLEMENTATION ISSUES: THE STRATEGIC MANAGEMENT OF CORE COMPETENCIES

Hamel and Prahalad (1994, pp. 224-236) identify six strategies by which the management of core competences may be undertaken. These strategies are described below.

Identify Core Competencies

The enterprise cannot manage or exploit its core competencies if its staff do not have an agreed view about what these core competences actually are. Hamel and Prahalad suggest (p. 224) that 'the first task in managing core competencies is therefore to produce' definitions and "inventories" of core competencies. Once this identification process has reached a degree of consensus, Hamel and Prahalad comment that 'companies (then) need to benchmark their core competencies with other firms' (p. 226) so that they are contained in a relevant and sector-comparative competitive framework.

Establish the Core Competence Acquisition Agenda

Specific goals for competence acquisition and deployment are described in Hamel and Prahalad's Figure 10.2 (1994, p. 227) reproduced here with permission as Figure 20.2. Core competence acquisition and deployment will vary according to position on the competence and market matrix shown in Figure 20.2. This matrix contains four strategies, being:

- ❑ "fill in the blanks" (existing competencies; existing markets).
- ❑ "premier plus 10" (new competencies; existing markets).
- ❑ "white spaces" (existing competencies; new markets).
- ❑ "mega-opportunities" (new competencies, new markets).

		Premier Plus 10	*Mega-opportunities*
CORE COMPETENCE	**New**	What new core competencies will we need to build to protect and extend our franchise in current markets?	What new core competencies will we need to build to participate in the most exciting markets of the future?
	Existing	*Fill in the blanks* What is the opportunity to improve our position in existing markets by better leveraging our existing core competencies?	*White spaces* What new products or services could we create by selectively redeploying or recombining our current core competencies?
		Existing	**New**

MARKET

Figure 20.2 Establishing the Core Competence Acquisition Agenda

Build New Core Competencies

Core competencies are a source of today's comparative or competitive advantage. Of equal importance is their role as the "gateway" to tomorrow's customers and tomorrow's markets.

Hamel and Prahalad advise enterprise management to establish and to stick to a long term and consistent consensus about which basic competencies the enterprise should build and support. They note (p. 231) that 'given that it may take five, ten, or more years to build world leadership in a core competence area, consistency of effort is key'. This consistency of pattern depends on consensus, and 'on the stability of the management teams charged with competence development'. Hamel and Prahalad comment that 'throwing money at a project, scrapping it when it doesn't yield short-term results, starting it up again when competitors appear to be moving ahead, and de-emphasising the project when a new CEO comes on board is a recipe for inefficient and ineffective competence development'. At the same time, the enterprise needs to build 'a community of people (across) the organization who view themselves as the "carriers" of core competencies', and see themselves as the stewards of a learning and developmental culture within the relationship architecture.

Deploying Core Competencies

The application of a core competence across a diversity of businesses, and into new markets, will require the deployment and redeployment of that competence internally across the enterprise. This issue has already been described above. It implies that competencies (and their mobility or transferability) are viewed as a *corporate* not a divisional or business unit resource. Hamel and Prahalad note (p. 234) that 'one Japanese company regularly publishes a list of the company's top market and product development priorities. Obviously, there is great status attached to working on a high-profile, critical programme. If an individual somewhere in the organization believes that he or she can contribute to one of the high priority projects, that individual can "self-promote" himself or herself onto the team. The team leader may not choose to take the applicant, but if the skills offered are critical to the project's success, the team leader can ask that the individual be transferred. At this point, the employee's boss has to justify why that individual's talents are of more value to the corporation in the current job than in the new job. As one might expect, the existence of such a system helps ensure that unit managers do their best to keep key people occupied with truly challenging projects. It also ensures that the best people end up working on the biggest potential opportunities'.

Defending and Protecting Core Competencies

Core competencies do not diminish with use. Unlike physical assets, which do deteriorate over time, knowledge and competencies are enhanced and developed as they are applied and shared. But competencies need to be nurtured and protected: knowledge and skill fade or lose their currency if they are not used. Worse, the competence base can be attacked or destroyed by crude downsizing and delayering activities that do not recognize people as the basic reservoirs of knowledge, skill, experience, culture and vision; and which eliminate them without any recognition of their role as constituents of basic enterprise competence.

Hamel and Prahalad suggest that protecting core competencies from erosion will require continuing and proactive vigilance, leadership, encouragement, and championing by the senior management of the enterprise. They comment (p. 235) that 'core competence leadership may be lost in many ways. Competencies may wither through lack of funding; become fragmented through divisionalisation, particularly where no single executive feels fully responsible for competence stewardship; be inadvertently surrendered to alliance partners; or be lost when an underperforming business is divested'. They suggest that senior managers should be assigned cross-corporate stewardship roles for particular competencies. These managers should be held responsible for the health of those competencies, and for carrying out regular "competence reviews" on a diagnostic and developmental basis over time.

Managing Obsolete Technologies and Technology Discontinuities

Technology discontinuities were described in Chapter 19. Enterprise management will need to remain vigilant to the possibility of the emergence of new competencies that might eventually replace and render obsolete the existing competence base. A number of examples of such obsolescence were given in Chapter 19. Hamel and Prahalad note (p. 229) that 'a company's competence-building agenda should include gaining an understanding of those new competencies that may one day supplant its traditional' knowledge, technology, and skill base.

Example: the displacement by the use of newer biotechnological competencies in drug development of older competences associated with the manipulation of chemical properties to produce pharmaceutical substances.

REVIEW QUESTIONS

1. What is a core competence? What is the significance of the concept?
2. What are the three tests of core competence?
3. How may the development and application of core competencies be co-ordinated and integrated within the organization?

4. What are the implications for management of ignoring the core competence concept?
5. Describe strategies by which the strategic management of core competencies may be undertaken.

TECHNIQUES OF CASE STUDY AND ANALYSIS

1. Identify core competencies (if any) from the case study.
2. Analyze and comment on how these core competencies yield competitive advantage.
3. Analyze the nature of the management of core competencies that is apparent from the case study. Comment on the implications of this management process for the case company.

PROJECT ASSIGNMENTS

1. Using available information, identify and comment on the core competencies of an organization in which you are interested.
2. Using available information, compare and contrast the core competencies of two or more organizations that operate in the same sector or market.
3. Using available information, compare and contrast the core competencies of two or more organizations that operate in the same sector or market, but are based in different countries, or are international in scope.

References

Hamel, G. and C.K. Prahalad (1990) "The core competence of the corporation", Harvard Business Review, May-June.
Hamel, G. and C.K. Prahalad (1994) *Competing For The Future*, Harvard Business School Press, Boston, Mass.
Hammer, H. and J. Champy (1993, 1995) *Re-engineering the Corporation*, Nicholas Brealey, London.
Kanter, R.M. (1990) *When Giants Learn to Dance*, Routledge, London.
Kay, J. (1993) *Foundations Of Corporate Success*, Oxford University Press, Oxford.
Morden, A.R. (2004) *Principles of Management (2nd Edition)*, Ashgate, Aldershot.
Pascale, R. (1994) "Changing face", *BusinessAge*, February.

Chapter 21

Resource Stretch and Leverage

This chapter analyzes the related concepts of "resource stretch" and "resource leverage". These strategic concepts may be used to formulate, to lead, and to realise an increasingly ambitious rate of enterprise performance. The concepts may be used to achieve significantly more output than at present with the knowledge and capability at the disposal of the organization.

The chapter recaps the concept of strategic intent introduced in Chapter 11. It describes Hamel and Prahalad's concept of strategy as resource stretch. It analyzes Hamel and Prahalad's concept of strategy as resource leverage, and it summarizes five major resource leverage strategies.

The copyrights of the material upon which this chapter is based are held variously by Gary Hamel and C.K. Prahalad, Harvard Business School Press, and the President and Fellows of Harvard College. Their permission to reproduce this copyright material is gratefully acknowledged.

ANTECEDENTS AND PARALLELS

Hamel and Prahalad (1994) conceptualize strategy formulation in terms of core competencies (described in Chapter 20), and in terms of resource stretch and leverage, described in this chapter. Hamel and Prahalad's discussion of stretch and leverage has such antecedents and parallels as:

❑ Stafford Beer's pioneering work *A Platform for Change* (1975).
❑ the work of Tom Peters *et al* (for instance 1982, 1986, 1989).
❑ Rosabeth Moss Kanter's (1985) analysis of empowerment.
❑ Rosabeth Moss Kanter's (1990) analysis of the post-entrepreneurial corporation, with its need for an architecture that includes co-operation and partnership; and a need to base enterprise resource management on "doing more with less". Reference is made to this concept in a later part of this chapter.

❑ the concept of re-engineering. For instance see Hammer and Champy (1993, 1995), Johannson *et al* (1993), McHugh *et al* (1995).
❑ the work of John Kay (1993).
❑ Tichy and Sherman's 1994 analysis of the US General Electric Company.
❑ the work of Collins and Porras (1996) described in Chapter 17.
❑ the work of Nonaka (1991) and Nonaka and Takeuchi (1995) described in Chapter 19.

STRATEGIC INTENT

Hamel and Prahalad's conceptualization of strategic intent was described in Chapter 11. Strategic intent is used to define and to communicate a *sense of direction* about the longer-term strategic position that the leadership of the enterprise wishes to achieve through its processes of objective setting and strategy formulation. Strategic intent comprises:

❑ *a sense of direction* - that is, a meaningful, consistent, and unifying sense of purpose and pattern that is to be maintained over time.
❑ *a sense of discovering* - that will provide opportunities to meet new challenges and explore the unfamiliar.
❑ *a sense of destiny* - that will create meaning, enthusiasm, inspiration, and commitment on the part of managers, employees, and stakeholders.

Hamel and Prahalad contend that strategic intent may imply the use of *resource stretch*. This means that (i) the present management and use of resources, and (ii) the current operating capabilities of the enterprise may both be deemed inadequate to meet the requirements of strategic intent. Both will need "stretching" in order to meet the needs specified by that strategic intent.

STRATEGY AS STRETCH

Stretch is the *gap* between:

❑ the knowledge, resources, willpower, capability, and competence currently available to the enterprise; *and*

❑ enterprise aspirations, and the degree to which its leadership desires to be more productive, more inventive, or more creative in the way in which the organization carries out its activities.

The degree of stretch that is deemed to be required by the organization is defined by:

❑ the strategic intent; and
❑ the nature of the *challenges* to the enterprise that are likely to face the organization in achieving that strategic intent, as established (i) by the forecasts and future scenarios that may affect the activities of that organization; and (ii) by external or competitive comparisons and benchmarks, for instance as defined by criteria of "excellence", "world class", "best value", or the ambition to be "number one" in the sector, etc.

Enterprise Challenges

Hamel and Prahalad conceptualize stretch in terms of focusing attention, effort, and willpower on challenges from which new capabilities or sources of competitive advantage may be built. Hamel and Prahalad comment that it is the job of leaders in the enterprise 'to focus the organization's attention on the next challenge, and the next after that. The first might be quality; the next, cycle time ... the next, mastery of a particular technology; and so on. In establishing the capability-building agenda, top management provides employees with a clear view of the next advantage to be constructed' (p. 136).

The definition and communication of corporate challenges thus provide a focal point for the building or enhancement of capability and competence in the near to medium-term future; and are an operational means of staging the acquisition of new competitive advantages.

Challenges are also seen as a means for harnessing and directing the intellectual and emotional energy that should flow from a proper commitment to the strategic intent of the enterprise. In this, Hamel and Prahalad define corporate challenges as milestones on the path from today to tomorrow.

They however note a caveat that 'employees are unlikely to rise to a particular challenge if they don't believe they will benefit proportionately from the firm's success. For challenges to take root, an atmosphere of "shared pain, shared gain" must prevail' (p. 143). Relative compensation levels for instance send powerful messages. Great disparities (and perceptions of top management greed) may kill off enthusiasm and commitment to the strategic intent.

Some of these issues were analyzed in their leadership context in Chapter 17 of this book.

Stretch

The gap between resources and aspirations is stretch. Where current resources and capabilities are unlikely to be adequate to meet the requirements of enterprise strategic intent, they will need stretching in order to meet the demands of that intent.

Hamel and Prahalad comment that 'we believe that it is essential for top management to set an aspiration that creates, by design, a chasm between ambition and resources ... managers must create a misfit between resources and ambitions. Medium term challenges should demand more of the organization than what it currently believes is possible' (p. 146).

A firm's strategic intent should represent an ambition that stretches far beyond the current resources and capabilities of the enterprise. A commitment to achieving that strategic intent may have to override the day-to-day constraints of strategic and business planning, capital budgeting (etc). 'The goal of strategic intent ... is to fold the future back into the present ... unless senior management is willing to commit to a goal that lies outside the planning horizon, there can be no strategic intent. The future will be discovered by someone else' (p. 146).

Hamel and Prahalad comment that the stretch implied in meeting corporate challenges may force enterprise management to abandon the 'orthodoxy of conventional wisdom' and an 'installed base of thinking'; and to involve and empower employees 'close to the action' in identifying issues and solving problems that arise. Stretch implies doing things differently and resourcefully, 'by fundamentally rethinking processes, roles, and responsibilities' (p. 137), or by re-engineering them.

The process of stretching aspirations and resources may be charted against, and compared with external market, competitor, or comparator benchmarks. Hamel and Prahalad comment that 'without external benchmarks, it is all too easy for employees to believe that it is top management, rather than competitive reality, that is applying the pressure for improvement'. At the same time, the enterprise and its competitors should be judged both on the resources available to them; and on the resourcefulness (creativity or imagination) with which they use these resources. Staff skill and enterprise resourcefulness may more than offset an apparent lack of resources and capability.

Hamel and Prahalad conclude that 'a view of strategy as stretch ... helps bridge the gap that exists between those who see strategy as "a grand plan, thought up by great minds", and those who see strategy as a pattern in a stream of incremental decisions. Strategy as stretch is strategy by design in the sense that top management does have a relatively clear view of the goal line and a broad agenda of the capability-building challenges that lie between today and tomorrow. Strategy as stretch is strategy by incrementalism to the extent that top management cannot predetermine every single step of the journey to the future. Strategy as stretch recognizes the ... paradox that while leadership cannot be entirely planned for, neither does it happen in the absence of a clearly articulated and widely shared aspiration.

Where fit is achieved by simply paring down ambitions, there will be no spur for such ingenuity and much of the firm's strategic potential will remain dormant. Tests of realism and feasibility must not be prematurely applied. Stretch and the creativity it engenders are the engine and fuel for corporate growth and vitality. This is why the genesis of the strategy process must be a purposefully created misfit between where the firm is and where it wants to be' (pp. 146-147).

STRATEGY AS LEVERAGE

Hamel and Prahalad suggest that enterprise management 'must find a way to close the gap between resources and aspirations that (the) strategic intent opens up'. This is achieved 'by leveraging resources, by travelling the maximum distance down the road to leadership, using the least possible amount of fuel. The goal is to challenge managers to become more ingenious both in multiplying the impact of the firm's resource base and enlarging it' (p. 147).

Using Resources

Hamel and Prahalad conceptualize the enterprise as a portfolio of knowledge, competencies, assets and resources (whether capital, technical, human, financial, operational or managerial).

They comment that a limitation to the level of knowledge and resource that is available to the enterprise is not necessarily an impediment to progress; nor are copious resources a guarantee of continued success. There may be significant differences between the impact that individual enterprises in any particular sector can generate with a given base of knowledge and resources. Some enterprises will be more creative, imaginative, inventive, resourceful and productive than others in the use of their knowledge, capability, and competence.

Strategy as Leverage

Hamel and Prahalad describe stretch and leverage as the two sides of the same coin. *Stretch relates to aspiration. Leverage relates to the use of capabilities and resources to achieve these aspirations.* Just as necessity begets invention and resourcefulness, so does stretch give rise to resource leverage. Creativity and inventiveness are the offspring of resource scarcity.

Hamel and Prahalad argue that in the absence of proper strategic intent, aspiration and focus, 'abundance is likely to be little more than a licence for carelessness in strategic decision-making ... resource abundance and the attendant ability to make multiple bets and to sustain multiple failures too often substitute for disciplined and creative strategic thinking' (p. 154). This is the opposite of stretch and leverage.

An enterprise that instead has a surfeit of ambition and a dearth of resources will quickly discover that it cannot imitate the advantages of more affluent competitors. Such an enterprise may have:

☐ to challenge the "orthodoxy" of the organization, to eliminate inflexible thinking, and to change established ways of doing things; *and:-*
☐ creatively to get the most from the limited resources it has; *and also:-*
☐ to proactively create new forms of competitive advantage for itself.

Doing More With What You Have

Resource leverage is defined by Hamel and Prahalad in terms of *doing more (or adding more value) with what you have.* This can be contrasted with Rosabeth Moss Kanter's (1990) dictum for the post-entrepreneurial corporation that enterprise management will need to "do more with less".

Hamel and Prahalad contend that leverage-based efficiency gains come primarily from 'raising the numerator' (such as revenue and profit) in productivity ratios, rather than from reducing the 'denominator' (such as capital employed or employee headcount).

Hamel and Prahalad argue that with the objective of 'reducing the buck for a given bang' rather than 'increasing the bang for a given buck', *denominator-driven* corporate restructuring programmes are more about cutting resources than leveraging them. An inefficient firm that downsizes, without improving its capacity for resource leverage, will find its productivity gains will be at best temporary in duration. It may instead embark on a destructive downward spiral of resource and capability attrition towards "corporate anorexia", entropy, and the potential for institutional decline and market vulnerability.

Resource leverage, on the other hand, implies creativity. Hamel and Prahalad comment that 'it is about the continual search for new, less resource-intensive means of achieving strategic objectives' (p. 159). Slimming down the work force and cutting back on investment are however intellectually less demanding for senior management than discovering ways to grow output on a static or slowly growing resource base: 'cutting the buck is easier than expanding the bang' (p. 159) for a leadership that is unimaginative, orthodox, short-termist in outlook, or just pure lazy.

ACHIEVING RESOURCE LEVERAGE

Hamel and Prahalad identify five major resource leverage strategies, as follow.

Concentrating Resources

Convergence - the pursuit over a long period of time of a clear strategic intent and an agreed objective will require the effort and willpower of the enterprise to converge consistently, collectively, and synergistically on that intent and that goal. Such convergence may not be possible where there are multiple, inconsistent, and competing objectives. Convergence requires that the enterprise decide how best its resources can be combined and orchestrated to achieve a stretch objective. Such convergence also requires a consistent pattern of direction over time, with an effective leadership "hand on the wheel" steering the same course.

Focus - which is the concentration of effort and resources on a very few objectives at any one time. Peters and Waterman (1982) call this "chunking". Focus in this sense implies concentrating a critical mass of willpower, effort, and work on the issue to hand until it is satisfactorily resolved; then (and only then) moving on to the next issue. Otherwise, effort will be diluted and dissipated. This is the opposite of resource leverage. Hamel and Prahalad comment (pp. 162-164) that:-

- 'put simply, the bigger the ... task and the smaller the resource base, the more critical is operational focus'.

- 'as a rule of thumb, no ... group of employees can attend to more than two key operational improvement goals at (any one) time'.
- 'mixed messages and conflicting signals prevent a sufficient head of steam from developing behind any improvement task'.
- '(to divide) meagre resources across a wide range of medium-term operational goals is a recipe for mediocrity across a broad front'.

Targeting - by which the enterprise targets effort and willpower on those activities which will yield the greatest benefit in terms of:-

- the potential improvement in customer perceptions of enterprise product or service offer that these activities represent.
- their relative opportunity cost.
- their relative competitive or comparative advantage.
- their relative value addition.

Hamel and Prahalad comment that resources may be most effectively leveraged when they are targeted in the areas that make the most difference to customers and stakeholders.

Accumulating Resources

Mining - Hamel and Prahalad comment that some organizations exploit their accumulated knowledge and experience more effectively than others. The authors contend that 'each new experience, each success or failure, must be seen as an opportunity to learn' (p. 165).

Some organizations are more adept at learning, absorbing, and applying new ideas than others. They are more open to new perceptions and conceptualizations; and less reluctant to challenge received wisdoms, orthodoxies, or 'installed bases of thinking'.

Borrowing - by which the enterprise variously gains access to, acquires, or internalizes competencies and resources from outside. It can do this through its network of relationships, and its architecture. This may for example involve:-

- the use of subcontractors in a de-integrated value chain, so as to exploit the internal sources of competitive advantage, excellence, creativity, and innovation of these subcontractors.
- inward licensing processes.
- strategic alliances (described in Chapter 27).
- other strategies of co-operation and partnership, such as sharing development activities with key competitors, customers, or suppliers.
- participating in international research consortia (that is, borrowing foreign taxpayers' money).
- 'harvesting the technology seeds planted in another nation' (p. 167).

- making use of more attractive factor markets (such as carrying out labour-intensive activities like bulk software programming in the Czech Republic, or locating call centre operations in India).

Hamel and Prahalad comment that borrowing can be used to multiply resources at any stage of the value chain. They also note that if borrowing is used, then the organization's absorptive capacity will be as important as its creative capacity. There will be no place for the negative "not invented here" syndrome described in Chapter 19.

Complementing Resources

Blending - by which resources are combined or integrated in ways that multiply the relative value of each. Hamel and Prahalad give the combined example of (i) technological integration; (ii) functional and operational integration; and (iii) the conceptualization, creation, specification, and development of new products or processes. Blending may create synergies amongst resources (for example on a cross-functional basis). Or it may yield benefits from new permutations and combinations of those resources that create new functionalities or new values (for instance by new combinations of technologies or the process of hybridization).

Kay comments similarly that the effectiveness of sources of competitive advantage is improved where they are represented in combination, such that the resources they represent are blended together. Kay in particular suggests that the more that enterprise architecture supports and complements innovation, corporate reputation, brand management or the maintenance of strategic assets, the more value will these sources of competitive advantage be capable of generating.

Balancing - by which a balanced array of resources and competencies are put in place that permit *all* necessary activities to be carried out with equal effectiveness. Hamel and Prahalad give as example the combined 'capacity to invent, make, and deliver' (p. 169), not just any one or two disproportionately. Hamel and Prahalad note that 'the leverage impact comes when, by gaining control over complementary resources, the firm is able to multiply the profits it can extract out of its own unique resources' (p. 170). Kay also deals with this issue in commenting on the need for mutually supporting sources of competence and competitive advantage, and in particular the need for a firm's activities to be supported by, and balanced with its relationship architecture.

Hamel and Prahalad note that 'a firm that has a strong product development capacity but is relatively weak in terms of brand or distribution or lacks the disciplines of cost and quality is unlikely to gain much of the profit stream that will ultimately accrue to its innovation. Although it can enter partnerships with firms that do possess critical complementary resources, the innovator is likely to find itself in a poor bargaining position with such firms when it comes to divvying up profits … in the international drinks industry, IDV, Seagrams, and Guinness once saw themselves as primarily brand creators and managers. Yet they now realize that to fully leverage the equity of brands like Smirnoff, Johnny Walker, and Chivas Regal, they must control distributors … this realization has set off a frenzied competition to buy up and consolidate distributors around the world' (p. 170).

Conserving Resources

Recycling - the more often a particular skill or competence is used, the greater the resource leverage and the more the competence is developed. This point was made in Chapters 19 and 20. It is the principle that underlies Tatsumo's mandala of creativity shown in Chapter 19. Hamel and Prahalad note for instance that 'Honda has recycled engine-related innovations across motorcycles, cars, outboard motors, generators, and garden tractors' (p. 171).

Co-opting - by which access to the resources of other enterprises is achieved through the relationship architecture of the enterprise on the basis of co-operation or partnership, in order to pursue a common objective. Such co-option may lead to such benefits as greater market access and scope; the achievement of critical mass; or the achievement of synergies; (etc). The principal of co-opting is fundamental to the establishment of the de-integrated value chains and network structures described in earlier chapters; and also to the establishment of the strategic alliances described in Chapter 27. Co-opting has become a classic Japanese strategy.

Protecting - by which the risk of value loss or damage to resources is avoided by the selection of appropriate competition strategies, as described in Chapter 22. Issues of value loss were also dealt with in earlier chapters of this book. The enterprise may choose, for example:-

- to avoid head-on confrontations with powerful opponents.
- to maintain strategies of defence or counter-attack.
- to enter new markets via undefended or poorly served segments, or 'loose bricks' (as Honda did with its first small motorcycles).
- to select strategic alliances and alliance partners with care, so that the relationship can be controlled and the transfer of competence between the partners equalized.

Recovering Resources

Expediting returns - by which the time between the expenditure of resources and the recovery of those resources ("return") is minimized. A rapid recovery process acts as a resource multiplier. An enterprise that can do anything twice as fast as its competitors, with a similar resource commitment, enjoys a twofold leverage advantage. Hence the widespread strategy of shortening product or process development times, compressing operational time scales, and carrying out related activities in parallel or synchrony rather than in sequence.

REVIEW QUESTIONS

1. Recap the concept of strategic intent (Chapter 11).
2. What is strategic stretch? On what basis may stretch objectives be established?
3. What is resource leverage?
4. Describe and comment on five major resource leverage strategies.

TECHNIQUES OF CASE STUDY AND ANALYSIS

1. Identify the mission and strategic intent (if any) of the case company.
2. Is there any evidence of stretch objectives in the case study?
3. Is there any evidence of resource leverage strategies in the case study?
4. Suggest stretch objectives that the case company could usefully establish for itself.
5. Suggest appropriate resource leverage strategies that the case company could usefully establish for itself.

PROJECT ASSIGNMENTS

1. Using available information, suggest some actual examples of strategic stretch. Look at a variety of sectors whether business, commercial, service, public, or not-for-profit.
2. Using available information from a variety of sectors, suggest some actual examples of resource leverage strategies.

References

Beer, S. (1975) *A Platform for Change*, Wiley, Chichester.

Collins, J.C. and J.I. Porras (1996) *Built to Last*, Century Business, London.

Hamel, G. and C.K. Prahalad (1994) *Competing for the Future*, Harvard Business School Press, Boston, Mass.

Hammer, H. and J. Champy (1993, 1995) *Reengineering the Corporation*, Nicholas Brealey, London.

Johansson, H.J., McHugh, P., Pendlebury, A.J., and W.A. Wheeler (1993) *Business Process Reengineering: Breakpoint Strategies for Market Dominance*, Wiley, Chichester.

Kanter, R.M. (1985) *The Change Masters*, Routledge, London.

Kanter, R.M. (1990) *When Giants Learn to Dance*, Routledge, London.

Kay, J. (1993) *Foundations of Corporate Success*, Oxford University Press, Oxford.

McHugh, P., Merli, G., and W.A. Wheeler (1995) *Beyond Business Process Reengineering*, Wiley, Chichester.

Morden, A.R. (1997) 'A strategic evaluation of re-engineering, restructuring, delayering and downsizing policies as flawed paradigm', *Management Decision*, Vol 35, No 3.

Nonaka, I. (1991) 'The knowledge-creating company', *Harvard Business Review*, November-December.

Nonaka, I. and H. Takeuchi (1995) *The Knowledge-Creating Company*, Oxford University Press, New York.

Peters, T.J. (1989) *Thriving on Chaos*, Pan, London.

Peters, T.J. and N. Austin (1986) *A Passion for Excellence*, Fontana, London.

Peters, T.J. and R.H. Waterman (1982) *In Search of Excellence*, Harper & Row, New York.

Tichy, N.M. and S. Sherman (1994) *Control Your Destiny or Someone Else Will*, Harper Business, New York.

Chapter 22

Competition Strategy

"Ahead of us are Darwinian shakeouts in every marketplace with no consolation prize for losing companies and nations".
Jack Welch - Former Chairman and CEO, the General Electric (GE) Corporation of the USA.

"I don't like the lust for failure in Britain. The only reason we don't have the death penalty in Britain is you're gone too quick - you can't jab people through the bars when they're dead". Billy Connolly

This chapter analyzes competition strategy. It also looks at how companies choose to position themselves in order to compete. The choice of competition strategy is a basic positioning decision in competitive environments. The role of *position* within strategy was described in Chapter 11.

The chapter summarizes a variety of competitive positions. It then describes alternative competition strategies or competitive ploys ranging from the proactive and the aggressive through the defensive to co-operation and partnership. The role of *ploy* within strategy was described in Chapter 11.

The nature of enterprise competition strategy will, in part, be determined by the prevailing competition policy or competition laws of the country in which the company is operating. Reference was made to these regulations in Chapters 5 and 6.

The nature of the competitive environment was described in Part One of this book, and in particular in Chapter 5. Business strategies that are used to implement enterprise competition strategies are dealt with in later chapters of Part Four.

COMPETITIVE POSITIONING

The enterprise may select, may work towards achieving, or may instead have forced upon it any of the *competitive positions* described immediately below. This competitive position will depend upon the relative strength of the enterprise within its competitive environment; and on its capability and its sources of competitive advantage.

Dominance - in which the enterprise is the outright leader. Its *deliberate* strategy is to maintain its position and to shape the nature of the trading environment in its own interest. Du Pont is for example often quoted as being dominant in a number of global chemical markets. Ultimately, dominance may take the form of oligopoly or monopoly if the prevailing competition laws will permit such a position in the sector or industry.

Leadership - in which the enterprise is "number one" in the perception of customer and trade alike. The leader acts as a benchmark for the sector. Leadership is likely to be based upon the possession and exploitation of very significant sources of competitive advantage, for instance as described in Chapter 4. A leadership position may, or may not be associated with a significant market share.

Seeking parity - where the enterprise attempts to maintain equality with its main competitors, ideally so that the emergence of any dominant or leading player is inhibited or discouraged. The enterprise however takes the nature of the competitive "game" as given. It plays the "same game" as its rivals. It is not likely to be in a strong enough position to shape or redefine the nature of that game.

This *required* strategy is for instance characteristic of mature markets for fast-moving consumer goods in which companies compete for relative market share.

Followership - where the enterprise follows the lead of dominant or leading competitors, playing the (*required*) game by the rules that these dominant or leading players have laid down. Followers may be *forced* to introduce "me too" products or campaigns that imitate the strategies of market leaders; or may instead be forced to calculate their price position relative to the leader's benchmark.

Low profile - in which the enterprise actively seeks to avoid the attentions of the main players in the market, thereby minimizing the risk of a head-on confrontation which would inevitably be damaging to the weaker party. This is a *self-imposed* strategy.

Complementary - where the existence of the enterprise is complementary to the competitive position of other organizations. For instance, markets characterized by an oligopoly situation based upon a small number of very powerful large players may also contain a range of mid-sized companies. The continued existence of these smaller companies is essential to their more powerful rivals in order to avoid statutory investigation or interference that could lead to an enforced increase in the number of significant competitive players.

Alternatively, the enterprise may supply its customers with products or services which those customers need, but which they do not wish to provide for themselves. This is the case for the development and manufacture of printers for the computer industry. The work of such companies as Canon and Hewlett-Packard is complementary to that of computer manufacturers, to the providers of microprocessors such as Intel, and to the providers of software such as Microsoft or Sage.

PROACTIVE, OFFENSIVE, OR ATTACKING COMPETITION STRATEGIES

Proactive, offensive, or attacking strategies are predicated upon an aggressive determination *to shape the nature of the competitive environment in the interest of the enterprise*; and where possible to disadvantage competitors. The enterprise "plays to win". Others may therefore lose.

The enterprise may attempt to shape the rules of the game (and the conditions in which it is played) in its own interest. Competitors will have to play the game by its rules, not by their own. A classic example is for enterprise management to use political and reputation advantages to ensure that *standards* are set (either or both by official standards institutions, or by market perceptions of benchmark quality and desirability):

❑ such that few, if any rivals can match these standards; *and*
❑ such that these standards constitute powerful barriers to entry; *and*
❑ such that the exit of weaker players is encouraged.

Where the enterprise is in a position to redefine the nature of the market or competition, or to establish a "new game", it will have the advantage of both (i) being able to be the first to move, and (ii) being free to choose the direction of that movement. This "first mover" advantage may then be used to establish leadership or dominance, since rivals will be placed in a position where as followers they may always be trying to catch up. The nature of the competitive game, and the strategy will both be *forced* upon them by the leader.

The ability of the enterprise to pursue proactive, attacking, or first-mover strategies may be strengthened where it has developed the long-term capability successfully to identify, invest in, bring to market, and exploit "winners". Its track record in *picking winners* may variously depend on:

❑ the depth and continuity of its leadership competence (Chapter 17) and its management skill.
❑ the strength of its sources of competitive advantage (Chapter 4).
❑ its core competencies (Chapter 20).
❑ its architecture (as described in Chapters 4 and 18).
❑ its ability financially to sustain consistent long term investment in new technologies, new processes, and new products or services (Chapter 13).
❑ its ability to manage technology and innovation; and to identify and exploit discontinuities (Chapter 19).
❑ its knowledge management capability, its creativity, and the depth of its experience and expertize (Chapter 19).
❑ its use of the business strategies described in later chapters of Part Four to implement its competition strategies.

Establishing Outright Market Leadership

Drucker (1985) describes the objective of this strategy as being to establish leadership in a new market or sector created or developed by the enterprise. The new market, and leadership of that market, are likely to be based on the possession and exploitation of some significant core competence, innovatory capability, or other source of competitive advantage.

The strategy aims to create new demands, new customers, and new markets which the originator then dominates. Drucker cites two examples:

❑ the acquisition and development of the first vitamin patents by Hoffman LaRoche during the 1920s; and that company's subsequent development and patenting of the tranquillizers Librium and Valium during the 1950s. Both developments established large new markets.
❑ the development and marketing by Du Pont of the synthetic fibre nylon.

Flanking or Segment Attack

Drucker describes this form of competition strategy in terms of "hitting the competition where it isn't". Alternatively, it may take the form of an attack on market segments or market niches that have been under-exploited or neglected by existing suppliers.

Products or services may be introduced that provide satisfaction within customer usage contexts not already adequately covered by existing suppliers. Or products may be introduced that outperform what is already available but perceived by customers to be unsatisfactory. Examples include the introduction by Sony of small, portable transistor radios; the development by Amstrad of efficient but low cost word processors; or the replacement of steam traction by diesel-electric railway locomotive technology.

The enterprise looks for market or process opportunities not yet recognized nor properly provided for by existing suppliers. Newcomers can use this route because the barriers to entry may not be high. Defensive tactics by existing suppliers may prove ineffective if the market is unsatisfied and the newcomer provides the value or satisfaction being sought by customers.

Drucker also points out that this strategy may be used as a form of *flanking attack* on existing suppliers. The enterprise concentrates at first on those parts of the market that are ineffectively provided for. But eventually the newcomer may be able to use its evolving and strengthening position to mount a wider or more general attack on the segment strongholds of existing suppliers, particularly where (i) these suppliers have become complacent; (ii) these suppliers have stopped investing in order to maximize short-term shareholder returns; or (iii) the newcomer is naïvely dismissed as insignificant.

The Prospector

Miles and Snow (1978) describe as "prospectors" those organizations that regularly search for new market opportunities, and experiment with potential responses to emerging trends within the technological or market environment. Prospectors are creators of change and uncertainty to which their competitors must respond. They conceptualize their environment as being characterized by dynamism and change. They believe that the parameters of that environment can be shaped in a *deliberate* and *opportunistic* manner in the interests of the enterprise.

COPYING AND CREATIVE IMITATION

Creative imitation implies the copying or the improvement of a product, process, or service first introduced by a competitor. The creative imitator copies or develops the competitor's offering, perhaps improving its specification or introducing it at a lower price level than the original. Examples include:

❑   the copying and development by Japanese manufacturers in the 1950s of British and American motor cycles; and the subsequent Japanese dominance of the world market.
❑   Seiko's adaptation of Swiss electronic quartz digital watch technology and its introduction into the mass watch market.

The strategy of creative imitation may contain less risk than that of innovation. It may also contain less risk than the strategy of attempting to establish outright market leadership already described above. The innovator or the originator of the product carries the burden and uncertainty (i) of developing the "new"; (ii) of familiarizing people with it; and (iii) of creating the market. The creative imitator can avoid these costs of origination and market creation; make improvements or cost reductions; and capitalize on the efforts of others.

Skilful imitators may be capable of rapid copying and *fast seconding* to the market. They are never far behind the leader in exploiting the market it is creating. The mass international toy market is characterized by a continuous cycle of new product introductions, market development, short product life cycles, imitation, and fast seconding.

THE STRATEGIC THINKING OF SUN TZU

Sun Tzu was an adviser to the Chinese Emperor Wu. His political dexterity and strategic ruthlessness helped his employer overwhelm the state of Chu, with whom the Emperor was in conflict. His teachings, compiled around 500 BC, are based on historical Chinese experience of fighting wars and handling the frequent conflicts that characterized the times.

Sun Tzu's book *The Art of War* (translated by Griffith, 1971; summarized by Min Chen, 1995; and, for instance, adapted by Krause, 1996) describes effective and ineffective strategies by which to fight wars or defeat opponents. The Chinese ideogram for "strategy" is the same as that for "war", so it is natural for the Chinese to perceive the two concepts in the same light. As a result, South East Asians tend to perceive the marketplace as a *battlefield*. The success or failure of a business or an economy directly affects the survival and well-being of the family or the nation. Strategies for waging war have therefore been applied to strategies for *waging business*. In competitive terms these strategies are summarized as follows.

Defeat Your Opponents by Strategy and Flexibility

The objective here should be to conquer the opponent by strategy not conflict. Conflict may ultimately benefit no-one. Defeating the opponent by strategy implies 'careful and detailed planning', that is, clear business strategy and proper strategic management. At the same time, given Sun Tzu's reminder that 'no plan survives contact with the enemy', enterprise strategy must be flexible and opportunistic according to the circumstances that present themselves.

Use Competitive Information

In order to win by strategy the enterprise needs to be well informed about its business environment and about its competitors. The manager needs to be in possession of the 'total picture of the situation'. Min Chen notes that 'to be competitive, an enterprise ... needs the information of its competitors, such as the development plan of its new products, operational plans and financial situation' (p. 48). Its rivals, meanwhile, would be well advised to put systems and incentives in place to ensure that such commercially sensitive information is kept secure and inaccessible!

Unite Your Own People in Purpose and Commitment

People who are in broad agreement with their ruler are more likely to be willing to accept the hazards of conflict than those who are in disagreement. In a competitive business situation, enterprise management may have to attempt to create meaningful and shared corporate goals 'so that all in the company come to view themselves as members of the group crossing the river in the same boat. They would be more likely [to] consider company affairs as their own and be willing to make personal sacrifices when needed ... as Sun Tzu said, "he whose ranks are united in purpose will win"' (Chen, p. 43).

Divide Your Opponents

Divided or fragmented opponents may provide the least resistance to your competition strategies. An unified opposition may instead be a force to be reckoned with. Hence, for instance, the individualism of western societies and a prevailing ethic of "going it alone" has in the past made difficult the establishment of the co-operation and partnership between companies described at various stages of this book. South East Asian companies, but especially the Japanese, have found it relatively easy to "pick off" industries (such as consumer electronics, heavy engineering, shipbuilding, or automotive) which were characterized (i) by intense and divisive national competition between fragmented and inward-looking companies, or (ii) restrictive competition laws as in the USA.

Use Climate and Conditions to Your Advantage

A good general knows how to exploit to his own advantage the uncontrollable elements of geographical conditions and climate in which his army finds itself. Thus did the Russian General Kutusov defeat Napoleon's troops with the help of the severe Russian winter. Similarly, the choice of business strategy needs to be appropriate to such prevailing environmental features of economic climate and business culture as:

- the prevailing political situation.
- demographic, social and cultural factors.
- on-going changes in consumer tastes and attitudes.
- economic conditions and trade cycles.
- the prevailing investment climate.

Better still, of course, if the enterprise can shape its environment in its own interest, for instance through controlling distribution outlets (as in the movie or alcoholic spirits markets); or through the effective political lobbying and persuasion of such institutions as national governments, the World Trade Organization (WTO), European Union (EU), or North American Free Trade Association (NAFTA), etc. This point has already been made above.

Play to Your Capabilities and Strengths

Like the general deploying his troops in battle order, the leader and his or her managers should concentrate personal and organizational capability, willpower, and enterprise experience where it is likely to prove most advantageous. At the same time, the enterprise will have to recognize the strengths of its rivals and avoid meeting them head on. It could lose such a confrontation.

Play to the Weaknesses of Competitors

At the same time the leader, like the general, may position enterprise strengths and capability against the weakest points of the competition. Thus, such was the difference in perceived quality between mass-produced Japanese cars and those made in the West during the 1970s and 1980s that Japanese manufacturers were able to capture a major slice of markets there.

DEFENSIVE OR REACTIVE COMPETITION STRATEGIES

Defensive or reactive strategies are used to defend enterprise position in the sector or market against the threat of competition from rivals, and in particular against the proactive, offensive or attacking strategies described above; or against strategies of creative imitation.

The enterprise will attempt to maintain its position, for instance by developing, reinforcing, exploiting, and protecting its various sources of competitive advantage. At the same time, it will attempt to block or neutralize attacking moves by competitors. Ries and Trout (1986) comment that a well-entrenched market or brand position, effectively reinforced and subject to continuous innovation and improvement, may be very difficult for a competitor to dislodge. Effective defenders include Unilever's Persil washing powder business; Du Pont, Coca-Cola, Guinness; Mercedes Benz automotive; and British Airways.

Segment Protection

A basic defensive strategy is that of *protecting existing segment provision*. The enterprise attempts to monitor threats to its position within the market segments from which it draws its business. It may then choose to:

❑ defend and enhance its presence in that market segment, for instance by undertaking activities that strengthen product and brand value, increase trade or customer loyalty, and so on.

❏ make entry harder or more expensive for would-be entrants or attackers, even where they may have achieved some initial platform of competitive advantage.

The potential for entrepreneurial or innovatory pressures from competitors is likely to make it sensible for the enterprise to undertake periodic reviews of its current segment provision. This may help to ensure that there is little or no potential "virgin territory" close to the business that a newcomer could use as the base for a later attack on the wider range of segments within which the enterprise operates.

Drucker describes a classic case of failure to protect existing segment provision. This was the change in the information technology market brought about by the first minicomputer and microcomputer manufacturers, and software houses. The innovations they introduced (and their concept of distributed processing) were initially ignored or rejected (for instance on the "not-invented here" basis described in Chapter 19) by the manufacturers of mainframe computers. Companies such as IBM eventually awoke to find that the mini and microcomputer manufacturers and producers of software had entered a variety of market segments; taken away much corporate business; and changed the entire direction in which the market was to develop.

The Defender

Miles and Snow describe as "defenders" those organizations which consciously and *deliberately impose on themselves* a restricted product-market mission or competence. They might be specialists in their field. They might instead take a limited view of what they do and how this fits within the external environment. The enterprise and its staff may be expert in a limited field of operation, and may be highly effective in the knowledge management that this expertize calls for. But enterprise management does not tend to search outside for new opportunities. They instead concentrate their efforts upon improving the efficiency and effectiveness of their existing operations.

Defenders are careful to protect their existing market segment provision and market share. They pursue strategies of innovation, stretch, and continuous improvement in order to maintain their leadership of a specialist area of operation. But such organizations tend to rely on the continuing stability of their market and external environment. The potential for major change in these external parameters may pose a significant threat for which they could be ill-prepared.

COUNTER-ATTACK STRATEGIES

An attack by one competitor on the market position of another may provoke a competitive response in the form of a counter-attack. Ries and Trout suggest that counter-attack strategies are particularly likely to be used where a position of market dominance is under threat from an attacker. The defender of that market position necessarily sees the need for a counter-attack as a *forced* or *self-imposed* strategic response. It considers that it is left with little choice but to commit resources to defend its market position. The resulting counter-attack may be based on any of:

❏ *head-hunting* (or poaching) key personnel currently employed by attackers.

❏ *exploiting competitor weaknesses* revealed during the attacking process. These weaknesses might include the technological or operational shortcomings of new processes or products; emergent shortages of finance; mismanagement, or overtrading.

❏ *embroiling the attacker in litigation* which, apart from the expense, may damage the attacker's corporate, brand and market reputation. This strategy was successfully used by Polaroid against Kodak when its rival attempted to introduce its own brand of instant photographic film on to the market.

❏ *using copying, creative imitation and fast seconding* in order rapidly to introduce better versions of the products, processes, or services introduced by competitors as the basis for the original attack.

❏ *outspending the attacker*. Ries and Trout suggest that the defender may be prepared to *expend more resources* in order to protect the position it holds than the attacker may be willing (or able) to commit to the attack. This may eventually place the attacker in a vulnerable position.

❏ *leapfrogging the attacker*, for instance by introducing better innovations, better processes, or moving further down the *experience curve* described in Chapter 23. This may have the effect of undermining or negating the advantage upon which the attack was originally based. If this strategy is combined with outspending (described immediately above), the result could potentially be highly damaging or even fatal to the original attacker.

MIXED COMPETITION STRATEGIES AND THE ANALYZER

Miles and Snow describe as "analyzers" those organizations that operate in two types of product-market. One type of product-market is relatively stable; the other is changing. In their stable markets, these organizations function as defenders, protecting their existing segment provision and seeking operational efficiency. In the more turbulent sectors, the enterprise monitors the performance of competitors (but especially the "prospectors" described above) and looks out for evidence of successful experimentation and innovation. They then adopt, copy or creatively imitate on an *opportunistic* basis those new ideas that appear to them to be proven and the most promising, using their operational efficiency or ability to "fast second".

THE REACTOR

Miles and Snow describe as "reactors" those organizations whose owners or senior managers do perceive change and uncertainty occurring within the external and market environment, but which are unable to make any effective response to it. The only competitive "strategy" of which such organizations *may* be capable would be adjustments made as a result of irresistible external and environmental pressures. Reactors may be at the mercy of rivals once they have reached or exceeded their limited (and often *self-imposed*) capacity for competitive response.

GOING IT ALONE

Competition strategy in this case may be based upon the maintenance of total independence of enterprise strategy formulation and implementation. This was once the basic strategy of IBM and Eastman Kodak. The "go it alone" independence may be culturally *self-imposed*.

This strategy may be predicated upon an ideology and value set of *aggression* towards rivals who compete in the same market or sector. Behaviour towards these competitors may be attacking or defensive as described above. It may be predatory where the prevailing competition laws permit. Or it may be focused on acquisition or take over as a prime business development strategy. Business development strategies are described in Chapter 27.

CO-OPERATION AND PARTNERSHIP

Strategy in this case is based upon the premise that the enterprise may benefit from the voluntary sharing with others of the risks and burdens of business, for instance:

❑ by being better able to compete with giant global corporations by jointly achieving a greater scope and scale of operation than that which could be achieved by any one individual player.

❑ by achieving the *synergy* that results from the combination and interaction of a variety and scale of resources that are unavailable to any one company. Synergy is a concept of joint effect.

Co-operation and partnership is also predicated upon an assumption that ongoing competition between rivals is not always or necessarily a good thing. Kay (1993), for instance, contends that there is no guarantee that the maximization of competition results in the maximization of utility for the consumer, or of profitability for the enterprises in the sector. Co-operation and partnership that reduces (or "takes out") competition may be an attractive strategic option to players in the field.

REVIEW QUESTIONS

1. What is competition strategy?
2. What is competitive position?
3. Analyze and compare the various alternative choices of competition strategy.
4. More specifically, compare and contrast proactive or attacking competition strategies with defensive strategies. What risks are associated with these different types of strategy?

TECHNIQUES OF CASE STUDY AND ANALYSIS

1. Identify the competitive positions evident from the case study. Are there leaders and followers? Are companies battling for market share, and so on?
2. Identify and analyze the competition strategies evident in the case study. Why have these strategies been chosen, and what are their implications for the case company, case companies, or competitors?

PROJECT ASSIGNMENTS

1. Using published data, categorize the various suppliers to a specific product-market or sector into their competitive position. Identify leaders, followers, and so on. Explain and comment on your findings.
2. Using published data, identify and categorize the various competition strategies evident within a particular product-market or sector. Analyze and compare these apparent strategies. How may they be explained?

References

Chen, Min (1995) *Asian Management Systems*, Routledge, London.
Drucker, P. (1985) *Innovation and Entrepreneurship*, Heinemann, London.
Griffith, S.B. (1971) Sun Tzu [tr] *The Art of War*, Oxford University Press, Oxford.
Hamel, G. and C.K. Prahalad (1994) *Competing for the Future*, Harvard Business School Press, Boston, Mass.
Kay, J. (1993) *Foundations of Corporate Success*, Oxford University Press, Oxford.
Krause, D.G. (1996) *Sun Tzu: the art of war for executives*, Nicholas Brealey, London.
Miles, R.E. and C.C. Snow (1978) *Organizational Strategy, Structure and Process*, McGraw-Hill, London.
Morden, A.R. (1993) *Elements of Marketing*, DP Publications, London.
Ries, A. and J. Trout (1986) *Marketing Warfare*, McGraw-Hill, Singapore.

Chapter 23

Volume and Cost-Based Strategies

This chapter analyzes types of strategic choice associated with volume and cost-based sources of competitive advantage. The implementation of enterprise competition strategy may in this case be based on the exploitation of volume and scale, market share advantage, or cost-efficiency throughout the value chain, or all three. The chapter analyzes the "experience effect". And it looks at enterprise achievement of cost-based advantages, or more proactively a cost leadership position, through a cost-orientated strategic management of the value chain. A variety of implementation issues are dealt with in the text of the chapter.

VOLUME STRATEGIES

Many organizations operate on a *volume basis*. This may be true whether they are in the private or the public sector. Their scope and scale of market or client provision is either *relatively* or *absolutely large*, or both. Such organizations include manufacturing companies, banks and building societies, trading companies, retailers, farms, central or local government authorities, educational institutions, and hospitals.

There are a number of reasons why these kinds of enterprise need to make use of volume strategies. These reasons include:

❑ the *spreading* of a large burden of essential fixed and other costs, interest payments, etc, across a wide range of revenues or income flows in order to support them. Fixed costs associated for example with the employment of specialist staff, research and development, or knowledge and technology management may be essential to the continuing effectiveness of operations.

❑ to achieve the reduction of manufacturing or operational costs.

❑ the ability to make *investments in ICTs or MIS* that will yield disproportionate gains in informational productivity or competitive advantage. Such systems include transaction processing systems, airline or hotel reservation systems, or customer and client databases in the financial services or healthcare sectors.

❑   *bulk-buying* and *purchase negotiation strength* relative to suppliers, for instance in retail buying, drug purchasing, healthcare provision, and government authorities.

❑   achieving the *absolute size of cash flows* needed to fund R&D, innovation, new product or process development, and developments in knowledge, competence, and technology.

❑   achieving the capacity to make certain types of *capital and staff investments* unavailable to smaller-scale enterprises; and thereby to achieve operational effectiveness or competitive advantage. Examples include the health sector, electronics and computing.

❑   the capacity to achieve *credibility with*, and to satisfy, very large customers such as government agencies or public utilities. At the same time, to be able to hold their own in negotiations with such customers over margins and price.

❑   to be able to *compete internationally*, and consistently and effectively to supply customers on a global scale.

CRITICAL MASS

It may be the case that the organization has to operate at or beyond a certain minimum volume or scale of capacity in order to be viable in certain types of activity or market. This is particularly true where it wishes to supply state agencies, or where it intends to compete internationally or globally.

This scale of operation is sometimes described in terms of *critical mass*. Ultimately, operational or competitive viability and business success may be dependent upon reaching such a critical volume of operations. If the enterprise cannot reach this point of critical mass *it may have to redefine its mission and scope*. It may have to restrict itself to a more limited provision, perhaps focusing on the *specialist segments* or *niches* described in more detail in Chapter 24.

The concept of critical mass may therefore be directly related to defining corporate mission, objectives, and strategies. This relationship is clearly evident in such sectors as electronics, computing and telecommunications; pharmaceuticals; advertizing; financial, insurance and investment services; distance learning provision; automotive manufacture; aircraft construction and avionics; global branding; and retail and distribution. These sectors may of necessity be characterized by a large or international scale of operations.

THE PIMS PRINCIPLE TWO: MARKET SHARE AND PROFITABILITY

The *"profit impact of market strategy"* or *PIMS Study* was originally established in the 1960s by Sidney Schoeffler of the US General Electric company. It was a corporate appraisal technique used to identify which strategic choices most influence cash flow and investment success. The scope of the study was extended in 1972 by Buzzell, Gale, *et al* of the Harvard Business School. The Strategic Planning Institute was then established in 1975 to develop PIMS for external clients on a consultancy basis.

The PIMS Study

PIMS is a computer model which draws upon a database containing information submitted by client companies. Buzzell and Gale (1987) noted that 'the approach we have used in the PIMS Program has been that of documenting the actual experiences of many businesses, operating in many different kinds of market and competitive settings. For each of these businesses we have collected three kinds of information:

❑ a description of the market conditions in which the business operates. These include such things as the distribution channels used by the (business), the number of its customers and their size, and rates of market growth and inflation.
❑ the business unit's competitive position in its marketplace. Measures of competitive position include market share, relative quality, prices and costs relative to competition, and degree of vertical integration relative to competition.
❑ measures of the (business's) financial and operating performance, on an annual basis, over periods ranging from 2 to 12 years.

By analyzing these kinds of information for a sufficiently large number of business units, we can find common patterns in the relationships among them' (p. 2).

The PIMS programme is designed to analyze the impact of a variety of strategic choices, strategic issues, and product-market, competitive and environmental influences on business performance.

It may then be used to advise or to guide the formulation and choice of strategies, using a set of generalized "PIMS Principles" derived from the evidence of the research base from which the performance analysis is carried out. Buzzell and Gale comment that 'our view...is that there *are* principles that can help managers understand and predict how strategic choices and market conditions will affect business performance. Some of these principles apply to virtually all kinds of businesses, while others apply only to specific types or under certain conditions. None of them constitutes a complete formula or prescription for any individual case because there are always situation-specific factors to consider in addition to the more general ones. The general principles must be calibrated to fit the distinctive features of a particular situation, and elements of the situation that are not covered by any general principle must also be taken into account' (p. 6).

PIMS Principle Two: Market Share and Profitability are Related

The PIMS database shows that businesses with large market shares enjoy a greater rate of return on investment than that of competitors with a smaller market share.

While this correlation may, in part, be explained by other features (such as more effective management or the possession of knowledge and competence unavailable to smaller competitors), Buzzell and Gale comment that 'the primary reason for the market-share/profitability linkage ... is that large-share businesses benefit from scale economies. They simply have lower per-unit costs than their smaller competitors. These cost advantages ... are directly reflected in higher profit margins' (p. 9).

This issue is explained in terms of the concept of the "experience effect", as follows.

THE EXPERIENCE EFFECT

In addition to analyzing the impact of volume and critical mass on the formulation of strategies, it is necessary here to consider the workings of the *experience effect*. The experience effect may under certain circumstances be the main determinant of the required scale of operation. It may therefore shape the nature of strategic choice for the enterprise.

The concept of experience was introduced in Chapter 19. The experience effect is defined below.

What is the Experience Effect?

The experience effect has its roots in the concept of the "learning curve". Researchers had discovered during the Second World War that it was possible to identify improvements in the rate of output of workers as they became more skilled in the processes and tasks on which they were occupied.

Subsequent work by Bruce Henderson, founder of the Boston Consulting Group (see Chapter 26), extended this concept by showing that it might be possible for all costs, not just production ones, to decrease at a given rate as the volume of output increases.

The experience effect concept assumes that *increases in the scale* on which an activity is carried out may yield both:

❑   proportionate decreases in the unit cost of production or provision; *and*
❑   a build-up of *experience,* the accumulation of which will also affect unit cost.

The concept postulates a relationship between total unit cost and the cumulative volume of units produced. For instance, in a manufacturing company, this states that costs of:

production or supply + marketing + distribution + capital provision

may decrease at a certain rate each time the volume of total output is doubled.

The *rate* at which unit cost decreases may decline as cumulative volume increases, and may eventually reach a zero value. At this point, decreases in cost may be offset by the emergence of diseconomies of scale (for instance of an organizational and managerial nature). The theory can be illustrated by a simple example of an *experience curve*, shown in Figure 23.1.

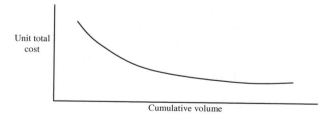

Figure 23.1 An Experience Curve

Sources of the Experience Effect

There are three potential sources of the experience effect. These are listed as follows.

Economies of scale - which yield proportionate decreases in the unit cost of production or provision as the scale of activity is increased. There are many examples, including (i) increases in the physical size, scale and volume of operation; and (ii) the absorption of fixed costs over a greater volume of output, thereby reducing the contribution required from each unit sold to pay for these fixed costs. Other examples were described above.

Gains in value-added - including:-

- *increases in labour productivity* resulting from downward movements on the learning curve. The more that an individual carries out the task, the more efficient he or she is likely to become at accomplishing it, and the greater is the productivity that may be achieved.

- *resource specialization*, for example in staff competence, manufacturing equipment, physical distribution systems, MIS, and so on.

- *new operational processes and improved methods*. For example the introduction of the "Chorleywood" process permitted the large scale baking of bread on a continuous flow basis, speeding up the manufacturing process and ending the need to leave large quantities of dough (working capital) waiting to prove and rise.

- *product and process standardization*, the effects of which are widely visible in car manufacture, where many parts are standardized and interchangeable between models and ranges, and between different manufacturers.

- *substitution in the product*, whereby cheaper but equally effective materials or processes are used to replace more expensive ones. Why use a bolt to secure a nut when a cheaper spring clip or a self-tapping screw will perform equally as well?

- *product redesign*, yielding cost decreases or value-added gains. Compare the electronic word-processor with the complex and heavy electro-mechanical typewriters of a decade or more ago. The electro-mechanical typewriter had reached its ultimate point of development, and was expensive to purchase and maintain. Technological changes have increased the capacity and options of text preparation, but decreased its relative cost.

Process re-engineering and Six Sigma - by which basic or core business processes are redesigned or re-configured to yield more value, or to decrease costs, or both.

Business process re-engineering (BPRE) was defined in Chapter 16 by Hammer and Champy (1995) as 'the fundamental rethinking and radical redesign of business processes to achieve dramatic improvements in critical ... measures of performance such as cost, quality, service and speed' (p. 32). Re-engineering implies abandoning long-established procedures and looking afresh at the work required to create a company's product or service, and thereby deliver value to the customer and shareholder or stakeholder. It means asking the question "if I were re-creating this company today, given what I know and given current technology, what would it look like?"

In focusing on core business processes, BPRE forces decision-makers to think about the relationship or "fit" (match or congruence) between (i) core processes and (ii) the strategies, resources, staffing, capability, systems, skills and competencies that are required by the enterprise to create value, provide competitive advantage, and achieve movement down the experience curve. Johansson *et al.* (1993) identify three types of BPRE. These are:-

- BPRE that is concentrated on *improving the performance* of individual business processes and functions. Such BPRE may be aimed at "doing more with less" (for instance achieving significant cost reductions and cost-based movement down the experience curve). Or it may instead be aimed at "doing more with what you have", that is moving down the experience curve by *stretching* resources and adding more value than before. This issue was dealt with in detail in Chapter 21.

- BPRE that aims to achieve *competitive parity*. Typically, the "best practice" benchmarks described in Chapter 16 are used as targets and comparators. Relative cost, relative value addition, and relative position on the experience curve must be comparable with the market leader, or with those enterprises classified in the sector as being of excellent or world class status.

- BPRE that is used to achieve a *breakpoint*. The objective here is to identify a level of customer or market values (such as performance, cost, value for money, quality, speed, flexibility of response, innovation capacity, or product and service variants offered) that, if realized by the enterprise, will yield significant gains in competitive advantage. Ultimately, the achievement of a breakpoint may permit the enterprise to redefine the rules and expectations of the sector or the market (and therefore the nature and shape of the experience curve itself) in its own favour. However, the achievement of such a breakpoint may instead be associated with the emergence of a new technology and its "S" curve ("S" curves were described in Chapter 19). The appearance of a new "S" curve may itself be associated with the occurrence of an experience curve discontinuity; and with the emergence of a *new experience curve* defined by that new technology. A later section below points out that such a development could be driven by newcomers who, as innovators, may be in a better position to exploit the new technology and new experience curve; and who may nullify the competitive advantage of existing players irrespective of the strength of their position on the old experience curve.

Six Sigma was defined in Chapter 16 as 'a set of ... tools for improving processes and products, and as an approach for improving both the process and people related aspects of business performance' (Bertels, 2003, p. 3). Bertels notes the US Honeywell Corporation's description of Six Sigma as a strategy 'to accelerate improvements in processes, products, and services, and to radically reduce manufacturing (or) administrative costs and improve quality' (p. 4). Six Sigma projects and processes are now widely used to achieve the kinds of BPRE objectives listed immediately above.

The Potential Volume, Cost and Market Share Relationship

The experience effect concept can in particular be applied to conditions *in which the products and services being marketed are broadly similar, or cannot be fully differentiated from each other.* The most extreme conditions to which it may apply are those in which the products or services are of a *commodity* nature. These cannot effectively be differentiated. Commodity type products include fresh and processed foodstuffs; basic house wares such as cleansers, detergents and polishes; standard bread lines; bulk industrial purchases of paint, steel and consumable items; standardized telecommunications services, standardized financial services, and so on.

The concept suggests that the manufacturer or supplier who is able to produce more units than its competitors *may,* given (i) the similarity between available products, and (ii) any particular level of market demand, *become the market share leader. This is because the supplier with the greatest volume of output is furthest down the industry's experience curve.* It has the lowest cost per unit, and can therefore enjoy a cost and price advantage.

The reasoning then becomes cyclical. The greater the supplier's volume of output, the lower the unit cost. The lower the unit cost, the lower can be the price per unit at which the product or service is offered for sale. The lower the price, the larger will be the sales and the greater will be the market share. The greater the market share, the greater the volume of manufacture or supply; and so on.

In theory, at least, the market share leader should then be able to steadily increase its market share at the expense of those competitors whose unit costs for producing a similar product are higher. This kind of pattern can be illustrated by the following examples:

❏ the UK bakery industry, which is dominated by two major companies.
❏ the manufacture and distribution of standard oil-based and vehicle fuel products which is carried out by a very small number of very large multinational companies.
❏ the manufacture and supply of standardized artificial fabric fibres such as nylon or polyester which is dominated in the West by such companies as Du Pont.

Experience Curve Pricing

Under market conditions where the product cannot effectively be differentiated, and where as a result competition centres around price, a manufacturer or supplier may follow a strategy of *experience curve pricing*. In order to maintain or increase market share, the supplier will base his or her price (and hence profit margin) *on the experience curve costs of the estimated sales volume to be obtained at that chosen market share.*

Thus, if it can calculate the experience curve, a company may be in a position to estimate its probable costs at any particular level of sales volume. By reducing price the supplier will be forced to accept lower profit margins in the short term (because of the lowered prices), but *may* gain a long-term increase in market share and profitability. This is shown in Figure 23.2. A reduction in price from price 1 to price 2 yields an increase in volume (and hence market share) from volume 1 to volume 2.

Three historical examples of experience curve pricing have been found in the markets for:

❏ integrated electronic circuits or "silicon chips".
❏ electronic calculators.
❏ electronic digital watches.

In each case the products were difficult to differentiate, the brand names were weak or unfamiliar, and increases in production volume yielded both economies of scale and gains in value added. Once into their growth stages, these markets grew rapidly in volume, and were characterized by substantial price reductions and the emergence of dominant manufacturers (such as Texas Instruments or Seiko), who came to hold significant market share.

In other words, where the supplier is distributing commodity-type products, or products and services capable of only ineffective differentiation, then the experience effect may be used to obtain market share increases or market share dominance. It may be essential, therefore, for other suppliers in such markets to monitor competitor activities and, if necessary, to match them. Where, however, such markets are inevitably *price sensitive*, supply may come to be dominated by a relatively small number of relatively large producers. If another business operating in such a market then finds itself unable to expand its market share because it is operating from a weak cost position, it may be advisable *to get out of that market altogether*, perhaps divesting (selling off) its interests to one of the dominant suppliers.

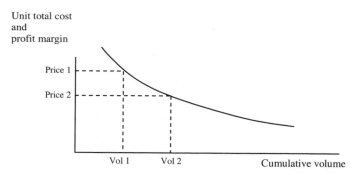

Figure 23.2 Experience Curve Pricing

The Experience Effect as a Barrier to Entry

Drucker (1985) suggests that a strategy of keeping prices *high* may 'hold an umbrella over potential competitors and encourage them' (p. 200).

On the other hand, the experience effect concept suggests that the strategy of lowering prices as a company's market share increases may discourage potential competitors. The increasing revenues obtained from an enhanced market share may allow a company (i) to depreciate the investment already made to achieve the additional output represented by that market share increase; and (ii) to finance further investment in operational capacity.

But the prospect of static or lowered prices may render that market unattractive to potential entrants. Given the start-up costs of entering the market and the likely prospects of these static or decreasing market prices, the investment would potentially be unviable. The newcomer would never make an adequate return, while at the same time being faced with a continuing need to invest in order to play "catch up". Drucker quotes the examples of Du Pont and 3M as companies who have employed this proactive competition strategy in the USA.

Porter (1979) suggests that the use of the experience curve as a barrier to entry may be reinforced where existing suppliers also control *access to experience*. This is particularly the case where the status of that experience may be kept *proprietary*, through the appropriate knowledge management strategies, patents or restrictions.

The control of patents, copyrights or registrations, or the recruitment and retention of the best staff may make replicating the experience level difficult or impossible. Potential competitors will not be able to gain adequate access to that experience (unless they take over the owner or purchase the rights to the experience, assuming that either of these courses of action are available to them).

Kay (1993) describes enterprise ability to exercise effective proprietary control over access to experience as a *strategic asset*. Strategic assets were described in Chapter 4. According to Kay's thesis, enterprise management may be able to use the experience effect as a barrier to entry where the relevant experience is based (i) on an ongoing process of *innovation* (which may reinforce the organization's position on the experience curve); (ii) on the possession of an *architecture* that cannot be imitated by others; and (iii) on the possession of such strategic assets as are described by Porter, above. The barrier to entry will be at its strongest where the enterprise has all three of these advantages working together.

Limitations of the Experience Effect Concept

The experience effect concept has a number of limitations as the basis for strategic choice associated with volume and the achievement of critical mass. These limitations include:

Diseconomies of scale - as institutions become larger they may meet administrative and informational problems associated with increasingly complex issues of leadership, communication, co-ordination, organization, and management. The result may be an upward turn in the experience curve, reflecting increasing costs caused by these organizational and managerial difficulties.

Efficiency and technical change - Porter (1979) suggests that:-

- where potential entrants can make use of more efficient *input resources* and gain *greater productivity or value per unit of that resource* than existing suppliers, the cumulative volume advantage of those suppliers may be nullified. In this case the new entrant's competitive advantage is his greater operational efficiency. "Catching-up" may not pose a problem. Market leadership may then depend on having the most efficient plant, rather than on producing the greatest cumulative volume in order to achieve cost decreases.

- where new entrants can *leapfrog* existing suppliers with technical advances or new technology which yield cost advantages, they may achieve competitive advantage. They are free of commitment to existing investments. It may be that existing suppliers are at a disadvantage, having to re-equip or adapt to the technological changes being implemented by newcomers.

- the experience curve as an entry barrier may be completely nullified by *product or process innovation*. This may give rise to new technology that creates *an entirely new experience curve*. New entrants can leapfrog the industry leaders where the latter are not in a strong position to make the transition.

This capacity to leapfrog over the existing competition will be enhanced where the newcomer has some kind of initial proprietary control over the source of the new technology. Such control has already been described above. It includes ownership of patents, design registration, or employment of staff skill and expertize. Foster (1987) suggests that this is what happened in the US tyre cord market. Du Pont's commitment to nylon cord made it vulnerable to Celanese's introduction of polyester fibres. These proved to be a more effective tyre cord material. Du Pont lost its dominant market position in the supply of tyre cords to a company that was free of existing commitments to products and plant associated with nylon. Concepts of leapfrogging and new technology were analyzed in more detail in Chapter 19.

The de-integrated value chain - the value chain concept and its linkages were described in Chapter 4. The de-integrated value chain was analyzed in Chapter 18. Operations management and value generation are conceptualized within the de-integrated value chain as a collective and co-operative process involving partners. These partners are independent enterprises but work in a co-ordinated and integrated manner as a coalition to manage the creation, production and distribution of goods and services, as if they were one enterprise. Thus, the joint effort and the joint effect created within the network may mean that it can compete as a *single entity* with competitors who are individually much larger than any one constituent of the de-integrated value chain. The unity and synergy created within the coalition may be enough to offset the apparent advantage of larger individual companies whose scale and resource base permits them directly to take advantage of the experience effect.

Thus, the companies that make up the de-integrated value chain may be able to combine and structure the available resources such that the network can compete in terms of:-

- a collective scale of market offering and price competitiveness.
- the combination of specialist skills, competencies, and distinctive capabilities to make available (i) a variety and diversity of market offering; (ii) a complexity of market offering (a coalition of resources may be in a better position to handle variety and complexity than a single enterprise with its individual culture and the potentially static or "installed base of thinking" that were described in Chapters 19 and 20); and (iii) a flexibility of segment positioning and market offer.

At the same time, the network may have an advantage over the large single competitor in terms of simpler organization structure. It may be able to avoid the establishment of a centralized bureaucracy with its heavy burden of fixed costs; at the same time being able to offer diversity and flexibility in response to changing knowledge management, technological, supply chain, and market demands.

Market segmentation and product differentiation - the experience effect may be less significant where markets are not strongly price-sensitive, and where market segmentation and product differentiation characterize the relevant product-markets. These issues are dealt with in detail in Chapter 24.

COST-BASED STRATEGIES AND THE VALUE CHAIN

The value chain was described in Chapter 4 to comprise:

- those activities categorized by Porter as "primary" and "supporting"; *and*
- linkages between these activities.

These two components, when conceptualized as a combined set of resources and architecture, may be used to generate value and advantage (i) for the customer or client, and (ii) for the enterprise supplying that customer or client.

Porter (1985) notes that 'value activities are ... the ... building blocks of competitive advantage. How each activity is performed combined with its economics will determine whether a firm is high or low cost relative to competitors ... comparing the value chains of competitors exposes differences that determine competitive advantage' (pp. 38-39).

The operation of the value chain in order to generate value will incur the costs of that operation. The value chain may therefore be specified or re-engineered:

□   to achieve its purpose at the lowest possible cost, that is to generate a given output value for the least consumption (expenditure) of resources relative to competitors.
□   to achieve the same (or a greater) level of output with the use of fewer resources than competitors; that is, to do more with less.
□   to do significantly more with the level of resources and architecture represented by the value chain, for instance by the use of the strategies of competence development, or stretch and leverage described in Chapters 20 and 21, when compared with competitors.
□   to make use of the supply chain management strategies described in Chapter 18.

The achievement of such cost positions may be based upon any or all of the methods described in this chapter (volume strategies; the achievement of critical mass; obtaining increases in market share; use of the experience effect). Additionally, the achievement of this cost position may be based on:

□   making resources and assets work harder ("sweating the assets") for instance (i) by improving the performance, profitability and asset utilization ratios described in Chapter 3; (ii) by increasing the speed of the working capital cycle; (iii) by decreasing the cost of capital as described in Chapter 13.
□   the achievement of cost reductions through short-term processes of organizational restructuring, delayering and downsizing; resource rationalization; limiting innovation or investment; outsourcing; or staff redundancy. This process is described as "taking out cost". More controversially it is sometimes termed "rightsizing". Carried to excess it may lead to the condition of long-term corporate weakening or "anorexia" (for instance see Morden 1996, 1997).

An enterprise that is better able to optimize or minimize the cost of value generation through the value chain, relative to its competitors, may use this capability as a key source of competitive advantage upon which to base its strategic choice. It will exploit its competitive advantage by pursuing *cost-based* or *cost-oriented* strategies.

These cost-based strategies are in particular likely to be espoused where the output of the value chain derives from a series of relatively standardized, repetitive or routinized processes and practices, irrespective of whether these are operationally categorized as (i) primary, (ii) support, or (iii) linking, relational, or architectural. Competitive advantage will be obtained by those enterprises that can achieve the requisite level, consistency and quality of output at a relatively lower cost than competitors. Relative to their competitors, such enterprises:

❑ may generate more output value per unit of input; *and/or*
❑ may be able to reduce price (or potentially to increase market share as described in earlier sections above); *and/or*
❑ may be more profitable. This implies offering the best returns in the sector to shareholders and stakeholders; whilst at the same time maintaining the necessary investment and innovation to reinforce the cost position and competitive advantage of the enterprise.

M.E. PORTER'S COST LEADERSHIP STRATEGY

M.E. Porter (1980) describes a cost leadership strategy as being 'to achieve overall cost leadership in an industry through a set of functional policies aimed at this basic objective. Cost leadership requires aggressive construction of efficient-scale facilities, vigorous pursuit of cost reductions from experience, tight cost and overhead control, (and) avoidance of marginal customer accounts' (p. 35).

The strategy implies the total and *deliberate* pursuit of *cost and volume effectiveness* in all value chain activities, whether procurement, supply chain management, operations and quality management, MIS, distribution, and so on.   Porter goes on to suggest that 'achieving a low overall cost position often requires a high relative market share, or other advantages such as favourable access to raw materials. It may well require designing products for ease in manufacturing, maintaining a wide line of related products to spread costs, and serving all major customer groups in order to build volume. In turn, implementing the low-cost strategy may require heavy up-front capital investment in state-of-the-art equipment, aggressive pricing, and start-up losses to build market share ... once achieved, the low-cost position provides high margins which can be reinvested in new equipment and modern facilities in order to maintain cost leadership' (p. 36).

The global automotive sector shows clear evidence of the implementation of cost leadership strategies. Large-scale manufacturers of middle-range hatchback, family and fleet saloon cars such as Toyota, General Motors, Ford, and Nissan, base their strategy on competitive pricing, and low cost international operations achieved through the various methods described in this chapter.

REVIEW QUESTIONS

1. What are volume strategies?
2. What is critical mass? What is its significance for strategic decision-making?
3. Why may market share and profitability be related?
4. What is the experience effect? Describe and comment on some of the sources of the experience effect.
5. What is the significance of the experience curve concept for volume, cost and market share decisions?
6. How may costs be reduced within the value chain?
7. Explain M.E. Porter's cost leadership strategy.

TECHNIQUES OF CASE STUDY AND ANALYSIS

1. Identify competition strategies (Chapter 22) evident in the case study.
2. Identify volume, cost, or market share based strategies (if any) in the case study. Analyze these business strategies. Explain their significance for competitive positioning and competition strategy.
3. Analyze the character of the cost management that is apparent within the value chain of the case company. Is there evidence of cost reduction, value enhancement, resource stretch and leverage, etc.?
4. Identify cost leadership strategies (if any) in the case study. Explain their significance within the context of competitive positioning and competition strategies evident in the case study.

PROJECT ASSIGNMENT

Using published data or key informant interviews, prepare an analysis and explanation of a national or international product-market or sector in which competition strategy is characterized by the implementation of any of the volume, market share, cost-based or cost leadership strategies described in this chapter. Present your findings.

References

Bertels, T. (ed.) (2003) *Rath & Strong's Six Sigma Leadership Handbook*, Wiley, Hoboken, NJ.

Buzzell, R.D. and B.T. Gale (1987) *The PIMS Principles*, Free Press, New York.

Drucker, P. (1985) *Innovation and Entrepreneurship*, Heinemann, London.

Foster, R. N. (1987) *Innovation: the Attacker's Advantage*, Pan, London.

Hammer, M. and J. Champy (1995) *Re-engineering the Corporation*, Nicholas Brealey, London.

Johansson, H.J., McHugh, P., Pendlebury, A.J. and W.A. Wheeler (1993) *Business Process Re-engineering: Breakpoint Strategies for Market Dominance*, Wiley, Chichester.

Kay, J. (1993) *Foundations of Corporate Success*, Oxford University Press, Oxford.

Morden, A.R. (1996) *Principles of Management*, McGraw-Hill, London.

Morden, A.R. (1997) "A strategic evaluation of re-engineering, restructuring, delayering and downsizing policies as flawed paradigm", *Management Decision*, Vol 35, No 3.

Porter, M.E. (1979) "How competitive forces shape strategy", *Harvard Business Review*, March-April.

Porter, M.E. (1980) *Competitive Strategy*, Free Press, New York.

Porter, M.E. (1985) *Competitive Advantage*, Free Press, New York.

Chapter 24

Differentiated, Focus, and Niche Strategies

The implementation of enterprise competition strategy may be based on the use of differentiated, focus, or niche strategies. This chapter analyzes strategic choice associated with differentiated, focus, and niche based sources of competitive advantage. It comments on the specification and management of the value chain to achieve these sources of competitive advantage.

It describes enterprise strategies that are focused closely on serving segment-specific or niche markets. Business strategy may alternatively be based on the process of product or service differentiation across a range of markets and market segments. Each type of strategy is compared and contrasted.

A variety of implementation issues are dealt with in the text of the chapter. Issues of brand and reputation as key sources of competitive advantage and product or service differentiation are then given detailed treatment in Chapter 25.

MARKET SEGMENTATION

Market segmentation was described in Chapter 6 as the analysis of a particular market or sector demand into its constituent parts, so that sets of buyers or clients can be differentiated. These sets of consumers or users may then be used as targets within the product-market against which appropriate products or services may be specified and positioned to meet segment customer demand.

Market segmentation will be needed as a key information input in order to relate the needs of users or customers to enterprise decision-making where strategic choice is to be based on the use of the differentiated, focus, or niche strategies described in this chapter.

UNDIFFERENTIATED PRODUCT-MARKET STRATEGIES

Organizations for example in the business, healthcare, and public sectors may not be *market orientated*. They may be "inward looking" or "production orientated". They may not be sensitive to the needs of their customers or clients. For instance, public sector, healthcare, or public service institutions may still perceive their role in the traditional terms of "administering" services to clients or customers. The views or concerns of these "recipients" are not seen as relevant to strategy formulation or decision-making within the organization.

These kinds of organization may therefore make little attempt to closely relate their product or service offer to the needs or expectations of users or customers. And where there is a lack of competition, for example in the public or healthcare sector, no attempt may be made to *differentiate* the product or service from that of any other provider. Customers or clients will just have to put up with whatever service is thought by others to be suitable for them.

The "strategy" being followed by such organizations can be described as *undifferentiated*. In the public or healthcare sectors, for instance, it may result from a lack of effective incentive or a lack of competition between providers, players, and relative customer powerlessness to do anything about the situation. In the business sector, it may result from product or customer familiarity, and the length of time for which the company has been trading in the market; on customer inertia; on a monopoly position; or on a lack of effective incentive or competition. *Companies will make what they think they can sell.* They may have considerable experience of the market, but the lack of market research and market analysis will result in an ineffective (or non-existent) market segmentation input to the business planning activity. And where there is a lack of market segmentation analysis, products or services may not properly be differentiated and positioned according to specific segment requirements.

There are several disadvantages attaching to such an undifferentiated product-market strategy. These include:

❑ *maximizing business risk* - success rates may be unpredictable since the enterprise has limited its use of market analysis in the business planning process. Its choice of strategies may in part depend on luck, past reputation, or past glory for their success.
❑ *maximizing new product or process development risk* - ineffective market analysis and product positioning is a major cause of new product or process failure.

❑ *volume-commodity business* - companies marketing undifferentiated products may be forced into the kind of high volume and low margin competition described in Chapter 23.

❑ *the manufacture of own brands* - companies who have been unable to position effectively differentiated products on clearly identified target segments may be forced to undertake the manufacture of distributor or retailer own-brands. This contains a high risk of loss of company identity and control, and the likelihood of depressed trading margins.

SEGMENT-SPECIFIC, FOCUS, AND NICHE STRATEGIES

Where an organization's product-market strategy is *segment-specific*, it will position one or a limited number of products or services on one or a small number of market segments. This specialized strategy is sometimes also described as a *concentrated, niche,* or *focus* strategy.

The strategy requires the enterprise to be highly sensitive to the requirements of the market segment it serves, and sensitive to changes in that requirement. And given the *dependence* of the enterprise on one or a small number of target market segments, an organization pursuing a segment-specific strategy may have to try to maintain the "number one" position in that market. This is necessary in order to minimize the risk attaching to such a limited market provision. The relevant competition strategies were described in Chapter 22.

The greatest risk attaches to a *one-product* or *one-service company* selling into one target market segment. The company must strive to maintain its position as market leader and most favoured supplier. And it has to assume, at least on the short term, that market demand will continue to exist. Otherwise its business may disappear entirely.

M.E. Porter's Focus Strategy

Porter (1980) describes focus as a 'strategy built around serving a particular target very well, and each functional policy is developed with this in mind. The strategy rests on the premise that the firm ... is able to serve its narrow strategic target more effectively or efficiently than competitors who are competing more broadly' (p. 38). The reward may potentially be "above-average returns", since effective focus strategies reinforce market position in the perception of segment customers, and provide effective segment protection (described in Chapter 22) against entrants.

Drucker's Niche Strategies

Drucker (1985) describes two forms of *niche* strategy. These are:

The use of speciality skill, expertize, or the possession of unique capacity -
the possession of specialized capacity puts the enterprise so far ahead in its
field that it is not really worthwhile for anyone else to try to compete,
particularly if the market is relatively restricted. Timing may be of the
essence in establishing this strong market position. Strength in the market
niche may have to be established at the beginning of a new market or
customer demand, or when a new trend appears within an existing demand.
An effective niche strategy also implies continuous self-improvement and
innovation to maintain the company's unique position. The company has
always to stay well ahead of any potential competition. It must always
remain the *only* serious supplier in the perception of market customers.

The use of speciality market knowledge - the key to this niche strategy is
the continuous and detailed monitoring and research of market and
customer needs. The enterprise maintains its pre-eminence within the niche
by its complete understanding of the market and its willingness to respond
quickly to changes in segment need. Drucker quoted the example of the UK
Baker Perkins Company who, along with a Danish competitor, at one time
supplied the majority of bread, cake and biscuit baking ovens to world
markets. While there is nothing very high technology about such ovens,
these two companies 'know the market: they know every single major
baker, and every single baker knows them. The market is just not big
enough or attractive enough to try to compete with these two, as long as
they remain satisfactory' (p. 223).

DIFFERENTIATED PRODUCT-MARKET STRATEGIES

In this case, a *variety* of products or services *containing appropriate
characteristics or "attributes"* are positioned or targeted upon a variety of
different market segments. Each may then be promoted by means of a
segment-specific promotional mix. This process of *differentiation* may be
achieved:

❑   by the accurate identification of the differences between the various
    market segments to be served; *and*

❑ by specifying the product or service so that it meets the need of *any one segment*; and varying it so that *at the same time* different product or service offerings meet the needs of a *variety of different segments*.

The use of differentiation as a strategy implies the building up of a market perception of *difference* or *uniqueness*. Sources of differentiation could include any of the following:

❑ product or service specification.
❑ operational or functional advantage.
❑ features of capability, competence, and leadership.
❑ customer service offering.
❑ product or service quality.
❑ distribution or access features.
❑ design or style.
❑ use of knowledge and intellectual capital.
❑ technology features.
❑ innovation features.
❑ supply chain features.
❑ international or global features and international capability.

Porter suggests that, ideally, the enterprise should differentiate along several dimensions at the same time. It should also attempt to increase the degree of uniqueness of the product or service. Kay (1993) suggests that enterprise management should seek to enhance *brand image* and *corporate reputation* as differentiating features. These are described in more detail in Chapter 25.

Competitive Implications

Effective product or service differentiation may provide insulation against competition because it increases the *brand preference* and *loyalty* of customers, and decreases their *sensitivity to price*. At the same time, it may lead to increased margins. Customers will perceive that an appropriately specified and positioned product or service offers them *added customer value*. They may be prepared to pay a higher price than would otherwise have been the case. Product differentiation may increase the barriers to entry to the market. Potential competitors may not be able to achieve the same level or quality of perceived uniqueness or service offer. Nor may they be able to decrease customer preference and loyalty to existing brands or suppliers.

In other words, product differentiation is used by the supplier (i) to enable customers to distinguish its products or services from competing offerings; (ii) to establish preference; and (iii) to decrease the sensitivity of those potential customers to price. The greater the utility or value of any product's perceived uniqueness, the less price-sensitive the buyer may be, and the more highly will he or she rate that offering in any ranking of personal or market priorities.

Otherwise the market may view ineffectively differentiated products or service as being broadly similar to other competing offerings; or worse, to be so similar as to be treated as the "commodity" described in Chapter 23. In such cases, the sale will go to the cheapest supplier.

Product Differentiation and Strategic Advantage

Differentiation may increase the perceived value of the offering, and mark it out from its competitors. At the same time, it may be used to:

❑ increase the appropriateness ("fit" or specification) of the product or service positioning to the customer usage context(s) for which it is being considered.

❑ increase the range of customer segments in which the product or service is perceived as being appropriate. This is of strategic advantage to the supplier, since he or she is able to avoid the dependence on the limited segment demand that is the fate of the focus or niche marketer described in an earlier section above. The focus or niche marketer maximizes risk since he or she is dependent on a customer patronage whose continuing existence may be beyond his or her control.

Hence, the argument can be put forward that product differentiation is a most desirable product-market strategy *in terms of the competitive advantage it offers*. It may combine the maximum *value advantage* with the maximum *strategic advantage*. This is illustrated in Figure 24.1.

Segment-specific and differentiated strategies may offer a *value advantage* over cost-based, commodity, and cost-leadership strategies. And differentiation strategies may offer *strategic advantage* over segment-specific strategies in that they offer equal opportunities for value-enhancement, but contain less risk of segment over-dependence.

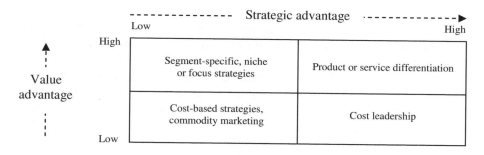

Figure 24.1 Strategic and Value Advantage in Product Markets

QUALITY AND THE PIMS PRINCIPLE ONE

The PIMS Principle One (Buzzell and Gale, 1987) states that "in the long run, the most important factor affecting a business unit's performance is the quality of its products and services, relative to those of its competitors".

The PIMS data show that products perceived to be of the highest quality achieve greater market acceptance, and yield a significantly better percentage return on investment than their competitors. Quality, therefore, is a critical source of competitive advantage by which to differentiate a product or service; or by which to achieve niche dominance in a segment-specific market.

DIFFERENTIATED, FOCUS, AND NICHE STRATEGIES AND THE VALUE CHAIN

The value chain was described in Chapter 4 to comprise:

❑ those activities categorized by Porter as "primary" and "supporting"; *and*
❑ linkages between activities

that, as a combined set of resources and architecture may be used to generate value (i) for the customer or client, and (ii) for the enterprise supplying that customer or client.

The activities that generate value, and the linkages between these value chain activities (its architecture) may be specified or managed to create features of competitive advantage as described throughout this book. These features may allow the enterprise effectively to differentiate its products or services relative to its competitors. Or they may facilitate the implementation of focus or niche strategies in the segment-specific markets already described above.

This implies that the specification, architecture, or management of the value chain to provide differentiation or focus may yield (i) significant value advantages or value-added from the viewpoint of the customer or the market; and (ii) success or profitability from the viewpoint of the enterprise. Some of these value advantages have already been described in an earlier section, above. They might for example take the form of:

❑ world class specification and quality (e.g. Mercedes Benz and Toyota cars; Boeing and Airbus aircraft; Kodak and Canon in imaging technologies).
❑ benchmark levels of customer service (e.g. Singapore Airlines and Virgin Atlantic in long-haul air transportation).
❑ innovation and new product development, such as that implemented by 3M, Sony, Philips, or Daimler Chrysler.
❑ the optimized forms of structure, architecture, and supply chain management described in Chapter 18.

REVIEW QUESTIONS

1. What are segment-specific, focus, or niche strategies? Give some illustrative examples.
2. What are the advantages to the enterprise of being able to pursue segment-specific, focus, or niche strategies? What, if any, are the disadvantages of these strategies?
3. What are differentiated product-market strategies? Give some illustrative examples.
4. What are the advantages to the enterprise of being able to pursue differentiated strategies? What, if any, are the disadvantages of these strategies?
5. Upon what sources of competitive advantage may segment-specific, focus, niche, or differentiated product-market strategies be based? Give some illustrative examples.

TECHNIQUES OF CASE STUDY AND ANALYSIS

1. Identify competition strategies evident in the case study.
2. Identify segment-specific, focus, or niche strategies (if any) in the case study. Analyze these product-market strategies. Explain their significance for competitive positioning and competition strategy. What sources of competitive advantage do they exploit?
3. Identify differentiated strategies (if any) in the case study. Analyze these product-market strategies. Explain their significance for competitive positioning and competition strategy. What sources of competitive advantage do they exploit?

PROJECT ASSIGNMENT

Using published data or key informant interviews, prepare an analysis and explanation of a national or international product-market or sector in which competition is characterized by the implementation of any of the segment-specific, focus, niche, or differentiated strategies described in this chapter. Present your findings.

References

Buzzell, R.D. and B.T. Gale (1987) *The PIMS Principles*, Free Press, New York.
Drucker, P. (1985) *Innovation and Entrepreneurship*, Heinemann, London.
Goldsmith, W. and D.Clutterbuck (1997) *The Winning Streak Mark II*, Orion Books, London.
Kay, J. (1993) *Foundations of Corporate Success*, Oxford University Press, Oxford.
Morden, A.R. (1985) "Market segmentation and practical policy formulation", *Quarterly Review of Marketing*, Vol. 10, No. 2.
Morden, A.R. (1993) *Elements of Marketing*, DP Publications, London.
Porter, M.E. (1980) *Competitive Strategy*, Free Press, New York.

Chapter 25

Brands, Reputation, and Corporate Identity

"Excellence comes as standard" - Robert Bosch Ltd

This chapter analyzes and illustrates selected aspects of the strategic management of brands, reputation, and corporate identity. Brands, reputation, and corporate identity may be assets of immense value and significance. They are key sources of product-market differentiation. Brands and companies such as Persil, Coca-Cola, Mercedes-Benz, Sony, Rolls Royce, Virgin, or Benetton are international household names. Indeed brands, reputation, or corporate identity have often become what Kay (1993) describes as strategic assets. These are major sources of competitive advantage upon which strategic choice may be based, but which it is largely impossible for competitors to imitate.

SECTION ONE – BRANDS AND BRANDING

THE ROLE OF THE BRAND

The use of brands and the process of branding were described in Chapter 24 as a key means of product or service *differentiation*. Differentiation was described in that chapter as a strategy whose aim is to create and secure a market perception of product or service as possessing:

❑ appropriateness to specific customer usage contexts within the relevant market segments; *and*
❑ difference or uniqueness as a characteristic or quality which can be directly compared with competing offerings.

Chapter 24 commented that effective product differentiation can provide an insulation against competition. It increases loyalty to the supplier and decreases customer sensitivity to price.

Brand image may be used to establish and to communicate the qualities of difference, uniqueness or appropriateness that identify the product or service and differentiate it from its competitors. The purpose of developing brand image is:

❑   to facilitate recognition by the customer or client.
❑   to establish an identity or character that communicates in an effective or persuasive manner the qualities and attributes of the product or service.
❑   to shape customer response to the product or service.
❑   to develop preference for the brand as compared with competing offerings.
❑   to secure loyalty to the brand, such that there is continued customer patronage over time.

Suppliers will attempt to use brand image to build up and to reinforce consistent brand-loyal trade and customer behaviour. This decreases the ability of competitors to take away business, and lessens the strategic importance of the cost-price relationship described in Chapter 23.

The creation and promotional support of brand identity and image is also a major factor in sustaining supplier capacity *to specify and to control the marketing of its goods*, for instance:

❑   in the face of buyer pressure from distributors and retailers, to whom the products of any one supplier (however large that supplier might be) may only be a relatively small constituent of the total market offering.
❑   in the face of retailer preference for own brands, as in the UK retail of foodstuffs and clothing. Companies such as Tesco, Asda-Walmart, or Marks and Spencer concentrate on their own brands, purchased on the basis of the volume-cost strategies described in Chapter 23.

KAY'S ANALYSIS OF BRANDING

Kay's (1993) analysis of branding as a source of competitive advantage was introduced in chapter 4. Kay analyzes:

❑   the value of a brand.

❑ the function of brands.
❑ brand success.

Each is described below.

The Value of a Brand

A brand is established when a branded item sells for more than a functionally equivalent product. The features of the brand, or its attributes, add value. They are the characteristic that distinguishes between a brand and the functionally equivalent product or service upon which it is based.

The more effective are the brand features or brand attributes in adding value, the higher the price that may be charged, and the more carefully will that brand be protected and its use controlled.

A brand with the recognition and recall of Coca-Cola, Levi's, Kodak, Guinness or Rolls Royce is a *strategic asset. It defines the market perception of the product, acts as a benchmark for that market, and is unavailable to any other competitor.* The brand itself becomes the key source of value addition and source of competitive advantage.

The Function of Brands

Kay describes five key functions of brands. These are:

Quality certification - the brand comes to be associated by purchasers with a certain perceived level of quality. Products or services carrying the brand are then seen to possess quality attributes which are of value to the purchaser (and for which they may be prepared to pay a premium). Examples include Price Waterhouse Coopers in accountancy and consultancy services; Marks and Spencer in foodstuffs retail; Persil and Ariel washing powders; Marriott hotels; and Robert Bosch in electrical consumer durable products.
Consistency and continuity - the brand comes to be associated by purchasers with consistency and continuity. Buyers perceive that the product or service will be the same today as it was yesterday. Its purchase can be made with confidence and certainty, as the customer believes that future purchase can be related to past experience with the product or service. Examples include Campbell's soup; Nescafé coffee; Mercedes Benz cars and trucks; or Walls ice creams.
Recipe, formulation or specification - the brand is used to represent and to communicate the particular formulation, use of technology, or knowledge

base which gives the product or service its distinctive features (or flavours). The brand may come to represent the product category, or act as its defining benchmark, as in the case of Coca-Cola and Pepsi-Cola, Lea and Perrins sauce, or Microsoft products in personal computing applications.

The more difficult it is for others to reproduce the recipe or formulation, the stronger the source of competitive advantage and the more valuable may be the brand as the market representation of that recipe or specification. Formulations and specifications based on architecture (the linkages and relationships described in Chapters 4 and 18) in areas of customer service may be impossible to imitate. This is a source of competitive advantage for instance in the better US hotel chains. Japanese manufacturing innovators also possess competitive advantage based upon interpersonal formulations based on relationship networks and architecture. *Signalling* - the purchase or consumption of a particular brand may be used as a means by which customers signal (communicate) information, intention or inference about themselves to other people; or indicate something about their taste.

Car buyers of a modest or conservative personal disposition, for instance, might not buy brands of sports-type cars, which they consider to be both "showy" and a powerful indicator of personal self-assertion, status, extroversion and aggression. Such vehicles (particularly if they are red!) may draw attention to the owner, which is not what purchasers of such a personal disposition want.

The more effective the brand is perceived to be at conveying the desired signals, the more value it will represent (and the more customers may become brand-loyal). Hence for example the global popularity of the Mercedes Benz marque with affluent car buyers of a conservative or understated taste. The ownership of a Mercedes Benz (perhaps painted in a dark colour) may be a discreet signal of personal power and success.

The purchase of a preferred brand may also reinforce *self-image*. The brand may be chosen because it reinforces the image that the person would like to convey, or that they would like to be. In this sense the purchase of the brand is *aspirational*, reinforcing personal value set or ambition. "People will think more highly of me if I drive a BMW than another brand. They will conclude that I am successful precisely because I drive a BMW". Brand strategies may be oriented to exploit these latent aspirations.

Kay comments (p. 263) that 'price may be the cost of the signal. It is no accident that signals of high status are generally expensive, and this puts the producer of such a (good) in a particularly strong position. The high price of the product actually enhances the value of a Rolls Royce. Manufacturers of expensive clothes or luggage have the same opportunity.

To ensure that the signal is immediately recognized, it may be reinforced by public display of the brand - the Burberry check or the Gucci logo'.

Examples of products or services whose brand strategy may be based on signalling features include cars, alcoholic drinks such as brandy and whisky, clothes, holiday locations, sports and leisure activities.

Incumbency - competitive advantage may derive from a long-established position in a market. This is incumbency. Incumbency advantages will be based on a positive track record of customer satisfaction with the product or service quality, continuity, specification and signalling aspects of the brand being described in this section. Incumbency advantages may lead to long-term brand loyal behaviour. This is one of the key purposes of seeking brand incumbency, which is a form of defensive competition strategy.

Kay suggests that whilst it might be easy enough to copy a product with strong brand incumbency, the obstacle to doing so lies in consumer inertia and resistance towards trying something new. At the same time the incumbent brand has the ongoing advantage of a high level of sunk costs incurred in the past to achieve its present level of distribution and customer recognition. The newcomer may have to make a similar level of investment, but with no guarantee that consumers will change their allegiance for the incumbent brand to the new, untried and untested one. The incumbency function of the brand reinforces brand-loyalty, strengthens market position, and discourages competition.

Incumbency is demonstrated by such chocolate confectionery brands as Mars, Kit Kat, Hershey, Suchard and Cadbury. It is also demonstrated by Mercedes Benz, Volvo, and Saab-Scania in the global heavy goods vehicle market.

Brand Success

Kay comments that 'the most successful brands are those which combine several of these purposes. One of the strengths of Coca-Cola is that you know it will be both pleasant to drink and fit to drink in environments where you cannot be sure that local products have either characteristic. Indeed, the world-wide reputation of Coca-Cola derives largely from its provision of precisely these quality certification characteristics for American GIs during the Second World War. Coca-Cola also provides continuity … it is important to customers that every bottle is the same. There is a distinctive recipe. The strength of Coca-Cola's distribution network, and the universal recognition of its name yield major incumbency advantages. And its very American associations give it a strong signalling function. Iranian Mullahs do not drink Coca-Cola; aspirant teenagers in less developed countries do' (p. 264).

Kay noted of Price Waterhouse Coopers that 'the Price Waterhouse brand is centred on quality certification, but gains strength from incumbency. It also benefits from signalling - many companies believe that having a prestigious adviser enhances their own reputation'.

BRAND VALUES

A key objective of brand management is to attribute to the product or service those *values* (or *utilities*) that:

❑   identify the product or service, and provide its character.
❑   create the desired image for the identity and character of the product or service.
❑   differentiate the product or service from its competitors.
❑   add value in the perceptions of both (i) the customer and (ii) the marketplace as represented by the relevant channels of distribution.
❑   establish preference in the minds of potential customers, such that the brand is selected from the alternatives available.
❑   establish and reinforce preference in the minds of existing customers, such that there is long-term brand loyalty and market incumbency.

Brand values must be consistent with:

❑   *the characteristics of the market segments* upon which the brand is to be positioned. In particular, the brand values should reflect, promote, and reinforce the positioning of the product's attributes on the usage context of the target customer segment. Are the brand's values consistent with the manner in which the customer will use or apply the service? Long-distance air travel is for example fast, convenient but generally uncomfortable (especially for tall people with long legs!). Long distance rail travel in the USA, Canada or Australia is slow but may be comfortable or even luxurious.
❑   *the unique selling propositions* of the product or service. For instance, the famous and successful "Relax" promotional campaign for the former British Rail "Intercity" brand stressed the safety, comfort and reliability of inter-city rail travel as against the use in bad weather of individual cars for long-distance passenger transportation.

GLOBAL BRANDS

Global brands are products or services (such as Pepsi-Cola, Visa credit cards, Disney merchandise, Kodak Film, or Benetton clothes) that are supplied on an international or global basis under a common brand identity. The product specification or its visual identity and packaging are virtually the same everywhere. The brands are often marketed in English. The product will have the same functional purpose, character, and emotional appeal to the customer, irrespective of where these customers are located (and maybe irrespective of the language they use).

Global brands are products or services which are relatively standardized. They possess the advantage of having similar consumption or usage contexts wherever they are purchased. Cars, photographic film, travel services, popular music, soft drinks, clothes, electrical goods, or accountancy and consultancy services have the same use everywhere. International differences in customer behaviour are largely irrelevant to the context within which the product is used, or the service availed of. The relative competitive advantage of global brands may be based on:

❑ market perceptions of effective performance or superior specification, leading to world class status and market leadership.

❑ a psychological or emotional appeal based on the superior performance described above, and associated with *the international character of the product*. The wearer of Benetton clothes or the customer at a Virgin Megastore, for instance, is associating themselves with western fashion and youth culture. This may be a prudent form of gentle rebellion against prevailing traditions and parental control, for instance in societies characterized by strong power distance, conservative or orthodox values, or family hierarchy. Global products also tend to be perceived as prestigious, particularly amongst brand-conscious consumer societies.

❑ an effective price-quality relationship such that customers will perceive that it is worth paying a relatively high or premium price. Kodak brand photographic film and paper, as the market leader, tends to be more expensive than its competitors for this reason. The same is true for Mercedes Benz and BMW cars in the UK.

The image and acceptance of global products may be reinforced by consistent and heavy international advertizing and promotion. The use of marketing and identity promotion to develop brand awareness and loyalty is a key component of strategic decision-making in globalized companies.

This may be true whether the company operates in consumer goods markets (such as for soft drinks or electronic goods); or in business-to-business markets (such as for IT based office and transaction processing systems, or railway equipment, or heavy road tractor and trailer units).

Some Advantages of Global Brands

The use of global branding has a number of strategic advantages. These include:

Obviating the need for regional variations - where global brands have become accepted, there may be no need for localized variations. Design, manufacturing and distribution may then be undertaken on a standardized global basis. This is related to:-

Taking advantage of economies of scale and the experience effect - as described in Chapters 23 and 28. The scale of manufacturing runs may be maximized, the need for variations may be reduced, and costs may thereby be minimized. This then leaves the supplier with significant revenue margins available to finance (i) the heavy and continuous investment in the innovation, design, and new product development that may be needed to maintain the product or process superiority and the operational capability upon which global market leadership depends; and (ii) the heavy and continuous investment in global advertizing and promotion already described above.

Optimizing manufacturing and operational capabilities - for instance as described in Chapter 28. Manufacturing or supply may be carried out in the most convenient or cost-effective locations, or in locations most suited to distribution arrangements. Manufacturing and supply may alternatively be based upon the network or de-integrated value chain structures described in Chapter 18; may make strategic use of the supply chain management process described in Chapter 18; and may focus on exploiting the competitive advantages of knowledge management and core competence described in Chapters 19 and 20.

For example, global manufacturers may concentrate on exploiting the capability that their knowledge base, experience, and core competencies give them, as in the case of Benetton (analyzed in Chapter 18). They then subcontract to ISO 9000 series quality-certified or world class benchmark firms in their supply chain those manufacturing activities in which they themselves choose not to make investments, or choose not to develop experience or competence.

Ultimately, the enterprise may choose not to make any investments at all in a manufacturing or distribution base. It may choose to focus solely on issues of design, distribution strategy, promotion and brand development. It will concentrate its use of knowledge and resources on developing and reinforcing the distinctive specification, creative, design, brand management, promotional and strategic distribution competencies upon which it considers its dominant market position is based. All other activities are subcontracted, or may instead be developed through the use of the processes of *franchising* and *licensing* described in Chapter 27. This is how the Italian motor cycle company Aprilia works. The ability (i) to avoid a potentially inflexible investment in manufacturing technology; and (ii) to subcontract to world class benchmark suppliers and distributors (market leaders in their own field) on a de-integrated supply or value chain basis, may yield both flexibility and competitive advantage. This advantage will stem from the capability to make rapid adaptations to changing demand patterns and prevailing environmental circumstances on a global as well as a local or regional scale.

Optimizing purchasing power over suppliers - the enterprise may be in a strong position to exercise buyer power over its suppliers. Suppliers may become more dependent upon it than it is dependent on them, particularly if there is a good international choice of alternatives.

Optimizing the relationship with distributors - the enterprise may be in a strong position relative to distributors. Its strong market position and the premium prices its products may command may offset the purchasing power of its larger distributors. Distributors may have little choice but to stock its products, and may be unable to create effective own brands because of the prestige attaching to the global brand. This is the case in international consumer electronics and alcoholic spirits markets. Ultimately, firms such as Sony and Guinness maintain their own distribution or retail networks. They do this in order to control the distribution process for their products, and to exercise leverage over other retailers who wish to stock these products.

Creating barriers to entry and defending market share - the prestige and loyalty attaching to a well-established global brand such as Coca-Cola, Kodak, or Johnny Walker whisky may constitute a powerful barrier to entry to newcomers. It may be very difficult to take market share from well-entrenched global brands, for instance for the reason of incumbency described in an earlier section above. And the cost (and risk) of entry by the newcomer may be disproportionate to the potential returns that may be obtained. Powerful global suppliers such as Microsoft or Kelloggs cereals are likely to defend their market position against attack by others with copious resources and great vigour. Competition strategies were analyzed in Chapter 22.

Some Disadvantages of Global Brands

The use of global branding has a number of disadvantages. These are listed below:

The brand, product or service may represent a compromise - such a compromise may for instance be specified to suit the optimum operations management needs of long-run or low-cost manufacturing, but may not actually meet the needs of any particular market or segment. Car design, for example, sometimes ignores differences in the height or build of people in different countries, their preferences for ride quality and seat softness (Germans like hard seats; the French and British like softer ones), or the quality of road infrastructure in different locations. US citizens can normally only drive their Volkswagen Golfs at a maximum speed of 55mph; German buyers of the same car may be permitted to drive at 100mph or more. Motorway road surfaces in the UK are smoother than those of freeways in Canada because winter conditions are less severe, and higher speeds are possible all year round.

The product over-competes - being specified to meet the most stringent of local market conditions (for instance as described by M.E. Porter's "diamonds" competition model analyzed in Chapter 28) the product may offer too many features or be over-specified for less demanding markets. This is a criticism made of Japanese consumer electronics products. It explains the success of South Korean manufacturers who have introduced less sophisticated electronic products to meet an unsatisfied global demand for a lower level of market specification (which as a result may be sold at a lower price).

The brand "trivializes" or is reduced to a meaningless lowest common denominator - the need to create universal global understanding may force the brand management process into creating a meaningless, stereotyped, or "dumbed-down" brand concept, using a few words of English or a set of what are perceived by advertizing copy writers to be "universal images". Buyers in any one locality may not be able to place the brand in their own context; may instead be unable to relate to it or to understand it; or worst of all may actually be insulted by it.

Local costs may reduce the cost advantage of a global brand - where a significant extra cost is added locally, the cost benefits described in an earlier section above may be negated. The imposition of local costs of adaptation or distribution, sales taxes, or import tariffs may erode the margins available. Or they may make the product prohibitively expensive relative to local products, thereby placing them at a disadvantage.

Damage to brand reputation - localized damage to the brand may have global repercussions. This is what happened to Shell in the case of the Brent Spar facility, and as a result of its necessary local dealings with a military regime in Nigeria. The enterprise will need to monitor the brand's management world-wide to ensure that potential local damage is avoided; or is instead limited in its international impact.

Inertia - it is possible that the structure and architecture of the management of a large global brand programme may be so widespread and so complex (and contain so many commitments and sunk costs) that it may develop inertia. This inertia may result in slowness to adapt in the face of changing local conditions. It may be very difficult to bring about rapid changes. The brand management programme may become like a great ship under full steam. It will be difficult to steer, slow to turn, and take many miles to stop! This syndrome may be exacerbated by:-

Unresponsive global strategy - global branding means global strategy. This may imply a high degree of central control. Centralized structures may get out of touch with the realities of the local situations faced by local managements, or be unresponsive to what the corporate centre judges to be "minor" or "unimportant" issues affecting the brand. Global strategy (and the brand management that depends on it) may become separated or dissociated from the local reality; and irrelevant to it.

The various forms of multinational company are analyzed in Chapter 28.

LOCALLY MODIFIED GLOBAL BRANDS

Market realities may mean that global brand propositions have to be tailored to meet local variations in the character of demand. The basic brand strategy and customer benefits described in the first four sections above of this chapter may be international or global, but local positioning adaptation is considered necessary in order to implement them. For instance:

The recipe, formulation or specification of the product may have to be modified - in order to suit local tastes and preferences. The product might be sweeter, lighter, darker, have a different perfume or smell, be more or less viscous, or contain design or packaging differences. Services might be presented or sold in different ways according to the prevailing customer service culture.

The brand name may differ by locality or country - for instance, Procter and Gamble's premium dishwashing liquid is specified as "mild". It is called "Fairy Liquid" in the UK, which name capitalizes on the caring values of the "Fairy Soap" name. But it is called "Ivory Liquid" in the USA, to capitalize on the mildness values of "Ivory Soap", a long-established incumbent American soap brand.

The content of promotional campaigns may be varied - according to local requirements. For instance, the production of television commercials for cosmetics, clothing, shampoo or hair colourants may employ blonde models for advertisements to be shown on some channels in the USA, the UK or Scandinavia; and darker models for advertisements to be shown in Italy, Spain, and on other channels in the USA. All of these variants might be filmed at one single production session.

A key skill in implementing locally modified global branding is to maintain the basic global strategy while at the same time tailoring specific implementation details to the requirement of local market conditions. The objective is to maximize local market appeal but to safeguard a significant proportion of the global economies (and profitability) of operational scale and scope.

LOCAL AND REGIONAL BRANDS

Social, aspirational, promotional, and economic pressures may lead variously to cultural convergence, "westernization", globalization, product homogeneity, or product standardization. However, there remain strong *localized forces* that may push buyer behaviour in a completely opposite direction. These forces might include:

❑ the continuing tenacity of national sentiment, as in Scotland, Ireland, Russia, and France.
❑ the continuing strength of the traditional cultures described in Chapter 28, and ongoing resistance to "western" and "consumerist" influences (for instance in Islamic countries).
❑ social fragmentation within some western countries based upon the development of strongly individualistic values, liberal-democratic social frameworks, and the popular rejection of "corporatism".

Such cultural and social features may make it difficult (or undesirable) to achieve the successful establishment of global brands and identities in regions in which these features are prevalent.

More specifically, global specifications may not be suitable for positioning on markets or segments characterized by:

❑ strong local or regional differences in culture, national orientations, or accustomed usage context. Local eating habits (and increasingly, the widespread and critical expression of medical concerns associated with issues of nutrition and obesity) may for instance influence market receptivity to international brands of processed foodstuffs or "fast food" offerings.

❑ loyalty to well-entrenched or incumbent local specialist brands such as "Oxo", "Lucozade" or "Marmite" (UK); or "Pernod" (France).

❑ distribution systems dominated by powerful wholesalers or retailers in which own brands are predominant over manufacturer or supplier brands. Similarly, the grip of trading houses on distribution in Japan may make it difficult for international brands to gain any significant level of representation in that country, relative to locally produced Japanese brands.

❑ distribution systems unsuited to meeting the supply, service or maintenance standards of global market leaders.

❑ relative price insensitivity, rendering supplier cost advantage irrelevant. This is the case for alcoholic spirit drinks sold in bars or restaurants. Local products may be as expensive (and therefore profitable) as international ones to the customer; price per drink bears no relationship to product cost. This is related to:-

❑ the imposition of government taxes or excise duties (such as those placed on alcoholic drinks, cars or imported luxuries) such that production or distribution cost advantage becomes irrelevant in establishing local market price.

Global brands may be inappropriate or unprofitable under such conditions.

They may instead be unacceptable because of social hostility toward the source country or region; or because of the prevailing xenophobia. For instance, things "American" are still not too popular in Iran! Both the Chinese and the South Koreans can still demonstrate an ambivalent attitude towards the Japanese, even if they are happy to buy many of their products. The local acceptance of international products may therefore be dependent on the creation of entirely new and locally appropriate specifications and images. These will have to accord closely with customary behaviour or consumption patterns (and may have to be locally manufactured).

SECTION TWO – REPUTATION

KAY'S ANALYSIS OF REPUTATION

Kay's analysis of *corporate, product and brand reputation* as a source of competitive advantage was introduced in Chapter 4.

Kay comments that 'reputation has been important to successful traders since pre-industrial society. Merchants were concerned to demonstrate the purity of their assays or the fullness of their measure. Craftsmen stressed the quality of their workmanship. But how were their ignorant customers to assess purity, fullness, or quality? Sometimes they looked to the state to regulate the market for them. In other cases, traders banded together in guilds to monitor each other's work and to establish an honest reputation for the whole group. Some craftsmen relied on their own name, or that of their family. All these mechanisms are still important today' (p. 87).

Kay suggests that reputation is the market's method of dealing with attributes of product or service quality which customers cannot easily monitor for themselves. It is a means of certifying quality, as described in an earlier section of this chapter, above. Reputation is a function of the product or service:

❑ *consistency and continuity*.
❑ reliability that is associated with successful long-term market position or *incumbency*.
❑ reliability that is associated with *specification, formulation or recipe*.
❑ *signalling*.

A strong corporate, product or service reputation, associated with the brand strength described earlier in this chapter, may generate value and act as a source of competitive advantage because:

❑ it reinforces the competitive position of the enterprise, especially where repeat purchase over time may be necessary.
❑ it establishes *preference* in the minds of customers, especially in markets where those customers cannot easily monitor or influence quality for themselves. Kay gives the examples of car hire and accountancy services in illustration. University education is another

example. Generations of would-be students (and their families) are faced each year with a significant (and expensive) decision choice about an entity of which by they may personally have limited prior experience. They may need to rely on the opinions and judgements of others as well as on their own perceptions of what to expect, and what as customers they think they will get out of a university education. Universities with strong reputations (however these reputations are established or defined) are therefore likely to find it easier to recruit. At the same time they can recruit the better students, the quality of whose eventual results will reinforce the reputation of the institution in a form of a virtuous circle.

❑ it enables the organization to charge premium prices or to earn greater profits.

Reputation may be established by any or all of:

❑ the making of promises of quality, reliability, and service which are *always fulfilled* in the perception of the customer.
❑ the making of a credible demonstration of long-term, consistent and continuous commitment to the market (for instance, "established in 1881 and still going strong").
❑ the association of new products or services with a strongly established reputation which already attaches to existing activities. Kay describes this as 'staking a reputation which has been acquired in another market' (p. 97). Kay quotes the successful introduction in 1988 by Marks and Spencer, a leading UK retailer of clothing and foodstuffs, of financial services products such as personal investments.

Kay suggests that reputation needs to have a name attached to it, whether it is the name of an individual, a profession, or an organization. Kay notes that in markets 'where quality standards are variable, names like Hertz or Avis, Price Waterhouse or Peat Marwick command large premiums' (p. 88). Kay comments that 'car hire and international accounting are both goods for which it is difficult for the customer to assess product quality in advance. Major firms with strong reputations and brand names have come to dominate these markets'.

The need for an appropriate reputation may in particular require the implementation of a strategy of the offer of consistent quality and reliability of product or service in markets characterized by long-term repeat purchase. Such markets might include medical services, holiday packages, financial services products, business services, cars and consumer durable goods.

Corporate reputation may also be crucial to the marketing of intangible goods or services that cannot be inspected and are consumed only once, such as pension plans, postgraduate education, weddings, and funeral services. Significantly, such services may have the additional (and important) characteristic of being associated with the "great moments and great deeds" of people's lives, to which great significance is justifiably attached. Fear of making the wrong decision will drive customers to reputable suppliers, even though they may be the most expensive in the market.

Kay notes, however, that the process of establishing reputation is likely to require a customer willingness to share their experience with others, for instance through interpersonal contact or "word of mouth". It will be in the interests of the enterprise to facilitate and encourage this process of sharing.

Kay concludes that reputation is usually associated with a variety of other sources of competitive advantage, such as functional specification, quality, a track record of successful innovation, or a customer-orientated architecture. These sources are often the initial source of reputation but in time may be reinforced by it. And they are needed to maintain the long-term reputation of the enterprise. Hence the need for the reliability, consistency, and continuity already described above.

SECTION THREE – CORPORATE IDENTITY

CORPORATE IDENTITY DEFINED

Hall (1989) defines corporate identity as the 'expression of who a company is, what it does and how it does it'. Olins (1989) adds that 'corporate identity tells the world ... just what the corporate strategy is' (p. 145). Corporate identity is *the outward face of the organization*. It communicates the personality behind the face, and gives an indication of the strategic intent described in earlier chapters.

Reference was made in Chapter 24 to the use of corporate identity to *differentiate* the enterprise from its competitors. Effective corporate identity is, for example, of particular importance in the market for business-to-business services such as consultancy, or in the processes of outsourcing and supply chain management described in earlier chapters. There may be no tangible product, so the supplier may have to rely on intangible or process features to differentiate its offer. This point has already been made in earlier sections of this chapter. Positive corporate identity and reputation must be inextricably linked in the mind of customers or clients in order to maximize the competitive advantage they represent.

Corporate identity gives a shape and form by which to visualize enterprise mission. Mission was described in Chapter 11 as a statement of corporate purpose and philosophy. A mission statement indicates what the organization stands for, what it is about, and how it is to go about its business. Corporate identity may be used to express and to communicate this statement of mission. It can be used to give colour and vitality to the mission statement, and to give it meaning in the outside world. Disney, for example, is associated with Mickey Mouse, with fun and entertainment, with family values, and with Disney's mission to "bring happiness to millions".

Olins suggests that, in order to be effective, *each organization needs to communicate a clear sense of purpose* that people can understand. This is true whether these people work in the enterprise, or are external customers or stakeholders.

People internal to the organization particularly need to be able to identify with the enterprise *in order to develop a sense of belonging*. Such a sense of belonging is a crucial motivating force. It may also be essential to the development of an effective customer and quality orientation within the enterprise.

THE ROLE OF CORPORATE IDENTITY

A basic role of corporate identity management is to develop and to communicate an *external image* for the organization, or to shape *external perceptions* about it. The external image might be "progressive" or "proactive", "customer-oriented", or "caring". The image is used to shape the perceptions of employees and managers; and those of customers, clients, opinion-formers, and stakeholders within the external environment. For example:

Employees and managers - corporate identity may be used by enterprise leaders to develop and communicate values, culture, and image within the organization and within its internal architecture. This internal culture or image might variously be customer or service-oriented, caring, values-based, employee-centred, innovative or creative (or whatever).

Customers and clients - the development of a strong corporate identity differentiates the enterprise (and its product or service offer) from its competition. An effective corporate identity reinforces brand image and company reputation. And the establishment of a positive corporate identity is likely to encourage customers to develop favourable perceptions about the organization as a *credible supplier*, for instance to world class buyers or to government agencies.

Customer perceptions are also likely to be important *in international markets*. Where product or service introductions are new, or where the enterprise is in the process of developing its position in any particular international market, it may be helpful if people in that territory already hold a favourable perception of the newcomer's identity. A prerequisite to establishing an effective product-market position may be some significant (and positive) development of local knowledge of what the enterprise is all about. Thus, for example, companies such as ABB, SKF, BP, Toyota or Ford are well-known internationally. They are widely regarded as efficient and well-managed global suppliers of quality products (as well as desirable employers to have in the country).

Otherwise, gaining a foothold in a new international market and achieving customer acceptance of expanded product-market operations therein may be much more difficult. Neither the supplier, nor its products, nor its reputation will be known. Its lack of identity will indicate a lack of presence and credibility. Establishing that presence is likely to be expensive. Advertizing, promotion, and test launches will be required in order to establish awareness and conviction among customer segments only familiar with well-established or incumbent market offerings. Before such customers can be "won over", a positive identity and image of the newcomer to the market may have to be built up. People are wary of buying from someone they do not know, and therefore do not feel they can yet trust.

Investors, financial institutions and the stock market - investors may be encouraged by a positive corporate identity to maintain their investment in the enterprise, and to contribute to further fund-raising when it is called for.

The creation of favourable perceptions amongst these shareholders will also be of relevance where mergers and acquisitions are used as forms of business development strategy described in Chapter 27. Positive external perceptions may, for instance, have the effect of discouraging threatened takeover bids. Stakeholder resistance to the threat they imply may be stiffened. Positive perceptions of the organization and what it stands for may diminish the apparent advantages being offered in exchange by the predator who wishes to attempt to make the takeover.

Buyers and the trade - maintaining trade image is essential to maintaining market position. And, as described above, it is vital when entering new markets. The trade needs to feel that the supplier is here to stay and can be trusted, before the newcomer will be accepted by it.

People and organizations within the external environment - decision-makers may feel the necessity to develop and maintain a favourable identity and image with those people and organizations external to the enterprise who may in some way be capable of exercising an influence over its affairs (such as opinion-formers, politicians, or the financial press), or who (for instance as potential employees) may have a future interest in them. Crisis management was analyzed in Chapter 10. The issues of business ethics, environmentalism, and social responsibility were analyzed in Chapter 12.

Corporate Identity and Competition

The development and communication of corporate identity may give rise to favourable external perceptions. The *intangible benefit* of such a positive external perception may be a source of competitive advantage. This point has already been made at various points in this chapter. Corporate identity (and the relationship architecture upon which it partly depends) is unique to the enterprise and cannot easily be imitated. Corporate identity can then be used effectively to differentiate the organization from its competitors, and to communicate to the customer the benefits of trading with it.

Corporate Identity and Quality

The PIMS data referred to in Chapters 23 and 24 suggested that products or services perceived to be of the highest *quality* may achieve the best returns on investment for their suppliers.

Corporate identity can be used to communicate and develop perceptions of quality amongst actual and potential customers, external stakeholders, and media influences. This communication may focus on:

❑ product or service specification and quality.
❑ brand position (because "good brand" perceptions may equal "good quality" perceptions).
❑ market position where reputation is based on the consistent offer of quality, reliability, and service; or is instead based on the duration of incumbency.
❑ corporate quality, where strategy formulation, decision-making, and strategic management processes are based on values that derive from a quality, customer-orientated, or caring culture and ethos in the organization.

MANAGING THE RELATIONSHIP BETWEEN CORPORATE AND BRAND IDENTITIES

The strategic management of brands was analyzed in earlier sections of this chapter. Brand and corporate identity are likely to be related. Each reinforces the other. Brand identity is used to differentiate the product or service. Brand identity is associated with the most favourable market values or characteristics of the product or service. Corporate identity has a wider role to play. It shapes perceptions of the organization as supplier or provider among a wider internal and external audience, as well as amongst customers.

Olins suggests that there are three main strategies by which to manage the relationship between corporate and brand identities. These are:

❑ the monolithic approach.
❑ endorsed identity.
❑ discrete brands.

Each is described below.

The monolithic approach - in which the parent company and all of its products or services carry the same strong, clear visual identity. Corporate and brand images are the same. Olins quotes Shell and Marks and Spencer as examples. Other examples include Orange, Prudential Insurance, Microsoft, and BMW. Every brand carries the company's image; the company and the brand are perceived to be the same.

It follows that every brand must live up to market or user expectations. Otherwise, both company and brand will suffer negative consequences.

Endorsed identity - in which an organization has a group of product-market activities or companies which it endorses with the group name and identity. Olins gives the examples of the US firms General Motors (who for instance make Chevrolet, Opel, Vauxhall, and Holden brand vehicles), and United Technologies (e.g. Pratt and Whitney aircraft engines). ABB Asea Brown Boveri (e.g. ABB Kent Controls) is a European example.

Olins suggests that this approach is appropriate to 'companies that have grown by acquisition' to establish that 'corporate identity is a way in which the organization can clearly articulate what it is; the way in which the acquiring company can clearly stake out its purpose' (p. 106).

Discrete brands - by which, for instance in the tradition of the fast-moving consumer goods sector, each brand carries its own individual values and identity. The brand does not necessarily identify the parent company. The organization operates through a series of brands which may appear to outsiders to be unrelated to each other. Olins quotes as a classic example the portfolio of Unilever brands, including "Sunlight", "Lifebuoy", "Vim", "Lux", and "Persil".

REVIEW QUESTIONS

1. What is a brand?
2. What is the strategic role of the brand?
3. Compare and contrast global brands, locally modified global brands, regional brands, and local brands. What are the roles of each type of brand? What are their relative advantages and disadvantages?
4. What is reputation?
5. What is the strategic role of reputation?
6. What is corporate identity?
7. What is the strategic role of corporate identity?
8. How may the enterprise manage the relationship between corporate and brand identities?

TECHNIQUES OF CASE STUDY AND ANALYSIS

1. Identify competition strategies (Chapter 22) evident in the case study.
2. Identify the nature and character of brand, or reputation, or corporate identity (or all three) in the case study.
3. Analyze brand, or reputation, or corporate identity (or all three) as sources of competitive advantage. In what ways do these sources of competitive advantage add value to the case company?
4. In what ways do brand, reputation, or corporate identity serve to differentiate the product-market offer of the case company from its competitors?
5. To what extent have brand, reputation, or corporate identity become strategic assets in the case company?

PROJECT ASSIGNMENTS

1. Using published information, advertisements and other appropriate material (i) draw up an analysis of the apparent brand portfolios and

brand strategies of the main competitors in a specific consumer (or business-to-business) market; (ii) compare these portfolios and strategies; and (iii) comment on the implications of the similarities and differences you can identify from this comparison.

2. Carry out an analysis of (i) a local or regional brand; and (ii) a global brand. Compare the two analyzes. Comment on the strategic implications of this comparison.

3. Using published information, advertisements and other appropriate material draw up an analysis and comparison of the brand strategy of (i) a named local or regional or national company; and (ii) a named international company, in a product-market with which you are familiar. Present your findings.

4. Using published information, carry out a comparative analysis of the reputation of two or more organizations in a particular industry or sector that is of interest to you. In what ways does reputation confer competitive advantage to these organizations, and how do they make use of this advantage?

5. Using published information or key informant interviews, draw up an analysis of the corporate identity and reputation of an organization with which you are familiar. What is the apparent purpose of the organization's strategies for identity and reputation? Present your findings.

References

Davidson, H. (1989) 'How to win the branding battle', *Annual Conference Proceedings*, The Marketing Society.

Hall, J. (1989) 'Corporate identity: asset or liability?', *Annual Conference Proceedings*, The Marketing Society.

Kay, J. (1993) *The Foundations of Corporate Success*, Oxford University Press, Oxford.

Menzies, D. (1996) 'A matter of identity', *The Financial Post Magazine*, November.

Olins, W. (1989) *Corporate Identity*, Thames & Hudson, London.

Chapter 26

Product-Market Development Strategies

A key area of strategic choice concerns decision-making about how to develop the product-market scope and position of the enterprise. For instance, should the enterprise continue to supply its existing products or services to its traditional markets? Should it develop new products; or move into new markets; or both? Might it instead decide to pursue strategies that are in some way different to what it has done before, for instance by following a strategy of diversification?

This chapter describes the alternative directions that this product-market development may take. The dynamics of this development are explained through the use of selected product-market matrices.

THE DIRECTION OF PRODUCT-MARKET DEVELOPMENT

The choice of volume, cost-based, focus, niche, and differentiated strategies has been described in Chapters 23, 24, and 25. The strategic choice described in those chapters must be made within the context of the desired direction and development of business strategy that enterprise management wishes to implement.

This chapter is concerned with product-market strategies. The direction in which these product-market strategies can be developed may be described in a number of ways. Two well-known frameworks for this analysis of strategic product-market direction and development form the content of this chapter. Each is based on a matrix form.

ANSOFF'S PRODUCT-MARKET MATRIX

A classic analysis of the choice of strategic product-market direction is given by H. Igor Ansoff (1968). His matrix suggests that there are *five* main product-market strategies. These are shown in Figures 26.1 and 26.2.

Ansoff's Five Product-Market Strategies

Consolidation - which implies a positive and active defence or reinforcement of existing market and segment provision, as described in Chapter 22.

Market penetration - which implies a strategy of increasing market share within existing markets and segments. Increasing promotional and sales expenditure might be used to achieve this objective. The enterprise might instead make use of the experience effect described in Chapter 23. Or the company might try to take over some of its competitors to add their market share to its own, especially where that market is mature or slow-growing. Acquisition strategy is dealt with in Chapter 27.

Product development - which calls for the effective management and development of existing products and brands; and for ongoing new product or process development (NPD) and new brand introductions (NBD).

Market development - which could be based upon new market research findings, or on the results of more detailed market segmentation and customer targeting. Or instead, advertising and promotion may be used to develop market demand from existing or latent needs that, up to now, have remained unsatisfied. New markets may also be opened up for new products that are derived from technological change and innovation. Market development may take place within either or both of national and international contexts.

Diversification - which has four choices, thus:-

- *horizontal integration* - in which the enterprise develops its business activities in a direction complementary or similar to its existing strategy. For instance, a retailer such as Tesco or Wal-Mart might internationalize its retail operations; or a shipping company might add a road haulage operation to its business. In this sense, the enterprise is choosing to stick to its core business as described in Chapters 18, 20, and 27.
- *concentric diversification* - in which the enterprise diversifies into closely related activities. A publishing company, for instance, might diversify into the making of programmes for television and radio for which it can produce stories and scripts. This form of diversification is also described in Chapters 18 and 27. It is sometimes referred to as "related-constrained" diversification.
- *vertical integration* - in which the enterprise diversifies *backwards* through its value chain into supply or manufacturing operations associated with its existing activities. Or it may instead diversify *forwards* through its value chain into further processing or distribution

of its products. Or it may integrate in both directions at the same time. Vertical integration was also described in Chapter 18.

- *conglomerate diversification* - in which the enterprise diversifies into unrelated activities to which it thinks it can apply particular capabilities or competencies (such as strong leadership, strategic, marketing, or financial management skills) in order to gain competitive advantage. Conglomerate diversification is also described in Chapters 18 and 27. Conglomerates such as the UK's BTR company are usually created by use of the acquisition strategies analyzed in Chapter 27. They may contain a variety of different activities across which the strategic intent is (i) to spread risk; or (ii) to make use of the Boston Consulting Group (BCG) market share and market growth rate matrix described in the next section below.

PRODUCT MARKET	EXISTING PRODUCTS		NEW PRODUCTS
EXISTING MARKETS	Consolidation	Market penetration	Product development
NEW MARKETS	Market development		Diversification

Figure 26.1 An Adaptation of Ansoff's Product-Market Matrix

THE BCG MARKET SHARE AND MARKET GROWTH RATE MATRIX

The *Boston Consulting Group* (BCG) approach to the strategic management of product-markets focuses on:

- ❑ the long-term enterprise share of target markets or segments; *and*
- ❑ the rate at which these markets are growing.

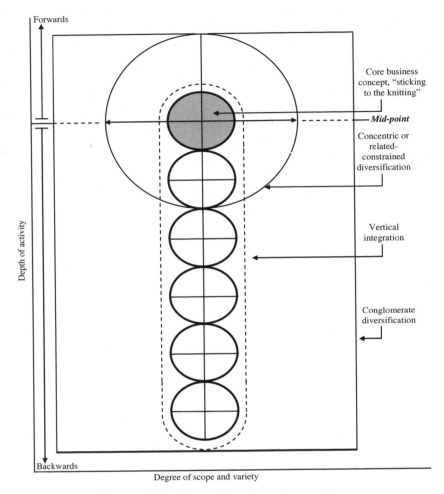

Figure 26.2 Diversification Alternatives

There are two basic justifications for the use of these market variables. The first justification is that business growth depends, in part, on *the prevailing rate of market growth.* For instance, where (i) a market is static, or is in the mature stage of the product life cycle; and (ii) a small number of dominant suppliers compete but cannot (for whatever reason) take each other over, then the prospects for growth in market share and profitability for any one of them will be limited. This is the case in the UK food manufacturing and retailing sector.

The second justification relates to product-markets described in Chapter 23 that may be characterized by (i) a need for high operational volume or the achievement of critical mass; or (ii) ineffective product differentiation; or (iii) commodity type products; or (iv) the experience effect implying movement down the experience curve. Chapter 23 suggested that in such markets the pursuit of *increased market share* (and possibly cost leadership) is seen to be a key to business survival and success. The apparent relationship between relative market share, enterprise profitability, and return on investment is a key finding of the PIMS study (Buzzell and Gale, 1987) quoted in Chapter 23.

The BCG's Four Product-Market Development Stages

The BCG identifies four potential development stages for any particular business activity. These development stages are defined by the growth rate of the market in which the activity takes place, and by its market share relative to competitors, as justified immediately above. These four development stages are described below, and illustrated in Figure 26.3.

"Stars" - which are high growth rate, high market share activities. They may be highly profitable (e.g. being at an early stage in the product life cycle) but require large cash inputs to finance their growth. Eventually their growth slows down, they become mature and, if they have a high share of what has become a low growth rate market, they become "cash cows".

"Cash cows" - which are low growth rate, high market share activities whose role is to generate cash flow to support innovative, technological, marketing and NPD activities taking place within the "stars" described above, or in the "question marks" described below.

"Question marks" - which are activities with a low share of a high growth rate market. Question marks consume finance (supplied by cash cows). Decision-makers have to make judgements based on experience and risk assessment as to whether these question-marks will develop into stars, or instead fail to fulfil their promise. In the latter case they would become "dogs".

"Dogs" - which are low market share activities in markets characterized by low growth rates. They may generate enough cash to support themselves, but worst of all, they may require financial support from other activities. Dogs might be products situated at an uncertain distance from the end of their life cycle, or potentially be threatened by the prospect of obsolescence.

The BCG's Four Product-Market Management Strategies

Boston Consulting Group specify *four management strategies* which can be used to achieve, maintain, or change the development stages described immediately above. These management strategies are listed as follows.

"Build" - which strategy aims to develop and improve to market position. This implies a willingness to provide the necessary financial resources from wherever these may be available (and in particular from cash cows). This strategy is particularly appropriate to stars (in order to ensure their eventual transition to cash cow status), and question marks (to achieve eventual star status).
"Hold" - which strategy is designed to preserve the long-term market position of an activity. This strategy is particularly appropriate for the management of cash cows, so that their capacity to yield large positive cash outflow is prolonged for as long as possible.
"Harvest" - which strategy aims to achieve the maximum short-term cash flow, regardless of the longer-term consequences. This strategy is appropriate for a weak cash cow near the end of its life cycle, and may be applied to question marks and dogs where it is thought that these have uncertain future prospects in the market.
"Divest" - which strategy is based upon selling off business activities and applying the resulting finance elsewhere, for instance being used to resource the growth of stars or question marks. The strategy is appropriate to dogs and question marks whose maintenance or growth the company decides to discontinue funding, and for which buyers can be found to whom the activity in question is more appropriate or desirable. Such activities might instead be sold off to their managers and employees, or established as independent specialist or venture companies.

Ideally, therefore, the BCG suggests that the development of the company's product-market strategies *should concentrate on developing stars and cash cows*, so that there is a movement over time concentrated on the upper and lower quadrants of the left-hand side of the matrix shown in Figure 26.3.

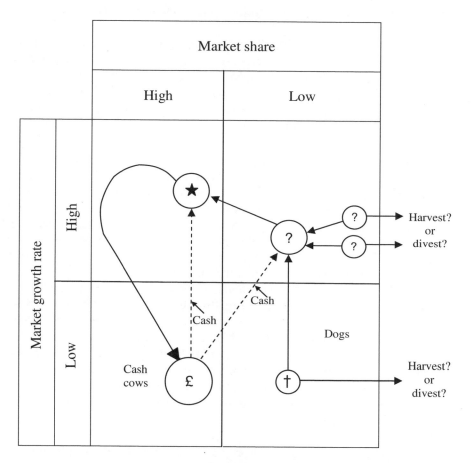

Figure 26.3 The BCG Market Share and Market Growth Rate Matrix

THE PIMS PRINCIPLES TWO AND FIVE

The PIMS Programme was described in Chapter 23 as a tool of market and competitive analysis. PIMS may be used on a client-specific basis for guiding the formulation and choice of the business strategies being described in this part of the book. It may also be used to predict how a particular combination of market conditions and strategic decisions might affect future business performance.

PIMS Principle Two - Market Share and Profitability are related

Chapter 23 noted that the PIMS results indicate that businesses with large market shares tend to enjoy a greater return on investment than that of competitors with a relatively smaller market share. Buzzell and Gale commented that this is due to the benefits of economies of scale and experience yielding lower unit costs and higher margins than may be available to smaller competitors.

Chapter 23 dealt with the interrelated issues of volume and cost, using analyzes of critical mass, experience, and the value chain. Strategies of cost minimization or cost leadership described in that chapter may be associated here with *the development and maintenance of growing or dominant market share positions.* The BCG describes these positions as "stars" and "cash cows" respectively. They are positioned in the market share and market growth rate matrix as key sources of investment profitability and funding for further product-market and business development. Business development strategies are described in Chapter 27.

Chapter 24 described focus and niche strategies whose long-term success is in part based on the use of differentiating features, innovation, quality, and excellence as key sources of competitive advantage by which to achieve and maintain a leading or dominant market share position. By definition such segment-specific or niche markets (such as those for specialized high-technology products or services) contain limited scope; it is essential for the supplier to obtain and consolidate its number one position. The business that remains for other, less successful competitors may be marginal in terms of volume or value.

PIMS Principle Five - Vertical Integration is a Profitable Strategy for Some Kinds of Business but not for Others

Ansoff describes vertical integration as one of the four main product-market diversification options. Vertical integration may be associated with either or both backwards or forward diversification movements through the value chain. It may be illustrated by global petrochemical companies vertically integrating from oil exploration and production through refining and distribution to the forecourt retailing of fuels, car accessories, maps, CTN (confectioner, tobacconist and newsagent) products, and foodstuffs.

Buzzell and Gale comment on the contingent relationship between strategy choice and the resulting performance. They suggest that 'whether increased vertical integration helps or hurts depends on the situation ... (as well as) on the cost of achieving it' (p. 12). The desirability and feasibility of vertical integration as a strategic choice may be influenced by such variables as:

- the prevailing views (or "fashions") about what forms of structure and architecture are desirable and feasible. Structure and architecture were described in Chapter 18. For instance, to what extent can a traditionally "control-oriented" management culture familiar with a monolithic integrated form of structure cope with the consequences of de-integrating the value chain? Do the necessary levels of trust prevail between network members in order to make a vertically de-integrated architecture or value chain, such as Benetton SpA, work?
- the degree to which the enterprise must develop core competencies at each stage of the value chain. Core competencies were described in Chapter 20. The greater the depth of activity, or the wider the scope and variety of the value chain (as described in Figure 26.2), the greater the number of core competencies that the enterprise may need. Chapter 20 noted Hamel and Prahalad's view that decision-makers may be wise to limit the number of core competencies that they must develop, in view of the knowledge, experience, and expense required to create any one of them. Hence the contemporary strategic preference for the de-integrated value chains or supply chain networks, described in Chapter 18, over the strategies described by Ansoff of deep backwards or forwards vertical integration, and based on a monolithic and internally integrated conceptualization of the value chain. On the other hand, where the enterprise already possesses the requisite core competencies throughout a vertically integrated and monolithic internal value chain (as in the international petrochemical, automotive and steel industries), its competitive advantage may be very great. It may be impossible for new entrants to replicate the value chains of existing players, or to match their experience and cost structures. The immense cost of establishing such a vertically integrated value chain would constitute a massive barrier to entry. And any attempt by new players to build up experience through a de-integrated value chain may be a slow, uncontrollable and unpredictable process, with no guarantee of success. The vertically integrated and monolithic value chains of existing suppliers (and the cost advantages they may yield) may under Kay's classification become *strategic assets* of enormous significance.
- the degree to which the enterprise must reach a point of *critical mass* at any or all of the stages in the value chain. Considerations of volume and cost (as described in Chapter 23) may require heavy capital

investment *at each of several stages of the value chain* rather than at one only of these stages. This increases the investment expense involved and increases the risk to the enterprise. But it also constitutes a source of competitive advantage to existing players in the sector who have already reached these points of critical mass; and provides a powerful barrier to entry to newcomers.

REVIEW QUESTIONS

1. Why is the direction of enterprise product-market development a key area of strategic choice?
2. Compare and contrast the strategic alternatives identified by Ansoff's product-market matrix.
3. Compare and contrast the strategic alternatives identified by the Boston Consulting Group (BCG) matrix.
4. Analyze and comment on the strategic implications of the PIMS Principles Two and Five (also see Chapter 23).

TECHNIQUES OF CASE STUDY AND ANALYSIS

1. Identify competition strategies evident in the case study.
2. Identify product-market development strategies (if any) evident in the case study. Analyze these product-market development strategies. Comment on their implications. Explain their significance for the competitive positioning and competition strategy of the case company/companies.

PROJECT ASSIGNMENT

Using published data or key informant interviews, present a past or current example (or examples) of company use of either of the product-market matrices described in this chapter. Explain the direction of development of company product-market strategy revealed by the use of these matrices. Comment on the apparent reasoning for the company's choice of direction and dynamic of development.

References

Ansoff, H.I. (1968) *Corporate Strategy*, Penguin Books, London.
Buzzell, R.D. and B.T. Gale (1987) *The PIMS Principles*, Free Press, New York.
Buzzell, R.D., B.T. Gale and R. Sultan (1975) "Market share: a key to profitability", *Harvard Business Review*, January-February.
Kay, J. (1993) *Foundations of Corporate Success*, Oxford University Press, Oxford.
Mantle, J. (1997) *Benetton*, Little, Brown & Co, London.

Chapter 27

Business Development Strategies and Strategic Alliances

Chapter 26 dealt with the development of strategies for product-market offer and position. This chapter looks at business development strategies and the use of strategic alliances.

An important area of strategic choice concerns decision-making about how to develop the business activity. Business development is also a key feature of the implementation of the enterprise competition strategy described in Chapter 22.

Business development may be based on a series of alternative strategic choices. These include the use of internally generated funds, co-operation and partnership, alliances, mergers, takeovers, licensing and franchising. The chapter also describes the alternative directions that the business development activity might take. A variety of implementation issues are dealt with in the text of the chapter.

THE OBJECTIVE OF BUSINESS DEVELOPMENT

There are a variety of objectives of the business development activity.

Some Strategic Requirements of Business Development

To consolidate, reinforce, or develop the existing position of the enterprise - the inevitable processes of market and environmental change described in earlier chapters means that the enterprise cannot stand still. Business development may be one way of "staying in the game" and maintaining competitive position.

The consolidation of existing position follows from the basic defensive competition strategies described in Chapter 22. It follows from the need to maintain and protect market share described in Chapters 23 and 26. And increasingly it implies the use of the strategies of stretch and leverage described in Chapter 21. The business development strategies associated with co-operation, partnership, and alliance described later in this chapter are now seen as key mechanisms of resource stretch and leverage.

The maintenance and protection of competitive position has for example become a key defensive strategy in the global automotive, media, and alcoholic spirit drinks sectors. Each is characterized by mature market conditions, slow growth, and increasing competition.

To achieve growth - for instance by gaining the market share increases described in Chapters 23 and 26. A business that stands still in a growing or changing market is often interpreted by its stakeholders as suffering from inertia, decline, or stagnation.

To achieve increases in scale - as described in Chapter 23.

To achieve critical mass - as described in Chapter 23.

To achieve changes or increases in the scope of business activity - for instance by applying new knowledge, adopting new technologies, or applying the innovation strategies as described in Chapter 19. In this case, business development may be associated with any of the forms of product-market development described in Chapters 24 and 26.

To access or reinforce knowledge, capability, competence and expertize - as described in Chapters 4, 19, 20, and 21. Business development strategies may be associated with enterprise needs to develop operational capability and resource efficiency. They may instead be based upon a belief that the enterprise may stretch and leverage the resources of merger or alliance partners, or takeover victims, more effectively than their former managements were able to.

To reinforce the knowledge management process - as described in Chapter 19. The objective of the business development process in this case is to gain access to, or to combine the knowledge base of the relevant players in order to enhance competitive advantage and strengthen competitive position. The combination of knowledge and experience may yield the *synergy* described in a later section of this chapter.

To achieve a change of direction - the enterprise may decide that changing market or environmental circumstances call for a radical departure from the existing line of business. Business development strategies such as acquisition or the use of licensing may allow the enterprise to achieve a rapid and significant change of direction. The Virgin Group for example sold *(divested)* some parts of its activities and moved into the airline business with the Virgin Atlantic company established for that purpose.

To internationalize or globalize the business - as described in Chapter 28. The rapid internationalization of business activities that has characterized the last two decades has been based on the use of all of the business development strategies described in this chapter, and in Chapter 28.

INCREASING THE CAPITAL AND RESOURCE BASE

The development or expansion of the business activity may require an expansion of the capital and resource base. The enterprise may need more funds or working capital; it needs more plant, equipment or information and communication technology facilities; or more investment in knowledge and competencies. There are a number of ways in which this expansion may be brought about. These are described below.

Organic Development and the Use of Internally Generated Funds

Business development based on the use of internally generated funds may be termed "organic" development. Funds generated and retained within the business are used to finance ongoing development and expansion.

Venture Capital

The provision of *venture capital* is usually associated with the establishment and development of new and entrepreneurial businesses. Specialist investors, for instance such as the UK's Investors In Industry ("3I") or the various government-sponsored enterprise agencies, provide funds and financial management skills to support the expansion of new and developing businesses. The providers of venture capital are often geared up to cope with:

❑ varying degrees of business risk, for example associated with innovation and new product development.
❑ varying degrees of investee maturity; and consequently:-
❑ varying degrees of post-investment involvement in the provision of skills of strategic, financial, operations, and marketing management.

Typically, the providers of venture capital are associated with the provision of relatively high risk capital for young, high growth companies at an early stage in their development. In many cases, this investment is accompanied by direct managerial support. This may be maintained until the investee company has acquired its own financial skills, and is judged to be in a position to raise further finance from more conventional funding sources.

Loan Finance

The use of loan finance from banks and financial institutions is a widely used and traditional means of financing business expansion and development. The lender and the borrower have to judge whether the returns from the investment will be sufficient to meet the required annual interest charges and the eventual capital repayment. The higher the interest charges, the less attractive may be the use of this kind of finance, in comparison with equity finance to which dividend payments are (at least in theory) not guaranteed.

The use of loan finance for instance in the UK and USA has, however, been associated with macroeconomic and political controversy over the prevailing level of interest rates. Some companies prefer to seek additional equity funding for new business development activity as this is perceived by them to carry less short-term risk.

However, in countries such as Germany, France, Spain, South Korea, and Japan the use of loan finance for business development and expansion is commonplace. There are often close interpersonal, structural, or ownership links between business and financial institutions. Banks and financial institutions may take a long-term view of client business development. They may be prepared to forego interest or capital repayments for lengthy periods of time while the venture becomes established. This is of particular advantage in situations of technological advance and innovation, where returns are unpredictable and where the use of equity funding might therefore be considered to be unviable.

The use of loan finance has been a critical factor in the international and global development of Japanese and South Korean industry since the 1950s.

Flotation and the Use of Equity Finance

Stock market flotation has been a traditional UK and US route to expanding the level of funds available for business development and growth. Flotation means the expansion of the ownership base so as to bring in additional funds. While there is relatively low risk attaching to these funds in the short term, shareholder expectations of an appropriate return provide a powerful incentive to the business to make its investments succeed. Failure, and the fall in share price that would accompany it, could lead to a takeover and the loss of ownership and control.

Indeed, the fear of loss of control has sometimes discouraged private businesses in the UK from seeking stock market representation. The alternative, which may be expensive loan finance commitments made available by institutions that lack the flexibility of their European or Japanese counterparts, may act as a major constraint on business development and expansion in these kinds of companies. It may place them at a considerable competitive disadvantage. Financial strategy was analyzed in Chapter 13.

CO-OPERATION AND PARTNERSHIP

Increasingly, business development has become predicated on strategies of co-operation and partnership. This is in particular true for international or global business development. Limitations on the scope, scale, resources, competence, or access available to any one enterprise may make desirable or sensible the establishment of some kind of development strategy based on such co-operation or partnership.

The de-integrated value chains, value adding partnerships, holonic networks, or virtual companies described in Chapter 18 provide examples of the structures by which strategies of co-operation and partnership may be implemented.

The use of co-operation or partnership to achieve resource leverage and joint effect was described in Chapter 21. Partnership or alliance strategies may also be used to achieve the *synergy* that is described in a later section of this chapter.

STRATEGIC ALLIANCES

Strategic alliances are a form of voluntary grouping between firms who come together for a specified period of time to achieve some common objective. They represent a type of strategic choice based on co-operation and partnership. Their use is now widespread, particularly on an international basis.

Definitions

An *alliance* may be defined as a voluntary association that furthers the common interests of the constituent members. A *strategic alliance* may be defined in terms of at least two companies or partners voluntarily combining value chain activities, architecture, and value chain linkages for the purpose of increasing individual and collective value addition, increasing competitive advantage, and achieving agreed or common objectives.

Yoshino and Rangan (1995, pp. 4-5) note that 'a strategic alliance links specific facets of the businesses of two or more firms. At its core, this link is a trading partnership that enhances the effectiveness of the competitive strategies of the participating firms by providing for the mutually beneficial trade of technologies, skills, or products based upon them. An alliance can take a variety of forms, ranging from an arm's-length contract to a joint venture. Because varied interpretations of the term exist, we define a strategic alliance as possessing simultaneously the following three *necessary* and *sufficient* characteristics:

❏ the two or more firms that unite to pursue a set of agreed-upon goals remain independent subsequent to the formation of the alliance.
❏ the partner firms share the benefits of the alliance and control over the performance of assigned tasks - perhaps the most distinctive characteristic of alliances and the one that makes them so difficult to manage.
❏ the partner firms contribute on a continuing basis in one or more key strategic areas, such as technology, products, and so forth.'

FOUR TYPES OF STRATEGIC ALLIANCE

Yoshino and Rangan describe four types of strategic alliance. Each is described below.

Pro-Competitive Alliances

Yoshino and Rangan suggest that pro-competitive alliances can be defined as 'inter-industry, vertical value chain relationships, as between manufacturers and their suppliers or distributors' (p. 19). The alliance partners are not rivals in direct competition with each other. They may for example work together to develop or improve products or processes, or to manage costs.

The attainment of added value or synergy, and the achievement of genetic variety and diversity (by using and combining the varying or different experience, capability and competence of partners) are key objectives of this kind of alliance. Partners may be able to re-conceptualize or re-define each other's problems in a non-threatening manner to achieve mutually advantageous or "win-win" solutions. For example, one leading

European steel-maker has an alliance with its key supplier of rollers. The quality of finished strip steel is dependent on the surface finish of the rollers used in the strip mill. The two companies are working together to improve the quality and durability of these rolls (which are expensive and constitute a major cost item to the steel-maker). At the same time, price negotiations for rolls are carried out on an "open book" basis so that both sides are satisfied that the roll-maker can make enough margin to re-invest in the necessary but costly research and development required to achieve the target improvements. The objective is a win-win situation for both parties under all of the technological, quality, and profitability criteria that define the alliance. Supply chain management issues were analyzed in Chapter 18.

Non-Competitive Alliances

These are intra-industry links among non-competing firms in the same sector. Whilst both partners operate in this sector, neither regards each other as a major rival. Partnership is seen as a source of synergy and competitive advantage, again in terms of mutuality and "win-win". Yoshino and Rangan suggest that the partners would tend to be different in character. Neither would want to become a major player in the particular market segments in which the other specializes. Alliances between Western and South Korean car manufacturers have for example been used to develop and manufacture low-cost cars for sale in Asia or South America. Such cars would not find ready acceptance in the more sophisticated (and regulated) car markets of North America or Europe.

Pre-Competitive Alliances

Yoshino and Rangan comment that pre-competitive alliances 'bring together firms from different, often unrelated industries to work on well-defined activities such as new technology development. Du Pont and Sony's co-operative development of optical memory-storage products is an example' (p. 20).

Yoshino and Rangan comment (pp. 20-21) that 'working together, the two firms, neither of which possesses the technological or market know-how to succeed alone' might expect to develop a product that they could manufacture and market independently of their partner if the alliance was subsequently terminated.

Such alliances may however have unpredictable consequences. Yoshino and Rangan comment that 'an important characteristic of these type of alliances is their capacity to transform ... to another. IBM's pre-competitive alliances with Intel and Microsoft are examples of such a transformation. The alliance that brought together IBM ... and the world's dominant chip maker and largest software company ... helped popularize and standardize the personal computer industry. But with success came mounting conflict. The erstwhile partners began to compete, each trying to cast itself in the role of standard setter. IBM's loss was its former partner's gain. A *Wall Street Journal* story called the IBM-Intel relationship one of "high technology's most tangled relationships"' (p. 21).

Certainly, companies may be careful not to expose too much of their core knowledge, capability, competence and experience to their alliance partners. The transfer of expertize and capability of an immense financial and competitive worth from Western to Japanese companies involved in pre-competitive alliances for instance in the electronics, computing and telecommunications sectors is the subject of extended (and controversial) comment by Hamel and Prahalad in their 1994 book *Competing for the Future*. Reference to the principle is made in Chapters 20 and 21 of this book. It is also relevant to the issue of knowledge management, described in Chapter 19. A knowledge resource that underpins competence but can be kept *tacit* may be denied to partners in a pre-competitive alliance, and rationed to them in a controlled manner. It may be much more difficult (or even impossible) to control the movement and assimilation of proprietary knowledge that has become fully *explicit* and shared within an organization or a profession.

Competitive Alliances

In this case, partners are likely to be direct competitors in the same sector. For example, the Advanced Photographic System (APS) was jointly developed by a consortium including the directly competing photographic film makers Kodak and Fuji.

Partners are likely to be well aware that each will, in their own interest, use the experience of the alliance to learn as much as possible about the others involved in it. In consequence, the participants will be concerned to protect their knowledge base, experience, capability and competence from unnecessary "leakage" to their partners, given the inevitably close relationship between them that is called for by such an alliance.

The usefulness of a competitive alliance will therefore be measured in terms of relative advantage to the individual participants. The disadvantages and risks of establishing a partnership with a direct competitor must be seen to be more than offset by the relative advantages that are described in the next section, below.

Yoshino and Rangan give as an example the ties between General Motors and Toyota who have jointly developed new car models. A number of competing car manufacturers share joint assembly facilities in different countries, thereby saving on investment cost, reducing risk, and optimizing manufacturing productivity at the same time as gaining enhanced market access.

SOME PURPOSES OF STRATEGIC ALLIANCES

Strategic alliances serve a variety of purposes. Some of these purposes are described as follow.

To Enhance Capability and Competence

Strategic alliances may be used specifically to combine and to enhance the knowledge, technology, experience, skill and competence of the partners. Such blending of these resources may yield synergy or critical mass. The alliance may be able to achieve a level or type of competence unavailable to individual partners; or to match the capability of larger competitors who have built up a critical mass of resources in-house.

Such large-scale competitors, for instance, may be capable of achieving the consistent rate of innovation that has been described at various points of this book. This ongoing innovation is a key source of competitive advantage and may facilitate market leadership. It is based on the possession of, or ready access to the competencies required to maintain continuous innovation. The use of strategic alliances by competitors may permit the partners to put in place (and to vary as necessary) an architecture which contains the skills to match the market leader, and also to achieve the operational scale described above. De-integrated value chains and network structures were described in Chapter 18. Such structures may be able to exploit opportunities that can only be accessed by the assembly and integration of multiple competencies, and by their variation to meet new market needs. Specific objectives under this heading include:

❑ the construction of alliances based on the process of knowledge and technology management described in Chapter 19. Different categories of knowledge may need for example to be blended in order to create a new technology "S" curve.

❑ to transfer skills and competencies between partners. Universities, for instance, have developed marketing and consultancy skills from alliances with companies and consultants with whom they have worked to fulfil commercial contracts. The universities' partners, in turn, have been able to develop more sophisticated research skills and methodologies than they hitherto possessed.

❑ to implement alliances with the best available or world class partners so as to learn from such companies as well as to achieve the most desirable and marketable outcome to the relationship.

❑ to re-vitalize, or gain access to new or improved managerial competencies, practices and systems. This is a common objective of alliances between organizations from Central and East European countries and their Western partners.

❑ to gain benefit from the blending of complementary technologies, for instance to produce new products or processes. The combination of gallium arsenide technology, fibre optics, and electronic software was for example used to revolutionize data transmission systems using light as the carrier of information bits. The blending of entities implies the implementation of diversity, and the potential for the creation of new concepts or methodologies.

❑ to exploit market and technological opportunities that require combinations of systems and relationship architecture to be integrated across a number of constituent partners in order to be functional. Operating on an individual basis is not viable, since the mixing of technologies and competencies comprises the source of competitive advantage. Examples include computer-based reservation systems, "hub and spoke" airline or freight handling systems, or the virtual companies and holonic networks described in Chapter 18.

To Enhance Value Generation

Strategic alliances may be used by their participants to enhance value generation by means of the sharing and joint use of knowledge, experience, resources and competence. At the same time, unnecessary or wasteful duplication of operational resources can be avoided where such sharing takes place. Publishing, for instance, is increasingly based on the international sharing of commissioning, production, and marketing activities in different territories.

Strategic alliances may be used to achieve the economies of scale, movements down the experience curve, and critical mass described in Chapter 23. They may also be used to achieve synergies that would otherwise be unavailable to individual partners. Such synergies may be based upon the achievement of diversity and variety that can only result from the coming together of different organizations with different capabilities.

To Leverage Resources

Hamel and Prahalad (1994) suggest that strategic alliances may be used to:

❑ concentrate resources.
❑ accumulate resources.
❑ complement resources.
❑ conserve resources.
❑ recover resources.

These strategies were described in detail in Chapter 21.

To Enhance Market Position and Achieve Business Development

The use of strategic alliances as a form of business development may permit alliance partners to achieve expansion and growth whilst at the same time maintaining their individual existence and identity. The strategic alliance may be of particular value in enabling small to medium sized enterprises to widen their scope of activity and to bid for large scale contracts. Various professional agencies have for instance formed European alliances in order to achieve international credibility and to bid for European contracts made available under open EU tender rules.

Strategic alliances may instead be used by their participants to gain access to a wider range of customers (for instance where the alliance comprises a group of national companies operating on an international basis). Alliance partners may gain access to new markets and new opportunities, or instead be in a position to market a global brand. Similarly, the alliance partners may be able to put together a wide range of products (perhaps marketed under one brand name) across which customers in any one country can shop. Such a range of products, especially if it possesses the prestige of an international brand name, would be beyond the capability of any one of the partners.

These features are usefully illustrated by the case of the international IVECO™ consortium of freight vehicle manufacturers whose individual product ranges, brand strength, competitive position and product-market scope would, on their own, be limited.

To Achieve Globalization

The use of strategic alliances has become a key feature of international or global business development strategies. Matsushita's "VHS" video format for instance achieved global acceptance and application through a series of alliances with European and US consumer electronics companies such as Philips and RCA. Strategic alliances may be used to:

❑ facilitate market access and international business growth.
❑ access international networks and distribution. This is the case of the international alcoholic spirits market in which competitors use each others' distribution networks on a global scale. Companies such as Seagram and United Distillers and Vintners (UDV) have established competing portfolios of "white" and "brown" spirit drinks (such as whisky, brandy and vodka) containing each others' products so as to maximize the available distribution.
❑ establish regional or continental manufacturing or distribution (or both) using large scale, world class quality facilities whose scale and cost would be beyond the resources and capability of any one of the partners. This is increasingly the case in specialist engineering sectors such as those associated with oil and gas exploration and extraction. International business strategy is described in Chapter 28.

Strategic Alliances and International Business Development

Clarke and Brennan (1988) suggest that the use of strategic alliances as a co-operative form of international business development has been encouraged because:

❑ the cost of building a presence in many markets simultaneously may be prohibitive, being beyond the resources and managerial capability of any one organization.
❑ the process of the organic development of this wider presence from the current base of operations may take too long, especially where larger global players are able to develop their activities more rapidly because of the scale of resources and capability available to them. This is the case of the international electrical engineering industry, which was forced into a series of competitive strategic alliances in order to react to the establishment in 1988 of the new ABB Asea Brown Boveri Company.

The use of *acquisition* as a strategy for business development is described in a later section of this chapter. Clarke and Brennan comment that the desire to make acquisitions assumes that:

❑ the right kinds of company are available for sale. This however cannot be taken for granted, especially in Europe, South Korea, and Japan where many enterprises are privately owned, or where takeover by a foreign company will meet hostile government reaction. Clarke and Brennan note that 'in Germany, Switzerland, Italy, Spain and France, being able to bid for the target company of one's choice is a comparatively rare event'. Indeed, Morden and Bowles (1998) comment on the refusal of the French government to sanction the purchase by Daiwoo of the Thomson CSF company after agreement in principle had been reached between the two companies that the acquisition should go ahead. The French government blocked the deal, in spite of the 'strong and hostile public reaction' in South Korea and in spite of the significant tension between the two governments that followed.
❑ the price is not prohibitive.
❑ the buyer will be able (i) to cope with international variations in business and corporate culture; and (ii) be willing to expend the time and resources on hammering its victim into the shape needed to achieve the objectives for which it was taken over in the first place. Reference is made in a later section to the potentially damaging effects (on both parties) of any so-called "harmonization" process that may be required.

Where these assumptions cannot be made, the co-operative use of alliances may be the preferred strategic choice.

Risk Management

Partnership arrangements, whether they are based on any of the four types of strategic alliance described above, may be used to manage and to spread risk. For instance, the risk of investments made in the strategies of expanded market access, globalization, technological development, or business development analyzed at various points in this chapter may be spread across the participants to the alliance, thereby reducing the risk to any one of them.

More specifically, strategic alliances may be used to maximize the inputs of competence and experience to projects that are in any way novel, uncertain, or ambiguous. These projects contain the maximum of risk, since their outcomes are unpredictable. This risk will be shared amongst the partners, any one of which would be unlikely to be prepared to shoulder the entire burden on its own. Such projects include advanced high technology projects associated with electronics and transaction processing systems, oil and gas exploration, aviation and avionics (aviation electronics), or space exploration.

The process of risk assessment was analysed in Chapter 8.

SOME IMPLEMENTATION ISSUES ASSOCIATED WITH STRATEGIC ALLIANCES

The usefulness of the alliance as a strategy for market, technology, or business development will in part depend on *whether the enterprise is able to identify and join forces with appropriate partners*. It may have to make use of agencies that specialize in putting together partnership arrangements if it is unsure about who the best participants might be.

Once the alliance is established, it will be important that there is at least some degree of *shared vision amongst the partners* about what can be achieved. It will also be necessary that a *consensus exists about the necessary degree of commitment and persistence* that the participants need to demonstrate. Partnerships will not work for long where some members are enthusiastic, whilst others are non-committal about the whole process and are not prepared to "pull their weight".

There will need to be some degree of *co-ordination of strategic direction and strategic management amongst the partners*. Otherwise the participants could go off at a variety of tangents to each other, making it impossible to integrate their efforts.

Achieving a consistency of strategic direction and strategic management amongst the partners may in turn depend on:

❑   the relative value sets of the partners; and the extent to which shared values and a shared purpose can be established and accepted. For instance, can the profit-orientated and short-termist time-scales of Western shareholder corporations be reconciled with the longer-term and technologically oriented view of South East Asian companies, or private European ones, between whom a technology development partnership exists?

❑   the establishment of trust, and an effective structure and relationship architecture within the alliance. In other words, can the participants create a sensible and effective organization by which to make viable the work of the alliance? This is related to:-

❑ the establishment of common and consistent codes of practice amongst the partners. The alliance will have to establish common languages, common methodologies (such as for software, costing, or financial management) and common approaches as to how to go about running the business. For instance, to what extent can companies familiar with high power distance, managerially-dominant cultures and hierarchical forms of control accommodate to the more flexible, low power distance forms of empowered team-based management process that are currently fashionable in Western corporations?

There is evidence that strategic alliances are likely to be successful where the participants already know each other (or know about each other); are familiar with each other's culture and way of working; or contain well-established business relationships or personal friendships amongst the decision-makers of the companies involved. Success may be correlated with a strong perception of common ground and identity; and a clear acceptance of the mutuality and interdependence of everyone's interests. All those involved should be convinced that success must favour everyone equally, and that failure will damage everyone equally.

MERGERS

Business development is achieved in this case by the *direct merger* between two or more enterprises. The *identity* of each constituent is subordinated to the identity of the newly merged organization, or disappears altogether.

The partners to the merger may be of the view that a union between them should allow the constituents for instance:

❑ to eliminate unnecessary competition between them.
❑ mutually to augment and reinforce strengths and capability, and to offset weaknesses in each constituent's structure and performance.
❑ to combine or harmonize knowledge, capabilities, competencies, experience, and market access.
❑ to achieve joint effect by any or all of (i) cutting or eliminating costs which would otherwise be duplicated; (ii) achieving the resource leverage described in Chapter 21; (iii) increasing scale, scope and critical mass, as described in Chapter 23; (iv) achieving the synergy described in a later section below.

In general terms, companies that seek to achieve a successful union would appear to require:

❑ a clear *logic* to the merger, that is one where the contribution of each participant is mutually compatible and adds value to the outcome.
❑ a mutual willingness to make the merger succeed.
❑ compatible, flexible, and adaptable cultures, such that change may be facilitated and eventual *harmonization* between the parties may be achieved.
❑ mutually compatible organization structures, and styles of leadership and management such that change may be facilitated and harmonization achieved.

ABB Asea Brown Boveri

Two large electrical engineering companies, Asea AB of Sweden and Brown Boveri Ltd of Switzerland, came together in a merger in 1988. The result was a new European organization, dominated by neither of the original parent companies, called ABB Asea Brown Boveri. The merged company has developed a powerful new identity and reputation within the international markets it serves. It has become a key player in the markets for power and electrical engineering products. Neither of its original constituents, on their own, could have achieved this objective.

Mergers as a Defensive Strategy

Two or more enterprises may also seek a merger with the specific objective of pre-empting a hostile takeover of any or all of the parties involved. The merged and enlarged enterprise may be much more difficult (or even too large) for a potential predator to attack, especially if one of its constituents (or its place of company registration) is based in a country that restricts the opportunity for hostile takeovers.

ACQUISITION AND TAKEOVER

Business development in this case is based on *the direct acquisition or takeover of other companies*. The acquiring company takes on the ownership of the company it has purchased, whilst the company it has bought loses its independent identity. The company purchased may continue to exist as a subsidiary or as a brand name, or it may disappear altogether.

The use of acquisition and takeover as a business development strategy is particularly common in Anglo-Saxon countries such as the USA, the UK, and Canada where many companies are publicly quoted on the stock market.

There are a number of basic justifications for the use of the takeover as a strategy for business development. These include:

❑ managing competitive position.
❑ achieving expansion and growth.
❑ achieving diversification.

Each of these justifications is analyzed below.

Managing Competitive Position

The enterprise may use acquisitions in a number of ways in order to manage its competitive position. These are listed as follows:

❑ to eliminate competitors.
❑ to pre-empt hostile takeover by another competitor.
❑ to consolidate or secure market position or market share (especially in mature markets), or to implement the defensive competition strategies described in Chapter 22.
❑ to build market position, or to achieve market leadership.
❑ to gain access to markets in which the takeover victim is already operating. This may be a favoured (and relatively speedy) strategy for companies that wish to increase the international scope of their business.
❑ to acquire innovations or innovators.
❑ to secure access to knowledge, resources, skills, competences or markets. This might mean taking over suppliers or distributors. Or instead it might mean implementing the strategy of vertical integration described in Chapters 18 and 26.

Achieving Expansion and Growth

Acquisition and takeover are widely used to implement strategies of expansion and growth. Such strategies include:

❑ achieving expansion or growth more rapidly, or at a lower cost (or both), as compared with what might be possible using the organic growth strategy described in an earlier section above.

❑ increasing national or international market share: the enterprise increases its relative market share by absorbing the market share of those companies it has acquired. This strategy is of particular importance in mature markets characterized by low (or non-existent) rates of growth, in which organic growth may not be feasible or where voluntary merger or alliance partners cannot be found.

❑ acquiring potential stars, cash cows, or question marks as identified by the Boston Consulting Group matrix described in Chapter 26. Where strategic management is based on the use of the BCG matrix, the use of acquisition may be regarded as a key strategy for managing the dynamics of the portfolio of businesses represented by the matrix. Cash cows may for instance be purchased in order to fund R&D, innovation, or new product or brand development. Examples of such acquisitions include hotel chains and other cash-flow based businesses such as fast-moving consumable goods, travel and tourism, or transportation and logistics.

❑ meeting shareholder expectations of the investment returns described in Chapter 13 that demonstrate growth in dividend yield and capital value. For example, shareholder expectations have been a key driving force of company use of acquisition and takeover during the last two decades in Anglo-Saxon countries whose economies are characterized by mature markets and slow economic growth.

Achieving Diversification

Reference was made in Chapter 26 to product-market strategies based on diversification. Diversification strategies may be used (i) to spread risk; (ii) to offset the effect of recession in any one market; and (iii) to attempt to stabilize the pattern of returns to investment over time.

Conglomerate businesses may make use of this strategy. They acquire a variety of companies, which may be PIMS-type market leaders. The objective is to construct a portfolio of businesses, any one of which is unlikely to be affected by conditions of boom or recession in the same way or at the same time as other business units in the portfolio.

Acquisitions Strategy Assumptions

Companies that plan to use strategies of acquisition and takeover may be faced with making a variety of assumptions. These assumptions may be directly relevant to the success (or otherwise) of the takeover activity. It may have to be assumed that:

❏ *the right potential candidates are actually available*, and that their price is appropriate. Potential acquisition prices may become unviable where there are too many would-be buyers and too few potential victims of any quality. The excessive bid premiums then needed to secure strongly-contested takeovers may represent poor investment value for money and constitute a severe drain on the resources of the acquirer.

❏ the buyer *can identify good and bad acquisition targets.* Can the buyer, and his or her advisers correctly appraise the potential target acquisition and the relative risk it represents? Is the target in fact a "well-packaged reject" or an over-priced "pig in a poke" with its owner just waiting for an ill-thought out, hurried, or opportunistic bid to come along in order to cash in on an overpriced bid for what will eventually prove to be significantly over-valued assets? The UK Ferranti Company was for example dragged down by an extremely unfortunate US acquisition that should have been rejected at the planning stage. The UK's Marks and Spencer Company instead had its corporate fingers burned with its earliest ventures into North American acquisitions.

❏ the acquisition can be *absorbed* and the total activity *harmonized* without the takeover process damaging the buyer. This is particularly the case where international takeovers are concerned. To what extent may international differences in leadership culture and management process be properly and efficiently reconciled? How much senior management time and company expenditure will be required to achieve the necessary co-ordination and harmonization?

❏ the planned (or hoped-for) *joint effects* or *synergies will be achieved.* Synergy was defined in Chapter 4, and is described in a later section below. The logic (or payoff) of the takeover may be based on anticipated synergies. To what extent are these synergies likely to emerge and what is their value relative to the cost of acquisition?

The Feasibility and Viability of Acquisition Strategy

Acquisition may be judged to be a feasible and viable means of business development where (i) the enterprise has developed effective skills of acquisition identification, risk assessment, and takeover capability; and (ii) where it considers that it possesses superior management skill and the capacity to improve on the existing performance of the companies it acquires.

The enterprise then has to live with the consequences of its actions. The use of acquisition and takeover as a strategy for business development remains controversial. Research study results are inconclusive. For instance, some studies of the after-effects of acquisitions in the UK have found the results to be disappointing. There is no consistent evidence that companies necessarily perform better after making acquisitions, while many have fared worse. And in many cases the share values of acquirers perform less well after their acquisitions than before these takeovers were made. Acquisitions may in any case be difficult to make where:

❑   a country's economy is dominated by private or close-held companies, as in Japan, South Korea, France, Spain, and Italy.
❑   the local company law is hostile to the takeover process; or hostile to acquisition by foreign companies (as was the case in India where local companies normally held majority shareholdings in enterprises).
❑   there are strong anti-trust laws (such as in the US) making certain types of takeover illegal. Some forms of vertical integration as described in Chapters 18 and 26 are not permitted in the US.
❑   the already concentrated nature of the sector (such as automotive, alcoholic beverages, or food manufacturing) means that further concentration by either merger or takeover would be deemed by national governments to be against the public interest.

Acquisition and Company Structure in the EU

Each EU country has its own company laws, practices, and organization structures, some of which differ from those currently prevailing in the UK. EU countries maintain the basic distinction between public and private companies. Member countries have stock exchanges on which company shares may be traded. But these exchanges may be smaller than that in the UK, because:

- there are relatively more family-owned and private enterprises of a medium to large scale than in the UK.
- fewer companies are listed on the national stock exchange. Other companies tend to raise equity capital directly by the means of private *placings* with large investors and investment trusts.
- widespread use is made of debenture and loan financing.
- banks in many EU countries invest heavily and directly in companies (for instance in Germany and Spain). Representatives of these banks therefore occupy seats on company boards and help to control the business.
- two-tier boards of directors, and compulsory worker participation in supervisory boards may (i) restrict the ability of would-be predators to make bids, or (ii) restrict the ability of the enterprise to consider merger suggestions.

Acquisition and Company Structure in Japan

Banks and corporate cross-holdings are used, making successful acquisition by outsiders relatively uncommon. Many Japanese companies are grouped together under the system of *keiretsu* or "business grouping". A small number of very large separate industrial groups, such as Mitsubishi or Mitsui, are each based around *their own core bank.* Each core bank has its own associated financial institutions. The group comprises an *integrated* collection of companies that operate in a wide variety of fields of manufacturing and service activity. This concept of integrated manufacturing and operations management is largely without parallel in the West.

Breaking into this closely-knit and integrated structure may be impossible for an outsider. Core bank investment and corporate cross-holdings amongst member companies of the same *keiretsu* may render them virtually immune from the threat of outside takeover.

Business development in Japan, or with Japanese companies, effectively means making use of the established national trading companies as *agents,* or establishing strategic alliances with individual *keiretsu* members or the many family-dominated companies that operate in Japan.

FRANCHISING

Business development takes place by the *franchising* of the right to use a *specified business format.* The owner or *franchisor* establishes a contractual relationship with another enterprise that, as *franchisee*, then has the right to make use of that business format during the lifetime of the contract. The franchisee may (i) have to supply the start-up capital; and (ii) have to pay a royalty to make use of the franchise during the lifetime of the contract.

The business format is developed and subsequently controlled by the owner or franchisor. The franchisee purchases the right to market a product or service under the franchisor's name and trademark, and to utilize the business format and methods specified in the franchise agreement.

Advantages to the Franchisor

The use of franchising as a method of business development means that the franchisor may be able relatively speedily to expand his or her business using a high proportion of other people's capital. At the same time there will (in theory) be a guaranteed return on the franchisor's investment by way of:

❏   royalty payments received.
❏   a contractual requirement to purchase certain types of inputs from the parent at prices determined by it, for example meat and buns for hamburgers, ingredients for soft drinks, copier and printing supplies, and so on.
❏   the mark-up on supplies sold to franchisees that have been purchased on a bulk basis, perhaps on an international scale.

It may also be the case that, while the franchisee usually carries most of the cost deriving from the establishment of the business, he or she assumes most of the risk.

Advantages to the Franchisee

The franchisee in return:

❏   obtains a well-known brand name supported by national or international marketing and advertising.
❏   has immediate competition restricted as the franchisor will not normally franchise more than one outlet within an particular locality.
❏   receives a package of supplementary services, such as loan finance, technical advice, quality control systems, accounting and management control systems, etc.

❑ receives standardized training in business management and administration.

Bennett (1991, p. 69) notes that franchising 'has allowed many people to start businesses that otherwise would not have been possible through lack of finance, business knowledge and technical expertise. Franchisees are sheltered under a protective umbrella of specialist skills, resources and experience already possessed by the parent organization'.

LICENSING

Business development in this case takes place on the basis of a *licence agreement* in which the originator or *licensor* grants rights to another company, the *licensee,* to manufacture, assemble or otherwise use a proprietary product, service patent, brand name or business format. The licensee pays a licence fee, and pays commission or royalty to the licensor calculated on the basis of unit volume or sales value achieved. Dudley (1989) suggests that licences can be granted for the use of:

❑ protected or proprietary intellectual property such as patents, registered copyrights and designs, or brand names.
❑ technical, manufacturing, or marketing expertize which, although not classified as protected or proprietary intellectual property, is controlled by the licensor and would not otherwise be available to the licensee.

Licensing may be used as a form of business development or *mode of entry into an international market* where:

❑ the *worldwide protection of patents and intellectual property* is seen as a prime corporate objective, particularly where foreign manufacturers might otherwise ignore trade mark or patent rights and produce illegal copies or "fakes". This is a problem for instance for the manufacturers of branded sports shoes and watches, which have been illegally copied and exported from a number of countries in South East Asia.
❑ the *cost of entry* into another market (and of developing the business there) would otherwise be too great. Licensing may provide access to one or a number of foreign markets without investment in operational capacity or international structures.
❑ *local market access* is limited by high rates of import duty, import quotas, or legislative prohibitions on foreign companies.

❏   the competitive and marketing advantages of *licensing to a major local organization* outweigh the benefits of any possible alternative modes of entry into that market.

❏   international licensing provides the fastest route to developing and exploiting a new business opportunity in conditions of (i) rapid technological innovation, dispersion, and change; or (ii) short product life-cycles; or (iii) the incidence of rapid copying or the introduction of "me too" products by competitors.

DIVESTMENT

Business development strategies may also involve the process of *divestment*. The enterprise may choose to close down, sell off, or otherwise get rid of business activities that are no longer perceived to be appropriate or viable. Reasons for divestment include:

❏   the disposal or sale of declining or under-performing businesses, for example to their management and employees who may be able to run them more cost-effectively without the burden of corporate fixed or R&D costs that would otherwise be incurred.

❏   clarifying the logic or balance of the total business portfolio. Some business activities may no longer be defined as appropriate to the strategic intent or core business described in a later section below, and also in Chapters 11, 18, 20, or 26.

❏   disposing of *question marks* and *dogs* described in Chapter 26 in which the enterprise wishes to cease investment. These may be sold off to other companies who consider that they have more appropriate competences with which to make a success of these activities, and to whom these activities carry a higher priority.

❏   the realization of the *value* of some of the business units in order to release funds for business development or for investment in innovation, R&D and new product or process development. This strategy may be pursued by companies to whom technological and product-market advance is seen as the basic rationale for the business activity.

❏   the deliberate encouragement of autonomy and *new venture management* outside of the company. The partial sale of some businesses may permit local managements to re-introduce a plethora of innovative and intrapreneurial activities that would otherwise be discouraged by role-dominated or bureaucratic cultures within the parent company. These venture companies may later be brought "back into the fold" as models or examples of *how to implement change and innovation.*

SYNERGY

Synergy was defined in Chapter 4 as a concept of joint effect. The concept of synergy is based on the assumption that the process of combining resources may yield an output that is greater than the sum of those input resources. Such synergy may be represented by the equation:

$$2 + 2 = 5 \text{ or more}$$

where that synergy is *positive.* The achievement of synergy as an outcome of joint effect is one of the key objectives of such business development strategies as the co-operation and partnership, strategic alliances, mergers, and acquisitions being described in this chapter. Synergy may also be achieved by increasing the capital or resource base of the enterprise. In this case, decision-makers may judge that an increase in the capacity of the enterprise will take it over some crucial operational threshold, or allow it to reach a point of critical mass. Some examples of positive synergy could include:

❑ scale effects or movement down the experience curve.
❑ capability enhancements that permit the enterprise to compete in wider national or international markets.
❑ entry to markets that were hitherto inaccessible.
❑ the ability to employ more highly specialized and productive capacity and personnel. This, in turn, may lead to the development of new and distinctive competences that again increase the scope or scale of the operation, or yield competitive advantage.
❑ increased investments in knowledge management, competence development, research and development, innovation, and new product or process development. These may yield disproportionate gains in market share and profitability.

Ansoff (1968) suggests, however, that the process can work both ways. *Negative* synergy can result in an effect of:

$$2 + 2 = 3 \text{ (or less)}$$

This has been a common result of past merger and acquisition activity. Many such unions failed to yield the joint effect that was the stated object of the exercise in the first place! There were problems of harmonization; organizational and cultural incompatibility; and cross-border difficulties. All of these combined to offset the potential advantage of the merger or acquisition.

Ansoff notes of *management synergy* that 'management in different types of industry faces different strategic, organizational, and operating problems. If upon entering a new industry management finds the new problems to be similar to the ones it has encountered in the past, it is in a position to provide forceful and effective guidance to the newly acquired venture. Since competent top-level management is a scarce commodity very positive enhancement of performance can result in the combined enterprise ... if, on the other hand, the problems in the acquired area are new and unfamiliar ... there is a distinct danger of a negative effect of top-management decisions' (p. 76).

Such negative synergy could result for example from the acquisition by an enterprise that operates in business or industrial markets of a company established in a consumer or service market with which it has had no previous contact or experience. Senior managers will have to spend time "learning the business". They also run the risk of making strategic mistakes that derive from unfamiliarity, cultural incompatibility, or an inability to grasp the basic philosophy that underlies the direction of the enterprise they have taken over.

THE DIRECTION OF BUSINESS DEVELOPMENT

The process of business development, and the strategies described in the preceding sections that are used to implement it, may take a variety of different directions. Three main categories may be used to summarize the alternatives available to decision-makers. Each category is described below.

Diversification Growth

Diversification as a product-market strategy was analyzed in Chapter 26. During the 1960s, 1970s, and 1980s many Anglo-Saxon companies sought to develop and expand their business on the basis of diversification options, for instance as described by Ansoff. In making this choice these companies hoped to spread risk. They also hoped to realize significant synergy gains across their portfolio of varied activities. This synergy would, it was assumed, be generated (i) by the combination of assets acquired; and (ii) by the application of the superior management competencies, skills of financial management, and skills of marketing or operations management that the conglomerate had convinced itself that it possessed.

This strategy of diversification growth produced mixed results. Business development based on *vertical integration* sometimes worked, and sometimes it did not. The reasons were given in Chapter 26. Some companies had the necessary core competencies at each of the vertical stages and gained the hoped-for synergies. Others expended so much of their resources and management time in learning or putting in place the requisite expertize that the decision was counter-productive. The result was the negative synergy described above.

Much of the *conglomerate* type diversification was also unsuccessful. The mergers or acquisitions used to establish the diversified portfolio produced negative synergy. Harmonizing the acquisitions soaked up an inordinate amount of resources and top management energy, without necessarily producing the hoped-for results. This is what happened when the former UK Imperial Tobacco Company took over the US Howard Johnson ("HoJo") hotel chain. Imperial Tobacco knew nothing about running hotels, still less about hotel keeping in North America. Its subsidiary performed poorly and was eventually sold off at a loss.

At the same time, the implementation of conglomerate strategies tended to divert management attention from the original core business. It also tended to dilute the original mission and strategic intent of both acquirer and acquired. Worse, leading executives and intrapreneurs in the victim companies taken-over tended to suffer dismissal or to leave, taking their knowledge, inspiration and expertize with them.

Ultimately, it may have subsequently been the case that *the conglomerate became worth more if broken up* into its constituent parts than it was worth as a conglomerate. A strategy of diversification growth had created negative synergy, and had consumed value rather than generating or adding to it as had been the original intention.

Controlled Diversity

A series of studies carried out in the 1970s at the Harvard Business School showed that successful US and UK companies had restricted their use of diversification as a business development strategy to a process of *controlled diversity*. Studies such as that of Channon (1973) for the UK, and Rumelt (1974) for the US indicated that the more successful companies had deliberately limited their business development to a strategy of only entering those fields of business that draw strength from, and build upon the core strength or competence of the enterprise. Mergers or acquisitions, for instance, would have clearly to be seen (i) to augment existing strengths and capability, (ii) to develop existing knowledge and competencies, and (iii) to enhance enterprise reputation within an acknowledged field of operation.

Rumelt categorized these successful business development strategies under two headings, thus:

❑ *related-constrained diversification* - in which there would be close relationships between the types of business entered. While technologies or modes of operations management may differ, there will always be a similar mission or strategic intent. The electrical engineering and financial services industries provides some good examples of related-constrained diversification.

❑ *dominant-constrained diversification* - in which business development is closely related to one or a handful of skills, capabilities or competencies. The company does not stray outside of this narrow definition of what its business should be about. Retailers, for instance, tend to stick to retailing. Whilst they may carry out a variety of different types of retail (such as men's or women's clothing) they do not normally get involved with wholesaling or manufacture.

The companies studied by Rumelt, Channon, and others had diversified by building on some particular capability or resource associated with an original and dominant core activity. Whilst such companies frequently develop new products or enter new businesses, they concentrate on the area of specialization that they have defined for themselves (and in which they possess highly developed expertize). They avoid areas with which they are unfamiliar. Business development may then be based on:

❑ the use of internally funded or organic growth.
❑ the acquisition of smaller specialist companies in similar or related fields from which new technological and market developments may speedily be obtained, and with which an obvious potential for synergy can be demonstrated.
❑ the merger with very similar companies, as for instance has happened in the pharmaceutical and aircraft manufacturing industries.

Concentrating on the Core Business, or "Sticking to the Knitting"

In this case, the enterprise focuses its business development closely on its core competence and its core business, attempting to further develop its expertize and seeking quality, excellence and a world class reputation. Peters and Waterman anticipated this strategy in their famous 1982 book *In Search of Excellence*. They noted that their sample of companies:

❑ did not acquire businesses that they would not know how to run.
❑ restricted acquisitions to smaller but related businesses that could readily be assimilated without changing the character of the acquiring institution.
❑ cut their losses early in the event of failure with an acquisition. Early divestment or write-off would minimize the financial damage that might otherwise result. Ultimately, an unsuccessful acquisition can be divested by means of a *management buy-out*. This means that it is sold to its managers and employees, possibly on preferential terms.

Peters and Waterman described the retreat from diversification strategies that has characterized recent decades. Extensive programmes of divestment, "de-cluttering" and "de-acquisitioning" have heralded a return to a clear focus on the core business. Peters and Waterman call this process "sticking to the knitting". Business development strategies focus on the core business. The enterprise aims to achieve excellence within its specialized field. This means concentrating on developing world class attributes of *quality, reliability, customer service* and *value for money* (QRSV) in everything that the business does. This concept was described in Chapter 16.

Strength in quality and market position may, in turn, be correlated with profitability, according to the PIMS findings described in earlier chapters. Internally funded development, partnerships, strategic alliances, or acquisitions are concentrated on and around the core business, so that the enterprise becomes a strong (or the strongest) force within its product-market. UK companies that have espoused this approach to their business include Wedgwood in ceramics, Diageo in brewing and spirits, and British Airways in air travel.

The interrelationship between the core competence and the core business was analyzed in Chapter 20.

REVIEW QUESTIONS

1. Compare and contrast the alternative business development strategies described in this chapter. What are their advantages and disadvantages?
2. What is a strategic alliance?
3. Analyze and illustrate some of the purposes of strategic alliances.
4. Why is the direction of enterprise business development a key area of strategic choice?

TECHNIQUES OF CASE STUDY AND ANALYSIS

1. Identify competition strategies (Chapter 22) evident in the case study.
2. Identify business development strategies (if any) evident in the case study. Analyze these business development strategies. Comment on their implications for the case company. Explain their significance for competitive positioning and competition strategy.
3. Identify strategies of co-operation, partnership and alliance (if any) evident in the case study. Analyze these strategies of co-operation, partnership and alliance. What is their apparent purpose? Comment on their implications for the case company. Explain their significance for competitive positioning and competition strategy.

PROJECT ASSIGNMENT

Using published data or key informant interviews, present a past or current case example (or case examples) of company use of any of the business development strategies described in this chapter. Explain the direction of company business development strategy. Comment on the apparent reasoning for the company's choice of type and direction of its business development. *Alternatively*, using published information or key informant interviews, identify and analyze a strategic alliance in an industry or sector that is of interest to you. Write your analysis in the form of a case study.

References

Ansoff, H.I. (1968) *Corporate Strategy*, Penguin Books, London.
Bennett, R. (1991) *Management*, Pitman, London
Buzzell, R.D. & B.T. Gale (1987) *The PIMS Principles*, Free Press, New York.
Channon, D. (1973) *Strategy and Structure of British Enterprise*, Macmillan, London.
Clarke, C. and K. Brennan (1988) "Allied forces", *Management Today*, November.

Dixon, R. (1991) "What do venture capitalists look for?", *ACCA Newsletter*, May.

Dudley, J.W. (1989) *1992: Strategies for the Single Market*, Kogan Page, London.

Goldsmith, W. and D. Clutterbuck (1997) *The Winning Streak Mark II*, Orion Books, London.

Hamel, G. & C.K. Prahalad (1994) *Competing for the Future*, Harvard Business School Press, Boston, Mass.

Morden, A.R. and D. Bowles (1998) "Management in South Korea: a review", *Management Decision*, Vol 36, No 5.

Peters, T.J. and R.H. Waterman (1982) *In Search of Excellence*, Harper & Row, New York.

Rumelt, R. (1974) *Strategy, Structure and Economic Performance*, Graduate School of Business Administration, Harvard University, Boston, Mass.

Yoshino, M.Y. and U.S. Rangan (1995) *Strategic Alliances*, Harvard Business School Press, Boston, Mass.

Young, D. and P. Scott (2004) *Having Their Cake*, Kogan Page, London.

Chapter 28

International Business Strategy

This chapter deals with the process of strategic management within an international context. It discusses the strategic implications of M E Porter's model of comparative national advantage. It summarizes some of the types of international operation and modes of entry available to enterprises. It analyzes the multinational company, describing its various forms and listing some of its key strategies. The chapter concludes with a discussion of a variety of implementation issues.

THE IMPORTANCE OF LOCATION

M.E. Porter (1990) suggests that, at an international level, *locational factors* will influence:

❑ the resources and capability available to enterprises.
❑ the degree of competitive advantage available to enterprises.
❑ the available and desirable choice of strategies.

That is, locational factors will to a greater or lesser degree confer comparative advantage on the enterprises of a nation. Porter suggests that locational comparative advantage is a function of four factors. He describes these factors as "diamonds". These *diamonds* are:

❑ factor conditions.
❑ demand conditions.
❑ sector rivalry and competition.
❑ related and supporting industries.

They are reproduced in Figure 28.1.

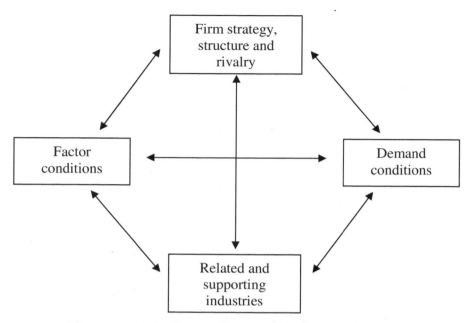

Figure 28.1 The Determinants of National Advantage

Factor Conditions

International and enterprise competitive advantage will be based upon access to, or the possession of such factors as:

Human resource competence and skill - the quality and expertize of the country's work force; the experience and expertize it has accumulated (for instance as described in Chapters 19 and 20); its education and training; and its technology-orientation are all critical determinants of international and enterprise competitiveness.

Geographical location, physical resources, and sources of energy - which include such features as geographical position, climate, and the availability of useful resources which may confer comparative advantage.

Individual countries (and their enterprises) may exploit these advantages; or will instead have to deal with their paucity or non-availability. The absence of key resources may provide a powerful strategic stimulus. Dutch expertize in horticulture and greenhouse technology, for example, is in part explained by poor climate and the positive (and energetic) Dutch attitude to land management. The availability of agricultural land in the Netherlands is a key limiting factor. Farmland has had to be reclaimed, and is actively protected from flooding or damage from salt water.

Knowledge resources - which comprise intellectual capital, social capital, and the prevailing level of trust in society. Such resources underpin all economic and business activity. They provide the context for the issues of architecture, technology, organization, and management described in earlier chapters of this book. Knowledge management was for example described in Chapter 19. Core competencies were analyzed in Chapter 20.

Countries and enterprises that understand the strategic value of the knowledge resource may attempt to manage access to vital proprietary knowledge; to subject it to protection; and to obtain a market or political lead from its exploitation prior to allowing any wider dissemination.

Capital resources - that are required to finance and sustain economic and business development. The level of capital available is a function of such variables as:-

- past history: for instance the UK and France accumulated wealth through their colonial power.
- the relative priority of savings and investment in the economy compared with expenditure and consumption.
- the structure and sophistication of capital markets; and the relative time scales of required return.
- the prevailing character of economic management, including interest rates, fiscal and monetary management, employment, social welfare, and the balance of payments.

Infrastructure - such as transportation, information and communication systems, financial systems, and construction capability. Of equal importance are systems of education, training, and health care. These will shape the quality and competence of the country's human resources.

Countries that maintain their natural beauty and heritage; possess an attractive housing stock; possess effective cultural and political institutions; offer a safe and secure environment to their citizens; and espouse sensible policies of personal taxation may be in a strong position to keep (and also to attract) people with expertize to live and work. This enhances a nation's competitive advantage.

Demand Conditions

Porter suggests that there will be a direct relationship between (i) the relative strength and sophistication of demand for the products or services of any particular sector in a country; and (ii) the likely dominance of the country's industry within international markets. Thus, the strength of the

US, Japan, and the UK in the entertainment, home entertainment and music industries; the UK in construction, financial services and garden tools; France, Italy, Switzerland, Germany and Japan in railway engineering; the US, Australia and the UK in the media industries; or Italy, Germany and the UK in clothing, all reflect the domestic importance and sophistication of these sectors in people's life-style and scale of priorities within the home country.

Sector Rivalry and Competition

Sector rivalry and competition are shown on Porter's "diamonds" model as *firm strategy, structure and rivalry*. The level of sector rivalry and competition within any one country may be described by Porter's "five forces" competition model shown in Chapter 5 of this book. This level of sector rivalry and competition is likely to provide a stimulus to the international competitiveness of that sector. The more competitive is the sector within the country, the more competent may that country's industry be to cope with (or to dominate) competition within a wider international context.

This in part explains the success of the Japanese consumer durables manufacturing sector; the US aviation and electronics industries; or the UK confectionery industry. The international competitiveness of these industries derives from the intense rivalry experienced in the home market; and from the competitive and marketing capability and competence built up by the individual participants as a response.

Related and Supporting Industries

Porter suggests that a country is likely to gain competitive advantage from the existence of *clusters of related and supporting industries*. Activities within these clusters support and stimulate activities elsewhere, for instance by creating supply chains from which manufacturers may gain competence, value and competitive advantage. This issue was dealt with in Chapter 18.

The global position of the City of London, Toronto, Hong Kong, Frankfurt or New York as financial centres is, in part, a function of the variety of inter-related national activities and expertize associated with banking, insurance, stock brokerage, futures and commodities trading, and other financial services that support them.

THE IMPLICATIONS OF PORTER'S "DIAMONDS" MODEL FOR STRATEGY

There are a number of implications of Porter's model of international competitive advantage for enterprise strategy (and related national policy). These include:

- the encouragement of the creation, sustaining, and enhancement of factors and factor conditions within the territory. This encouragement may be based upon market forces, deliberate enterprise policy, government intervention (or all three) depending upon the prevailing value set and ideology of the location.
- the stimulation of the development of local and national clusters of related and supporting industries. For example, the UK's One North East (ONE, a regional development agency) has developed a leading edge expertize in the development of localized clusters and supply chains of world class providers of manufactured and service inputs. These clusters support the many large international companies located in the North East of England. Stimulation of the development of local and national clusters of related and supporting industries may again be based upon market forces, deliberate enterprise policy, government intervention (or all three) depending upon the prevailing value set and ideology of the location.
- the placing of emphasis (both by government policy and individual enterprise strategic choice) on related or related-constrained development around core knowledge, core technologies, core capacities, core competence, and core reputation. *Enterprise strategy may concentrate on, and develop areas of greatest strength, capability, reputation and competitive advantage.* Such an approach to strategic management has been described in detail at various points in this book, for instance in Chapter 27.
- gaining access to the markets of advanced buyers. This access may be achieved by foreign direct investment, strategic alliances, or acquisition of suppliers local to the territory. The objective is to achieve exposure to the requirements of the most sophisticated and most demanding customers, so that the enterprise can learn, develop its capabilities, and gain experience which can be applied in the form of competitive advantage elsewhere.
- attempting to encounter foreign rivals "head on" in their own strongest markets, with the objective of reducing their local dominance and global strength (Chapter 22 comments on the risk of such "attacking"

strategies; and on the likely need for adequate and sustained investment in order to offset the almost inevitable and well-resourced counter-attack by a powerful defender entrenched in his or her home stronghold).

❑ maximizing the autonomy of the company's foreign subsidiaries, such that each one can (i) reap the benefits of their own local "diamonds"; and (ii) pass on this benefit to other parts of the enterprise elsewhere. Such intra-company transfer of knowledge, experience and expertize may have the added bonus of containing *synergy* from which all can benefit.

❑ locating or re-locating operational activities according to the features of national comparative advantage described by the "diamonds" model. This may represent an optimizing strategy, particularly where conditions of free trade apply, as for example in the EU or NAFTA. It may instead mean the transfer of low-technology or labour-intensive manufacturing and service activities to areas of low labour cost, where transportation costs and the value of import duties are more than outweighed by the savings that can be achieved.

❑ relocating the home base or corporate centre of the enterprise to a more favourable national "diamond" if that home location lacks competitive or comparative advantage (or worse is actually relatively disadvantageous). Again, such moves are more likely in areas of free trade; or may instead occur *to* areas of free trade. Porter describes this as an ultimate act of international strategy. *It may create a transnational corporation.* Transnational corporations are described in a later section below.

TYPES OF INTERNATIONAL OPERATION AND MODES OF ENTRY

There are a variety of types of international operation and modes of entry available to the enterprise. These types of international operation and modes of entry may be based on any or all of:

❑ the forms of co-operation and partnership described in Chapters 18 and 22.

❑ the business development strategies and strategic alliances described in Chapter 27.

❑ any form of foreign direct investment (FDI) by the enterprise in other countries.

Home Base

International operations and entry modes carried out from a home base are usually categorized as *export*. Exporters make use of:

❑ home-based staff visiting international customers.
❑ export houses or agencies offering specialized international trade and transportation services to client companies.
❑ buying agencies who act on behalf of international customers, for instance by publishing tenders and inviting closed competitive bids from potential suppliers. The UK Crown Agents is a well-known example of a buying agency that operates on behalf of Commonwealth countries in the purchase of goods and services.
❑ local agents who as independent intermediaries sell an exporter's products within a particular territory, or act as his or her representative. Agents receive commission or fees but do not handle stock or physical distribution. Dudley (1989) notes that agents 'are particularly useful in dealing with government contracts - particularly in sensitive areas (such as) the Middle East where their ability to make and sustain contacts is the basis of their livelihoods' (p. 164).
❑ local distributors who as independent intermediaries buy goods on their own account from suppliers and re-sell them through the distribution channels in their markets. Such distributors handle stock and physical distribution, offer promotional support and carry out the usual range of sales and marketing activities associated with the distribution activity in any country.
❑ joint marketing ventures in which the importing partner takes the exporting partner's products into its own range and treats them as if they were its own. The advantage to both partners lies (i) in the ability of the exporting partner to reinforce the importing partner's local market position with products that might otherwise have been unavailable (or whose development costs would have been beyond the resources of that partner), and from which it can gain competitive and product-market advantage; (ii) from the market access and promotional support that might otherwise be unavailable to the exporter; (iii) from avoiding unnecessary duplication of expenditure and resources, for instance in product development; and (iv) from the potential for synergy that may come from the combination of enterprise capabilities and product ranges. Strategic alliances were described in Chapter 27.

International Base

Operations and entry modes which have an international or global base include:

❏ local branch offices situated within foreign markets. Such branches represent the parent company and are a part of its organization. They also act as information monitors. They feed back communications to the home base about local market, competitive, and environmental conditions.

❏ partly-owned or shared subsidiaries in which investment requirements and business risk are carried jointly. This may ease (or spread) the burden of resource commitment on the parent company; or allow it to meet prevailing government regulations concerning the level of local ownership by foreign firms.

❏ wholly-owned subsidiaries of the company. The relative degree of autonomy of such subsidiaries will depend on the level of decentralized authority permitted as a feature of the parent company's policy. At one extreme such subsidiaries will have no independence, following home company dictates and minimizing their adaptation to local conditions. At the other extreme such subsidiaries will operate as independent companies. Each will establish and implement locally-adapted strategies and policies according to their own judgements about what are the most "situationally-relevant" course of action to implement.

❏ joint ventures and strategic alliances as described in Chapter 27, by which products, services, capabilities, and competencies are shared. Such arrangements pool resources and may achieve a level of synergy unavailable to any one partner. They may be used to allow each partner access to a variety of national or local markets which would be unavailable to any one individual.

❏ licensing and franchising arrangements, in which one company (the *licensor* or the *franchisor*) grants contractual rights to another company (the *licensee* or *franchisee*) to make use of a particular business activity, to manufacture or to distribute certain products, or to use certain brand names. In return the licensee or franchisee compensates the owner by making annual payments of licence fees, royalties, or commission. Dudley describes the advantages of licensing and franchising to include (i) facilitating market access where otherwise the cost and risk of market entry would be too great for the company; (ii) its use as a mode of entry where government regulations, quota restrictions, or excessive import duties would otherwise render exporting an impractical strategy; (iii) allowing market access where the *volume-value relationship* would render international transportation uneconomic, which is the case with soft drinks and beer; (iv) obtaining market representation through licensees or franchisees who are themselves market leaders in their own locality, and whose competitive and market positioning could never be achieved by the licensor or the franchisor (and particularly if their eventual acquisition is not likely to be an available option for the licensor or franchisor); and (v) permitting the speedy international marketing and distribution of innovations or products which have short life-cycles or are likely to face rapid "me-too" copying, such as toys and electronic items. Licensing and franchising as forms of business development strategy were described in Chapter 27.

FORMS OF INTERNATIONAL ORGANIZATION

Morden (2004) describes forms of international organization to include the following:

☐ *Export function* - in which the international activities described immediately above are serviced from a home base by an export department.

☐ *International territories* - in which sales and marketing activities are carried out from the branch offices (described above) located within the geographical territories to which they relate. Organizational issues may be seen from a territory or sales management perspective. Decision-making will be centralized to the home base.

☐ *Parent company and wholly or partly owned subsidiary companies* - in which foreign direct investment may be carried out. Issues of management and control are resolved (i) on the basis of company policy towards the relationships with subsidiaries (and on the degree of decentralization and autonomy permitted by that policy); and (ii) on company policy towards the objectives and performance evaluation of subsidiaries.

The nature of the relationship between parent and subsidiary may also be determined by local features of company law, for instance restricting the degree of ownership by foreign organizations of local companies; or establishing the necessary forms of corporate governance (perhaps by requiring the establishment of supervisory boards).

❏ *Corporate international division* - based at the corporate centre and directly responsible for the strategic management of international sales and business development throughout the company.
❏ *International, multinational, or global company structure* - whose structure and strategy are described in the next section of this chapter, below.

THE MULTINATIONAL COMPANY

A multinational company (MNC) is an enterprise that owns or controls production, process, service, distribution, or marketing capacity outside of the country in which it is based. It earns at least 30 percent of its revenue from its international operations. It considers itself to be international in scope, and it manages its home and foreign activities in an integrated manner to pursue local, international, and global opportunities.

A key issue for a multinational company is the decision on *the appropriate degree of decentralization* to implement. Decisions have to be made as to:

❏ which functions and activities should be retained in the home country or at the corporate centre/head office.
❏ the extent to which strategy formulation, decision-making authority, and operational responsibility should be delegated to foreign subsidiaries or divisions.
❏ the form and criteria of performance measurement, evaluation, and control that should be applied across the company.

A critical determinant of the outcome of these decisions is the company's view of the *trade-off* that it may have to make between (i) the efficiency gains to be obtained from global integration, and (ii) the benefits to be achieved from the local differentiation that may arise from a significant degree of multi-domestic decentralization.

The choice of degree of decentralization may also depend on the relevant contingencies. For instance:

❏ in industries such as semiconductors, electronics, cosmetics and toiletries, car and motorcycle manufacture, or consumer durables, (i) the potential for standardization and global branding (described in Chapter 25); and (ii) the importance of scale economies and experience (Chapter 23); coupled with a lack of significant local differences in customer requirements or usage context, may lead to a preference for global co-ordination.

❑ in industries such as branded foodstuffs processing, construction and civil engineering, electrical and electronic engineering, personal financial services, clothing and fashion, travel and tourism, retail and entertainment, (etc), responsiveness to local customer preferences may take precedence over international considerations.

SOME FORMS OF THE MULTINATIONAL COMPANY

Four types of multinational company are described below.

The Centralized Hub

In this case, the company pursues its international ambitions from a centralized home base. This structure has in the past been characteristic of Japanese and South Korean corporations.

Key value adding activities, such as research and development, design, and the manufacture or processing of critical items containing proprietary sources of knowledge, competence and competitive advantage, are concentrated within the home country. These are likely to be based on the carefully guarded (and retained) levels of high value tacit and explicit knowledge described in Chapter 19. At the same time, there may be a preference for the home-based establishment of manufacturing plants and transportation facilities at a large operational scale in order to service global demand on an export and global brand basis. This may yield the significant competitive advantages of cost efficiency and experience described in detail in Chapter 23.

Overseas subsidiaries (if any) are (at least initially) likely to be established as assembly ("screwdriver"), sales, distribution, and service operations containing relatively low levels of proprietary advantage. These are likely to be based on low-level explicit knowledge with limited value advantage.

The Decentralized Federation

The enterprise takes the form of a "federation" of decentralized companies and subsidiaries owned (or part-owned) by the parent. *Multi-domestic strategies* are pursued in which national subsidiaries are permitted a high degree of independence from the parent company in determining their own product-market, brand, marketing, supply chain, manufacturing, and operational strategies. Parent-subsidiary relationships would concentrate on such issues as:

❑   the formulation of broad areas of corporate and business strategy for the enterprise as a whole.
❑   the authorization of major capital expenditure.
❑   managing the pattern and dynamics of inter-company financial movements, and smoothing the effects of foreign currency exchange variations using in-house corporate treasury management functions.
❑   the appointment of senior managers to subsidiaries.

The advantage of the decentralized federation is its ability to respond to the requirements and usage contexts of individual local and regional markets. At the same time, the federation can make available on a "one-stop shopping" basis all of the relevant product or service ranges of all of the companies in the federation. In other words it can make available to all the synergy advantages that derive from a combined product-market mix offer. Decentralized federations may also demonstrate the characteristics of the *co-ordinated federation* described next.

The Co-ordinated Federation

This structure retains the high level of local autonomy and operational independence of the decentralized federation described immediately above. Additional features may include:

❑   its use of the *knowledge management strategies* described in Chapter 19, and in particular the management and controlled dissemination of high value tacit and explicit knowledge. This may take the form of:-
❑   its use of knowledge and technology uplift from, and transfer across the constituents of the federation.
❑   its co-ordinated use of research and development (R&D), innovation, and new product or process development within the federation.
❑   its use of brand or image uplift and transfer within the federation.
❑   its use of reputation uplift and transfer within the federation.

The co-ordinated federation is therefore characterized by the development and sharing of knowledge, experience, technologies, products, brands and identities. This is a key source of its competitive advantage. Each constituent has access to continuing flows of new concepts, new products, new brands, new process technologies, new manufacturing and distribution opportunities. This flow is treated as a total capability which all may share, and from which all should benefit.

Examples of co-ordinated federations include ABB Asea Brown Boveri, Ford Motor Company, Shell, and British Petroleum.

The Trans-national Organization

This is an integrated network or architecture of interdependent organizations and capabilities. Each constituent is capable of adding value independently, but at the same time contributes to the synergy represented by the whole. Distinguishing features of the trans-national organization include:

❑ its achievement of operational and cost efficiency through high levels of global integration, and through the local positioning of its capability against the most favourable factor and other location conditions available to it, as described by M.E. Porter in an earlier section, above.

❑ its national and local responsiveness in terms of local product or brand differentiation; local generation of value; and ability to accommodate to (or "manage") local pressures to "influence" the affairs of the MNC. The political objective of these local pressures will be to maximize the local advantage to be gained from the operations of the MNC in that country.

❑ its capacity to develop and exploit its knowledge and competence on a global basis. This implies an integrated approach to the knowledge and technology management process described in Chapter 19, and to the development of competencies analyzed in Chapter 20.

❑ its global capacity to develop its technology and to innovate. Technological advantage and innovation are transferred throughout the company, and are used to maintain competitive position within local and global markets. Grant (1991, pp. 297-298) notes that the achievement of outstanding innovation 'requires simultaneous pursuit of global integration and local responsiveness. The generation of product, process, and organizational innovation is best encouraged by a high degree of decentralization which encourages creativity and participation throughout the organization ... conversely, the effective global introduction of innovation is likely to require a high degree of integration' in order to capitalize on the potential competitive advantage to be gained, and to fund further research and development.

❑   its use of the resources represented by each national unit as a source of capability and competence that can be harnessed *for the benefit of the organization as a whole.*

❑   the achievement of regional, international, or global scale and efficiency by each national unit in at least one (or a number of) specific products, processes, or functions. Each national unit will be a regional, continental, or global leader in its field; and therefore a major institutional contributor in at least this particular area.

❑   the creation of an organizational and cultural context in which (i) basic core values and ideologies are agreed and disseminated that serve to provide vision and unity; (ii) mechanisms are in place to resolve conflicts and settle intra-organizational differences; (iii) managerial, informational, decision-making, and communication mechanisms are in place to achieve the necessary organizational and operational co-ordination and integration; and (iv) managers and technical specialists as repositories of knowledge and competence can as decision-makers develop broad national and international perspectives within a positive and supportive environment.

MULTINATIONAL STRATEGIES

Multinational strategies may be summarized to include:

❑   optimizing locational choice, for instance as described above, in order to maximize competitive advantage, knowledge and value generation, technology and market access, political relationships and so on. This might mean locating (or outsourcing) cost-sensitive manufacturing activities to areas of low-cost labour; or instead locating high value adding activities to countries with the appropriate high technology infrastructure, education, skills and competencies.

❑   optimizing currency exchange relationships and treasury management capability. At the same time, the MNC may wish to avoid (or minimize) its exposure to avoidable foreign currency risks such as unpredictable variations over time in the value of any particular currency.

❑   taking advantage of favourable national laws and taxation policies; and optimizing inward investment subsidies made available by national governments, the EU, and so on. American, Japanese, and South Korean multinationals have, for example, been the recipients of major government subsidies when locating plants to the UK.

❑ more generally, accommodating to (or "managing") localized political pressures on the affairs of the MNC.

❑ avoiding locations with unfavourable environmental conditions or "hostile" laws; or instead using intermediaries therein to do business.

❑ attempting to achieve international or global economies of scale, critical mass, experience, and cost-effectiveness, for instance (i) to achieve synergy in the total capability available to the enterprise; (ii) to exploit knowledge, capability, competence and experience across the enterprise; (iii) to optimize the use of technology and technology transfer world-wide; (iv) to seek advantages of value generation and quality through the value chain as a whole; and (v) to achieve low cost, or cost-efficiency advantages. The automotive sector, for instance, has seen the establishment of large continental manufacturing plants supplying models on both a regional basis (e.g. to Europe), and on a global basis. The Nissan plant in the UK for example fulfils both of these manufacturing roles. Japanese and South Korean consumer electronics companies may source their entire global manufacturing output of certain products from one only manufacturing facility, thereby achieving significant economies of scale and reducing costs to the minimum.

❑ putting in place world class aspirations, policy, culture and quality.

❑ putting in place international systems of operations and supply chain management, manufacturing, logistics, distribution and service. Favoured locations in Europe for such systems include Northern France and The Netherlands.

❑ putting in place appropriate structures and architectures of relationships, communication, information management; and management processes of decision-making, integration, co-ordination and control within the organization.

❑ disseminating and reinforcing core values and ethos, especially where a degree of international cultural difference or the need for "polycentricity" is accepted. The concept of polycentricity is described in a later section of this chapter, below.

❑ putting in place the international or global management of research and development, innovation, new product and process development, and brand development, in order (i) to develop global ranges of products, services and brands; (ii) to develop regional or local modifications of global products, services and brands; (iii) to develop regionally or locally specific products, services and brands.

❑ achieving operational effectiveness, quality, and cost-efficiency through appropriate structure and architecture; through appropriate levels of global integration; and through positioning against the most favourable factor conditions available to the MNC.

❏ using each national unit as a source of capability and competence to the benefit and competitive advantage of the MNC as a whole.

❏ establishing regional or continental centres of specialization and excellence, each concentrating on particular activities in which they must develop world class status, and which they make available or supply on an international basis. These centres may correspond with the locational features of Porter's national "diamonds".

❏ establishing a requisite degree of local, national, or regional sensitivity or responsiveness in terms (i) of product, process or brand differentiation; and (ii) of the local generation of value.

❏ putting in place mechanisms to resolve differences and conflicts within the MNC or its relationship architecture.

❏ putting in place an appropriately harmonized language capability and terminology across the MNC. ABB Asea Brown Boveri, for instance, operates in English and German as its two common languages.

❏ developing and supporting a cadre of leaders, managers, and technical specialists capable of managing the operations of the MNC; and capable of dealing with cross-cultural matters that arise. These issues are described in detail in a later section, below.

MANAGING LOCALLY

Implicit in the implementation of international business strategy must be an *enterprise capacity for effective local management*. International strategies are actually implemented on a local or national scale, within the context of individual economies and cultures. The formalization of international business strategies and the localized implementation of those strategies are the two sides of the same coin.

The process of managing locally has a number of key elements, some of which are analyzed below.

Knowledge of the Country and its International Context

The implementation of localized management is dependent upon effective local knowledge. International managers may need to know and understand:

❏ national geography and history; local political and economic management; international trade and competition policy; knowledge and technological development; and socio-cultural features.

❏ the international context within which the country may be placed. For instance, is the country categorized as "traditional" or "third world"; "developing", "achieving", or a "lesser developed country" (LDC); or "industrialized", "affluent", or "westernized"?

❏ the prevailing local level of political, social and economic stability; and the degree of risk incurred in carrying out business activities, or undertaking foreign direct or inward investment, and so on.

❏ the current reputation of the enterprise (if any) within the local markets in which it wishes to establish itself.

❏ how business is actually done within the territory. *Business culture* is analyzed later in this section.

Knowledge of the Country's Language and Communication Patterns

International managers may need to understand and adapt to localized types of language use and expectation; to the prevailing level of education and literacy; and to the type of literacy. Being able to communicate in a second or third language may be an essential competence.

There is likely to be a relationship between language capacity and knowledge of local market conditions. A limited linguistic capacity may be associated with a restricted mind-set. This may limit the capacity of the individual to deal with cultural diversity, and in consequence restrict understanding of foreign markets and the buying behaviour of the people who make them up.

At the same time, multilingual capacity may yield competitive advantage in any form of business negotiation. The individual is not dependent on others for translation or interpretation of the subtleties of the bargaining process. And the negotiator can follow the developing train of thought of his or her fellow negotiators if he or she can follow their interactions in their own language.

International managers may also need to come to terms with the communication media and modes available for business use, and the promotional media available for marketing use. In some developing countries, for instance, television and radio rather than printed media are the most widely accessible methods for marketing communications, especially where levels of literacy are low or rural populations dispersed.

Traditional, Achieving, and Affluent Cultures

Local cultures may be categorized as *traditional, achieving, or affluent.* Each is described below.

Traditional cultures - are rooted in the past. Such cultures may be characterized by a strong deference to long-established religious and moral customs, traditional hierarchies of authority and family relationships, strongly established social stratification, and entrenched class structures. Behaviour, work and consumption patterns may be firmly anchored in customary habits; and changes may be very slow to take place.

Achieving cultures - are cultures that have begun to break away from the traditions of the past, in order to develop and grow. Where achieving cultures are growing out of traditional ones, there will inevitably be tension and conflict between the two. Enterprise management must be wary of causing or inciting such conflict, since the consequences for the enterprise are likely to be unpredictable and uncontrollable.

Affluent cultures - include the industrial societies of North America, Europe, and South East Asia. Such cultures place varied emphasis upon individualism, personal achievement, material possession, family support, or the provision of social welfare systems for those who are disadvantaged by the essentially competitive nature of such cultures.

Each country's culture gives rise to a variety of prevailing life-styles. Life-style, or pattern of customary behaviour, is a manifestation of the cultural, behavioural, and social variables that characterize the society. Culture and life-style then influence patterns of consumption, manufacturing, agriculture, service, distribution and investment.

Similarly, each country's culture and life-style shape attitudes towards the relative priority of *personal saving* and *national investment* as opposed to *personal consumption.* The degree of cultural emphasis on personal consumption will determine the political and economic priority of investment in consumer goods manufacture and distribution, and on the provision of services, as opposed to agricultural, industrial, or infrastructure development.

Knowledge and Understanding of National Culture

National culture is defined by Fukuyama (1995) as *inherited ethical habit.* It is defined by Hofstede (1980, 1991) as *the collective mental programming* of a society. The people of any particular nationality are conditioned (and their values established) by particular patterns of socialization, ideology, education, and life experience. Hofstede maintains that cultural conditioning is relatively stable and resistant to change. This is because national culture resides (i) collectively in the mental make-up of the people in the society; (ii) in their institutions (family, education, religion, forms of government, communal institutions and associations, law, work organizations, literature, settlement patterns, towns and cities, buildings, etc); and (iii) in their values, ideologies, paradigms, scientific theories, and technology.

Models that aid the international understanding of, and adaptation to the prevailing national culture include the following:

Hofstede's model - which identifies five key dimensions of national culture. These are its:-

- "power distance" - by which the culture deals with inequality and the relative distribution of power and authority amongst its people.
- "uncertainty avoidance" - by which the culture deals with situations of uncertainty and ambiguity.
- "individualism versus collectivism" - by which people's behaviour is shaped by a collective (or communitarian) orientation, or instead an individualistic one. Western societies (but in particular Anglo-Saxon ones) have tended to be more individualistic than European or South East Asian ones.
- "masculinity versus femininity" - by which the dominant values of a society are masculine (assertive, acquisitive or competitive) or feminine (caring; or concerned with people, the quality of life or the environment).
- "term orientation" - by which a society perceives time and the value of time, and how it makes use of that time.

References to Hofstede's model are also made in earlier chapters.

Hampden-Turner and Trompenaars' (1994) model - which identifies eight "value dilemmas" by which national cultural features associated with knowledge management, social interaction, and work behaviour may be compared and contrasted. These eight value dilemmas are:-

- a strict emphasis on rules and standardization; *or instead* the acceptance of flexibility and exceptions.
- the analysis or breaking-down of concepts or events (deconstructionism); *or instead* the integration of these concepts and events into wholes with a search for relationships or patterns amongst them (constructionism).
- the use of a communal (or collective/communitarian) focus, in which the desires of the individual are subordinated to the needs of family,

clan or society; *or instead* an emphasis on the individual and his or her autonomy. Hofstede also recognizes this fundamental cultural dilemma.

- an internal and inwardly-directed focus on the society or on the organization (inner-direction); *or instead* an external orientation of people to their environment and the potential for change that environment is likely to contain (outer-direction).

- the conceptualization of time as a linear sequence; *or instead* as a cycle with no real beginning or end.

- the ascription of status on the basis of some accepted (or imposed) criteria such as age, seniority, education, gender, class or race; *or instead* the making available of opportunity to allow individuals to achieve status on the basis of their own capability or merit, irrespective of who or what they are.

- an emphasis on hierarchy (and the status differences that go with it); *or instead* an emphasis on equality within the community. Hofstede also deals with this cultural issue.

- the cultural difference between societies that demonstrate patterns of "affective" *or instead* "neutral" behaviour, particularly within the context of interpersonal dynamics. Affective cultures may openly display expressive or emotional behaviour, for instance during business transactions or negotiations. Neutral cultures instead subdue and control emotions, separating them from the process of thought, reasoning, and interaction.

References to Hampden-Turner and Trompenaars' model are also made in earlier chapters.

Lessem and Neubauer's (1994) model - which identifies four paradigms of Anglo-Saxon and European culture. These paradigms can also be applied to other Western societies originally or in part derived from Anglo-Saxon or European roots. Lessem and Neubauer's paradigms are described in terms of:-

- a "pragmatic" approach to the development and application of concepts and experience, which is based on opportunism, experimentation, learning and entrepreneurship. Pragmatism is an Anglo-Saxon characteristic.

- a "rationalistic" philosophy, which is grounded in a dominant belief in reason, logic, mathematics and science as the source of certainty in knowledge and technology. Rationalism is typically French, but is widely found in Northern Europe and North America.

- a "holistic" philosophy in which individual entities and concepts are to be seen within a wider context of the whole or society of which they are a subsidiary part. Holism is characteristic of Germanic countries, Northern Europe, and to a degree Canada.

- a "humanistic" philosophy, in which actions and events are perceived opportunistically from the viewpoint of family and community; and from the viewpoint of the importance of "taste" and conviviality as "good things in life". Humanism is characteristic of Italy; also of Spain, Portugal, Greece and Ireland.

Fukuyama's model - which differentiates between two types of national culture. These are:-

- the "low trust culture" which is characteristic of strongly hierarchical or authoritarian societies, or societies dominated by powerful family structures. People (and their motivations) are not trusted (particularly if they are strangers with no bonds of family or kin), so they must be coerced and controlled by systems of rules and regulations laid down by a higher authority. Such societies may have a problem with interpersonal association, knowledge management, and innovation that goes outside of the established rules. Change may be difficult to achieve without outside intervention.
- the "high trust culture" which is characteristic of open and empowered societies that share similar values. The prevailing consensus and commitment means that the society can achieve and develop its goals without external or hierarchical intervention; and is free of the inevitable mental and conceptual (or ideological) limitations that characterize the dominant thinking of the autocrats who control low trust societies.

References to Fukuyama's model are also made in earlier chapters.

Historic influences on South East Asian management - which are summarized to include the following:-

- "Taoism".
- "Confucianism", heirarchy, role, responsibility, and communitarianism.
- the role of the "mandarin" and the "taipan".
- the nature of friendship and favour ("guanxi").
- the obligations associated with interpersonal relationships ("renqing").
- the need to maintain "face".
- the "five cardinal relationships", and the roles associated therewith.
- the strategic thinking of Sun Tzu, analysed in a competitive context in Chapter 22.
- developing political and military concepts.
- the interpretation and adaptation of Western influences.

These historic influences on South East Asian management are, *inter alia*, described in detail in the classic 1995 study written by Min Chen.

Issues of national culture are given extended and detailed treatment in the author's Ashgate text *Principles of Management* (2004).

Knowledge and Understanding of Business Culture

Business culture can usefully be defined as "the way we do things here". International managers will need to know how business is carried out in its local context. Business culture can be analyzed under two headings, as follows.

The task and decision-making level - which is determined by the nature of the trading and business infrastructure of the locality; and by the determinant commercial and competitive attitudes. For instance, is competition or co-operation the dominant paradigm? Will de-integrated value or supply chain architectures work? Are stakeholders more or less important than shareholders? How important are family businesses and family connections? How important is a network of influential contacts and intermediaries?

The task level is shaped by local attitudes to such key variables as time, customer service, quality, technology, entrepreneurship, performance evaluation, or employee relations. It will also be shaped by the prevailing patterns of influence and decision-making. Some business cultures, such as South Korea, are characterized by autocratic (high power distance) decision-making by company proprietors or senior managers. Others may instead involve many staff on a consultative (low power distance) basis, emphasizing equality, knowledge dissemination, professional contribution, and personal expertize irrespective of hierarchical status.

The level of the organization - local business culture will be shaped by the prevailing organizational and managerial paradigms. These paradigms will determine how strategies are formulated, decisions are made, and business plans put into practice. They will determine the choice of organization structure and style, communication, and leadership patterns. They will determine the issue of organization culture and style of management; as well as the conceptualization of how enterprise capability, value generation, and competitive advantage may be best achieved.

Issues of *organization structure*, *organization culture*, and *international management style* are given detailed and extended treatment in the author's Ashgate text *Principles of Management*.

DEVELOPING THE INTERNATIONAL MANAGER

Enterprises operating in an international or global context may have to make a choice from three alternative approaches to selecting and developing their local and international managers. These are the:

❑   ethnocentric.
❑   polycentric.
❑   geocentric.

Each is described below.

Ethnocentric approach - which places emphasis on selecting and developing leaders, managers, and technical specialists from the "home" country or culture of the parent organization (or from a national cultural background that is similar to that of the home country). This approach is held to have operational advantages in its likely consistency in patterns and conceptualizations of language, communication, operations and control. Value set, ethos, education and methodology may be similar; and the behaviour of the *essentially similar* kinds of staff involved may be predictable and controllable. However, the use of an ethnocentric approach may raise such issues as:-

• the degree of international staff sensitivity and adaptation to the local situation. This may, for instance be a problem for Anglo-Saxons or Europeans working in the Middle East or mainland China.

• the motivation of local staff who may otherwise perceive (i) that only limited management development or promotional opportunities are likely to be available to local nationals; or (ii) that dual standards of available employment terms and promotion opportunities exist between expatriates and local nationals.

An ethnocentric approach may be correlated with the use of the centralized hubs described in an earlier section of this chapter, above.

Polycentric approach - in which there is an interchangeable appointment and training of staff from both the home country or culture, and local nationals within the territories in which the enterprise operates. Such an approach has the advantage of increasing local sensitivity and adaptability, while at the same time offering equal incentive and opportunity to local nationals. Additionally, its use accords with the *requisite variety* and *genetic diversity* argument described in Chapter 19. The use of a polycentric approach, in this case to the issues of strategic management being analyzed in this book, may as a source of external and novel stimuli lead to the introduction of new ideas and concepts from which the enterprise may benefit, and which may offset inertia, complacency, obsolescence and entropy in the knowledge and paradigm base. The use of a polycentric approach may however raise such developmental issues as:-

- the need to develop common (and consistent) language and communication skills; common terminologies; and common methodologies amongst enterprise staff.
- the need to develop appropriate mechanisms to ensure the necessary degree of organizational and operational co-ordination and integration.
- the need to train staff to deal with localized inconsistencies and uncertainties.
- the need to train leaders and managers to deal with local variations in value set and priority.
- the need to train leaders and managers to deal with (that is, to harmonize) local variations in performance expectations, measurement, and control.

A polycentric approach may be correlated with the use of the decentralized and co-ordinated federations, and the trans-national organizations described in an earlier section of this chapter, above.

Geocentric approach - enterprise policy aims in this case to create an "international cadre" of management and technical staff who can move freely and interchangeably about the company's locations as strategic and operational needs, promotional opportunities, and local immigration laws permit. This cadre may come from any nationality or national culture; its focus and loyalty lie with the company not the location. The development of such an international cadre may require:-

- socialization, teamwork, conditioning, cultural development, and reward that reduces the tendency of individual members of staff to identify with local units and localities; but encourages them instead to identify with the company as a global entity. Companies such as ABB Asea Brown Boveri, IBM, Shell, Sony and Michelin appear to pursue such an approach.
- the training and conditioning of managerial and technical staff to internalize and represent to others in a leadership role the corporate values and culture of the enterprise, irrespective of location or issue.
- the training of enterprise staff to achieve consistent levels of operational effectiveness and efficiency, irrespective of unit location or "difficulty".

A geocentric approach may be correlated with the use of the co-ordinated federations and the trans-national organizations described in an earlier section of this chapter, above.

REVIEW QUESTIONS

1. In what ways may strategy formulation and strategic decision-making be determined by the needs of international business?
2. What is the significance of location to decisions on international business strategy?
3. What are some of the implications of M.E. Porter's "diamonds" model for international business strategy?
4. Describe some of the alternative types of international operation and modes of entry available to the enterprise.
5. Describe some of the alternative forms of international organization available to the enterprise.
6. Compare and contrast the four types of multinational company.
7. Describe and explain a variety of multinational strategies.
8. Outline and comment on some of the key elements of the localized implementation of international business strategy.
9. Compare and contrast the three approaches to developing the international manager.

TECHNIQUES OF CASE STUDY AND ANALYSIS

1. Identify and analyze the international context of the case study.
2. Carry out an analysis of locational comparative advantage using M.E. Porter's "diamonds" model. What are the implications of this analysis for the case company?
3. Identify, analyze, and explain the international business strategies evident in the case study.
4. Identify, analyze, and explain the multinational strategies (if any) evident in the case study.
5. What relevant implementation issues are evident in the case study?

PROJECT ASSIGNMENTS

1. Using M.E. Porter's "diamonds" model of comparative national advantage, carry out an analysis of an industry or sector in your country that is of interest to you, and for which appropriate information may be obtained. What are the implications of this analysis for enterprise strategy?
2. Compare and contrast the types of international operation, modes of entry, and forms of international organization used by selected enterprises in your country who are involved in international business.
3. Compare and contrast the organization and strategy of any two (or more) of (i) a centralized hub; (ii) a decentralized or co-ordinated federation; and (iii) a trans-national organization for which appropriate information is available to you.
4. Using published information, describe and analyze the international business strategy of a multinational company that is of interest to you.

References

Chen, M. (1995) *Asian Management Systems*, Routledge, London.
Cragg, C. (1995) *The New Taipans*, Century Business, London.
Dudley, J.W. (1989) *1992: Strategies for the Single Market*, Kogan Page, London.
Fukuyama, F. (1995) *Trust – the Social Values and the Creation of Prosperity*, Hamish Hamilton, London.
Grant, R.M. (1991) *Contemporary Strategy Analysis*, Blackwell, Oxford.
Hampden-Turner, C. and F. Trompenaars (1994) *The Seven Cultures of Capitalism*, Piatkus, London.
Hofstede, G. (1980) *Cultures Consequences*, Sage, London.
Hofstede, G. (1991) *Cultures and Organizations*, McGraw-Hill, London.
Lessem, R. and F. Neubauer (1994) *European Management Systems*, McGraw-Hill, London.
Morden, A.R. (1999) "Models of national culture: a management review", *Cross Cultural Management*, Vol 6, No 1.
Morden, A.R. (2004) *Principles of Management (2nd Edition)*, Ashgate, Aldershot.
Morden, A.R. and D. Bowles (1998) "Management in South Korea: a review", *Management Decision*, Vol 36, No 5.
Porter, M.E. (1990) *The Competitive Advantage of Nations*, Macmillan, London.

Glossary

Acquisition - this is a business development strategy based on the direct purchase of another company. The acquiring company takes on the ownership of the company it has taken over, whilst the enterprise that has been purchased loses its independent existence and identity. The company acquired may continue to exist as a subsidiary, or as a brand name; or it may disappear altogether.

Ansoff's product-market matrix - a classic analysis of product-market development alternatives based on a matrix comprising the four variables (i) existing products, (ii) new products, (iii) existing markets, and (iv) new markets. Ansoff's matrix suggests five main product-market development alternatives. These are consolidation, market penetration, product development, market development, and diversification.

Architecture - architecture (or "social architecture") is defined as the structure of relationships within an organization; and the structure of relationships between the organization and its external customers, clients, suppliers, investors, partners, and other stakeholders. The successful enterprise is one which (i) creates a distinctive and positive character within the structure of these relationships; (ii) creates uniqueness within these relationships (such that it can do things that comparators or competitors cannot do, or cannot do so effectively); and (iii) creates conditions in which the value that can be generated from these relationships is maximized by the enterprise, its customers or clients, its partners, its investors and its other stakeholders.

Architecture and trust - Fukuyama suggests that the most effective architecture and relationships (such as those of the "high trust workplace") are likely to be based on a community of shared values. Such communities of shared values do not require extensive contractual, legal or bureaucratic regulation of their relations and social architecture because a strong moral consensus gives members of the group a basis for mutual trust and co-operation.

Balanced Scorecard - Kaplan and Norton comment that 'the Balanced Scorecard translates an organization's mission and strategy into a comprehensive set of performance measures that provide the framework for a strategic measurement and management system. The Balanced Scorecard retains an emphasis on achieving financial objectives, but also includes the performance drivers of these financial objectives'.

Basis of strategy formulation - Mintzberg and his colleagues categorize the basis of strategy formulation under the seven headings of the "forced", the "self-imposed", the "required", the "rationalistic", the "deliberate", the "logically incremental", and the "opportunistic".

BCG product-market matrix - the Boston Consulting Group (BCG) product-market matrix (or "Boston Box") comprises a market growth rate axis, and a market share axis. The BCG matrix identifies four potential development stages for any particular product-market activity. These are (i) "stars", (ii) "cash cows", (iii) "question marks", and (iv) "dogs". The BCG then specify four management strategies by which to achieve, maintain, or change these development stages. These management strategies are (i) "build", (ii) "hold", (iii) "harvest", and (iv) "divest".

Benchmark - performance measurement indicator used for comparison purposes. Typically based on "best in class" comparators or competitors.

Best fit approach - a contingency or situational approach to analysis and implementation in which variables or solutions are chosen that most closely match (are congruent with) the particular situation under consideration. It is axiomatic to this "equifinal" approach that there is no "one best way" of doing things.

Best Value - is defined by the UK Government as a mandatory duty on publicly-funded agencies so to manage their affairs as to deliver services to clearly stated standards of achievement, or to benchmarked performance indicators ("PIs"). These performance standards are defined in terms of such criteria as effectiveness, quality, efficiency, economy, and cost.

Brand - may be defined as the proprietary name or "make" of a good or service, or of their provider. It is a form of proprietary identity given to the product or service by its provider that incorporates the values or qualities attributed to that product or service (or its maker), and differentiates it from its comparators or competitors.

Brand image - used to establish and communicate the values and the qualities of appropriateness, uniqueness, or difference that identify and position the product or service, and differentiate it from its competitors in the market-place.

Budget - may be defined as a quantitative and financial plan of an activity or strategy to be pursued during the forthcoming financial year to achieve that year's objectives.

Budgetary plan - is a detailed financial framework by which to manage the implementation of a business plan. A budgetary plan will be based on appropriate performance measurement indicators such as market share, sales revenue, number of staff employed, cost of operating, and so on. The budgetary plan will be associated with quantifiable mechanisms of monitoring, feedback and review to ensure the achievement of the required performance outcomes, or to facilitate the revision of the plan to take account of changed operating parameters. Budgetary plans are typically written on an annual basis.

Budgetary planning and control - the process of budgetary planning and control may be defined as the establishment of budgets that relate the responsibilities of departments and individuals to the requirements of strategies and plans; and the continuous monitoring and comparison of actual results with the budgeted targets, so that these targets may be achieved or amendments made to the objectives upon which they were based.

Business culture - may be defined as "the way we do things around here". International managers will need to know how business is carried out in its local context. Business culture is evident at the level of the society, the task, and the organization. Business culture is shaped by the society's values, standards, expectations, and perceptions of necessity and priority.

Business development strategy - may be defined as a strategy that determines the approach of the enterprise to developing or growing the business activity. Business development can be based on a series of alternative strategic choices. These include (i) increasing the capital and resource base, (ii) co-operation and partnership, (iii) strategic alliances, (iv) mergers, (v) acquisition and takeover, (vi) franchising, (vii) licensing, and (viii) divestment. Business development strategies are used to implement enterprise competition strategy.

Business ethics - may be defined as the application of general ethical principles to business behaviour. In order to be considered "ethical", the enterprise and its management must draw concepts of what is proper behaviour from the same sources as everyone else, not constructing its own definitions of what is right or wrong behaviour. People who work in business or administrative organizations, however powerful, are bound by the same ethical principles that apply to others.

Business plan - is a short to medium-term plan (for instance lasting for one to three years in duration) which is used to organize and implement the detailed operational or business unit activities required to accomplish the longer-term strategic vision or strategic plan from which it is derived. A business plan is likely to contain mechanisms of monitoring, feedback and review to ensure the achievement of the necessary performance outcomes. Achievement will in turn be measured by the appropriate performance indicators.

Business planning - defined as a strategic process in which the priority, timing, and sequence of events are arranged from their starting point to move towards the future time horizon to which the enterprise is working, in order that it may achieve its objectives for that time period.

Business process - a logically interrelated and integrated group of responsibilities, tasks, workflows, transactions, skills and competences that have a clear interface with other processes and which, taken together, produce a result of value to a customer or add value to something else. The business process has a set of inputs that it processes so as to add value, and create identifiable sets of outputs or outcomes.

Business process re-engineering (BPRE or BPR) - is defined by Hammer and Champy as 'the fundamental rethinking and radical redesign of business processes to achieve dramatic improvements in critical … measures of performance such as cost, quality, service and speed'.

Capability and capacity - describe what the organization is (or is not) capable of using its resources to achieve. Strategic decisions must be based on knowing what can realistically be achieved by the enterprise, or on knowing what new capabilities must instead be developed in order to reach new or extended goals.

Capital structure - comprises the various sources of finance used in a business or administrative organization, in whatever proportions they are represented and however they are combined.

Cash cow - is a low growth, high market share activity whose role is to generate cash outflows to support ongoing investment in product-market, process, or business development activities elsewhere in the enterprise.

Centralization - a process by which the authority to make strategic decisions which commit the organization's people and resources is retained by senior decision-makers ("top management") at the corporate centre. The degree of centralization is manifest in the degree to which (if at all) decision-making authority and the control of resources are delegated downwards and outwards within the management structure.

Centralized structure - is one in which power and authority are retained by senior decision-makers at the corporate centre or strategic apex. Commands and decisions flow downwards through the scalar chain; strategies and policies are implemented by middle-level or unit management; and control information flows back up the hierarchy. All issues for decision or sanction must be referred upwards through the hierarchy.

Champion - a prime leadership role of champion will be to implement, to nurture and as role model to reinforce a culture and process in which the values and mission of the organization can take root and prosper; in which the strategic intent of the enterprise can be achieved; and in which purposes, responsibilities and tasks can successfully be implemented and brought to fruition. The champion encourages and facilitates the work of others, smoothing the implementation process and protecting it from negative influences.

Charismatic leadership processes - describe conditions in which the possession of certain personal qualities ("charisma") by the leader enables him or her to exercise influence over others by force of personality, charm, or personal values. Charisma may be described as "a fire that ignites followers' energy and commitment, producing results above and beyond the call of duty".

Commodity product - may be defined as a standard product or service which it is difficult or impossible to differentiate effectively (such as polyester fibres, sheet steel, or call-centre operations), and which is likely to be sold on the basis of cost, volume, market share, or price.

Comparative international advantage - defined by Porter in terms of the relative competitive advantage enjoyed by the enterprises of any one nation as compared with those of another. The level of comparative advantage is determined by key locational factors.

Competence - defined as a single or discrete skill, capability, or technological capacity; or a "bundle" or integration of such skills, capabilities and capacities. In particular, staff, personnel, or leadership competence is a basic resource (and constraint) upon which the process of strategic management ultimately depends. The availability of the right people or the right leaders often constitutes a key limiting factor in the strategic decision-making and implementation processes of the enterprise. The philosophy, character, direction, and quality of human resource strategy and management may be critical success factors within the strategic management process.

Competition strategy - may be defined in terms of the "positioning" and "ploy" elements of strategy. Competition strategy determines the sector or product-market positioning (for example "number one in a global market"; "leader of a national niche market" and so on) that the enterprise wishes to achieve or maintain (or instead has forced on it). It also determines the "game plan" or competitive ploys of the enterprise, whether these be attacking, defensive, reactive, copying, based on co-operation and partnership, and so on.

Competitive analysis - is a key component of the process of strategic analysis. It comprises the appraisal and evaluation of the competitive situation which faces the enterprise in its markets or sectors. Enterprise strategic choice will be strongly influenced by the competitive situation with which the organization has to deal.

Competitive or comparative advantage - is a concept which describes the relative advantage (or the degree of relative advantage) possessed by an enterprise within its markets or sectors as compared with other organizations with which it competes or with which it may be compared, for instance on a benchmarking basis.

Conglomerate diversification - is a strategy in which the enterprise diversifies into unrelated activities to which it thinks it can apply particular capabilities or competencies (such as strong strategic, marketing or financial management skills) in order to add value or to gain competitive advantage.

Contingency approach - is based on the equifinal view that the specification of strategic, leadership, managerial, and organizational practice is likely to be effective in terms of performance outcomes only if account is taken of relevant contingent or situational circumstances prevailing at the time. The contingency approach contends that there are neither "universal standards" nor any "one best way" by which to determine issues of strategic, leadership, organizational, and managerial practice. Decision-makers need to assess and to weigh up the situational implications of the particular contingencies that happen to confront them. They must also accept that different people will perceive issues of strategic, leadership, organizational, and managerial process in different ways; and will therefore create the required performance outcomes in differing ways. Key contextual contingencies facing leaders, decision-makers, and managers include national, business, and organizational culture; the external, regulatory and political environments; the market or sector; the competitive environment; knowledge and technology; staff and resource availability; and the pressures for internationalization and globalization. These contingencies are determinant and variable parameters for which allowance and adjustment must be made in the processes of concept formulation, problem and issue identification, strategic and management practice, and the establishment of paths to problem-solving and the handling of issues.

Controlling - wherever any forward planning is carried out or operational objectives are established, enterprise management will require appropriate control systems (i) to measure and monitor actual performance; (ii) to ensure that the agreed objectives and strategies are implemented and achieved; or if necessary (iii) to put in place corrective action to deal with performance which has varied unacceptably from the standard or benchmark set for it.

Core business - may be defined as that chosen product-market activity or those chosen product-market activities in which the firm's resources, capability and competence give it the greatest competitive or comparative advantage, and in which its choice of competition strategy will be most effective.

Core competence - is defined by Hamel and Prahalad as 'the sum of learning across individual skill sets and individual organizational units'. Core competences are represented by the collective and accumulated learning and experience of the organization and its staff. Core competencies are defined as those capabilities that are most fundamental to the successful operation of the enterprise. They represent activities that the organization must be good at performing, or in which it must possess competitive advantage in order to achieve its objectives. Core competences include the co-ordination, integration, and management of technologies; the management of knowledge and experience; leadership, managerial, organizational, and operational skills; the management of culture and value sets; capacities to manage knowledge, innovation, and change; the understanding of customers, sectors, markets, and their potential; and the management of architecture and the relevant external environments.

Core ideology - is defined by Collins and Porras in terms of the basic values and sense of purpose that guide, inspire, and motivate people associated with the enterprise, whether these people are internal or external to it.

Corporate appraisal - is that component of the process of strategic analysis which comprises the appraisal and analysis of the capacity, state or condition in which the enterprise currently finds itself.

Corporate governance - may be defined as a process whose purpose is to shape, to direct, and to supervise corporate actions. It comprises (i) the setting of strategic purpose and direction; (ii) the selection, development, and compensation of senior management; (iii) the supervision of leadership and executive action through the strategic management process; (iv) the creation as appropriate of accountability to owners, primary beneficiaries, and stakeholders; and (v) the performance monitoring and evaluation of the capability, competence and leadership record of decision-makers and managers. The governance role is not concerned directly with the operations of the organization, but instead focuses (i) on the process by which directors or governors (etc) give leadership and direction; (ii) on overseeing and controlling the executive actions of management in implementing strategy and achieving enterprise objectives; and (iii) on satisfying the legitimate expectations of shareholders or stakeholders for proper regulation and accountability.

Corporate identity - is defined by Hall as 'the expression of who a company is, what it does, and how it does it'. Corporate identity is the outward face of the organization. It communicates the personality and character of that organization, and gives an indication of its purpose and intent. A basic role of the management of corporate identity is to develop and communicate a positive external image, and proactively to shape external perceptions of the enterprise and its activities.

Corporate mission - a fundamental statement of enterprise purpose, which defines the place and position of the organization within its external environment.

Cost leadership - a cost leadership strategy is described by Porter in terms of the achievement of 'overall cost leadership in an industry ... (requiring) aggressive construction of efficient-scale facilities, vigorous pursuit of cost reductions from experience, tight cost and overhead control, (and the) avoidance of marginal customer accounts'. This product-market strategy implies the total and deliberate pursuit of cost and volume effectiveness in all value chain activities, whether procurement, supply chain management, operations and quality management, MIS, distribution, and so on.

Cost of capital - the cost of the capital employed or invested in an enterprise may be represented by the weighted average cost to it of all those capital components from which that enterprise has drawn its financing. These capital components might include investor or shareholder equity, loan finance, and earnings retained in the business.

Crisis management - in which enterprise management has to plan for, or to deal with what Rosenthal defines as any 'serious threat to the basic structures or the fundamental values and norms' of the organization as a social system. The concept of crisis management may be analysed on the basis of any or all of "emergencies", "crises", "disasters", or "induced catastrophes" as categories or subsets. Crisis management may also be termed "business continuity planning".

Critical mass - may be defined as a minimum level or volume of capacity or activity below which operations are unviable. It may be the case that the organization has to operate at or beyond this level of critical mass in order to be viable, for instance in cost terms.

Critical Success Factor (CSF) - is a key indicator or determinant of corporate success. Critical success factors will have a predominant impact on the achievement of (or the failure to achieve) enterprise objectives. The achievement of effective performance under these headings is of fundamental importance to the enterprise. The identification and achievement of critical success factors is therefore likely to take priority in the ordering of the organization's affairs. The failure to identify, understand, or respond to critical success factors is likely instead to be correlated with a disproportionate degree of risk and the potential for enterprise failure.

Cultural conditioning - by which theories, prescriptions, or the processes of concept formulation reflect the cultural environment from which they originate. For instance, Hofstede notes that 'not only organizations are culture bound; theories about organizations are equally culture bound. The professors who wrote the theories are children of a culture ... their experiences represent the material on which their thinking and writing have been based. Scholars are as human and as culturally biased as other mortals'. This implies, therefore, that there is no guarantee that concepts and theories developed within the cultural context of one country can with good effect be applied in another. This means that it is not possible for such theories to be universally valid.

Customer service - may be defined in terms of a wide concept encompassing any or all of the following meanings: operating the enterprise so as to be "close" to the customer or client in order to understand his or her needs (and changes in those needs); "taking constant care of customers" and their requirements; placing client, customer or recipient needs at the top of the organization's priorities; focusing internal activities in a customer-orientated manner; placing as much emphasis on the intangible element of service content as on its tangible components ("delight the customer", etc.).

Decentralization - describes a situation in which power, the authority to make decisions, and the control of resources are to some degree delegated downwards and outwards within the management structure. Mintzberg notes that 'when all the power rests at a single point in an organization, we call its structure centralized; to the extent that power is dispersed among many individuals, we call it relatively decentralized'.

Decentralized structure - characterized by some degree of decentralization. Ultimately, totally decentralized organizations are characterized by the diffusion of power throughout the structure, as in co-operatives and empowered work teams. Decentralized structures are often established on the basis of a process of divisionalization.

Decision-making - the choice of a course of action from among the available alternatives. The making of decisions implies the commitment of resources, the direction of enterprise action, and the acceptance of the risk and the responsibility associated with the decision.

De-integrated value chain - where a value chain is de-integrated (or "disaggregated"), key value generating activities take place across units or locations within any number of independent organizations, for instance acting as suppliers or distributors within a network architecture or structure as the progress of creation of the product or service moves towards its final outcome or market exchange. The de-integrated value chain may operate routinely across time or across an ongoing series of events; or it may instead be formed for specific purposes or contracts.

Delegation - the process by which an individual manager allocates responsibility and authority to a subordinate, in order that a certain task or activity may be carried out by that subordinate on behalf of the organization. The level of delegated authority must be commensurate with (equivalent to) the level of responsibility associated with the task.

Differentiated product-market strategy - in which a variety of products or services containing appropriate differentiating characteristics or attributes are positioned (or targeted) on a variety of different market segments. Each product or service may then be promoted by means of a segment-specific promotional mix. This process of differentiation may be achieved (i) by the accurate identification of the differences between the various market segments to be served; and (ii) by specifying the product or service so that it meets the need of any one segment, and varying it so that different product or service offerings meet the needs of a variety of different segments at the same time. Sources of differentiation include product or service specification, quality, operational or functional advantage, technology features, innovation features, brand, reputation, customer service offerings, and so on.

Direction of business development - the process of business development, and the strategies that are used to implement it, may take a variety of different directions. The three main categories described in this book are (i) diversification or diversification growth, (ii) controlled diversity, and (iii) concentrating on the core business (or "sticking to the knitting").

Diversification - is a product-market strategy based on a new product or new service offer (or offers) in a new market (or markets). Diversification takes the product-market positioning of the enterprise into new directions.

Divestment - is a product-market and business development strategy based on selling off or otherwise disposing of unwanted business activities, perhaps applying the resulting finance elsewhere within the enterprise.

Divisionalization - is the establishment of semi-autonomous organization structures or responsibility centres. The process of divisionalization is a widely used mechanism by which to achieve some degree of decentralization. The level of decentralization inherent in any particular pattern of divisionalization is represented by the degree to which strategic decision-making authority and the control of resource allocation is vested in divisional not corporate management.

Entropy - is the tendency for all systems (but especially "closed" systems) to deteriorate or to wear out over time. The tendency towards entropic behaviour may however be halted or offset if the system takes in new resources, knowledge, energy, or other value inputs from the external environment.

Environmental or external analysis - is a key component of the process of strategic analysis. It comprises the appraisal and evaluation of the external circumstances within which the enterprise must operate. This is because enterprise strategic choice will be influenced by the external situation within which the organization has to work. The process of environmental analysis may be used to identify external opportunities and threats facing the enterprise, however these are categorized.

Environmental stability - the concept of environmental stability is used to identify and analyse the relative degree of stability and the relative rate of change that characterize the external and competitive environments in which the enterprise operates.

Environmentalism - may be defined as an internal and external focus on the physical, ecological and psychological environments in which industrial, consumer and agricultural societies operate. Environmentalism is concerned with the impact of these societies on the external environments described immediately above, and with the proper or most effective way to manage or minimize that impact. Environmentalism is also concerned with human impact on the wider biosphere in which these three specific environments are located. Environmentalism cannot be separated from issues of social responsibility or ethics.

Equifinality - is a systems concept predicated on the assumption that open systems can achieve their objectives in a variety of different ways. There is no one best way to achieve organizational or operational objectives. Similar ends can be achieved by different paths and from different starting points, for instance depending on the character of the contingencies prevailing within the relevant internal and external environments. A practical consequence of equifinality is that leaders, managers and administrators have greater scope and discretion in deciding how to achieve their objectives than would be suggested by other, more prescriptive schools of management thought and culture or concept formulation.

Ethics - underpin the ethos and values of the enterprise, and of the people who work within it. Ethics can be defined as a conception of right or wrong conduct. Ethics tells us when our actions are "moral" or "immoral". Ethics provide a guide to moral behaviour, and to what is "morally acceptable" or "morally unacceptable". Ethical principles underlie the basic rules of social behaviour that are essential to the preservation and continuing of social and organized life.

Ethnocentricity - is the taking of a restricted "single nation" approach, or a "home country" orientation to management paradigms and issues within an international context.

Ethos - is defined by Argenti as 'how an organization behaves toward its employees and all other people or groups ... with whom it interacts. These include ... the state, the local community, employees, suppliers and so on ... the way in which it has decided to behave constrains and modifies the means it uses to achieve its purposes'.

European Foundation for Quality Management (EFQM ®) "Excellence" Model - is a proprietary framework for achieving "sustainable excellence" within the organization. The model is based on eight "fundamental concepts of excellence", these being (i) results orientation, (ii) customer focus, (iii) leadership and constancy of purpose, (iv) management by processes and facts, (v) people development and involvement, (vi) continuous learning, innovation, and improvement, (vii) partnership development, and (viii) public responsibility. The achievement of excellence will be "enabled" by the leadership, the strategy and policy, the people, the partnerships and the resources, and the processes of the organization.

Event characteristics - the definition, characteristics, or categorization of events about which decisions have to be made are likely (in some degree) to shape the nature and outcome of the decision-making process, and the level of resource committed to that decision-making process.

Excellence - defined in terms of the achievement of very high or "world class" standards of enterprise performance, as measured against objective external standards or benchmarks. Excellence may be measured in terms of benchmarks for quality, reliability, customer service or client satisfaction, clinical success, voter satisfaction, value-addition, perceived value-for-money, or cost management (etc).

Experience - is a key component of knowledge. Experience is built up by iterative processes of repetition, trial and error, feeling, observation, analysis, interpretation, categorization, evaluation, learning, application or practice, and feedback. Experience and judgement are related. The greater the accumulation of experience and knowledge the more effective may be personal or collective judgements about how to deal (i) with repeated situations of which we have already had past experience; and (ii) with new situations characterized for example by novelty, ambiguity, risk, uncertainty, complexity, or unpredictability.

Experience curve - shows the relationship between unit total cost and the cumulative volume of enterprise output that may result from the application of the experience effect. Unit total cost may typically decrease significantly (but at a proportionately declining or diminishing rate of decrease) each time the total cumulative volume is doubled.

Experience effect - which is based on the learning curve concept. The accumulation, retention, and application over time of an increasing level of individual and organizational experience may be used by the enterprise to achieve significant productivity gains or cost reductions as the volume of its output increases.

Explicit knowledge - is the formalized and systematic collective knowledge or intellectual capital of the enterprise. It can be communicated and shared, whether in product specifications, scientific formulae, technical data, organization policies and procedures, or programmes of socialization and training.

Familism - a philosophy in which processes and practices of leadership and management in the enterprise are conceptualized, shaped, or dominated by family (or familistic) relationships, values, and priorities.

Finance - which is a basic resource and constraint upon which the process of strategic management ultimately depends. The availability of finance usually constitutes a key limiting factor in the strategic decision making of the enterprise.

Financial appraisal - is that component of the process of strategic analysis which comprises the appraisal and analysis of the financial state and capacity of the organization. Financial appraisal is described in this book as the "financial health check". Where the published accounts of a business are available, the process of financial appraisal may be based on the analysis of accounting ratios. It may also be based on the analysis of internal margin of safety calculations, or on the technique of zero based budgeting.

Financial strategy and management - the paradigms of financial strategy and management upon which enterprise mission, objectives, strategy, and performance evaluation are based are crucial determinants of the nature and outcomes of the strategy process. And the philosophy, character, direction, and quality of financial strategy and management are usually critical success factors within the strategic management process.

Fit - decisions on the choice of current and future strategies will have to be based on judgements as to whether the objectives and strategy to be implemented are congruent with, or "fit" the resource base of the enterprise as represented by its leadership; its financial, human, and physical assets; its knowledge and competence; its capability; its willpower; and its operational capacity. In other words, has the organization actually got the desire, the capability, and the resources to put its chosen strategies into effect and to deliver the required results?

Forecasting - a process in which an attempt is made to visualize and to quantify the way in which market, risk, and other relevant variables will behave during the planning period or "time horizon" within which the enterprise is working into the future. The process of forecasting aims to create a picture of the kind of future environment in which enterprise plans and activities are likely to be implemented.

Franchising - a business development strategy based on the franchise to use a specified business format (eg McDonald's). The owner of the franchise (the franchisor) establishes a contractual relationship with another (usually separate) enterprise which, as a franchisee, then has the right to make use of that business format during the lifetime of the contract.

Functional authority - the right of functional specialists (such as strategic planners) to use their expert power to give orders in pre-specified functional areas (such as strategic management) to unit or line managers, who must comply with these orders. Functional authority is used in areas of the organization's work where enterprise-wide policies are to be applied in all departments on a consistent and unified basis.

Geocentricity - may be defined as the combination and synthesis of the localized cultural and managerial variations or paradigms that are to be found in the different countries in which an international company operates. Ultimately, an international or multinational company may develop and apply its own or "homogenized" culture right across the local enterprises and subsidiaries that make up its global organization.

Global brand - is a product or service that is supplied on an international or global basis under a common brand name. This brand name is used everywhere. Examples: Kodak film, Hertz car rental.

Globalization - may be defined as the process of internationalizing the scope, scale, and mindset of enterprise strategic management. Enterprise leadership espouses the belief that a "one-world" approach to doing business is the key to strategic direction, to operational efficiency, and to cost minimization. Strategies of globalization (i) rationalize and unify operations throughout the world; (ii) establish synergies between ranges of national and international activities and competencies; (iii) facilitate "shopping across the range" (thereby optimizing product availability and customer choice on an international basis); and (iv) establish consistent levels of operations and quality management that may be world class. Strategies of globalization are often associated with the offer throughout the world of relatively standardized products, services, or brands, each with a global appeal. At the same time, however, the multinational company may develop the capacity to segment local markets, and then to specify and position locally relevant but world class quality products or services on them in order to compete effectively with local suppliers.

Groupthink - may be defined as a mental set in which personal attitudes conform to a collective norm from which individuals are reluctant to deviate. For instance, if the prevailing mental set is hostile to the need for innovation, then group attitudes (and the decisions based on them) are likely to impede the process of innovation. Groupthink and conformity may be reinforced where the enterprise is conceptualized as either or both a closed system or a monolithic structure. The enterprise may come to suffer from a lack of inputs of a "requisite variety" and a "genetic diversity"; a lack of novelty, creativity and adaptability; an increasingly inward, bureaucratic and systematized orientation; and an increasing reluctance to accommodate to changing external conditions.

High trust society or community - a society or community in which strong bonds of trust may develop between people who are not related to each other. The relationship between non-kin is characterized by spontaneous sociability, that is a willingness to co-operate with others outside of the family, tribe, or clan. Such spontaneous sociability may give rise to greater social capital and organizational efficiency than is possible in low trust societies. The relative degree of trust in a society has major implications for the implementation component of the strategic management process being described in this book.

High trust workplace - in which (i) there is an assumption of totally co-operative and trustworthy behaviour on the part of all parties involved in the work of the organization; and (ii) in which responsibility and authority are delegated to the organizational location in which they are needed, and staff given discretion to act as is deemed necessary in order to carry out their work. "Lean manufacturing", for instance as exemplified by Toyota, is often quoted as a classic illustration of the high trust workplace.

Innovation - defined by the OED as 'something newly introduced, a novel practice or method; the alteration of what is already established; a change made by innovating; a renewal, something that favours change'. Rosabeth Moss Kanter defines innovation in terms of a comprehensive 'process of bringing any new, problem-solving idea into use … innovation is the generation, acceptance, and implementation of new ideas, processes, products, or services … application and implementation are central to this definition; it involves the capacity to change or adapt'.

Integrated value chain - where a value chain is integrated (or "monolithic" or "aggregated"), key value generating activities take place mainly within one organization; or within a group of closely interdependent and interrelated organizations functioning routinely and seamlessly over time as an integrated value chain.

Intellectual capital - is represented by the value addition that results from the generation and development of ideas, knowledge, experience, expertize, capability, creativity, innovation, intrapreneurship and entrepreneurship.

Intrapreneur - is an internal or corporate entrepreneur who promotes and organizes innovation, new business development, or adaptation to change within the organization.

Intrapreneurship - is the practice and promotion of entrepreneurial values and entrepreneurship within an existing business, not-for-profit, or public sector organization.

Knowledge base - the knowledge base of the enterprise comprises the concepts, theories, methodologies and paradigms by which the organization goes about its business and manages its affairs. The knowledge base includes accumulated experience, received wisdoms ("this is the way we would expect to do this"), technologies or "ways of doing the work", values and cultures, mindsets and attitudes.

Knowledge management - is a strategic process of developing and managing the "tacit" and "explicit" components of the enterprise knowledge base so as to create intellectual capital, competitive advantage, and value generation.

Kondriatev Wave - describes a period of intense innovation and change in a knowledge or technology base. Such waves may be followed by a period of consolidation during which the fruits of the new developments are diffused, applied, and brought to their maturity. The incidence of Kondriatev Waves provide a basic parameter and context for strategic processes of knowledge, technology, or change management within the enterprise.

Leadership - may be defined as a shared enterprise resource by which things get done by means of the use of the voluntary or willing co-operation of other people. Leadership may be analyzed variously in terms of dynamic "transactional", "charismatic", or "transformational" processes in which an individual influences others to contribute to the achievement of a group or collective task. This influence will be perceived as fully legitimate by those people who are responding to the leadership process.

Leadership and strategy - leadership is a key issue for the long-term strategic direction and survival of the enterprise. The organization's leadership has a strategic responsibility to focus attention towards and to develop the knowledge and technology base, the architecture and the relationships, the core competencies, the resources, the sources of competitive or comparative advantage, and the wider strategic management processes upon which the efforts of the enterprise ultimately depend. Leadership is a key strategic competence.

Leverage - is defined by Hamel and Prahalad as the process of achieving significantly more outputs than hitherto with the input knowledge, resources and competencies available to the enterprise, in order to achieve the "stretch" objectives that may be associated with strategic intent and strategy implementation. Resource and competence leverage may be achieved by any or all of the processes of concentrating, accumulating, complementing, conserving, and recovering resources.

Licensing - a business development strategy based on a licence agreement in which the originator or licensor grants rights to the licensee to manufacture, assemble, market or otherwise use a product, patent, brand name, or business format that remains the property of the licensor.

Limiting factor - limiting factors are those influences which directly shape and limit the strategies, strategic choices, and operations of the enterprise. Limiting factors internal to the enterprise will be associated with resource capability and capacity, knowledge, technology, competence, finance, cash flow, and operations management issues. Limiting factors external to the enterprise will be associated with legislative, regulatory, distributional, market or competitive limitations.

Local brand - may be specified to meet the specific demand characteristics of a particular local market. Example: "Pernod" (France).

Localization - implies the ability to adjust to, or absorb "local" (country or region-specific) cultures, customs, and practices. It also implies the capacity and competence to accurately segment local markets; and to specify and position products, services, or brands on these segments within the prevailing conditions of local competition or regulation. It may also imply the re-specification of global or generic products and brands to meet local requirements.

Locally modified global brand - is a global brand which is subject to significant local modification in order to meet local variations in the character of market demand. Example: variations in the recipe, formulation, specification or presentation of a product to suit localized tastes and preferences.

Low trust society or community - a society or community in which there may be strong bonds of trust between family members, relatives, clan members, or kin; but in which there are weak bonds of trust between people who are unrelated to each other (non-kin), resulting in a low development of social capital.

Management By Wandering Around (MBWA) - is a process in which decision-makers are involved in widespread processes of listening and consultation throughout the organization about strategic management issues before decisions are made. Decision makers may be exposed to, and must listen to comment and criticism about their past actions and future plans. MBWA is associated with consultative styles of leadership and management.

Management processes - these are concerned with establishing and reinforcing the values, competences, capabilities, attitudes, behaviours, and perceptions of priority of the managers, employees, value chain partners, and other relevant stakeholders of the organization. These values, competences, and behaviours are associated with the achievement of the objectives and tasks of individuals, groups, and functions (etc).

Managing locally - implicit in the implementation of international business strategy must be an enterprise capacity for effective local management. International strategies are actually implemented on a local, national, or regional scale, within the context of individual economies and cultures. The formulation of international business strategies and the localized implementation of those strategies are the two sides of the same coin.

Market segmentation - is defined as the analysis of a particular market demand into its constituent parts, so that sets of buyers can be differentiated and targeted.

Merger - is a business development strategy in which there is a direct merger or union between two (or more) enterprises. The separate identity of each is subordinated to the identity of the newly merged organization, or disappears altogether into it.

Mission - is a fundamental statement of purpose, direction, and intent, which defines the place and position of the organization within its environment. This statement of purpose and direction distinguishes the enterprise from others of its type, and separates it from its competitors.

Multinational company - may be defined as an enterprise that owns or controls production, service, distribution, or marketing capacity outside of the country in which it is based. It will earn at least 30% of its revenue from its international operations. It considers itself to be international in scope, and it manages its home and foreign activities in an integrated manner to pursue local, international, and global opportunities.

National culture - is defined by Hofstede as the 'collective mental programming' of the people of any particular nationality. People are collectively conditioned by particular patterns of history, socialization, education, and life experience. National culture resides (i) collectively in the mental makeup of the people of the society; (ii) in their institutions and enterprises; and (iii) in their ideologies, paradigms, technologies, scientific theories, and modes of concept formation.

Negotiation - a process of agreeing terms, or finding an accommodation between two or more parties who have a difference or conflict of interest which they wish to resolve.

Not Invented Here (NIH) - this syndrome is demonstrated by the deliberate rejection by the enterprise of ideas or innovations which are relevant to it, and which may affect it. Ideas or innovations not created or developed within the enterprise may be rejected by it precisely because it did not invent them. The NIH syndrome reflects a negative (and potentially risky) management attitude to external (and possibly "inconvenient") developments.

Objective - specifies and quantifies the goals or outcomes towards which leadership, effort, willpower, the investment of resources, and the use of capability are to be directed in order to achieve enterprise mission and strategic intent. Objectives specify the sequence, the time scale, or the time frame for those activities designed to achieve the necessary outcomes.

Open system - is an entity that is described as interacting with its external environment, from which it receives essential inputs of information, energy and resources. The capacity of an open system to incorporate knowledge and resources from the external environment allows it to adapt to the changing needs of that environment, to accumulate and to synthesize knowledge and experience, to learn, and to avoid the process of "entropy" or deterioration. Organizations as social systems are always regarded by systems thinkers as open systems. The strategic management process is predicated on the categorization of the enterprise as an open system.

Operational planning - comprises detailed programmes, procedures, rules and regulations, business plans and budgetary plans implemented at the functional or departmental level.

Opportunity cost - the opportunity cost of an enterprise resource is that use which represents the best available investment return or the optimum value that it can be used to generate. The opportunity cost of a resource is therefore frequently treated as its performance benchmark, for instance in calculating shareholder or stakeholder value.

Organization culture - may be defined as the collective mental programming of the enterprise and its members. Organization culture is apparent "in the way we do things around here", as compared with the way things are done in any other organization. Organization culture comprises such interrelated variables as value judgements, vision, value system, behavioural standards and norms, and perceptions of necessity, priority and desirability. Organization culture, strategic intent, and issues of strategy implementation are closely related.

Outsourcing - may be defined as a practice by which one organization engages another to undertake specified services or to make particular products for it. Typically this is done where an enterprise decides that it cannot, or should not undertake activities that other companies (i) can do better or at a lower cost, (ii) to which these outsourced activities represent the core business, and (iii) for which their capability to provide the required outsourcing is their core competence.

Pareto Principle - by which (say) 80 percent of the available resource is concentrated on managing the 20 percent of events that are most significant to the effective operation of the organization, and to the achievement of the desired outcomes. The remaining 20 percent of the resource is applied to dealing with the 80 percent of events that are defined to be less important in the achievement of objectives and outcomes.

Performance gap analysis - is the process of identifying gaps between what the enterprise intended to happen (what was planned), and what it actually achieved during the time period under consideration. Where the gap can be quantified, or the reasons for it explained, then new or revised strategies may be put in place to "close the gap".

PIMS - the acronym PIMS stands for the "Profit Impact of Market Strategy" programme and principles.

Planning - may be defined as a process in which events or activities are placed in their sequence, and ordered over time. Planning may take place within current time scales; it may take place in future time scales; it may be based on longitudinal or lifecycle sequence; or it may be based on cyclical or continuous sequence.

Planning period - see time horizon.

Planning style - is the approach taken by enterprise management to the process and direction of strategy formulation and decision-making. The strategy process may be "top-down" or "planning down" in style; or it may be "bottom up" or "planning up" in style; or it may be "negotiated" or "negotiative". Planning style correlates with features of organization structure and style of management as means of implementing strategy.

Policy - may be defined as a predetermined course of action. Policy is used to establish "contingent decision". Such decisions anticipate and lay down before the event the type and range of required responses to particular situations which are known with a degree of certainty to recur. Policy is used to guide and to standardize the action of people and departments, so as to achieve a consistent and predictable pattern of response to these recurring situations. Clearly understood policies reduce the total need for decision-making, and eliminate the need to repeat any particular decision-making process once it has been completed and accepted as appropriate. Policy decisions are also likely to incorporate and be improved by the repeated learning and accumulation of experience about events that recur. The greater the experience of the enterprise with a particular recurring event, the greater will be the certainty with which it can formulate accurate policy decisions as to how to deal with that event, and the more effectively and economically it will be able to deal with it.

Polycentricity - by which a multinational enterprise accepts and absorbs the localized influence of national cultures and characteristics within its local, regional, and global operations. Enterprise policies may as a result be characterized by local variations. Polycentricity may therefore be a source of requisite variety and genetic diversity.

Post-entrepreneurial corporation - described by Kanter as a hybrid type of organization that combines (i) the best of a creative and intrapreneurial approach with (ii) the discipline, focus, and teamwork of an agile and innovative corporation in which a necessary level of requisite bureaucracy will ensure effective functioning, financial control, and cost-efficiency.

Power distance - indicates (i) the extent to which a society accepts the fact that power in institutions and organizations (as well as in society in general) is (or should or should not be) distributed unequally; and (ii) applies that acceptance in interpersonal, leadership and managerial relationships.

Procurement - see supply chain management.

Product-market strategy - may be defined as a strategy that determines the approach of the enterprise to the provision of its products or services to the markets in which it has chosen to operate. Product-market strategies are typically based on cost and volume, differentiation, or segment-specificity (focus or niche). Product-market strategies are used to implement enterprise competition strategy.

Purchasing - see supply chain management.

Purpose - is defined by Argenti as 'the reason why the organization was formed or why it now exists. All organizations are originally formed to provide a specific benefit for specific groups of beneficiaries' or stakeholders. Enterprise purpose will shape the formulation of mission and objectives within the enterprise.

QRSV - the acronym QRSV stands for "quality, reliability, service, and value for money" as key market and performance indicators. Companies which achieved a competitively dominant reputation for the high level of their QRSV were described by Tom Peters as "excellent".

Relationship architecture - see architecture.

Representative leadership roles and championing - the role of the leader may include (i) acting as a champion within the organization; (ii) acting as a role model and exemplar within the organization; (iii) acting as ambassador, figurehead, and representative within the organization; and (iv) acting as ambassador, figurehead, champion, and representative within the organization's external environment.

Reputation - is a means of indicating quality as a differentiating feature. Kay suggests that reputation is a market's method of dealing with attributes of product or service quality which customers cannot easily monitor for themselves. Reputation is a function of the reliability, consistency, continuity and incumbency features of the product or service.

Requisite variety and genetic diversity - requisite variety and genetic diversity are concepts that represent the critical level or critical mass of novel or external stimuli to which an open system must be exposed in order (i) to update the knowledge base, mindset, paradigms, and technology of the entity; (ii) to offset obsolescence and entropy within that paradigm, knowledge, and technology base; and (iii) to facilitate ongoing or continuous creativity, adaptability, innovation and change.

Resource allocation - an end product of the strategy hierarchy, and a key outcome of the process of strategy formulation and strategic decision-making will be the allocation of finance, people, and resources to those activities by which the enterprise implements its strategies and attempts to achieve its objectives. Processes of resource allocation include the drawing up of business and budgetary plans, capital budgeting, the use of return targets or thresholds, investment appraisal techniques, the post-audit of capital investments, zero-based budgeting, re-engineering, and Six Sigma. Resource allocation processes may in turn be based for instance on the formal presentation of resource commitment proposals to, and their discussion with decision makers; competitive bidding and the making of a "business case"; negotiation amongst those who control the allocation of resources and those who seek to invest them; power interplays, lobbying, and political behaviour.

Resource base - comprises such economic factors as people and their skills, capital, and land. In practical terms the resource base will be represented by such tangible and intangible assets as human skills and capabilities, leadership abilities, cash and finance, brands, reputation, machinery and equipment, buildings, operational processes, information systems and so on. It will also be represented by knowledge, experience, technology, competencies and relationships. The resource base may in strategic terms be managed so as to achieve a desired level of value generation and customer satisfaction, and to yield the optimum competitive or comparative advantage.

Risk management - the process of making strategic decisions, and allocating resources to the implementation of strategies and plans will give rise to risk or the chance of loss of status, reputation, or value. This risk will have to be managed and, where possible, decreased by strategies of risk avoidance or risk reduction.

Segment-specific, focus, or niche strategies - where an organization's product-market strategy is segment-specific, focused, or niche based, it will market one only or a limited range of products or services into one only or a small number of market segments.

Sensitivity (or "what if?") analysis - a problem solving or forecasting methodology, based upon the iterative or repeated manipulation of variables to examine their behaviour or outcome as values are changed or the balance of the variables is altered. Used for example in scenario planning, business forecasting, budgetary planning, and network analysis modelling.

Six Sigma - may be defined as a mathematical methodology whose purpose is to improve 'the process and people-related aspects' of such business performance variables as cost, revenue, quality, and customer service. Six Sigma is based on the following components (i) the DMAIC process (define, measure, analyse, improve, control); (ii) listen to the voice of the customer (VOC); (iii) the identification and elimination of variation; (iv) the DFSS process (design for Six Sigma). Six Sigma is based on the statistic that nearly 100 percent of all performance outcome values will lie within six standard deviations around the average or mean of a normal distribution curve.

Social capital - is the value that derives from the willingness and ability of people to work together for a common purpose within the context of groups, organizations and communities. Fukuyama suggests that in calculating comparative and competitive advantage, strategists need to take into account the relative prevailing endowment of social capital, as well as the more conventionally described forms of resources and capital. Fukuyama also suggests that the incidence of social capital is not distributed uniformly amongst societies and nations. The development of social capital depends on the strength of adherence to the moral norms of community, and to the virtues of trust, loyalty, honesty, and dependability. The prevailing "stock" of social capital may be damaged by the excessive growth of personal individualism, self-centredness, materialism, or greed.

Social responsibility - enterprise management may be deemed to have social responsibility where its mission, objectives and strategy are perceived to accord with the values and culture of the wider society of which it is a part. Expectations of socially responsible behaviour imply that managers should interact with the various stakeholders, with whose interests they are confronted, in a responsible and ethical manner, refraining from questionable practices and doing no harm.

Stakeholder - may be defined as a person or an institution either internal or external to the organization who has an investment of some kind in that organization; or who instead has some kind of involvement or interest in it; or who is in some way directly affected by its activities or its processes. Stakeholders can, to a varying degree according to their relative power, exercise influence over the formulation of mission, objectives and strategy, and exercise influence over the strategic management of the organization.

Strategic alliance - is a form of voluntary grouping between organizations who come together for a specified period of time to achieve some common objective. They represent a form of product-market, business development, or technology development strategy that is based on co-operation and partnership. A strategic alliance is defined in this book as 'at least two companies or partners voluntarily combining value chain activities, architecture, and value chain linkages for the purpose of increasing individual and collective value addition, increasing competitive advantage, and achieving agreed or common objectives'.

Strategic analysis - is a process by which the enterprise analyses its own internal or corporate characteristics and capabilities; and identifies the features of the external legislative, and competitive environments within which it operates.

Strategic asset - defined by Kay as a feature of competitive advantage that is unavailable or inaccessible to competitors. It may be impossible to copy or replicate this asset.

Strategic decision-making - Mintzberg defines strategic decision making to comprise four decision roles, namely the "entrepreneurial" role, the "disturbance" handler role, the "resource allocator" role, and the "negotiator" role.

Strategic intent - is defined by Hamel and Prahalad as the nature or features of the direction that needs to be taken in order to attain the long term strategic position that the enterprise wishes to achieve. Hamel and Prahalad argue that if decision makers can clearly define and communicate this strategic intent, the activities of the organization should be characterized by a clear and consistent purpose which all those people involved with it should be able to understand.

Strategic management - may as a paradigm be defined in terms of the derivation and implementation of fundamental decisions about (i) what the enterprise is; (ii) what its mission, purpose, and intent is to be; and (iii) how its performance should be measured and evaluated. The strategic management process provides the framework for the process of planning for the enterprise as a whole into the medium to long term future. It is concerned with anticipating that future, establishing a vision and framework by which to reach it, and giving leadership and direction to the implementation of its achievement. The process of strategic management comprises four interrelated elements. These are strategic analysis, strategy formulation and strategic decision-making, strategy choice, and strategy implementation. The strategic management approach places emphasis on issues of leadership, management process, and operational implementation.

Strategic plan - is a long-term plan (for instance lasting for between two to five years in duration) which is used to shape, and to act as a blueprint for the implementation of the achievement of the broad strategic purpose or intent of the organization over that time scale. Strategic plans are sometimes termed "corporate" or "long-range" plans.

Strategic time management - in which time is managed by the enterprise variously as (i) a critical success factor; (ii) a finite resource; (iii) a limiting factor; (iv) a contingency or constraint; (v) a management variable subject to short and long-term interpretations; (vi) a linear, sequential, or cyclical construct; (vii) a concept capable of synchronization and leverage; (viii) a key national cultural variable; and (ix) a potential source of competitive advantage.

Strategies - may be defined in terms of the means (or "rules of the game") by which the enterprise attempts to achieve its objectives. Strategies indicate the path, route, or method by which the organization will go about attempting to attain its desired goals. Strategies act as "ground rules" or guides for action, and define the nature and occasion of the decisions needed to achieve and to implement enterprise objectives. Strategies provide the focus by which the enterprise will attempt to deal with or to manage the impact of the various internal and external forces that are likely to impinge upon it. Strategy is defined by Mintzberg as comprising five elements, namely perspective, plan, pattern, position and ploy. Issues of power and politics may be added to this list of components. Strategies have their risk content and their time scale. In summary, strategies determine how the enterprise intends to carry out its business during the time horizons to which it is working.

Strategy choice - the process of strategy choice identifies the alternative courses of action that, given its critical success factors, constraints and limiting factors, its available resources, its capability and its sources of competitive or comparative advantage, are likely to be available to the enterprise over the time scale and time horizon to which it operates, and from which a choice may be made by strategic decision makers in order that mission and objectives may be achieved.

Strategy formulation and strategic decision-making - these processes are used to establish enterprise mission, intent, objectives and strategy. These, in turn, will derive from the vision, values and interactions of the enterprise, its leaders and decision-makers, its managers, and its stakeholders.

Strategy hierarchy - the process of strategy formulation and implementation takes place at three levels within the strategy hierarchy. These are the "strategic", the "tactical", and the "operational".

Strategy implementation - describes the process by which the chosen strategies of the enterprise are put into operation within the internal context and constraints of the people, the governance mechanisms, the structure, the resources, the capability, the limiting factors, and the culture of the organization; and within the context, values and constraints of the external, legislative and competitive environments. The implementation of strategic choice will in addition take place within the context of those people and organizations external to the enterprise but with whom it has some kind of operational, supply, trading or partnership relationship. The enterprise will have to decide how to formulate its plans and strategies, who is to be involved in governance and decision-making, and how to make decisions about the allocation of finance and resources that are required to put these strategies and plans into operation. Decision-makers will therefore have to know how to identify and describe the alternative courses of action, policies and paradigms that are likely to be available to the enterprise. They will also have to put into place criteria by which to judge whether these alternative courses of action, policies or paradigms are appropriate and feasible; whether they meet the requirements of critical success factors; and whether it will be worthwhile to put them into practice.

Strategy process - describes the practice of establishing missions and intents, setting objectives, formulating and agreeing strategy, and making strategic decisions within the organization.

Stretch - is defined by Hamel and Prahalad as the gap between the knowledge, resources, capability and competence currently available to the enterprise; and the aspirations of the enterprise as defined by its mission, objectives and strategic intent. The degree of desired stretch will be indicated by the degree to which enterprise decision-makers want the organization to be more creative, inventive and resourceful in the way that it carries out its activities. Stretch objectives are deliberately intended to introduce incongruence or mismatch into the concept of "fit" defined above.

Supply chain - the chain of internal and/or external suppliers through which inputs and outputs flow, costs are accumulated, and value is added by productive, operational, distributive, or service processes. Issues of partnership, trust, quality, efficiency, speed, control, and cost are crucial to understanding effective supply chain management.

Supply chain management - the process of purchasing, procurement, and supply chain management links (i) organizations who as customers are purchasing goods and services for their business activity or operations; and (ii) enterprises that supply these goods and services. The supply chain management concept represents the rethinking of the process of purchasing and supply. It implies the positive and strategic management of customer-supplier relationships, for instance on the basis of high trust status, value-adding partnership architecture, co-operation, resource stretch and leverage, "win-win", and mutual benefit.

Sustainability - is a key environmental and ecological issue. It raises the fundamental question as to whether the operations of the enterprise (and therefore the nature of its strategic choices) are environmentally sustainable, or whether instead the enterprise exploits its environment on an irrecoverable basis, leaving that environment impoverished, damaged, or un-restored.

SWOT analysis - is a basic component of the process of strategic analysis. It comprises the identification and analysis of internal "strengths" and "weaknesses" based on corporate and financial appraisal; and the identification and analysis of external "opportunities" and "threats" based on environmental appraisal.

Synchrony - in which the management of events is synchronized over time, such that the achievement of those events is co-ordinated, and co-ordinate with other events which are related within a wider context. Hampden-Turner and Trompenaars give the example of Toyota's invention of the system of lean manufacturing which as an operational technique depends chiefly on the synchronization of supply chain and operational events to achieve its objectives.

Synergy - is defined as a concept of joint effect, based on the assumption that a combination of resources or value chains may yield an output which is greater than the sum of those input resources. Such "positive synergy" may be indicated by the equation $2 + 2 =$ more than 4. (The process may however work both ways; "negative synergy" may be shown by the equation $2 + 2 =$ less than 4).

Tacit knowledge - is a rich, subtle, and complex knowledge or expertize developed and internalized by an individual person over time. Tacit knowledge comprises the accumulated learning, experience, and judgement of that individual.

Tactical planning - determines the functional and departmental contribution to the achievement of enterprise objectives, and to the implementation of strategies. It shapes the detailed decisions as to how the resources and capability of the enterprise will be allocated, organized and managed that are the remit of operational plans within the strategy hierarchy.

Takeover - see acquisition.

Technology - may be defined as "belonging to or relating to, or systematically characteristic of a particular art, science, profession or occupation ... also pertaining to the mechanical arts and applied science, the science of industrial arts" (OED). Technology defines how things are done, for instance "in the manner of performance in the mechanical or industrial arts, skill or capacity" (OED). Technology widely defines processes, products, services, or the manner in which an organization completes its tasks or carries out its business. It is not a narrow technical or scientific concept.

Technology discontinuity - is a period of change from one prevailing technology to another. There is a break or gap between the "S" curve of the former or prevailing technology, and the "S" curve of the new technology that will eventually obsolete or replace its predecessor.

Technology limit - the technology "S" curve described immediately below implies technological limits. As any particular technology approaches a limit, the cost of making further progress may accelerate significantly, whilst the returns from that investment may decrease significantly. Eventually the technology reaches a point where no worthwhile further enhancements in performance may be achieved.

Technology S curve - Foster describes the technology "S" curve as "a graph of the relationship between the effort put into improving a product or process, and the results one gets back for that investment". The shape of the "S" curve may show learning curve effects at the lower left hand end, and the onset of diminishing returns at the upper right hand end or limit of the curve.

Term orientation - defined as the degree to which a society or an organization takes a predominately "short-term" or instead a "long-term" view of future time and events.

Time horizon - the current and future time scales (i) over which the implementation of strategies and plans are specified by the enterprise to take place; and (ii) over which the measurement and evaluation of performance against plan is to be based.

Time span of discretion - defined by Jaques as the relative length of time over which managers are required to exercise discretion, or for which they have the responsibility to make decisions. The higher up in the management hierarchy is the executive, the longer will be the time span for which he or she is responsible as decision-maker. These time spans will vary on a scale from the "immediate" (day-to-day) at one end; to the "strategic", the "environmental", and the "visionary" (long-term; future-orientated) at the other end. Jaques believes that the willingness and capacity to look far ahead is a crucial aspect of leadership potential. Long-term time orientation is therefore perceived as an indicator of high-level leadership status.

Transactional leadership processes - focus on the interactions or exchanges that occur between leaders and followers in the task or goal achievement context within the organization. These exchanges are used to seek to achieve or to optimize the relative mutual benefit of the outcome to be secured from the transaction.

Transformational leadership - is based on a process of accessing the needs and motives of followers as well as leaders so as better to achieve the goals of the leader and the organization. This implies that the leader engages in a dynamic with subordinates that creates an increased motivation and performance through a positive change in the values, attitudes, and willpower of those followers. Daft suggests that, in particular, transformational leaders 'are distinguished by their special ability to bring about innovation and change'.

Trans-national organization - may be defined as an integrated international network or architecture of interdependent organizations and capabilities. Each constituent is capable of adding value independently, but at the same time contributes to the synergy represented by the whole.

Trust - is the expectation within a community that there will be consistent, open, and co-operative behaviour amongst all members. This trust will be based on commonly shared standards, norms of behaviour, values, and beliefs. Trust should lead to individual and collective behaviour that is characterized by honesty, moral and ethical obligation, reciprocity, and a duty towards the community that transcends individual interest. Fukuyama differentiates between "high trust" and "low trust" societies.

Uncertainty avoidance - defines how a society copes with uncertainty about the future, and deals with the realities of risk. Indicators of uncertainty avoidance show the extent to which a society or an organization feels threatened by uncertain, ambiguous, or risky situations (or instead sees them as a source of opportunity); and tries to pre-empt (or to manage) these situations by the use of avoidance or stabilizing mechanisms and methodologies.

Value chain - a series or chain of interrelated activities specified to produce an output or outcome, across which decisions must be made, resources will be consumed, costs will be accumulated, and outcome value generated. The effectiveness with which the value chain and its connecting linkages are established and managed will variously be indicated by output or outcome measures of value added, competitive advantage, customer or client satisfaction, improvement in the relevant performance indicator, margin, or profit/contribution earned (etc). The value chain concept was first described by Porter. Value chains may be "integrated" or "de-integrated".

Value generation - indicates the level of value generated or value added by the chosen use of the enterprise's resource base.

Values - derive from prevailing ethical or philosophical principles. They are moral principles, ideologies, or core beliefs. Enterprise values may act as a driving or motivating force that underpin the organization's choice of strategies and activities. Values create or give rise to required expectations and standards of behaviour within the enterprise. In particular they shape attitudes as to what things should be done, and how those things should be done.

Vertical integration - is a diversification strategy in which the enterprise diversifies "backwards" or "downstream" through its value chain into supply or manufacturing operations associated with its existing activities. It may instead diversify "forwards" or "upstream" through its value chain into further processing or distribution of its products, or into service activities associated therewith. Or it may integrate in both a backwards and a forwards direction at the same time.

Vision - may be defined as an organized perception or phenomenon. It represents an imagined or perceived pattern of communal possibility to which others can be drawn into long-term commitment, given the necessary enthusiasm and inspiration on the part of the leader who is promulgating that vision. Vision acts as a "glue" which holds together sets of value judgements and ideologies within the value system of the enterprise. It provides a focus, framework and direction for the future development of the organization and its strategy.

What business we are in - the enterprise needs to base its strategic decision-making on a clear and accepted understanding of what business it is in. Levitt suggests that this understanding must primarily be based on the view of the customer or client, and on the benefits or values sought by that customer from the enterprise.

Win-win - describes a relationship between two or more parties which is characterized by the achievement of mutual benefit. Both parties are better off as a result of their relationship than they were before they established it.

World class - may be defined as an ultimate performance benchmark that indicates "excellence" or "best in class" reputation when compared with all other international or global competitors.

Zero based budgeting - is a formalized process of setting and reviewing budgets for the activities of an organization as if each of these activities were being performed for the first time, that is from a "zero base" of experience or resource allocation.

Index